ROCK ON™
ALMANAC
Second Edition

The First Four Decades of Rock 'n' Roll: A Chronology

NORM N. NITE
"Mr. Music"

HarperPerennial
A Division of HarperCollinsPublishers

This book is dedicated to both my mother, Jean, and the loving memory of my late father, Jim, and my grandmother, Catherine, whose love and inspiration enabled me to develop my interest in music, which eventually led to my first three books and now this one becoming a reality.

A portion of the royalties from this book is being donated to the National Music Foundation.

Photo acknowledgments follow the index.

Designed by Joan Greenfield

Library of Congress Cataloging-in-Publication Data
Nite, Norm N.
   Rock on almanac : the first four decades of rock 'n'roll : a chronology / Norm N. Nite, "Mr. Music."—2nd ed.
      p.   cm.
   Includes indexes.
   ISBN 0-06-271555-0 (hc)—ISBN 0-06-273157-2 (pbk.)
   1. Rock music—Chronology.   I. Title.
ML3534.N58   1992
781.66'09—dc20   92-52544
                                                              MN

92 93 94 95 96 DT/MPC 10 9 8 7 6 5 4 3 2 1
92 93 94 95 96 DT/MPC 10 9 8 7 6 5 4 3 2 1

CONTENTS

FOREWORD TO THE FIRST EDITION

by Dick Clark

Several years ago, my friend Norm N. Nite asked me to write the introduction to a new book he planned to call *Rock On.* Though I did not realize it at the time, that book was to become an almost daily part of my life.

Those of us who have been around since the first days of rock are expected somehow to recall all of the details. People constantly ask me to come up with the names, dates, song titles, and whereabouts of artists involved in the rock era. Obviously, it is flattering to be known as an authority. I invariably find myself turning to *Rock On* as one of the first sources of accurate information.

I am truly a history buff in all respects. I treasure our American musical roots—*American Bandstand,* The American Music Awards, and the thousands of hours of musical programming in which we have been involved have touched millions of people's lives. Over the years, we have been able to gather what is probably the world's largest film and tape musical archives. Its invaluable visual library of music is just one more effort to preserve our rich musical past.

In *Rock On Almanac,* Norm N. Nite has undertaken to publish the definitive encyclopedia of rock music. I have known the author for many years. He is an extraordinarily devoted researcher and writer. In all honesty, I do not know of anyone who has the knowledge and patience that he has.

This book is not just for the music fan, but also for the researcher and teacher. The wonderful thing about this publication is that it is not only fun to read, but it leaves you with the historical facts and some of the color behind today's music. Music truly does touch all of us in our personal lives. We wrap our memories in it and we share those moments of history.

When I first became associated with the music of the fifties, the critics of the day cynically suggested it would never last. The musical assassins set about to kill it. There were many of us who fought to keep it alive. Fortunately, we succeeded.

Thanks, Norm N. Nite, for helping to further preserve our musical heritage.

Opening scene from American Bandstand *(photo: Ron Wolfson)*

1989 American Music Awards: Michael Jackson and Eddie Murphy

ACKNOWLEDGMENTS

After many long years of exhaustive research, the book that I have always wanted to write is finally complete. This history of rock 'n' roll would not have been able to be written had it not been for the efforts put forth by my cousin Ken Zychowski and the computer software we both developed, called RockCom, the rock 'n' roll database containing four decades of information on the artists and the music.

A very special thanks goes to my dear friend Dick Clark for his foreword to the book and for the advice he has shared over the years about the business of rock 'n' roll. To my researchers Dennis Falcone and Renee Mocny and my attorney Bruce Mielziner. To Anastasia Pantsios for the many wonderful photos that she took over years and supplied for this book. And to copy editors Eric Wirth and Bruce Emmer and to Jane Scott of the Cleveland *Plain Dealer* for their help in this mammoth project.

Heartfelt appreciation to Ahmet Ertegun, Linda Moran, Noreen Wood, Peter Lopez, and John Westin, Atlantic Records; Kenneth Powell and John McHugh, A & M Records; Bob Young and Dave Morrell, Capitol Records; Danny Wynn and Jerry Lembo, Columbia Records; Bob Krasnow, Virginia Vasquez, Gary Casson, and Ed Simpson, Elektra Records; Terry Cohen, Epic Records; Susan Allen, Bobby Shor, and Nicole Dorato, MCA Records; Eric Hodge, Mercury Records; Beebe Jennings and Kay Kline, Polygram Records; Beth M. Schillinger and David Ross, RCA Records; Seymour Stein, Sire Records; and Carol Fenelon and Valarie Goodman, Warner Bros. Records. Thanks also to Donald Durma; Carol Cohen and Helen Moore, Harper & Row; Richard Turk, Colony Records; Brian Bierne, KRTH-FM; Richard Lorenzo, ABC Radio Network; Hank LoConti, the Agora Nite Club; Arthur Levy and Mel Phillips, Columbia Records; Bob Leszczak, United Stations; Bobby Jay, Jeff Mazzei, "Cousin" Bruce Morrow, Don K. Reed, and Bob Shannon, CBS-FM; Tony DeLauro, Charlie Crespo, Ursula Kadziela, Steve Petryszyn, Steve Piazza and Wolfman Jack and to the folks at MTV.

Special thanks to *Billboard* magazine, *Rolling Stone* magazine, *Goldmine* magazine, *Radio and Records* magazine, the Cleveland *Plain Dealer*, and the Cleveland Public Library. Also to Frank Rezek of Warner Bros.; Jann S. Wenner; Alan Spitzer; Bob Sagendorf; Renee Casis; Joe Smith; Dianne Pupillo; Loretta, Chris, and Jeannie Zychowski; Bill Randle; Carl Reece; Beverly George; Chuck Rambaldo; David Fishof; Joel Lind; Bill Brown; Harry Harrison; Ron Lundy; Max Kinkel; Bob Porter; Vince DeFini; Edward and Tony Durma; and Frank T. Cammarata, Jr.

Thanks also to my family and friends, Catherine Cichocki; Mary Abrahamowicz; Ken Levy; Carolyn and Joe Lascko; Barb and Rich Durma; Frank Lanziano; Joe Contorno; Joe Corace; Jim Swingos; Marc Wiener; Sanford Fisher; Tom Long; Mike and John Zappone; Jim Paponetti; Tom Jones; Jay Riggio; Rod Calarco; Joe McCoy; Charlie Scimeca; Bill Smith; Jack Soden; Michel Landron; Donna Mathers; Suzan Evans; Rick Newman; Suzy Baldwin; Suzy Phalin; Little Steven Van Zandt; John Lanigan; Joe Rock; Don Imus; Dick Fox; Richard Nader; Hank Niedzwiecki; Mary Ellen Wright; Stu Mintz; Patrick A. Terrail; Nick Verbitsky; Ed Salamon; Denise Oliver; Tony Garcia; John Valdastri; Patrick A. Sweeney; Dino Lucarelli; K. Michael Benz; Bill Wendling; Fred Strasser; Richard F. Celeste; George V. Voinovich; Mary Rose Oakar; James Karnback; Gary Kabat; Bruce Mielziner; Jon Sobel; Jules and Mike Belkin; Larry Benjamin; Kari Clark; Kay Keller; Rick, Michael, and Tim Durma; and Linda, Lisa, and Marc Lascko; Robin Belfer; Bonnie Z. Oviatt, Rock 'N' Roll Hall of Fame; Judith Richardson-Haimes, National Music Foundation; Angela Corio, R.I.A.A.; Ann Marie Picardo, BMI; Andrew Schwartz, Epic Records; Bernie and Mike Sokolowski; Martha Robi and Bill Sabatini.

INTRODUCTION

Rock 'n' roll. For close to four decades, this unique phrase has had a very special meaning to millions of fans throughout the world. No one can be sure of the origin of the phrase, but we do know the lasting effect the music has had upon millions of teenagers over the years. To every one of us rock 'n' roll has been a special part of our lives and has given us some wonderful memories of our growing-up years to look back upon.

It was because of the very strong feelings that I have about rock 'n' roll that I wrote my first book, *Rock On, Volume 1.* It was published in 1974, and since then I have had two other volumes published by Harper & Row on the history of rock 'n' roll and its performers. The focus of my three previous books was the history, performers, music, and memories of rock 'n' roll. With these volumes behind me, I wanted to do a book that would encompass the full scope of rock 'n' roll, containing material not only on the performers and their music but also on the trends, the innovations, the styles, and the various influential elements that have emerged since its beginning. I was able to accomplish this goal in this new book. I have chronicled how rock 'n' roll began, what happened in it, and how it evolved into the enormous business it is today. Admittedly there are a number of books available dealing with the same subject matter, but I wanted to produce a book that had all the elements of rock 'n' roll: the music, the films, the top albums, the top singles, the events that occurred in our lives. This book could then become the source for all facts dealing with rock 'n' roll.

Rock On Almanac: The First Four Decades of Rock 'n' Roll is a musical scrapbook filled with memories of the greatest music and events from 1950 to early 1989. The purpose of this book is to show chronologically the history, events, music, and people that helped shape rock 'n' roll into what it is today.

Since 1950 there have been thousands of artists who recorded tens of thousands of songs both locally and nationally. It is virtually impossible to capture all of these artists and all of their songs in one book. What I have embodied in this book are those artists and recordings that obtained national popularity over the years. The basis for the information assembled in this book is RockCom, a computer software product developed by myself and Ken Zychowski in 1983. This product is currently used by many top radio stations throughout the world as an informational database dealing with the history of rock 'n' roll. The database combines information from all three *Rock On* volumes with chart and playlist data and personal information about the various artists. The database contains more than 3,000 artists and over 19,000 song titles.

There are some facts you should know about how I assembled the information in this book. I carefully selected 15 of the most popular recordings that debuted in each month of every year in the rock 'n' roll era. My selection was guided by the national charts, airplay lists, and the data stored in RockCom. In identifying the debut month of a recording, I used the date a song

Elvis Presley, Elvis *(1956)* **album cover**

Little Richard & His Band, Little Richard *(1958)* **album cover**

The Beatles, Sgt. Pepper's Lonely Hearts Club Band *(1967) album* **cover**

Hair *(1968) album cover*   **Boston** *(1976) album*
                                   cover

Billy Joel, 52nd Street
(1978) album cover

became popular, not the date it was released by the recording company. It generally takes some time for a song to be added to the radio stations' playlists, where it can start to get the most listener attention and work its way onto and upward within the national charts. Using information from the Recording Industry Association of America (RIAA), the organization that certifies the gold and platinum status of recordings, I labeled the recordings that were certified. It should be noted that the recording companies must apply for these certifications and that many successful recording companies, like Motown, did not apply for certification for many years. The platinum award was not instituted until 1976. See under Music Highlights of 1976 and 1988 for more about the RIAA certifications.

Rock On Almanac begins with a survey of singles from the 1940s that developed the sound that would become rock 'n' roll. From 1950 through 1953, the book shows artists who debuted on the national music charts each year, along with a sampling of some of the biggest hits. From 1954 through early 1989, each year comprises a different chapter of the book containing these elements:

⇨ Each chapter (year) begins with news highlights, showing a sampling from the top stories of that year.
⇨ Next are the top sports winners for the year, indicating who played in and won the World Series, the football and basketball championships, and the Stanley Cup playoff in hockey.
⇨ Each chapter contains approximately 10 photos of some of the debut artists of that year, debut album covers, and concert performances. Over 425 photos appear in this book.
⇨ A list in each year focuses on the current music highlights, noting facts like when the first rock 'n' roll concert was held and who was on the bill; the years in which *American*

Bandstand, MTV, and VH-1 debuted; when and where Elvis, the Beatles, the Who, and others played their first or last concerts; when stars married, recorded a monumental song, launched a major concert, or did something controversial; and the introduction of new technological advances in music. This section alone contains hundreds of documented facts, or, if you will, trivia.

⇨ Each chapter shows the artists and groups who debuted on the national charts that year. This category is broken into major and minor debuts. Major debut artists are ones who would go on to have no fewer than six national hits during their careers. These songs would all have to be nationally charted. The debut single of major debut artists is shown with the label it was released on. Major group members' names at the time of the released single are listed. Minor debut artists in each year are simply listed by name.
⇨ Each chapter lists by month some of the biggest and most popular songs of that year. The song titles are arranged in alphabetical order within each month. For the sake of brevity I introduced the following simplified coding for some data. A star (☆) next to a song title indicates that it obtained number one status. A ⑥ identifies the songs that were certified gold, and a ⑫ marks those that went platinum. Every year contains at least 180 hit songs. This means that from January 1954 through December 1991 a total of 6,840 songs is documented. To this add the sampling from the 1940s and 1950–1953 and the hits of the early months of 1992, and the new total is over 7,000 songs. Starting in January 1989, the Recording Industry Association of America changed the award status of singles to 500,000 for a Gold Award and 1,000,000 for a Platinum Award.
⇨ The portion of each chapter that deals with

Bruce Springsteen, Born In The U.S.A. *(1984) album cover*

Michael Jackson, Bad *(1987) album cover*

hit music ends with the top ten singles and albums of that year, in alphabetical sequence. The performing artists and the recording labels are identified for all these recordings. In addition to the 7,000 singles mentioned above, I have noted 760 singles and albums popular between 1954 and 1991.

⇨ Beginning in 1958, the Grammy winners are provided. Shown are not only winning songs, names, and labels, in many categories, but also when and where the ceremonies were held and who was the host each year.

⇨ Beginning in 1986, the Rock and Roll Hall of Fame inductions are completely documented, with who was inducted and when and where the ceremony was held. Birth dates and, where appropriate, death dates and group members' names for each inductee are listed.

⇨ Chapters contain birth and/or death information about performers and other notables in the year of their birth or death. Not only the date but also the day (i.e., Monday, Tuesday, etc.) is given. Death information includes age at and cause of death.

⇨ Each chapter describes outstanding rock movies of the day, listing who starred in them and some of the biggest rock hits featured in the film. In later years soundtracks and concert films are also listed. Popular nonrock movies are cited as well.

⇨ Chapters end with the Motion Picture Academy Award winners in the Actor, Actress, Picture, and Song categories and the most popular television shows of the year, based on the Nielsen ratings.

Rock On Almanac ends with a glossary of many of the terms associated with rock music, such as *charts, demo, disco, heavy metal, mix, overdub, reggae, soul,* and *Tin Pan Alley.*

It has been my goal in my three previous books and now in this new book to be able somehow to put into perspective this wonderful music known as rock 'n' roll. This is a music that has thrilled, entertained, and excited millions of fans throughout the world for close to four decades. It is the music that I have spent my life researching, writing about, and enjoying. I acknowledge that volumes 1, 2, and 3 of *Rock On* and this *Rock On Almanac* would not have been possible if it had not been for the total cooperation of hundreds of people in the industry and so many of the recording artists I have been privileged to know and become friendly with over the years.

Rock 'n' roll music is something I have always loved and will continue to love. May the music, the memories, the performers, and the fans all ROCK ON forever!

THE
EARLY
YEARS

MUSIC HIGHLIGHTS OF THE EARLY YEARS

⇨ In July 1940, *Billboard* magazine begins charting pop records. The very first number one national hit is "I'll Never Smile Again" by Tommy Dorsey on Victor records.

⇨ In June 1948, Columbia introduces the long-playing (LP) record with the microgroove, which plays at 33⅓ revolutions per minute. Until this time, albums consisted of collections of 12-inch 78-rpm discs that featured one or two selections on each side.

⇨ RCA Victor develops the 45-rpm single and presses the very first one in April 1949. The first pressed single is "Gaïté Parisienne" by the Boston Pops Orchestra, Arthur Fiedler, conductor, record no. 49-0100. The first pop 45 is also pressed in April 1949 by RCA Victor: "The Waltz You Saved For Me" by Wayne King and His Orchestra, record no. 47-2715.

⇨ Disc jockey Alan Freed, the man who popularized the expression "rock 'n' roll" in Cleveland, Ohio, in 1950, gathers popular rhythm and blues performers of the time for his Moondog Coronation Ball, the first rock 'n' roll stage show, held at the Cleveland Arena on Friday, March 21, 1952. Acts include the Dominoes, Varetta Dillard, Danny Cobb, Tiny Grimes, and the Paul Williams Orchestra.

⇨ In July 1950, *Your Hit Parade,* the popular radio show that since 1935 has featured the popular hits of the day, moves to television.

⇨ In November 1952, the *New Musical Express,* a British music magazine, begins to chart pop singles.

⇨ In 1953, Bill Haley & His Comets' "Crazy Man, Crazy," on Essex Records, becomes the first rock 'n' roll record to appear on the pop music charts.

1940s

The 1940s had some ground-breaking singles that helped pave the way for rock 'n' roll.

1945

Caldonia	Erskine Hawkins	Bluebird
Rock Me Mama	Arthur "Big Boy" Crudup	Bluebird
That's The Stuff You Gotta Watch	Buddy Johnson	Decca

The Ravens

1946

Buzz Me	Louis Jordan	Decca
I've Got A Right To Cry	Joe Liggins	Excelsior
Let The Good Times Roll	Louis Jordan	Decca
R.M. Blues	Roy Milton	Juke Box

1947

Bobby Sox Blues	Johnny Moore	Excelsior
I Love You, Yes I Do	Bull Moose Jackson	King
Open The Door Richard	Dusty Fletcher	National
True Blues	Roy Milton	Specialty

1948

Bye Bye Baby Blues	The Ravens	Savoy
Elevator Boogie	Mabel Scott	Excelsior
Good Rockin' Tonight	Wynonie Harris	King
Pleasing You (As Long As I Live)	Lonnie Johnson	King

1949

Boogie At Midnight	Roy Brown	De Luxe
Boogie Children	Johnny Lee Hooker	Modern
Deacon's Hop	Big Jay McNeeley	Savoy
D' Natural Blues	Lucky Millinder	RCA Victor
Don't Put Me Down	Joe Liggins	Specialty
Drinkin' Wine Spo-Dee-O-Dee	Stick McGhee	Atlantic
Empty Arm Blues	Amos Milburn	Aladdin
Homesick Blues	Charles Brown	Aladdin
It's Midnight	Little Willie Littlefield	Modern
Pot Likker	Todd Rhodes	King
Saturday Night Fish Fry	Louis Jordan	Decca

1950

DEBUT ARTISTS OF 1950

Ray Anthony	Mario Lanza
Eileen Barton	Little Esther Phillips
Teresa Brewer	Dean Martin
Joe "Fingers" Carr	Mitch Miller
Mindy Carson	Guy Mitchell
Don Cherry	Les Paul & Mary Ford
Fats Domino	Joe Turner
Percy Faith	The Weavers
Eddie Fisher	Hugo Winterhalter
Georgia Gibbs	Victor Young
Phil Harris	

Fats Domino in concert (photo: Anastasia Pantsios)

POP HITS OF 1950

☆ ⑥ All My Love	Patti Page	Mercury
☆ ⑥ Chattanooga Shoe Shine Boy	Red Foley	Decca
☆ ⑥ The Cry Of The Wild Goose	Frankie Laine	Mercury
☆ ⑥ Goodnight Irene	The Weavers	Decca
☆ ⑥ Harbor Lights	Sammy Kaye & His Orchestra	RCA Victor
☆ ⑥ I Can Dream, Can't I	The Andrews Sisters	Decca
☆ ⑥ If I Knew You Were Comin'	Eileen Barton	National
☆ ⑥ Mona Lisa	Nat "King" Cole	Capitol
☆ ⑥ Music! Music! Music!	Teresa Brewer	London
☆ ⑥ Peter Cottontail	Mervin Shiner	Decca
☆ ⑥ Rag Mop/Sentimental Me	The Ames Brothers	Coral
☆ ⑥ Tennessee Waltz	Patti Page	Mercury
☆ ⑥ The Thing	Phil Harris	RCA Victor
☆ ⑥ Third Man Theme	Anton Karas	London
☆ ⑥ Third Man Theme	Guy Lombardo & the Royal Canadians	Decca

Eddie Fisher   *Dean Martin (photo: Kier)*   *Mitch Miller*

4

Guy Mitchell

Mary Ford and Les Paul (photo: *Bruno of Hollywood*)

Joe Turner

R&B HITS OF 1950

Double Crossing Blues	Johnny Otis, Little Esther & Mel Walker	Savoy
⑥ **Hard Luck Blues**	Roy Brown	De Luxe
⑥ **I Almost Lost My Mind**	Ivory Joe Hunter	MGM
⑥ **Pink Champagne**	Joe Liggins	Specialty
Well, Oh, Well	Tiny Bradshaw	King

1951

DEBUT ARTISTS OF 1951

Les Baxter
Tony Bennett
Earl Bostic
Ray Charles
Rosemary Clooney
The Clovers
The Dominoes
The Five Keys
The Fontane Sisters
The Four Aces

The Four Knights
Stan Freberg
Bill Haley & His Comets
Eddy Howard
B. B. King
Mantovani
Johnnie Ray
The Swallows
Muddy Waters
Howlin' Wolf

Tony Bennett

Rosemary Clooney

Johnnie Ray (photo: Maurice Seymour)

The Dominoes (top l to r: Billy Ward, Bill Brown; bottom l to r: Joe Lamont, Clyde McPhatter, Charlie White; photo: Kriegsmann)

The Four Aces (top: Al Alberts; bottom l to r: Dave Mahoney, Sod Vaccaro, Lou Silvestri; photo: Kier)

POP HITS OF 1951

	Song	Artist	Label
⑥	Aba Daba Honeymoon	Carleton Carpenter & Debbie Reynolds	MGM
☆ ⑥	Because Of You	Tony Bennett	Columbia
☆ ⑥	Be My Love	Mario Lanza	RCA Victor
⑥	Charmaine	Mantovani & His Orchestra	London
☆ ⑥	Cold, Cold Heart	Tony Bennett	Columbia
☆ ⑥	Come On-A My House	Rosemary Clooney	Columbia
☆ ⑥	Cry	Johnnie Ray	Okeh
☆ ⑥	How High The Moon	Les Paul & Mary Ford	Capitol
☆ ⑥	If	Perry Como	RCA Victor
⑥	Mockin' Bird Hill	Patti Page	Mercury
⑥	My Truly, Truly Fair	Guy Mitchell	Columbia
⑥	On Top Of Old Smoky	The Weavers	Decca
⑥	Sin	The Four Aces	Victoria

Bill Haley & His Comets (top l to r: Rudy Pompelli, Al Rey, Bill Haley; bottom l to r: Ralph Jones, John Grande, Francis Beecher, Billy Williamson; photo: Kriegsmann)

Ray Charles

☆ ⑥ Sin   Eddie Howard & His Orchestra   Mercury

☆ ⑥ Too Young   Nat "King" Cole   Capitol

R&B HITS OF 1951

Black Night	Charles Brown	Aladdin
⑥ Chains Of Love	Joe Turner	Atlantic
Glory Of Love	The Five Keys	Aladdin
Rocket 88	Jackie Brenston	Chess
⑥ Sixty Minute Man	The Dominoes	Federal

1952

DEBUT ARTISTS OF 1952

Johnny Ace
Leroy Anderson
Jimmy Boyd
Don Cornell
The "5" Royales
The Four Freshmen
The Four Lads
The Gaylords
The Hilltoppers

Joni James
Steve Lawrence
Smiley Lewis
Al Martino
Robert Maxwell
Lloyd Price
Tex Ritter
Shirley & Lee
Chuck Willis

POP HITS OF 1952

☆ ⑥ Blue Tango   Leroy Anderson   Decca

☆   Delicado   Percy Faith   Columbia

☆ ⑥ Don't Let The Stars Get In Your Eyes   Perry Como   RCA Victor

The Four Lads (clockwise from top: Jimmy Arnold, Connie Codarini, Bernie Toorish, Frankie Busseri; photo: Kier)

Johnny Ace

7

Joni James (photo: Kier)

Steve Lawrence

Lloyd Price (photo: Bruno of Hollywood)

☆ ⑥ The Glow Worm	The Mills Brothers	Decca
☆ ⑥ A Guy Is A Guy	Doris Day	Columbia
☆ ⑥ Half As Much	Rosemary Clooney	Columbia
☆ ⑥ I Saw Mommy Kissing Santa Claus	Jimmy Boyd	Columbia
☆ ⑥ I Went To Your Wedding	Patti Page	Mercury
☆ ⑥ Kiss Of Fire	Georgia Gibbs	Mercury
☆ ⑥ Slow Poke	Pee Wee King & His Golden West Cowboys	RCA Victor
☆ ⑥ Till I Waltz Again With You	Teresa Brewer	Coral
☆ ⑥ Wheel Of Fortune	Kay Starr	Capitol
☆ ⑥ Why Don't You Believe Me	Joni James	MGM
☆ ⑥ Wish You Were Here	Eddie Fisher	RCA Victor
☆ ⑥ You Belong To Me	Jo Stafford	Columbia

R&B HITS OF 1952

⑥ Goin' Home	Fats Domino	Imperial
Have Mercy, Baby	The Dominoes	Federal
⑥ Lawdy, Miss Clawdy	Lloyd Price	Specialty
Night Train	Jimmy Forrest	United
One Mint Julep	The Clovers	Atlantic

Shirley & Lee, The Sweethearts of the Blues (l to r: Shirley Pixley, Leonard Lee)

Chuck Willis

A typical in-store promotion, at B&M Records on 125th Street in Harlem, New York City, by a recording star of the time, Earl Bostic (photo: *Seymour*)

Record Rendezvous, 300 Prospect Avenue, Cleveland, Ohio, the record store where Alan Freed and proprietor Leo Mintz decided to call the music Freed played "rock 'n' roll" (photo: *Stu Mintz*)

"The Moondog Show." In Cleveland, disc jockey Alan Freed called himself Moondog after the blind New York street poet Moondog, whose recordings appeared on Temple Records. When Freed moved to WINS in New York, the "Viking" poet won an injunction against Freed's using the name. (photo: *Stu Mintz*)

The first rock 'n' roll poster, announcing the first rock 'n' roll concert. Alan Freed hosted and broadcast the Moondog Coronation Ball on March 21, 1952. (photo: *Cleveland Plain Dealer*)

Alan Freed presiding over one of his popular Moondog Dances, in the Cleveland area (photo: *Norm N. Nite*)

Red Buttons

Julius LaRosa (photo: Kriegsmann)

1953

DEBUT ARTISTS OF 1953

Faye Adams
Red Buttons
The Drifters
The Flamingos
The Four Tunes
The Harptones
Richard Hayman

Eartha Kitt
Julius LaRosa
Ralph Marterie
The Moonglows
The Spaniels
Willie Mae Thornton
June Valli

POP HITS OF 1953

☆ ⑥ **Doggie In The Window**
  ⑥ **Ebb Tide**

Patti Page
Frank Chacksfield & His
   Orchestra

Mercury
London

The Drifters (clockwise from top: Charlie Hughes, Johnny Moore, Gerhart Thrasher, Tommy Evans, Jimmy Oliver; photo: Kriegsmann)

The Flamingos (top l to r: Jake Carey, Johnny Carter, Paul Wilson; bottom l to r: Nate Nelson, Zeke Carey)

The Harptones, featuring Willie Winfield (top: Willie Winfield; middle l to r: William (Dempsey) James, Nicky Clark, Billy Brown, William (Dicey) Galloway; bottom: Raol Cita; photo: Kriegsmann)

	⑥ Eh Cumpari	Julius LaRosa	Cadence
	⑥ Have You Heard	Joni James	MGM
☆	⑥ I'm Walking Behind You	Eddie Fisher	RCA Victor
	⑥ Kaw-Liga/Your Cheatin' Heart	Hank Williams & His Drifting Cowboys	MGM
☆	No Other Love	Perry Como	RCA Victor
	⑥ Pretend	Nat "King" Cole	Capitol
	⑥ P.S. I Love You	The Hilltoppers	Dot
☆	⑥ Rags To Riches	Tony Bennett	Columbia
☆	⑥ Song From "Moulin Rouge"	Percy Faith	Columbia
☆	⑥ St. George And The Dragonet	Stan Freberg	Capitol
	⑥ That's Amore	Dean Martin	Capitol
☆	⑥ Vaya Con Dios	Les Paul & Mary Ford	Capitol
	⑥ You, You, You	The Ames Brothers	RCA Victor

R&B HITS OF 1953

The Clock	Johnny Ace	Duke
⑥ Crying In The Chapel	The Orioles	Jubilee

The Moonglows (top l to r: Prentiss Barnes, Bobby Lester, Alexander "Pete" Graves, Harvey Fuqua; bottom: Billy Johnson; photo: Kriegsmann)

ROCK ON ALMANAC

The Spaniels (James "Pookie" Hudson, Ernest Warren, Willis C. Jackson, Opal Courtney, Jr., Gerald Gregory [order in photo unknown])

Hound Dog	Willie Mae Thornton	Peacock
⑤ **(Mama) He Treats Your Daughter Mean**	Ruth Brown	Atlantic
⑤ **Shake A Hand**	Faye Adams	Herald

1954

ROCK ON ALMANAC

⇨ Movie star Marilyn Monroe weds baseball player Joe DiMaggio.

⇨ Dr. Jonas Salk's polio vaccine is administered the first time, to children in Pittsburgh.

⇨ Four Puerto Rican terrorists shoot five Congressmen in the U.S. House of Representatives.

⇨ Despite critics, Juan Perón is re-elected president of Argentina.

⇨ The U.S. Supreme Court outlaws racial segregation in public schools.

⇨ France and China reach an agreement on independence for the states of Indochina.

⇨ The first four-engine airliner, the Boeing 707, debuts.

⇨ President Eisenhower signs a bill to destroy the American Communist Party as a political and legal entity.

⇨ Some 250,000 North Vietnamese leave their Communist-controlled homeland for South Vietnam.

⇨ The Western Allies approve West Germany's admission to NATO.

⇨ Ed Sullivan signs a 20-year contract with CBS as host of *Toast of the Town.*

⇨ Ernest Hemingway wins the Nobel Prize for Literature.

⇨ The Sheppard murder case draws national attention. Dr. Sam Sheppard is ultimately convicted, on dubious evidence, of murdering his wife. He serves 10 years in prison before the Supreme Court overturns his conviction.

⇨ U.S.S. *Nautilus,* the first atomic-powered submarine, is launched.

⇨ RCA begins selling the first color TV sets.

⇨ Young women begin wearing ponytails, while young men begin wearing flat-tops and ducktail haircuts.

SPORTS WINNERS

Baseball   The New York Giants beat the Cleveland Indians 4 games to 0 to win the World Series.

Football   The Cleveland Browns beat the Detroit Lions 56–10 for the NFL championship in Cleveland.

Basketball   Minneapolis beats the Syracuse Nationals 4 games to 3 to win the NBA title.

Hockey   The Detroit Red Wings win the Stanley Cup over the Montreal Canadiens in 7 games.

MUSIC HIGHLIGHTS OF 1954

⇨ Multiple versions of the same song begin to appear. If a recording is popular, many artists record it, and thus many versions of each song appear on the charts at the same time. "Three Coins In The Fountain," "The High And The Mighty," "Stranger In Paradise," and "Let Me Go, Lover" are among the hits that reached the Top 10 in more than one version.

⇨ "Cover" records also make their debut. If a song is successful by a black artist, a white artist on a major record label "covers" the song by recording a similar version. "Shake, Rattle And Roll" by Joe Turner is covered by Bill Haley & His Comets, "Sh-Boom" by the Chords is covered by the Crew Cuts, "Goodnight Sweetheart, Goodnight" by the Spaniels and "Sincerely" by the Moonglows are covered by the McGuire Sisters, "Tweedle Dee" by LaVern Baker is covered by Georgia Gibbs, and "Little Things Mean A Lot" by the Dominoes is covered by Kitty Kallen.

⇨ The song "Sh-Boom" by the Chords crosses over from the R&B charts to the pop charts and becomes a number one national hit for the Crew Cuts, making it the first major crossover record. This breakthrough resulted in many more R&B records getting airplay on pop music stations.

⇨ On Monday, April 12, at the Pythian Temple Studio in New York City, Bill Haley & His Comets record "(We're Gonna) Rock Around The Clock." The song is moderately pop-

Alan Freed at the time he left radio station WJW in Cleveland to take over his new spot on WINS in New York (photo: Kriegsmann)

1954

ular when released a few months later, but after being featured in the film *The Blackboard Jungle* in 1955, it would go on to become the most successful rock 'n' roll song of all time, selling over 23 million copies.

⇨ The 45-rpm record starts to gain in popularity, beginning the phaseout of the 78.

⇨ *The Record Mirror,* a British music magazine, begins publication.

⇨ On Monday, July 5, Elvis Presley, Scotty Moore, and Bill Black enter Sam Phillips's Memphis Sound Services studio at 706 Union Avenue in Memphis and record several songs including Arthur "Big Boy" Cruddup's "That's All Right (Mama)," which would be Elvis's first release for Sun Records and the song to launch the Elvis phenomenon.

⇨ In September, Alan Freed leaves Cleveland, Ohio, to begin work at WINS radio in New York City, beginning a five-year term in New York that would help change the direction of rock 'n' roll forever. This was done through his radio show, live stage concerts, films, and television shows, which brought black recording artists to the forefront of rock 'n' roll.

⇨ Lead singer of the Drifters, Clyde McPhatter, leaves the group to enter the military. His replacement is a young man named David Baughan.

⇨ On Friday, December 24, while playing Russian roulette backstage at the City Auditorium in Houston, Texas, Johnny Ace accidentally shoots himself. He dies the next day at the age of 25, making him the first fatality of the rock 'n' roll era. His song "Pledging My Love" goes on to become one of the big hits of early 1955.

DEBUT ARTISTS OF 1954

MAJOR ARTISTS	Debut Single	Label
LaVern Baker	Tweedle Dee ⑥	Atlantic
The Cadillacs (Earl Carroll, Robert Phillips, Laverne Drake, Gus Willingham, Papa Clark)	Gloria	Josie
The Chordettes (Lynn Evans, Margie Needham, Janet Ertel, Carol Bushman)	Mr. Sandman ☆ ⑥	Cadence
The Crew Cuts (John Perkins, Pat Barrett, Rudi Maugeri, Ray Perkins)	Crazy 'Bout You, Baby	Mercury
The Crows (Daniel "Sonny" Norton, Harold Major, William Davis, Gerald Hamilton)	Gee	Rama
Sammy Davis, Jr.	Hey There	Decca
The De Castro Sisters (Peggy, Babette, Cherie)	Teach Me Tonight	Abbott
Roy Hamilton	You'll Never Walk Alone	Epic
Kitty Kallen	Little Things Mean A Lot ☆ ⑥	Decca

15

LaVern Baker

Roy Hamilton

Kitty Kallen

The McGuire Sisters (Chris, Dotty, Phyllis)	Goodnight Sweetheart, Goodnight	Coral
The Midnighters (Hank Ballard, Lawson Smith, Norman Thrasher, Billy Davis, Henry Booth)	Work With Me Annie ⑥	Federal
Jaye P. Morgan	That's All I Want From You	RCA Victor
The Platters (Tony Williams, Zola Taylor, David Lynch, Paul Robi, Herb Reed)	Tell The World	Federal
Elvis Presley	That's All Right (Mama)	Sun
Billy Vaughn	Melody Of Love ☆	Dot

OTHER ARTISTS

Archie Bleyer	Hugo & Luigi
Rusty Bryant	The Jewels
David Carroll	Richard Maltby
The Charms	Marvin & Johnny
The Cheers	The Medallions
The Chords	Lou Monte
The De John Sisters	The Penguins
The Diablos	The Spiders
The El Dorados	Joan Weber
Gene & Eunice	Frank Weir
Leroy Holmes	David Whitfield

HITS OF 1954

JANUARY

⑥	**Answer Me, My Love**	Nat "King" Cole	Capitol
	Bimbo	Pee Wee King	RCA Victor
⑥	**Changing Partners**	Patti Page	Mercury
⑥	**Ebb Tide**	Frank Chacksfield & His Orchestra	London
	I'm Just Your Fool	Buddy Johnson	Mercury
	The Jones Boy	The Mills Brothers	Decca
☆ ⑥	**Oh, Mein Papa**	Eddie Calvert	Essex
⑥	**Oh! My Pa-Pa**	Eddie Fisher	RCA Victor
⑥	**Ricochet**	Teresa Brewer	Coral

Santa Baby	Eartha Kitt	RCA Victor
Saving My Love For You	Johnny Ace	Duke
⑥ Stranger In Paradise	Tony Bennett	Columbia
⑥ Stranger In Paradise	The Four Aces	Decca
Such A Night	The Drifters	Atlantic
What It Was, Was Football	Deacon Andy Griffith	Capitol

FEBRUARY

At The Darktown Strutters' Ball	Lou Monte	RCA Victor
The Breeze And I	Vic Damone	Mercury
⑥ Cross Over The Bridge	Patti Page	Mercury
From The Vine Came The Grape	The Gaylords	Mercury
The Gang That Sang "Heart Of My Heart"	The Four Aces	Decca
⑥ I Get So Lonely (When I Dream About You)	The Four Knights	Capitol
Lovey Dovey	The Clovers	Atlantic
☆ ⑥ Make Love To Me!	Jo Stafford	Columbia
☆ ⑥ Secret Love	Doris Day	Columbia
Somebody Bad Stole De Wedding Bell	Eartha Kitt	RCA Victor
⑥ The Things That I Used To Do	Guitar Slim	Specialty
Till Then	The Hilltoppers	Dot
☆ ⑥ Wanted	Perry Como	RCA Victor
Woman	Johnny Desmond	Coral
⑥ Young At Heart	Frank Sinatra	Capitol

MARCH

Cuddle Me	Ronnie Gaylord	Mercury
Gee	The Crows	Rama
A Girl, A Girl	Eddie Fisher	RCA Victor
Goodnight Sweetheart, Goodnight	The Spaniels	Vee Jay
Here	Tony Martin	RCA Victor
⑥ Honey Hush	Joe Turner	Atlantic

The Cadillacs (top: Earl Carroll; bottom l to r: Earl Wade, Robert Phillips, Charles Brooks, Laverne Drake; photo: Kriegsmann)

Jilted	Teresa Brewer	Coral
Life Is But A Dream	The Harptones	Paradise
☆ ⑥ Little Things Mean A Lot	Kitty Kallen	Decca
Man With The Banjo	The Ames Brothers	RCA Victor
There'll Be No Teardrops Tonight	Tony Bennett	Columbia
Y'All Come	Bing Crosby	Decca
You Done Me Wrong	Fats Domino	Imperial
You'll Never Walk Alone	Roy Hamilton	Epic
You're My Everything	Joni James	MGM

APRIL

All Night Long	Rusty Bryant	Dot
Anema E Core	Eddie Fisher	RCA Victor
The Happy Wanderer	Frank Weir	London
If You Love Me (Really Love Me)	Kay Starr	Capitol
I Really Don't Want To Know	Les Paul & Mary Ford	Capitol
Isle Of Capri	The Gaylords	Mercury
Isle Of Capri	Jackie Lee	Coral
My Memories Of You	The Harptones	Bruce
Poor Butterfly	The Hilltoppers	Dot
Rose-Marie	Slim Whitman	Imperial
Secret Love	The Moonglows	Chance
Shake, Rattle And Roll	Joe Turner	Atlantic
Such A Night	Johnnie Ray	Columbia
Till We Two Are One	Georgie Shaw	Decca
⑥ Work With Me, Annie	The Midnighters	Federal

MAY

Crazy 'Bout You, Baby	The Crew Cuts	Mercury
Heartbreaker	The Crows	Rama
Hernando's Hideaway	Archie Bleyer	Cadence
⑥ Honey Love	The Drifters	Atlantic
If I Loved You	Roy Hamilton	Epic
It Should've Been Me	Ray Charles	Atlantic
⑥ I Understand Just How You Feel	The Four Tunes	Jubilee
Kid's Last Fight	Frankie Laine	Columbia
Man Upstairs	Kay Starr	Capitol

The Chordettes (l to r: Jinny Osborn, Lynn Evans, Carol Bushman, Janet Ertel)

1954

The Crew Cuts (l to r: Rudy Maugeri, John Perkins, Pat Barrett, Ray Perkins)

The McGuire Sisters (from top: Chris, Dotty, Phyllis; photo: Kier)

⑥ Oh, Baby Mine	The Four Knights	Capitol
Point Of Order	Stan Freberg	Capitol
Sh-Boom	The Chords	Cat
Steam Heat	Patti Page	Mercury
☆ ⑥ Three Coins In The Fountain	The Four Aces	Decca
Three Coins In The Fountain	Frank Sinatra	Capitol

JUNE

Gloria	The Cadillacs	Josie
Green Years	Eddie Fisher	RCA Victor
Hernando's Hideaway	Johnnie Ray	Columbia
⑥ The High And The Mighty	Leroy Holmes	MGM
⑥ In The Chapel In The Moonlight	Kitty Kallen	Decca
Joey	Betty Madigan	MGM
Just Make Love To Me	Muddy Waters	Chess
The Little Shoemaker	The Gaylords	Mercury
⑥ Sexy Ways	Midnighters	Federal
☆ ⑥ Sh-Boom	The Crew Cuts	Mercury
Some Day	Frankie Laine	Columbia
Sway	Dean Martin	Capitol
Wedding Bells (Are Breaking Up That Old Gang Of Mine)	The Four Aces	Decca
(We're Gonna) Rock Around the Clock	Bill Haley & His Comets	Decca
The Wind	The Diablos	Fortune

JULY

⑥ Cara Mia	David Whitfield	London
Cherry Pie	Marvin & Johnny	Modern
Cinnamon Sinner	Tony Bennett	Columbia

19

The Midnighters with Hank Ballard (photo: Suggs Photo)

Gilly, Gilly, Ossenfeffer, Katzenellen Bogen By The Sea	The Four Lads	Columbia
Goodnight Sweetheart, Goodnight	The McGuire Sisters	Coral
☆ Ⓖ Hey There/This Ole House	Rosemary Clooney	Columbia
Hey There	Sammy Davis, Jr.	Decca
Hit And Run Affair	Perry Como	RCA Victor
Ⓖ I Don't Hurt Anymore	Hank Snow & the Rainbow Ranch Boys	RCA Victor
If You Love Me (Really Love Me)	Vera Lynn	London
I'm A Fool To Care	Les Paul & Mary Ford	Capitol
Oh What A Dream	Ruth Brown	Atlantic
Please Forgive Me	Johnny Ace	Duke
Ⓖ Shake, Rattle And Roll	Bill Haley & His Comets	Decca
Your Cash Ain't Nothin' But Trash	The Clovers	Atlantic

AUGUST

Ⓖ Annie Had A Baby	The Midnighters	Federal
Happy Days And Lonely Nights	The Fontane Sisters	Dot
The High And The Mighty	Victor Young	Decca
Ⓖ Hold My Hand	Don Cornell	Coral
I Cried	Patti Page	Mercury
If I Didn't Care	The Hilltoppers	Dot
In The Chapel In The Moonlight	The Orioles	Jubilee
Little Things Mean A Lot	The Dominoes	King
Skokiaan	The Four Lads	Columbia
Skokiaan	Ralph Marterie	Mercury
Smile	Nat "King" Cole	Capitol
Tell The World	The Platters	Federal
That's All Right (Mama)	Elvis Presley	Sun
They Were Doing The Mambo	Vaughn Monroe	RCA Victor
Untrue	The Crows	Rama

SEPTEMBER

Count Your Blessings	Eddie Fisher	RCA Victor
Dream	The Four Aces	Decca
⑥ Hearts of Stone	The Charms	De Luxe
Hearts of Stone	The Jewels	Imperial
The High And The Mighty	Les Baxter	Capitol
☆ ⑥ I Need You Now	Eddie Fisher	RCA Victor
It's A Woman's World	The Four Aces	Decca
I Want You All To Myself	Kitty Kallen	Decca
Muskrat Ramble	The McGuire Sisters	Coral
Oop Shoop	The Crew Cuts	Mercury
⑥ Papa Loves Mambo	Perry Como	RCA Victor
Pink Champagne	Rusty Bryant	Dot
That's All I Want From You	Jaye P. Morgan	RCA Victor
You Upset Me Baby	B. B. King	RPM
Zippity Zum	The Chords	Cat

OCTOBER

Annie's Aunt Fanny	The Midnighters	Federal
Bip Bam	The Drifters	Atlantic
⑥ Earth Angel	The Penguins	Dootone
Good Rockin' Tonight	Elvis Presley	Sun
Hurt	Roy Hamilton	Epic
Ling, Ting, Tong	The Five Keys	Capitol
The Mama Doll Song	Patti Page	Mercury
⑥ Mambo Italiano	Rosemary Clooney	Columbia
☆ ⑥ Mr. Sandman	The Chordettes	Cadence
Sh-Boom	Stan Freberg	Capitol
Sincerely	The Moonglows	Chess
Teach Me Tonight	The De Castro Sisters	Abbott
Teach Me Tonight	Jo Stafford	Columbia
Whither Thou Goest	Les Paul & Mary Ford	Capitol
Whole Lotta' Love	B. B. King	RPM

NOVEMBER

(Bazoom) I Need Your Lovin'	The Cheers	Capitol
Buick 59/The Letter	The Medallions	Dootone
Dim, Dim The Lights	Bill Haley & His Comets	Decca
Hajji Baba	Nat "King" Cole	Capitol
☆ ⑥ Hearts of Stone	The Fontane Sisters	Dot

The Penguins (l to r: Curtis Williams, Cleve Duncan, Dexter Tisby, Bruce Tate)

21

Home For The Holidays	Perry Como	RCA Victor
Mood Indigo	The Norman Petty Trio	X
⑥ More And More	Webb Pierce	Decca
⑥ The Naughty Lady of Shady Lane	The Ames Brothers	RCA Victor
The Naughty Lady of Shady Lane	Archie Bleyer	Cadence
Runaround	The Chuckles	X
Skokiaan	Ray Anthony	Capitol
That's What I Like	Don, Dick, & Jimmy	Crown
⑥ Tweedle Dee	LaVern Baker	Atlantic
White Christmas	The Drifters	Atlantic

DECEMBER

I Love You Madly	The Four Coins	Epic
Ko Ko Mo	Gene & Eunice	Combo
⑥ Let Me Go, Lover	Teresa Brewer	Coral
Let Me Go, Lover	Patti Page	Mercury
☆ ⑥ Let Me Go, Lover	Joan Weber	Columbia
Make Yourself Comfortable	Sarah Vaughan	Mercury
Mambo Baby	Ruth Brown	Atlantic
A Man Chases A Girl	Eddie Fisher	RCA Victor
Melody Of Love	The Four Aces	Decca
Pledging My Love	Johnny Ace	Duke
Rain, Rain, Rain	Frankie Laine	Columbia
Rock-A-Beatin' Boogie	The Esquire Boys	Guyden
Santo Natale	David Whitfield	London
☆ ⑥ Sincerely	The McGuire Sisters	Coral
Teach Me Tonight	Dinah Washington	Mercury

TOP SINGLES OF 1954

⑥ Hey There	Rosemary Clooney	Columbia
⑥ I Need You Now	Eddie Fisher	RCA Victor
⑥ Little Things Mean A Lot	Kitty Kallen	Decca
⑥ Make Love To Me!	Jo Stafford	Columbia
⑥ Mr. Sandman	The Chordettes	Cadence
⑥ Oh! My Pa-Pa	Eddie Fisher	RCA Victor
⑥ Secret Love	Doris Day	Columbia
⑥ Sh-Boom	The Crew Cuts	Mercury
⑥ This Ole House	Rosemary Clooney	Columbia
⑥ Wanted	Perry Como	RCA Victor

TOP ALBUMS OF 1954

Calamity Jane	Doris Day/Howard Keel	Columbia
May I Sing To You	Eddie Fisher	RCA Victor
Music For Lovers Only	Jackie Gleason	Capitol
Music, Martinis And Memories	Jackie Gleason	Capitol
Music To Make You Misty	Jackie Gleason	Capitol
Selections From The Glenn Miller Story	Glenn Miller & His Orchestra	RCA Victor

Seven Brides For Seven Brothers	Soundtrack	MGM
Songs For Young Lovers	Frank Sinatra	Capitol
The Student Prince	Mario Lanza	RCA Victor
Two In Love	Nat "King" Cole	Capitol

1954

BIRTHS AND DEATHS IN 1954

MUSIC PERFORMERS BORN IN 1954

Adrian Vandenberg (Vandenberg),
    January 31
John Travolta, February 18
Pat Travers, April 12
Debora Iyall (Romeo Void), April 29
Ray Parker, Jr., May 1
Dan Hill, June 3
Jorge Santana (Malo), June 13
Terri Gibbs, June 15
David Paich (Toto), June 25

Debbie Sledge (Sister Sledge), July 9
Patrice Rushen, September 30
Bob Geldof, October 5
Adam Ant (Stuart Goddard), November 3
Chris Difford (Squeeze), November 4
Rickie Lee Jones, November 8
Jermaine Jackson, December 11
Steve Forbert, December 13
Annie Lennox (Eurythmics), December 25

MUSIC PERFORMERS AND MUSIC INDUSTRY NOTABLES WHO DIED IN 1954

Johnny Ace, Saturday, December 25 (gunshot; 25)

OTHERS WHO DIED IN 1954

Lionel Barrymore
Sidney Greenstreet
Sir Cedric Hardwicke

Grantland Rice
Glenn Scobey "Pop" Warner

POPULAR MOVIES OF 1954

Beachhead
The Caine Mutiny

The Country Girl
The Creature from the Black Lagoon

The Platters (top l to r: David Lynch, Paul Robi; middle: *Tony Williams, Herb Reed;* bottom: *Zola Taylor)*

23

ROCK ON ALMANAC

Elvis Presley

Dial M for Murder
Executive Suite
Go Man, Go!
On the Waterfront
Rear Window
Seven Brides for Seven Brothers

A Star Is Born
Them!
Three Coins in the Fountain
The Wild One
Woman's World

ACADEMY AWARD WINNERS OF 1954

Best Actor: Marlon Brando, *On the Waterfront*
Best Actress: Grace Kelly, *The Country Girl*
Best Picture: *On the Waterfront*
Best Song: "Three Coins In The Fountain," *Three Coins in the Fountain* (music by Jule
   Styne, lyrics by Sammy Cahn)

TOP TELEVISION SHOWS OF 1954

Disneyland
Dragnet
Ford Theater
The George Gobel Show
I Love Lucy

The Jack Benny Show
The Jackie Gleason Show
The Martha Raye Show
Toast of the Town
You Bet Your Life

1955

ROCK ON ALMANAC

⇨ After nine months of development, no-iron Dacron is put on the market.

⇨ Under George Meany, the AFL and CIO labor unions merge.

⇨ In Belgrade, Yugoslavia, Communist Party Secretary Nikita Khrushchev makes up with Yugoslav President Tito.

⇨ In the worst auto racing accident ever, 80 die at Le Mans raceway southwest of Paris.

⇨ In Anaheim, California, Disneyland opens.

⇨ In Geneva, the Big Four summit meeting is a success.

⇨ Walt Disney's new program *The Mickey Mouse Club* has children donning mouse ears and chanting "M-I-C-K-E-Y M-O-U-S-E."

⇨ Billing it as the "world's most popular airplane," Cessna unveils its 172 Skyhawk, a single-engine light aircraft.

⇨ Eddie Fisher marries actress Debbie Reynolds.

⇨ *The Honeymooners,* one of early television's most popular sitcoms, ends after 39 episodes.

⇨ The *Village Voice,* the first official "underground" newspaper, debuts.

⇨ Americans enjoy TV game shows, Davy Crockett hats, and the mambo.

SPORTS WINNERS

Baseball   The Brooklyn Dodgers beat the New York Yankees 4 games to 3.

Football   The Cleveland Browns beat the Los Angeles Rams 38–14 for the NFL championship in Los Angeles.

Basketball   The Syracuse Nationals beat the Fort Wayne Pistons 4 games to 3 to win the NBA title.

Hockey   The Detroit Red Wings beat the Montreal Canadiens 4 games to 3 to win the Stanley Cup.

MUSIC HIGHLIGHTS OF 1955

⇨ On Friday and Saturday, January 14 and 15, Alan Freed holds his first Rock 'n' Roll Party stage show in New York at the St. Nicholas Arena, drawing over 15,000 paid admissions, at the time making it the greatest advance sale in the history of American dance promotions. The lineup of performers includes Joe Turner, the Clovers, Fats Domino, the Moonglows, the Harptones, the Drifters, Ella Johnson, Danny Overbea, Dakota Staton, Red Prysock, Nolan Lewis, and the Buddy Johnson Orchestra.

⇨ Because of the popularity of the number one hits "Cherry Pink And Apple Blossom White" by Perez Prado and "The Ballad Of Davy Crockett" by Bill Hayes, teens and adults are learning the mambo and the cha-cha and kids are clamoring for Davy Crockett "coonskin" caps.

⇨ Cover records continue to flourish with Pat Boone, Gale Storm, and Perry Como covering hits of Little Richard, Fats Domino, Ivory Joe Hunter, Smiley Lewis, and the Penguins.

⇨ The movie *Blackboard Jungle* premieres. "(We're Gonna) Rock Around The Clock" by Bill Haley & His Comets is heard at both the beginning and end of the film. It is the first rock 'n' roll song to be featured in a movie and also the first, after being re-released by Decca, to become a number one national hit.

⇨ Small independent labels like Atlantic, Savoy, King, Federal, De Luxe, Chess, Checker, Vee Jay, Specialty, Modern, and RPM begin to rival the majors like Columbia, Decca, RCA Victor, Mercury, and Capitol and take a commanding lead in the sale of rock 'n' roll records.

⇨ On Tuesday, November 22, Steve Sholes of RCA Victor records signs Elvis Presley for a reported $35,000, paid to Sam Phillips of Sun Records for releasing Elvis from his contract. (Elvis himself received a $5,000 bonus). RCA also acquired all five previously released Sun singles and an unspecified number of unreleased recordings. Elvis's new manager, Colonel Tom Parker, negotiated the deal.

⇨ "The Royalty of Rock" make it big this year, with Elvis, Bill Haley, Fats Domino, and newcomers Chuck Berry, Little Richard, and Bo Diddley paving the way for a new direction in rock 'n' roll.

1955

DEBUT ARTISTS OF 1955

MAJOR ARTISTS

MAJOR ARTISTS	Debut Single	Label
Chuck Berry	Maybellene ⓖ	Chess
Pat Boone	Two Hearts	Dot
The Dells (Johnny Funches, Marvin Junior, Verne Allison, Mike McGill, Chuck Barksdale)	Tell The World	Vee Jay
Bo Diddley (Ellas McDaniel)	Bo Diddley	Checker
The Four Coins (George Mantalis, Jim Gregorakis, Michael James, George James)	I Love You Madly	Epic
Al Hibbler	Unchained Melody ⓖ	Decca
Etta James	The Wallflower (Dance With Me Henry)	Modern
Little Richard (Penniman)	Tutti-Frutti ⓖ	Specialty
Little Willie John	All Around The World	King
Clyde McPhatter	Seven Days	Atlantic
Jimmy Reed	You Don't Have To Go	Vee Jay
Gale Storm	I Hear You Knocking ⓖ	Dot
The Turbans (Al Banks, Matthew Platt, Charles Williams, Andrew Jones)	When You Dance	Herald
Roger Williams	Autumn Leaves ☆ ⓖ	Kapp

OTHER ARTISTS

Boyd Bennett
Lillian Briggs

Nappy Brown
Kit Carson

Chuck Berry (photo: **Norm N. Nite**)

Lillian Briggs (photo: **Alan Freed**)

Bo Diddley (photo: **Kriegsmann**)

27

ROCK ON ALMANAC

Al Hibbler (photo: *Kriegsmann*)

Little Richard

Little Willie John (photo: *Kriegsmann*)

The Colts	Julie London
Cowboy Church Sunday School	Bonnie Lou
Lenny Dee	Gloria Mann
The Dream Weavers	Chuck Miller
The Four Deuces	The Nutmegs
The Four Fellows	Fess Parker
Barry Gordon	Red Prysock
Gogi Grant	The Rainbows
Bill Hayes	The Robins
The Hearts	Bobby Scott
The Jacks	The Sensations
The Jodimars	Somethin' Smith & the Redheads
Bubber Johnson	The Valentines
Don Julian & the Meadowlarks	

HITS OF 1955

JANUARY

	Baby Doll	The Crows	Rama
☆ ⑤	**Cherry Pink And Apple Blossom White**	Perez Prado	RCA Victor
	Close Your Eyes	The Five Keys	Capitol
⑤	**Crazy Otto Medley**	Johnny Maddox	Dot
	Darling Je Vous Aime Beaucoup	Nat "King" Cole	Capitol
⑤	**How Important Can It Be?**	Joni James	MGM
	I've Got A Woman	Ray Charles	Atlantic
	Ko Ko Mo	The Crew Cuts	Mercury
☆ ⑤	**Melody Of Love**	Billy Vaughn	Dot
	No More	The De John Sisters	Epic
	Ookey Ook	The Penguins	Dootone
	Open Up Your Heart	Cowboy Church Sunday School	Decca
	Plantation Boogie	Lenny Dee	Decca
⑤	**Tweedle Dee**	Georgia Gibbs	Mercury
	You're A Heartbreaker	Elvis Presley	Sun

28

FEBRUARY

The Ballad Of Davy Crockett	Tennessee Ernie Ford	Capitol
☆ ⑥ The Ballad Of Davy Crockett	Bill Hayes	Cadence
Blue Velvet	The Clovers	Atlantic
⑥ Dance With Me Henry	Georgia Gibbs	Mercury
Don't You Know	Fats Domino	Imperial
⑥ Flip, Flop And Fly	Joe Turner	Atlantic
It's A Sin To Tell A Lie	Somethin' Smith & the Redheads	Epic
Ko Ko Mo	Perry Como	RCA Victor
Ling, Ting, Tong	The Charms	De Luxe
Mambo Rock	Bill Haley & His Comets	Decca
No More	The McGuire Sisters	Coral
Pledging My Love	Teresa Brewer	Coral
Rock Love	The Fontane Sisters	Dot
The Sand And The Sea	Nat "King" Cole	Capitol
The Wallflower (Dance With Me Henry)	Etta James	Modern

MARCH

Birth Of The Boogie	Bill Haley & His Comets	Decca
⑥ A Blossom Fell	Nat "King" Cole	Capitol
Boom Boom Boomerang	The De Castro Sisters	Abbott
Bop Ting-A-Ling	LaVern Baker	Atlantic
Don't Be Angry	Nappy Brown	Savoy
Don't Be Angry	The Crew Cuts	Mercury
Earth Angel	Gloria Mann	Sound
⑥ Every Day I Have The Blues	B. B. King	RPM
It May Sound Silly	The McGuire Sisters	Coral
Lonely Nights	The Hearts	Baton
Tell The World	The Dells	Vee Jay
This Is My Story	Gene & Eunice	Aladdin
Two Hearts	Pat Boone	Dot
Two Hearts	The Charms	De Luxe
What'cha Gonna Do	The Drifters	Atlantic

APRIL

⑥ Ain't It A Shame	Fats Domino	Imperial
The Ballad Of Davy Crockett	Fess Parker	Columbia
Bo Diddley	Bo Diddley	Checker
⑥ The Breeze And I	Caterina Valente	Decca
Heart	Eddie Fisher	RCA Victor
Heart	The Four Aces	Decca
Heaven And Paradise	Don Julian & the Meadowlarks	Dootone
⑥ Honey Babe	Art Mooney	MGM
If I May	Nat "King" Cole	Capitol
Most Of All	The Moonglows	Chess
Play Me Hearts And Flowers	Johnny Desmond	Coral
☆ ⑥ Unchained Melody	Les Baxter	Capitol
Unchained Melody	Roy Hamilton	Epic
⑥ Unchained Melody	Al Hibbler	Decca
Whatever Lola Wants	Sarah Vaughan	Mercury

29

ROCK ON ALMANAC

MAY

Baby, Let's Play House	Elvis Presley	Sun
Hey, Mr. Banjo	The Sunnysiders	Kapp
The House Of Blue Lights	Chuck Miller	Mercury
If It's The Last Thing I Do	Dinah Washington	Mercury
I Gotta New Car	Big Boy Groves	Spark
⑥ Learnin' The Blues	Frank Sinatra	Capitol
Most Of All	Don Cornell	Coral
Something's Gotta Give	The McGuire Sisters	Coral
A Story Untold	The Nutmegs	Herald
Unchained Melody	June Valli	RCA Victor
The Verdict	The Five Keys	Capitol
☆ ⑥ (We're Gonna) Rock Around The Clock	Bill Haley & His Comets	Decca
Whatever Lola Wants	Dinah Shore	RCA Victor
Why Don't You Write Me?	The Jacks	RPM
You Don't Have To Go	Jimmy Reed	Vee Jay

JUNE

⑥ Ain't That A Shame	Pat Boone	Dot
Chee Chee Oo Chee	Perry Como & Jaye P. Morgan	RCA Victor
Domani	Julius La Rosa	Cadence
Eating Goober Peas	Rusty Draper	Mercury
Feel So Good	Shirley & Lee	Aladdin
I'll Never Stop Loving You	Doris Day	Columbia
⑥ Moments To Remember	The Four Lads	Columbia
My One Sin	Nat "King" Cole	Capitol
Razzle Dazzle	Bill Haley & His Comets	Decca
Rollin' Stone	The Fontane Sisters	Dot
Silver Dollar	Teresa Brewer	Coral
Soldier Boy	The Four Fellows	Glory
A Story Untold	The Crew Cuts	Mercury
That Old Black Magic	Sammy Davis, Jr.	Decca
☆ ⑥ The Yellow Rose Of Texas	Mitch Miller	Columbia

JULY

Alabama Jubilee	The Ferko String Band	Media
Bible Tells Me So	Nick Noble	Wing
⑥ Cattle Call	Eddy Arnold	RCA Victor
Gum Drop	The Crew Cuts	Mercury
Gum Drop	Otis Williams & His New Group	De Luxe
Hummingbird Song	Les Paul & Mary Ford	Capitol
Life Is But A Dream	The Harptones	Paradise
Love Me Or Leave Me	Lena Horne	RCA Victor
⑥ Maybellene	Chuck Berry	Chess
⑥ Only You	The Platters	Mercury
Seventeen	Boyd Bennett	King
Seventeen	The Fontane Sisters	Dot
Tina Marie	Perry Como	RCA Victor
When You Dance	The Turbans	Herald
W-P-L-J	The Four Deuces	Music City

Clyde McPhatter

Jimmy Reed (photo: *Kriegsmann*)

1955

AUGUST

At My Front Door	Pat Boone	Dot
At My Front Door	The El Dorados	Vee Jay
Day By Day	The Four Freshman	Capitol
A Fool For You	Ray Charles	Atlantic
Forgive My Heart/Someone You Love	Nat "King" Cole	Capitol
Hard To Get	Gisele MacKenzie	X
It's Love, Baby	Ruth Brown	Atlantic
Love Is A Many Splendored Thing	Don Cornell	Coral
☆ ⑥ Love Is A Many Splendored Thing	The Four Aces	Decca
My Bonnie Lassie	The Ames Brothers	RCA Victor
Mystery Train	Elvis Presley	Sun
Nip Sip	The Clovers	Atlantic
Pet Me, Poppa	Rosemary Clooney	Columbia
Song Of The Dreamer	Eddie Fisher	RCA Victor
Wake The Town And Tell The People	Les Baxter	Capitol

SEPTEMBER

☆ ⑥ Autumn Leaves	Roger Williams	Kapp
⑥ Band Of Gold	Don Cherry	Columbia
Black Denim Trousers	The Cheers	Capitol
Hand Clappin'	Red Prysock	Mercury
He	Al Hibbler	Decca
I Hear You Knocking	Smiley Lewis	Imperial
⑥ I Hear You Knocking	Gale Storm	Dot
I Want You To Be My Baby	Lillian Briggs	Epic
The Longest Walk	Jaye P. Morgan	RCA Victor
My Boy Flat-Top	Boyd Bennett	King
Pete Kelly's Blues	Ray Anthony	Capitol
Shifting, Whispering Sands	Billy Vaughn Orchestra	Dot
☆ ⑥ Sixteen Tons	Tennessee Ernie Ford	Capitol
Suddenly There's A Valley	Jo Stafford	Columbia
There Goes That Train	Rollie McGill	Mercury

ROCK ON ALMANAC

Gale Storm

Roger Williams (photo: Kriegsmann)

OCTOBER

	Adorable	The Colts	Vita
	Adorable	The Drifters	Atlantic
	All Around The World	Little Willie John	King
⑥	Cry Me A River	Julie London	Liberty
⑥	It's Almost Tomorrow	The Dream Weavers	Decca
	The Kentuckian Song	Eddy Arnold	RCA Victor
⑥	Love And Marriage	Frank Sinatra	Capitol
	Nite Owl	Tony Allen	Specialty
	Rock-A-Beatin' Boogie	Bill Haley & His Comets	Decca
	Smokey Joe's Cafe	The Robins	Atco
	Speedo	The Cadillacs	Josie
	Thirty Days	Chuck Berry	Chess
⑥	Tutti-Frutti	Little Richard	Specialty
	A Woman In Love	The Four Aces	Decca
	You Are My Love	Joni James	MGM

NOVEMBER

	Burn The Candle	Bill Haley & His Comets	Decca
	Come Home	Bubber Johnson	King
	Convicted	Oscar McLollie	Modern
	Crazy For You	The Heartbeats	Hull
	Croce Di Oro (Cross Of Gold)	Patti Page	Mercury
⑥	Dungaree Doll	Eddie Fisher	RCA Victor
	Gee Whittakers	Pat Boone	Dot
	Lily Maebelle	The Valentines	Rama
	Lovely Lies	The Manhattan Brothers	London
☆ ⑥	Memories Are Made Of This	Dean Martin	Capitol
	Same Ole Saturday Night	Frank Sinatra	Capitol
⑥	Shifting, Whispering Sands	Rusty Draper	Mercury
	Well Now, Dig This	The Jodimars	Capitol
	Witchcraft	The Spiders	Imperial
	Yes Sir, That's My Baby	The Sensations	Atco

32

Band Of Gold	Kit Carson	Capitol
Chicken An' The Hawk	Joe Turner	Atlantic
Daddy-O	The Fontane Sisters	Dot
Devil Or Angel	The Clovers	Atlantic
Drown In My Own Tears	Ray Charles	Atlantic
In My Diary	The Moonglows	Chess
⑥ **Nuttin' For Christmas**	Barry Gordon	MGM
Play It Fair	LaVern Baker	Atlantic
Seven Days	Clyde McPhatter	Atlantic
So Fine	The Sheiks	Federal
Teen Age Prayer	Gale Storm	Dot
Tutti-Frutti	Pat Boone	Dot
Wanting You	Roger Williams	Kapp
The Wedding	The Chordettes	Cadence
Young Abe Lincoln	Don Cornell	Coral

TOP SINGLES OF 1955

⑥ **The Ballad Of Davy Crockett**	Bill Hayes	Cadence
⑥ **Cherry Pink And Apple Blossom White**	Perez Prado	RCA Victor
⑥ **Hearts Of Stone**	The Fontane Sisters	Dot
⑥ **Let Me Go, Lover**	Joan Weber	Columbia
⑥ **Love Is A Many Splendored Thing**	The Four Aces	Decca
⑥ **Sincerely**	The McGuire Sisters	Coral
⑥ **Sixteen Tons**	Tennessee Ernie Ford	Capitol
⑥ **Unchained Melody**	Les Baxter	Capitol
⑥ **(We're Gonna) Rock Around The Clock**	Bill Haley & His Comets	Decca
⑥ **The Yellow Rose Of Texas**	Mitch Miller	Columbia

TOP ALBUMS OF 1955

By Request	The McGuire Sisters	Coral
Crazy Otto	Crazy Otto	Decca

The Turbans (l to r: Charlie Williams, Andrew Jones, Matthew Platt, Al Banks; photo: Kriegsmann)

Deep In My Heart	Soundtrack	MGM
In The Wee Small Hours	Frank Sinatra	Capitol
Lonesome Echo	Jackie Gleason	Capitol
Love Me Or Leave Me	Soundtrack	Columbia
⑥ Merry Christmas	Bing Crosby	Decca
Music To Remember Her	Jackie Gleason	Capitol
So Smooth	Perry Como	RCA Victor
Starring Sammy Davis, Jr.	Sammy Davis, Jr.	Decca

BIRTHS AND DEATHS IN 1955

MUSIC PERFORMERS BORN IN 1955

Mike Reno (Loverboy), January 8
Howard Jones, February 23
Randy Jackson (Zebra), February 29
Dale Bozzio (Missing Persons), March 2
Dee Snider (Twisted Sister), March 15
Randy Vanwarmer, March 30
John Schneider, April 8
Louis Johnson (The Brothers Johnson), April 13
Van McLain (Shooting Star), May 3

Rosanne Cash, May 24
Joey Scarbury, June 7
John Waite, July 4
Taco (Taco Ockerse), July 21
Joe Jackson, August 11
Elvis Costello, August 25
David Lee Roth, October 10
Kevin DuBrow (Quiet Riot), October 29
Billy Idol, November 30

MUSIC PERFORMERS AND MUSIC INDUSTRY NOTABLES WHO DIED IN 1955

Charlie "Bird" Parker, Saturday, March 12 (drug abuse; 34)

OTHERS WHO DIED IN 1955

Theda Bara
Dale Carnegie
James Dean
Albert Einstein

Carmen Miranda
Honus Wagner
Cy Young

34

Bill Randle, the legendary Cleveland disc jockey who discovered Pat Boone, Johnny Ray, and Tony Bennett, among others, and who is most famous for introducing Elvis Presley into the Midwest. In January 1956, he introduced Elvis to the nation on the Tommy and Jimmy Dorsey television show.

Peter Pan *album cover*

Oklahoma! *album cover*

1955

MOVIES OF 1955

MOVIES FEATURING A POP MUSIC SOUNDTRACK

Blackboard Jungle "(We're Gonna) Rock Around The Clock" by Bill Haley & His Comets was featured during the opening and closing credits of the film, the very first to use rock 'n' roll music.

OTHER POPULAR MOVIES OF 1955

Bad Day at Black Rock
The Bridges at Toko-Ri
Davy Crockett, King of the Wild Frontier
East of Eden
Guys and Dolls
Love Is a Many Splendored Thing
Love Me or Leave Me
The Man with the Golden Arm
Marty

Mister Roberts
The Night of the Hunter
Oklahoma!
Picnic
Rebel Without a Cause
The Rose Tattoo
The Seven Year Itch
To Catch a Thief
To Hell and Back

ACADEMY AWARD WINNERS OF 1955

Best Actor: Ernest Borgnine, *Marty*
Best Actress: Anna Magnani, *The Rose Tattoo*
Best Picture: *Marty*
Best Song: "Love Is A Many Splendored Thing," *Love Is a Many Splendored Thing* (music by Sammy Fain, lyrics by Paul Francis Webster)

TOP TELEVISION SHOWS OF 1955

December Bride
Disneyland
Dragnet
I Love Lucy
I've Got a Secret

The Jack Benny Show
The Millionaire
The $64,000 Question
Toast of the Town
You Bet Your Life

1956

⇨ Blacks boycott buses in Montgomery, Alabama, triggering large, dramatic protests that ultimately lead to the end of segregation in public transportation.

⇨ George L. Wright III, 14, wins $100,000 on the TV quiz show *The Big Surprise.*

⇨ *My Fair Lady,* the Lerner and Loewe musical, debuts on Broadway.

⇨ Rebellious Archbishop Makarios is driven from Cyprus.

⇨ Heavyweight boxing champion Rocky Marciano retires undefeated.

⇨ In a Roman Catholic ceremony, actress Grace Kelly marries Ranier, Prince of Monaco.

⇨ Thomas J. Watson, Sr., developer of IBM, dies of a heart attack at the age of 82 in New York.

⇨ In a long speech to the 20th Congress of the Communist Party, Soviet Leader Nikita Khrushchev denounces Stalin.

⇨ A U.S. Senate panel charges the three national TV networks with hindering the development of other broadcasters.

⇨ The Swedish ocean liner *Stockholm* and the Italian liner *Andrea Doria* collide off Nantucket. Neither ship sinks, but 52 people are left dead or missing.

⇨ President Dwight Eisenhower and Vice President Richard Nixon are renominated as a team. In a landslide victory over Democrat Adlai E. Stevenson, they win a second term.

⇨ Dr. Albert B. Sabin of the University of Cincinnati tests an oral polio vaccine.

⇨ At the tender age of 21, Floyd Patterson takes the heavyweight title.

⇨ Actress Marilyn Monroe marries playwright Arthur Miller.

⇨ The Winter Olympics are held in Cortina di Ampezzo, Italy, and the Summer Olympics in Melbourne, Australia.

SPORTS WINNERS

Baseball   The New York Yankees beat the Brooklyn Dodgers 4 games to 3.

Football   The New York Giants beat the Chicago Bears 47–7 for the NFL championship in New York.

Basketball   The Philadelphia Warriors beat the Fort Wayne Pistons 4 games to 1 to win the NBA title.

Hockey   The Montreal Canadiens beat the Detroit Red Wings 4 games to 1 to win the Stanley Cup.

MUSIC HIGHLIGHTS OF 1956

⇨ 1956 is the year of Elvis Presley. His accomplishments this year are monumental: He has 17 charted songs, five of which go to number one, spending 25 weeks there, 16 of them consecutive. He makes 11 national television appearances and stars in a major movie. No other performer in the history of rock 'n' roll will come close to matching this.

Harry Belafonte

Almost single-handedly, Presley causes rock 'n' roll to become big business. His influence over millions of fans spans the world.

⇨ On Saturday, January 28, Elvis Presley makes his first of six live television appearances on CBS's *Jackie Gleason Stage Show,* hosted by Tommy and Jimmy Dorsey. He sings "Blue Suede Shoes" and "Heartbreak Hotel." This appearance launches Elvis mania and propels him to instant stardom.

⇨ In Elvis's second TV appearance, Saturday, February 4, again on the *Jackie Gleason Stage Show,* he sings "Tutti-Frutti" and "I Was The One." The latter song is the flip side of his first single for RCA Victor, "Heartbreak Hotel," which in April becomes the first of his 18 number one national hits, a record surpassed only by the Beatles, with 20.

⇨ Elvis's third appearance on the *Jackie Gleason Stage Show* is on Saturday, February 11. He sings "Shake, Rattle And Roll," "Flip, Flop And Fly," and "I Got A Woman."

⇨ Elvis's last three appearances on the Gleason show are on Saturday, February 18, March 17, and March 24. He sings new songs like "Baby, Let's Play House" and "Money Honey" and reprises hits like "Tutti-Frutti," "Blue Suede Shoes," and "Heartbreak Hotel."

⇨ "Doo-wop" music (group harmonies of primarily black singing groups) gains popularity with young record buyers thanks to groups like the Cleftones, Frankie Lymon & the Teenagers, the Spaniels, the Five Satins, the El Dorados, the Cadillacs, the Charms, the Platters, and the Drifters.

⇨ On Tuesday, April 3, Elvis appears on the *Milton Berle Show* live from the flight deck of the U.S.S. *Hancock* anchored in New York. He sings "Heartbreak Hotel," "Blue Suede Shoes," and "Money Honey."

⇨ The CBS radio network offers disc jockey Alan Freed a chance to do a national broadcast of his radio show, *Rock 'n' Roll Dance Party.* This show, coupled with his debut film *Rock Around the Clock,* gives Freed national exposure and makes him a very powerful figure in rock 'n' roll.

⇨ On Monday, April 23, Elvis plays Las Vegas for the first time, at the Venus Room at the Frontier Hotel. The show bombs, and he plays only one week of a scheduled two-week engagement.

⇨ On Tuesday, June 5, Elvis makes a final appearance on the Berle show, singing "I Want You, I Need You, I Love You" and "Hound Dog." This performance causes a national furor because of his wild gyrations, witnessed by millions. He becomes known as Elvis the Pelvis, a name he disliked immensely.

The Cleftones (top: Berman Patterson; middle l to r: Herb Cox, William "Buzzy" McClain; bottom l to r: Warren Corbin, Charles James)

The Coasters (top l to r: Bobby Nunn, Carl Gardner; bottom l to r: Leon Hughes, Billy Guy)

⇨ In response to critics urging him to tone down his image, on Sunday, July 1, Elvis appears on the *Steve Allen Show* dressed in white tie and black tails singing "Hound Dog" to a dog sitting on a stool. He immediately regrets this decision, feeling he was letting his fans down.

⇨ The next day, Monday, July 2, Elvis records "Hound Dog," "Don't Be Cruel," and "Anyway You Want Me." It is the first time he records in New York studios and the first time he uses the Jordanaires as background singers. "Hound Dog" and "Don't Be Cruel" become a double-sided number one hit and his biggest-selling record.

⇨ Studio 51, London's first rock 'n' roll club, opens during the summer.

⇨ On Sunday, September 9, Elvis makes his first of three appearances on Ed Sullivan's *Toast of the Town* show. He sings "Don't Be Cruel," "Hound Dog," "Ready Teddy," and "Love Me Tender." On his next appearance, on Sunday, October 28, he sings four songs, three from his first appearance and "Love Me" replacing "Ready Teddy."

⇨ On Friday, November 16, 20th Century Fox releases Elvis's debut film *Love Me Tender*. The title song becomes another number one hit.

⇨ Harry Belafonte's "Jamaica Farewell" launches the "calypso" sound.

DEBUG ARTISTS OF 1956

MAJOR ARTISTS	Debut Single	Label
Harry Belafonte	Jamaica Farewell	RCA Victor
James Brown	Please, Please, Please Ⓖ	Federal
Johnny Cash	I Walk The Line Ⓖ	Sun
The Channels (Earl Lewis, Larry Hampden, Billy Morris, Edward Doulphin, Clifton Wright)	The Closer You Are	Whirlin' Disc
The Cleftones (Herb Cox, Berman Patterson, Warren Corbin, Charles James, William McClain)	You Baby You	Gee
The Coasters (Carl Gardner, Billy Guy, Leon Hughes, Bobby Nunn)	Down In Mexico	Atco
The Diamonds (Dave Somerville, Bill Reed, Ted Kowalski, Phil Leavitt)	Why Do Fools Fall In Love	Mercury
Bill Doggett	Honky Tonk Ⓖ	King
The Five Satins (Fred Paris, Rich Freeman, Wes Forbes, Lewis Peeples, Sy Hopkins)	In The Still Of The Night Ⓖ	Ember
The Four Preps (Bruce Belland, Glen Larson, Ed Cobb, Marv Ingram)	Dreamy Eyes	Capitol
Eydie Gorme	Too Close For Comfort	ABC Paramount
George Hamilton IV	A Rose And A Baby Ruth	ABC Paramount
The Heartbeats (James "Shep" Sheppard, Wally Roker, Vernon Seavers, Robbie Brown, Albert Crump)	Crazy For You	Hull
Clarence "Frogman" Henry	Ain't Got No Home	Argo
Dick Jacobs	Main Title And Molly-O	Coral
Betty Johnson	I'll Wait	Bally
Frankie Lymon & the Teenagers (Frankie Lymon, Herman Santiago, Jimmy Merchant, Joe Negroni, Sherman Garnes)	Why Do Fools Fall In Love Ⓖ	Gee

ROCK ON ALMANAC

Roy Orbison	Ooby Dooby	Sun
Carl Perkins	Blue Suede Shoes ⑥	Sun
Marty Robbins	Singing The Blues	Columbia
Eileen Rodgers	Miracle Of Love	Columbia
David Seville	Armen's Theme	Liberty
Billy Stewart	Billy's Blues	Chess
Jerry Vale	Innamorata	Columbia
Andy Williams	Walk Hand In Hand	Cadence
Billy Williams	A Crazy Little Palace	Coral

OTHER ARTISTS

Russell Arms	Jim Lowe
Sil Austin	The Magnificents
Jesse Belvin	The Manhattan Brothers
The Bonnie Sisters	Vince Martin with the Tarriers
Buchanan & Goodman	Billy May
The Cadets	Mickey & Sylvia
Cathy Carr	Jane Morgan
George Cates	Nino & the Ebb Tides
Sanford Clark	Nervous Norvus
The Cliques	Patience & Prudence
Chris Connor	Mike Pedicin
Eddie Cooley & the Dimples	Joe Reisman
Jill Corey	Don Robertson
Bob Crewe	Don Rondo
Lonnie Donegan	The Rover Boys
The Four Esquires	The Schoolboys
The Four Lovers	The Six Teens
The Four Voices	Cyril Stapleton
The Gallahads	Morris Stoloff
The G-Clefs	Sylvia Syms
Screamin' Jay Hawkins	The Teen Queens
Eddie Heywood	The Three Friends
Dick Hyman	Joe Valino
The Jayhawks	Leroy Van Dyke
Grace Kelly	Gene Vincent & His Blue Caps
Sonny Knight	Otis Williams & His New Group
Eddie Lawrence	The Willows
The Lennon Sisters	Helmut Zacharias
Jerry Lewis	

HITS OF 1956

JANUARY

	Angels In The Sky	The Crew Cuts	Mercury
	Charmaine	The Four Freshmen	Capitol
	Daddy-O	Bonnie Lou	King
	Go On With The Wedding	Patti Page	Mercury
☆ ⑥	The Great Pretender	The Platters	Mercury
	I'll Be Home	The Flamingos	Checker
☆ ⑥	Lisbon Antigua	Nelson Riddle	Capitol
	Memories Of You	The Four Coins	Epic
⑥	No, Not Much	The Four Lads	Columbia

☆ ⑥ The Poor People Of Paris	Les Baxter	Capitol
☆ ⑥ Rock And Roll Waltz	Kay Starr	Victor
Teen Age Prayer	Gloria Mann	Sound
⑥ Why Do Fools Fall In Love	Frankie Lymon & the Teenagers	Gee
The Yellow Rose Of Texas	Stan Freberg	Capitol
You Baby You	The Cleftones	Gee

FEBRUARY

⑥ Bo Weevil	Fats Domino	Imperial
⑥ Chain Gang	Bobby Scott	ABC Paramount
Chicken	The Cheers	Capitol
Cry Baby	The Bonnie Sisters	Rainbow
Eddie My Love	The Teen Queens	RPM
If You Can Dream	The Four Aces	Decca
(Love Is) The Tender Trap	Frank Sinatra	Capitol
Main Title (Theme From *The Man with the Golden Arm*)	Billy May	Capitol
Ninety-Nine Years	Guy Mitchell	Columbia
No Money Down	Chuck Berry	Chess
Penny Nickel Dime Quarter (On A Teenage Date)	Bob Crewe	Spotlight
⑥ Rock Island Line	Lonnie Donegan	London
Rock 'N' Roll Party	Red Prysock	Mercury
⑥ See You Later, Alligator	Bill Haley & His Comets	Decca
That's Your Mistake	Otis Williams & His New Group	De Luxe

MARCH

⑥ Blue Suede Shoes	Carl Perkins	Sun
Church Bells May Ring	The Willows	Melba
Down In Mexico	The Coasters	Atco

The Diamonds (clockwise from top: Mike Douglas, Bill Reed, Dave Somerville, Ted Kowalski)

The Heartbeats (l to r: Robbie Brown, Wally Roker, James Sheppard, Vernon Seavers, Albert Crump; photo: Kriegsmann)

41

☆ ⑥ Heartbreak Hotel/I Was The One	Elvis Presley	RCA Victor
Hi-Lili, Hi-Lo	The Dick Hyman Trio	MGM
☆ ⑥ Hot Diggity	Perry Como	RCA Victor
Ivory Tower	Cathy Carr	Fraternity
A Kiss From Your Lips	The Flamingos	Checker
⑥ Long Tall Sally/Slippin' And Slidin'	Little Richard	Specialty
Look Homeward Angel	The Four Esquires	London
R-O-C-K	Bill Haley & His Comets	Decca
⑥ A Tear Fell	Teresa Brewer	Coral
Too Young To Go Steady	Nat "King" Cole	Capitol
Woe Is Me	The Cadillacs	Josie
(You've Got) The Magic Touch	The Platters	Mercury

APRIL

Blue Suede Shoes	Elvis Presley	RCA Victor
⑥ Corrine Corrina	Joe Turner	Atlantic
Girl Of My Dreams	The Cliques	Modern
⑥ The Happy Whistler	Don Robertson	Capitol
⑥ I'm In Love Again/My Blue Heaven	Fats Domino	Imperial
Innamorata	Dean Martin	Capitol
I Want You To Be My Girl	Frankie Lymon & the Teenagers	Gee
Little Girl Of Mine	The Cleftones	Gee
☆ ⑥ Moonglow And Theme From Picnic	Morris Stoloff	Decca
Mr. Wonderful	Sarah Vaughan	Mercury
⑥ On The Street Where You Live	Vic Damone	Columbia
⑥ Please, Please, Please	James Brown	Federal
Standing On The Corner	The Four Lads	Columbia
⑥ Treasure Of Love	Clyde McPhatter	Atlantic
☆ ⑥ The Wayward Wind	Gogi Grant	Era

MAY

⑥ Allegheny Moon	Patti Page	Mercury
⑥ Be-Bop-A-Lula	Gene Vincent & His Blue Caps	Capitol
Church Bells May Ring	The Diamonds	Mercury
Glendora	Perry Como	RCA Victor
Graduation Day	The Rover Boys	ABC Paramount
Hot Dog Buddy Buddy	Bill Haley & His Comets	Decca
How Little We Know	Frank Sinatra	Capitol
☆ ⑥ I Almost Lost My Mind	Pat Boone	Dot
I Could Have Danced All Night	Rosemary Clooney	Columbia
It Only Hurts For A Little While	The Ames Brothers	RCA Victor
☆ ⑥ I Want You, I Need You, I Love You/My Baby Left Me	Elvis Presley	RCA Victor
⑥ Picnic	The McGuire Sisters	Coral
Right Now, Right Now	Alan Freed & His Rock 'N' Roll Band	Coral

1956

Sonny James (photo: *Kier*)   **Roy Orbison**   **Carl Perkins**

Ruby Baby	The Drifters	Atlantic
Second Fiddle	Kay Starr	RCA Victor

JUNE

Blanche	The Three Friends	Lido
Boppin' The Blues	Carl Perkins	Sun
Can't We Be Sweethearts	The Cleftones	Gee
Can You Find It In Your Heart	Tony Bennett	Columbia
It's Too Late	Chuck Willis	Atlantic
Ka-Ding-Dong	The G-Clefs	Pilgrim
Love, Love, Love	The Clovers	Atlantic
☆ ⓖ **My Prayer/Heaven On Earth**	The Platters	Mercury
Ooby Dooby	Roy Orbison	Sun
ⓖ **Roll Over Beethoven**	Chuck Berry	Chess
A Sweet Old Fashioned Girl	Teresa Brewer	Coral
Transfusion	Nervous Norvus	Dot
Walk Hand In Hand	Tony Martin	RCA Victor
We Go Together	The Moonglows	Chess
ⓖ **Whatever Will Be, Will Be** **(Que Sera, Sera)**	Doris Day	Columbia

JULY

Born To Be With You	The Chordettes	Cadence
A Casual Look	The Six Teens	Flip
The Closer You Are	The Channels	Whirlin' Disc
ⓖ **Fever**	Little Willie John	King
The Fool	Sanford Clark	Dot
☆ ⓖ **Hound Dog/Don't Be Cruel**	Elvis Presley	RCA Victor
ⓖ **In The Still Of The Night**	The Five Satins	Ember
I Promise To Remember	Frankie Lymon & the Teenagers	Gee
ⓖ **Rip It Up/Ready Teddy**	Little Richard	Specialty
Stranded In The Jungle	The Cadets	Modern
Stranded In The Jungle	The Jayhawks	Flash
That's All There Is To That	Nat "King" Cole	Capitol
Up On The Mountain	The Magnificents	Vee Jay

When My Dreamboat Comes Home/So-Long	Fats Domino	Imperial
You Don't Know Me	Jerry Vale	Columbia

AUGUST

	After The Lights Are Down Low	Al Hibbler	Decca
Ⓖ	Canadian Sunset	Hugo Winterhalter	RCA Victor
Ⓖ	Flying Saucer	Buchanan & Goodman	Luniverse
Ⓖ	Friendly Persuasion (Thee I Love)	Pat Boone	Dot
Ⓖ	Honky Tonk	Bill Doggett	King
	In A Shanty In Old Shanty Town	Somethin' Smith & the Redheads	Epic
	I Only Know I Love You	The Four Aces	Decca
Ⓖ	Oh, What A Night	The Dells	Vee Jay
	The Old Philosopher	Eddie Lawrence	Coral
	Portuguese Washerwoman	Joe "Fingers" Carr	Capitol
	The Shrine Of St. Cecilia	The Harptones	Rama
	Somebody Up There Likes Me	Perry Como	RCA Victor
	Theme From The Proud Ones	Nelson Riddle	Capitol
Ⓖ	Tonight You Belong To Me	Patience & Prudence	Liberty
	Voices	The Fontane Sisters	Dot

SEPTEMBER

	Blue Moon	Elvis Presley	RCA Victor
	The Bus Stop Song (A Paper Of Pins)	The Four Lads	Columbia
	Canadian Sunset	Andy Williams	Cadence
	Cindy, Oh Cindy	Vince Martin with the Tarriers	Glory
Ⓖ	I Walk The Line	Johnny Cash	Sun
Ⓖ	Just Walking In The Rain	Johnnie Ray	Columbia
Ⓖ	Let The Good Times Roll	Shirley & Lee	Aladdin
	Mama From The Train	Patti Page	Mercury
	Now Is The Hour	Gale Storm	Dot
	See Saw/When I'm With You	The Moonglows	Chess
	Song For A Summer Night	Mitch Miller	Columbia
Ⓖ	True Love	Bing Crosby & Grace Kelly	Capitol
	Tumbling Tumbleweeds	Roger Williams	Kapp
	When The Lilacs Bloom Again	Helmut Zacharias	Decca
	You'll Never Know/It Isn't Right	The Platters	Mercury

OCTOBER

Ⓖ	Blueberry Hill	Fats Domino	Imperial
	From The Bottom Of My Heart	The Clovers	Atlantic
	Garden Of Eden	Joe Valino	Vik
	Gonna Get Along Without Ya Now	Patience & Prudence	Liberty
☆ Ⓖ	The Green Door	Jim Lowe	Dot
	Hey! Jealous Lover	Frank Sinatra	Capitol
	Jamaica Farewell	Harry Belafonte	RCA Victor

44

Frankie Lymon & the Teenagers (top l to r: Jimmy Merchant, Herman Santiago, Joe Negroni, Sherman Garnes; bottom: Frankie Lymon; photo: Kriegsmann)

Gene Vincent & His Blue Caps (clockwise from top: Jumpin' Jack Neal, Be-Bop Harrell, Gene Vincent, Wee Willie Williams, Galloping Cliff Gallup; photo: Bruno of Hollywood)

1956

	Just In Time	Tony Bennett	Columbia
☆ ⑥	Love Me Tender/Anyway You Want Me	Elvis Presley	RCA Victor
	Out Of Sight, Out Of Mind	The Five Keys	Capitol
	Priscilla	Eddie Cooley & the Dimples	Roost
	Rudy's Rock	Bill Haley & His Comets	Decca
☆ ⑥	Singing The Blues	Guy Mitchell	Columbia
	Too Much Monkey Business/ Brown Eyed Handsome Man	Chuck Berry	Chess
⑥	Two Different Worlds	Don Rondo	Jubilee

NOVEMBER

	The ABC's Of Love	Frankie Lymon & the Teenagers	Gee
⑥	The Auctioneer	Leroy Van Dyke	Dot
	Buchanan And Goodman On Trial	Buchanan & Goodman	Luniverse
	Confidential	Sonny Knight	Dot
	I Feel Good	Shirley & Lee	Aladdin
	I Put A Spell On You	Screamin' Jay Hawkins	Okeh
	I Saw Esau	The Ames Brothers	RCA Victor
⑥	Love Is Strange	Mickey & Sylvia	Groove
	Love Me/When My Blue Moon Turns To Gold Again	Elvis Presley	RCA Victor
⑥	Rock-A-Bye Your Baby	Jerry Lewis	Decca
	A Rose And A Baby Ruth	George Hamilton IV	ABC Paramount
⑥	Since I Met You, Baby	Ivory Joe Hunter	Atlantic
	Slow Walk	Sil Austin	Mercury
	A Thousand Miles Away	The Heartbeats	Hull
	Written On The Wind	The Four Aces	Decca

ROCK ON ALMANAC

DECEMBER

Ain't Got No Home	Clarence "Frogman" Henry	Argo
Cindy, Oh Cindy	Eddie Fisher	RCA Victor
Dreamy Eyes	The Four Preps	Capitol
I Dreamed	Betty Johnson	Bally
I Miss You So	Chris Connor	Atlantic
I'm Not A Juvenile Delinquent	Frankie Lymon & the Teenagers	Gee
ⓖ Mary's Boy Child	Harry Belafonte	RCA Victor
ⓖ Moonlight Gambler	Frankie Laine	Columbia
Night Lights	Nat "King" Cole	Capitol
Old Shep	Elvis Presley	RCA Victor
On My Word Of Honor	The Platters	Mercury
Poor Boy	Elvis Presley	RCA Victor
What's The Reason I'm Not Pleasing You	Fats Domino	Imperial
Without Love (There Is Nothing)	Clyde McPhatter	Atlantic
You Gave Me Peace Of Mind	The Spaniels	Vee Jay

TOP SINGLES OF 1956

ⓖ Don't Be Cruel/Hound Dog	Elvis Presley	RCA Victor
ⓖ Heartbreak Hotel	Elvis Presley	RCA Victor
ⓖ I Want You, I Need You, I Love You	Elvis Presley	RCA Victor
ⓖ Lisbon Antigua	Nelson Riddle	Capitol
ⓖ Love Me Tender	Elvis Presley	RCA Victor
ⓖ Memories Are Made Of This	Dean Martin	Capitol
ⓖ My Prayer	The Platters	Mercury
ⓖ The Poor People Of Paris	Les Baxter	Capitol

Dick Clark, with scooters

Paramount Theater (photo: Herb Cox)

My Fair Lady *album cover*   The King And I *album cover*

1956

ⓖ Singing The Blues   Guy Mitchell   Columbia
ⓖ The Wayward Wind   Gogi Grant   Era

TOP ALBUMS OF 1956

Ballads Of The Day	Nat "King" Cole	Capitol
ⓖ Belafonte	Harry Belafonte	RCA Victor
ⓖ Calypso	Harry Belafonte	RCA Victor
The Eddy Duchin Story	Soundtrack	Decca
ⓖ Elvis Presley	Elvis Presley	RCA Victor
ⓖ The King And I	Soundtrack	Capitol
ⓖ My Fair Lady	Original Cast	Columbia
ⓖ Oklahoma!	Soundtrack	Capitol
The Platters	The Platters	Mercury
ⓖ Songs For Swingin' Lovers!	Frank Sinatra	Capitol

BIRTHS AND DEATHS IN 1956

MUSIC PERFORMERS BORN IN 1956

Gary Portnoy, January 1
Paul Young, January 17
Tom Bailey (Thompson Twins), January 18
Peter Schilling, January 28

Debby Boone, September 22
Mike Score (A Flock of Seagulls),
   November 5

MUSIC PERFORMERS AND MUSIC INDUSTRY NOTABLES WHO DIED IN 1956

Victor Young, Sunday, November 11 (heart
   attack; 56)

Tommy Dorsey, Monday, November 26
   (choking; 51)

OTHERS WHO DIED IN 1956

Fred Allen
Bela Lugosi

Connie Mack
Babe Didrikson Zaharias

MOVIES OF 1956

MOVIES FEATURING POP MUSIC ARTISTS

Don't Knock the Rock *Stars:* Disc jockey Alan Freed, Alan Dale. *Featured songs:*
   "Don't Knock The Rock" and "Hot Dog Buddy Buddy" by Bill Haley & His Comets,

47

"Tutti-Frutti" and "Long Tall Sally" by Little Richard. *Other musical performers:* The Treniers, Dave Appell & His Applejacks. Sequel to *Rock Around the Clock*.

The Girl Can't Help It   *Stars:* Jayne Mansfield, Tom Ewell, Edmond O'Brien. *Featured songs:* "Cry Me A River" by Julie London, "The Girl Can't Help It," "She's Got It," and "Ready Teddy" by Little Richard, "Blue Monday" by Fats Domino, "You'll Never Know" by the Platters, "Be-Bop-A-Lula" by Gene Vincent & His Blue Caps, and "Twenty Flight Rock" by Eddie Cochran. *Other musical performers:* Ray Anthony, Barry Gordon, the Three Chuckles, Eddie Fontaine, Abbey Lincoln, the Treniers. First rock movie shot in color.

Love Me Tender   *Stars:* Elvis Presley (in his very first motion picture), Richard Egan, Debra Paget. *Featured songs:* "Love Me Tender," "Poor Boy."

Rock Around the Clock   *Stars:* Disc jockey Alan Freed, Alan Dale. *Featured songs:* "Rock Around The Clock," "Rudy's Rock," "See You Later, Alligator," "Rock-A-Beatin' Boogie," "Mambo Rock," "Razzle Dazzle," and "R-O-C-K" by Bill Haley & His Comets, "Only You" and "The Great Pretender" by the Platters. *Other musical performers:* Freddy Bell & the Bellboys, Tony Martinez. The very first movie about rock 'n' roll that starred rock acts of the time. The title of this film came as a result of the popularity of the song "Rock Around The Clock," featured in the 1955 film *Blackboard Jungle*.

Rock, Rock, Rock   *Stars:* Disk jockey Alan Freed, Teddy Randazzo, newcomer Tuesday Weld. *Featured songs:* "Baby Baby" and "I'm Not A Juvenile Delinquent" by Frankie Lymon & the Teenagers, "Tra La La" by LaVern Baker, "Over And Over Again" by the Moonglows, "Right Now, Right Now" by Alan Freed & His Rock 'N' Roll Band. *Other musical performers:* Chuck Berry, the Three Chuckles, the Johnny Burnette Trio, the Flamingos, Cirino & the Bowties, Jimmy Cavallo & the House Rockers.

Shake, Rattle and Rock   *Stars:* Touch (Mike) Connors, Margaret Dumont, Sterling Holloway. *Featured songs:* "Ain't It A Shame," "I'm In Love Again," and "Honey Chile" by Fats Domino, "Lipstick, Powder And Paint" by Joe Turner.

OTHER POPULAR MOVIES OF 1956

Around the World in 80 Days
Baby Doll
Bus Stop
Davy Crockett and the River Pirates
Forbidden Planet
Friendly Persuasion
Giant
Invasion of the Body Snatchers

The King and I
Lust for Life
The Man in the Gray Flannel Suit
The Rack
The Searchers
The Ten Commandments
Trapeze

ACADEMY AWARD WINNERS OF 1956

Best Actor: Yul Brynner, *The King and I*
Best Actress: Ingrid Bergman, *Anastasia*
Best Picture: *Around the World in 80 Days*
Best Song: "Whatever Will Be, Will Be (Que Sera, Sera)," *The Man Who Knew Too Much* (music and lyrics by Jay Livingston and Ray Evans)

TOP TELEVISION SHOWS OF 1956

Alfred Hitchcock Presents
December Bride
General Electric Theater
Gunsmoke
I Love Lucy

I've Got a Secret
The Jack Benny Show
The Perry Como Show
The $64,000 Question
Toast of the Town

1957

NEWS HIGHLIGHTS OF 1957

⇨ Andrei Gromyko replaces Dmitri T. Shepilov as Soviet foreign minister.

⇨ Ghana, formerly the British colony known as the Gold Coast, achieves independence as the first new nation in Africa in the 20th century, marking the beginning of the end of the British Empire.

⇨ A panel appointed by the American Heart Association, the American Cancer Society, and the National Heart and Cancer Institutes reports a direct cause-and-effect relationship between smoking and lung cancer.

⇨ In its first test, an Atlas intercontinental missile explodes shortly after takeoff from Cape Canaveral, Florida.

⇨ The Reverend Dr. Billy Graham attracts 100,000 people, the largest crowd in Yankee Stadium's history.

⇨ Armed for another civil war, federal troops escort blacks into schools in Little Rock, Arkansas.

⇨ The Soviet Union launches into orbit the first artificial satellite, *Sputnik I.*

⇨ The Soviet Union launches a second space satellite carrying a dog named Laika.

⇨ In a rivetingly unique role, Joanne Woodward plays three parts in one character in *The Three Faces of Eve.* She later wins an Oscar for her portrayal.

⇨ Jimmy Hoffa is elected president of the powerful Teamsters labor union.

⇨ President Eisenhower suffers a stroke.

⇨ Gangland leaders are arrested at a Mafia meeting at Apalachin, New York.

⇨ The Ford Motor Company introduces the Edsel, ballyhooed as the best-engineered automobile ever designed. It would become the most famous flop in automotive history.

⇨ Baseball's Giants play their last season in New York, and the Dodgers their last season in Brooklyn.

SPORTS WINNERS

Baseball   The Milwaukee Braves beat the New York Yankees 4 games to 3.

Football   The Detroit Lions beat the Cleveland Browns 54–14 for the NFL championship in Detroit.

Basketball   The Boston Celtics beat the St. Louis Hawks 4 games to 3 to win the NBA title.

Hockey   The Montreal Canadiens beat the Boston Bruins 4 games to 1 to win the Stanley Cup.

MUSIC HIGHLIGHTS OF 1957

⇨ On Sunday, January 6, Elvis makes his last appearance on Ed Sullivan's *Toast of the Town.* This would also be his last live televised appearance for more than three years. He sings seven songs: "Love Me Tender," "Hound Dog," "Don't Be Cruel," "Heartbreak Hotel," "Too Much," "When My Blue Moon Turns To Gold Again," and "Peace In The Valley."

⇨ For the very first time in rock 'n' roll, two versions of the same song become number one national hits: "Young Love" by Sonny James on Capitol and by Tab Hunter on Dot.

⇨ The Cavern Club opens in Liverpool, England. The Beatles would become the house band four years later.

⇨ John Lennon and Paul McCartney meet for the first time at a church picnic and discover a common interest in American rock 'n' roll.

⇨ The National Academy of Recording Arts and Sciences (NARAS) is established.

⇨ The popular singing group Frankie Lymon & the Teenagers disbands, with young Frankie going out as a solo performer.

⇨ Pat Boone makes his acting debut in *Bernardine.*

⇨ On Monday, August 5, from 3:00 to 4:30 P.M., ABC television launches 28-year-old Dick

Clark's *American Bandstand* show. A staple on local WFIL television in Philadelphia since 1952, this show would go on to become a major force in the growth of rock 'n' roll. The very first record played on the show is Buddy Holly's group the Crickets doing "That'll Be The Day." Dick's very first guest is Billy Williams, singing his hit "I'm Gonna Sit Right Down And Write Myself A Letter."

⇨ On Saturday, October 5, while appearing in Sydney, Australia, Little Richard announces to his band members that he is giving up show business and going back to God. He says that the Russian satellite *Sputnik,* launched the night before, is a sign from God to give up the evils of rock 'n' roll. To show band member Clifford Burks he is serious about this, Richard tosses several rings worth thousands of dollars into a river.

⇨ *The Adventures of Ozzie and Harriet* television show features 17-year-old Ricky Nelson singing songs like "A Teenager's Romance" and "I'm Walking." He is the first of a flock of new singers, the teen idols. Others like Paul Anka, Frankie Avalon, Fabian, and Bobby Rydell were quick to follow.

DEBUT ARTISTS OF 1957

MAJOR ARTISTS	Debut Single	Label
Paul Anka	Diana ☆ Ⓖ	ABC Paramount
Bobby "Blue" Bland	Farther Up The Road	Duke
The Chantels (Arlene Smith, Sonia Goring, Lois Harris, Jackie Landry, Renee Minus)	He's Gone	End
Patsy Cline	Walkin' After Midnight	Decca
Eddie Cochran	Sittin' In The Balcony	Liberty
Sam Cooke	You Send Me ☆ Ⓖ	Keen
The Crests (Johnny Maestro, Jay Carter, Harrold Torres, Tommy Gough)	Sweetest One	Joyce
The Crickets (Buddy Holly, Joe B. Mauldin, Jerry Allison)	That'll Be The Day ☆ Ⓖ	Brunswick
Danny & the Juniors (Danny Rapp, Dave White, Frank Maffei, Joe Terranova)	At The Hop ☆ Ⓖ	ABC Paramount
Bobby Day	Little Bitty Pretty One	Class
Jimmy Dean	Deep Blue Sea	Columbia
The Del Vikings (Norman Wright, Corinthian "Kripp" Johnson, Donald "Gus" Bakus, David Lerchey, Clarence E. Quick)	Come Go With Me Ⓖ	Dot

Paul Anka (photo: Kier)

Eddie Cochran

Sam Cooke

The Dubs (Richard Blandon, Cleveland Still, Cordell Brown, Tommy Grate, James Miller)	Don't Ask Me To Be Lonely	Gone
The Everly Brothers (Don and Phil)	Bye, Bye Love ⑥	Cadence
Bobby Helms	Fraulein	Decca
Buddy Holly	Peggy Sue/Everyday ⑥	Coral
Tab Hunter	Young Love ☆ ⑥	Dot
Sonny James	Young Love ☆ ⑥	Capitol
The Jesters (Lennie McKay, Adam Jackson, Jimmy Smith, Melvin Lewis, Donald Lewis)	Love No One But You	Winley
Buddy Knox	Party Doll ☆ ⑥	Roulette
Brenda Lee	One Step At A Time	Decca
Jerry Lee Lewis	Whole Lot Of Shakin' Going On ⑥	Sun
Little Junior Parker	Next Time You See Me	Duke
Johnny Mathis	Wonderful! Wonderful! ⑥	Columbia
Johnny Nash	A Very Special Love	ABC Paramount
Ricky Nelson	A Teenager's Romance/ I'm Walking	Verve
Ray Price	My Shoes Keep Walking Back To You	Columbia
Della Reese	And That Reminds Me	Jubilee
Jimmie Rodgers	Honeycomb ☆ ⑥	Roulette
Tommy Sands	Teen-Age Crush	Capitol
Conway Twitty	I Need Your Lovin'	Mercury
Jackie Wilson	Reet Petite	Brunswick

OTHER ARTISTS

The Chuck Alaimo Quartet
Lee Andrews & the Hearts
Doc Bagby
Joe Bennett & the Sparkletones
Billy & Lillie
The Bobbettes

Jimmy Bowen
Jo-Ann Campbell
The Cellos
The Charts
Ray Conniff
The Crescendos

Buddy Holly & the Crickets (clockwise from top: Buddy Holly, Joe B. Mauldin, Jerry Allison; photo: Kriegsmann)

The Del Vikings (top: "Kripp" Johnson; middle l to r: "Gus" Bakus, Clarence Quick, Dave Lerchey; bottom: Norman Wright)

1957

Jimmy Dee
Johnny Dee
Tommy Edwards
Ernie Freeman
Paul Gayten
Terry Gilkyson & the Easy Riders
The Gladiolas
Ron Goodwin
Charlie Gracie
Bonnie Guitar
Russ Hamilton
Thurston Harris
Dale Hawkins
Johnny Heartsman
The Hollywood Flames
Ferlin Husky
The Jive Bombers
Johnnie & Joe
Bill Justis
Annie Laurie
Little Joe & the Thrillers
Hank Locklin
The Mello-Kings

The Mello-Tones
Sal Mineo
Billy Myles
The Paragons
Webb Pierce
Marvin Rainwater
Margie Rayburn
The Rays
Debbie Reynolds
Timmie Rogers
Jodie Sands
The Shepherd Sisters
Huey "Piano" Smith & the Clowns
Randy Starr
Nick Todd
Tom & Jerry
The Tune Weavers
The Valiants
The Velours
Noble "Thin Man" Watts
Andre Williams
Larry Williams

HITS OF 1957

JANUARY

⑥ **Banana Boat (Day-O)**	Harry Belafonte	RCA Victor
The Banana Boat Song	The Tarriers	Glory
⑥ **Blue Monday**	Fats Domino	Imperial
⑥ **Come Go With Me**	The Del Vikings	Dot
Don't Knock The Rock	Bill Haley & His Comets	Decca
The Girl Can't Help It	Little Richard	Specialty
⑥ **Gone**	Ferlin Husky	Capitol

53

The Everly Brothers (l to r: Don Everly, Phil Everly; photo: Kriegsmann)   *Brenda Lee (photo: Bruno of Hollywood)*

⑥	Jim Dandy	LaVern Baker	Atlantic
	Love Is Strange	Mickey & Sylvia	Groove
⑥	Marianne	Terry Gilkyson & the Easy Riders	Columbia
☆ ⑥	Too Much/Playing For Keeps	Elvis Presley	RCA Victor
	Wisdom Of A Fool	The Five Keys	Capitol
⑥	Wonderful! Wonderful!	Johnny Mathis	Columbia
☆ ⑥	Young Love	Tab Hunter	Dot
☆ ⑥	Young Love	Sonny James	Capitol

FEBRUARY

	Bad Boy	Jive Bombers	Savoy
⑥	Butterfly	Charlie Gracie	Cameo
☆ ⑥	Don't Forbid Me/Anastasia	Pat Boone	Dot
	Fools Fall In Love	The Drifters	Atlantic
	I'm Sorry/He's Mine	The Platters	Mercury
⑥	I'm Sticking With You	Jimmy Bowen	Roulette
⑥	I'm Walkin'	Fats Domino	Imperial
	Just Because	Lloyd Price	KRC
⑥	Little Darlin'	The Diamonds	Mercury
⑥	Lucky Lips	Ruth Brown	Atlantic
☆ ⑥	Party Doll	Buddy Knox	Roulette
⑥	Sittin' In The Balcony	Eddie Cochran	Liberty
⑥	Teen-Age Crush	Tommy Sands	Capitol
	Teenage Love/Paper Castles	Frankie Lymon & the Teenagers	Gee
	Who Needs You	The Four Lads	Columbia

MARCH

☆ ⑥	All Shook Up/That's When Your Heartaches Begin	Elvis Presley	RCA Victor
	Banana Boat (Day-O)	Stan Freberg	Capitol
	C. C. Rider	Chuck Willis	Atlantic
	Chantez Chantez	Dinah Shore	RCA Victor
⑥	It's Not For Me To Say	Johnny Mathis	Columbia
⑥	Lucille/Send Me Some Lovin'	Little Richard	Specialty
	Matchbox	Carl Perkins	Sun
	My Girl Friend	The Cadillacs	Josie

Rock-A-Billy	Guy Mitchell	Columbia
☆ ⑥ Round And Round	Perry Como	RCA Victor
⑥ School Day/Deep Feeling	Chuck Berry	Chess
Shirley	The Schoolboys	Okeh
⑥ So Rare	Jimmy Dorsey	Fraternity
Walkin' After Midnight	Patsy Cline	Decca
⑥ Why Baby Why?	Pat Boone	Dot

APRIL

Crazy Love	Frank Sinatra	Capitol
Dark Moon	Bonnie Guitar	Dot
⑥ Empty Arms	Ivory Joe Hunter	Atlantic
⑥ Four Walls	Jim Reeves	RCA Victor
Freight Train	Rusty Draper	Mercury
Gonna Find Me A Bluebird	Marvin Rainwater	MGM
⑥ Mama Look-A Booboo	Harry Belafonte	RCA Victor
Ninety-Nine Ways	Charlie Gracie	Cameo
One Step At A Time	Brenda Lee	Decca
Over The Mountain, Across The Sea	Johnnie & Joe	Chess
Peace In The Valley	Elvis Presley	RCA Victor
Rosie Lee	The Mello-Tones	Gee
⑥ Start Movin'	Sal Mineo	Epic
There Oughta Be A Law	Mickey & Sylvia	Vik
⑥ A White Sport Coat (And A Pink Carnation)	Marty Robbins	Columbia

MAY

⑥ Bye, Bye Love	The Everly Brothers	Cadence
Everyone's Laughing	The Spaniels	Vee Jay
Florence	The Paragons	Winley
I Like Your Kind Of Love	Andy Williams	Cadence
⑥ I'm Gonna Sit Right Down And Write Myself A Letter	Billy Williams	Coral
⑥ It's You I Love	Fats Domino	Imperial
Jim Dandy Got Married	LaVern Baker	Atlantic
Long Lonely Nights	Lee Andrews & the Hearts	Chess
☆ ⑥ Love Letters In The Sand/ Bernardine	Pat Boone	Dot
Rang Tang Ding Dong	The Cellos	Apollo
⑥ Searchin'/Young Blood	The Coasters	Atco
Send For Me	Nat "King" Cole	Capitol
⑥ Stardust	Billy Ward & His Dominoes	Liberty
Susie-Q	Dale Hawkins	Checker
A Teenager's Romance/I'm Walkin'	Ricky Nelson	Verve

JUNE

Around The World	Victor Young	Decca
Arrow Of Love	The Six Teens	Flip

Can I Come Over Tonight	The Velours	Onyx
Don't Ask Me To Be Lonely	The Dubs	Gone
Flying Saucer The 2nd	Buchanan & Goodman	Luniverse
Goody Goody	Frankie Lymon	Gee
⑥ Jenny, Jenny/Miss Ann	Little Richard	Specialty
⑥ Old Cape Cod	Patti Page	Mercury
Rainbow	Russ Hamilton	Kapp
Shangri-La	The Four Coins	Epic
⑥ Short Fat Fannie	Larry Williams	Specialty
Tonite, Tonite	The Mello-Kings	Herald
Valley Of Tears	Fats Domino	Imperial
Whispering Bells	The Del Vikings	Dot
⑥ Whole Lotta Shakin' Going On	Jerry Lee Lewis	Sun

JULY

Cool Shake	The Del Vikings	Mercury
Deserie	The Charts	Everlast
☆ ⑥ Diana	Paul Anka	ABC Paramount
A Fallen Star	The Hilltoppers	Dot
Farther Up The Road	Bobby "Blue" Bland	Duke
☆ ⑥ (Let Me Be Your) Teddy Bear/ Loving You	Elvis Presley	RCA Victor
Lotta Lovin'	Gene Vincent & His Blue Caps	Capitol
Mr. Lee	The Bobbettes	Atlantic
Oh Baby Doll	Chuck Berry	Chess
Remember You're Mine	Pat Boone	Dot
⑥ Rocking Pneumonia And The Boogie Woogie Flu	Huey "Piano" Smith & the Clowns	Ace
Sweetest One	The Crests	Joyce
☆ ⑥ Tammy	Debbie Reynolds	Coral
☆ ⑥ That'll Be The Day	The Crickets	Brunswick
To The Aisle	The Five Satins	Ember

AUGUST

Alone	The Shepherd Sisters	Lance
And That Reminds Me	Della Reese	Jubilee
Black Slacks	Joe Bennett & the Sparkletones	ABC Paramount
☆ ⑥ Chances Are/Twelfth Of Never	Johnny Mathis	Columbia
Dumplin's	Doc Bagby	Okeh
⑥ Fascination	Jane Morgan	Kapp
Happy, Happy Birthday Baby	The Tune Weavers	Checker
☆ ⑥ Honeycomb	Jimmie Rodgers	Roulette
Hula Love	Buddy Knox	Roulette
⑥ In The Middle Of An Island	Tony Bennett	Columbia
Love Me To Pieces	Jill Corey	Columbia
Swingin' Sweethearts	Ron Goodwin	Capitol
⑥ White Silver Sands	Don Rondo	Jubilee
You're My One And Only Love	Ricky Nelson	Verve
Zip Zip	The Diamonds	Mercury

SEPTEMBER

	An Affair To Remember	Vic Damone	Columbia
Ⓖ	All The Way/Chicago	Frank Sinatra	Capitol
	Back To School Again	Timmie Rogers	Cameo
Ⓖ	Be-Bop Baby	Ricky Nelson	Imperial
	He's Gone	The Chantels	End
☆ Ⓖ	Jailhouse Rock/Treat Me Nice	Elvis Presley	RCA Victor
	Just Between You And Me	The Chordettes	Cadence
Ⓖ	Keep A Knockin'	Little Richard	Specialty
Ⓖ	Little Bitty Pretty One	Thurston Harris	Aladdin
	Love Me Forever	The Four Esquires	Paris
Ⓖ	Melodie D'Amour	The Ames Brothers	RCA Victor
Ⓖ	My Special Angel	Bobby Helms	Decca
	Peanuts	Little Joe & the Thrillers	Okeh
Ⓖ	Silhouettes/Daddy Cool	The Rays	Cameo
☆ Ⓖ	Wake Up Little Suzy	The Everly Brothers	Cadence

OCTOBER

☆ Ⓖ	April Love	Pat Boone	Dot
Ⓖ	Bony Moronie	Larry Williams	Specialty
	Buzz-Buzz-Buzz	The Hollywood Flames	Ebb
	Deep Purple	Billy Ward & His Dominoes	Liberty
	I'm Available	Margie Rayburn	Liberty
	The Joker	Billy Myles	Ember
Ⓖ	Peggy Sue/Everyday	Buddy Holly	Coral
	Pretend You Don't See Her	Jerry Vale	Columbia
Ⓖ	Raunchy	Bill Justis	Philips
	Reet Petite	Jackie Wilson	Brunswick
Ⓖ	Rock And Roll Music	Chuck Berry	Chess
	Soft	Bill Doggett	King
	Tear Drops	Lee Andrews & the Hearts	Chess
	Wait And See	Fats Domino	Imperial
☆ Ⓖ	You Send Me	Sam Cooke	Keen

Jerry Lee Lewis

57

ROCK ON
ALMANAC

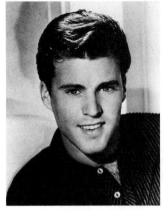

Ricky Nelson (photo: *Kier*)

Jackie Wilson (photo: *Kier*)

NOVEMBER

	After New Year's Eve	The Heartbeats	Gee
☆ ⑥	At The Hop/Sometimes When I'm All Alone	Danny & the Juniors	ABC Paramount
	The Big Beat	Fats Domino	Imperial
	Could This Be Magic	The Dubs	Gone
⑥	Great Balls Of Fire	Jerry Lee Lewis	Sun
	Hard Times (The Slop)	Noble "Thin Man" Watts	Baton
	Hey, Schoolgirl	Tom & Jerry	Big
⑥	I'll Come Running Back To You	Sam Cooke	Specialty
⑥	Kisses Sweeter Than Wine	Jimmie Rodgers	Roulette
	My Juanita	The Crests	Joyce
	Nervous Boogie	Paul Gayten	Argo
	Oh, Boy!/Not Fade Away	The Crickets	Brunswick
	Put A Light In The Window	The Four Lads	Columbia
	This Is The Night	The Valiants	Keen
	Wun'erful, Wun'erful!	Stan Freberg	Capitol

DECEMBER

	Dance To The Bop	Gene Vincent & His Blue Caps	Capitol
	Do What You Did	Thurston Harris	Aladdin
	Idol With The Golden Head	The Coasters	Atco
	I Want You To Know	Fats Domino	Imperial
⑥	Jingle Bell Rock	Bobby Helms	Decca
	Jingle Bells	Perry Como	RCA Victor
⑥	La Dee Dah	Billy & Lillie	Swan
	No Love (But Your Love)/ Wild Is The Wind	Johnny Mathis	Columbia
⑥	Oh Julie	The Crescendos	Nasco
	Santa & The Satellite	Buchanan & Goodman	Luniverse
⑥	Stood Up/Waitin' In School	Ricky Nelson	Imperial
⑥	The Stroll	The Diamonds	Mercury
	Wait A Minute	Jo-Ann Campbell	Gone
⑥	Why Don't They Understand?	George Hamilton IV	ABC Paramount
⑥	You Are My Destiny	Paul Anka	ABC Paramount

1957

TOP SINGLES OF 1957

⑥ All Shook Up	Elvis Presley	RCA Victor
⑥ April Love	Pat Boone	Dot
⑥ Jailhouse Rock	Elvis Presley	RCA Victor
⑥ (Let Me Be Your) Teddy Bear	Elvis Presley	RCA Victor
⑥ Love Letters In The Sand	Pat Boone	Dot
⑥ Tammy	Debbie Reynolds	Coral
⑥ Too Much	Elvis Presley	RCA Victor
⑥ Wake Up Little Suzy	The Everly Brothers	Cadence
⑥ Young Love	Tab Hunter	Dot
⑥ You Send Me	Sam Cooke	Keen

TOP ALBUMS OF 1957

Around The World In 80 Days	Soundtrack	Decca
⑥ Calypso	Harry Belafonte	RCA Victor
⑥ Elvis	Elvis Presley	RCA Victor
⑥ Elvis' Christmas Album	Elvis Presley	RCA Victor
⑥ An Evening With Belafonte	Harry Belafonte	RCA Victor
⑥ Love Is The Thing	Nat "King" Cole	Capitol
⑥ Loving You	Elvis Presley	RCA Victor
⑥ My Fair Lady	Original Cast	Columbia
A Swingin' Affair	Frank Sinatra	Capitol
Where Are You?	Frank Sinatra	Capitol

BIRTHS AND DEATHS IN 1957

MUSIC PERFORMERS BORN IN 1957

Teena Marie, January 1
Falco, February 19
Stephanie Mills, March 22
Jimmy McShane (Baltimora), May 23
Brad Gillis (Night Ranger), June 15
Patty Smyth (Scandal), June 26
Laura Branigan, July 3
Robbie Grey (Modern English), July 24
Doug Fieger (The Knack), August 20
Siobhan Fahey (Bananarama), September 10
Howard Hewett (Shalamar), October 1
Donny Osmond, December 9
Cy Curnin (The Fixx), December 12

MUSIC PERFORMERS AND MUSIC INDUSTRY NOTABLES WHO DIED IN 1957

Jimmy Dorsey, Wednesday, June 12 (cancer; 53)

Arturo Toscanini, Wednesday, January 16 (natural causes; 89)

OTHERS WHO DIED IN 1957

Humphrey Bogart
Richard E. Byrd
Oliver Hardy
Louis B. Mayer
Joseph McCarthy
Erich von Stroheim

MOVIES OF 1957

MOVIES FEATURING POP MUSIC ARTISTS

Bernardine *Stars:* Pat Boone (film debut), Terry Moore, Janet Gaynor, Dean Jagger. *Featured song:* "Bernardine."

Brooklyn Paramount theater (photo: Herb Cox)

The Big Beat   *Stars:* Gogi Grant, William Campbell, Rose Marie, Hans Conried. *Featured songs:* "Come Go With Me" by the Del Vikings, "Little Darlin' " by the Diamonds, "The Big Beat" and "I'm Walkin' " by Fats Domino. *Other musical performers:* The Four Aces, Harry James, the Mills Brothers.

Carnival Rock   *Stars:* Susan Cabot, Dick Miller. *Featured song:* "Remember When" by the Platters. *Other musical performers:* David Houston, Bob Luman.

Jailhouse Rock   *Stars:* Elvis Presley, Judy Tyler, Mickey Shaughnessy, Dean Jones. *Featured songs:* "Jailhouse Rock," "Treat Me Nice."

Jamboree   *Stars:* Kay Medford, Robert Pastine, Paul Carr. *Featured songs:* "Great Balls Of Fire" by Jerry Lee Lewis, "Hula Love" by Buddy Knox. *Other musical performers:* Fats Domino, Jimmy Bowen, Charlie Gracie, the Four Coins, Jodie Sands, Carl Perkins, Slim Whitman, Lewis Lymon & the Teenchords, Connie Francis, Frankie Avalon. The film also featured many of the nation's top disc jockeys in cameo roles.

Loving You   *Stars:* Elvis Presley (in his first color film), Lizabeth Scott, Dolores Hart, Wendell Corey, James Gleason. *Featured songs:* "Loving You," "(Let Me Be Your) Teddy Bear," "Got A Lot O' Livin' To Do," and "Mean Woman Blues."

Mister Rock and Roll   *Stars:* Disc jockey Alan Freed, Teddy Randazzo, Rocky Graziano. *Featured songs:* "Lucille" and "Keep A Knockin' " by Little Richard, "Oh, Baby Doll" by Chuck Berry. *Other musical performers:* Frankie Lymon & the Teenagers, LaVern Baker, Clyde McPhatter, Brook Benton, Ferlin Husky, the Moonglows, Lionel Hampton & His Band.

Rock All Night   *Stars:* Abby Dalton, Dick Miller. *Featured song:* "I'm Sorry" by the Platters.

OTHER POPULAR MOVIES OF 1957

And God Created Woman
Boy on a Dolphin
The Bridge on the River Kwai

The Delicate Delinquent
The Delinquent
Funny Face

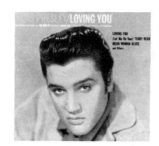

Elvis Presley, Loving You
album cover

1957

Gunfight at the O.K. Corral
The Incredible Shrinking Man
Les Girls
Paths of Glory
Peyton Place
The Prince and the Showgirl

Sayonara
Silk Stockings
Sweet Smell of Success
Tammy and the Bachelor
The Three Faces of Eve
Witness for the Prosecution

ACADEMY AWARD WINNERS OF 1957

Best Actor: Alec Guinness, *The Bridge on the River Kwai*
Best Actress: Joanne Woodward, *The Three Faces of Eve*
Best Picture: *The Bridge on the River Kwai*
Best Song: "All The Way," *The Joker Is Wild* (music by James Van Heusen, lyrics by Sammy Cahn)

TOP TELEVISION SHOWS OF 1957

December Bride
General Electric Theater
Gunsmoke
Have Gun, Will Travel
I've Got a Secret

The Life and Legend of Wyatt Earp
Make Room for Daddy
The Restless Gun
Tales of Wells Fargo
You Bet Your Life

61

1958

NEWS HIGHLIGHTS OF 1958

⇨ In Venezuela, the dictatorship of General Marcos Perez Jimenez is overthrown during riots.

⇨ The *Explorer* satellite is launched from Cape Canaveral.

⇨ Elvis Presley reports to Local Draft Board 86 in Memphis, Tennessee.

⇨ The winner of the Soviet Union's international Tchaikovsky piano competition is a young American, Van Cliburn.

⇨ Vice President Richard M. Nixon and his wife are threatened, spat on, and stoned while touring Latin America.

⇨ The Mackinac Bridge, linking Michigan's upper and lower peninsulas, is dedicated. It is the world's longest suspension bridge, featuring the second-longest span (the Golden Gate is longer).

⇨ President Eisenhower sends 5,000 troops to Beirut to protect the Lebanese government against a possible coup.

⇨ In Peking, Soviet Premier Nikita Khrushchev meets Chinese Communist Party Chief and Chairman Mao Tse-tung for talks.

⇨ A ticker-tape parade in New York honors the crew of the nuclear submarine *Nautilus* for making history's first undersea voyage across the North Pole.

⇨ White smoke rising from a chimney above the Sistine Chapel at the Vatican announces that Angelo Giuseppe Roncalli has been elevated to the papacy as Pope John XXIII.

⇨ Jeweler Harry Winston gives the $1.5 million steel-blue Hope diamond to the Smithsonian Institution in Washington, D.C.

⇨ A popular sedative called thalidomide causes birth defects in about 7,000 infants and is banned around the world.

⇨ Charles de Gaulle becomes the new French president.

⇨ The sack dress debuts.

⇨ Rock singer Jerry Lee Lewis marries his 13-year-old cousin, causing a scandal contributing to the decline of his popularity.

⇨ The first quiz show scandals surface with relevations that contestants on *Twenty-One* and *The $64,000 Question* had been given their answers.

⇨ Hula hoops are the rage.

SPORTS WINNERS

Baseball   The New York Yankees beat the Milwaukee Braves 4 games to 3.

Football   The Baltimore Colts beat the New York Giants 23–17 for the NFL championship in overtime in New York.

Basketball   The St. Louis Hawks beat the Boston Celtics 4 games to 3 to win the NBA title.

Hockey   The Montreal Canadiens beat the Boston Bruins 4 games to 2 to win the Stanley Cup.

MUSIC HIGHLIGHTS OF 1958

⇨ On Saturday, February 15, ABC television launches *The Dick Clark Saturday Night Show*. Broadcast live from the 498-seat Little Theater in New York City, the fast-paced weekly half-hour rock 'n' roll stage show features the hottest current performers lip-synching their hits. The first show features Johnnie Ray, the Royal Teens singing "Short Shorts," Jerry Lee Lewis performing "Great Balls Of Fire," Connie Francis singing "Who's Sorry Now," and Pat Boone singing "A Wonderful Time Up There."

⇨ On Monday, March 24, Elvis Presley reports to Local Draft Board 86 in Memphis, Tennessee, and goes from being the king of rock 'n' roll to Army private US53310761.

⇨ The National Academy of Recording Arts and Sciences (NARAS) awards the first Grammys for excellence in recorded music.

ROCK ON ALMANAC

⇨ Alan Freed leaves WINS radio and joins WABC in New York, doing both a radio show and a local television show called *The Big Beat,* which will be seen Monday through Friday.

⇨ On Thursday, August 14, Elvis's mother, Gladys, age 46, dies of a heart attack, complicated by hepatitis. She is buried on August 16, the date on which Elvis will die 19 years later.

⇨ Columbia Records introduces the first stereo album, Ray Conniff's *'S Awful Nice,* no. CS 8001.

⇨ Folk music gets hot as the Kingston Trio's hit "Tom Dooley" rises to number one. The song awakens a new nostalgia for the banjo-flavored vocal sound of traditional American music.

⇨ John Lennon, Paul McCartney, and George Harrison begin playing around Liverpool, England, as the Quarrymen.

⇨ Hank Ballard writes a song called "The Twist," which would become a major hit for Chubby Checker two years later.

DEBUT ARTISTS OF 1958

MAJOR ARTISTS	Debut Single	Label
Frankie Avalon	Dede Dinah	Chancellor
Brook Benton	A Million Miles From Nowhere	Vik
The Champs (Dave Burgess, Dale Norris, Chuck Rio, Ben Norman, Gen Alden)	Tequila ☆ ⑥	Challenge
The Chipmunks (David Seville)	The Chipmunk Song ☆ ⑥	Liberty
Jimmy Clanton	Just A Dream ⑥	Ace
Dee Clark	Nobody But You	Abner
Floyd Cramer	Flip, Flop And Bop	RCA Victor
Bobby Darin	Splish Splash ⑥	Atco
Dion & the Belmonts (Dion DiMucci, Angelo D'Aleo, Freddie Milano, Carlo Mastrangelo)	I Wonder Why	Laurie
Duane Eddy	Moovin' N' Groovin'	Jamie
Tommy Edwards	It's All In The Game ☆ ⑥	MGM
Connie Francis	Who's Sorry Now ⑥	MGM
Bobby Freeman	Do You Want To Dance?	Josie

Frankie Avalon (photo: *Kier*)

Don Gibson	Oh, Lonesome Me ⑥	RCA Victor
Earl Grant	The End	Decca
The Kingston Trio (Bob Shane, Nick Reynolds, Dave Guard)	Tom Dooley ☆ ⑥	Capitol
Little Anthony & the Imperials (Anthony Gourdine, Tracy Lord, Ernest Wright, Clarence Collins, Glouster Rogers)	Tears On My Pillow ⑥	End
The Miracles (William "Smokey" Robinson, Claudette Rodgers Robinson, Ronald White, Robert Rodgers, Warren "Pete" Moore)	Got A Job	End
The Olympics (Walter Ward, Eddie Lewis, Charles Fizer, Melvin King)	Western Movies	Demon
The Playmates (Donny Conn, Morey Carr, Chic Hetti)	Jo-Ann	Roulette
Jack Scott	My True Love/Leroy ⑥	Carlton
Neil Sedaka	The Diary	RCA Victor
The Shirelles (Shirley Alston, Beverly Lee, Addie "Micky" Harris, Doris Kenner)	I Met Him On A Sunday	Decca
Joe South	The Purple People Eater Meets The Witch Doctor	NRC
Johnny Tillotson	Well, I'm Your Man	Cadence
Ritchie Valens	Come On, Let's Go	Del-Fi
Jerry Wallace	How The Time Flies	Challenge

OTHER ARTISTS

The Accents
Lee Allen & His Band
The Applejacks
The Aquatones
The Big Bopper
The Casuals
The Chanters
Eugene Church & the Fellows
Cozy Cole

The Danleers
Joe Darensbourg & the Dixie Flyers
Hutch Davie
Don & Dewey
Dicky Doo & the Don'ts
The Edsels
The Elegants
The Five Blobs
The Five Discs

Brook Benton

Bobby Darin (photo: Kriegsmann)

Frank Gallop
The Gone All Stars
Billy Grammer
Gerry Granahan
Bobby Hendricks
Ersel Hickey
The Honeycones
Ivan
The Jamies
Jan & Arnie
The Kalin Twins
Bob Kayli
The Kingsmen
The Kirby Stone Four
The Moe Koffman Quartette
The Kuf-Linx
Kathy Linden
Laurie London
Robin Luke
The Mark IV
Jimmy McCracklin
Robert Mitchum
Domenico Modugno
The Monotones
The Nu Tornados
Reg Owen
Donnie Owens
Bill Parsons

The Pastels
The Pets
Eddie Platt
The Playboys
The Poni-Tails
The Quaker City Boys
The Quin-Tones
Teddy Randazzo
Jody Reynolds
The Rinky-Dinks
The Rivieras
Robert & Johnny
The Royal Teens
The Royaltones
The Shields
The Silhouettes
The Harry Simeone Chorale
The Slades
The Teddy Bears
Art & Dotty Todd
Ed Townsend
The Tune Rockers
The Voxpoppers
Sheb Wooley
Link Wray & the Wray Men
Faron Young
John Zacherle

HITS OF 1958

JANUARY

⑥	**Dede Dinah**	Frankie Avalon	Chancellor
	Do What You Did	Thurston Harris	Aladdin
☆ ⑥	**Get A Job**	The Silhouettes	Ember
	Henrietta	Jimmie Dee	Dot
	(I Love You) For Sentimental Reasons	Sam Cooke	Keen
	Jo-Ann	The Playmates	Roulette
	Magic Moments	Perry Como	RCA Victor

Dion & the Belmonts (l to r: Freddie Milano, Dion DiMucci, Carlo Mastrangelo, Angelo D'Aleo)

Duane Eddy

Connie Francis (photo: Kier)

1958

⑥	March From The River Kwai And Colonel Bogey	Mitch Miller	Columbia
⑥	Maybe	The Chantels	End
	Put A Light In The Window	The Four Lads	Columbia
⑥	Sail Along Silvery Moon	Billy Vaughn	Dot
☆ ⑥	Sugartime	The McGuire Sisters	Coral
⑥	Twenty-Six Miles	The Four Preps	Capitol
	Walkin' With Mr. Lee	Lee Allen	Ember

FEBRUARY

	Are You Sincere	Andy Williams	Cadence
	Ballad Of A Teen-Age Queen	Johnny Cash	Sun
	Betty And Dupree	Chuck Willis	Atlantic
☆ ⑥	Catch A Falling Star	Perry Como	RCA Victor
	Click Clack	Dickey Doo & the Don'ts	Swan
☆ ⑥	Don't/I Beg Of You	Elvis Presley	RCA Victor
⑥	Good Golly Miss Molly	Little Richard	Specialty
⑥	Oh-Oh, I'm Falling In Love Again	Jimmie Rodgers	Roulette
	Shake A Hand	The Mike Pedicin Quintet	Cameo
	Short Shorts	The Royal Teens	ABC Paramount
⑥	Sweet Little Sixteen	Chuck Berry	Chess
	The Swingin' Shepherd Blues	The Moe Koffman Quartette	Jubilee
	A Wonderful Time Up There/It's Too Soon To Know	Pat Boone	Dot
	Yellow Dog Blues	Joe Darensbourg & His Dixie Flyers	Lark
	Yes, My Darling	Fats Domino	Imperial

MARCH

	Been So Long	The Pastels	Argo
⑥	Breathless	Jerry Lee Lewis	Sun
	Dinner With Drac	John Zacherle	Cameo
⑥	Don't You Just Know It	Huey "Piano" Smith & the Clowns	Ace

Little Anthony & the Imperials (top: Anthony Gourdine; bottom l to r: Glouster Rogers, Tracy Lord, Clarence Collins, Ernest Wright; photo: Kriegsmann)

☆ ⑥ He's Got The Whole World In His Hands	Laurie London	Capitol
⑥ Lollipop	The Chordettes	Cadence
⑥ Oh, Lonesome Me	Don Gibson	RCA Victor
The Plea	The Jesters	Winley
Rock And Roll Is Here To Stay	Danny & the Juniors	ABC Paramount
"7-11"	The Gone All Stars	Gone
So Tough	The Casuals	Backbeat
☆ ⑥ Tequila	The Champs	Challenge
The Walk	Jimmy McCracklin	Checker
We Belong Together	Robert & Johnny	Old Town
⑥ Who's Sorry Now	Connie Francis	MGM

APRIL

⑥ Believe What You Say	Ricky Nelson	Imperial
Billy	Kathy Linden	Felsted
⑥ Book of Love	The Monotones	Argo
⑥ Chanson D'Amour	Art & Dotty Todd	Era
Crazy Love	Paul Anka	ABC Paramount
For Your Love	Ed Townsend	Capitol
Looking Back	Nat "King" Cole	Capitol
⑥ Maybe Baby	The Crickets	Brunswick
⑥ Return To Me	Dean Martin	Capitol
Skinny Minnie	Bill Haley & His Comets	Decca
⑥ Talk To Me, Talk To Me	Little Willie John	King
To Be Loved	Jackie Wilson	Brunswick
☆ ⑥ Twilight Time	The Platters	Mercury
⑥ Wear My Ring Around Your Neck/Doncha' Think It's Time	Elvis Presley	RCA Victor
☆ ⑥ Witch Doctor	David Seville	Liberty

MAY

☆ ⑥	All I Have To Do Is Dream	The Everly Brothers	Cadence
	Big Man	The Four Preps	Capitol
	Dizzy, Miss Lizzy	Larry Williams	Specialty
	Do You Want To Dance?	Bobby Freeman	Josie
	Endless Sleep	Jody Reynolds	Demon
	Every Night	The Chantels	End
	Hang Up My Rock And Roll Shoes	Chuck Willis	Atlantic
	I Met Him On A Sunday	The Shirelles	Decca
	I Wonder Why	Dion & the Belmonts	Laurie
	Jennie Lee	Jan & Arnie	Arwin
⑥	Johnny B. Goode	Chuck Berry	Chess
	Rumble	Link Wray & the Wray Men	Cadence
⑥	Secretly	Jimmie Rodgers	Roulette
	Witchcraft	Frank Sinatra	Capitol
	You	The Aquatones	Fargo

JUNE

	Don't Go Home	The Playmates	Roulette
	For Your Precious Love	Jerry Butler & the Impressions	Abner
	Guess Things Happen That Way	Johnny Cash	Sun
☆ ⑥	Hard Headed Woman/Don't Ask Me Why	Elvis Presley	RCA Victor
⑥	High School Confidential	Jerry Lee Lewis	Sun
⑥	Kewpie Doll	Perry Como	RCA Victor
	Ooh! My Soul	Little Richard	Specialty
☆ ⑥	Patricia	Perez Prado	RCA Victor
☆ ⑥	The Purple People Eater	Sheb Wooley	MGM
	Rave On	Buddy Holly	Coral
	Sick And Tired	Fats Domino	Imperial
	Sugar Moon	Pat Boone	Dot
	The Things I Love	The Fidelities	Baton
	Try The Impossible	Lee Andrews & the Hearts	United Artists
☆ ⑥	Yakety Yak	The Coasters	Atco

The Miracles (l to r: William "Smokey" Robinson, Claudette Rodgers Robinson, Ronald White, Robert Rodgers, Warren "Pete" Moore)

JULY

Born Too Late	The Poni-Tails	ABC Paramount
A Certain Smile	Johnny Mathis	Columbia
⑥ Fever	Peggy Lee	Capitol
Ginger Bread	Frankie Avalon	Chancellor
I Love You So	The Chantels	End
⑥ Just A Dream	Jimmy Clanton	Ace
☆ ⑥ Little Star	The Elegants	APT
⑥ My True Love/Leroy	Jack Scott	Carlton
One Summer Night	The Danleers	Mercury
☆ ⑥ Poor Little Fool	Ricky Nelson	Imperial
⑥ Rebel Rouser	Duane Eddy	Jamie
⑥ Splish Splash	Bobby Darin	Atco
Western Movies	The Olympics	Demon
⑥ When	The Kalin Twins	Decca
Willie And The Hand Jive	The Johnny Otis Show	Capitol

AUGUST

☆ ⑥ Bird Dog/Devoted To You	The Everly Brothers	Cadence
⑥ Chantilly Lace	The Big Bopper	Mercury
Early In The Morning	The Rinky-Dinks	Atco
Everybody Loves A Lover	Doris Day	Columbia
Itchy Twitchy Feeling	Bobby Hendricks	Sue
☆ ⑥ It's All In The Game	Tommy Edwards	MGM
⑥ Rockin' Robin/Over And Over	Bobby Day	Class
Somebody Touched Me	Buddy Knox	Roulette
Stupid Cupid	Connie Francis	MGM
Summertime Blues	Eddie Cochran	Liberty
⑥ Susie Darlin'	Robin Luke	Dot
⑥ Tears On My Pillow	Little Anthony & the Imperials	End
Think It Over	The Crickets	Brunswick
☆ ⑥ Volare (Nel Blu Dipinto Di Blu)	Domenico Modugno	Decca
You Cheated	The Shields	Dot

SEPTEMBER

Carol	Chuck Berry	Chess
Down The Aisle Of Love	The Quin-Tones	Hunt
The End	Earl Grant	Decca

*Neil Sedaka (photo: **Kriegsmann**)*

1958

The Green Mosquito	The Tune-Rockers	United Artists
How The Time Flies	Jerry Wallace	Challenge
☆ ⑤ It's Only Make Believe	Conway Twitty	MGM
Lazy Summer Night	The Four Preps	Capitol
Near You	Roger Williams	Kapp
No One Knows	Dion & the Belmonts	Laurie
Summertime, Summertime	The Jamies	Epic
⑤ Tea For Two Cha Cha	The Tommy Dorsey Orchestra	Decca
The Ten Commandments Of Love	Harvey & the Moonglows	Chess
There Goes My Heart	Joni James	MGM
⑤ Topsy II	Cozy Cole	Love
Win Your Love For Me	Sam Cooke	Keen

OCTOBER

Call Me	Johnny Mathis	Columbia
The Day The Rains Came	Jane Morgan	Kapp
Firefly	Tony Bennett	Columbia
Forget Me Not	The Kalin Twins	Decca
Hideaway	The Four Esquires	Paris
The Hula Hoop Song	Georgia Gibbs	Roulette
I Got A Feeling/Lonesome Town	Ricky Nelson	Imperial
Mexican Hat Dance	The Applejacks	Cameo
Need You	Donnie Owens	Guyden
Non Dimenticar	Nat "King" Cole	Capitol
Poor Boy	The Royal Tones	Jubilee
⑤ Queen Of The Hop	Bobby Darin	Atco
This Little Girl's Gone Rockin'	Ruth Brown	Atlantic
☆ ⑤ To Know Him Is To Love Him	The Teddy Bears	Dore
☆ ⑤ Tom Dooley	The Kingston Trio	Capitol

NOVEMBER

⑤ Beep Beep	The Playmates	Roulette
Bimbombey	Jimmie Rodgers	Roulette
The Blob	The Five Blobs	Columbia
Cannonball	Duane Eddy	Jamie
Come On, Let's Go	Ritchie Valens	Del-Fi
Fallin'	Connie Francis	MGM
⑤ I Got Stung/One Night	Elvis Presley	RCA Victor
I'll Wait For You	Frankie Avalon	Chancellor
Love Is All We Need	Tommy Edwards	MGM
⑤ A Lover's Question	Clyde McPhatter	Atlantic
⑤ Problems	The Everly Brothers	Cadence
☆ ⑤ Smoke Gets In Your Eyes	The Platters	Mercury
⑤ That Old Black Magic	Louis Prima & Keely Smith	Capitol
Walking Along	The Diamonds	Mercury
⑤ Whole Lotta Loving	Fats Domino	Imperial

DECEMBER

☆ ⑤ The Chipmunk Song	The Chipmunks	Liberty
C'mon Everybody	Eddie Cochran	Liberty

71

The Diary	Neil Sedaka	RCA Victor
¿Donde Esta Santa Claus?	Augie Rios	Metro
⑥ Donna/La Bamba	Ritchie Valens	Del-Fi
Goodbye Baby	Jack Scott	Carlton
⑥ Gotta Travel On	Billy Grammer	Monument
Green Chritma	Stan Freberg	Capitol
⑥ I Cried A Tear	LaVern Baker	Atlantic
⑥ The Little Drummer Boy	The Harry Simeone Chorale	20th Century–Fox
⑥ Lonely Teardrops	Jackie Wilson	Brunswick
Love You Most Of All	Sam Cooke	Keen
Peek-A-Boo	The Cadillacs	Josie
Philadelphia U.S.A.	The Nu Tornados	Carlton
⑥ 16 Candles	The Crests	Coed

TOP SINGLES OF 1958

⑥ All I Have To Do Is Dream/ Claudette	The Everly Brothers	Cadence
⑥ At The Hop	Danny & the Juniors	ABC Paramount
⑥ Don't/I Beg Of You	Elvis Presley	RCA Victor
⑥ Hard Headed Woman/Don't Ask Me Why	Elvis Presley	RCA Victor
⑥ It's All In The Game	Tommy Edwards	MGM
⑥ Poor Little Fool	Ricky Nelson	Imperial
⑥ The Purple People Eater	Sheb Wooley	MGM
⑥ Tequila	The Champs	Challenge
⑥ To Know Him Is To Love Him	The Teddy Bears	Dore
⑥ Volare (Nel Blu Dipinto Di Blu)	Domenico Modugno	Decca

TOP ALBUMS OF 1958

Come Fly With Me	Frank Sinatra	Capitol
⑥ Frank Sinatra Sings For Only The Lonely	Frank Sinatra	Capitol

The Shirelles in concert, 1968 (photo: Norm N. Nite)

South Pacific
soundtrack album cover

1958

⑥	**Gigi**	Soundtrack	MGM
℗	**Johnny's Greatest Hits**	Johnny Mathis	Columbia
	King Creole	Elvis Presley	RCA Victor
⑥	**The Kingston Trio**	The Kingston Trio	Capitol
⑥	**The Music Man**	Original Cast	Capitol
⑥	**Sing Along With Mitch**	Mitch Miller	Columbia
⑥	**South Pacific**	Soundtrack	RCA Victor
⑥	**Tchaikovsky: Piano Concerto No. 1**	Van Cliburn	RCA Victor

GRAMMY WINNERS IN 1958

The first Grammy Awards ceremony was held at the Beverly Hilton Hotel in Los Angeles on Monday, May 4, 1959. Mort Sahl was the host.

Record of the Year: "Volare (Nel Blu Dipinto Di Blu)," Domenico Modugno (Decca)
Song of the Year: "Volare (Nel Blu Dipinto Di Blu)" (music and lyrics by Domenico Modugno)
Album of the Year: *The Music From Peter Gunn,* Henry Mancini (RCA Victor)
Best Vocal Performance, Female: *Ella Fitzgerald Sings The Irving Berlin Songbook,* Ella Fitzgerald (Verve)
Best Vocal Performance, Male: "Catch A Falling Star," Perry Como (RCA Victor)
Best Vocal Performance, Group: "That Old Black Magic," Louis Prima & Keely Smith (Capitol)
Best Comedy Performance: "The Chipmunk Song," The Chipmunks (Liberty)

BIRTHS AND DEATHS IN 1958

MUSIC PERFORMERS BORN IN 1958

Mike Peters (The Alarm), February 25
Andy Gibb, March 5
Gary Numan, March 8
Martin Fry (ABC), March 9
Oran "Juice" Jones, March 28
Prince (Prince Rogers Nelson), June 7
Kate Bush, July 30

Belinda Carlisle, August 17
Michael Jackson, August 29
David Lewis (Atlantic Starr), September 8
Freddie Jackson, October 2
Tanya Tucker, October 10
Thomas Dolby, October 14
Simon Le Bon (Duran Duran), October 27

MUSIC PERFORMERS AND MUSIC INDUSTRY NOTABLES WHO DIED IN 1958

W.C. Handy, Friday, March 28 (bronchial pneumonia; 84)

Chuck Willis, Thursday, April 10 (heart attack; 30)

OTHERS WHO DIED IN 1958

Ronald Colman
Christian Dior

Tyrone Power
Mike Todd

MOVIES OF 1958

MOVIES FEATURING POP MUSIC ARTISTS

Go, Johnny Go! *Stars:* Disc jockey Alan Freed, Jimmy Clanton, Sandy Stewart, Chuck Berry. *Featured songs:* "Johnny B. Goode," "Little Queenie," and "Memphis" by Chuck Berry, "You'd Better Know It" by Jackie Wilson, and "Jay Walker" and "Please Mr. Johnson" by the Cadillacs. Ritchie Valens makes his only film appearance singing "Ooh, My Head." *Other musical performers:* Jo-Ann Campbell, Eddie Cochran, the Flamingos, Jimmy Clanton, Harvey Fuqua, Sandy Stewart.

Hot Rod Gang *Stars:* John Ashley, Gene Vincent. *Featured song:* "Dance To The Bop" by Gene Vincent & His Blue Caps.

King Creole *Stars:* Elvis Presley, Carolyn Jones, Dolores Hart, Dean Jagger, Walter Matthau, Vic Morrow. *Featured songs:* "King Creole," "Trouble," "Hard Headed Woman."

Let's Rock *Stars:* Julius LaRosa, Phyllis Newman, Conrad Janis. *Featured songs:* "At The Hop" by Danny & the Juniors, "Short Shorts" by the Royal Teens. *Other musical performers:* Paul Anka, Roy Hamilton, Julius La Rosa, Della Reese.

Sing, Boy, Sing *Stars:* Tommy Sands, Edmond O'Brien, Nick Adams, John McIntire. *Featured songs:* "Sing, Boy, Sing" and "Teenage Crush" by Tommy Sands. Began as a *Kraft TV Playhouse* production called "The Singing Idol" and was expanded into a feature film.

OTHER POPULAR MOVIES OF 1958

Auntie Mame
Cat on a Hot Tin Roof
The Defiant Ones
Gigi
High School Confidential
Horror of Dracula
Hot Spell

The Inn of the Sixth Happiness
Separate Tables
The Sheepman
Some Came Running
South Pacific
Underwater Warrior
Vertigo

ACADEMY AWARD WINNERS OF 1958

Best Actor: David Niven, *Separate Tables*
Best Actress: Susan Hayward, *I Want to Live*
Best Picture: *Gigi*
Best Song: "Gigi," *Gigi* (music by Frederick Loewe, lyrics by Alan Jay Lerner)

TOP TELEVISION SHOWS OF 1958

Gunsmoke
Have Gun, Will Travel
I've Got a Secret
The Life and Legend of Wyatt Earp
Make Room for Daddy

Maverick
The Real McCoys
The Rifleman
Tales of Wells Fargo
Wagon Train

1959

NEWS HIGHLIGHTS OF 1959

⇨ Charismatic rebel leader Fidel Castro and his supporters conquer Cuba.

⇨ After a 42-year struggle for statehood, Alaska becomes the 49th and largest state.

⇨ Two monkeys survive a 1,700-mile American space trip.

⇨ Swede Ingemar Johansson kayoes Floyd Patterson to become the first non-American in 25 years to hold the world heavyweight championship.

⇨ At the opening of the American National Exhibition in Moscow, U.S. Vice President Richard Nixon engages Soviet Premier Nikita Khrushchev in a heated discussion that comes to be known as the "Kitchen Debate" because it took place in a model kitchen.

⇨ Hawaii becomes the 50th state.

⇨ The Soviet Union launches the *Lunik II* spacecraft, which becomes the first object originating on earth to land on the moon.

⇨ Conceding failure, Ford discontinues production of the Edsel.

⇨ Twelve nations sign a treaty setting the Antarctic continent aside as a preserve for scientific research.

⇨ Soviet Premier Nikita Khrushchev tours the United States.

⇨ The St. Lawrence Seaway opens along the U.S.-Canada border to facilitate shipping on the St. Lawrence River between Montreal and Lake Superior.

⇨ The reverse side of the Lincoln penny is redesigned, with the Lincoln Memorial in Washington, D.C., replacing the words "ONE CENT."

⇨ At Thanksgiving, reports of contaminated cranberries frighten millions of Americans.

SPORTS WINNERS

Baseball   Los Angeles Dodgers beat the Chicago White Sox 4 games to 2.

Football   The Baltimore Colts beat the New York Giants 31–16 in Baltimore for the NFL championship.

Basketball   The Boston Celtics beat the Minneapolis Lakers 4 games to 0 to win the NBA title.

Hockey   The Montreal Canadiens beat the Toronto Maple Leafs 4 games to 1 to win the Stanley Cup.

MUSIC HIGHLIGHTS OF 1959

⇨ Calico records of Pittsburgh, Pennsylvania, releases the Skyliners' hit ballad "Since I Don't Have You," the first rock song to feature strings in the arrangement.

⇨ On Tuesday, February 3, a small chartered plane carrying Buddy Holly, Ritchie Valens, and J.P. "Big Bopper" Richardson crashes shortly after takeoff, killing the three rock

Hank Ballard

Freddy Cannon

Fabian

Chubby Checker

stars and the plane's pilot. The crash occurs near Mason City, Iowa, as the plane was en route to Fargo, North Dakota. The performers were part of a tour that had just played Clear Lake, Iowa, on its swing through the Midwest. The crash caused millions of fans to go into mourning. Don McLean referred to the date as "the day the music died" in his 1971 hit "American Pie."

⇨ On Saturday, April 25, the television version of the radio classic *Your Hit Parade* has its last broadcast.

⇨ Dick Clark launches his Dick Clark Caravan of Stars live stage shows, which appeal to his *American Bandstand* audience. The show follows a simple formula: Dick would book as many acts as he could afford, have each do two or three songs, all backed up by the same band, and Dick would be the MC. The show travels the country playing to capacity crowds.

⇨ Cliff Richard becomes one of the first teen idols in England.

⇨ Payola scandals gain notoriety, informing the public that disc jockeys are alleged to be taking money to play records. Alan Freed, caught in the middle of the investigations, is fired from New York's WABC radio and television for refusing to sign a statement that he never took money for playing records on the air.

⇨ Chuck Berry is convicted, under the Mann Act, of transporting a minor across state lines for immoral purposes. Berry serves a few months in prison for his offense.

DEBUT ARTISTS OF 1959

MAJOR ARTISTS	Debut Single	Label
Annette (Funicello)	Tall Paul	Disneyland
Hank Ballard & the Midnighters	Teardrops On Your Letter/The Twist	King
Bill Black's Combo	Smokie—Part 2	Hi
The Blue Notes (Theodore Pendergrass, Harold Melvin, Bernard Wilson, Lawrence Brown, Lloyd Parks)	I Don't Know What It Is	Brooke
The Browns (Jim Edward, Maxine, and Bonnie)	The Three Bells ☆ ⑥	RCA Victor
Anita Bryant	Till There Was You	Carlton
Freddy Cannon	Tallahassee Lassie ⑥	Swan
Chubby Checker (Ernest Evans)	The Class	Parkway
Dave "Baby" Cortez	The Happy Organ ☆ ⑥	Clock
James Darren	Gidget	Colpix
Fabian (Forte)	I'm A Man	Chancellor

77

The Fireballs (George Tomsco, Stan Lark, Jimmy Gilmer, Eric Budd)	Torquay	Top Rank
The Fleetwoods (Gary Troxel, Barbara Ellis, Gretchen Christopher)	Come Softly To Me ☆ ⑥	Dolphin
Johnny Horton	The Battle Of New Orleans ☆ ⑥	Columbia
The Isley Brothers (Ronald, Rudolph, and O'Kelly)	Shout—Part 1	RCA Victor
Jan & Dean (Jan Berry, Dean Torrance)	Baby Talk	Dore
Johnny & the Hurricanes (Johnny Paris, Paul Tesluk, Dave Yorko, Lionel "Butch" Mattice, Tony Kaye)	Crossfire	Warwick
Marv Johnson	Come To Me	United Artists
Sandy Nelson	Teen Beat ⑥	Original Sound
Ray Peterson	The Wonder Of You	RCA Victor
Cliff Richard	Living Doll	ABC Paramount
Bobby Rydell	Kissin' Time	Cameo
Santo & Johnny (Farina)	Sleep Walk ☆ ⑥	Canadian-American
The Skyliners (Jimmy Beaumont, Janet Rapp, Wally Lester, Joe Verscharen, Jack Taylor)	Since I Don't Have You	Calico
Bobby Vee	Suzie Baby	Liberty
Baby Washington	The Time	Neptune

OTHER ARTISTS

Chris Barber's Jazz Band
Richard Barrett
Bob Beckham
The Bell Notes
Rod Bernard
Edward (Edd) Byrnes
Bobby Comstock
Don Costa
Tommy Dee
Martin Denny
Mark Dinning
Carl Dobkins, Jr.
Preston Epps
The Eternals
Paul Evans
Tommy Facenda
The Falcons
Ernie Fields
The Fiestas
The Fireflies
Toni Fisher
Frankie Ford
John Fred & His Playboy Band
Don French
Jerry Fuller
The Genies
Rocco Granata
Billy Graves

Larry Hall
Wilbert Harrison
Ronnie Hawkins
The Hot-Toddys
The Impalas
The Intruders
Stonewall Jackson
Damita Jo
Jerry Keller
Rod Lauren
Arthur Lyman
Wink Martindale
Big Jay McNeely
The Megatrons
The Mickey Mozart Quintet
The Mystics
The Nutty Squirrels
The Passions
Pat & the Satellites
Phil Phillips
Frank Pourcel
Johnny Preston
The Revels
Ivo Robic
Floyd Robinson
The Rock-A-Teens
Ray Sharpe
Nina Simone

Skip & Flip
The Spacemen
Dodie Stevens
Gary Stites
Billy Storm
The Tempos

Travis & Bob
Sammy Turner
The Virtues
The Wailers
Thomas Wayne

1959

HITS OF 1959

JANUARY

The All American Boy	Bill Parsons	Fraternity
(All Of A Sudden) My Heart Sings	Paul Anka	ABC Paramount
Don't Pity Me	Dion & the Belmonts	Laurie
Don't You Know Yockomo	Huey "Piano" Smith & the Clowns	Ace
Goodbye Baby	Jack Scott	Carlton
⑥ The Hawaiian Wedding Song	Andy Williams	Cadence
I'm A Man	Fabian	Chancellor
Lucky Ladybug	Billy & Lillie	Swan
Manhattan Spiritual	Reg Owen	Palette
May You Always	The McGuire Sisters	Coral
⑥ My Happiness	Connie Francis	MGM
⑥ Peter Gunn Theme	Ray Anthony	Capitol
☆ ⑥ Stagger Lee	Lloyd Price	ABC Paramount
Tall Paul	Annette	Disneyland
With The Wind And The Rain In Your Hair	Pat Boone	Dot

FEBRUARY

Apple Blossom Time	Tab Hunter	Warner Bros.
⑥ Charlie Brown	The Coasters	Atco
⑥ The Children's Marching Song	Cyril Stapleton	London
Don't Take Your Guns To Town	Johnny Cash	Columbia
I Got A Wife	The Mark IV	Mercury
I've Had It	The Bell Notes	Time
The Lonely One	Duane Eddy	Jamie

The Fleetwoods (l to r: Gretchen Christopher, Gary Troxel, Barbara Ellis)

79

 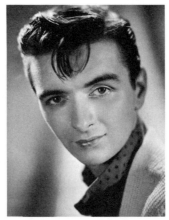 

Marv Johnson (photo: Kriegsmann) **Ray Peterson** (photo: Maurice Seymour) **Bobby Rydell**

	Lovers Never Say Goodbye	The Flamingos	End
⑥	Petite Fleur	Chris Barber's Jazz Band	Laurie
	Plain Jane	Bobby Darin	Atco
	She Say (Oom Dooby Doom)	The Diamonds	Mercury
	Since I Don't Have You	The Skyliners	Calico
⑥	Tragedy	Thomas Wayne	Fernwood
	Try Me	James Brown	Federal
☆ ⑥	Venus	Frankie Avalon	Chancellor

MARCH

⑥	Alvin's Harmonica	David Seville & the Chipmunks	Liberty
☆ ⑥	Come Softly To Me	The Fleetwoods	Dolphin
	Everybody Likes To Cha Cha Cha	Sam Cooke	Keen
⑥	A Fool Such As I/I Need Your Love Tonight	Elvis Presley	RCA Victor
☆ ⑥	The Happy Organ	Dave "Baby" Cortez	Clock
⑥	It Doesn't Matter Anymore/ Raining In My Heart	Buddy Holly	Coral
⑥	It's Just A Matter Of Time	Brook Benton	Mercury
⑥	Never Be Anyone Else But You/ It's Late	Ricky Nelson	Imperial
⑥	Pink Shoelaces	Dodie Stevens	Crystalette
	Please Mr. Sun	Tommy Edwards	MGM
	Pretty Girls Everywhere	Eugene Church & the Fellows	Class
⑥	Sea Cruise	Frankie Ford	Ace
	Tell Him No	Travis & Bob	Sandy
	Where Were You (On Our Wedding Day)?	Lloyd Price	ABC Paramount

APRIL

Almost Grown	Chuck Berry	Chess
Come To Me	Marv Johnson	United Artists
Guess Who	Jesse Belvin	RCA Victor

	I Miss You So	Paul Anka	ABC Paramount
☆ ⑥	Kansas City	Wilbert Harrison	Fury
⑥	Kookie, Kookie (Lend Me Your Comb)	Edward Byrnes & Connie Stevens	Warner Bros.
⑥	Only You	Frank Pourcel	Capitol
⑥	Quiet Village	Martin Denny	Liberty
	So Fine	The Fiestas	Old Town
⑥	Sorry (I Ran All The Way Home)	The Impalas	Cub
⑥	A Teenager In Love	Dion & the Belmonts	Laurie
	That's Why	Jackie Wilson	Brunswick
	Turn Me Loose	Fabian	Chancellor

MAY

☆ ⑥	The Battle of New Orleans	Johnny Horton	Columbia
	Bongo Rock	Preston Epps	Original
	Crossfire	Johnny & the Hurricanes	Warwick
⑥	Dream Lover	Bobby Darin	Atco
	Endlessly	Brook Benton	Mercury
	Goodbye, Jimmy, Goodbye	Kathy Linden	Felsted
	Hushabye	The Mystics	Laurie
	Just Keep It Up	Dee Clark	Abner
⑥	Lipstick On Your Collar/Frankie	Connie Francis	MGM
⑥	Personality	Lloyd Price	ABC Paramount
⑥	Tallahassee Lassie	Freddy Cannon	Swan
	Tall Cool One	The Wailers	Golden Crest
	What A Diff'rence A Day Makes	Dinah Washington	Mercury
	The Wonder Of You	Ray Peterson	RCA Victor
⑥	You're So Fine	The Falcons	Unart

JUNE

	Along Came Jones	The Coasters	Atco
	Back In The U.S.A.	Chuck Berry	Chess
	Bobby Sox To Stockings	Frankie Avalon	Chancellor
	Forty Days	Ronnie Hawkins	Roulette
	Forty Miles Of Bad Road/The Quiet Three	Duane Eddy	Jamie
	I'll Be Satisfied	Jackie Wilson	Brunswick
	I'm Ready	Fats Domino	Imperial
	I Only Have Eyes For You	The Flamingos	End
	Lavender Blue	Sammy Turner	Big Top
☆ ⑥	Lonely Boy	Paul Anka	ABC Paramount
	M.T.A.	The Kingston Trio	Capitol
	Only Sixteen	Sam Cooke	Keen
⑥	Tiger	Fabian	Chancellor
⑥	Waterloo	Stonewall Jackson	Columbia

JULY

| | Alimony | Frankie Ford | Ace |
| ☆ ⑥ | A Big Hunk O' Love/My Wish Came True | Elvis Presley | RCA Victor |

1959

81

⑥ Here Comes Summer	Jerry Keller	Kapp
It Was I	Skip & Flip	Brent
Just A Little Too Much/Sweeter Than You	Ricky Nelson	Imperial
Lonely Guitar	Annette	Vista
⑥ Ragtime Cowboy Joe	David Seville & the Chipmunks	Liberty
Remember When	The Platters	Mercury
⑥ Sea Of Love	Phil Phillips	Mercury
Small World	Johnny Mathis	Columbia
Thank You Pretty Baby	Brook Benton	Mercury
⑥ There Goes My Baby	The Drifters	Atlantic
⑥ What'd I Say (Part I)	Ray Charles	Atlantic
What Is Love	The Playmates	Roulette
The Whistling Organ	Dave "Baby" Cortez	Clock

AUGUST

The Angels Listened In	The Crests	Coed
Baby Talk	Jan & Dean	Dore
⑥ Broken-Hearted Melody	Sarah Vaughan	Mercury
I'm Gonna Be A Wheel Someday	Fats Domino	Imperial
⑥ I'm Gonna Get Married	Lloyd Price	ABC Paramount
⑥ Just Ask Your Heart	Frankie Avalon	Chancellor
Linda Lu	Ray Sharpe	Jamie
Makin' Love	Floyd Robinson	RCA Victor
Mona Lisa	Conway Twitty	MGM
⑥ Morgen	Ivo Robic	Laurie
⑥ Poison Ivy	The Coasters	Atco
⑥ Red River Rock	Johnny & the Hurricanes	Warwick
☆ ⑥ Sleep Walk	Santo & Johnny	Canadian-American
☆ ⑥ The Three Bells	The Browns	RCA Victor
⑥ ('Til) I Kissed You	The Everly Brothers	Cadence

SEPTEMBER

Come On And Get Me/Got The Feeling	Fabian	Chancellor
⑥ Deck Of Cards	Wink Martindale	Dot
Hey Little Girl	Dee Clark	Abner
I Ain't Never	Webb Pierce	Decca
Lonely Street	Andy Williams	Cadence
☆ ⑥ Mack The Knife	Bobby Darin	Atco
☆ ⑥ Mr. Blue	The Fleetwoods	Dolton
⑥ Primrose Lane	Jerry Wallace	Challenge
Put Your Head On My Shoulder	Paul Anka	ABC Paramount
Shortnin' Bread	The Bell Notes	Madison
Somethin' Else	Eddie Cochran	Liberty
⑥ Teen Beat	Sandy Nelson	Original
A Worried Man	The Kingston Trio	Capitol
You Better Know It	Jackie Wilson	Brunswick
You Were Mine	The Fireflies	Ribbon

The Skyliners (top l to r: Joe Verscharen,
Jack Taylor; bottom l to r: Wally Lester,
Janet Rapp, Jimmy Beaumont)

1959

OCTOBER

Danny Boy	Conway Twitty	MGM
⑥ Don't You Know	Della Reese	RCA Victor
☆ ⑥ Heartaches By The Number	Guy Mitchell	Columbia
If I Give My Heart To You	Kitty Kallen	Columbia
⑥ In The Mood	Ernie Fields	Rendezvous
Love Potion No. 9	The Clovers	United Artists
⑥ Misty	Johnny Mathis	Columbia
⑥ Oh! Carol	Neil Sedaka	RCA Victor
Say Man	Bo Diddley	Checker
⑥ (Seven Little Girls) Sittin' In The Back Seat	Paul Evans & the Curls	Guaranteed
⑥ Shout—Part 1	The Isley Brothers	RCA Victor
So Many Ways	Brook Benton	Mercury
Unforgettable	Dinah Washington	Mercury
⑥ We Got Love	Bobby Rydell	Cameo
Woo-Hoo	The Rock-A-Teens	Roulette

NOVEMBER

Always	Sammy Turner	Big Top
⑥ Among My Souvenirs	Connie Francis	MGM
⑥ Believe Me	The Royal Teens	Capitol
Be My Guest	Fats Domino	Imperial
The Big Hurt	Toni Fisher	Signet
⑥ Dance With Me	The Drifters	Atlantic
High School U.S.A.	Tommy Facenda	Atlantic
Hound Dog Man/This Friendly World	Fabian	Chancellor
It Happened Today	The Skyliners	Calico
It's Time To Cry	Paul Anka	ABC Paramount
Pretty Blue Eyes	Steve Lawrence	ABC Paramount
Reveille Rock	Johnny & the Hurricanes	Warwick
⑥ Way Down Yonder In New Orleans	Freddy Cannon	Swan
☆ ⑥ Why/Swingin' On A Rainbow	Frankie Avalon	Chancellor
⑥ You Got What It Takes	Marv Johnson	United Artists

83

DECEMBER

Go, Jimmy, Go	Jimmy Clanton	Ace
The Happy Reindeer	Dancer, Prancer & Nervous	Capitol
⑥ He'll Have To Go	Jim Reeves	RCA Victor
I Wanna Be Loved	Ricky Nelson	Imperial
☆ ⑥ Running Bear	Johnny Preston	Mercury
Sandy	Larry Hall	Strand
⑥ Smokie—Part 2	Bill Black's Combo	Hi
Swingin' On A Rainbow	Frankie Avalon	Chancellor
Talk That Talk	Jackie Wilson	Brunswick
Tear Drop	Santo & Johnny	Canadian-American
☆ ⑥ Teen Angel	Mark Dinning	MGM
Uh! Oh! Part 2	The Nutty Squirrels	Hanover
The Village Of St. Bernadette	Andy Williams	Cadence
A Year Ago Tonight	The Crests	Coed

TOP SINGLES OF 1959

⑥ The Battle of New Orleans	Johnny Horton	Columbia
⑥ Come Softly To Me	The Fleetwoods	Dolphin
⑥ Heartaches By The Number	Guy Mitchell	Columbia
⑥ Kansas City	Wilbert Harrison	Fury
⑥ Lonely Boy	Paul Anka	ABC Paramount
⑥ Mack The Knife	Bobby Darin	Atco
⑥ Smoke Gets In Your Eyes	The Platters	Mercury
⑥ Stagger Lee	Lloyd Price	ABC Paramount
⑥ The Three Bells	The Browns	RCA Victor
⑥ Venus	Frankie Avalon	Chancellor

TOP ALBUMS OF 1959

⑥ Come Dance With Me!	Frank Sinatra	Capitol
Exotica	Martin Denny	Liberty

***Bobby Vee* (photo: *Kier*)**

Henry Mancini, The Music From Peter Gunn *album cover*

⑥	**Flower Drum Song**	Original Cast	Columbia
⑥	**From The Hungry i**	The Kingston Trio	Capitol
⑫	**Heavenly**	Johnny Mathis	Columbia
⑥	**Here We Go Again!**	The Kingston Trio	Capitol
	Inside Shelley Berman	Shelley Berman	Verve
⑥	**The Kingston Trio At Large**	The Kingston Trio	Capitol
⑥	**The Music From Peter Gunn**	Henry Mancini	RCA Victor
	No One Cares	Frank Sinatra	Capitol

GRAMMY WINNERS IN 1959

The Grammys were awarded at the Beverly Hilton Hotel in Los Angeles on Sunday, November 29, 1959. Meredith Willson was the host.

Record of the Year: "Mack The Knife," Bobby Darin (Atco)
Song of the Year: "The Battle Of New Orleans" (music and lyrics by Jimmy Driftwood)
Album of the Year: *Come Dance With Me,* Frank Sinatra (Capitol)
Best Vocal Performance, Female: "But Not For Me," Ella Fitzgerald (Verve)
Best Vocal Performance, Male: *Come Dance With Me!* Frank Sinatra (Capitol)
Best Vocal Performance, Group: (no award)
Best New Artist of the Year: Bobby Darin
Best Comedy Performance: (spoken) *Inside Shelley Berman,* Shelley Berman (Verve); (musical) "The Battle of Kookamonga," Homer & Jethro (RCA Victor)
Best Soundtrack Album from a Motion Picture or Television: *Anatomy Of A Murder,* Duke Ellington (Columbia)

BIRTHS AND DEATHS IN 1959

MUSIC PERFORMERS BORN IN 1959

Irene Cara, March 18
Sheena Easton, April 27
Steven Pearcy (Ratt), July 3
Jim Kerr (Simple Minds), July 9
Kurtis Blow, August 9
Tony DeFranco (The DeFranco Family), August 31
Shaun Cassidy, September 27

Jack Wagner, October 3
Neil Tennant (Pet Shop Boys), October 4
Julian Cope, October 10
Marie Osmond, October 13
"Weird Al" Yankovic, October 23
Bryan Adams, November 5
Sheila E., December 12
Tracey Ullman, December 30

ROCK ON ALMANAC

MUSIC PERFORMERS AND MUSIC INDUSTRY NOTABLES WHO DIED IN 1959

The Big Bopper, Tuesday, February 3 (plane crash; 23)

Buddy Holly, Tuesday, February 3 (plane crash; 22)

Ritchie Valens, Tuesday, February 3 (plane crash; 17)

Mario Lanza, Wednesday, October 7 (heart attack; 38)

OTHERS WHO DIED IN 1959

Ethel Barrymore
Lou Costello
Cecil B. De Mille
Errol Flynn

Duncan Hines
George Reeves
Frank Lloyd Wright

MOVIES OF 1959

MOVIES FEATURING POP MUSIC ARTISTS

Girls Town   *Stars:* Mamie Van Doren, Mel Torme, Elinor Donahue. *Featured song:* "Lonely Boy" by Paul Anka. *Other musical performers:* The Platters.

Hound Dog Man   *Stars:* Fabian, Stuart Whitman, Carol Lynley, Arthur O'Connell. *Featured songs:* "Hound Dog Man" and "This Friendly World" by Fabian.

Juke Box Rhythm   *Stars:* Jack Jones, Brian Donlevy, George Jessel, Hans Conried. *Featured song:* "Willie And The Hand Jive" by Johnny Otis. *Other musical performers:* The Earl Grant Trio, the Treniers.

OTHER POPULAR MOVIES OF 1959

Anatomy of a Murder
Ben Hur
The Best of Everything
Gidget
Hercules
Imitation of Life
North by Northwest
The Nun's Story
On the Beach

Pillow Talk
Rio Bravo
Some Came Running
Some Like It Hot
Strangers When We Meet
Suddenly, Last Summer
A Summer Place
The World, the Flesh, and the Devil

ACADEMY AWARD WINNERS OF 1959

Best Actor: Charlton Heston, *Ben Hur*
Best Actress: Simone Signoret, *Room at the Top*
Best Picture: *Ben Hur*
Best Song: "High Hopes," *A Hole in the Head* (music by James Van Heusen, lyrics by Sammy Cahn)

TOP TELEVISION SHOWS OF 1959

Father Knows Best
Gunsmoke
Have Gun, Will Travel
Make Room for Daddy
Perry Mason

The Price Is Right
The Red Skelton Show
77 Sunset Strip
Wagon Train
Wanted: Dead or Alive

1960

NEWS HIGHLIGHTS OF 1960

➪ An artificial kidney is introduced that can operate continuously without human monitoring.

➪ In Squaw Valley, California, the Soviet Union wins the Winter Olympics.

➪ Senator John F. Kennedy of Massachusetts is nominated as Democratic Party presidential candidate on the first ballot.

➪ The United States places in orbit the first satellite capable of taking pictures of the earth's weather systems.

➪ The Republican nomination for president is won by Vice President Richard Nixon.

➪ British, Turkish, and Greek officials sign a charter granting Cyprus independence of British rule.

➪ Americans dominate the track and swimming events in the Summer Olympics in Rome.

➪ In Chicago, Kennedy and Nixon meet in the first televised debate between presidential candidates.

➪ Nikita Khrushchev disrupts a meeting at the UN by banging on the podium with his shoe.

➪ John F. Kennedy is elected president by a narrow margin.

➪ An American U-2 spy plane is shot down over Russia. Its pilot, Francis Gary Powers, is captured and imprisoned.

➪ Americans are so concerned about nuclear attacks that they begin building bomb shelters in their basements and backyards.

➪ Convicted murderer and author Caryl Chessman is executed. The publicity around this event draws attention to the many protests against capital punishment occurring worldwide.

➪ *The Howdy Doody Show* comes to an end.

➪ Lucille Ball and Desi Arnaz end their marriage.

SPORTS WINNERS

Baseball   The Pittsburgh Pirates beat the New York Yankees 4 games to 3.

Football

NFL: The Philadelphia Eagles beat the Green Bay Packers 17–13 in Philadelphia.

AFL: (first championship): The Houston Oilers beat the Los Angeles Chargers 24–16 in Houston.

Basketball   The Boston Celtics beat the St. Louis Hawks 4 games to 3 for the NBA title.

Hockey   The Montreal Canadiens beat the Toronto Maple Leafs 4 games to 0 to win the Stanley Cup.

MUSIC HIGHLIGHTS OF 1960

➪ In March, Elvis Presley is discharged from the Army and goes to Nashville, Tennessee, to record "Stuck On You" and "Fame And Fortune," his first stereo release for RCA Victor. The record is rushed to hungry fans, who make it a number one national hit. He proceeds to Miami, Florida, to tape the *Frank Sinatra Timex Show* for ABC television. The show, which airs May 12, features Sinatra, Presley, Sammy Davis, Jr., Joey Bishop, and Nancy Sinatra. This is Elvis's first national appearance in over three years and marks his comeback as an entertainer.

➪ Rock 'n' roll really needs Elvis's presence, since many of the major figures of the fifties are not on the charts. Buddy Holly, Ritchie Valens, the Big Bopper, Jesse Belvin, and Eddie Cochran are dead. Little Richard is in the ministry, Chuck Berry is in jail, and Alan Freed is under investigation for taking payola.

➪ Lead singer Tony Williams leaves the Platters and is replaced by Sonny Turner. Neither Williams as a solo nor the Platters as a group comes close to the success they had together in the fifties with songs like "The Great Pretender," "My Prayer," "Smoke Gets In Your Eyes," and "Twilight Time."

1960

- A 30-year-old from Detroit, Michigan, named Berry Gordy, Jr., writes a song called "Money," which becomes a hit for Barrett Strong on the Anna label. Thanks to this fledgling success, Gordy is able to raise enough money to form his own label, Tamla, the first step in the Motown success story, sustained by early hits like "Way Over There" by the Miracles.
- The Beatles begin to make appearances beyond Liverpool, including several in Hamburg, Germany.
- Dion & the Belmonts dissolve the group, with Dion going on as a solo on Laurie records and Freddie Milano, Carlo Mastrangelo, and Angelo D'Aleo continuing as the Belmonts on Sabrina Records.
- On Thursday, December 1, rock star Bobby Darin marries movie queen Sandra Dee in the living room of a New Jersey magistrate.
- *Bye Bye Birdie* opens, the first rock musical on Broadway.
- After seven straight hits as the lead voice of the Drifters with songs like "There Goes My Baby" and "Save The Last Dance For Me," Ben E. King leaves the group to go out as a solo performer. His replacement is Rudy Lewis.

DEBUT ARTISTS OF 1960

MAJOR ARTISTS	Debut Single	Label
Gary "U.S." Bonds	New Orleans	Legrand
The Brothers Four (Bob Flick, Mike Kirkland, John Paine, Richard Foley)	Greenfields ⑥	Columbia
Johnny Burnette	Dreamin'	Liberty
Jerry Butler	He Will Break Your Heart	Vee Jay
The Chiffons (Judy Craig, Barbara Lee, Patricia Bennett, Sylvia Peterson)	Tonight's The Night	Big Deal
Skeeter Davis	(I Can't Help You) I'm Falling Too	RCA Victor
Dion (DiMucci)	Lonely Teenager	Laurie
Ferrante & Teicher (Arthur Ferrante, Louis Teicher)	Theme From The Apartment ⑥	United Artists
Brian Hyland	Itsy Bitsy Teenie Weenie Yellow Polka Dot Bikini ☆ ⑥	Leader
Bert Kaempfert	Wonderland By Night ☆ ⑥	Decca

Gary "U.S." Bonds (photo: *John Apostole*)

89

The Brothers Four (l to r: John Paine, Mike Kirkland, Richard Foley, Bob Flick)

Henry Mancini	Mr. Lucky	RCA Victor
Charlie Rich	Lonely Weekends Ⓖ	Phillips
Ike & Tina Turner	A Fool In Love Ⓖ	Sue
The Ventures (Nokie Edwards, Don Wilson, Bob Bogle, Howie Johnson)	Walk—Don't Run Ⓖ	Dolton
Adam Wade	Tell Her For Me	Coed
Lenny Welch	You Don't Know Me	Cadence

OTHER ARTISTS

The Beau-Marks	Joiner, Arkansas, Junior High School Band
Jeanne Black	Jimmy Jones
Billy Bland	Joe Jones
Johnny Bond	The Knockouts
James Booker	The Little Dippers
Walter Brennan	Lolita
Donnie Brooks	Bob Luman
Buster Brown	Bobby Marchan
Al Brown's Tunetoppers	Gary Miles
Ray Bryant	Gary Mills
Bud & Travis	The Paradons
Dorsey Burnette	Rosie & the Originals
Al Caiola	Spencer Ross
Jimmy Charles	Charlie Ryan
The Chimes	The Safaris
Dante & the Evergreens	The Shells
The Demensions	Ray Smith
Harold Dorman	Joanie Sommers
The Fendermen	The Statues
Johnny Ferguson	Connie Stevens
Frank Gari	Barrett Strong
Dean Hawley	The Temptations
Jessie Hill	Larry Verne
Ron Holden	The Viscounts
The Hollywood Argyles	Maurice Williams & the Zodiacs
The Ivy Three	Kathy Young and the Innocents
Wanda Jackson	

1960

JANUARY

The Big Hurt	Toni Fisher	Signet
Bulldog	The Fireballs	Top Rank
Down By The Station	The Four Preps	Capitol
☆ ⑥ El Paso	Marty Robbins	Columbia
⑥ Handy Man	Jimmy Jones	Cub
⑥ Honey Hush *(re-entry)*	Joe Turner	Atlantic
How About That	Dee Clark	Abner
I Can't Say Goodbye	The Fireflies	Ribbon
If I Had A Girl	Rod Lauren	RCA Victor
Let It Be Me	The Everly Brothers	Cadence
Shimmy, Shimmy, Ko-Ko Bop	Little Anthony & the Imperials	End
⑥ Sweet Nothin's	Brenda Lee	Decca
☆ ⑥ Theme From A Summer Place	Percy Faith	Columbia
Tracy's Theme	Spencer Ross	Columbia
Where Or When	Dion & the Belmonts	Laurie

FEBRUARY

⑥ Baby (You Got What It Takes)	Dinah Washington & Brook Benton	Mercury
⑥ Beyond The Sea	Bobby Darin	Atco
Forever	The Little Dippers	University
Harbor Lights	The Platters	Mercury
Lady Luck	Lloyd Price	ABC Para-mount
Midnight Special	Paul Evans	Guaranteed
⑥ Money	Barrett Strong	Anna
O Dio Mio	Annette	Vista
⑥ Puppy Love	Paul Anka	ABC Para-mount
⑥ Rockin' Little Angel	Ray Smith	Judd
String Along/About This Thing Called Love	Fabian	Chancellor
Tall Oak Tree	Dorsey Burnette	Era
This Magic Moment	The Drifters	Atlantic
⑥ What In The World's Come Over You	Jack Scott	Top Rank
⑥ Wild One/Little Bitty Girl	Bobby Rydell	Cameo

MARCH

Angela Jones	Johnny Ferguson	MGM
Big Iron	Marty Robbins	Columbia
Chattanooga Shoe Shine Boy	Freddy Cannon	Swan
Clementine	Bobby Darin	Atco
Footsteps	Steve Lawrence	ABC Para-mount
⑥ Greenfields	The Brothers Four	Columbia
I Love The Way You Love	Marv Johnson	United Artists
⑥ Mama	Connie Francis	MGM
⑥ Night/Doggin' Around	Jackie Wilson	Brunswick

91

The Old Lamplighter	The Browns	RCA Victor
Outside My Window	The Fleetwoods	Dolton
Sink The Bismarck	Johnny Horton	Columbia
Step By Step	The Crests	Coed
Teenage Sonata	Sam Cooke	RCA Victor
⑥ White Silver Sands	Bill Black's Combo	Hi

APRIL

Cherry Pie	Skip & Flip	Brent
Cradle Of Love	Johnny Preston	Mercury
⑥ Good Timin'	Jimmy Jones	Cub
Just A Closer Walk With Thee	Jimmie Rodgers	Roulette
⑥ Lonely Weekends	Charlie Rich	Phillips
Love You So	Ron Holden	Donna
The Madison	Al Brown's Tunetoppers	Amy
Mountain Of Love	Harold Dorman	Rita
Mr. Lucky	Henry Mancini	RCA Victor
⑥ Paper Roses	Anita Bryant	Carlton
Ruby	Adam Wade	Coed
Shazam!	Duane Eddy	Jamie
Stairway To Heaven	Neil Sedaka	RCA Victor
☆ ⑥ Stuck On You/Fame And Fortune	Elvis Presley	RCA Victor
The Ties That Bind	Brook Benton	Mercury

MAY

Another Sleepless Night	Jimmy Clanton	Ace
Barbara	The Temptations	Goldisc
☆ ⑥ Cathy's Clown	The Everly Brothers	Warner Bros.
☆ ⑥ Everybody's Somebody's Fool	Connie Francis	MGM
Happy-Go-Lucky Me	Paul Evans	Guaranteed
⑥ He'll Have To Stay	Jeanne Black	Capitol
Jump Over	Freddy Cannon	Swan
Nobody Loves Me Like You	The Flamingos	End

Skeeter Davis

Brian Hyland (photo: **Maurice Seymour**)

A Rockin' Good Way	Dinah Washington & Brook Benton	Mercury
⑥ Swingin' School/Ding-A-Ling	Bobby Rydell	Cameo
Think	James Brown & the Famous Flames	Federal
When You Wish Upon A Star	Dion & the Belmonts	Laurie
⑥ Wonderful World	Sam Cooke	Keen
(Won't You Come Home) Bill Bailey	Bobby Darin	Atco
Young Emotions	Ricky Nelson	Imperial

JUNE

☆ ⑥ Alley-Oop	The Hollywood Argyles	Lute
⑥ Because They're Young	Duane Eddy	Jamie
Clap Your Hands	The Beau-Marks	Shad
Down Yonder	Johnny & the Hurricanes	Big Top
Ebb Tide	The Platters	Mercury
Image Of A Girl	The Safaris	Eldo
☆ ⑥ I'm Sorry/That's All You Gotta Do	Brenda Lee	Decca
Mule Skinner Blues	The Fendermen	Soma
⑥ My Home Town	Paul Anka	ABC Paramount
National City	The Joiner, Arkansas, Junior High School Band	Liberty
Ooh Poo Pah Doo (Part 2)	Jessie Hill	Minit
Pennies From Heaven	The Skyliners	Calico
Please Help Me, I'm Falling	Hank Locklin	RCA Victor
⑥ Walking To New Orleans	Fats Domino	Imperial
Walkin' The Floor Over You	Pat Boone	Dot

JULY

Feel So Fine	Johnny Preston	Mercury
⑥ Finger Poppin' Time	Hank Ballard & the Midnighters	King
⑥ In My Little Corner Of The World	Anita Bryant	Carlton
☆ ⑥ It's Now Or Never/A Mess Of Blues	Elvis Presley	RCA Victor
☆ ⑥ Itsy Bitsy Teenie Weenie Yellow Polka Dot Bikini	Brian Hyland	Leader
⑥ Josephine	Bill Black's Combo	Hi
Look For A Star	Garry Mills	Imperial
⑥ Only The Lonely	Roy Orbison	Monument
Question	Lloyd Price	ABC Paramount
Red Sails In The Sunset	The Platters	Mercury
Tell Laura I Love Her	Ray Peterson	RCA Victor
This Bitter Earth	Dinah Washington	Mercury
Trouble In Paradise	The Crests	Coed
Volare	Bobby Rydell	Cameo
When Will I Be Loved	The Everly Brothers	Cadence

93

AUGUST

⑥ Devil Or Angel	Bobby Vee	Liberty
⑥ Dreamin'	Johnny Burnette	Liberty
Hot Rod Lincoln	Johnny Bond	Republic
I Shot Mr. Lee	The Bobbettes	Triple-X
Kiddio	Brook Benton	Mercury
Little Bitty Pretty One	Frankie Lymon	Roulette
A Million To One	Jimmy Charles	Promo
Over The Rainbow	The Demensions	Mohawk
Pineapple Princess	Annette	Vista
⑥ Theme From The Apartment	Ferrante & Teicher	United Artists
☆ ⑥ The Twist	Chubby Checker	Parkway
⑥ Walk—Don't Run	The Ventures	Dolton
Yogi	The Ivy Three	Shell
You Mean Everything To Me	Neil Sedaka	RCA Victor
(You Were Made For) All My Love/A Woman, A Lover, A Friend	Jackie Wilson	Brunswick

SEPTEMBER

⑥ Chain Gang	Sam Cooke	RCA Victor
Diamonds And Pearls	The Paradons	Milestone
⑥ Don't Be Cruel	Bill Black's Combo	Hi
⑥ A Fool In Love	Ike & Tina Turner	Sue
☆ I Want To Be Wanted/Just A Little	Brenda Lee	Decca
Let's Have A Party	Wanda Jackson	Capitol
⑥ Move Two Mountains	Marv Johnson	United Artists
☆ ⑥ Mr. Custer	Larry Verne	Era
Nice 'N' Easy	Frank Sinatra	Capitol
☆ ⑥ Save The Last Dance For Me	The Drifters	Atlantic
Shimmy Like Kate	The Olympics	Arvee
Sleep	Little Willie John	King
So Sad/Lucille	The Everly Brothers	Warner Bros.
Three Nights A Week	Fats Domino	Imperial
You Talk Too Much	Joe Jones	Ric

Jimmy Jones (photo: **Bruno of Hollywood**)

Henry Mancini

OCTOBER

Alone At Last	Jackie Wilson	Brunswick
Artificial Flowers	Bobby Darin	Atco
⑥ Blue Angel	Roy Orbison	Monument
☆ ⑥ Georgia On My Mind	Ray Charles	ABC Para-mount
The Hucklebuck	Chubby Checker	Parkway
⑥ Last Date	Floyd Cramer	RCA Victor
⑥ Let's Go, Let's Go, Let's Go	Hank Ballard & the Midnighters	King
Let's Think About Livin'	Bob Luman	Warner Bros.
New Orleans	U.S. Bonds	LeGrand
⑥ North To Alaska	Johnny Horton	Columbia
⑥ Poetry In Motion	Johnny Tillotson	Cadence
☆ ⑥ Stay	Maurice Williams & the Zodiacs	Herald
Summer's Gone	Paul Anka	ABC Para-mount
⑥ Tonight's The Night	The Shirelles	Scepter
Twistin' U.S.A.	Danny & the Juniors	Swan

NOVEMBER

☆ ⑥ Are You Lonesome Tonight?/ I Gotta Know	Elvis Presley	RCA Victor
Exodus	Ferrante & Teicher	United Artists
Fools Rush In	Brook Benton	Mercury
He Will Break Your Heart	Jerry Butler	Vee Jay
I'll Save The Last Dance For You	Damita Jo	Mercury
Lonely Teenager	Dion	Laurie
⑥ Many Tears Ago	Connie Francis	MGM
My Girl Josephine	Fats Domino	Imperial
⑥ Perfidia	The Ventures	Dolton
⑥ Sailor (Your Home Is The Sea)	Lolita	Kapp
Sway	Bobby Rydell	Cameo
A Thousand Stars	Kathy Young & the Innocents	Indigo
Wait For Me	The Playmates	Roulette
☆ ⑥ Wonderland By Night	Bert Kaempfert	Decca
⑥ You're Sixteen	Johnny Burnette	Liberty

Charlie Rich

Adam Wade

Lenny Welch (photo: *Bruno of Hollywood*)

DECEMBER

	Angel Baby	Rosie & the Originals	Highland
☆ ⓖ	Calcutta	Lawrence Welk	Dot
	Calendar Girl	Neil Sedaka	RCA Victor
	Christmas Auld Lang Syne	Bobby Darin	Atco
	Corinna, Corinna	Ray Peterson	Dunes
	I Count The Tears	The Drifters	Atlantic
	The Magnificent Seven	Al Caiola	United Artists
	Once In A While	The Chimes	Tag
ⓖ	Rockin' Around The Christmas Tree	Brenda Lee	Decca
	Rubber Ball	Bobby Vee	Liberty
	Sad Mood	Sam Cooke	RCA Victor
ⓖ	Shop Around	The Miracles	Tamla
	There She Goes	Jerry Wallace	Challenge
	Twistin' Bells	Santo & Johnny	Canadian-American
☆ ⓖ	Will You Love Me Tomorrow	The Shirelles	Scepter

TOP SINGLES OF 1960

ⓖ	Alley-Oop	The Hollywood Argyles	Lute
ⓖ	Are You Lonesome Tonight?	Elvis Presley	RCA Victor
ⓖ	Cathy's Clown	The Everly Brothers	Warner Bros.
ⓖ	I'm Sorry	Brenda Lee	Decca
ⓖ	It's Now Or Never	Elvis Presley	RCA Victor
ⓖ	My Heart Has A Mind Of Its Own	Connie Francis	MGM
ⓖ	Save The Last Dance For Me	The Drifters	Atlantic
ⓖ	Stuck On You	Elvis Presley	RCA Victor
ⓖ	Theme From A Summer Place	Percy Faith	Columbia
ⓖ	The Twist	Chubby Checker	Parkway

TOP ALBUMS OF 1960

ⓖ	The Button-Down Mind Of Bob Newhart	Bob Newhart	Warner Bros.

96

	Elvis Is Back!	Elvis Presley	RCA Victor
⑥	**Faithfully**	Johnny Mathis	Columbia
	Italian Favorites	Connie Francis	MGM
	Music From Mr. Lucky	Henry Mancini	RCA Victor
⑥	**Nice 'N' Easy**	Frank Sinatra	Capitol
⑥	**Sold Out**	The Kingston Trio	Capitol
⑥	**The Sound Of Music**	Original Cast	Columbia
⑥	**String Along**	The Kingston Trio	Capitol
⑥	**Theme From A Summer Place**	Billy Vaughn	Dot

1960

GRAMMY WINNERS IN 1960

The Grammys were awarded at the Beverly Hilton Hotel in Los Angeles on Wednesday, April 12, 1961. Mort Sahl was the host.

Record of the Year: "Theme From A Summer Place," Percy Faith (Columbia)
Song of the Year: "Theme From Exodus" (music and lyrics by Ernest Gold)
Album of the Year: *The Button-Down Mind Of Bob Newhart,* Bob Newhart (Warner Bros.)
Best Vocal Performance, Female: (single) "Mack The Knife," Ella Fitzgerald (Verve); (album) *Ella In Berlin,* Ella Fitzgerald (Verve)
Best Vocal Performance, Male: (single) "Georgia On My Mind," Ray Charles (ABC Paramount); (album) *The Genius Of Ray Charles,* Ray Charles (ABC Paramount)
Best Vocal Performance, Group: *We Got Us,* Steve Lawrence & Eydie Gorme (ABC Paramount)
Best New Artist of the Year: Bob Newhart
Best Comedy Performance: (spoken) *The Button-Down Mind Strikes Back!* Bob Newhart (Warner Bros.); (musical) *Jonathan And Darlene Edwards In Paris,* Jonathan and Darlene Edwards (Columbia)
Best Soundtrack Album from a Motion Picture or Television: *Exodus,* Ernest Gold (RCA Victor)

BIRTHS AND DEATHS IN 1960

MUSIC PERFORMERS BORN IN 1960

Holly Johnson (Frankie Goes To Hollywood), February 19
Laurie Sargent (Face To Face), March 22
Brian Setzer (Stray Cats), April 10

Bono Vox (Paul Hewson of U2), May 10
John Butcher, June 5
John Taylor, June 20
Evelyn "Champagne" King, July 1

Presenting Dion and the Belmonts *album cover*

Mark Holmes (Platinum Blonde), July 26
Madonna (Madonna Louise Ciccone),
    August 16
Joan Jett, September 22

Jennifer Holliday, October 19
Kim Wilde, November 18
Rick Savage (Def Leppard), December 2

MUSIC PERFORMERS AND MUSIC INDUSTRY NOTABLES WHO DIED IN 1960

Jesse Belvin, Saturday, February 6 (car
    crash; 26)
Eddie Cochran, Sunday, April 17 (car
    crash; 21)

Oscar Hammerstein II, Tuesday, August
    23 (stomach cancer; 65)
Johnny Horton, Saturday, October 5 (car
    crash; 33)

OTHERS WHO DIED IN 1960

Clark Gable
Emily Post

John D. Rockefeller, Jr.
Mack Sennett

MOVIES OF 1960

MOVIES FEATURING POP MUSIC ARTISTS

Because They're Young   *Stars:* Dick Clark (film debut), Michael Callan, Tuesday Weld, Doug McClure, James Darren. *Featured songs:* "Shazam!" by Duane Eddy & the Rebels, "Swingin' School" by Bobby Rydell (who does not appear).
Flaming Star   *Stars:* Elvis Presley, Barbara Eden, Steve Forrest, John McIntire. *Featured song:* "Flaming Star."
G.I. Blues   *Stars:* Elvis Presley, Juliet Prowse, James Douglas. *Featured songs:* "G.I. Blues," "Wooden Heart."

OTHER POPULAR MOVIES OF 1960

The Alamo
The Apartment
Butterfield 8
Can-Can
Elmer Gantry
Exodus
Inherit the Wind

The Magnificent Seven
Never on Sunday
North to Alaska
Psycho
Spartacus
The Time Machine
Where the Boys Are

ACADEMY AWARD WINNERS OF 1960

Best Actor: Burt Lancaster, *Elmer Gantry*
Best Actress: Elizabeth Taylor, *Butterfield 8*
Best Picture: *The Apartment*
Best Song: "Never On Sunday," *Never on Sunday* (music and lyrics by Manos Hadjidakis)

TOP TELEVISION SHOWS OF 1960

The Andy Griffith Show
Candid Camera
Gunsmoke
Have Gun, Will Travel
The Jack Benny Show

The Price Is Right
Rawhide
The Real McCoys
The Untouchables
Wagon Train

1961

NEWS HIGHLIGHTS OF 1961

⇨ The recipient of the Nobel Peace Prize is South African civil rights leader Albert Luthuli.

⇨ Crown Prince Moulay Hassan is the new king of Morocco.

⇨ The U.S. Peace Corps is formed to aid developing nations.

⇨ The Soviets win the race to place a man in space by sending Major Yuri Gagarin into orbit.

⇨ The first American in space, Navy Lieutenant Commander Alan B. Shepard, Jr., makes a 15-minute flight 115 miles above the earth.

⇨ President Kennedy and Soviet Premier Khrushchev hold a two-day summit meeting in Vienna.

⇨ The Communist occupation administration in East Berlin erects a wall to separate the Soviet eastern sector of the city from the three Western-occupied sectors.

⇨ The Soviet Communist Party votes for the removal of Stalin from Lenin's tomb.

⇨ Former Nazi Adolf Eichmann is sentenced to death in Israel.

⇨ Scientist Harry Hess of Princeton University advances the revolutionary new theory of continental drift.

SPORTS WINNERS

Baseball   The New York Yankees beat the Cincinnati Reds 4 games to 1.
Football
  NFL: The Green Bay Packers beat the New York Giants 37–0 in Green Bay, Wisconsin.
  AFL: The Houston Oilers beat the San Diego Chargers 10–3 in San Diego.
Basketball   The Boston Celtics beat the St. Louis Hawks 4 games to 1 to nab the NBA title.
Hockey   The Chicago Black Hawks beat the Detroit Red Wings 4 games to 2 to take the Stanley Cup.

MUSIC HIGHLIGHTS OF 1961

⇨ "The Second Time Around" is the debut single on Frank Sinatra's new Reprise label.

⇨ In March, the Beatles make their first appearance at the Cavern Club in Liverpool.

⇨ Bob Dylan makes his debut concert appearance at Gerde's Folk City in New York's Greenwich Village.

⇨ The Liverpool fan magazine *Mersey Beat* debuts.

⇨ America goes dance crazy with songs like "Pony Time," "The Fly," and "The Twist" by Chubby Checker, "Peppermint Twist" by Joey Dee & the Starliters, "Bristol Stomp" by the Dovells, and "The Majestic" by Dion.

The Crystals (photo: Bruno of Hollywood)

1961

⇨ Writer-producer Phil Spector launches the Philles label (the name combines Spector's first name with that of his partner, Lester Sill). First release is the Crystals' "There's No Other," a precursor of Spector's trademark "wall of sound," dense, Latin-flavored orchestrations with a heavy beat he used for performers like the Crystals, the Ronettes, Darlene Love, Bob B. Soxx & the Blue Jeans, and the Righteous Brothers.

⇨ "Those Oldies But Goodies" by Little Caesar & the Romans unleashes a wave of nostalgia for the fifties. The word *oldies* becomes associated with the hits of the past, and doo-wop groups like the Cleftones with "Heart And Soul," the Marcels with "Blue Moon," the Regents with "Barbara Ann," and the Capris with "There's A Moon Out Tonight" enjoy chart success.

⇨ FM stereo becomes available for the first time.

DEBUT ARTISTS OF 1961

MAJOR ARTISTS	Debut Single	Label
The Angels (Linda Jansen, Barbara Allbut, Phyllis "Jiggs" Allbut)	'Til	Caprice
The Belmonts (Angelo D'Aleo, Freddie Milano and Carlo Mastrangelo)	Tell Me Why	Sabrina
Maxine Brown	All In My Mind	Nomar
Solomon Burke	Just Out of Reach	Atlantic
Glen Campbell	Turn Around, Look At Me	Crest
Johnny Crawford	Daydreams	Del-Fi
The Crystals (Mary Thomas, Dee Dee Kennibrew, Lala Brooks, Barbara Alston, Pat Wright)	There's No Other (Like My Baby)	Philles
Vic Dana	Little Altar Boy	Dolton
Joey Dee & the Starliters (Joey Dee, Carlton Latimor, Willie Davis, Larry Vernieri, David Brigati)	Peppermint Twist ☆ Ⓖ	Roulette
Dick & Dee Dee (Dick St. John, Dee Dee Sperling)	The Mountain's High Ⓖ	Liberty
Ral Donner	Girl Of My Best Friend	Gone
Lee Dorsey	Ya Ya Ⓖ	Fury
The Dovells (Len Barry, Jerry Summers Gross, Mike Dennis, Arnie Satin, Danny Brooks)	Bristol Stomp Ⓖ	Parkway
The Earls (Larry Chance, Robert Del Din, Eddie Harder, Larry Palumbo, John Wray)	Life Is But A Dream	Rome
Aretha Franklin	Won't Be Long	Columbia
Dickie Goodman	The Touchables	Mark X
The Impressions (Curtis Mayfield, Sam Gooden, Fred Cash)	Gypsy Woman	ABC Paramount
Chuck Jackson	I Don't Want To Cry	Wand
Ben E. King	Spanish Harlem/First Taste Of Love	Atco
Gladys Knight & the Pips (Gladys Knight, Merald "Bubba" Knight, William Guest, Edward Patten)	Every Beat Of My Heart Ⓖ	Fury/Vee Jay
The Lettermen (Bob Engemann, Tony Butala, Jim Pike)	The Way You Look Tonight	Capitol
Gloria Lynne	Impossible	Everest

101

The Marvelettes (Gladys Horton, Katherine Anderson, Georgeanna Tillman, Juanita Cowart, Wanda Young)	Please Mr. Postman ☆ ⑤	Tamla
Gene McDaniels	A Hundred Pounds Of Clay ⑤	Liberty
Tony Orlando	Halfway To Paradise	Epic
Gene Pitney	(I Wanna) Love My Life Away	Musicor
Paul Revere & the Raiders (Paul Revere, Mark Lindsay, Drake Levin, Phil Volk, Mike Smith)	Like Long Hair	Gardena
Linda Scott	I've Told Every Little Star	Canadian-American
Del Shannon	Runaway ☆ ⑤	Big Top
Shep & the Limelites (James "Shep" Sheppard, Clarence Bassett, Charles Baskerville)	Daddy's Home	Hull
The Spinners (Robert Smith, Phillippe Wynn, Billy Henderson, Henry Fambrough, Pervis Jackson)	That's What Girls Are Made For	Tri-Phi
Ray Stevens	Jeremiah Peabody's Poly Unsaturated Quick Dissolving Fast Acting Pleasant Tasting Green And Purple Pills	Mercury
Carla Thomas	Gee Whiz (Look At His Eyes)	Atlantic
Sue Thompson	Sad Movies (Make Me Cry) ⑤	Hickory
The Tokens (Jay Siegal, Mitchell Margo, Philip Margo, Hank Medress)	Tonight I Fell In Love ⑤	Warwick
Mary Wells	Bye Bye Baby	Motown
Timi Yuro	Hurt	Liberty

Aretha Franklin in concert (photo: **Anastasia Pantsios**)

The Impressions (l to r: Sam Gooden, Fred Cash, Curtis Mayfield)

OTHER ARTISTS

Ann-Margret
B. Bumble & the Stingers
H. B. Barnum
Joe Barry
The Blue Jays
Dave Brubeck
Ace Cannon
The Capris
Andrea Carroll
The Castells
Cathy Jean & the Roommates
Buzz Clifford
The Corsairs
Don Covay & the Goodtimers
Kenny Dino
Paul Dino
Joe Dowell
The Dreamlovers
The Duals
The Echoes
Bobby Edwards
Jimmy Elledge
The Flares
Shelby Flint
The Frogmen
Barbara George
Janie Grant
The Halos
Slim Harpo
Eddie Harris
The Highwaymen
Eddie Hodges
Jorgen Ingmann
Bullmoose Jackson
The Jarmels
Jose Jimenez
The Jive Five
Ernie K-Doe
Chris Kenner
Adrian Kimberly

Claude King
Freddy King
Kokomo
Curtis Lee
Bobby Lewis
The Limeliters
Little Caesar & the Romans
John D. Loudermilk
The Ly-Dells
Johnny Maestro
Barry Mann
The Marathons
The Marcels
The Mar-Keys
Phil McLean
Hayley Mills
Matt Monro
Bob Moore
The Paris Sisters
The Pentagons
The Quotations
The Ramrods
James Ray
The Regents
Rick & the Keens
Rochell & the Candles
The Sevilles
Troy Shondell
The Showmen
The Sims Twins
The Stereos
The String-A-Longs
Tico & the Triumphs
The Time-Tones
Titus Turner
The Phil Upchurch Combo
The Velvets
The Vibrations
Si Zentner

ROCK ON ALMANAC

Ben E. King (photo: *Maurice Seymour*)

HITS OF 1961

JANUARY

	Angel Baby	Rosie & the Originals	Highland
	Apache	Jorgen Ingmann	Atco
	Baby Sittin' Boogie	Buzz Clifford	Columbia
	Dedicated To The One I Love	The Shirelles	Scepter
	Don't Worry	Marty Robbins	Columbia
	Emotions	Brenda Lee	Decca
	Good Time Baby	Bobby Rydell	Cameo
	Havin' Fun	Dion	Laurie
	If I Knew	Nat "King" Cole	Capitol
☆ ⑥	Pony Time	Chubby Checker	Parkway
	Ruby	Ray Charles	ABC Paramount
	Spanish Harlem/First Taste Of Love	Ben E. King	Atco
	There She Goes	Jerry Wallace	Challenge
⑥	Wheels	The String-A-Longs	Warwick
⑥	Where The Boys Are	Connie Francis	MGM

FEBRUARY

	Angel On My Shoulder	Shelby Flint	Valiant
	Asia Minor	Kokomo	Felsted
	But I Do	Clarence "Frogman" Henry	Argo
	Ebony Eyes/Walk Right Back	The Everly Brothers	Warner Bros.
	Gee Whiz (Look At His Eyes)	Carla Thomas	Atlantic
	I Don't Want To Cry	Chuck Jackson	Wand
	(I Wanna) Love My Life Away	Gene Pitney	Musicor
	Lazy River	Bobby Darin	Atco
	Little Boy Sad	Johnny Burnette	Liberty
	My Empty Arms	Jackie Wilson	Brunswick
	Please Love Me Forever	Cathy Jean & the Roommates	Valmor
☆ ⑥	Surrender/Lonely Man	Elvis Presley	RCA Victor
	There's A Moon Out Tonight	The Capris	Old Town
	To Be Loved (Forever)	The Pentagons	Donna
	You Can Have Her	Roy Hamilton	Epic

104

MARCH

1961

	Baby Blue	The Echoes	Segway
☆ ⑥	Blue Moon	The Marcels	Colpix
	Bumble Boogie	B. Bumble & the Stingers	Rendezvous
	Daddy's Home	Shep & the Limelites	Hull
	Funny	Maxine Brown	Nomar
	Hearts Of Stone	Bill Black's Combo	Hi
	Hideaway	Freddy King	Federal
⑥	A Hundred Pounds Of Clay	Gene McDaniels	Liberty
⑥	I've Told Every Little Star	Linda Scott	Canadian-American
☆	Mother-In-Law	Ernie K-Doe	Minit
⑥	One Mint Julep	Ray Charles	Impulse
⑥	On The Rebound	Floyd Cramer	RCA Victor
	Portrait Of My Love	Steve Lawrence	United Artists
☆ ⑥	Runaway	Del Shannon	Big Top
⑥	Tonight I Fell In Love	The Tokens	Warwick

APRIL

	Breakin' In A Brand New Broken Heart	Connie Francis	MGM
	California Sun	Joe Jones	Roulette
	(Dance The) Mess Around	Chubby Checker	Parkway
	Exodus (In Jazz)	Eddie Harris	Vee Jay
	Flaming Star	Elvis Presley	RCA Victor
	Girl Of My Best Friend	Ral Donner	Gone
	Glory Of Love	The Roommates	Valmor
⑥	I'm A Fool To Care	Joe Barry	Smash
	Little Egypt	The Coasters	Atco

Gladys Knight and the Pips (l to r: William Guest, Merald Knight, Edward Patten, Gladys Knight; photo: Kriegsmann)

105

Mama Said	The Shirelles	Scepter
Peanut Butter	The Marathons	Arvee
☆ ⑥ Running Scared	Roy Orbison	Monument
☆ ⑥ Tossin' And Turnin'	Bobby Lewis	Beltone
Tragedy	The Fleetwoods	Dolton
☆ ⑥ Travelin' Man/Hello Mary Lou	Ricky Nelson	Imperial

MAY

Barbara Ann	The Regents	Gee
⑥ The Boll Weevil Song	Brook Benton	Mercury
⑥ Every Beat Of My Heart	Gladys Knight & the Pips	Fury/Vee Jay
Halfway To Paradise	Tony Orlando	Epic
I Fall To Pieces	Patsy Cline	Decca
⑥ I Feel So Bad/Wild In The Country	Elvis Presley	RCA Victor
Little Devil	Neil Sedaka	RCA Victor
☆ ⑥ Moody River	Pat Boone	Dot
⑥ Raindrops	Dee Clark	Vee Jay
Stand By Me	Ben E. King	Atco
Tell Me Why	The Belmonts	Sabrina
That Old Black Magic	Bobby Rydell	Cameo
Those Oldies But Goodies	Little Caesar & the Romans	Del-Fi
The Writing On The Wall	Adam Wade	Coed
You Always Hurt The One You Love	Clarence "Frogman" Henry	Argo

JUNE

Big Boss Man	Jimmy Reed	Vee Jay
Cupid	Sam Cooke	RCA Victor
Dance On Little Girl	Paul Anka	ABC Paramount
Dum Dum	Brenda Lee	Decca
⑥ Hats Off To Larry	Del Shannon	Big Top
Heart And Soul	The Cleftones	Gee
⑥ I Like It Like That	Chris Kenner	Instant
My Kind Of Girl	Matt Monro	Warwick
Please Stay	The Drifters	Atlantic
☆ ⑥ Quarter To Three	U.S. Bonds	Legrand
Sacred	The Castells	Era
Summertime	The Marcels	Colpix
Tonight (Could Be The Night)	The Velvets	Monument
Yellow Bird	Arthur Lyman	Hi Fi
⑥ You Can't Sit Down, Part 2	The Phil Upchurch Combo	Boyd

JULY

Don't Bet Money Honey	Linda Scott	Canadian-American
Heart And Soul	Jan & Dean	Challenge
Last Night	The Mar-Keys	Satellite

⑥ Let's Twist Again	Chubby Checker	Parkway
☆ ⑥ Michael	The Highwaymen	United Artists
My True Story	The Jive Five	Beltone
Nag	The Halos	Seven Arts
Pretty Little Angel Eyes	Curtis Lee	Dunes
Runaround	The Regents	Gee
School Is Out	Gary (U.S.) Bonds	LeGrand
A Tear	Gene McDaniels	Liberty
That's What Girls Are Made For	The Spinners	Tri-Phi
Time Was	The Flamingos	End
☆ ⑥ Wooden Heart	Joe Dowell	Smash
You Don't Know What You've Got (Until You Lose It)	Ral Donner	Gone

AUGUST

Amor	Ben E. King	Atco
Bless You	Tony Orlando	Epic
⑥ Crying/Candy Man	Roy Orbison	Monument
Hurt	Timi Yuro	Liberty
It's Gonna Work Out Fine	Ike & Tina Turner	Sue
Let The Four Winds Blow	Fats Domino	Imperial
A Little Bit Of Soap	The Jarmels	Laurie
⑥ Little Sister/(Marie's The Name) His Latest Flame	Elvis Presley	RCA Victor
Lover's Island	The Blue Jays	Milestone
⑥ The Mountain's High	Dick & DeeDee	Liberty
☆ ⑥ Take Good Care Of My Baby	Bobby Vee	Liberty
When We Get Married	The Dreamlovers	Heritage
Who Put The Bomp (In The Bomp, Bomp, Bomp)	Barry Mann	ABC Paramount
Without You	Johnny Tillotson	Cadence
Wizard Of Love	The Ly-Dells	Master

SEPTEMBER

⑥ Bristol Stomp	The Dovells	Parkway
☆ ⑥ Hit The Road Jack	Ray Charles	ABC Paramount
I Love How You Love Me	The Paris Sisters	Gregmark

Gene Pitney

Del Shannon (photo: Kriegsmann)

Mary Wells (photo: McGhee's Studio)

(I Love You) For Sentimental Reasons	The Cleftones	Gee
Juke Box Saturday Night	Nino & the Ebb Tides	Madison
Let's Get Together	Hayley Mills	Vista
Look In My Eyes	The Chantels	Carlton
One Track Mind	Bobby Lewis	Beltone
☆ ⑥ Please Mr. Postman	The Marvelettes	Tamla
⑥ Sad Movies (Make Me Cry)	Sue Thompson	Hickory
Sweets For My Sweet	The Drifters	Atlantic
⑥ Take Five	Dave Brubeck	Columbia
The Way You Look Tonight	The Lettermen	Capitol
You Must Have Been A Beautiful Baby	Bobby Darin	Atco
You're The Reason	Bobby Edwards	Crest

OCTOBER

☆ ⑥ Big Bad John	Jimmy Dean	Columbia
Everlovin'/A Wonder Like You	Rick Nelson	Imperial
⑥ The Fly	Chubby Checker	Parkway
Fool #1/Anybody But Me	Brenda Lee	Decca
⑥ Goodbye Cruel World	James Darren	Colpix
Heartaches	The Marcels	Colpix
I Really Love You	The Stereos	Cub
I Understand (Just How You Feel)	The G-Clefs	Terrace
⑥ Moon River	Jerry Butler	Vee Jay
☆ ⑥ Runaround Sue	Dion	Laurie
September In The Rain	Dinah Washington	Mercury
⑥ This Time	Troy Shondell	Liberty
'Til	The Angels	Caprice
⑥ Tonight	Ferrante & Teicher	United Artists
Tower Of Strength	Gene McDaniels	Liberty
⑥ Ya Ya	Lee Dorsey	Fury

NOVEMBER

Crazy	Patsy Cline	Decca
Gypsy Woman	The Impressions	ABC
		Paramount

Happy Birthday, Sweet Sixteen	Neil Sedaka	RCA Victor
It Will Stand	The Showmen	Minit
Let There Be Drums	Sandy Nelson	Imperial
☆ ⑥ The Lion Sleeps Tonight	The Tokens	RCA Victor
☆ ⑥ Peppermint Twist	Joey Dee & the Starliters	Roulette
⑥ Run To Him	Bobby Vee	Liberty
School Is In	Gary (U.S.) Bonds	LeGrand
There's No Other (Like My Baby)	The Crystals	Philles
☆ ⑥ The Twist (re-entry)	Chubby Checker	Parkway
⑥ Town Without Pity	Gene Pitney	Musicor
⑥ Walk On By	Leroy Van Dyke	Mercury
When I Fall In Love	The Lettermen	Capitol
When The Boy In Your Arms (Is The Boy In Your Heart)	Connie Francis	MGM

DECEMBER

Baby It's You	The Shirelles	Scepter
⑥ Can't Help Falling In Love/ Rock-A-Hula Baby	Elvis Presley	RCA Victor
Dear Lady Twist	Gary (U.S.) Bonds	LeGrand
Do-Re-Mi	Lee Dorsey	Fury
Irresistible You/Multiplication	Bobby Darin	Atco
Jambalaya	Fats Domino	Imperial
Little Altar Boy	Vic Dana	Dolton
A Little Bitty Tear	Burl Ives	Decca
Maria	Johnny Mathis	Columbia
⑥ Norman	Sue Thompson	Hickory
Peppermint Twist	Danny Peppermint & the Jumping Jacks	Carlton
Pocketful Of Miracles	Frank Sinatra	Reprise
Turn On Your Love Light	Bobby Bland	Duke
Unchain My Heart	Ray Charles	ABC Paramount
The Wanderer/The Majestic	Dion	Laurie

Shep & the Limelites (top to bottom: *Charles Baskerville, Clarence Bassett, James "Shep" Sheppard;* photo: *Kreigsmann*)

109

ROCK ON
ALMANAC

Chubby Checker and Dick Clark, with Checker's first gold record
(photo: *Norm N. Nite*)

TOP SINGLES OF 1961

⑥ Big Bad John	Jimmy Dean	Columbia
⑥ Blue Moon	The Marcels	Colpix
⑥ The Lion Sleeps Tonight	The Tokens	RCA Victor
⑥ Michael	The Highwaymen	United Artists
⑥ Pony Time	Chubby Checker	Parkway
⑥ Runaround Sue	Dion	Laurie
⑥ Runaway	Del Shannon	Big Top
⑥ Surrender	Elvis Presley	RCA Victor
⑥ Take Good Care Of My Baby	Bobby Vee	Liberty
⑥ Tossin' And Turnin'	Bobby Lewis	Beltone

TOP ALBUMS OF 1961

⑥ Blue Hawaii	Elvis Presley	RCA Victor
⑥ Calcutta!	Lawrence Welk	Dot
⑥ Camelot	Original Cast	Columbia
⑥ Exodus	Soundtrack	RCA Victor
⑥ G.I. Blues	Elvis Presley	RCA Victor
⑥ Judy At Carnegie Hall	Judy Garland	Capitol
Portrait Of Johnny	Johnny Mathis	Columbia
Something For Everybody	Elvis Presley	RCA Victor
Stars For A Summer Night	Various Artists	Columbia
⑥ Wonderland By Night	Bert Kaempfert	Decca

GRAMMY WINNERS IN 1961

The Grammys were awarded at the Beverly Hilton Hotel in Los Angeles on Tuesday, May 29, 1962. Carl Reiner was the host.

Record of the Year: "Moon River," Henry Mancini (RCA Victor)
Song of the Year: "Moon River" (music by Henry Mancini, lyrics by Johnny Mercer)
Album of the Year: *Judy At Carnegie Hall,* Judy Garland (Capitol)
Best Vocal Performance, Female: *Judy At Carnegie Hall,* Judy Garland (Capitol)
Best Vocal Performance, Male: "Lollipops And Roses," Jack Jones (Kapp)

110

Best Vocal Performance, Group: "High Flying," Lambert, Hendricks & Ross (Columbia)

Best Rock 'n' Roll Recording: "Let's Twist Again," Chubby Checker (Parkway)

Best New Artist of the Year: Peter Nero

Best Comedy Performance: *An Evening With Mike Nichols And Elaine May,* Mike Nichols and Elaine May (Mercury)

Best Soundtrack Album from a Motion Picture or Television: *Breakfast At Tiffany's,* Henry Mancini (RCA Victor)

BIRTHS AND DEATHS IN 1961

MUSIC PERFORMERS BORN IN 1961

Vince Neil (Mötley Crüe), February 8
Andy Taylor, February 16
Eddie Murphy, April 3
El DeBarge, June 4
Boy George (Culture Club), June 14

Martin Gore (Depeche Mode), July 23
Fiona (Flanagan), September 13
Leif Garrett, November 8
Eugene Wilde, December 6

NOTABLES WHO DIED IN 1961

Ty Cobb
Gary Cooper
Marion Davies
Dag Hammarskjöld

Moss Hart
George S. Kaufman
Chico Marx
James Thurber

MOVIES OF 1961

MOVIES FEATURING POP MUSIC ARTISTS

Blue Hawaii *Stars:* Elvis Presley, Angela Lansbury, Joan Blackman. *Featured songs:* "Blue Hawaii," "Can't Help Falling In Love," "Rock-A-Hula Baby," "Hawaiian Wedding Song."

Hey, Let's Twist! *Stars:* Joey Dee, Greg Garrison, Teddy Randazzo, Jo-Ann Campbell. *Featured songs:* "Hey, Let's Twist!" "Shout!" and "Peppermint Twist" by Joey Dee & the Starliters. *Other musical performers:* Teddy Randazzo, Jo-Ann Campbell.

Teenage Millionaire *Stars:* Jimmy Clanton, Zasu Pitts, Rocky Graziano. *Featured songs:* "Let's Twist Again" by Chubby Checker, "Smokie" by Bill Black's Combo. *Other musical performers:* Dion, Jackie Wilson, Marv Johnson.

Twist Around the Clock *Stars:* Chubby Checker, Clay Cole, Vicki Spencer. *Featured songs:* "Twistin' USA" by Chubby Checker, "Runaround Sue," "The Wanderer," and "The Majestic" by Dion, and "Blue Moon" by the Marcels. This film was a remake of the 1956 film *Rock Around the Clock.*

Wild in the Country *Stars:* Elvis Presley, Hope Lange, Tuesday Weld, Rafer Johnson. *Featured songs:* "Wild In The Country," "Lonely Man."

OTHER POPULAR MOVIES OF 1961

Breakfast at Tiffany's
The Devil at 4 O'Clock
The Errand Boy
Goodbye Again
The Guns of Navarone
The Hoodlum Priest
The Hustler

Judgment at Nuremberg
King of Kings
The Misfits
Misty
The Music Man
Splendor in the Grass
West Side Story

ROCK ON ALMANAC

West Side Story
album cover

ACADEMY AWARD WINNERS OF 1961

Best Actor: Maximilian Schell, *Judgment at Nuremberg*
Best Actress: Sophia Loren, *Two Women*
Best Picture: *West Side Story*
Best Song: "Moon River," *Breakfast at Tiffany's* (music by Henry Mancini, lyrics by Johnny Mercer)

TOP TELEVISION SHOWS OF 1961

The Andy Griffith Show
Bonanza
Candid Camera
Dr. Kildare
Gunsmoke

Hazel
Make Room for Daddy
Perry Mason
The Red Skelton Show
Wagon Train

1962

ROCK ON ALMANAC

NEWS HIGHLIGHTS OF 1962

⇨ A $4 billion merger is proposed between the Pennsylvania and New York Central railroads. (It is authorized four years later.)

⇨ Lieutenant Colonel John H. Glenn, Jr., is the first American to orbit the earth.

⇨ At New York City's Madison Square Garden, a rally for Republican Senator Barry Goldwater raises $80,000 for conservative causes.

⇨ The Lenin Peace Prize is awarded to artist Pablo Picasso.

⇨ President Kennedy signs a bill authorizing $32 million to expand educational television.

⇨ Brazil's soccer team retains the World Cup championship in Chile.

⇨ The *Telstar* communications satellite transmits the first worldwide TV show.

⇨ Richard Nixon opens his drive for California's governorship.

⇨ The Nobel Prize for Literature is awarded to John Steinbeck.

⇨ Close-up photos of Venus are sent back to earth by the *Mariner 2* spacecraft.

SPORTS WINNERS

Baseball   The New York Yankees beat the San Francisco Giants 4 games to 3.
Football
   NFL: The Green Bay Packers beat the New York Giants 16–7 in New York.
   AFL: The Dallas Texans beat the Houston Oilers in overtime 20–17 in Houston.
Basketball   The Boston Celtics beat the L.A. Lakers 4 games to 3 to win the NBA title.
Hockey   The Toronto Maple Leafs beat the Chicago Black Hawks 4 games to 2 to take the Stanley Cup.

MUSIC HIGHLIGHTS OF 1962

⇨ In January, "The Twist," by Chubby Checker becomes the first (and still only) former number one pop record to have a second chart run all the way to number one.

⇨ The Beatles sign a contract with a 27-year-old record store owner named Brian Epstein to act as their manager.

⇨ Stuart Sutcliffe, an original Beatles member who left the group in 1961, dies of a brain hemorrhage at the age of 22.

⇨ Chris Blackwell founds Island Records, a company originally devoted to West Indian music, including what became Jamaican reggae.

⇨ School friends Keith Richards and Mick Jagger begin sitting in with a band called Alexis Korner's Blues Incorporated. The band's drummer is Charlie Watts, and the three eventually come together with Brian Jones and Bill Wyman as the Rolling Stones. They build a substantial cult following at R&B clubs in London like the Marquee, the Flamingo, and the Crawdaddy.

⇨ Original Beatles drummer Pete Best is asked to leave the group and is replaced by the former drummer for Rory Storm & the Hurricanes, Ringo Starr.

⇨ The California-based Beach Boys' hits "Surfin' " and "Surfin' Safari" give rise to a new fad in rock 'n' roll, "surf music."

⇨ In honor of the first transmission of live television pictures from Europe via the *Telstar* communications satellite, British recording engineer and producer Joe Meek composes an instrumental song called "Telstar" that is recorded by a studio group called the Tornadoes. It tops the charts on both sides of the Atlantic, becoming the first English rock song to reach number one in the United States.

⇨ Female voices dominate the charts. The airwaves are filled with the sounds of Little Eva, Barbara George, Connie Francis, Brenda Lee, Sue Thompson, Ketty Lester, Shelley Fabares, Dee Dee Sharp, Patsy Cline, Claudine Clark, Barbara Lynn, Timi Yuro, and Mary Wells, along with groups like the Ikettes, the Marvelettes, the Shirelles, the Crystals, the Orlons, the Cookies, and the Exciters.

The Beach Boys (clockwise from top: Carl Wilson, Brian Wilson, Mike Love, Al Jardine, Dennis Wilson; photo: Kier)

Booker T. & the MG's (l to r: Donald "Duck" Dunn, Booker T. Jones, Steve Cropper, Al Jackson)

1962

⇨ Peter, Paul & Mary give a major boost to a rekindled interest in folk music and lay the groundwork for a new form of music, protest songs that draw attention to the ills of society.

⇨ "Soul" music begins to get attention thanks to performers like Sam Cooke, Solomon Burke, Otis Redding, Aretha Franklin, and Carla Thomas.

⇨ In October, in Great Britain, the Beatles release their very first record, "Love Me Do," on Parlophone Records no. R4949. It goes to number 17 on the British charts. Beatlemania is still six months away.

DEBUT ARTISTS OF 1962

MAJOR ARTISTS	Debut Single	Label
Steve Alaimo	Mashed Potatoes	Checker
Herb Alpert & the Tijuana Brass	The Lonely Bull ⓖ	A & M
Bobby Bare	Shame On Me	RCA Victor
The Beach Boys (Brian, Carl, and Dennis Wilson, Mike Love, David Marks)	Surfin'	Candix
Booker T. & the MG's (Booker T. Jones, Steve Cropper, Donald "Duck" Dunn, Al Jackson)	Green Onions ⓖ	Stax
Richard Chamberlain	Theme From Dr. Kildare	MGM
Gene Chandler	Duke of Earl ☆ ⓖ	Vee Jay
The Contours (Billy Gordon, Billy Hoggs, Joe Billingslea, Sylvester Potts, Hubert Johnson, Huey Davis)	Do You Love Me ⓖ	Gordy
King Curtis	Soul Twist	Enjoy
The Duprees (Joey Vann, Joe Santollo, John Salvato, Mike Arnone, Tom Bialaglow)	You Belong To Me	Coed

115

The Four Seasons (clockwise from top: *Frankie Valli, Nick Massi, Bob Gaudio, Tommy DeVito;* photo: *Kier)*

The Exciters (Brenda Reid, Carol Johnson, Lilian Walker, Herbert Rooney)	Tell Him	United Artists
The Four Seasons (Frankie Valli, Bob Gaudio, Nick Massi, Tommy DeVito)	Sherry ☆ ⑥	Vee Jay
Marvin Gaye	Stubborn Kind Of Fellow	Tamla
Bobby Goldsboro	Molly	Laurie
Jay & the Americans (Jay Traynor [replaced by Jay Black], Sandy Yaguda, Kenny Vance, Marty Sanders, Howie Kane)	She Cried	United Artists
Jack Jones	Lollipops And Roses	Kapp
Carole King	It Might As Well Rain Until September	Dimension
Dickey Lee	Patches ⑥	Smash
Barbara Lynn	You'll Lose A Good Thing	Jamie
Chris Montez	Let's Dance	Monogram
The New Christy Minstrels	This Land Is Your Land	Columbia
The Orlons (Shirley Brickley, Rosetta Hightower, Marlena Davis, Steve Caldwell)	The Wah Watusi ⑥	Cameo
Peter, Paul & Mary (Peter Yarrow, Paul Stookey, Mary Travers)	Lemon Tree	Warner Bros.
Paul Petersen	She Can't Find Her Keys	Colpix
Jerry Reed	Goodnight Irene	Columbia
Tommy Roe	Sheila ☆ ⑥	ABC Para-mount
Dee Dee Sharp	Mashed Potato Time ⑥	Cameo
Jimmy Smith	Midnight Special, Part I	Blue Note
The Supremes (Diana Ross, Florence Ballard, Mary Wilson)	Your Heart Belongs To Me	Motown
The Tams (Charles and Joseph Pope, Robert Smith, Floyd Ashton, Horace Key)	Untie Me	Arlen

Nino Tempo & April Stevens Sweet And Lovely Atco
Bobby Vinton Roses Are Red ☆ ⑥ Epic
Dionne Warwick Don't Make Me Over Scepter

OTHER ARTISTS

Arthur Alexander
Rex Allen
Kenny Ball & His Jazzmen
William Bell
Mr. Acker Bilk
Billy Joe & the Checkmates
Marcie Blane
The Blue-Belles
Bob B. Soxx & the Blue Jeans
Tommy Boyce
Bob Braun
Bruce Channel
Claudine Clark
Mike Clifford
The Cookies
Les Cooper
Bobby Curtola
Don & Juan
Charlie Drake
The Excellents
Shelly Fabares
Bent Fabric
Larry Finnegan
Gabriel & the Angels
Don Gardner & Dee Dee Ford
Stan Getz & Charlie Byrd
Robert Goulet
Buddy Greco
Bobby Gregg & His Friends
The Vince Guaraldi Trio
Joe Harnell
Joe Henderson
Eddie Holland

Frank Ifield
The Ikettes
Kris Jensen
The Lafayettes
Ketty Lester
Little Eva
Little Joey & the Flips
The Majors
Ernie Maresca
The Marketts
Nathaniel Mayer
Ned Miller
The Chad Mitchell Trio
Johnnie Morisette
The Pastel 6
Emilio Pericoli
Bobby "Boris" Pickett
The Rivingtons
The Rockin' Rebels
Ronnie & the Hi-Lites
The Routers
Saverio Saridis
The Sherrys
Jimmy Soul
The Springfields
Sandy Stewart
Johnny Thunder
The Tornadoes
Mark Valentino
The Valentinos
Valjean
Vito & the Salutations
The Volumes

Marvin Gaye

117

ROCK ON ALMANAC

JANUARY

Break It To Me Gently/So Deep	Brenda Lee	Decca
Dear Ivan	Jimmy Dean	Columbia
☆ ⑥ Duke Of Earl	Gene Chandler	Vee Jay
Go On Home	Patti Page	Mercury
The Greatest Hurt	Jackie Wilson	Brunswick
I Know	Barbara George	AFO
I'm Blue (The Gong-Gong Song)	The Ikettes	Atco
Let Me In	The Sensations	Argo
A Little Bitty Tear	Burl Ives	Decca
Shadrack	Brook Benton	Mercury
She's Everything	Ral Donner	Gone
Smoky Places	The Corsairs	Tuff
Tequila Twist	The Champs	Challenge
Tuff	Ace Cannon	Hi
Twist-Her	Bill Black's Combo	Hi

FEBRUARY

Cajun Queen	Jimmy Dean	Columbia
Chip Chip	Gene McDaniels	Liberty
Crying In The Rain	The Everly Brothers	Warner Bros.
☆ ⑥ Don't Break The Heart That Loves You	Connie Francis	MGM
Her Royal Majesty	James Darren	Colpix
☆ ⑥ Hey! Baby	Bruce Channel	Smash
Hey, Let's Twist	Joey Dee & the Starliters	Roulette
Midnight In Moscow	Kenny Ball & His Jazzmen	Kapp
My Boomerang Won't Come Back	Charlie Drake	United Artists
Percolator (Twist)	Billy Joe & the Checkmates	Dore
She's Got You	Patsy Cline	Decca
Twistin' Postman	The Marvelettes	Tamla
Twistin' The Night Away	Sam Cooke	RCA Victor
What's Your Name	Don & Juan	Big Top
Where Have All The Flowers Gone	The Kingston Trio	Capitol

MARCH

Anything That's Part Of You	Elvis Presley	RCA Victor
Come Back Silly Girl	The Lettermen	Capitol
⑥ Dream Baby	Roy Orbison	Monument
☆ ⑥ Good Luck Charm	Elvis Presley	RCA Victor
I've Got Bonnie	Bobby Rydell	Cameo
☆ ⑥ Johnny Angel	Shelley Fabares	Colpix
⑥ Love Letters	Ketty Lester	Era
Love Me Warm And Tender	Paul Anka	RCA Victor
Lover, Please	Clyde McPhatter	Mercury
⑥ Mashed Potato Time	Dee Dee Sharp	Cameo

Our Anniversary	Shep & the Limelites	Hull
Please Don't Ask About Barbara	Bobby Vee	Liberty
⑥ Slow Twistin'	Chubby Checker	Parkway
When My Little Girl Is Smiling	The Drifters	Atlantic
Young World	Rick Nelson	Imperial

APRIL

⑥ Dear One	Larry Finnegan	Old Town
Funny Way Of Laughin'	Burl Ives	Decca
I Wish That We Were Married	Ronnie & the Hi-Lites	Joy
Lovers Who Wander	Dion	Laurie
P.T. 109	Jimmy Dean	Columbia
She Can't Find Her Keys	Paul Petersen	Colpix
She Cried	Jay & the Americans	United Artists
Shout! Shout! (Knock Yourself Out)	Ernie Maresca	Seville
☆ ⑥ Soldier Boy	The Shirelles	Scepter
Soul Twist	King Curtis	Enjoy
☆ ⑥ Stranger On The Shore	Mr. Acker Bilk	Atco
Tell Me	Dick & DeeDee	Liberty
Twistin' Matilda	Jimmy Soul	SPQR
Twist, Twist, Senora	Gary U.S. Bonds	LeGrand
Uptown	The Crystals	Philles

MAY

Any Day Now	Chuck Jackson	Wand
Don't Play That Song (You Lied)	Ben E. King	Atco
Follow That Dream	Elvis Presley	RCA Victor
☆ ⑥ I Can't Stop Loving You	Ray Charles	ABC Para- mount
I Love You	The Volumes	Chex

1962

The Orlons (l to r: Steve Caldwell, Marlena Davis, Shirley Brickley, Rosetta Hightower; photo: Kriegsmann)

It Keeps Right On A-Hurtin'	Johnny Tillotson	Cadence
⑥ The Man Who Shot Liberty Valance	Gene Pitney	Musicor
Moon River	Henry Mancini	RCA Victor
Old Rivers	Walter Brennan	Liberty
The One Who Really Loves You	Mary Wells	Motown
⑥ Palisades Park	Freddy Cannon	Swan
Playboy	The Marvelettes	Tamla
So This Is Love	The Castells	Era
That's Old Fashioned	The Everly Brothers	Warner Bros.
Village Of Love	Nathaniel Mayer	Fortune/U.A.

JUNE

⑥ Al Di La'	Emilio Pericoli	Warner Bros.
Bristol Twistin' Annie	The Dovells	Parkway
Gravy	Dee Dee Sharp	Cameo
Having A Party	Sam Cooke	RCA Victor
I'll Never Dance Again	Bobby Rydell	Cameo
Lemon Tree	Peter, Paul & Mary	Warner Bros.
☆ ⑥ Roses Are Red	Bobby Vinton	Epic
⑥ Sealed With A Kiss	Brian Hyland	ABC Paramount
Sharing You	Bobby Vee	Liberty
Snap Your Fingers	Joe Henderson	Todd
⑥ Speedy Gonzales	Pat Boone	Dot
☆ ⑥ The Stripper	David Rose	MGM
⑥ Twist And Shout	The Isley Brothers	Wand
⑥ The Wah Watusi	The Orlons	Cameo
⑥ Wolverton Mountain	Claude King	Columbia

JULY

⑥ Ahab The Arab	Ray Stevens	Mercury
Bongo Stomp	Little Joey & the Flips	Joy
☆ ⑥ Breaking Up Is Hard To Do	Neil Sedaka	RCA Victor

Jay & the Americans (clockwise from top: Sandy Yaguda, Jay Black, Marty Sanders, Kenny Vance; photo: Kier)

	Dancing Party	Chubby Checker	Parkway
	(Girls, Girls, Girls) Were Made To Love	Eddie Hodges	Cadence
	I Need Your Loving	Don Gardner & Dee Dee Ford	Fire
	Little Diane	Dion	Laurie
☆ ⑥	**The Loco-Motion**	Little Eva	Dimension
	Party Lights	Claudine Clark	Chancellor
	Route 66 Theme	Nelson Riddle	Capitol
	Seven Day Weekend	Gary U.S. Bonds	LeGrand
	Theme From Doctor Kildare	Richard Chamberlain	MGM
	West Of The Wall	Toni Fisher	Big Top
	You'll Lose A Good Thing	Barbara Lynn	Jamie

AUGUST

⑥	**Alley Cat**	Bent Fabric	Atco
	Come On Little Angel	The Belmonts	Sabrina
	Devil Woman	Marty Robbins	Columbia
	I Left My Heart In San Francisco	Tony Bennett	Columbia
	Make It Easy On Yourself	Jerry Butler	Vee Jay
	Point Of No Return	Gene McDaniels	Liberty
⑥	**Ramblin' Rose**	Nat "King" Cole	Capitol
	Rinky Dink	Dave "Baby" Cortez	Chess
☆ ⑥	**Sheila**	Tommy Roe	ABC Paramount
⑥	**She's Not You**	Elvis Presley	RCA Victor
	Teen Age Idol	Rick Nelson	Imperial
	Vacation	Connie Francis	MGM
	What's A Matter Baby	Timi Yuro	Liberty
	You Belong To Me	The Duprees	Coed
	You Don't Know Me	Ray Charles	ABC Paramount

SEPTEMBER

	Beechwood 4-5789	The Marvelettes	Tamla
⑥	**Green Onions**	Booker T. & the MG's	Stax
	Hully Gully Baby	The Dovells	Parkway
	If I Had A Hammer	Peter, Paul & Mary	Warner Bros.
⑥	**Let's Dance**	Chris Montez	Monogram
⑥	**Limbo Rock/Popeye The Hitchhiker**	Chubby Checker	Parkway
	Papa-Oom-Mow-Mow	The Rivingtons	Liberty
⑥	**Patches**	Dickey Lee	Smash
	Send Me The Pillow You Dream On	Johnny Tillotson	Cadence
☆ ⑥	**Sherry**	The Four Seasons	Vee Jay
	Silver Threads And Golden Needles	The Springfields	Philips
	Surfin' Safari/409	The Beach Boys	Capitol
⑥	**Venus In Blue Jeans**	Jimmy Clanton	Ace
	A Wonderful Dream	The Majors	Imperial
	You Beat Me To The Punch	Mary Wells	Motown

1962

121

ROCK ON ALMANAC

The Supremes (top l to r: *Diana Ross, Cindy Birdsong*; bottom: *Mary Wilson*)

OCTOBER

⑥	All Alone Am I	Brenda Lee	Decca
☆ ⑥	Big Girls Don't Cry	The Four Seasons	Vee Jay
⑥	Bobby's Girl	Marcie Blane	Seville
	The Cha-Cha-Cha	Bobby Rydell	Cameo
	Close To Cathy	Mike Clifford	United Artists
⑥	Don't Hang Up	The Orlons	Cameo
⑥	Do You Love Me	The Contours	Gordy
	Gina	Johnny Mathis	Columbia
☆ ⑥	He's A Rebel	The Crystals	Philles
⑥	I Remember You	Frank Ifield	Vee Jay
☆ ⑥	Monster Mash	Bobby "Boris" Pickett	Garpax
	Next Door To An Angel	Neil Sedaka	RCA Victor
⑥	Only Love Can Break A Heart	Gene Pitney	Musicor
⑥	Return To Sender	Elvis Presley	RCA Victor
	Ride!	Dee Dee Sharp	Cameo

NOVEMBER

	Chains	The Cookies	Dimension
	Dear Lonely Hearts	Nat "King" Cole	Capitol
⑥	Desafinado	Stan Getz & Charlie Byrd	Verve
	Eso Beso	Paul Anka	RCA Victor
☆ ⑥	Go Away Little Girl	Steve Lawrence	Columbia
	Keep Your Hands Off My Baby	Little Eva	Dimension
	Let's Go	The Routers	Warner Bros.
⑥	The Lonely Bull	The Tijuana Brass	A & M
	Love Came To Me	Dion	Laurie
	My Own True Love	The Duprees	Coed
⑥	Release Me	Little Esther Phillips	Lenox
	Stubborn Kind Of Fellow	Marvin Gaye	Tamla
☆ ⑥	Telstar	The Tornadoes	London
	Wiggle Wobble	Les Cooper	Everlast
	Zip-A-Dee-Doo-Dah	Bob B. Soxx & the Blue Jeans	Philles

DECEMBER

Coney Island Baby	The Excellents	Blast
Don't Make Me Over	Dionne Warwick	Scepter
Everybody Loves A Lover	The Shirelles	Scepter
Half Heaven—Half Heartache	Gene Pitney	Musicor
I Saw Linda Yesterday	Dickey Lee	Smash
It's Up To You	Rick Nelson	Imperial
My Dad	Paul Petersen	Colpix
⑥ The Night Has A Thousand Eyes	Bobby Vee	Liberty
⑥ Pepino The Italian Mouse	Lou Monte	Reprise
Remember Then	The Earls	Old Town
Santa Claus Is Coming To Town	Four Seasons	Vee Jay
Tell Him	The Exciters	United Artists
That's Life	Gabriel & the Angels	Swan
⑥ Two Lovers	Mary Wells	Motown
⑥ Up On The Roof	The Drifters	Atlantic

TOP SINGLES OF 1962

⑥ Big Girls Don't Cry	The Four Seasons	Vee Jay
⑥ Duke of Earl	Gene Chandler	Vee Jay
⑥ Good Luck Charm	Elvis Presley	RCA Victor
⑥ Hey! Baby	Bruce Channel	Smash
⑥ I Can't Stop Loving You	Ray Charles	ABC Paramount
⑥ Peppermint Twist	Joey Dee & the Starliters	Roulette
⑥ Roses Are Red	Bobby Vinton	Epic
⑥ Sheila	Tommy Roe	ABC Paramount
⑥ Sherry	The Four Seasons	Vee Jay
⑥ Soldier Boy	The Shirelles	Scepter

TOP ALBUMS OF 1962

⑥ Blue Hawaii	Elvis Presley	RCA Victor
⑥ Breakfast At Tiffany's	Henry Mancini	RCA Victor
College Concert	The Kingston Trio	Capitol

Bobby Vinton

Dionne Warwick (photo: Kier)

⑥ Modern Sounds In Country And Western Music	Ray Charles	ABC Paramount
⑥ My Son, The Folk Singer	Allan Sherman	Warner Bros.
℗ Peter, Paul & Mary	Peter, Paul & Mary	Warner Bros.
⑥ Stranger On The Shore	Mr. Acker Bilk	Atco
⑥ The Stripper And Other Fun Songs For The Family	David Rose	MGM
℗ West Side Story	Soundtrack	Columbia
Your Twist Party	Chubby Checker	Parkway

GRAMMY WINNERS IN 1962

The Grammys were awarded at the Beverly Hilton Hotel in Los Angeles on Wednesday, May 15, 1963. Soupy Sales was the host.

Record of the Year: "I Left My Heart In San Francisco," Tony Bennett (Columbia)
Song of the Year: "What Kind Of Fool Am I" (music by Leslie Bricusse, lyrics by Anthony Newley)
Album of the Year: *The First Family,* Vaughn Meader (Cadence)
Best Vocal Performance, Female: *Ella Fitzgerald Swings With Nelson Riddle,* Ella Fitzgerald (Verve)
Best Vocal Performance, Male: *I Left My Heart In San Francisco,* Tony Bennett (Columbia)
Best Vocal Performance, Group: "If I Had A Hammer," Peter Paul & Mary (Warner Bros.)
Best Rock 'n' Roll Recording: "Alley Cat," Bent Fabric (Atco)
Best New Artist of the Year: Robert Goulet
Best Comedy Performance: *The First Family,* Vaughn Meader (Cadence)
Best Soundtrack Album from a Motion Picture or Television: (no award)

BIRTHS AND DEATHS IN 1962

MUSIC PERFORMERS BORN IN 1962

Foster Sylvers (The Sylvers), February 25
Jon Bongiovi (Bon Jovi), March 2

John Griffith (Red Rockers), April 3
Stanley Burrell (Hammer), March 30

NOTABLES WHO DIED IN 1962

William Faulkner
Ernie Kovacs
Charles Laughton

Marilyn Monroe
Eleanor Roosevelt

MOVIES OF 1962

MOVIES FEATURING POP MUSIC ARTISTS

Don't Knock the Twist *Stars:* Chubby Checker, Mari Blanchard, Lang Jeffries. *Featured songs:* "The Fly" by Chubby Checker, "Slow Twistin' " by Chubby Checker & Dee Dee Sharp, "Duke of Earl" by Gene Chandler, "Mashed Potato Time" by Dee Dee Sharp, "Little Altar Boy" by Vic Dana, "Bristol Stomp" by the Dovells. *Other musical performer:* Linda Scott.
Follow That Dream *Stars:* Elvis Presley, Arthur O'Connell, Anne Helm, Jack Kruschen. *Featured song:* "Follow That Dream."

Peter, Paul and Mary
album cover

1962

Follow the Boys   *Stars:* Connie Francis, Paula Prentiss, Russ Tamblyn. *Featured song:* "Follow The Boys" by Connie Francis.

Girls! Girls! Girls!   *Stars:* Elvis Presley, Stella Stevens, Jeremy Slate. *Featured song:* "Return To Sender."

Kid Galahad   *Stars:* Elvis Presley, Gig Young, Charles Bronson, Lola Albright. *Featured song:* "King Of The Whole Wide World."

Ring-a-Ding Rhythm   *Stars:* Craig Douglas, Felix Fulton, Arthur Mullard. *Featured song:* "Seven Day Weekend" by Gary U.S. Bonds. *Other musical performers:* Chubby Checker, Gene McDaniels, Del Shannon, Gene Vincent. This was British director Richard Lester's first feature film (he later directed *A Hard Day's Night* for the Beatles). In England, it was released as *It's Trad, Dad!*

OTHER POPULAR MOVIES OF 1962

Birdman of Alcatraz
Days of Wine and Roses
Experiment in Terror
Gypsy
The Horizontal Lieutenant
Lawrence of Arabia

Lolita
The Longest Day
The Manchurian Candidate
The Miracle Worker
To Kill a Mockingbird
What Ever Happened to Baby Jane?

ACADEMY AWARD WINNERS OF 1962

Best Actor: Gregory Peck, *To Kill a Mockingbird*
Best Actress: Anne Bancroft, *The Miracle Worker*
Best Picture: *Lawrence of Arabia*
Best Song: "Days Of Wine And Roses," *Days of Wine and Roses* (music by Henry Mancini, lyrics by Johnny Mercer)

TOP TELEVISION SHOWS OF 1962

The Andy Griffith Show
Ben Casey
Beverly Hillbillies
Bonanza
Candid Camera

The Dick Van Dyke Show
Gunsmoke
The Lucy Show
Make Room for Daddy
The Red Skelton Show

1963

⇨ A tennis racquet with a frame of steel rather than wood is patented by former French champion René Lacoste.

⇨ New York newspapers roll off the presses for the first time in 114 days due to strikes.

⇨ Alcatraz in San Francisco Bay is no longer a prison with the removal of the last 27 prisoners.

⇨ President Kennedy receives an extraordinary welcome as more than a million West Berliners turn out to cheer him at the Berlin wall.

⇨ The Soviet Union puts the first woman in space.

⇨ An earthquake in Yugoslavia claims more than 1,000 lives.

⇨ Dr. Martin Luther King, Jr., speaks of justice and equality to more than 200,000 peaceful demonstrators in Washington, D.C.

⇨ A diplomatic "hot line" between Moscow and Washington is made operational.

⇨ President Kennedy authorizes the sale of some 150 million bushels of wheat to the Soviet Union for $250 million.

⇨ President Kennedy is assassinated while riding in a motorcade in Dallas, plunging the nation into mourning. His interment in National Cemetery is watched tearfully on TV by tens of millions.

⇨ With a single .38-caliber bullet, Jack Ruby kills presidential assassin Lee Harvey Oswald as millions watch on TV.

SPORTS WINNERS

Baseball   The Los Angeles Dodgers beat the New York Yankees 4 games to 0.
Football
   NFL: The Chicago Bears beat the New York Giants 14–10 in Chicago.
   AFL: The San Diego Chargers beat the Boston Patriots 51–10 in San Diego.
Basketball   The Boston Celtics beat the Los Angeles Lakers 4 games to 3 to win their fifth consecutive NBA championship.
Hockey   The Toronto Maple Leafs beat the Detroit Red Wings 4 games to 1.

MUSIC HIGHLIGHTS OF 1963

⇨ Los Angeles gets its first rock club with the opening of the Whiskey-a-Go-Go.

⇨ The first Beatles record to arrive in the United States is "Please Please Me," released on Chicago-based Vee Jay Records. It "bubbles under" the national charts.

⇨ An aspiring young manager named Andrew Loog Oldham, in partnership with Eric Easton, begins handling the Rolling Stones and obtains a recording contract with British Decca. The group's first release for Decca is "Come On" (no. F11675). It reaches number 21 on the British charts.

⇨ Car songs become very popular, with tunes like "Shut Down" and "Little Deuce Coupe" by the Beach Boys, "Hey Little Cobra" by the Rip Chords, and "Drag City" by Jan & Dean leading the way.

⇨ Bobby Darin becomes the first rock singer to be nominated for an Academy Award with his best supporting actor nomination in the film *Captain Newman, M.D.*

⇨ Two foreign-language songs become number one hits in America: the Japanese hit "Sukiyaki" by Kyu Sakamoto in June and the French hit "Dominique" by Belgium's Singing Nun in December.

⇨ A British television show similar to Dick Clark's *American Bandstand* makes its debut. *Ready, Steady, Go!* features guest hosts introducing the top recording acts of the day, lip-synching their hits before a live studio audience.

⇨ Fanned by the hits "Love Me Do," "Please Please Me," "From Me To You," and "She Loves You," Beatlemania sweeps England. Capitol Records, the U.S. EMI affiliate, decides to release the Beatles' "I Want To Hold Your Hand" as the group's first "official" single in America. It hits the airwaves at the end of the year; by mid-January it is number one.

DEBUT ARTISTS OF 1963

MAJOR ARTISTS	Debut Single	Label
Joan Baez	We Shall Overcome	Vanguard
Mel Carter	When A Boy Falls In Love	Derby
Lou Christie	The Gypsy Cried ⑥	Roulette
Jackie De Shannon	Faded Love	Liberty
Shirley Ellis	The Nitty Gritty	Congress
Betty Everett	You're No Good	Vee Jay
Lesley Gore	It's My Party ☆ ⑥	Mercury
Dobie Gray	Look At Me	Cor Dak
The Kingsmen (Lynn Easton, Gary Abbott, Don Gallucci, Mike Mitchell, Norm Sundholm)	Louie Louie ⑥	Wand
Major Lance	The Monkey Time	Okeh
Barbara Lewis	Hello Stranger	Atlantic
Trini Lopez	If I Had A Hammer	Reprise
Martha & the Vandellas (Martha Reeves, Roslyn Ashford, Annette Beard)	Come And Get These Memories	Gordy
Garnet Mimms & the Enchanters (Garnet Mimms, Zola Pearnell, Sam Bell, Charles Boyer)	Cry Baby	United Artists
Wayne Newton	Heart	Capitol
The O'Jays (Walter Williams, Eddie Levert, William Powell)	The Lonely Drifter	Imperial
Wilson Pickett	If You Need Me	Double-L
Otis Redding	These Arms Of Mine	Volt
The Righteous Brothers (Bobby Hatfield, Bill Medley)	Little Latin Lupe Lu	Moonglow
The Ronettes (Veronica Bennett Spector, Estelle Bennett, Nedra Talley)	Be My Baby	Philles

Lou Christie

Shirley Ellis

Lesley Gore   *Major Lance*

Ruby & the Romantics (Ruby Nash, Edward Roberts, Robert Mosley, Leroy Fann, George Lee)	Our Day Will Come ☆ ⑥	Kapp
Freddy Scott	Hey Girl	Colpix
Rufus Thomas	The Dog	Stax
The Tymes (Donald Banks, Al Berry, Norman Bennett, George Hilliard, George Williams, Jr.)	So Much In Love ☆ ⑥	Parkway
Nancy Wilson	Tell Me The Truth	Capitol
Little Stevie Wonder	Fingertips—Part 2 ☆ ⑥	Tamla

OTHER ARTISTS

Bill Anderson
Ray Barretto
Barry & the Tamerlanes
Jan Bradley
The Caravelles
The Cascades
The Chantays
The Classics
Johnny Cymbal
Dale & Grace
The Dartells
Dean & Jean
The Dixiebelles
Dave Dudley
The Essex
The Five Du-Tones
Inez & Charlie Foxx
Jimmy Gilmer & the Fireballs
Tom Glazer & the Children's Chorus
The Glencoves
Rolf Harris
Joe Hinton
The Jaynetts
Patti LaBelle & the Blue Belles
Little Peggy March
Los Indios Tabajaras
Darlene Love
Lonnie Mack

The Matys Brothers
The Murmaids
Jack Nitzsche
Joey Powers
Bill Pursell
The Raindrops
The Ran-Dells
Boots Randolph
Randy & the Rainbows
Diane Ray
The Rip Chords
The Rocky Fellers
The Rooftop Singers
Kyu Sakamoto
Mongo Santamaria
The Sapphires
The Secrets
Allan Sherman
The Singing Nun
Sunny & the Sunglows
The Surfaris
The Trashmen
Doris Troy
The Village Stompers
Robin Ward
Kim Weston
Kai Winding

HITS OF 1963

JANUARY

Boss Guitar	Duane Eddy	RCA Victor
Cast Your Fate To The Wind	The Vince Guaraldi Trio	Fantasy
Fly Me To The Moon (Bossa Nova)	Joe Harnell	Kapp
⑥ From A Jack To A King	Ned Miller	Fabor
He's Sure The Boy I Love	The Crystals	Philles
☆ ⑥ Hey Paula	Paul & Paula	Philips
Little Town Flirt	Del Shannon	Big Top
Loop De Loop	Johnny Thunder	Diamond
Mama Didn't Lie	Jan Bradley	Chess
My Coloring Book	Sandy Stewart	Colpix
⑥ Rhythm Of The Rain	The Cascades	Valiant
Shutters And Boards	Jerry Wallace	Challenge
☆ ⑥ Walk Right In	The Rooftop Singers	Vanguard
Wild Weekend	The Rockin' Rebels	Swan
You've Really Got A Hold On Me	The Miracles	Tamla

FEBRUARY

⑥ Blame It On The Bossa Nova	Eydie Gorme	Columbia
⑥ The End Of The World	Skeeter Davis	RCA Victor
Every Day I Have To Cry	Steve Alaimo	Checker
Greenback Dollar	The Kingston Trio	Capitol
⑥ The Gypsy Cried	Lou Christie	Roulette
⑥ In Dreams	Roy Orbison	Monument
I Wanna Be Around	Tony Bennett	Columbia
⑥ One Broken Heart For Sale	Elvis Presley	RCA Victor
☆ ⑥ Our Day Will Come	Ruby & the Romantics	Kapp
Our Winter Love	Bill Pursell	Columbia
Ruby Baby	Dion	Columbia
Send Me Some Lovin'	Sam Cooke	RCA Victor
☆ ⑥ Walk Like A Man	The Four Seasons	Vee Jay
What Will Mary Say	Johnny Mathis	Columbia
You're The Reason I'm Living	Bobby Darin	Capitol

Little Peggy March

MARCH

Baby Workout	Jackie Wilson	Brunswick
⑥ Can't Get Used To Losing You	Andy Williams	Columbia
Days Of Wine And Roses	Henry Mancini	RCA Victor
Do The Bird	Dee Dee Sharp	Cameo
☆ ⑥ He's So Fine	The Chiffons	Laurie
☆ ⑥ I Will Follow Him	Little Peggy March	RCA Victor
Mr. Bass Man	Johnny Cymbal	Kapp
On Broadway	The Drifters	Atlantic
Pipeline	The Chantays	Dot
⑥ Puff The Magic Dragon	Peter, Paul & Mary	Warner Bros.
Sandy	Dion	Laurie
⑥ South Street	The Orlons	Cameo
⑥ Surfin' U.S.A./Shut Down	The Beach Boys	Capitol
Twenty Miles/Let's Limbo Some More	Chubby Checker	Parkway
Why Do Lovers Break Each Other's Heart?	Bob B. Soxx & the Blue Jeans	Philles

APRIL

Another Saturday Night	Sam Cooke	RCA Victor
Foolish Little Girl	The Shirelles	Scepter
Hot Pastrami	The Dartells	Dot
☆ ⑥ If You Wanna Be Happy	Jimmy Soul	S.P.Q.R.
Killer Joe	The Rocky Fellers	Specter
Linda	Jan & Dean	Liberty
⑥ Losing You	Brenda Lee	Decca
Mecca	Gene Pitney	Musicor
Reverend Mr. Black	The Kingston Trio	Capitol
⑥ Take These Chains From My Heart	Ray Charles	ABC Paramount
(Today I Met) The Boy I'm Gonna Marry	Darlene Love	Philles
⑥ Two Faces Have I	Lou Christie	Roulette
Young And In Love	Dick & DeeDee	Warner Bros.
Young Lovers	Paul & Paula	Philips

MAY

Blue On Blue	Bobby Vinton	Epic
⑥ Da Doo Ron Ron	The Crystals	Philles
18 Yellow Roses	Bobby Darin	Capitol
El Watusi	Ray Barretto	Tico
The Good Life	Tony Bennett	Columbia
Hello Stranger	Barbara Lewis	Atlantic
☆ ⑥ It's My Party	Lesley Gore	Mercury
My Whole World Is Falling Down	Brenda Lee	Decca
Still	Bill Anderson	Decca
☆ ⑥ Sukiyaki	Kyu Sakamoto	Capitol
Sweet Dreams (Of You)	Patsy Cline	Decca
Those Lazy-Hazy-Crazy Days Of Summer	Nat "King" Cole	Capitol
What A Guy	The Raindrops	Jubilee

Martha & the Vandellas (Martha Reeves, Roslyn Ashford, Annette Beard; photo: Kriegsmann)

Wildwood Days	Bobby Rydell	Cameo
You Can't Sit Down	The Dovells	Parkway

JUNE

☆ ⑥	**Easier Said Than Done**	The Essex	Roulette
⑥	**Falling**	Roy Orbison	Monument
	Harry The Hairy Ape	Ray Stevens	Mercury
	Just One Look	Doris Troy	Atlantic
⑥	**Memphis**	Lonnie Mack	Fraternity
	One Fine Day	The Chiffons	Laurie
	On Top Of Spaghetti	Tom Glazer & the Children's Chorus	Kapp
	Pride And Joy	Marvin Gaye	Tamla
⑥	**Ring Of Fire**	Johnny Cash	Columbia
⑥	**Six Days On The Road**	Dave Dudley	Golden Wing
☆ ⑥	**So Much In Love**	The Tymes	Parkway
	String Along	Rick Nelson	Decca
☆ ⑥	**Surf City**	Jan & Dean	Liberty
	Swinging On A Star	Big Dee Irwin	Dimension
	Tie Me Kangaroo Down, Sport	Rolf Harris	Epic

JULY

	Abilene	George Hamilton IV	RCA Victor
⑥	**Blowin' In The Wind**	Peter, Paul & Mary	Warner Bros.
	Candy Girl/Marlena	The Four Seasons	Vee Jay
	Denise	Randy & the Rainbows	Rust
⑥	**Detroit City**	Bobby Bare	RCA Victor
☆ ⑥	**Fingertips—Part 2**	Little Stevie Wonder	Tamla
⑥	**Green, Green**	The New Christy Minstrels	Columbia
	Hopeless	Andy Williams	Columbia
	I (Who Have Nothing)	Ben E. King	Atco
	Judy's Turn To Cry	Lesley Gore	Mercury
	More	Kai Winding	Verve
	Not Me	The Orlons	Cameo

Till Then	The Classics	Music Note
⑥ Wipe Out	The Surfaris	Dot
⑥ (You're The) Devil In Disguise	Elvis Presley	RCA Victor

AUGUST

☆ ⑥ Blue Velvet	Bobby Vinton	Epic
⑥ Heat Wave	Martha & the Vandellas	Gordy
Hello Muddah, Hello Fadduh	Allan Sherman	Warner Bros.
Hey Girl	Freddie Scott	Colpix
⑥ If I Had A Hammer	Trini Lopez	Reprise
The Kind Of Boy You Can't Forget	The Raindrops	Jubilee
⑥ Mickey's Monkey	The Miracles	Tamla
⑥ Mockingbird	Inez & Charlie Foxx	Symbol
The Monkey Time	Major Lance	Okeh
☆ ⑥ My Boyfriend's Back	The Angels	Smash
⑥ Surfer Girl/Little Deuce Coupe	The Beach Boys	Capitol
⑥ Then He Kissed Me	The Crystals	Philles
Wait 'Til My Bobby Gets Home	Darlene Love	Philles
Why Don't You Believe Me	The Duprees	Coed
Wonderful! Wonderful!	The Tymes	Parkway

SEPTEMBER

⑥ Be My Baby	The Ronettes	Philles
Blue Bayou	Roy Orbison	Monument
⑥ Busted	Ray Charles	ABC Paramount
⑥ Cry Baby	Garnet Mimms & the Enchanters	United Artists
☆ ⑥ Deep Purple	Nino Tempo & April Stevens	Atco
Donna The Prima Donna	Dion	Columbia
Don't Think Twice, It's All Right	Peter, Paul & Mary	Warner Bros.
Fools Rush In	Rick Nelson	Decca
I Can't Stay Mad At You	Skeeter Davis	RCA Victor
Only In America	Jay & the Americans	United Artists
Sally Go 'Round The Roses	The Jaynetts	Tuff
☆ ⑥ Sugar Shack	Jimmy Gilmer & the Fireballs	Dot

Wilson Pickett (photo: Kriegsmann)

133

Talk To Me	Sunny & the Sunglows	Tear Drop
That Sunday, That Summer	Nat "King" Cole	Capitol
A Walkin' Miracle	The Essex	Roulette

OCTOBER

⑥ Bossa Nova Baby	Elvis Presley	RCA Victor
Crossfire	The Orlons	Cameo
(Down At) Papa Joe's	The Dixiebelles	Sound Stage 7
Down The Aisle	Patti Labelle & the Blue Belles	Newtown
Everybody	Tommy Roe	ABC Paramount
500 Miles Away From Home	Bobby Bare	RCA Victor
The Grass Is Greener	Brenda Lee	Decca
Hey Little Girl	Major Lance	Okeh
☆ ⑥ I'm Leaving It Up To You	Dale & Grace	Montel
It's All Right	The Impressions	ABC Paramount
I Wonder What She's Doing Tonight	Barry & the Tamerlanes	Valiant
September Song	Jimmy Durante	Warner Bros.
She's A Fool	Lesley Gore	Mercury
Walking The Dog	Rufus Thomas	Stax
Washington Square	The Village Stompers	Epic

NOVEMBER

⑥ Be True To Your School/In My Room	The Beach Boys	Capitol
Can I Get A Witness	Marvin Gaye	Tamla
☆ ⑥ Dominique	The Singing Nun	Philips
Drip Drop	Dion	Columbia
⑥ Forget Him	Bobby Rydell	Cameo
Have You Heard	The Duprees	Coed
Loddy Lo/Hooka Tooka	Chubby Checker	Parkway
⑥ Louie Louie	The Kingsmen	Wand
Midnight Mary	Joey Powers	Amy
The Nitty Gritty	Shirley Ellis	Congress
Since I Fell For You	Lenny Welch	Cadence
⑥ Twenty-Four Hours From Tulsa	Gene Pitney	Musicor
Wives And Lovers	Jack Jones	Kapp
Wonderful Summer	Robin Ward	Dot
You Don't Have To Be A Baby To Cry	The Caravels	Smash

DECEMBER

⑥ Anyone Who Had A Heart	Dionne Warwick	Scepter
The Boy Next Door	The Secrets	Philips
Daisy Petal Pickin'	Jimmy Gilmer & the Fireballs	Dot
I Have A Boyfriend	The Chiffons	Laurie
The Marvelous Toy	The Chad Mitchell Trio	Mercury
Popsicles And Icicles	The Murmaids	Chattahoochee
Pretty Paper	Roy Orbison	Monument

Otis Redding

1963

Somewhere	The Tymes	Parkway
Stewball	Peter, Paul & Mary	Warner Bros.
Surfin' Bird	The Trashmen	Garrett
Talk Back Trembling Lips	Johnny Tillotson	MGM
That Lucky Old Sun	Ray Charles	ABC Para-mount
Tra La La La Suzy	Dean & Jean	Rust
Walking Proud	Steve Lawrence	Columbia
When The Lovelight Starts Shining Through His Eyes	The Supremes	Motown

TOP SINGLES OF 1963

⑥ Blue Velvet	Bobby Vinton	Epic
⑥ Dominique	The Singing Nun	Philips
⑥ Fingertips—Part 2	Little Stevie Wonder	Tamla
⑥ He's So Fine	The Chiffons	Laurie
⑥ Hey Paula	Paul & Paula	Philips
⑥ I Will Follow Him	Little Peggy March	RCA Victor
⑥ My Boyfriend's Back	The Angels	Smash
⑥ Sugar Shack	Jimmy Gilmer & the Fireballs	Dot
⑥ Sukiyaki	Kyu Sakamoto	Capitol
⑥ Walk Like A Man	The Four Seasons	Vee Jay

TOP ALBUMS OF 1963

Bye Bye Birdie	Soundtrack	RCA Victor
⑥ Days Of Wine And Roses	Andy Williams	Columbia
⑥ The First Family	Vaughn Meader	Cadence
Ingredients In A Recipe For Soul	Ray Charles	ABC Para-mount
⑥ In The Wind	Peter, Paul & Mary	Warner Bros.
Lawrence of Arabia	Soundtrack	Colpix
⑥ Moving	Peter, Paul & Mary	Warner Bros.
My Son, The Nut	Allan Sherman	Warner Bros.
⑥ Songs I Sing On The Jackie Gleason Show	Frank Fontaine	ABC Para-mount
⑥ Trini Lopez At PJ's	Trini Lopez	Reprise

135

GRAMMY WINNERS IN 1963

The Grammys were awarded at the Beverly Hilton Hotel in Los Angeles on Tuesday, May 12, 1964. Stan Freberg was the host.

Record of the Year: "Days Of Wine And Roses," Henry Mancini (RCA Victor)
Song of the Year: "Days Of Wine And Roses" (music by Henry Mancini, lyrics by Johnny Mercer)
Album of the Year: *The Barbra Streisand Album,* Barbra Streisand (Columbia)
Best Vocal Performance, Female: *The Barbra Streisand Album,* Barbra Streisand (Columbia)
Best Vocal Performance, Male: "Wives And Lovers," Jack Jones (Kapp)
Best Vocal Performance, Group: "Blowin' In The Wind," Peter, Paul & Mary (Warner Bros.)
Best Rock 'n' Roll Recording: "Deep Purple," Nino Tempo & April Stevens (Atco)
Best New Artist of the Year: The Swingle Singers
Best Comedy Performance: "Hello Muddah, Hello Fadduh," Allan Sherman (Warner Bros.)
Best Soundtrack Album from a Motion Picture or Television: *Tom Jones,* John Addison (United Artists)

BIRTHS AND DEATHS IN 1963

MUSIC PERFORMERS BORN IN 1963

Julian Lennon, April 8
"Little" Jimmy Osmond, April 16
George Michael, June 25

Kristy McNichol, September 9
Joey Tempest (Europe), September 19

MUSIC PERFORMERS AND MUSIC INDUSTRY NOTABLES WHO DIED IN 1963

Patsy Cline, Tuesday, March 5 (plane crash; 30)

Dinah Washington, Saturday, December 14 (drug overdose; 39)

The Ronettes (top to bottom: Estelle Bennett, Nedra Talley, Veronica Bennett Spector)

Stevie Wonder (photo: *Kriegsmann*)

1963

OTHERS WHO DIED IN 1963

Robert Frost
Rogers Hornsby
Pope John XXIII (Angelo Giuseppi Roncalli)

John F. Kennedy
Dick Powell

MOVIES OF 1963

MOVIES FEATURING POP MUSIC ARTISTS

Beach Party *Stars:* Frankie Avalon, Annette Funicello, Bob Cummings, Dorothy Malone, Harvey Lembeck. Although Frankie Avalon, Annette Funicello, and Dick Dale & the Deltones performed in the film, the movie produced no significant hits. First in a long series of "beach" movies starring Frankie and Annette.

Fun in Acapulco *Stars:* Elvis Presley, Ursula Andress, Paul Lukas. *Featured song:* "Bossa Nova Baby."

It Happened at the World's Fair *Stars:* Elvis Presley, Joan O'Brien, Gary Lockwood, Vicky Tiu. *Featured song:* "One Broken Heart For Sale."

Just for Fun *Stars:* Mark Wynter, Cherry Roland, Richard Vernon. *Featured song:* "The Night Has A Thousand Eyes" by Bobby Vee. *Other musical performers:* Freddy Cannon, Ketty Lester, Johnny Tillotson, the Crickets, the Springfields, the Tremeloes.

OTHER POPULAR MOVIES OF 1963

The Birds
Charade
Cleopatra
How the West Was Won
Hud

Irma La Douce
It's a Mad Mad Mad Mad World
Lilies of the Field
Tom Jones

ACADEMY AWARD WINNERS OF 1963

Best Actor: Sidney Poitier, *Lilies of the Field*
Best Actress: Patricia Neal, *Hud*
Best Picture: *Tom Jones*
Best Song: "Call Me Irresponsible," *Papa's Delicate Condition* (music by James Van Heusen, lyrics by Sammy Cahn)

ROCK ON ALMANAC

TOP TELEVISION SHOWS OF 1963

The Andy Griffith Show
The Beverly Hillbillies
Bonanza
Candid Camera
The Dick Van Dyke Show

The Ed Sullivan Show
The Lucy Show
Make Room for Daddy
My Favorite Martian
Petticoat Junction

1964

ROCK ON ALMANAC

⇨ Beatlemania invades America.

⇨ Jack Ruby, killer of President Kennedy's accused assassin Lee Harvey Oswald, is sentenced to death.

⇨ For the fourth time, golfer Arnold Palmer wins the Masters.

⇨ The Ford Mustang rolls into the showrooms, featuring sporty looks and an enticing sticker price of $2,368.

⇨ India's first prime minister, Jawaharlal Nehru, dies.

⇨ President Johnson signs the most sweeping civil rights legislation in the history of the nation.

⇨ The Warren Commission issues a report on the assassination of President Kennedy, concluding that no conspiracy was involved.

⇨ Robert Kennedy resigns as attorney general to run for the Senate.

⇨ Leonid Brezhnev replaces Nikita Khrushchev, ousted by the Soviet Union's Communist Party.

⇨ Lyndon Johnson defeats Barry Goldwater for the presidency in one of the most lopsided elections in American history.

⇨ At age 35, Dr. Martin Luther King, Jr., is the youngest Nobel Peace Prize recipient.

⇨ The Winter Olympics are held in Innsbruck, Austria; the Summer Olympics, in Tokyo, Japan.

SPORTS WINNERS

Baseball   The St. Louis Cardinals beat the New York Yankees 4 games to 3.
Football
    NFL: The Cleveland Browns beat the Baltimore Colts 27–0 in Cleveland.
    AFL: The Buffalo Bills beat the San Diego Chargers 20–7 in Buffalo.
Basketball   The Boston Celtics beat the San Francisco Warriors 4 games to 1.
Hockey   The Toronto Maple Leafs beat the Detroit Red Wings 4 games to 3.

MUSIC HIGHLIGHTS OF 1964

⇨ *Top of the Pops,* a pop music television show, debuts on the BBC in England.

⇨ Capitol Records releases the Beatles' debut album for the label, *Meet The Beatles!* It is the group's first album available in America.

⇨ On Friday, February 7, at New York's John F. Kennedy Airport, 25,000 screaming Beatles fans await the arrival of their heroes. Mass hysteria erupts as John Lennon, Paul McCartney, George Harrison, and Ringo Starr step from the plane to their awaiting limousines. The British invasion had begun.

⇨ On Sunday, February 9, the Beatles make their first American television appearance on *The Ed Sullivan Show,* causing the same sensation among teenagers that Elvis had caused on the same show eight years earlier.

⇨ On Tuesday, February 11, the Beatles play their first American concert in Washington, D.C. The next day, they return to New York to play the famed Carnegie Hall. Adoring audience reaction to the shows dramatizes the Beatles' impact on America's youth.

⇨ Demand for Beatles information is so intense that a press conference held by Brian Epstein in the ballroom of New York's Plaza Hotel attracts more than 250 reporters.

⇨ On Monday, March 2, several weeks after their return from America, the Beatles begin work on their first feature-length film, *A Hard Day's Night.*

⇨ In March, Dick Clark moves his *American Bandstand* operations from Philadelphia to Los Angeles.

⇨ In the April 4 issue of *Billboard* magazine, the Beatles occupy the top five positions on the Hot 100, the only time in the history of *Billboard*'s charts that this feat has ever been accomplished. The top five songs were "Can't Buy Me Love" on Capitol, "Twist And

The Beatles (l to r: John Lennon, Ringo Starr, Paul McCartney, George Harrison)

1964

Shout" on Tollie, "She Loves You" on Swan, "I Want To Hold Your Hand" on Capitol, and "Please Please Me" on Vee Jay.

⇨ Madame Tussaud's Wax Museum in London casts the Beatles in wax, the first time this has ever been done for pop music stars.

⇨ On Monday, June 1, the Rolling Stones land at Kennedy Airport in New York to embark on their first American tour. This ties in directly with their first single release in America on London Records, Buddy Holly's hit "Not Fade Away."

⇨ *Crawdaddy,* the first magazine devoted exclusively to rock music, begins publication.

⇨ On Monday, July 6, the Beatles' first film, *A Hard Day's Night,* premieres in London. Thousands of fans gather outside the theater.

⇨ On Tuesday, August 18, the Beatles' plane lands in San Francisco, first stop on their first American tour. The four-week engagement beginning the next day at San Francisco's Cow Palace encompasses 30 shows in 24 cities. The last show of the tour, on Sunday, September 20, is a charity concert at the Paramount Theater in Brooklyn. On the same show are singers Steve Lawrence and Eydie Gorme. This tour solidifies the lasting effect the Beatles would have on America's teenagers. Young men begin to let their hair grow into the famous "moptop" look, and almost every band begins to use the Beatles' instrumentation of three guitars and a drum.

⇨ On Friday, September 4, the Animals debut in America at Brooklyn's famous Paramount Theater. Their debut single, "House Of The Rising Sun," rises to number one, the first post-Beatles British recording to do so.

⇨ On Wednesday, September 16, ABC television premieres the weekly rock music show *Shindig.* Host Jimmy O'Neil uses this forum to showcase many of the top recording acts of the time. The career of the Righteous Brothers zooms as a result of the exposure they get each week as regulars on the show.

⇨ In their first year on the national charts in America, the Beatles score six number one hits, more than any other debut act in the history of rock 'n' roll. Their tally of 15 chart singles in one calendar year also still stands as an all-time record that is unlikely ever to be broken.

DEBUT ARTISTS OF 1964

MAJOR ARTISTS	Debut Single	Label
The Animals (Eric Burdon, Hilton Valentine, Alan Price, Bryan "Chas" Chandler, John Steel)	The House Of The Rising Sun ☆ ⑥	MGM
The Bachelors (Con Cluskey, Declan Stokes, John Stokes)	Diane ⑥	London

141

The Beatles (John Lennon, Paul McCartney, George Harrison, Ringo Starr)	I Want To Hold Your Hand ☆ ⑤	Capitol
Chad & Jeremy (Chad Stuart, Jeremy Clyde)	Yesterday's Gone	World Artists
The Ray Charles Singers	Love Me With All Your Heart	Command
The Dave Clark Five (Dave Clark, Lenny Davidson, Rick Huxley, Denis Payton, Mike Smith)	Glad All Over ⑤	Epic
Petula Clark	Downtown ☆ ⑤	Warner Bros.
The Dixie Cups (Barbara Ann Hawkins, Joan Marie Johnson, Rosa Lee Hawkins)	Chapel of Love ☆ ⑤	Red Bird
Ronnie Dove	Say You	Diamond
The Four Tops (Levi Stubbs, Abdul "Duke" Fakir, Renaldo "Obie" Benson, Lawrence Payton)	Baby, I Need Your Loving ⑤	Motown
Gerry & the Pacemakers (Gerry Marsden, Leslie Maguire, Leslie Chadwick, Fred Marsden)	Don't Let The Sun Catch You Crying ⑤	Laurie
Herman's Hermits (Peter Noone, Karl Anthony Greene, Keith Hopwood, Derek "Lek" Leckenby, Barry Whitman)	I'm Into Something Good ⑤	MGM
Al Hirt	Java ⑤	RCA Victor
The Hollies (Allan Clarke, Anthony Hicks, Graham Nash, Eric Haydock, Robert Elliott)	Just One Look	Imperial
Brenda Holloway	Every Little Bit Hurts	Tamla
The Kinks (Ray Davies, Dave Davies, Peter Quaife, Mick Avory)	You Really Got Me ⑤	Reprise
Billy J. Kramer & the Dakotas (Billy J. Kramer, Michael Maxfield, Michael Green, Ray Jones, Tony Mansfield)	Little Children/Bad To Me ⑤	Imperial

The Ramsey Lewis Trio (Ramsey Lewis, Eldee Young, Isaac "Red" Holt)	Something You Got	Argo
Lulu (Marie McDonald, McLaughlin Lawrie)	Shout	Parrot
Manfred Mann (Manfred Mann, Paul Jones, Michael Vickers, David Richmond, Michael Huggs)	Do Wah Diddy Diddy ☆ ⑥	Ascot
Jody Miller	He Walks Like A Man	Capitol
Roger Miller	Dang Me ⑥	Smash
Willie Mitchell	20-75	Hi
The Newbeats (Lawrence Henley, Marcus Mathis, Lewis "Dean" Mathis)	Bread And Butter	Hickory
Peter & Gordon (Peter Asher, Gordon Waller)	A World Without Love ☆ ⑥	Capitol
Johnny Rivers	Memphis ⑥	Imperial
The Rolling Stones (Mick Jagger, Keith Richards, Brian Jones, Bill Wyman, Charlie Watts)	Not Fade Away	London
The Searchers (Anthony Jackson, Michael Pendergast, John McNally, Chris Curtis)	Needles And Pins ⑥	Kapp
The Shangri-Las (Mary and Betty Weiss, Mary Anne and Marge Ganser)	Remember (Walkin' In The Sand) ⑥	Red Bird
Dusty Springfield	I Only Want To Be With You ⑥	Philips
Barbra Streisand	People	Columbia
The Temptations (David Ruffin, Eddie Kendricks, Otis Williams, Melvin Franklin, Paul Williams)	The Way You Do The Things You Do	Gordy
Joe Tex	Hold What You've Got	Dial
The Zombies (Rod Argent, Paul Atkinson, Hugh Grundy, Colin Blunstone, Chris White)	She's Not There ⑥	Parrot

The Four Tops (l to r: "Duke" Fakir, Lawrence Payton, Levi Stubbs, "Obie" Benson; photo: *Kriegsmann)*

143

The Hollies (l to r: Allan Clarke, Robert Elliott, Graham Nash, Bernard Calver, Anthony Hicks)

OTHER ARTISTS

Cilla Black	The Premiers
Candy & the Kisses	P.J. Proby
The Ray Conniff Singers	The Reflections
The Detergents	Diane Renay
The Devotions	Rene & Rene
Marianne Faithfull	The Rivieras
Lefty Frizzell	Julie Rogers
Gale Garnett	Ronny & the Daytonas
Stan Getz & Astrud Gilberto	Jackie Ross
Lorne Greene	The Serendipity Singers
The Hondells	Sandie Shaw
The Honeycombs	Jumpin' Gene Simmons
Jimmy Hughes	The Simon Sisters
The Jelly Beans	Millie Small
Bobby Martin	Terry Stafford
George Martin	The Swingin' Blue Jeans
Robert Maxwell	Irma Thomas
The Monarchs	Tommy Tucker
The Nashville Teens	Danny Williams
Patty & the Emblems	J. Frank Wilson & the Cavaliers

HITS OF 1964

JANUARY

As Usual	Brenda Lee	Decca
Baby I Love You	The Ronettes	Philles
Doo-Wah-Diddy	The Exciters	United Artists
Drag City	Jan & Dean	Liberty
A Fool Never Learns	Andy Williams	Columbia
For You	Rick Nelson	Decca
Hey Little Cobra	The Rip Chords	Columbia
☆ ⓖ **I Want To Hold Your Hand/I Saw Her Standing There**	The Beatles	Capitol
ⓖ **Java**	Al Hirt	RCA Victor
ⓖ **Out Of Limits**	The Marketts	Warner Bros.
Quicksand	Martha & the Vandellas	Gordy
☆ ⓖ **There, I've Said It Again**	Bobby Vinton	Epic
Um, Um, Um, Um, Um, Um	Major Lance	Okeh

144

Whispering	Nino Tempo & April Stevens	Atco
ⓖ You Don't Own Me	Lesley Gore	Mercury

FEBRUARY

Abigail Beecher	Freddy Cannon	Warner Bros.
California Sun	The Rivieras	Riviera
Dawn (Go Away)	The Four Seasons	Philips
Good News	Sam Cooke	RCA Victor
☆ ⓖ Hello, Dolly!	Louis Armstrong	Kapp
Hi-Heel Sneakers	Tommy Tucker	Checker
ⓖ I Only Want To Be With You	Dusty Springfield	Philips
ⓖ Kissin' Cousins	Elvis Presley	RCA Victor
Navy Blue	Diane Renay	20th Century Fox
ⓖ Please Please Me/From Me To You	The Beatles	Vee Jay
☆ ⓖ She Loves You	The Beatles	Swan
Southtown U.S.A.	The Dixiebelles	Sound Stage 7
Stop And Think It Over	Dale & Grace	Montel
Talking About My Baby	The Impressions	ABC Paramount
Who Do You Love	The Sapphires	Swan

MARCH

☆ ⓖ Can't Buy Me Love/You Can't Do That	The Beatles	Capitol
Dead Man's Curve	Jan & Dean	Liberty
Don't Let The Rain Come Down (Crooked Little Man)	The Serendipity Singers	Philips
ⓖ Fun, Fun, Fun	The Beach Boys	Capitol
ⓖ Glad All Over	The Dave Clark Five	Epic
My Bonnie	The Beatles	MGM
My Heart Belongs To Only You	Bobby Vinton	Epic
ⓖ Needles And Pins	The Searchers	Kapp
Rip Van Winkle	The Devotions	Roulette
The Shoop Shoop Song (It's In His Kiss)	Betty Everett	Vee Jay
Stay	The Four Seasons	Vee Jay

The Kinks (l to r: Ray Davies, Dave Davies, John Gosling, Mick Avory; photo: David Gahr)

145

⑥	Suspicion	Terry Stafford	Crusader
⑥	Twist And Shout/There's A Place	The Beatles	Tollie
	The Way You Do The Things You Do	The Temptations	Gordy
	You're A Wonderful One	Marvin Gaye	Tamla

APRIL

	⑥	Bits And Pieces	The Dave Clark Five	Epic
	⑥	Do You Want To Know A Secret/ Thank You Girl	The Beatles	Vee Jay
		Hey, Bobba Needle	Chubby Checker	Parkway
		Hippy Hippy Shake	The Swinging Blue Jeans	Imperial
	⑥	It's Over	Roy Orbison	Monument
		(Just Like) Romeo And Juliet	The Reflections	Golden World
		The Matador	Major Lance	Okeh
		Money	The Kingsmen	Wand
☆	⑥	My Guy	Mary Wells	Motown
		Nadine	Chuck Berry	Chess
		Ronnie	The Four Seasons	Philips
		Shangri-La	Robert Maxwell	Decca
		Stay Awhile	Dusty Springfield	Philips
		That's The Way Boys Are	Lesley Gore	Mercury
		White On White	Danny Williams	United Artists

MAY

☆	⑥	Chapel Of Love	The Dixie Cups	Red Bird
	⑥	Diane	The Bachelors	London
	⑥	Do You Love Me	The Dave Clark Five	Epic
		Every Little Bit Hurts	Brenda Holloway	Tamla
	⑥	Little Children/Bad To Me	Billy J. Kramer & the Dakotas	Imperial
☆	⑥	Love Me Do/P.S. I Love You	The Beatles	Tollie
		Love Me With All Your Heart	The Ray Charles Singers	Command
		People	Barbra Steisand	Columbia
		Rock Me Baby	B.B. King	Kent
		Today	The New Christy Minstrels	Columbia
		The Very Thought Of You	Rick Nelson	Decca
	⑥	Viva Las Vegas/What'd I Say	Elvis Presley	RCA Victor

Johnny Rivers

146

The Rolling Stones (l to r: Charlie Watts, Mick Jagger, Ron Wood, Bill Wyman, Keith Richards)

1964

	Walk On By	Dionne Warwick	Scepter
⑥	Wish Someone Would Care	Irma Thomas	Imperial
☆ ⑥	A World Without Love	Peter & Gordon	Capitol

JUNE

	Alone	The Four Seasons	Vee Jay
	Beans In My Ears	The Serendipity Singers	Philips
⑥	Can't You See That's She's Mine	The Dave Clark Five	Epic
⑥	Dang Me	Roger Miller	Smash
⑥	Don't Let The Sun Catch You Crying	Gerry & the Pacemakers	Laurie
	Don't Throw Your Love Away	The Searchers	Kapp
⑥	The Girl From Ipanema	Getz/Gilberto	Verve
☆ ⑥	I Get Around/Don't Worry Baby	The Beach Boys	Capitol
⑥	Memphis	Johnny Rivers	Imperial
⑥	My Boy Lollipop	Millie Small	Smash
	No Particular Place To Go	Chuck Berry	Chess
☆ ⑥	Rag Doll	The Four Seasons	Philips
	Tell My Why	Bobby Vinton	Epic
	Wishin' And Hopin'	Dusty Springfield	Philips
	Yesterday's Gone	Chad & Jeremy	World Artists

JULY

	C'mon And Swim	Bobby Freeman	Autumn
	Do I Love You	The Ronettes	Philles
☆ ⑥	Everybody Loves Somebody	Dean Martin	Reprise
	Good Times	Sam Cooke	RCA Victor
☆ ⑥	A Hard Day's Night/I Should Have Known Better	The Beatles	Capitol
	How Do You Do It?	Gerry & the Pacemakers	Laurie
	I Wanna Love Him So Bad	The Jelly Beans	Red Bird
	Keep On Pushing	The Impressions	ABC Paramount
	The Little Old Lady (From Pasadena)	Jan & Dean	Liberty
	Nobody I Know	Peter & Gordon	Capitol
	Steal Away	Jimmy Hughes	Fame

147

Under The Boardwalk	The Drifters	Atlantic
☆ ⑥ Where Did Our Love Go	The Supremes	Motown
(You Don't Know) How Glad I Am	Nancy Wilson	Capitol
⑥ You're My World	Cilla Black	Capitol

AUGUST

Ain't She Sweet	The Beatles	Atco
⑥ Because	The Dave Clark Five	Epic
⑥ Bread And Butter	The Newbeats	Hickory
⑥ G.T.O.	Ronny & the Daytonas	Mala
☆ ⑥ The House Of The Rising Sun	The Animals	MGM
In The Misty Moonlight	Jerry Wallace	Challenge
It Hurts To Be In Love	Gene Pitney	Musicor
Maybe I Know	Lesley Gore	Mercury
Mixed-Up, Shook-Up Girl	Patty & the Emblems	Herald
People Say	The Dixie Cups	Red Bird
Selfish One	Jackie Ross	Chess
Such A Night	Elvis Presley	RCA Victor
Tell Me	The Rolling Stones	London
⑥ Walk—Don't Run '64	The Ventures	Dolton
You Never Can Tell	Chuck Berry	Chess

SEPTEMBER

⑥ Baby, I Need Your Loving	The Four Tops	Motown
⑥ Dancing In The Streets	Martha & the Vandellas	Gordy
☆ ⑥ Do Wah Diddy Diddy	Manfred Mann	Ascot
Funny	Joe Hinton	Back Beat
Girl (Why You Wanna Make Me Blue)	The Temptations	Gordy
Haunted House	Jumpin' Gene Simmons	Hi
I'm On The Outside (Looking In)	Little Anthony & the Imperials	DCP
⑥ Last Kiss	J. Frank Wilson & the Cavaliers	Josie
Let It Be Me	Betty Everett & Jerry Butler	Vee Jay
☆ ⑥ Oh, Pretty Woman	Roy Orbison	Monument
⑥ Remember (Walkin' In The Sand)	The Shangri-Las	Red Bird
Save It For Me	The Four Seasons	Philips
A Summer Song	Chad & Jeremy	World Artists
⑥ We'll Sing In The Sunshine	Gale Garnett	RCA Victor
When I Grow Up (To Be A Man)	The Beach Boys	Capitol

OCTOBER

☆ ⑥ Baby Love	The Supremes	Motown
⑥ Chug-A-Lug	Roger Miller	Smash
Come A Little Bit Closer	Jay & the Americans	United Artists
The Door Is Still Open To My Heart	Dean Martin	Reprise
Everybody Knows	The Dave Clark Five	Epic
⑥ Have I The Right?	The Honeycombs	Interphon

148

Dusty Springfield

Joe Tex

1964

ⓖ I'm Into Something Good	Herman's Hermits	MGM
☆ ⓖ Leader Of The Pack	The Shangri-Las	Red Bird
Little Honda	The Hondells	Mercury
Ride The Wild Surf	Jan & Dean	Liberty
ⓖ She's Not There	The Zombies	Parrot
Tobacco Road	The Nashville Teens	London
Who Can I Turn To	Tony Bennett	Columbia
You Must Believe Me	The Impressions	ABC Paramount
ⓖ You Really Got Me	The Kinks	Reprise

NOVEMBER

Big Man In Town	The Four Seasons	Philips
☆ ⓖ Come See About Me	The Supremes	Motown
Dance, Dance, Dance	The Beach Boys	Capitol
Goin' Out Of My Head	Little Anthony & the Imperials	DCP
I Like It	Gerry & the Pacemakers	Laurie
I'm Gonna Be Strong	Gene Pitney	Musicor
The Jerk	The Larks	Money
Mountain Of Love	Johnny Rivers	Imperial
☆ ⓖ Mr. Lonely	Bobby Vinton	Epic
Reach Out For Me	Dionne Warwick	Specter
Right Or Wrong	Ronnie Dove	Diamond
☆ ⓖ Ringo	Lorne Greene	RCA Victor
ⓖ Sha La La	Manfred Mann	Ascot
ⓖ Time Is On My Side	The Rolling Stones	London
Walking In The Rain	The Ronettes	Philles

DECEMBER

Amen	The Impressions	ABC Paramount
Ask Me/Ain't That Loving You Baby	Elvis Presley	RCA Victor
As Tears Go By	Marianne Faithfull	London
☆ ⓖ Downtown	Petula Clark	Warner Bros.
How Sweet It Is	Marvin Gaye	Tamla
☆ ⓖ I Feel Fine/She's A Woman	The Beatles	Capitol

Barbra Streisand

⑥ Keep Searchin'	Del Shannon	Amy
Leader Of The Laundromat	The Detergents	Roulette
Love Potion Number Nine	The Searchers	Kapp
My Love Forgive Me (Amore, Scusami)	Robert Goulet	Columbia
Oh No, Not My Baby	Maxine Brown	Wand
Saturday Night At The Movies	The Drifters	Atlantic
Too Many Fish In The Sea	The Marvelettes	Tamla
⑥ The Wedding	Julie Rogers	Mercury
Willow Weep For Me	Chad & Jeremy	World Artists

TOP SINGLES OF 1964

⑥ Baby Love	The Supremes	Motown
⑥ Can't Buy Me Love	The Beatles	Capitol
⑥ Chapel Of Love	The Dixie Cups	Red Bird
⑥ A Hard Day's Night	The Beatles	Capitol
⑥ The House Of The Rising Sun	The Animals	MGM
⑥ I Get Around	The Beach Boys	Capitol
⑥ I Want To Hold Your Hand	The Beatles	Capitol
⑥ Oh, Pretty Woman	Roy Orbison	Monument
⑥ Rag Doll	The Four Seasons	Philips
⑥ There, I've Said It Again	Bobby Vinton	Epic

TOP ALBUMS OF 1964

⑥ The Beatles' Second Album	The Beatles	Capitol
⑥ Everybody Loves Somebody	Dean Martin	Reprise
⑥ A Hard Day's Night	The Beatles	United Artists
⑥ Hello, Dolly!	Louis Armstrong	Kapp
⑥ Honey In The Horn	Al Hirt	RCA Victor
⑥ In The Wind	Peter, Paul & Mary	Warner Bros.
⑥ Introducing . . . The Beatles	The Beatles	Vee Jay
⑥ Meet The Beatles!	The Beatles	Capitol
⑥ People	Barbra Streisand	Columbia
⑥ The Singing Nun	The Singing Nun	Philips

GRAMMY WINNERS IN 1964

The Grammys were awarded at the Beverly Hilton Hotel in Los Angeles on Tuesday, April 13, 1965. Donald O'Connor was the host.

Record of the Year: "The Girl From Ipanema," Stan Getz & Astrud Gilberto (Verve)
Song of the Year: "Hello, Dolly!" (music and lyrics by Jerry Herman)
Album of the Year: *Getz/Gilberto,* Stan Getz & João Gilberto (Verve)
Best Vocal Performance, Female: "People," Barbra Streisand (Columbia)
Best Vocal Performance, Male: "Hello, Dolly!" Louis Armstrong (Kapp)
Best Vocal Performance, Group: "A Hard Day's Night," The Beatles (Capitol)
Best Rock 'n' Roll Recording: "Downtown," Petula Clark (Warner Bros.)
Best New Artist of the Year: The Beatles
Best Comedy Performance: *I Started Out As A Child,* Bill Cosby (Warner Bros.)
Best Soundtrack Album from a Motion Picture or Television: *Mary Poppins,*
   Richard M. Sherman & Roger B. Sherman (Buena Vista)

BIRTHS AND DEATHS IN 1964

MUSIC PERFORMERS BORN IN 1964

Kennedy Gordy (Rockwell), March 15

MUSIC PERFORMERS AND MUSIC INDUSTRY NOTABLES WHO DIED IN 1964

Jack Teagarden, Wednesday, January 15
   (pneumonia; 58)
Jim Reeves, Friday, July 31 (plane crash;
   39)
Johnny Burnette, Saturday, August 15
   (fishing accident; 30)

Eddie Cantor, Saturday, October 10 (heart
   attack; 72)
Cole Porter (composer), Friday, October
   16 (kidney stones; 71)
Sam Cooke, Friday, December 11
   (gunshot; 29)

OTHERS WHO DIED IN 1964

Gracie Allen
William Bendix
Jimmie Dodd
Ian Fleming
Sir Cedric Hardwicke
Herbert Hoover

Alan Ladd
Peter Lorre
Douglas MacArthur
Harpo Marx
Alvin C. York

MOVIES OF 1964

MOVIES FEATURING POP MUSIC ARTISTS

Bikini Beach   *Stars:* Frankie Avalon, Annette Funicello, Harvey Lembeck, Don Rickles,
   Keenan Wynn. *Featured song:* "Fingertips" by Little Stevie Wonder. *Other musical
   performers:* The Exciters, the Pyramids, Donna Loren.
Get Yourself a College Girl   *Stars:* Mary Ann Mobley, Nancy Sinatra, Chad Everett.
   No significant hits. *Musical performers:* The Animals, the Dave Clark Five, Donnie
   Brooks, Freddy Bell & the Bellboys, the Jimmy Smith Trio, the Standells.
A Hard Day's Night   *Stars:* The Beatles (film debut), Wilfred Brambell, Victor Spinetti,
   Norman Rossington. *Featured songs:* "A Hard Day's Night," "I'll Cry Instead," "I
   Should Have Known Better," "Can't Buy Me Love," "If I Fell," "And I Love Her," "I'm
   Happy Just To Dance With You," "Ringo's Theme (This Boy)," "Tell Me Why."

ROCK ON ALMANAC

Kissin' Cousins *Stars:* Elvis Presley, Arthur O'Connell, Jack Albertson, Glenda Farrell. *Featured song:* "Kissin' Cousins."

The Lively Set *Stars:* James Darren, Pamela Tiffin, Doug McClure, Joanie Sommers. No significant hits. *Musical performers:* James Darren, Joanie Sommers, the Surfaris.

Muscle Beach Party *Stars:* Frankie Avalon, Annette Funicello, Morey Amsterdam, Buddy Hackett, Don Rickles, Peter Lupus. No significant hits. *Musical performers:* Frankie Avalon, Annette Funicello, Dick Dale & the Deltones, Little Stevie Wonder (film debut). Sequel to 1963's *Beach Party.*

Pajama Party *Stars:* Annette Funicello, Tommy Kirk, Harvey Lembeck, Buster Keaton, Elsa Lanchester, Dorothy Lamour, Jody McCrea. No significant hits or performers.

Roustabout *Stars:* Elvis Presley, Barbara Stanwyck, Leif Erickson, Pat Buttram. *Featured song:* "Little Egypt."

Surf Party *Stars:* Bobby Vinton, Jackie De Shannon, Patricia Morrow, Kenny Miller. No significant hits. *Musical performers:* Bobby Vinton, Jackie De Shannon, the Routers.

Viva Las Vegas *Stars:* Elvis Presley, Ann-Margret, William Demarest, Nicky Blair. *Featured song:* "Viva Las Vegas."

POP MUSIC CONCERTS ON FILM

The T.A.M.I. Show This show, taped at California's Santa Monica Civic Auditorium in October 1964, was a historic documentary featuring the best American and British rock acts of the time (T.A.M.I. stands for Teenage Awards Music International). Filmed in "Electronovision" video and later transferred to film, this was the first major rock concert recorded for showing to the general public. Performers included the Beach Boys, Chuck Berry, James Brown & the Famous Flames, the Barbarians, Marvin Gaye, Gerry & the Pacemakers, Lesley Gore, Jan & Dean, Billy J. Kramer & the Dakotas, Smokey Robinson & the Miracles, the Supremes, and the Rolling Stones.

OTHER POPULAR MOVIES OF 1964

Becket
The Carpetbaggers
Dr. Strangelove or: How I Learned to Stop Worrying and Love the Bomb
Goldfinger
Mary Poppins
My Fair Lady
Seven Days in May
Zorba the Greek

ACADEMY AWARD WINNERS OF 1964

Best Actor: Rex Harrison, *My Fair Lady*
Best Actress: Julie Andrews, *My Fair Lady*
Best Picture: *My Fair Lady*
Best Song: "Chim, Chim, Cher-ee," *Mary Poppins* (music and lyrics by Richard B. Sherman & Robert B. Sherman)

TOP TELEVISION SHOWS OF 1964

The Andy Griffith Show
Bewitched
Bonanza
Combat
The Dick Van Dyke Show
The Fugitive
Gomer Pyle, U.S.M.C.
The Lucy Show
Peyton Place II
The Red Skelton Show

1965

ROCK ON ALMANAC

⇨ The Johnson administration orders air strikes against targets in North Vietnam.

⇨ Two battalions of U.S. marines are ordered into South Vietnam to help protect a major air base at Danang.

⇨ Some 25,000 civil rights demonstrators conduct a 50-mile walk for freedom from Selma, Alabama, to the state capitol in Montgomery.

⇨ Soviet cosmonaut Aleksei A. Leonov becomes the first human to leave an orbiting spacecraft and float in space.

⇨ The world's biggest air-conditioned arena, the Houston Astrodome, opens.

⇨ Marines and men from the 82nd Airborne Division are sent to the Dominican Republic to prevent a Communist takeover.

⇨ President Johnson signs a bill increasing Social Security benefits and creating Medicare.

⇨ President Johnson sends 50,000 more men to South Vietnam.

⇨ Racial tension in the Watts neighborhood of Los Angeles explodes in a five-day bloodbath of rioting, looting, and arson.

⇨ The FBI arrests David Miller, the first person charged with burning his draft card.

⇨ Ferdinand E. Marcos is sworn in as the sixth president of the Republic of the Philippines.

SPORTS WINNERS

Baseball The Los Angeles Dodgers beat the Minnesota Twins 4 games to 3.
Football
  NFL: The Green Bay Packers beat the Cleveland Browns 23–12 in Green Bay.
  AFL: The Buffalo Bills beat the San Diego Chargers 23–0 in San Diego.
Basketball The Boston Celtics beat the Los Angeles Lakers 4 games to 1.
Hockey The Montreal Canadiens beat the Chicago Black Hawks 4 games to 3.

MUSIC HIGHLIGHTS OF 1965

⇨ On Wednesday, January 20, disc jockey Alan Freed, the man who popularized the phrase "rock 'n' roll" in the fifties and considered the "father" of rock 'n' roll, dies of uremic poisoning in Palm Springs, California, at the age of 42.

⇨ NBC television counters ABC's black-and-white music show *Shindig* with a similar show called *Hullabaloo* in glorious color.

⇨ Filmmakers Kit Lambert and Chris Stamp (brother of actor Terence Stamp) begin pushing a new group they are managing called the Who. The group's debut single in America is "I Can't Explain" on Decca.

⇨ The Yardbirds (a slang term for bums who survive by hitching trains) rank among the most important of the British bands, and its members would ultimately emerge as major figures in rock. The family tree of this group reads like a "Who's Who" of British rock. This year Eric Clapton leaves the group and is replaced by Jeff Beck just prior to recording "For Your Love," the group's first hit. Other members to join the group eventually are future Led Zeppelin members Robert Plant, Jimmy Page, John Paul Jones, and John Bonham.

⇨ Bob Dylan makes his first appearance at London's Royal Albert Hall.

⇨ The Byrds emerge in May as the first group to play electronically amplified folk music, creating an entirely new direction in popular music known as folk rock. Their debut single, Bob Dylan's "Mr. Tambourine Man," goes to number one.

⇨ This summer, Bob Dylan begins to turn toward rock and is subjected to bitter criticism by his former fans. The cause is his album *Bringing It All Back Home,* which for the first time features electric instrumentation and musicians like Al Kooper and Paul Butterfield. When Dylan displays his new electric sound live at the Newport Folk Festival, he is booed by the crowd.

⇨ In July, Columbia Records releases Dylan's "Like A Rolling Stone," rock's first single to

The Byrds (clockwise from top: Roger McGuinn, Gene Clarke, Chris Hillman, Michael Clark, David Crosby)

1965

be over 5 minutes in length. Although the record was released as Parts 1 and 2, many radio stations play the entire cut.

⇨ Former New Christy Minstrels lead singer Barry McGuire launches his solo career with a number one hit, P. F. Sloan's "Eve Of Destruction." The record rapidly becomes one of the anthems of the mid-sixties protest movement.

⇨ On Thursday, July 29, the Beatles' second film, *Help!*, which is shot in color, debuts in London.

⇨ Paul McCartney writes the song "Yesterday" (originally titled "Scrambled Eggs"), which goes on to become a number one hit for the Beatles and the single most recorded song in history, with over 2,600 cover versions.

⇨ On Friday, August 13, the Beatles arrive in New York to begin their third concert tour of America, which would take them to nine cities for 13 shows. On Sunday, August 15, a hot, humid night, they rock a crowd of over 56,000 screaming fans into a frenzy at New York's Shea Stadium.

⇨ In August, while playing Los Angeles during their tour, the Beatles are invited to Elvis Presley's Bel-Air mansion. On their one and only meeting, these rock legends talk and play rock music for several hours.

⇨ The last concert of the Beatles' tour is held at San Francisco's Cow Palace on Tuesday, August 31.

⇨ Marty Balin and Paul Kantner form the Jefferson Airplane in San Francisco with vocalist Signe Anderson, musicians Jorma Kaukonen and Jack Casady, and drummer Skip Spence and begin to play at the Club Matrix. A short time later, Anderson would leave the group and be replaced by an ex-model, Grace Slick.

⇨ ABC television premieres *The Beatles,* a half-hour cartoon show seen on Saturday mornings.

⇨ Columbia Records releases a folk album called *Wednesday Morning, 3 A.M.* by a new duo called Simon & Garfunkel, who immediately develop an almost cultish following.

⇨ In December, the Beatles release *Rubber Soul,* marking their shift from commercial rock 'n' roll to more serious music.

DEBUT ARTISTS OF 1965

MAJOR ARTISTS	Debut Single	Label	
Ed Ames	Try To Remember	RCA Victor	
Len Barry	Lip Sync	Decca	155

The Beau Brummels (Sal Valentino, Ronald Elliot, Ronald Meagher, John Peterson, Declan Mulligan)	Laugh, Laugh	Autumn
The Byrds (Roger McGuinn, David Crosby, Gene Clarke, Chris Hillman, Michael Clark)	Mr. Tambourine Man ☆ Ⓖ	Columbia
Dino, Desi & Billy (Dean Martin, Jr., Desiderio Arnaz IV, William Hinsche)	I'm A Fool	Reprise
Donovan (Donovan Phillip Leitch)	Catch The Wind	Hickory
Bob Dylan (Robert Zimmerman)	Subterranean Homesick Blues	Columbia
The Fortunes (Barry Pritchard, Glen Dale, Rod Allen, David Carr, Andrew Brown)	You've Got Your Troubles	Press
The Gentrys (Larry Raspberry, James Hart, Bruce Bowles, Robert Fisher, James Johnson, Pat Neal, Lawrence Wall)	Keep On Dancing Ⓖ	MGM
The Guess Who (Randy Bachman, Burton Cummings, Jim Kale, Garry Peterson)	Shakin' All Over	Scepter
Leon Haywood	She's With Her Other Love	Imperial
Roy Head	Treat Her Right	Back Beat
Tom Jones	It's Not Unusual Ⓖ	Parrot
Gary Lewis & the Playboys (Gary Lewis, Al Ramsey, John R. West, David Walker, David Costell)	This Diamond Ring ☆ Ⓖ	Liberty
Little Milton (Milton Campbell)	Blind Man	Checker
The Lovin' Spoonful (John Sebastian, Zal Yanovsky, John Stephen Boone, Joe Butler)	Do You Believe In Magic	Kama Sutra
The Manhattans (Winfred "Blue" Lovett, Edward "Sonny" Bivens, Kenneth "Wally" Kelly, Richard "Ricky" Taylor, George Smith)	I Wanna Be	Carnival
Barbara Mason	Yes, I'm Ready	Arctic
The McCoys (Rick Derringer [Zehringer], Ronnie Brandon, Randy Hobbs, Randy Zehringer)	Hang On Sloopy ☆ Ⓖ	Bang

Donovan

156

1965

The Moody Blues (Denny Laine, Ray Thomas, Michael Pinder, Clint Warwick, Graeme Edge)	Go Now ⑥	London
Lou Rawls	Three O'Clock In The Morning	Capitol
Billy Joe Royal	Down In The Boondocks	Columbia
Mitch Ryder & the Detroit Wheels (Mitch Ryder, James McCarty, Joe Kubert, Earl Elliot, "Little" John Badanjek)	Jenny Take A Ride ⑥	New Voice
Sam the Sham & the Pharoahs (Sam [Domingo Samudio], Ray Stinnet, David Martin, Jerry Patterson, Butch Gibson)	Wooly Bully ⑥	MGM
Simon & Garfunkel (Paul Simon, Art Garfunkel)	The Sounds of Silence ☆ ⑥	Columbia
Nancy Sinatra	So Long Babe	Reprise
Sonny & Cher (Salvatore "Sonny" Bono, Cherilyn Sakisian LaPierre)	I Got You Babe ☆ ⑥	Atco
Edwin Starr	Agent Double-O-Soul	Ric Tic
The Three Degrees (Fayette Pinkney, Linda Turner, Shirley Porter)	Gee Baby	Swan
The Turtles (Howard Kaylan, Mark Volman, G. Allan Nichol, James Ray Tucker, Charles M. Portz, Donald Ray Murray)	It Ain't Me Babe	White Whale
The Vogues (Bill Burkette, Hugh Geyer, Charles Blasko, Don Miller)	You're The One	Co & Ce
Junior Walker & the All Stars (Junior Walker [Autrey DeWalt, Jr.], Willie Woods, Vic Thomas, James Graves)	Shotgun	Soul
The Who (Roger Daltrey, Pete Townshend, John Entwistle, Keith Moon)	I Can't Explain	Decca
The Yardbirds (Keith Relf, Anthony "Top" Topham, Chris Dreja, Paul "Sam" Samwell-Smith, James McCarty)	For Your Love ⑥	Epic

The Guess Who (l to r: Burton Cummings, Gary Peterson, Jim Kale, Domenic Troiano)

The Young Rascals (Felix Cavaliere, Gene Cornish, Eddie Brigati, Dino Danelli)

I Ain't Gonna Eat Out My Heart Anymore | Atlantic

OTHER ARTISTS

Cannonball Adderley
The Ad Libs
Jewel Akens
Shirley Bassey
Fontella Bass
Cannibal & the Headhunters
Alvin Cash & the Crawlers
The Castaways
"Little" Jimmy Dickens
Mike Douglas
Patty Duke
Georgie Fame
Wayne Fontana & the Mindbenders
Freddie & the Dreamers
Noel Harrison
Horst Jankowski
Jonathan King
The Knickerbockers
The Larks
Jackie Lee
The Marvelows
Barry McGuire
Arthur Prysock

Eddie Rambeau
Reparata & the Delrons
The Royalettes
The San Remo Golden Strings
The Seekers
The Silkie
Sir Douglas Quintet
Sounds Orchestral
The Statler Brothers
The Strangeloves
Koko Taylor
The T-Bones
Them
The Toys
The Trade Winds
Unit 4 + 2
The Walker Brothers
We Five
Ian Whitcomb
The Wonder Who
Glenn Yarbrough
Barry Young

HITS OF 1965

JANUARY

All Day And All Of The Night | The Kinks | Reprise
Cry | Ray Charles | ABC Para-mount

The 81 | Candy & the Kisses | Cameo
Give Him A Great Big Kiss | The Shangri-Las | Red Bird

158

Heart Of Stone	The Rolling Stones	London
⑥ Hold What You've Got	Joe Tex	Dial
I Go To Pieces	Peter & Gordon	Capitol
I'll Be There	Gerry & the Pacemakers	Laurie
The "In" Crowd	Dobie Gray	Charger
Let's Lock The Door (And Throw Away The Key)	Jay & the Americans	United Artists
☆ ⑥ My Girl	The Temptations	Gordy
Shake	Sam Cooke	RCA Victor
Tell Her No	The Zombies	Parrot
☆ ⑥ This Diamond Ring	Gary Lewis & the Playboys	Liberty
☆ ⑥ You've Lost That Lovin' Feelin'	The Righteous Brothers	Philles

FEBRUARY

Ask The Lonely	The Four Tops	Motown
The Boy From New York City	The Ad Libs	Blue Cat
Bye Bye Baby	The Four Seasons	Philips
⑥ Can't You Hear My Heartbeat	Herman's Hermits	MGM
☆ ⑥ Eight Days A Week/I Don't Want To Spoil The Party	The Beatles	Capitol
⑥ Goldfinger	Shirley Bassey	United Artists
Hurts So Bad	Little Anthony & the Imperials	DCP
The Jolly Green Giant	The Kingsmen	Wand
⑥ King Of The Road	Roger Miller	Smash
Laugh, Laugh	The Beau Brummels	Autumn
New York's A Lonely Town	The Trade Winds	Red Bird
⑥ Red Roses For A Blue Lady	Bert Kaempfert	Decca
Shotgun	Junior Walker & the All Stars	Soul
☆ ⑥ Stop! In The Name Of Love	The Supremes	Motown
⑥ Yeh, Yeh	Georgie Fame	Imperial

Tom Jones

159

MARCH

⑥	The Birds And The Bees	Jewel Akens	Era
	Cast Your Fate To The Wind	Sounds Orchestral	Parkway
	Come Home	The Dave Clark Five	Epic
	Do You Wanna Dance?	The Beach Boys	Capitol
☆ ⑥	Game Of Love	Wayne Fontana & the Mindbenders	Fontana
⑥	Go Now	The Moody Blues	London
	I Know A Place	Petula Clark	Warner Bros.
	I'll Be Doggone	Marvin Gaye	Tamla
☆ ⑥	I'm Telling You Now	Freddie & the Dreamers	Tower
	Land Of 1000 Dances	Cannibal & the Headhunters	Rampart
⑥	Little Things	Bobby Goldsboro	United Artists
	Nowhere To Run	Martha & the Vandellas	Gordy
	People Get Ready	The Impressions	ABC Para-mount
	Tell Her No	The Zombies	Parrot
⑥	Tired Of Waiting For You	The Kinks	Reprise

APRIL

	Count Me In	Gary Lewis & the Playboys	Liberty
	I Do Love You	Billy Stewart	Chess
	Iko Iko	The Dixie Cups	Red Bird
⑥	I'll Never Find Another You	The Seekers	Capitol
	It's Gonna Be Alright	Gerry & the Pacemakers	Laurie
⑥	It's Not Unusual	Tom Jones	Parrot
	Just A Little	The Beau Brummels	Autumn
	Just Once In My Life	The Righteous Brothers	Philles
⑥	The Last Time	The Rolling Stones	London
☆ ⑥	Mrs. Brown, You've Got A Lovely Daughter	Herman's Hermits	MGM
	Ooo Baby Baby	The Miracles	Tamla
	She's About A Mover	Sir Douglas Quintet	Tribe
⑥	Silhouettes	Herman's Hermits	MGM
☆ ⑥	Ticket To Ride/Yes It Is	The Beatles	Capitol
⑥	Wooly Bully	Sam the Sham & the Pharoahs	MGM

MAY

☆ ⑥	Back In My Arms Again	The Supremes	Motown
	Concrete And Clay	Unit 4 + 2	London
⑥	Crying In The Chapel	Elvis Presley	RCA Victor
	Do The Freddie	Freddie & the Dreamers	Mercury
	Engine, Engine #9	Roger Miller	Smash
⑥	For Your Love	The Yardbirds	Epic
☆ ⑥	Help Me Rhonda	The Beach Boys	Capitol
	Hush, Hush Sweet Charlotte	Patti Page	Columbia
☆ ⑥	I Can't Help Myself	The Four Tops	Motown
	Last Chance To Turn Around	Gene Pitney	Musicor
	Queen Of The House	Jody Miller	Capitol

1965

Shakin' all Over	The Guess Who	Scepter
Subterranean Homesick Blues	Bob Dylan	Columbia
True Love Ways	Peter & Gordon	Capitol
⑥ **A Walk In The Black Forest**	Horst Jankowski	Mercury

JUNE

Cara Mia	Jay & the Americans	United Artists
Catch The Wind	Donovan	Hickory
Here Comes The Night	Them	Parrot
☆ ⑥ **(I Can't Get No) Satisfaction**	The Rolling Stones	London
I Do	The Marvelows	ABC Paramount
Laurie	Dickey Lee	TCF-Hall
A Little Bit Of Heaven	Ronnie Dove	Diamond
☆ ⑥ **Mr. Tambourine Man**	The Byrds	Columbia
(Remember Me) I'm The One Who Loves You	Dean Martin	Reprise
Seventh Son	Johnny Rivers	Imperial
What The World Needs Now Is Love	Jackie De Shannon	Imperial
⑥ **Wonderful World**	Herman's Hermits	MGM
A World Of Our Own	The Seekers	Capitol
Yes, I'm Ready	Barbara Mason	Arctic
You Turn Me On	Ian Whitcomb	Tower

JULY

California Girls	The Beach Boys	Capitol
Down In The Boondocks	Billy Joe Royal	Columbia
⑥ **Hold Me, Thrill Me, Kiss Me**	Mel Carter	Imperial
☆ ⑥ **I Got You Babe**	Sonny & Cher	Atco
⑥ **I Like It Like That**	The Dave Clark Five	Epic
☆ ⑥ **I'm Henry VIII, I Am**	Herman's Hermits	MGM
I Want Candy	The Strangeloves	Bang
⑥ **Papa's Got A Brand New Bag**	James Brown	King

161

Sonny & Cher (l to r: Cher, Sonny Bono)

Save Your Heart For Me	Gary Lewis & the Playboys	Liberty
Since I Lost My Baby	The Temptations	Gordy
Sunshine, Lollipops And Rainbows	Lesley Gore	Mercury
Take Me Back	Little Anthony & the Imperials	DCP
⑥ Tracks Of My Tears	The Miracles	Tamla
Unchained Melody	The Righteous Brothers	Philles
⑥ What's New, Pussycat?	Tom Jones	Parrot

AUGUST

⑥ Catch Us If You Can	The Dave Clark Five	Epic
☆ ⑥ Eve Of Destruction	Barry McGuire	Dunhill
Heart Full Of Soul	The Yardbirds	Epic
☆ ⑥ Help!	The Beatles	Capitol
Houston	Dean Martin	Reprise
⑥ The "In" Crowd	The Ramsey Lewis Trio	Argo
⑥ In The Midnight Hour	Wilson Pickett	Atlantic
It Ain't Me Babe	The Turtles	White Whale
It's Gonna Take A Miracle	The Royalettes	MGM
It's The Same Old Song	The Four Tops	Motown
⑥ Like A Rolling Stone	Bob Dylan	Columbia
⑥ Nothing But Heartaches	The Supremes	Motown
We Gotta Get Out Of This Place	The Animals	MGM
⑥ You Were On My Mind	We Five	A & M

SEPTEMBER

Baby Don't Go	Sonny & Cher	Reprise
Do You Believe In Magic	The Lovin' Spoonful	Kama Sutra
☆ ⑥ Hang On Sloopy	The McCoys	Bang
I'm A Happy Man	The Jive Five	United Artists
Just A Little Bit Better	Herman's Hermits	MGM
⑥ Keep On Dancing	The Gentrys	MGM
Laugh At Me	Sonny	Atco
Liar, Liar	The Castaways	Soma
⑥ A Lover's Concerto	The Toys	DynoVoice
Make Me Your Baby	Barbara Lewis	Atlantic
Mohair Sam	Charlie Rich	Smash

162

Some Enchanted Evening	Jay & the Americans	United Artists	**1965**
Treat Her Right	Roy Head	Back Beat	
☆ ⑥ Yesterday/Act Naturally	The Beatles	Capitol	
You've Got Your Troubles	The Fortunes	Press	

OCTOBER

Ain't That Peculiar	Marvin Gaye	Tamla
Everybody Loves A Clown	Gary Lewis & the Playboys	Liberty
⑥ Everyone's Gone To The Moon	Jonathan King	Parrot
☆ ⑥ Get Off Of My Cloud	The Rolling Stones	London
I Knew You When	Billy Joe Royal	Columbia
⑥ I'm Yours	Elvis Presley	RCA Victor
⑥ Let's Hang On	The Four Seasons	Philips
My Girl Has Gone	The Miracles	Tamla
⑥ 1-2-3	Len Barry	Decca
⑥ Positively 4th Street	Bob Dylan	Columbia
⑥ Rescue Me	Fontella Bass	Checker
Run, Baby, Run	The Newbeats	Hickory
A Taste Of Honey/Third Man Theme	Herb Alpert & the Tijuana Brass	A & M
You're The One	The Vogues	Co & Ce
You've Got To Hide Your Love Away	The Silkie	Fontana

NOVEMBER

(All Of A Sudden) My Heart Sings	Mel Carter	Imperial
Don't Think Twice	The Wonder Who	Philips
England Swings	Roger Miller	Smash
Fever	The McCoys	Bang
⑥ I Got You (I Feel Good)	James Brown	King
☆ ⑥ I Hear A Symphony	The Supremes	Motown
I'm A Man	The Yardbirds	Epic
It's My Life	The Animals	MGM
⑥ Make It Easy On Yourself	The Walker Brothers	Smash
Make The World Go Away	Eddy Arnold	RCA Victor
May The Bird Of Paradise Fly Up Your Nose	Little Jimmy Dickens	Columbia
My Baby	The Temptations	Gordy
☆ ⑥ Over And Over	The Dave Clark Five	Epic
Something About You	The Four Tops	Motown
☆ ⑥ Turn! Turn! Turn!	The Byrds	Columbia

DECEMBER

Crying Time	Ray Charles	ABC Paramount
Ebb Tide	The Righteous Brothers	Philles
Five O'Clock World	The Vogues	Co & Ce
Flowers On The Wall	The Statler Brothers	Columbia
⑥ Jenny Take A Ride	Mitch Ryder & the Detroit Wheels	New Voice

163

Lies	The Knickerbockers	Challenge
The Little Girl I Once Knew	The Beach Boys	Capitol
A Must To Avoid	Herman's Hermits	MGM
No Matter What Shape (Your Stomach's In)	The T-Bones	Liberty
Puppet On A String	Elvis Presley	RCA Victor
She's Just My Style	Gary Lewis & the Playboys	Liberty
☆ ⑥ The Sounds Of Silence	Simon & Garfunkel	Columbia
Sunday And Me	Jay & the Americans	United Artists
☆ ⑥ We Can Work It Out/Day Tripper	The Beatles	Capitol
You Didn't Have To Be So Nice	The Lovin' Spoonful	Kama Sutra

TOP SINGLES OF 1965

⑥ Get Off My Cloud	The Rolling Stones	London
⑥ Help!	The Beatles	Capitol
⑥ Help Me Rhonda	The Beach Boys	Capitol
⑥ (I Can't Get No) Satisfaction	The Rolling Stones	London
⑥ I Got You Babe	Sonny & Cher	Atco
⑥ Mrs. Brown, You've Got A Lovely Daughter	Herman's Hermits	MGM
⑥ Stop! In The Name Of Love	The Supremes	Motown
⑥ Turn! Turn! Turn!	The Byrds	Columbia
⑥ Wooly Bully	Sam the Sham & the Pharaohs	MGM
⑥ Yesterday	The Beatles	Capitol

TOP ALBUMS OF 1965

⑥ Beatles VI	The Beatles	Capitol
⑥ Beatles '65	The Beatles	Capitol
Goldfinger	Soundtrack	United Artists
⑥ Help!	The Beatles	Capitol

The Vogues (top l to r: Don Miller, Hugh Geyer, Bill Burkette; bottom: Chuck Blasko; photo: Cardell)

The Who (l to r: Roger Daltrey, Keith Moon, Pete Townshend, John Entwistle)

1965

⑥ **Introducing Herman's Hermits**	Herman's Hermits	MGM
⑥ **Mary Poppins**	Soundtrack	Buena Vista
⑫ **My Name Is Barbra**	Barbra Streisand	Columbia
⑥ **Out Of Our Heads**	The Rolling Stones	London
Where Did Our Love Go	The Supremes	Motown
⑥ **Whipped Cream & Other Delights**	Herb Alpert & the Tijuana Brass	A & M

GRAMMY WINNERS IN 1965

The Grammys were awarded at the Beverly Hilton Hotel in Los Angeles on Tuesday, March 15, 1966. Jerry Lewis was the host.

Record of the Year: "A Taste Of Honey," Herb Alpert & the Tijuana Brass (A & M)
Song of the Year: "The Shadow Of Your Smile" (music by Johnny Mandel, lyrics by Paul Francis Webster)
Album of the Year: *September Of My Years,* Frank Sinatra (Reprise)
Best Vocal Performance, Female: *My Name Is Barbra,* Barbra Streisand (Columbia)
Best Vocal Performance, Male: "It Was A Very Good Year," Frank Sinatra (Reprise)
Best Vocal Performance, Group: *We Dig Mancini,* The Anita Kerr Singers (RCA)
Best Contemporary (Rock 'n' Roll) Single: "King Of The Road," Roger Miller (Smash)
Best New Artist of the Year: Tom Jones
Best Comedy Performance: *Why Is There Air?* Bill Cosby (Warner Bros.)
Best Soundtrack Album from a Motion Picture or Television: *The Sandpiper,* Johnny Mandel (Mercury)

DEATHS IN 1965

MUSIC PERFORMERS AND MUSIC INDUSTRY NOTABLES WHO DIED IN 1965

Alan Freed (disc jockey), Wednesday, January 20 (euremic poisoning; 42)
Nat "King" Cole, Monday, February 15 (cancer; 45)

Bill Black, Thursday, October 21 (brain tumor; 39)
Earl Bostic, Thursday, October 28 (heart attack; 45)

OTHERS WHO DIED IN 1965

Harry Blackstone
Clara Bow
Winston Churchill
T. S. Eliot
Judy Holliday

Stan Laurel
Edward R. Murrow
Albert Schweitzer
David O. Selznick
Adlai E. Stevenson

165

MOVIES OF 1965

MOVIES FEATURING POP MUSIC ARTISTS

Beach Ball   *Stars:* Edd Byrnes, Chris Noel, Gail Gilmore. *Featured song:* "Dawn" by the Four Seasons. *Other musical performers:* The Righteous Brothers, the Supremes, the Hondells, the Walker Brothers.

Beach Blanket Bingo   *Stars:* Frankie Avalon, Annette Funicello, Paul Lynde, Harvey Lembeck, Don Rickles, Linda Evans, Buster Keaton. No significant hits or performers. Probably the best known of all the "beach" movies.

Ferry Cross the Mersey   *Stars:* Gerry Marsden, Cilla Black, George Cooper. *Featured songs:* "It's Gonna Be Alright" and "Ferry Cross The Mersey" by Gerry & the Pacemakers. *Other musical performers:* Cilla Black, the Fourmost.

Girl Happy   *Stars:* Elvis Presley, Shelley Fabares, Gary Crosby, Mary Ann Mobley, Jackie Coogan. *Featured song:* "Puppet On A String."

Girls on the Beach   *Stars:* Martin West, Noreen Corcoran, Peter Brooks. No significant hits. *Musical performers:* The Beach Boys, Lesley Gore, the Crickets.

Harum Scarum   *Stars:* Elvis Presley, Mary Ann Mobley, Billy Barty, Fran Jeffries. No significant hits.

Help!   *Stars:* The Beatles, Leo McKern, Victor Spinetti. *Featured songs:* "Help!" "You're Gonna Lose That Girl," "You've Got To Hide Your Love Away," "Ticket To Ride," "I Need You," "Another Girl," "The Night Before." The Beatles' first color film.

How to Stuff a Wild Bikini   *Stars:* Frankie Avalon, Annette Funicello, Dwayne Hickman, Harvey Lembeck, Buster Keaton, Mickey Rooney, Brian Donlevy. No significant hits. *Musical performers:* Annette Funicello, the Kingsmen.

Ski Party   *Stars:* Frankie Avalon, Dwayne Hickman, Deborah Walley, Robert Q. Lewis. *Featured songs:* "I Got You" by James Brown, "Sunshine, Lollipops And Rainbows" by Lesley Gore.

Tickle Me   *Stars:* Elvis Presley, Jocelyn Lane, Julie Adams. No significant hits.

POP MUSIC CONCERTS ON FILM

Go Go Mania   Originally titled *Pop Gear,* this mock concert film, hosted by disc jockey Jimmy Saville, featured many of Britain's top acts lip-synching their big hits. Shot in

The Yardbirds (top l to r: *James McCarty, Chris Dreja, Paul Samwell-Smith;* middle: *Keith Relf;* bottom: *Jeff Beck)*

**Herb Alpert's Tijuana Brass,
Whipped Cream and Other
Delights** *album cover*

Technicolor, the major acts included the Beatles, the Animals, the Honeycombs, Herman's Hermits, the Nashville Teens, Billy J. Kramer & the Dakotas, Peter & Gordon, and the Spencer Davis Group.

OTHER POPULAR MOVIES OF 1965

Cat Ballou
The Collector
Doctor Zhivago
Hush . . . Hush, Sweet Charlotte
The Ipcress File

The Pawnbroker
Ship of Fools
The Sound of Music
A Thousand Clowns

ACADEMY AWARD WINNERS OF 1965

Best Actor: Lee Marvin, *Cat Ballou*
Best Actress: Julie Christie, *Darling*
Best Picture: *The Sound of Music*
Best Song: "The Shadow Of Your Smile," *The Sandpiper* (music by Johnny Mandel, lyrics by Paul Francis Webster)

TOP TELEVISION SHOWS OF 1965

The Andy Griffith Show
Batman
The Beverly Hillbillies
Bewitched
Bonanza

Gomer Pyle, U.S.M.C.
Green Acres
Hogan's Heroes
The Lucy Show
The Red Skelton Hour

1966

⇨ Nehru's daughter, Indira Gandhi, becomes the third prime minister of India.

⇨ The first docking in space is achieved by Gemini 8 astronauts Neil Armstrong and David Scott.

⇨ In Houston, Texas, Dr. Michael E. De Bakey implants the first artificial pump in a patient's heart.

⇨ The Great Proletarian Cultural Revolution in China is launched by Mao Tse-tung.

⇨ Outside Paris, Sophia Loren and Carlo Ponti finally wed.

⇨ The unmanned capsule *Surveyor 1* lands on the moon and sends back pictures of its surface.

⇨ Frank Sinatra and Mia Farrow are wed in a 5-minute ceremony in Las Vegas.

⇨ The New York *Herald-Tribune* newspaper runs into financial difficulties and announces it will cease publication.

⇨ President Johnson makes an unexpected visit to the soldiers in South Vietnam.

⇨ A devastating flood damages valuable art in Florence, Italy.

⇨ Ronald Reagan is elected governor of California.

⇨ Fashion model Twiggy popularizes the miniskirt.

SPORTS WINNERS

Baseball   The Baltimore Orioles beat the Los Angeles Dodgers 4 games to 0.

Football

NFL: The Green Bay Packers beat the Dallas Cowboys 34–27 in Dallas.

AFL: The Kansas City Chiefs beat the Buffalo Bills 31–7 in Buffalo.

Super Bowl I: The Green Bay Packers beat the Kansas City Chiefs 35–10 on January 15, 1967, at Memorial Coliseum in Los Angeles.

Basketball   The Boston Celtics beat the Los Angeles Lakers 4 games to 3.

Hockey   The Montreal Canadiens beat the Detroit Red Wings 4 games to 2.

MUSIC HIGHLIGHTS OF 1966

⇨ On Saturday, January 8, ABC television's *Shindig* is broadcast for the last time.

⇨ The Cavern Club in Liverpool, where the Beatles began, ceases operation.

⇨ A London newspaper quotes John Lennon as saying that the Beatles "are more popular than Jesus Christ." This comment engenders worldwide hostility to the Beatles, many people destroying Beatles records in retaliation.

⇨ In April, NBC television cancels *Hullabaloo*.

⇨ In the summer, the Beatles' controversial *"Yesterday"* . . . *And Today* album cover is pulled off the market. The original showed the Beatles with an assortment of bloodied baby dolls. A more conventional cover is substituted.

⇨ Indian musician Ravi Shankar introduces the sitar to George Harrison.

⇨ The tape cartridge, or cassette, invented in 1954, is introduced commercially.

⇨ Bob Dylan is involved in a serious accident while riding his motorcycle in Woodstock, New York. He remains in the hospital for over a month.

⇨ On Friday, August 11, the Beatles arrive at O'Hare Airport in Chicago for their final tour of America. That same night, John Lennon makes a public apology to reporters about the comment he made earlier in the year about the Beatles being more popular than Jesus Christ. He said he was misquoted and that he was not anti-Christ. After Chicago, the Beatles played Cleveland, Ohio; Washington, D.C.; Toronto, Canada; Memphis, Tennessee; Cincinnati, Ohio; New York City; and Seattle, Washington, among other cities. Their last public concert was on Monday, August 29, at San Francisco's Candlestick Park. In front of 25,000 screaming fans, the final song they performed was Little Richard's "Long Tall Sally."

⇨ Controversy erupts over the novelty record "They're Coming To Take Me Away, Ha-

169

Haaa!" by Napoleon XIV. Health groups protest that it ridiculed the mentally ill, and many radio stations and record stores abandon the disc, even though it is in the national Top 10.

⇨ Columbia Pictures decides to create a television series based on the concept of the Beatles' highly successful movie *A Hard Day's Night*. Michael Nesmith, Micky Dolenz, Peter Tork, and Davy Jones are chosen for the show, and with Don Kirshner at the helm as music director, *The Monkees* goes on the air in September and rapidly becomes a smash. The first single released by the made-in-Hollywood group zooms to number one and becomes the first of the Monkees' six successive gold records.

⇨ During the fall of the year, John Lennon meets a Japanese-American woman named Yoko Ono at an art exhibit she was giving at the Indica Gallery in London.

⇨ Chas Chandler, bass player for the Animals, brings American guitarist Jimi Hendrix to England and helps him establish a rhythm section consisting of Mitch Mitchell and Noel Redding. The new group, called the Experience, begins by recording the classic "Hey Joe," which is then sold to Polydor Records. After an appearance by the group on the *Ready, Steady, Go!* TV show, the record becomes a major British hit, launching Hendrix's career. Shortly thereafter, *Ready, Steady, Go!* goes off the air.

⇨ The Beatles' 13th album release in America, *Revolver*, becomes their ninth to go to number one on the national charts.

DEBUT ARTISTS OF 1966

MAJOR ARTISTS	Debut Single	Label
The Association (Russ Giguere, Gary Alexander, Jim Yester, Terry Kirkman, Brian Cole, Ted Bluechel, Jr.)	Along Comes Mary	Valiant
Judy Collins	Hard Loving Loser	Elektra
The Cyrkle (Donald Dannemann, Thomas Dawes, Martin Fried, Earl Pickens)	Red Rubber Ball ⑥	Columbia
Neil Diamond	Solitary Man	Bang
The Five Americans (Michael Rabon, Leonard Goldsmith, Robert Rambo, James Grant, James Wright)	I See The Light	HBR
The Five Stairsteps (Aloha, Clarence, James, Dennis, and Kenneth Burke)	You Waited Too Long	Windy C
Eddie Floyd	Knock On Wood	Stax
The Grass Roots (Creed Bratton, Warren Entner, Rob Grill, Rick Coonce)	Where Were You When I Needed You	Dunhill

The Buckinghams (l to r: Dennis Tufano, Dennis Miccoli, Jon Jon Paulos, Carl Giamarese, Nicholas Fortune)

The Blues Magoos (Ronald Gilbert, Ralph Scala, Emil "Peppy" Theilhelm, Michael Esposito, Jeffrey Daking [order in photo unknown])

1966

The Happenings (Robert Miranda, Ralph DeVito, David Libert, Tom Giuliano)	See You In September ⑤	B.T. Puppy
The Intruders (Phil Terry, Robert "Big Sonny" Edwards, Samuel "Little Sonny" Brown, Eugene "Bird" Daughtry)	United	Gamble
Tommy James & the Shondells (Tommy James, Joe Kessler, Ron Rosman, Michael Vale, Vince Pietropaoli, George Magura)	Hanky Panky ☆ ⑤	Roulette
The Mamas & the Papas (John Phillips, Denny Doherty, Michelle Gilliam Phillips, Cass Elliott)	California Dreamin' ⑤	Dunhill
Herbie Mann	Philly Dog	Atlantic
Sergio Mendes & Brasil '66 (Sergio Mendes, Lani Hall, Karen Phillipp, Sebastião Neto, Dom Um Rãomão, Rubens Bassini)	Mas Que Nada	A & M
The Monkees (Davy Jones, Peter Tork, Michael Nesmith, Micky Dolenz)	Last Train To Clarksville ☆ ⑤	Colgems
The New Colony Six (Gerry Van Kollenberg, Ronald Rice, Charles Jobes, Patrick McBride, Les Kummel, William Herman)	I Confess	Centaur
Peaches & Herb (Francine Barker, Herb Feemster)	Let's Fall In Love	Date
The Pozo-Seco Singers (Don Williams, Susan Taylor, Lofton Kline)	Time	Columbia
James & Bobby Purify (James Purify, Bobby Lee Dickey)	I'm Your Puppet ⑤	Bell
The Royal Guardsmen (Chris Nunley, Tom Richards, Barry "Snoopy" Winslow, Bill Balogh, Bill Taylor, John Burdette)	Snoopy Vs. The Red Baron ⑤	Laurie
Jimmy Ruffin	What Becomes Of The Brokenhearted	Soul
Sam & Dave (Sam Moore, Dave Prater)	You Don't Know Like I Know	Soul
Joe Simon	Teenager's Prayer	Sound Stage 7
Percy Sledge	When A Man Loves A Woman ☆ ⑤	Atlantic

B.J. Thomas (Billy Joe Thomas)		
	I'm So Lonesome I Could Cry	Scepter
Frankie Valli	Hurt Yourself	Smash

OTHER ARTISTS

The Arbors	Tommy McLain
Darrell Banks	Mrs. Miller
The Blues Magoos	The Mindbenders
The Brass Ring	The Music Machine
The Count Five	Napoleon XIV (Jerry Samuels)
The Bob Crewe Generation	Aaron Neville
The Critters	The New Vaudeville Band
The Crusaders	The Outsiders
The Cryan' Shames	Robert Parker
David & Jonathan	The Poppies
The Spencer Davis Group	Sandy Posey
The Electric Prunes	? (Question Mark) & the Mysterians
The Bobby Fuller Four	The Googie Rene Combo
Bobby Hebb	SSgt. Barry Sadler
Neal Hefti	The Sandpipers
Don Ho	The Seeds
Eddie Holman	The Shades of Blue
Richard "Groove" Holmes	The Shadows of Knight
David Houston	The Sopwith "Camel"
The Ides of March	Red Sovine
The Innocence	The Standells
Deon Jackson	Crispian St. Peters
J. J. Jackson	The Swingin' Medallions
The Jazz Crusaders	The Syndicate of Sound
Keith (James Barry Keefer)	Norma Tanega
Terry Knight & the Pack	Tammi Terrell
Bob Kuban & the In-Men	The Troggs
The Leaves	Spyder Turner
The Left Banke	Walter Wanderley
Bob Lind	Brian Wilson
Shorty Long	The Youngbloods
Los Bravos	Young-Holt Unlimited

Judy Collins

Neil Diamond

Sam & Dave (Sam Moore, Dave Prater)

The Monkees (l to r: Michael Nesmith, Micky Dolenz, Peter Tork, Davy Jones)

1966

HITS OF 1966

JANUARY

As Tears Go By	The Rolling Stones	London
Attack	The Toys	DynoVoice
ⓖ Barbara Ann	The Beach Boys	Capitol
Don't Mess With Bill	The Marvelettes	Tamla
ⓖ Going To A Go-Go	The Miracles	Tamla
It Was A Very Good Year	Frank Sinatra	Reprise
☆ ⓖ Lightnin' Strikes	Lou Christie	MGM
Like A Baby	Len Barry	Decca
The Men In My Little Girl's Life	Mike Douglas	Epic
☆ ⓖ My Love	Petula Clark	Warner Bros.
ⓖ My World Is Empty Without You	The Supremes	Motown
One Has My Name	Barry Young	Dot
☆ ⓖ These Boots Are Made For Walkin'	Nancy Sinatra	Reprise
Working My Way Back To You	The Four Seasons	Philips
Zorba The Greek	Herb Alpert & the Tijuana Brass	A & M

FEBRUARY

Baby Scratch My Back	Slim Harpo	Excello
☆ ⓖ The Ballad Of The Green Berets	SSgt. Barry Sadler	RCA Victor
Batman Theme	The Marketts	Warner Bros.
ⓖ California Dreamin'	The Mamas & the Papas	Dunhill
The Cheater	Bob Kuban & the In-Men	Musicland, U.S.A.
Elusive Butterfly	Bob Lind	World Pacific
Homeward Bound	Simon & Garfunkel	Columbia
I Fought The Law	The Bobby Fuller Four	Mustang
ⓖ Listen People	Herman's Hermits	MGM
Love Is All We Need	Mel Carter	Imperial
ⓖ 19th Nervous Breakdown	The Rolling Stones	London
634-5789	Wilson Pickett	Atlantic
ⓖ Uptight (Everything's Alright)	Stevie Wonder	Tamla
Woman	Peter & Gordon	Capitol
You Baby	The Turtles	White Whale

173

ROCK ON ALMANAC

MARCH

	Bang Bang	Cher	Imperial
⑥	Daydream	The Lovin' Spoonful	Kama Sutra
	Get Ready	The Temptations	Gordy
⑥	I'm So Lonesome I Could Cry	B.J. Thomas & the Triumphs	Specter
⑥	It's Too Late	Bobby Goldsboro	United Artists
	Kicks	Paul Revere & the Raiders	Columbia
	Magic Town	The Vogues	Co & Ce
⑥	Nowhere Man/What Goes On	The Beatles	Capitol
⑥	Secret Agent Man	Johnny Rivers	Imperial
	Shake Me, Wake Me (When It's Over)	The Four Tops	Motown
⑥	Spanish Flea	Herb Alpert & the Tijuana Brass	A & M
	Sure Gonna Miss Her	Gary Lewis & the Playboys	Liberty
	This Old Heart Of Mine (Is Weak For You)	The Isley Brothers	Tamla
⑥	Time Won't Let Me	The Outsiders	Capitol
☆ ⑥	(You're My) Soul And Inspiration	The Righteous Brothers	Verve

APRIL

	Eight Miles High	The Byrds	Columbia
⑥	Gloria	The Shadows of Knight	Dunwich
⑥	A Groovy Kind Of Love	The Mindbenders	Fontana
	How Does That Grab You, Darlin'?	Nancy Sinatra	Reprise
	Leaning On The Lamp Post	Herman's Hermits	MGM
	Love Is Like An Itching In My Heart	The Supremes	Motown
	Message To Michael	Dionne Warwick	Scepter
☆ ⑥	Monday, Monday	The Mamas & the Papas	Dunhill
	Nothing's Too Good For My Baby	Stevie Wonder	Tamla
	Rainy Day Women #12 & 35	Bob Dylan	Columbia

B.J. Thomas

Frankie Valli

Rhapsody In The Rain	Lou Christie	MGM	**1966**
A Sign Of The Times	Petula Clark	Warner Bros.	
⑥ Sloop John B	The Beach Boys	Capitol	
The Sun Ain't Gonna Shine (Anymore)	The Walker Brothers	Smash	
☆ ⑥ When A Man Loves A Woman	Percy Sledge	Atlantic	

MAY

⑥ Barefootin'	Robert Parker	Nola
Cool Jerk	The Capitols	Karen
Did You Ever Have To Make Up Your Mind?	The Lovin' Spoonful	Kama Sutra
Don't Bring Me Down	The Animals	MGM
Double Shot (Of My Baby's Love)	The Swingin' Medallions	Smash
Green Grass	Gary Lewis & the Playboys	Liberty
⑥ Hold On! I'm Comin'	Sam & Dave	Stax
I Am A Rock	Simon & Garfunkel	Columbia
Oh How Happy	The Shades of Blue	Impact
Opus 17 (Don't Worry 'Bout Me)	The Four Seasons	Philips
☆ ⑥ Paint It, Black	The Rolling Stones	London
⑥ Red Rubber Ball	The Cyrkle	Columbia
☆ ⑥ Strangers In The Night	Frank Sinatra	Reprise
Sweet Talkin' Guy	The Chiffons	Laurie
⑥ You Don't Have To Say You Love Me	Dusty Springfield	Philips

JUNE

Ain't Too Proud To Beg	The Temptations	Gordy
Along Comes Mary	The Association	Valiant
☆ ⑥ Hanky Panky	Tommy James & the Shondells	Roulette
I Love You 1,000 Times	The Platters	Musicor
The Impossible Dream	Jack Jones	Kapp
It's A Man's, Man's, Man's World	James Brown	King
⑥ Lil' Red Riding Hood	Sam the Sham & the Pharoahs	MGM
Little Girl	The Syndicate of Sound	Bell
The More I See You	Chris Montez	A & M
☆ ⑥ Paperback Writer/Rain	The Beatles	Capitol
The Pied Piper	Crispian St. Peters	Jamie
Popsicle	Jan & Dean	Liberty
Somewhere My Love	Ran Coniff & the Singers	Columbia
⑥ Sweet Pea	Tommy Roe	ABC Paramount
Younger Girl	The Critters	Kapp

JULY

I Couldn't Live Without Your Love	Petula Clark	Warner Bros.

I Saw Her Again	The Mamas & the Papas	Dunhill
I Want You	Bob Dylan	Columbia
⑥ **Love Letters**	Elvis Presley	RCA Victor
⑥ **Mother's Little Helper/Lady Jane**	The Rolling Stones	London
Over Under Sideways Down	The Yardbirds	Epic
⑥ **See You In September**	The Happenings	B.T. Puppy
☆ ⑥ **Summer In The City**	The Lovin' Spoonful	Kama Sutra
⑥ **Sunny**	Bobby Hebb	Philips
Sweet Dreams	Tommy McLain	MSL
⑥ **They're Coming To Take Me Away, Ha-Haaa!**	Napoleon XIV	Warner Bros.
This Door Swings Both Ways	Herman's Hermits	MGM
Trains And Boats And Planes	Dionne Warwick	Scepter
☆ ⑥ **Wild Thing**	The Troggs	Atco
You Better Run	The Young Rascals	Atlantic

AUGUST

Blowin' In The Wind	Stevie Wonder	Tamla
⑥ **Born A Woman**	Sandy Posey	MGM
⑥ **Bus Stop**	The Hollies	Imperial
Guantanamera	The Sandpipers	A & M
⑥ **Land Of 1000 Dances**	Wilson Pickett	Atlantic
Mr. Dieingly Sad	The Critters	Kapp
My Heart's Symphony	Gary Lewis & the Playboys	Liberty
Respectable	The Outsiders	Capitol
Summertime	Billy Stewart	Chess
Sunny Afternoon	The Kinks	Reprise
☆ ⑥ **Sunshine Superman**	Donovan	Epic
Turn Down Day	The Cyrkle	Columbia
Wouldn't It Be Nice/God Only Knows	The Beach Boys	Capitol
⑥ **Yellow Submarine/Eleanor Rigby**	The Beatles	Capitol
☆ ⑥ **You Can't Hurry Love**	The Supremes	Motown

SEPTEMBER

B-A-B-Y	Carla Thomas	Stax
Beauty Is Only Skin Deep	The Temptations	Gordy
⑥ **Black Is Black**	Los Bravos	Press
☆ ⑥ **Cherish**	The Association	Valiant
⑥ **Cherry, Cherry**	Neil Diamond	Bang
It Hurts Me	Bobby Goldsboro	United Artists
I've Got You Under My Skin	The Four Seasons	Philips
Just Like A Woman	Bob Dylan	Columbia
☆ ⑥ **Last Train To Clarksville**	The Monkees	Colgems
☆ ⑥ **96 Tears**	? (Question Mark) & the Mysterians	Cameo
Psychotic Reaction	The Count Five	Double Shot
☆ ⑥ **Reach Out I'll Be There**	The Four Tops	Motown
Summer Wind	Frank Sinatra	Reprise
There Will Never Be Another You	Chris Montez	A & M

The Troggs (top: Reg Presley; bottom l to r: Tony Murray, Ronnie Bond, Colin Fletcher)

1966

What Becomes Of The Brokenhearted	Jimmy Ruffin	Soul

OCTOBER

	Ain't Gonna Lie	Keith	Mercury
	Born Free	Roger Williams	Kapp
	Coming On Strong	Brenda Lee	Decca
	Dandy	Herman's Hermits	MGM
	Devil With The Blue Dress On & Good Golly Miss Molly	Mitch Ryder & the Detroit Wheels	New Voice
	Fa-Fa-Fa-Fa-Fa (Sad Song)	Otis Redding	Volt
⑥	Go Away, Little Girl	The Happenings	B.T. Puppy
⑥	Have You Seen Your Mother, Baby, Standing In The Shadow?	The Rolling Stones	London
	Hooray For Hazel	Tommy Roe	ABC
	If I Were A Carpenter	Bobby Darin	Atlantic
⑥	I'm Your Puppet	James & Bobby Purify	Bell
	Love Is A Hurtin' Thing	Lou Rawls	Capitol
	Mas Que Nada	Sergio Mendes & Brasil '66	A & M
☆ ⑥	Poor Side Of Town	Johnny Rivers	Imperial
⑥	Walk Away Renee	The Left Banke	Smash

NOVEMBER

	But It's Alright	J.J. Jackson	Calla
☆ ⑥	Good Vibrations	The Beach Boys	Capitol
	A Hazy Shade Of Winter	Simon & Garfunkel	Columbia
	(I Know) I'm Losing You	The Temptations	Gordy
	I'm Ready For Love	Martha & the Vandellas	Gordy
⑥	Lady Godiva	Peter & Gordon	Capitol
⑥	Mellow Yellow	Donovan	Epic
⑥	Mustang Sally	Wilson Pickett	Atlantic
	Rain On The Roof	The Lovin' Spoonful	Kama Sutra
⑥	Stop Stop Stop	The Hollies	Imperial
⑥	Sugar Town	Nancy Sinatra	Reprise
	That's Life	Frank Sinatra	Reprise

177

	Whispers	Jackie Wilson	Brunswick
☆ ⑥	Winchester Cathedral	The New Vaudeville Band	Fontana
☆ ⑥	You Keep Me Hangin' On	The Supremes	Motown

DECEMBER

⑥	Georgy Girl	The Seekers	Capitol
	Hello Hello	The Sopwith "Camel"	Kama Sutra
	I Had Too Much To Dream (Last Night)	The Electric Prunes	Reprise
☆ ⑥	I'm A Believer/(I'm Not Your) Steppin' Stone	The Monkees	Colgems
	I've Passed This Way Before	Jimmy Ruffin	Soul
	Nashville Cats	The Lovin' Spoonful	Kama Sutra
⑥	98.6	Keith	Mercury
⑥	Single Girl	Sandy Posey	MGM
⑥	Snoopy Vs. The Red Baron	The Royal Guardsmen	Laurie
	Stand By Me	Spyder Turner	MGM
⑥	Standing In The Shadows Of Love	The Four Tops	Motown
⑥	Tell It Like It Is	Aaron Neville	Parlo
	Tell It To The Rain	The Four Seasons	Philips
	(We Ain't Got) Nothin' Yet	The Blues Magoos	Mercury
	Words Of Love/Dancing In The Street	The Mamas & the Papas	Dunhill

TOP SINGLES OF 1966

⑥	The Ballad Of The Green Berets	SSgt. Barry Sadler	RCA Victor
⑥	Cherish	The Association	Valiant
⑥	Hanky Panky	Tommy James & the Shondells	Roulette
⑥	Monday, Monday	The Mamas & the Papas	Dunhill
⑥	Paint It, Black	The Rolling Stones	London
⑥	Summer In The City	The Lovin' Spoonful	Kama Sutra
⑥	Wild Thing	The Troggs	Fontana
⑥	Winchester Cathedral	The New Vaudeville Band	Fontana
⑥	You Can't Hurry Love	The Supremes	Motown
⑥	(You're My) Soul And Inspiration	The Righteous Brothers	Verve

The Beach Boys, Pet Sounds album cover

TOP ALBUMS

⑤ Aftermath	The Rolling Stones	London
⑤ Ballads Of The Green Berets	SSgt. Barry Sadler	RCA Victor
⑤ Big Hits (High Tide And Green Grass)	The Rolling Stones	London
⑤ Doctor Zhivago	Soundtrack	MGM
⑤ If You Can Believe Your Eyes And Ears	The Mamas & the Papas	Dunhill
⑤ The Monkees	The Monkees	Colgems
⑤ Revolver	The Beatles	Capitol
⑤ Rubber Soul	The Beatles	Capitol
⑤ What Now My Love	Herb Alpert & the Tijuana Brass	A & M
⑤ "Yesterday" . . . And Today	The Beatles	Capitol

GRAMMY WINNERS IN 1966

The Grammys were awarded at the Beverly Hilton Hotel in Los Angeles on Thursday, March 2, 1967. Bill Dana was the host.

Record of the Year: "Strangers In The Night," Frank Sinatra (Reprise)
Song of the Year: "Michelle" (music and lyrics by Paul McCartney and John Lennon)
Album of the Year: *Sinatra: A Man And His Music,* Frank Sinatra (Reprise)
Best Vocal Performance, Female: "If He Walked Into My Life," Eydie Gorme (Columbia)
Best Vocal Performance, Male: "Strangers In The Night," Frank Sinatra (Reprise)
Bst Vocal Performance, Group: "A Man And A Woman," The Anita Kerr Singers (Warner Bros.)
Best Contemporary (Rock 'n' Roll) Recording: "Winchester Cathedral," The New Vaudeville Band (Fontana)
Best New Artist of the Year: (no award)
Best Comedy Performance: *Wonderfulness,* Bill Cosby (Warner Bros.)
Best Soundtrack Album from a Motion Picture or Television: *Doctor Zhivago,* Maurice Jarre (MGM)

BIRTHS AND DEATHS IN 1966

MUSIC PERFORMERS BORN IN 1966

Janet Jackson, May 16

Stacy Lattisaw, November 25

MUSIC PERFORMERS AND MUSIC INDUSTRY NOTABLES WHO DIED IN 1966

Sophie Tucker, Tuesday, February 8 (lung cancer; 82)

Bobby Fuller (Bobby Fuller Four), Monday, July 18 (asphyxiation; 22)

OTHERS WHO DIED IN 1966

Lenny Bruce
Montgomery Clift
Walt Disney
William Frawley
Hedda Hopper

Buster Keaton
S.S. Kresge
Chester Nimitz
Clifton Webb
Ed Wynn

ROCK ON ALMANAC

MOVIES OF 1966

MOVIES FEATURING POP MUSIC ARTISTS

Frankie and Johnny   *Stars:* Elvis Presley, Donna Douglas, Harry Morgan, Robert Strauss. *Featured song:* "Frankie And Johnny."

Ghost in the Invisible Bikini   *Stars:* Tommy Kirk, Deborah Walley, Nancy Sinatra, Harvey Lembeck, Basil Rathbone, Boris Karloff, Francis X. Bushman, Jesse White, Patsy Kelly. Last in a series of "beach" movies; featured the only film appearance of the Bobby Fuller Four.

Hold On!   *Stars:* Peter Noone (of Herman's Hermits), Sue Ann Langdon, Shelley Fabares. *Featured songs:* "A Must To Avoid" and "Leaning On The Lamp Post" by Herman's Hermits.

Out of Sight   *Stars:* Jonathan Daly, Karen Jensen, Robert Pine. No significant hits. *Musical performers:* Freddie & the Dreamers, Dobie Gray, the Turtles, Gary Lewis & the Playboys, the Knickerbockers.

Paradise Hawaiian Style   *Stars:* Elvis Presley, Suzanna Leigh, James Shigeta. No significant hits.

Spinout   *Stars:* Elvis Presley, Shelley Fabares, Deborah Walley, Carl Betz, Cecil Kellaway. No significant hits.

Wild, Wild Winter   *Stars:* Gary Clarke, Chris Noel, Don Edmonds. No significant hits. *Musical performers:* The Beau Brummels, Jay & the Americans, Dick & Dee Dee.

POP MUSIC CONCERTS ON FILM

The Big T.N.T. Show   With David McCallum as host, this show, a "sequel" to the T.A.M.I. show of 1964, was shot with the same Electronovision video process. Staged in a concert setting in Los Angeles, the show featured the Byrds, Bo Diddley, Joan Baez, the Ronettes, Ray Charles, Donovan, the Lovin' Spoonful, and Ike & Tina Turner. In 1984, both the T.A.M.I. show and the T.N.T. show were combined and released as a video under the name *That Was Rock*.

OTHER POPULAR MOVIES OF 1966

Alfie
Born Free
The Fortune Cookie
Georgy Girl
Harper

Khartoum
A Man for All Seasons
The Professionals
Who's Afraid of Virginia Woolf?

ACADEMY AWARD WINNERS OF 1966

Best Actor: Paul Scofield, *A Man for All Seasons*
Best Actress: Elizabeth Taylor, *Who's Afraid of Virginia Woolf?*
Best Picture: *A Man for All Seasons*
Best Song: "Born Free," *Born Free* (music by John Barry, lyrics by Don Black)

TOP TELEVISION SHOWS OF 1966

The Andy Griffith Show
The Beverly Hillbillies
Bewitched
Bonanza
Daktari

Gomer Pyle, U.S.M.C.
Green Acres
The Jackie Gleason Show
The Lucy Show
The Red Skelton Hour

1967

ROCK ON ALMANAC

⇨ Three astronauts are killed in a flash fire that engulfs their *Apollo I* spacecraft.

⇨ Svetlana Alliluyeva, daughter of the late Soviet dictator Stalin, defects to the West.

⇨ Muhammad Ali is stripped of his world heavyweight boxing championship when he refuses to be inducted into the military service.

⇨ In Montreal, the 700-acre Canada Expo '67 opens.

⇨ The Six-Day War in the Middle East is an enormous victory for Israel but for the Arab world a defeat without honor.

⇨ Egypt closes the Suez Canal to all shipping.

⇨ French President de Gaulle causes a controversy when he pledges to liberate French Canadians.

⇨ Thurgood Marshall is the first black appointed to the U.S. Supreme Court.

⇨ Novelist Norman Mailer and some other 250 protesters are arrested while storming the Pentagon, rallying against the Vietnam War.

⇨ Antiwar protester and singer Joan Baez is arrested in California for trying to block the doors of an army induction center.

⇨ The celebration of the 50th anniversary of the Russian Revolution opens with a huge military parade in Moscow's Red Square that unveils five new types of missiles.

⇨ Dr. Christiaan Barnard and a team of surgeons in Cape Town, South Africa, transplant a young woman's heart into the body of Louis Washkansky, who survives 18 days before succumbing to pneumonia.

⇨ The first microwave oven for consumers makes fast food at home in an instant.

SPORTS WINNERS

Baseball The St. Louis Cardinals beat the Boston Red Sox 4 games to 3.

Football

NFL: The Green Bay Packers beat the Dallas Cowboys 21–17 in Green Bay.

AFL: The Oakland Raiders beat the Houston Oilers 40–7 in Oakland.

Super Bowl II: The Green Bay Packers beat the Oakland Raiders 33–14 on January 14, 1968, at the Orange Bowl in Miami.

Basketball The Philadelphia 76ers beat the San Francisco Warriors 4 games to 2.

Hockey The Toronto Maple Leafs beat the Montreal Canadiens 4 games to 2.

MUSIC HIGHLIGHTS OF 1967

⇨ In early March, the Bee Gees sign a management agreement with Robert Stigwood, an executive with the Beatles' NEMS Enterprises, and their first recording, "Spicks And Specks," is released. Their second recording, "New York Mining Disaster 1941," issued

The Bee Gees (l to r: Robin Gibb, Maurice Gibb, Barry Gibb)

simultaneously in the United States on Atco Records, becomes a Top 10 hit and establishes their success internationally.

⇨ Steve Winwood announces that he is leaving the Spencer Davis Group to start up a band called Traffic with Chris Wood, Dave Mason, and Jim Capaldi. Soon afterward, the Spencer Davis Group disbands.

⇨ Underground radio begins on KMPX in San Francisco, playing progressive rock music.

⇨ On Monday, May 1, Elvis Presley marries Priscilla Ann Beaulieu in a private suite of the Aladdin Hotel in Las Vegas, Nevada. Joe Esposito is Elvis's best man; Priscilla's sister Michelle is maid of honor.

⇨ In June, the Beatles' monumental *Sgt. Pepper's Lonely Hearts Club Band,* the first "concept" album, is released and becomes the group's biggest all-time seller.

⇨ The Monterey Pop Festival in Monterey, California, has a profound effect on rock music by introducing such superstars as Janis Joplin, Otis Redding, and Jimi Hendrix. That performance sends Hendrix on his way to becoming rock's reigning guitarist.

⇨ Scott McKenzie's "San Francisco (Be Sure To Wear Flowers In Your Hair)" becomes a virtual anthem for the "flower power" movement in the Haight-Ashbury district of San Francisco.

⇨ The Beatles' manager, Brian Epstein, dies of an overdose of sleeping pills on Sunday, August 27, at the age of 32.

⇨ Kenny Rogers leaves the New Christy Minstrels to form a new band called the First Edition. The group debuts at Ledbetter's in Los Angeles, where they meet Ken Kragen, who gets them a contract with Reprise Records.

⇨ The Who tours America for the first time. A few months later, Pink Floyd arrives in America for the first time as well. Floyd is the first British rock band to use a light show as part of its act.

⇨ On Thursday, November 9, the first issue of *Rolling Stone* magazine is published, featuring John Lennon on the cover.

⇨ Ginger Baker, Jack Bruce, and Eric Clapton form Cream, the first of the "supergroups" to emerge during the late sixties.

DEBUT ARTISTS OF 1967

MAJOR ARTISTS	Debut Single	Label
The Bar-Kays (James King, Ronald Caldwell, Phalon Jones, Benjamin Cauley, James Alexander, Carl Cunningham)	Soul Finger	Volt
The Bee Gees (Barry, Robin, and Maurice Gibb)	New York Mining Disaster 1941 Ⓖ	Atco
The Box Tops (Alex Chilton, Gary Talley, William Cunningham, Daniel Smythe, John Evans)	The Letter ☆ Ⓖ	Mala
Brenda & the Tabulations	Dry Your Eyes	Dionn
The Buckinghams (Dennis Tufano, Dennis Miccoli, Nicholas Fortune, Carl Giamerese, Jon Jon Paulos)	Kind Of A Drag ☆ Ⓖ	USA
The Buffalo Springfield (Stephen Stills, Neil Young, Richie Furay, Dewey Martin, Bruce Palmer)	For What It's Worth Ⓖ	Atco
Vikki Carr	It Must Be Him Ⓖ	Liberty
Clarence Carter	Thread The Needle	Fame
The Classics IV (Dennis Yost, James Cobb, Wally Eaton, Joseph Wilson, Kim Venable)	Spooky Ⓖ	Imperial

ROCK ON ALMANAC

The Doors (l to r: Jim Morrison, John Densmore, Robbie Krieger, Ray Manzarek)

Arthur Conley	Sweet Soul Music ⑥	Atco
Bill Cosby	Little Ole Man (Uptight —Everything's Alright) ⑥	Warner Bros.
The Cowsills (John, Robert, Barry, William, Paul, Richard, and Barbara Cowsill)	The Rain, The Park And Other Things ⑥	MGM
The Doors (Jim Morrison, Robbie Krieger, Ray Manzarek, John Densmore)	Light My Fire ☆ ⑥	Elektra
The 5th Dimension (Marilyn McCoo, Florence La Rue, Billy Davis, Jr., Ron Townson, Lamonte McLemore)	Go Where You Wanna Go	Soul City
Bobbie Gentry	Ode To Billie Joe ☆ ⑥	Capitol
Al Green	Back Up Train	Hot Line
The Jimi Hendrix Experience (Jimi Hendrix, Noel Redding, John "Mitch" Mitchell)	Purple Haze	Reprise
Engelbert Humperdinck	Release Me (And Let Me Love Again) ⑥	Parrot
The Jefferson Airplane (Grace Slick, Marty Balin, Paul Kantner, Jorma Kaukonen, Jack Casady, Spencer Dryden)	Somebody To Love	RCA Victor
Van Morrison	Brown Eyed Girl ⑥	Bang
The Nitty Gritty Dirt Band (Jeff Hanna, Glen Grosclose, Ralph Barr, Les Thompson, Bruce Kunkel, David Hanna)	Buy For Me The Rain	Liberty
The Ohio Express (Dale Powers, Douglas Grassel, James Pfayler, Dean Kastran, Tim Corwin)	Beg, Borrow And Steal	Cameo
Gary Puckett & the Union Gap (Gary Puckett, Dwight Bement, Gary Withem, Kerry Chater, Paul Wheatbread)	Woman, Woman ⑥	Columbia
Spanky & Our Gang (Elaine "Spanky" McFarlane, Lefty Baker, Malcom Hale, Geoffrey Myers, John Seiter, Nigel Pickering, Oz Bach)	Sunday Will Never Be The Same ⑥	Mercury

The Staple Singers (Roebuck "Pop," Cleo, Mavis, Yvonne, and Pervis Staples)	Why? (Am I Treated So Bad)	Epic
Johnnie Taylor	Somebody's Been Sleeping In My Bed	Stax
Vanilla Fudge (Tom Bogert, Mark Stein, Vince Martell, Carmine Appice)	You Keep Me Hanging On	Atco
The Watts 103rd Street Rhythm Band (Charles Wright, Al McKay, William Cannon, "Big" John Rayford, Gabriel Flemings, Joseph Banks, Ray Jackson, Melvin Dunlap, James Gadson)	Spreading Honey	Keymen

OTHER ARTISTS

The American Breed	Miriam Makeba
Henson Cargill	Hugh Masekela
The Casinos	Scott McKenzie
Jimmy Castor	The Music Explosion
The Choir	Kenny O'Dell
Country Joe & the Fish	The Parliaments
Senator Everett McKinley Dirksen	Procol Harum
Dyke & the Blazers	The Rose Garden
The Easybeats	Lalo Schifrin
The Esquires	Senator Bobby
Every Mother's Son	Bunny Sigler
Fantastic Johnny C	The Small Faces
The Fifth Estate	Whistling Jack Smith
The Foundations	The Soul Survivors
Gene & Debbie	The Stone Poneys
Harpers Bizarre	The Strawberry Alarm Clock
The Hombres	The Sunshine Company
The Human Beinz	The Sweet Inspirations
Janis Ian	Traffic
Jay & the Techniques	The Tremeloes
Jerry Jaye	Billy Vera & Judy Clay
Linda Jones	Brenton Wood
Robert Knight	Bill Wyman
The Lemon Pipers	Yellow Balloon
Victor Lundberg	

HITS OF 1967

JANUARY

⑥ **The Beat Goes On**	Sonny & Cher	Atco
Color My World	Petula Clark	Warner Bros.
Gallant Men	Senator Everett McKinley Dirksen	Capitol
⑥ **Gimme Some Lovin'**	The Spencer Davis Group	United Artists
Good Thing	Paul Revere & the Raiders	Columbia
Green, Green Grass Of Home	Tom Jones	Parrot
Hey, Leroy, Your Mama's Calling You	Jimmy Castor	Smash

185

⑥ Indescribably Blue	Elvis Presley	RCA Victor
It Takes Two	Marvin Gaye & Kim Weston	Tamla
☆ ⑥ Kind Of A Drag	The Buckinghams	U.S.A.
Knight In Rusty Armour	Peter & Gordon	Capitol
Mercy, Mercy, Mercy	Cannonball Adderley	Capitol
Music To Watch Girls By	The Bob Crewe Generation	DynoVoice
Pretty Ballerina	The Left Banke	Smash
Wild Thing	Senator Bobby	Parkway

FEBRUARY

Baby I Need Your Lovin'	Johnny Rivers	Imperial
California Nights	Lesley Gore	Mercury
Darlin' Be Home Soon	The Lovin' Spoonful	Kama Sutra
⑥ For What It's Worth	The Buffalo Springfield	Atco
Go Where You Wanna Go	The 5th Dimension	Soul City
☆ ⑥ Happy Together	The Turtles	White Whale
I've Been Lonely Too Long	The Young Rascals	Atlantic
Let's Fall In Love	Peaches & Herb	Date
☆ ⑥ Love Is Here And Now You're Gone	The Supremes	Motown
My Cup Runneth Over	Ed Ames	RCA Victor
☆ ⑥ Ruby Tuesday/Let's Spend The Night Together	The Rolling Stones	London
Sock It To Me—Baby!	Mitch Ryder & the Detroit Wheels	New Voice
Then You Can Tell Me Goodbye	The Casinos	Fraternity
⑥ There's A Kind Of Hush/No Milk Today	Herman's Hermits	MGM
You Got To Me	Neil Diamond	Bang

MARCH

Beggin'	The Four Seasons	Philips
Bernadette	The Four Tops	Motown
⑥ Dedicated To The One I Love	The Mamas & the Papas	Dunhill
Dry Your Eyes	Brenda & the Tabulations	Dionn

Engelbert Humperdinck

Van Morrison

Janis Ian

1967

Epistle To Dippy	Donovan	Epic
The 59th Street Bridge Song (Feelin' Groovy)	Harpers Bizarre	Warner Bros.
The Hunter Gets Captured By The Game	The Marvelettes	Tamla
⑥ I Think We're Alone Now	Tommy James & the Shondells	Roulette
Jimmy Mack	Martha & the Vandellas	Gordy
☆ ⑥ Penny Lane/Strawberry Fields Forever	The Beatles	Capitol
☆ ⑥ Somethin' Stupid	Frank & Nancy Sinatra	Reprise
⑥ Sweet Soul Music	Arthur Conley	Atco
⑥ This Is My Song	Petula Clark	Warner Bros.
Western Union	The Five Americans	Abnak
With This Ring	The Platters	Musicor

APRIL

At The Zoo	Simon & Garfunkel	Columbia
Close Your Eyes	Peaches & Herb	Date
⑥ Friday On My Mind	The Easybeats	United Artists
Girl, You'll Be A Woman Soon	Neil Diamond	Bang
☆ ⑥ Groovin'	The Young Rascals	Atlantic
☆ ⑥ The Happening	The Supremes	Motown
⑥ Here Comes My Baby	The Tremeloes	Epic
⑥ I Got Rhythm	The Happenings	B.T. Puppy
⑥ I'm A Man	The Spencer Davis Group	United Artists
⑥ I Never Loved A Man The Way I Love You	Aretha Franklin	Atlantic
⑥ A Little Bit You, A Little Bit Me/ The Girl I Knew Somewhere	The Monkees	Colgems
⑥ On A Carousel	The Hollies	Imperial
⑥ Release Me (And Let Me Love Again)	Engelbert Humperdinck	Parrot
Somebody To Love	Jefferson Airplane	RCA Victor
You Got What It Takes	The Dave Clark Five	Epic

187

MAY

Ain't No Mountain High Enough	Marvin Gaye & Tammi Terrell	Tamla
All I Need Is You	The Temptations	Gordy
Come On Down To My Boat	Every Mother's Son	MGM
Creeque Alley	The Mamas & the Papas	Dunhill
Happy Jack	The Who	Decca
Him Or Me—What's It Gonna Be?	Paul Revere & the Raiders	Columbia
⑥ I Was Kaiser Bill's Batman	Whistling Jack Smith	Deram
⑥ Let's Live For Today	The Grass Roots	Dunhill
⑥ Little Bit O' Soul	The Music Explosion	Laurie
⑥ Mirage	Tommy James & the Shondells	Roulette
My Girl Josephine	Jerry Jaye	Hi
☆ ⑥ Respect	Aretha Franklin	Atlantic
⑥ She'd Rather Be With Me	The Turtles	White Whale
⑥ Sunday Will Never Be The Same	Spanky & Our Gang	Mercury
☆ ⑥ Windy	The Association	Warner Bros.

JUNE

⑥ Can't Take My Eyes Off You	Frankie Valli	Philips
C'mon Marianne	The Four Seasons	Philips
Ding Dong! The Witch Is Dead	The Fifth Estate	Jubilee
Don't Sleep In The Subway	Petula Clark	Warner Bros.
⑥ I Was Made To Love Her	Stevie Wonder	Tamla
☆ ⑥ Light My Fire	The Doors	Elektra
Mercy, Mercy, Mercy	The Buckinghams	Columbia
More Love	Smokey Robinson & the Miracles	Tamla
⑥ New York Mining Disaster 1941	The Bee Gees	Atco
⑥ San Francisco (Be Sure To Wear Some Flowers In Your Hair)	Scott McKenzie	Ode
7 Rooms Of Gloom	The Four Tops	Motown
Society's Child	Janis Ian	Verve
The Tracks Of My Tears	Johnny Rivers	Imperial
⑥ Up-Up And Away	The 5th Dimension	Soul City
White Rabbit	Jefferson Airplane	RCA Victor

JULY

⑥ Baby I Love You	Aretha Franklin	Atlantic
⑥ Carrie Ann	The Hollies	Epic
For Your Love	Peaches & Herb	Date
A Girl Like You	The Young Rascals	Atlantic
I Like The Way	Tommy James & the Shondells	Roulette
In The Chapel In The Moonlight	Dean Martin	Reprise
I Thank The Lord For The Night Time	Neil Diamond	Bang
(I Wanna) Testify	The Parliaments	Revilot
Jackson	Nancy Sinatra & Lee Hazelwood	Reprise
⑥ My Mammy	The Happenings	B.T. Puppy

⑥ Pleasant Valley Sunday/Words	The Monkees	Colgems
⑥ Silence Is Golden	The Tremeloes	Epic
⑥ There Goes My Everything	Engelbert Humperdinck	Parrot
To Love Somebody	The Bee Gees	Atco
⑥ A Whiter Shade Of Pale	Procol Harum	Deram

AUGUST

☆ ⑥ All You Need Is Love/Baby You're A Rich Man	The Beatles	Capitol
⑥ Brown Eyed Girl	Van Morrison	Bang
⑥ Come Back When You Grow Up	Bobby Vee & the Strangers	Liberty
Fakin' It	Simon & Garfunkel	Columbia
⑥ Funky Broadway	Wilson Pickett	Atlantic
⑥ Gimme Little Sign	Brenton Wood	Double Shot
Heroes And Villains	The Beach Boys	Brother
☆ ⑥ The Letter	The Box Tops	Mala
☆ ⑥ Ode To Billie Joe	Bobbie Gentry	Capitol
⑥ Reflections	Diana Ross & the Supremes	Motown
San Franciscan Nights	Eric Burdon & the Animals	MGM
There Is A Mountain	Donovan	Epic
You Know What I Mean	The Turtles	White Whale
You're My Everything	The Temptations	Gordy
(Your Love Keeps Lifting Me) Higher And Higher	Jackie Wilson	Brunswick

SEPTEMBER

⑥ Apples, Peaches, Pumpkin Pie	Jay & the Techniques	Smash
⑥ Dandelion/We Love You	The Rolling Stones	London
⑥ Expressway To Your Heart	The Soul Survivors	Crimson
Get On Up	The Esquires	Bunky
Gettin' Together	Tommy James & the Shondells	Roulette
How Can I Be Sure	The Young Rascals	Atlantic
⑥ It Must Be Him	Vikki Carr	Liberty
Let It Out (Let It All Hang Out)	The Hombres	Verve Forecast

The Nitty Gritty Dirt Band (l to r: Jeff Hanna, Jimmie Fadden, John McEuen, Jim Ibbotson)

189

⑥ Little Ole Man (Uptight—Everything's Alright)	Bill Cosby	Warner Bros.
Making Every Minute Count	Spanky & Our Gang	Mercury
⑥ Never My Love	The Association	Warner Bros.
People Are Strange	The Doors	Elektra
⑥ Soul Man	Sam & Dave	Stax
☆ ⑥ To Sir With Love	Lulu	Epic
Your Precious Love	Marvin Gaye & Tammi Terrell	Tamla

OCTOBER

Boogaloo Down Broadway	Fantastic Johnny C	Phil-L.A. of Soul
Everlasting Love	Robert Knight	Rising Sons
Hey Baby (They're Playing Our Song)	The Buckinghams	Columbia
Holiday	The Bee Gees	Atco
I Can See For Miles	The Who	Decca
⑥ I Heard It Through The Grapevine	Gladys Knight & the Pips	Soul
I'm Wondering	Stevie Wonder	Tamla
☆ ⑥ Incense And Peppermints	The Strawberry Alarm Clock	Uni
⑥ I Say A Little Prayer	Dionne Warwick	Scepter
Kentucky Woman	Neil Diamond	Bang
⑥ Lazy Day	Spanky & Our Gang	Mercury
A Natural Woman	Aretha Franklin	Atlantic
Pata Pata	Miriam Makeba	Reprise
Please Love Me Forever	Bobby Vinton	Epic
⑥ The Rain, The Park And Other Things	The Cowsills	MGM

NOVEMBER

By The Time I Get To Phoenix	Glen Campbell	Capitol
☆ ⑥ Daydream Believer	The Monkees	Colgems
Different Drum	The Stone Poneys	Capitol
Honey Chile	Martha Reeves & the Vandellas	Gordy
In And Out Of Love	Diana Ross & the Supremes	Motown
⑥ I Second That Emotion	Smokey Robinson & the Miracles	Tamla
⑥ Keep The Ball Rollin'	Jay & the Techniques	Smash
⑥ (The Lights Went Out In) Massachusetts	The Bee Gees	Atco
Neon Rainbow	The Box Tops	Mala
⑥ An Open Letter To My Teenage Son	Victor Lundberg	Liberty
She's My Girl	The Turtles	White Whale
⑥ Skinny Legs And All	Joe Tex	Dial
Summer Rain	Johnny Rivers	Imperial
⑥ Woman, Woman	Gary Puckett & the Union Gap	Columbia
You Better Sit Down Kids	Cher	Imperial

DECEMBER

⑥	Bend Me, Shape Me	The American Breed	Acta
⑥	Chain Of Fools	Aretha Franklin	Atlantic
	Goin' Out Of My Head/Can't Take My Eyes Off You	The Lettermen	Capitol
☆ ⑥	Green Tambourine	The Lemon Pipers	Buddah
☆ ⑥	Hello Goodbye/I Am The Walrus	The Beatles	Capitol
	If I Could Build My Whole World Around You	Marvin Gaye & Tammi Terrell	Tamla
⑥	Itchycoo Park	The Small Faces	Immediate
	It's Wonderful	The Young Rascals	Atlantic
☆ ⑥	Judy In Disguise (With Glasses)	John Fred & His Playboy Band	Paula
	My Baby Must Be A Magician	The Marvelettes	Tamla
	Next Plane To London	The Rose Garden	Atco
	The Other Man's Grass Is Always Greener	Petula Clark	Warner Bros.
⑥	Spooky	The Classics IV	Imperial
	Susan	The Buckinghams	Columbia
	Wear Your Love Like Heaven	Donovan	Epic

TOP SINGLES OF 1967

⑥	Daydream Believer	The Monkees	Colgems
⑥	Groovin'	The Young Rascals	Atlantic
⑥	Happy Together	The Turtles	White Whale
⑥	I'm A Believer	The Monkees	Colgems
⑥	The Letter	The Box Tops	Mala
⑥	Light My Fire	The Doors	Elektra
⑥	Ode To Billie Joe	Bobbie Gentry	Capitol
⑥	Somethin' Stupid	Frank & Nancy Sinatra	Reprise
⑥	To Sir With Love	Lulu	Epic
⑥	Windy	The Association	Warner Bros.

Spanky & Our Gang

191

ROCK ON ALMANAC

TOP ALBUMS OF 1967

⑥ Between The Buttons	The Rolling Stones	London
⑥ Headquarters	The Monkees	Colgems
⑥ I Never Loved A Man The Way I Love You	Aretha Franklin	Atlantic
⑥ More Of The Monkees	The Monkees	Colgems
⑥ Ode To Billy Joe	Bobbie Gentry	Capitol
⑥ Pisces, Aquarius, Capricorn & Jones Ltd.	The Monkees	Colgems
⑥ Revenge	Bill Cosby	Warner Bros.
⑥ Sgt. Pepper's Lonely Hearts Club Band	The Beatles	Capitol
⑥ S.R.O.	Herbert Alpert & the Tijuana Brass	A & M
⑥ Surrealistic Pillow	The Jefferson Airplane	RCA Victor

GRAMMY WINNERS IN 1967

The Grammys were awarded at a new location, the Century Plaza Hotel in Los Angeles, on Thursday, February 29, 1968. Stan Freberg was the host.

Record of the Year: "Up-Up And Away," The 5th Dimension (Soul City)
Song of the Year: "Up-Up And Away" (music and lyrics by Jim Webb)
Album of the Year: *Sgt. Pepper's Lonely Hearts Club Band,* The Beatles (Capitol)
Best Vocal Performance, Female: "Ode To Billie Joe," Bobbie Gentry (Capitol)
Best Vocal Performance, Male: "By The Time I Get To Phoenix," Glen Campbell (Capitol)
Best Vocal Performance, Group: "Up-Up And Away," The 5th Dimension (Soul City)
Best Contemporary Single: "Up-Up And Away," The 5th Dimension (Soul City)
Best New Artist of the Year: Bobbie Gentry
Best Comedy Performance: *Revenge,* Bill Cosby (Warner Bros.)
Best Soundtrack Album from a Motion Picture or Television: *Mission: Impossible,* Lalo Shifrin (Dot)

DEATHS IN 1967

MUSIC PERFORMERS AND MUSIC INDUSTRY NOTABLES WHO DIED IN 1967

John Coltrane, Monday, July 17 (liver ailment; 40)
Brian Epstein (Beatles' manager), Sunday, August 27 (sleeping pill overdose; 32)
Woody Guthrie, Tuesday, October 3 (Huntington's chorea; 55)
The Bar-Kays (James King, Ronald Caldwell, Phalon Jones, Carl Cunningham), Sunday, December 10 (plane crash)
Otis Redding, Sunday, December 10 (plane crash; 26)
Paul Whiteman, Friday, December 29 (heart attack; 77)

OTHERS WHO DIED IN 1967

Dan Duryea
Dorothy Gish
Vivien Leigh
Jayne Mansfield
Ramon Novarro

Claude Rains
Basil Rathbone
Carl Sandburg
Spencer Tracy

Johnnie Taylor *Dennis Yost* (photo: *Kriegsmann*)

MOVIES OF 1967

MOVIES FEATURING POP MUSIC ARTISTS

Clambake *Stars:* Elvis Presley, Shelley Fabares, Will Hutchins, Bill Bixby, Gary Merrill.
Featured songs: "Guitar Man," "Big Boss Man."

C'mon Let's Live a Little *Stars:* Bobby Vee, Jackie De Shannon, Eddie Hodges, Bo
Belinsky, Patsy Kelly, Kim Carnes. No significant hits.

Double Trouble *Stars:* Elvis Presley, Annette Day, John Williams. No significant hits.

Easy Come, Easy Go *Stars:* Elvis Presley, Dodie Marshall, Pat Harrington, Skip Ward,
Frank McHugh, Elsa Lanchester. No significant hits.

Good Times *Stars:* Sonny & Cher, George Sanders, Larry Duran. *Featured songs:*
"I Got You Babe" by Sonny and Cher, "Bang Bang" by Cher.

It's a Bikini World *Stars:* Tommy Kirk, Deborah Walley, Bob (Bobby "Boris") Pickett,
Suzie Kaye. *Featured song:* We Gotta Get Out Of This Place" by the Animals. *Other
musical performers:* The Castaways, the Toys, the Gentrys.

Magical Mystery Tour *Stars:* The Beatles (on a bus tour doing their big hits), Victor
Spinetti. *Featured songs:* "Magical Mystery Tour," "I Am The Walrus," "The Fool On
The Hill," "All You Need Is Love," "Baby You're A Rich Man," "Hello Goodbye,"
"Penny Lane," "Strawberry Fields Forever."

POP MUSIC CONCERTS ON FILM

Festival Film of the Newport Folk Festival from 1963 to 1966, edited down to an hour-
and-a-half documentary capturing the biggest folk and blues performers of the time.
Shot in color, it shows a historic performance from 1966 of Bob Dylan doing "electric"
folk-rock songs that shocked his audience. *Other musical performers:* Joan Baez,
Donovan, the Paul Butterfield Blues Band, Judy Collins, Buffy Sainte-Marie, the Staple
Singers.

The Jimi Hendrix Experience,
Are You Experienced?
album cover

193

MOVIES FEATURING A POP MUSIC SOUNDTRACK

The Graduate   *Stars:* Dustin Hoffman, Anne Bancroft, Katherine Ross, Murray
   Hamilton. *Featured songs:* "The Sounds Of Silence," "Scarborough Fair," and "Mrs.
   Robinson" by Simon & Garfunkel.

OTHER POPULAR MOVIES OF 1967

Bonnie and Clyde
Camelot
Cool Hand Luke
The Dirty Dozen
Doctor Doolittle

The Good, the Bad and the Ugly
Guess Who's Coming to Dinner
In Cold Blood
In the Heat of the Night
Reflections in a Golden Eye

ACADEMY AWARD WINNERS OF 1967

Best Actor: Rod Steiger, *In the Heat of the Night*
Best Actress: Katherine Hepburn, *Guess Who's Coming to Dinner*
Best Picture: *In the Heat of the Night*
Best Song: "Talk To The Animals," *Doctor Doolittle* (music and lyrics by Leslie Bricusse)

TOP TELEVISION SHOWS OF 1967

The Andy Griffith Show
Bonanza
The Dean Martin Show
A Family Affair
Gomer Pyle, U.S.M.C.

Gunsmoke
The Jackie Gleason Show
The Lucy Show
The Red Skelton Show
Saturday Night at the Movies

1968

ROCK ON ALMANAC

NEWS HIGHLIGHTS OF 1968

➪ In Grenoble, France, Jean-Claude Killy wins three medals in the Olympic Alpine ski events.

➪ President Johnson announces that he will not accept renomination as president.

➪ Dr. Martin Luther King, Jr., is fatally shot outside his room at the Lorraine Motel in Memphis, Tennessee.

➪ France is nearly paralyzed by protesters and near-revolution in the streets.

➪ The section of San Francisco near the intersection of Haight and Ashbury streets becomes a haven for hippies during the "Summer of Love."

➪ Senator Robert F. Kennedy is shot to death in California. Sirhan Sirhan is indicted for first-degree murder for this assassination.

➪ Billie Jean King wins her third straight Wimbledon championship.

➪ The Summer Olympics are held in Mexico City.

➪ Soviet tanks invade Czechoslovakia to prevent liberalization.

➪ Jacqueline Kennedy marries shipping magnate Aristotle Onassis on the island of Skorpios.

➪ Richard Milhous Nixon is elected president.

➪ Three Apollo 8 astronauts are the first men to orbit the moon.

SPORTS WINNERS

Baseball   The Detroit Tigers beat the St. Louis Cardinals 4 games to 3.

Football

NFL: The Baltimore Colts beat the Cleveland Browns 34–0 in Cleveland.

AFL: The New York Jets beat the Oakland Raiders 27–23 in New York.

Super Bowl III: The New York Jets beat the Baltimore Colts 16–7 on January 12, 1969, at the Orange Bowl.

Basketball   The Boston Celtics beat the Los Angeles Lakers 4 games to 2.

Hockey   The Montreal Canadiens beat the St. Louis Blues 4 games to 0.

MUSIC HIGHLIGHTS OF 1968

➪ In January, Bob Dylan makes his first public appearance in several years at New York's Carnegie Hall at a benefit concert for Woodie Guthrie, who died on October 3, 1967.

➪ On Thursday, February 1, Elvis Presley's wife, Priscilla, gives birth to their only child, daughter Lisa Marie, in Memphis, Tennessee.

➪ On Friday, March 8, West Coast concert promoter Bill Graham opens the Fillmore East rock theater in New York City, a direct counterpart to the already successful Fillmore West in San Francisco.

➪ On Monday, April 29, the off-Broadway musical *Hair* opens at the Biltmore Theater on New York's Broadway. Billed as an "American tribal love-rock musical," it is very controversial but will run for 1,742 performances and will later be turned into a motion picture.

➪ In July, the Yardbirds disband and Jimmy Page, left with the ownership of the group's name and several concert obligations to fulfill, assembles a new group known at first as the New Yardbirds. Beginning with John Paul Jones, a good friend and a leading British session musician, Page rounded out the lineup by recruiting Robert Plant and John Bonham from the Band of Joy. Once assembled, the group changed its name to Led Zeppelin at the suggestion of Page's friend Keith Moon of the Who.

➪ British rockers Ritchie Blackmore, Ian Paice, Nicholas Simper, Rod Evans, and Jon Lord form the now legendary Deep Purple, a name they took from a 1963 hit song by Nino Tempo & April Stevens. They release an album called *Shades Of Deep Purple,* distributed in America by Tetragrammaton Records, a label partially owned by comedian Bill Cosby and marketed by Warner Brothers. This yields a single titled "Hush," a remake of a Joe South song that had been a hit for Billy Joe Royal in 1967.

➪ Mike Clark, David Crosby, and Gram Parsons depart from the Byrds at different times during the year. Crosby eventually joins forces with Stephen Stills and Graham Nash, while Parsons forms the Flying Burrito Brothers.

⇨ The Beatles found Apple Records. The label's first release is "Hey Jude," which becomes the year's biggest hit and the Beatles' biggest hit as well.

⇨ Rock entrepreneur Don Kirshner creates *The Archies,* a Saturday morning animated television program conceived as a musical version of the comic-strip "Archie." Kirshner hires Ron Dante, a studio singer, to be the key voice in the studio group called the Archies. Its sound was aimed squarely at the preteen market and became known as "bubblegum" music.

⇨ Other purveyors of the bubblegum sound—groups such as the 1910 Fruitgum Company, the Ohio Express, and the Kasenetz-Katz Singing Orchestral Circus—swamp the charts.

⇨ John Sebastian leaves the Lovin' Spoonful to embark on a solo career, marking the end of the group.

⇨ The strain of having three dominant musical personalities in the same group proves too great, causing the supergroup Cream to dissolve. Ginger Baker and Eric Clapton go on to form Blind Faith, while Jack Bruce becomes a member of West, Bruce & Laing.

⇨ On Tuesday, December 3, the Singer Sewing Machine Company sponsors a one-hour Elvis Christmas special called *Elvis.* The show, taped in Burbank, California, on June 29 and shown on NBC, marks Elvis's first television appearance in over eight years. Originally scheduled to close the show singing "Silent Night," Elvis opts for "If I Can Dream," which becomes a major comeback hit for him.

DEBUT ARTISTS OF 1968

MAJOR ARTISTS	Debut Single	Label
Herb Alpert	This Guy's In Love With You ☆ Ⓖ	A & M
The Archies (Ron Dante)	Bang Shang-A-Lang	Calendar
The Band (Robbie Robertson, Richard Manuel, Rick Danko, Garth Hudson, Levon Helm)	The Weight	Capitol
Archie Bell & the Drells (Archie Bell, James Wise, Willie Pernell)	Tighten Up ☆ Ⓖ	Atlantic
The Brooklyn Bridge (Johnny Maestro, Les Cauchi, Fred Ferrara, Jim Rosica, Mike Gregorio, Tom Sullivan, Carolyn Wood, Richie Macioce, Artie Cantanzarita, Shelly Davis, Joe Ruvio)	Worst That Could Happen Ⓖ	Buddah

The Band (l to r: Garth Hudson, Robbie Robertson, Rick Danko, Richard Manuel, Levon Helm)

197

Joe Cocker	With A Little Help From My Friends	A & M
Cream (Ginger Baker, Jack Bruce, Eric Clapton)	Sunshine Of Your Love ⑥	Atco
Creedence Clearwater Revival (John Fogerty, Tom Fogerty, Stuart Cook, Doug Clifford)	Suzie Q.	Fantasy
Tyrone Davis	Can I Change My Mind ⑥	Dakar
Deep Purple (Ritchie Blackmore, Jon Lord, Ian Paice, Rod Evans, Nicholas Simper)	Hush ⑥	Tetragrammaton
The Delfonics (William Hart, Wilbert Hart, Randy Cain)	La-La Means I Love You ⑥	Philly Groove
The Detroit Emeralds (Abraham Tilmon, Ivory Tilmon, James Mitchell)	Show Time	Ric Tic
Jose Feliciano	Light My Fire	RCA Victor
The First Edition (Kenny Rogers, Mike Settle, Terry Benson Williams, Thelma Camacho, Mickey Jones)	Just Dropped In (To See What Condition My Condition Was In)	Reprise
Mary Hopkin	Those Were The Days ⑥	Apple
Robert John (Robert Pedrick, Jr.)	If You Don't Want My Love	Columbia
Andy Kim	How'd We Ever Get This Way	Steed
Mama Cass (Cass Elliott)	Dream A Little Dream Of Me	Dunhill
Bill Medley	I Can't Make It Alone	MGM
The Steve Miller Band	Living In The U.S.A.	Capitol
The Moments (Al Goodman, Harry Ray, William Brown)	Not On The Outside	Stang
The 1910 Fruitgum Company (Chuck Travis, "Mark," Lawrence Ripley, Bruce Shay, Rusty Oppenheimer)	Simon Says ⑥	Buddah
The Bob Seger System	Ramblin' Gamblin' Man	Capitol
Sly & the Family Stone (Sylvester "Sly" Stewart, Fred Stone, Cynthia Robinson, Jerry Martini, Rose Stone, Lawrence Graham, Jr., Gregg Errico)	Dance To The Music	Epic

Joe Cocker

Tyrone Davis

1968

O. C. Smith	The Son Of Hickory Holler's Tramp	Columbia
Steppenwolf (John Kay, Michael Monarch, Goldy McJohn, Rushton Moreve, Jerry Edmonton)	Born To Be Wild Ⓖ	Dunhill
Al Wilson	The Snake	Soul City
Bobby Womack	Fly Me To The Moon	Minit
Betty Wright	Girls Can't Do What The Guys Do	Alston
Tammy Wynette	D-I-V-O-R-C-E	Epic

OTHER ARTISTS

The Amboy Dukes
Balloon Farm
Madeline Bell
Big Brother & the Holding Company
Blue Cheer
Canned Heat
Carl Carlton
The Chambers Brothers
The Crazy World of Arthur Brown
Derek
The Equals
Don Fardon
Four Jacks & a Jill
Friend & Lover
Richard Harris
The Irish Rovers
Iron Butterfly
The Kasenetz-Katz Singing Orchestral Circus

Leapy Lee
Michele Lee
The Magic Lanterns
Pigmeat Markham
Paul Mauriat
Hugo Montenegro
Cliff Nobles & Company
The O'Kaysions
The People
Jeannie C. Riley
Merilee Rush & the Turnabouts
Grace Slick
The Status Quo
Bobby Taylor & the Vancouvers
Tiny Tim
Jerry Jeff Walker
Mason Williams

HITS OF 1968

JANUARY

Ⓖ	**Baby, Now That I've Found You**	The Foundations	Uni
	Bottle Of Wine	The Fireballs	Atco
	Darlin'	The Beach Boys	Capitol
	Everybody Knows	The Dave Clark Five	Epic

199

Deep Purple (l to r: Glenn Hughes, Ritchie Blackmore, Ian Paice, Jon Lord, David Coverdale; photo: Kriegsmann)

⑥ I Wish It Would Rain	The Temptations	Gordy
⑥ I Wonder What She's Doing Tonight	Tommy Boyce & Bobby Hart	A & M
Just As Much As Ever	Bobby Vinton	Epic
☆ ⑥ Love Is Blue (L'Amour Est Bleu)	Paul Mauriat	Philips
Monterey	Eric Burdon & the Animals	MGM
Nobody But Me	The Human Beinz	Capitol
No Sad Songs	Joe Simon	Sound Stage
Some Velvet Morning	Nancy Sinatra & Lee Hazelwood	Reprise
Sunday Mornin'	Spanky & Our Gang	Mercury
Too Much Talk	Paul Revere & the Raiders	Columbia
We Can Fly	The Cowsills	MGM

FEBRUARY

⑥ The Ballad Of Bonnie And Clyde	Georgie Fame	Epic
Dance To The Music	Sly & the Family Stone	Epic
Everything That Touches You	The Association	Warner Bros.
Guitar Man	Elvis Presley	RCA Victor
I'm Gonna Make You Love Me	Madeline Bell	Philips
⑥ I Thank You	Sam & Dave	Stax
Just Dropped In (To See What Condition My Condition Was In)	The First Edition	Reprise
⑥ La-La Means I Love You	The Delfonics	Philly Groove
⑥ Simon Says	The 1910 Fruitgum Company	Buddah
☆ ⑥ (Sittin' On) The Dock Of The Bay	Otis Redding	Volt
⑥ Sunshine Of Your Love	Cream	Atco
(Theme From) Valley Of The Dolls	Dionne Warwick	Scepter
There Is	The Dells	Cadet

| Walk Away Renee | The Four Tops | Motown |
| ⑥ Words | The Bee Gees | Atco |

1968

MARCH

Cab Driver	The Mills Brothers	Dot
⑥ Cry Like A Baby	The Box Tops	Mala
☆ ⑥ Honey	Bobby Goldsboro	United Artists
I Got The Feelin'	James Brown & the Famous Flames	King
Jennifer Juniper	Donovan	Epic
Kiss Me Goodbye	Petula Clark	Warner Bros.
⑥ Lady Madonna	The Beatles	Capitol
Love Is All Around	The Troggs	Fontana
⑥ Mighty Quinn (Quinn The Eskimo)	Manfred Mann	Mercury
Playboy	Gene & Debbe	TRX
Scarborough Fair	Simon & Garfunkel	Columbia
⑥ (Sweet Sweet Baby) Since You've Been Gone	Aretha Franklin	Atlantic
⑥ Valleri/Tapioca Tundra	The Monkees	Colgems
Will You Love Me Tomorrow?	The Four Seasons	Philips
⑥ Young Girl	Gary Puckett & the Union Gap	Columbia

APRIL

Ain't Nothing Like The Real Thing	Marvin Gaye & Tammi Terrell	Tamla
Ain't No Way	Aretha Franklin	Atlantic
⑥ A Beautiful Morning	The Rascals	Atlantic
⑥ Cowboys To Girls	The Intruders	Gamble
Do You Know The Way To San Jose	Dionne Warwick	Scepter
I Will Always Think About You	The New Colony Six	Mercury
Like To Get To Know You	Spanky & Our Gang	Mercury
⑥ Mony Mony	Tommy James & the Shondells	Roulette
☆ ⑥ Mrs. Robinson	Simon & Garfunkel	Columbia
Red Red Wine	Neil Diamond	Bang

Jose Feliciano

201

Shoo-Be-Doo-Be-Doo-Da-Day	Stevie Wonder	Tamla
The Son Of Hickory Holler's Tramp	O.C. Smith	Columbia
Summertime Blues	Blue Cheer	Philips
☆ ⑥ Tighten Up	Archie Bell & the Drells	Atlantic
The Unicorn	The Irish Rovers	Decca

MAY

⑥ **Angel Of The Morning**	Merilee Rush & the Turnabouts	Bell
How'd We Ever Get This Way	Andy Kim	Steed
I Could Never Love Another (After Loving You)	The Temptations	Gordy
If I Were A Carpenter	The Four Tops	Motown
The Look Of Love	Sergio Mendes & Brasil '66	A & M
⑥ **MacArthur Park**	Richard Harris	Dunhill
A Man Without Love (Quando M'Innamora)	Engelbert Humperdinck	Parrot
Master Jack	Four Jacks & a Jill	RCA Victor
Never Give You Up	Jerry Butler	Mercury
Reach Out Of The Darkness	Friend & Lover	Verve Forecast
She's Lookin' Good	Wilson Pickett	Atlantic
⑥ **Think/You Send Me**	Aretha Franklin	Atlantic
☆ ⑥ **This Guy's In Love With You**	Herb Alpert	A & M
Time For Livin'	The Association	Warner Bros.
⑥ **Yummy, Yummy, Yummy**	The Ohio Express	Buddah

JUNE

D.W. Washburn/It's Nice To Be With You	The Monkees	Colgems
Folsom Prison Blues	Johnny Cash	Columbia
☆ ⑥ **Grazing In The Grass**	Hugh Masekela	Uni
Here Comes The Judge	Shorty Long	Soul
⑥ **The Horse**	Cliff Nobles & Co.	Phil-L.A. of Soul

Mama Cass *Steve Miller*

	Indian Lake	The Cowsills	MGM
Ⓖ	Jumpin' Jack Flash	The Rolling Stones	London
Ⓖ	Lady Willpower	Gary Puckett & the Union Gap	Columbia
	Licking Stick	James Brown & the Famous Flames	King
	She's A Heartbreaker	Gene Pitney	Musicor
	Sky Pilot	Eric Burdon & the Animals	MGM
	Some Things You Never Get Used To	Diana Ross & the Supremes	Motown
Ⓖ	Stoned Soul Picnic	The 5th Dimension	Soul City
	Tip-Toe Thru The Tulips With Me	Tiny Tim	Reprise
Ⓖ	Turn Around, Look At Me	The Vogues	Reprise

1968

JULY

	Autumn Of My Life	Bobby Goldsboro	United Artists
Ⓖ	Born To Be Wild	Steppenwolf	Dunhill
Ⓖ	Classical Gas	Mason Williams	Warner Bros.
	D-I-V-O-R-C-E	Tammy Wynette	Epic
	Don't Take It So Hard	Paul Revere & the Raiders	Columbia
	Dream A Little Dream Of Me	Mama Cass	Dunhill
☆ Ⓖ	Hello, I Love You	The Doors	Elektra
	Hurdy Gurdy Man	Donovan	Epic
	Journey To The Center Of Your Mind	The Amboy Dukes	Mainstream
☆ Ⓖ	People Got To Be Free	The Rascals	Atlantic
	Soul Limbo	Booker T. & the MG's	Stax
	Stay In My Corner	The Dells	Cadet
Ⓖ	Sunshine Of Your Love	Cream	Atco
	With Pen In Hand	Billy Vera	Atlantic
	(You Keep Me) Hangin' On	Vanilla Fudge	Atco

AUGUST

	Do It Again	The Beach Boys	Capitol
	The Eyes Of A New York Woman	B. J. Thomas	Scepter
	The Fool On The Hill	Sergio Mendes & Brasil '66	A & M
☆ Ⓖ	Harper Valley P.T.A.	Jeannie C. Riley	Plantation
Ⓖ	The House That Jack Built/I Say A Little Prayer	Aretha Franklin	Atlantic
Ⓖ	Hush	Deep Purple	Tetragrammaton
	I Can't Stop Dancing	Archie Bell & the Drells	Atlantic
Ⓖ	Light My Fire	Jose Feliciano	RCA Victor
Ⓖ	Little Green Apples	O.C. Smith	Columbia
	Magic Bus	The Who	Decca
	Mr. Businessman	Ray Stevens	Monument
Ⓖ	1, 2, 3, Red Light	The 1910 Fruitgum Company	Buddah
Ⓖ	Slip Away	Clarence Carter	Atlantic

203

Tuesday Afternoon (Forever Afternoon)	The Moody Blues	Deram
You're All I Need To Get By	Marvin Gaye & Tammi Terrell	Tamla

SEPTEMBER

	All Along The Watchtower	The Jimi Hendrix Experience	Reprise
	Down On Me	Big Brother & the Holding Company	Mainstream
	Elenore	The Turtles	White Whale
⑥	Fire	The Crazy World of Arthur Brown	Atlantic
⑥	Girl Watcher	The O'Kaysions	ABC
	Help Yourself	Tom Jones	Parrot
☆ ⑥	Hey Jude/Revolution	The Beatles	Apple
	Hold Me Tight	Johnny Nash	JAD
⑥	I've Gotta Get A Message To You	The Bee Gees	Atco
⑥	Midnight Confessions	The Grass Roots	Dunhill
	My Special Angel	The Vogues	Reprise
⑥	Over You	Gary Puckett & the Union Gap	Columbia
	Suzie Q.	Creedence Clearwater Revival	Fantasy
	Time Has Come Today	The Chambers Brothers	Columbia
	The Weight	The Band	Capitol

OCTOBER

⑥	Abraham, Martin And John	Dion	Laurie
⑥	Baby, Come Back	The Equals	RCA Victor
	Chained	Marvin Gaye	Tamla
⑥	Chewy Chewy	The Ohio Express	Buddah
	Hi-Heel Sneakers	Jose Feliciano	RCA Victor
⑥	In-A-Gadda-Da-Vida	Iron Butterfly	Atco
⑥	Little Arrows	Leapy Lee	Decca
☆ ⑥	Love Child	Diana Ross & the Supremes	Motown
⑥	Magic Carpet Ride	Steppenwolf	Dunhill
	Quick Joey Small (Run Joey Run)	The Kasenetz-Katz Singing Orchestral Circus	Buddah
	Ride My See-Saw	The Moody Blues	Deram
	Sweet Blindness	The 5th Dimension	Soul City
⑥	Those Were The Days	Mary Hopkin	Apple
⑥	White Room	Cream	Atco
⑥	Who's Making Love	Johnnie Taylor	Stax

NOVEMBER

	Both Sides Now	Judy Collins	Elektra
	Cinnamon	Derek	Bang
⑥	Cloud Nine	The Temptations	Gordy

Cycles	Frank Sinatra	Reprise
⑥ For Once In My Life	Stevie Wonder	Tamla
☆ ⑥ I Heard It Through The Grapevine	Marvin Gaye	Tamla
⑥ I Love How You Love Me	Bobby Vinton	Epic
Les Bicyclettes De Belsize	Engelbert Humperdinck	Parrott
Promises, Promises	Dionne Warwick	Scepter
⑥ See Saw/My Song	Aretha Franklin	Atlantic
Shame, Shame	The Magic Lanterns	Atlantic
⑥ Stormy	The Classics IV	Imperial
The Straight Life	Bobby Goldsboro	United Artists
⑥ Too Weak To Fight	Clarence Carter	Atlantic
⑥ Wichita Lineman	Glen Campbell	Capitol

DECEMBER

⑥ Can I Change My Mind	Tyrone Davis	Dakar
☆ ⑥ Crimson And Clover	Tommy James & the Shondells	Roulette
☆ ⑥ Everyday People	Sly & the Family Stone	Epic
Going Up The Country	Canned Heat	Liberty
Hey Jude	Wilson Pickett	Atlantic
⑥ Hooked On A Feeling	B.J. Thomas	Scepter
⑥ If I Can Dream	Elvis Presley	RCA Victor
⑥ I'm Gonna Make You Love Me	Diana Ross & the Supremes	Motown
I Started A Joke	The Bee Gees	Atco
Ready Or Not Here I Come (Can't Hide From Love)	The Delfonics	Philly Groove
Son-Of-A Preacher Man	Dusty Springfield	Atlantic
⑥ Soulful Strut	Young-Holt Unlimited	Brunswick
⑥ Stand By Your Man	Tammy Wynette	Epic
(There's Gonna Be A) Showdown	Archie Bell & the Drells	Atlantic
⑥ Worst That Could Happen	The Brooklyn Bridge	Buddah

TOP SINGLES OF 1968

⑥ Hello, I Love You	The Doors	Elektra
⑥ Hey Jude	The Beatles	Apple

Bob Seger in concert (photo: Anastasia Pantsios)

⑥ Honey	Bobby Goldsboro	United Artists
I Heard It Through The Grapevine	Marvin Gaye	Tamla
⑥ Judy In Disguise (With Glasses)	John Fred & His Playboy Band	Paula
⑥ Love Is Blue (L'Amour Est Bleu)	Paul Mauriat	Philips
⑥ Mrs. Robinson	Simon & Garfunkel	Columbia
⑥ People Got To Be Free	The Rascals	Atlantic
⑥ (Sittin' On) The Dock Of The Bay	Otis Redding	Volt
⑥ This Guy's In Love With You	Herb Alpert	A & M

TOP ALBUMS OF 1968

⑫ Axis: Bold As Love	The Jimi Hendrix Experience	Reprise
⑥ Blooming Hits	Paul Mauriat & His Orchestra	Philips
⑫ Bookends	Simon & Garfunkel	Columbia
⑫ Cheap Thrills	Big Brother & the Holding Company	Columbia
⑥ The Graduate	Soundtrack	Columbia
⑥ Lady Soul	Aretha Franklin	Atlantic
⑥ Magical Mystery Tour	The Beatles	Capitol
⑥ Time Peace/Greatest Hits	The Rascals	Atlantic
⑫ Waiting For The Sun	The Doors	Elektra
⑥ Wheels Of Fire	Cream	Atco

GRAMMY WINNERS IN 1968

The Grammys were awarded at the Century Plaza Hotel in Los Angeles on Wednesday, March 12, 1969. Gary Owens was the host.

Record of the Year: "Mrs. Robinson," Simon & Garfunkel (Columbia)
Song of the Year: "Little Green Apples" (music and lyrics by Bobby Russell)
Album of the Year: *By The Time I Get To Phoenix,* Glen Campbell (Capitol)

Sly Stone

*Tiny Tim (photo: **Kriegsmann**)*

1968

Best Contemporary/Pop Vocal Performance, Female: "Do You Know The Way To San Jose," Dionne Warwick (Scepter)

Best Contemporary/Pop Vocal Performance, Male: "Light My Fire," Jose Feliciano (RCA Victor)

Best Contemporary/Pop Vocal Performance, Group: "Mrs. Robinson," Simon & Garfunkel (Columbia)

Best New Artist of the Year: Jose Feliciano

Best Comedy Performance: *To Russell, My Brother, Whom I Slept With,* Bill Cosby (Warner Bros.)

Best Soundtrack Album from a Motion Picture or Television: *The Graduate,* Paul Simon (Columbia)

BIRTHS AND DEATHS IN 1968

MUSIC PERFORMERS BORN IN 1968

Ralph Tresvant (New Edition), May 16

MUSIC PERFORMERS AND MUSIC INDUSTRY NOTABLES WHO DIED IN 1968

Frankie Lymon, Tuesday, February 27 (drug overdose; 25)

Little Willie John, Sunday, May 26 (pneumonia; 30)

OTHERS WHO DIED IN 1968

Tallulah Bankhead
Nelson Eddy
Edna Ferber

Robert F. Kennedy
Martin Luther King, Jr.
Ann Sheridan

MOVIES OF 1968

MOVIES FEATURING POP MUSIC ARTISTS

Head *Stars:* The Monkees, Terri Garr, Frank Zappa, Jack Nicholson, Sonny Liston, Annette Funicello, Victor Mature. No significant hits.

Live a Little, Love a Little   *Stars:* Elvis Presley, Michele Carey, Don Porter, Rudy Vallee, Dick Sargent, Sterling Holloway. *Featured song:* "A Little Less Conversation."

Mrs. Brown, You've Got a Lovely Daughter   *Stars:* Herman's Hermits, Stanley Holloway, Lance Percival, Mona Washbourne. *Featured songs:* "Mrs. Brown, You've Got A Lovely Daughter" and "There's A Kind Of Hush" by Herman's Hermits.

Psych-Out   *Stars:* Jack Nicholson, Susan Strasberg, Bruce Dern, Dean Stockwell, Max Julien. *Featured songs:* "Pushin' Too Hard" by the Seeds, "Incense And Peppermints" by the Strawberry Alarm Clock.

Speedway   *Stars:* Elvis Presley, Nancy Sinatra, Bill Bixby, Gale Gordon. *Featured song:* "Let Yourself Go."

Stay Away Joe   *Stars:* Elvis Presley, Burgess Meredith, Joan Blondell, Thomas Gomez, Katy Jurado. No significant hits.

Yellow Submarine   The first animated film that featured rock music. This psychedelic voyage to Pepperland included the following Beatles hits: "Yellow Submarine," "Eleanor Rigby," "When I'm Sixty-Four," "Nowhere Man," "Lucy In The Sky With Diamonds," "Sgt. Pepper's Lonely Hearts Club Band," "All You Need Is Love."

POP MUSIC CONCERTS ON FILM

You Are What You Eat   A semidocumentary approach to live performances, showing the "flower power" and "hippie" look of the sixties. *Musical performers:* Tiny Tim, Peter Yarrow, Paul Butterfield, David Crosby, Harpers Bizarre, Barry McGuire.

MOVIES FEATURING A POP MUSIC SOUNDTRACK

I Love You, Alice B. Toklas   *Stars:* Peter Sellers, Jo Van Fleet, Leigh Taylor-Young, Joyce Van Patten. No significant hits. Featured music by Harpers Bizarre, the Strawberry Alarm Clock.

Up Tight   *Stars:* Raymond St. Jacques, Ruby Dee, Roscoe Lee Browne. Featured score by Booker T. & the MG's, including the hit "Time Is Tight."

OTHER POPULAR MOVIES OF 1968

Charly	The Producers
Funny Girl	Romeo and Juliet
The Lion in Winter	Rosemary's Baby
Oliver!	The Thomas Crown Affair
Planet of the Apes	2001: A Space Odyssey

ACADEMY AWARD WINNERS OF 1968

Best Actor: Cliff Robertson, *Charly*
Best Actress: Katharine Hepburn, *The Lion in Winter;* Barbra Streisand, *Funny Girl*
Best Picture: *Oliver!*
Best Song: "The Windmills Of Your Mind," *The Thomas Crown Affair* (music by Michel Legrand, lyrics by Alan & Marilyn Bergman)

TOP TELEVISION SHOWS OF 1968

The Beverly Hillbillies	Gunsmoke
Bonanza	Here's Lucy
The Dean Martin Show	Julia
A Family Affair	Mayberry R.F.D.
Gomer Pyle, U.S.M.C.	Rowan & Martin's Laugh-In

1969

ROCK ON ALMANAC

NEWS HIGHLIGHTS OF 1969

⇨ Thousands of New Yorkers pile food on the steps of St. Patrick's Cathedral for the millions of people starving in Biafra, a state that had seceded from Nigeria.

⇨ Yasir Arafat is acknowledged at a Cairo conference as leader of the Palestine Liberation Organization.

⇨ In Toulouse, France, the world's fastest commercial airplane, the Concorde, makes its maiden flight.

⇨ Golda Meir is elected Israel's fourth premier.

⇨ Dr. Denton A. Cooley implants the world's first entirely artificial heart. The recipient lives four days.

⇨ Georges Pompidou succeeds Charles de Gaulle as president of France

⇨ Neil Armstrong and Edwin Aldrin, Jr., pilot their lunar module, named *Eagle,* to land on the moon. Television cameras beam the event back to earth.

⇨ Mary Jo Kopechne drowns in a car driven accidentally off a bridge by Senator Edward Kennedy.

⇨ Young people, estimated at close to 400,000, gather for the Woodstock festival.

⇨ In a bloodless coup, Colonel Muammar Khadafy becomes the ruler of Libya.

⇨ Pandemonium erupts at Shea Stadium as the New York Mets win their first World Series.

⇨ The government bans the use of cyclamates as artificial sweeteners.

⇨ Some 567 residents of My Lai, South Vietnam, are reportedly slaughtered by an American platoon.

⇨ After 147 years, the *Saturday Evening Post* ceases publication.

SPORTS WINNERS

Baseball   The New York Mets beat the Baltimore Orioles 4 games to 1.
Football
   NFL: The Minnesota Vikings beat the Cleveland Browns 27–7 in Minnesota.
   AFL: The Kansas City Chiefs beat the Oakland Raiders 17–7 in Oakland.
   Super Bowl IV: The Kansas City Chiefs beat the Minnesota Vikings 23–7 on January 11, 1970, in New Orleans.
Basketball
   NBA: The Boston Celtics beat the Los Angeles Lakers 4 games to 3.
   ABA: The Oakland Oaks beat the Indiana Pacers 4 games to 2.
Hockey   The Montreal Canadiens beat the St. Louis Blues 4 games to 0.

MUSIC HIGHLIGHTS OF 1969

⇨ In January, Elvis Presley returns to Memphis to record for the first time in that city since his Sun Records days in 1954 and 1955. He goes to the American Sound Studios at 827

Blood, Sweat & Tears
(photo: *Kriegsmann*)

1969

Thomas Street, a studio founded by record producer Chips Moman, who was recording artists like Neil Diamond, Dusty Springfield, Merilee Rush, the Box Tops, the Gentrys, and Aretha Franklin, and makes a recording comeback. From January 13 to 23 and from February 17 to 22, Elvis records a half-dozen million-selling singles and two albums. "In The Ghetto," "Suspicious Minds," "Don't Cry Daddy," and "Rubberneckin' " are a few of the songs he recorded during that period.

⇨ In January, while filming the documentary film *Let It Be,* the Beatles give their final concert on the rooftop of Apple Studios at 3 Saville Row in London. Captured on film, this would be their last performance as a group.

⇨ On Wednesday, March 12, Paul McCartney marries Linda Eastman; eight days later, on Thursday, March 20, John Lennon marries Yoko Ono.

⇨ After months of wrangling over the show's anti-Establishment tone and its showcasing of anti–Vietnam War singers, CBS-TV pulls the plug on *The Smothers Brothers.*

⇨ Jim Morrison, lead singer of the Doors, is arrested in Miami, for exposing himself on stage.

⇨ The Who's *Tommy,* the world's first rock opera, comes to the fore in the spring. A major best seller for the group in album form, the work is later performed on stages around the world and is finally made into a star-studded film by Ken Russell.

⇨ Rhythm guitarist Brian Jones leaves the Rolling Stones and is replaced by Mick Taylor. Shortly after his resignation, Jones is found drowned in the swimming pool of his home.

⇨ John Lennon, Yoko Ono, Eric Clapton, Alan White, and Klaus Voorman, recording as the Plastic Ono Band, make an album titled *Live Peace At Toronto.* This album yields Lennon's first solo hit single, an antiwar anthem called "Give Peace A Chance."

⇨ Summer rock festivals include Denver's Pop Festival, Toronto's Festival, and the Newport '69 Festival in California.

⇨ Sun Records founder Sam Phillips sells his company to Shelby Singleton of Nashville.

⇨ In July, for the first time since 1956, Elvis returns to Las Vegas. This is also his first live concert in more than eight years. From Saturday, July 26, until Thursday, August 28, at the International Hotel, he electrifies the crowds in a total of 57 fantastic shows.

⇨ From Friday, August 15, until Sunday, August 17, the greatest rock festival of all time takes place in upstate New York on Max Yasgur's farm in Woodstock. Over 400,000 fans come for three days of "peace, love, and music." They see dozens of performers, including the Who, the Grateful Dead, Jimi Hendrix, Sly & the Family Stone, Joe Cocker, Santana, and Joan Baez.

⇨ Bob Dylan appears at the Isle of Wight Festival in England.

⇨ Rumors begin to spread that Paul McCartney is dead. The controversy develops because of newspaper stories alleging that references to Paul's death can be found in clues on the *Sgt. Pepper* and *Abbey Road* album covers and in songs like "Strawberry Fields Forever." A few weeks later, McCartney surfaces to deny the allegations.

⇨ On Saturday, October 18, Richard Nader does his first oldies show at the Felt Forum at Madison Square Garden in New York City. The 1950's Rock 'n' Roll Revival stars Bill Haley & His Comets, Chuck Berry, the Platters, the Shirelles, Jimmy Clanton, the Coasters, and Sha Na Na.

⇨ On December 6, while acting as security guards for the Rolling Stones, in concert at California's Altamont Raceway, the infamous Hell's Angels stab a spectator, a gruesome spectacle captured on film by the makers of the feature *Gimme Shelter.*

DEBUT ARTISTS OF 1969

MAJOR ARTISTS	Debut Single	Label
Blood, Sweat & Tears (David Clayton-Thomas, Robert Colomby, James Fielder, Steven Katz, Richard Halligan, Fred Lipsius, Lewis Soloff, Charles Winfield, Jerry Hyman)	You've Made Me So Very Happy Ⓖ	Columbia

The Chi-Lites (top l to r: Robert Lester, Eugene Record; bottom l to r: Creadel Jones, Marshall Thompson; photo: Kriegsmann)

Chicago (Robert Lamm, Peter Cetera, Terry Kath, Lee Loughnane, Walter Parazaider, James Pankow, Daniel Seraphine) | Questions 67 & 68 | Columbia

The Chi-Lites (Eugene Record, Marshall Thompson, Robert Lester, Creadel Jones) | Give It Away | Brunswick

Roy Clark | Yesterday, When I Was Young | Dot

Rita Coolidge | Turn Around And Love You | Pepper

Crosby, Stills & Nash (David Crosby, Stephen Stills, Graham Nash) | Marrakesh Express | Atlantic

The Emotions (Sheila, Wanda, and Jeanette Hutchinson) | So I Can Love You | Volt

The Friends of Distinction (Floyd Butler, Harry Elston, Jessica Cleaves, Barbara Love) | Grazing In The Grass ⑤ | RCA Victor

Funkadelic (Edward Hazel, Lucas Tunia "Tawl" Ross, Bernard Worrell, Mickey Atkins, William Nelson, Jr., Ramon "Tiki" Fulwood) | I'll Bet You | Westbound

Grand Funk Railroad (Mark Farner, Mel Schacher, Don Brewer) | Time Machine | Capitol

Merle Haggard | Okie From Muskogee | Capitol

Isaac Hayes | Walk On By | Enterprise

The Honey Cone (Edna Wright, Shellie Clark, Carolyn Willis) | While You're Out Looking For Sugar | Hot Wax

The Jackson 5 (Michael, Marlon, Jermaine, Tito, and Jackie Jackson) | I Want You Back ☆ ⑤ | Motown

Waylon Jennings | MacArthur Park | RCA Victor

Janis Joplin | Kozmic Blues | Columbia

Kool & the Gang (Robert "Kool" Bell, Ronald Bell, Dennis "Dee Tee" Thomas, Claydes "Clay" Smith, Robert "Spike" Mickens, George "Funky" Brown, James "J.T." Taylor, Clifford Adams, Michael Ray) | Kool & The Gang | De-Lite

Led Zeppelin (Jimmy Page, Robert Plant, John Paul Jones, John "Bonzo" Bonham) | Good Times, Bad Times | Atlantic

Mark Lindsay	First Hymn From Grand Terrace	Columbia
The Meters (Leo Nocentelli, Art Neville, George Porter, Cyril Neville, Joseph Modliste)	Sophisticated Cissy	Josie
Buddy Miles	Memphis Train	Mercury
Nilsson (Harry Nilsson)	Everybody's Talkin'	RCA Victor
The Plastic Ono Band (John Lennon, Yoko Ono, Eric Clapton, Alan White, Klaus Voorman)	Give Peace A Chance	Apple
Billy Preston	That's The Way God Planned It	Apple
"Country" Charlie Pride	All I Have To Offer You (Is Me)	RCA Victor
David Ruffin	My Whole World Ended (The Moment You Left Me)	Motown
Santana (Devadip Carlos Santana, Gregg Rolie, Jose Chepito Areas, Michael Carabello, David Brown, Michael Shrieve)	Jingo	Columbia
Bobby Sherman	Little Woman ⑤	Metromedia
Candi Staton	I'd Rather Be An Old Man's Sweetheart	Fame
Three Dog Night (Chuck Negron, Danny Hutton, Cory Wells)	Try A Little Tenderness	Dunhill

OTHER ARTISTS

Blinky
Bubble Puppy
Cat Mother & the All Night Newsboys
The Checkmates Ltd.
Jimmy Cliff
The Clique
Crazy Elephant
Crow
The Cuff Links
Bill Deal & the Rhondels
Desmond Dekker & the Aces

Electric Indian
The Flaming Ember
The Flirtations
The Flying Machine
The Charles Randolph Grean Sound
R. B. Greaves
Arlo Guthrie
The Edwin Hawkins Singers
Jefferson
The Joe Jeffrey Group
Art Linkletter

Chicago (top l to r: James Pankow, Terry Kath, Laudir De Oliveira, Walter Parazaider, Peter Cetera, Daniel Seraphine; bottom l to r: Lee Loughnane, Robert Lamm)

"Moms" Mabley
John Mayall
Mel & Tim
Mercy
Dorothy Morrison
Motherlode
The Nazz
The Neon Philharmonic
Oliver
100 Proof Aged in Soul
The Originals
Orpheus
The Peppermint Rainbow
Quicksilver Messenger Service
Savoy Brown

John Sebastian
The Shocking Blue
Smith
The Spiral Starecase
Spirit
Steam
John Stewart
Thunderclap Newman
Vanity Fare
Vik Venus
Tony Joe White
Harlow Wilcox
Wind
The Winstons
Zager & Evans

HITS OF 1969

JANUARY

Baby, Baby Don't Cry	Smokey Robinson & the Miracles	Tamla
The Beginning Of My End	The Unifics	Kapp
⑥ Build Me Up, Buttercup	The Foundations	Uni
California Soul	The 5th Dimension	Soul City
Daddy Sang Bass	Johnny Cash	Columbia
Does Anybody Know I'm Here	The Dells	Cadet
Games People Play	Joe South	Capitol
Goodnight My Love	Paul Anka	RCA Victor
I've Gotta Be Me	Sammy Davis, Jr.	Reprise
Ramblin' Gamblin' Man	The Bob Seger System	Capitol
Sweet Cream Ladies	The Box Tops	Mala
Things I'd Like To Say	The New Colony Six	Mercury
⑥ This Magic Moment	Jay & the Americans	United Artists
⑥ Touch Me	The Doors	Elektra
You Showed Me	The Turtles	White Whale

FEBRUARY

But You Know I Love You	The First Edition	Reprise
Crossroads	Cream	Atco
☆ ⑥ Dizzy	Tommy Roe	ABC
Hot Smoke And Sassafras	Bubble Puppy	Int'l Artists
I'm Livin' In Shame	Diana Ross & the Supremes	Motown
⑥ Indian Giver	The 1910 Fruitgum Company	Buddah
May I	Bill Deal & the Rhondels	Heritage
My Whole World Ended (The Moment You Left Me)	David Ruffin	Motown
⑥ Proud Mary	Creedence Clearwater Revival	Fantasy
Run Away Child, Running Wild	The Temptations	Gordy
This Girl's In Love With You	Dionne Warwick	Scepter
⑥ Time Of The Season	The Zombies	Date

214

1969

⑥ Traces	The Classics IV	Imperial
Try A Little Tenderness	Three Dog Night	Dunhill
The Weight	Aretha Franklin	Atlantic

MARCH

☆ ⑥ Aquarius/Let The Sunshine In	The 5th Dimension	Soul City
Blessed Is The Rain	The Brooklyn Bridge	Buddah
Brother Love's Travelling Salvation Show	Neil Diamond	Uni
⑥ The Chokin' Kind	Joe Simon	Sound Stage
Don't Give In To Him	Gary Puckett & the Union Gap	Columbia
Don't Touch Me	Bettye Swan	Capitol
⑥ Galveston	Glen Campbell	Capitol
Gimme Gimme Good Lovin'	Crazy Elephant	Bell
I Can Hear Music	The Beach Boys	Capitol
I'll Try Something New	The Supremes & the Temptations	Motown
⑥ It's Your Thing	The Isley Brothers	T-Neck
⑥ Only The Strong Survive	Jerry Butler	Mercury
⑥ Rock Me	Steppenwolf	Dunhill
Twenty-Five Miles	Edwin Starr	Gordy
⑥ You've Made Me So Very Happy	Blood, Sweat & Tears	Columbia

APRIL

Atlantis	Donovan	Epic
The Boxer	Simon & Garfunkel	Columbia
⑥ Gitarzan	Ray Stevens	Monument
⑥ Hair	The Cowsills	MGM
⑥ Hawaii Five-O	The Ventures	Liberty
⑥ Love (Can Make You Happy)	Mercy	Sundi
Memories	Elvis Presley	RCA Victor
⑥ More Today Than Yesterday	The Spiral Starecase	Columbia
⑥ My Way	Frank Sinatra	Reprise
Nothing But A Heartache	The Flirtations	Deram
Pinball Wizard	The Who	Decca
⑥ Sweet Cherry Wine	Tommy James & the Shondells	Roulette

215

The Jackson 5 (l to r: Randy, Michael, Jackie, Tito, Marlon)

⑥ These Eyes	The Guess Who	RCA Victor
Time Is Tight	Booker T. & the MG's	Stax
Try A Little Tenderness	Three Dog Night	Dunhill

MAY

⑥ Bad Moon Rising	Creedence Clearwater Revival	Fantasy
Black Pearl	Sonny Charles & the Checkmates Ltd.	A & M
Don't Let The Joneses Get You Down	The Temptations	Gordy
Everyday With You Girl	The Classics IV	Imperial
☆ ⑥ Get Back/Don't Let Me Down	The Beatles	Apple
Goodbye	Mary Hopkin	Apple
⑥ Grazing In The Grass	The Friends of Distinction	RCA Victor
⑥ In The Ghetto	Elvis Presley	RCA Victor
⑥ The Israelites	Desmond Dekker & the Aces	Uni
Love Me Tonight	Tom Jones	Parrot
☆ ⑥ Love Theme From Romeo & Juliet	Henry Mancini	RCA Victor
Morning Girl	The Neon Philharmonic	Warner Bros.
⑥ Oh Happy Day	The Edwin Hawkins Singers	Pavillion
⑥ One	Three Dog Night	Dunhill
Too Busy Thinking About My Baby	Marvin Gaye	Tamla

JUNE

The April Fools	Dionne Warwick	Scepter
⑥ Baby, I Love You	Andy Kim	Steed
⑥ Color Him Father	The Winstons	Metromedia
⑥ Crystal Blue Persuasion	Tommy James & the Shondells	Roulette

216

⑥ Good Morning Starshine	Oliver	Jubilee	**1969**
Hushabye	Jay & the Americans	United Artists	
Let Me	Paul Revere & the Raiders	Columbia	
Moody Woman	Jerry Butler	Mercury	
⑥ My Cherie Amour	Stevie Wonder	Tamla	
The Popcorn	James Brown	King	
⑥ Spinning Wheel	Blood, Sweat & Tears	Columbia	
Welcome Me Love	The Brooklyn Bridge	Buddah	
What Does It Take To Win Your Love	Junior Walker & the All Stars	Soul	
Without Her	Herb Alpert	A & M	
With Pen In Hand	Vikki Carr	Liberty	

JULY

Abraham, Martin And John	"Moms" Mabley	Mercury
⑥ The Ballad Of John And Yoko	The Beatles	Apple
Don't Wake Me Up In The Morning, Michael	The Peppermint Rainbow	Decca
⑥ Get Together	The Youngbloods	RCA Victor
Good Old Rock 'N Roll	Cat Mother & the All Night Newsboys	Polydor
I'd Wait A Million Years	The Grass Roots	Dunhill
☆ ⑥ In The Year 2525 (Exordium & Terminus)	Zager & Evans	RCA Victor
It's Getting Better	Mama Cass	Dunhill
⑥ Laughing	The Guess Who	RCA Victor
My Pledge Of Love	The Joe Jeffrey Group	Wand
Polk Salad Annie	Tony Joe White	Monument
⑥ Put A Little Love In Your Heart	Jackie De Shannon	Imperial
⑥ Ruby, Don't Take Your Love To Town	Kenny Rogers & the First Edition	Reprise
⑥ Sweet Caroline (Good Times Never Seemed So Good)	Neil Diamond	Uni
Yesterday, When I Was Young	Roy Clark	Dot

AUGUST

⑥ A Boy Named Sue	Johnny Cash	Columbia
⑥ Easy To Be Hard	Three Dog Night	Dunhill
⑥ Give Peace A Chance	The Plastic Ono Band	Apple
⑥ Green River	Creedence Clearwater Revival	Fantasy
☆ ⑥ Honky Tonk Women	The Rolling Stones	London
Hot Fun In The Summertime	Sly & the Family Stone	Epic
Hurt So Bad	The Lettermen	Capitol
⑥ I'll Never Fall In Love Again	Tom Jones	Parrot
Keem-O-Sabe	The Electric Indian	United Artists
Lay Lady Lay	Bob Dylan	Columbia
Marrakesh Express	Crosby, Stills & Nash	Atlantic
⑥ Oh, What A Night	The Dells	Cadet
Soul Deep	The Box Tops	Mala
☆ ⑥ Sugar, Sugar	The Archies	Calendar
When I Die	Motherlode	Buddah

217

ROCK ON ALMANAC

SEPTEMBER

⑥ Baby It's You	Smith	Dunhill
Daddy's Little Man	O.C. Smith	Columbia
Everybody's Talkin'	Nilsson	RCA Victor
⑥ Going In Circles	The Friends of Distinction	RCA Victor
☆ ⑥ I Can't Get Next To You	The Temptations	Gordy
I'm Gonna Make You Mine	Lou Christie	Buddah
⑥ Jean	Oliver	Crewe
⑥ Little Woman	Bobby Sherman	Metromedia
Muddy Mississippi Line	Bobby Goldsboro	United Artists
The Nitty Gritty	Gladys Knight & the Pips	Soul
☆ ⑥ Suspicious Minds	Elvis Presley	RCA Victor
That's The Way Love Is	Marvin Gaye	Tamla
This Girl Is A Woman Now	Gary Puckett & the Union Gap	Columbia
What Kind Of Fool Do You Think I Am	Bill Deal & the Rhondels	Heritage

OCTOBER

⑥ And When I Die	Blood, Sweat & Tears	Columbia
Baby, I'm For Real	The Originals	Soul
⑥ Backfield In Motion	Mel & Tim	Bamboo
Ball Of Fire	Tommy James & the Shondells	Roulette
Cherry Hill Park	Billy Joe Royal	Columbia
Is That All There Is	Peggy Lee	Capitol
Ruben James	Kenny Rogers & the First Edition	Reprise
⑥ Smile A Little Smile For Me	The Flying Machine	Congress
☆ ⑥ Something/Come Together	The Beatles	Apple
Something In The Air	Thunderclap Newman	Track
Suite: Judy Blue Eyes	Crosby, Stills & Nash	Atlantic
⑥ Take A Letter Maria	R.B. Greaves	Atco
⑥ Tracy	The Cuff Links	Decca
☆ ⑥ Wedding Bell Blues	The 5th Dimension	Soul City
You'll Never Walk Alone	The Brooklyn Bridge	Buddah

Janis Joplin

John Lennon

1969

NOVEMBER

⑥ Down On The Corner	Creedence Clearwater Revival	Fantasy
Eleanor Rigby	Aretha Franklin	Atlantic
⑥ Eli's Coming	Three Dog Night	Dunhill
Heaven Knows	The Grass Roots	Dunhill
⑥ Holly Holy	Neil Diamond	Uni
I Guess The Lord Must Be In New York City	Nilsson	RCA Victor
☆ ⑥ Leaving On A Jet Plane	Peter, Paul & Mary	Warner Bros.
⑥ Midnight Cowboy	Ferrante & Teicher	United Artists
☆ ⑥ Na Na Hey Hey Kiss Him Goodbye	Steam	Fontana
☆ ⑥ Raindrops Keep Fallin' On My Head	B.J. Thomas	Scepter
☆ ⑥ Someday We'll Be Together	Diana Ross & the Supremes	Motown
Undun	The Guess Who	RCA Victor
Up On Cripple Creek	The Band	Capitol
We Love You, Call Collect	Art Linkletter	Capitol
⑥ Yester-Me, Yester-You, Yesterday	Stevie Wonder	Tamla

DECEMBER

⑥ Arizona	Mark Lindsay	Columbia
Baby Take Me In Your Arms	Jefferson	Janus
⑥ Don't Cry Daddy/Rubberneckin'	Elvis Presley	RCA Victor
⑥ Early In The Morning	Vanity Fare	Page One
I'll Never Fall In Love Again	Dionne Warwick	Scepter
☆ ⑥ I Want You Back	The Jackson 5	Motown
⑥ Jam Up Jelly Tight	Tommy Roe	ABC
⑥ Jingle Jangle	The Archies	Kirshner
⑥ La La La (If I Had You)	Bobby Sherman	Metromedia
One Tin Soldier	The Original Caste	TA
☆ ⑥ Venus	The Shocking Blue	Colossus
Walkin' In The Rain	Jay & the Americans	United Artists
⑥ Whole Lotta Love	Led Zeppelin	Atlantic
Winter World Of Love	Engelbert Humperdinck	Parrot
⑥ Without Love (There Is Nothing)	Tom Jones	Parrot

ROCK ON ALMANAC

TOP SINGLES OF 1969

Ⓖ Aquarius/Let The Sunshine In	The Fifth Dimension	Soul City
Ⓖ Dizzy	Tommy Roe	ABC
Ⓖ Everyday People	Sly & the Family Stone	Epic
Ⓖ Get Back	The Beatles	Capitol
Ⓖ Honky Tonk Women	The Rolling Stones	London
Ⓖ I Can't Get Next To You	The Temptations	Gordy
Ⓖ In The Year 2525	Zager & Evans	RCA
Ⓖ Na Na Hey Hey Kiss Him Goodbye	Steam	Fontana
Ⓖ Sugar, Sugar	The Archies	Calendar
Ⓖ Wedding Bell Blues	The Fifth Dimension	Soul City

TOP ALBUMS OF 1969

Ⓖ Abbey Road	The Beatles	Apple
Ⓖ The Age Of Aquarius	The Fifth Dimension	Soul City
Ⓖ The Beatles [White Album]	The Beatles	Apple
Ⓟ Blood, Sweat & Tears	Blood, Sweat & Tears	Columbia
Ⓖ Goodbye	Cream	Atco
Ⓖ Green River	Creedence Clearwater Revival	Fantasy
Ⓖ Hair	Original Cast	RCA
Ⓖ Led Zeppelin II	Led Zeppelin	Atlantic
Ⓟ Nashville Skyline	Bob Dylan	Columbia
Ⓖ Wichita Lineman	Glen Campbell	Capitol

GRAMMY WINNERS IN 1969

The Grammys were awarded at the Century Plaza Hotel in Los Angeles on Wednesday, March 11, 1970. Bill Cosby was the host.

Record of the Year: "Aquarius/Let The Sunshine In," The 5th Dimension (Soul City)
Song of the Year: "Games People Play" (music and lyrics by Joe South)
Album of the Year: *Blood, Sweat & Tears,* Blood, Sweat & Tears (Columbia)

Billy Preston

David Ruffin (photo: *Kriegsmann*)

Three Dog Night (top l to r: Joe Schermie, Floyd Sneed, Michael Allsup, Jimmy Greenspoon; bottom l to r: Danny Hutton, Cory Wells, Chuck Negron)

1969

Best Contemporary Vocal Performance, Female: "Is That All There Is," Peggy Lee (Capitol)

Best Contemporary Vocal Performance, Male: "Everybody's Talkin'," Harry Nilsson (RCA Victor)

Best Contemporary Vocal Performance, Group: "Aquarius/Let The Sunshine In," The 5th Dimension (Soul City)

Best New Artist of the Year: Crosby, Stills & Nash

Best Comedy Performance: *Bill Cosby,* Bill Cosby (Warner Bros.)

Best Soundtrack Album from a Motion Picture or Television: *Butch Cassidy & The Sundance Kid,* Burt Bacharach (A & M)

BIRTHS AND DEATHS IN 1969

MUSIC PERFORMERS BORN IN 1969

Bobby Brown, February 5

MUSIC PERFORMERS AND MUSIC INDUSTRY NOTABLES WHO DIED IN 1969

Shorty (Frederick) Long, Sunday, June 29 (boating accident; 29)

Brian Jones (The Rolling Stones), Thursday, July 3 (drowning; 27)

Roy Hamilton, Sunday, July 20 (stroke; 40)

Leonard Chess (record company head), Thursday, October 16 (heart attack; 52)

Tommy Edwards, Thursday, October 23 (natural causes; 47)

OTHERS WHO DIED IN 1969

Dwight D. Eisenhower
Judy Garland
Sonja Henie
Boris Karloff
Joseph P. Kennedy

Rocky Marciano
Drew Pearson
Thelma Ritter
Robert Taylor

MOVIES OF 1969

MOVIES FEATURING POP MUSIC ARTISTS

Alice's Restaurant *Stars:* Arlo Guthrie, Pat Quinn, James Broderick. In 1967, Arlo Guthrie wrote an autobiographical song called "Alice's Restaurant," based on his experiences of the previous two years with the Army and the police in Stockbridge,

Massachusetts. The song later became a worldwide anthem for the antidraft movement of the late sixties and also inspired the making of this film.

Change of Habit *Stars:* Elvis Presley, Mary Tyler Moore, Barbara McNair, Edward Asner. *Featured Song:* "Rubberneckin'."

The Trouble with Girls *Stars:* Elvis Presley (last full-length feature film), Marlyn Mason, Vincent Price, Sheree North, Joyce Van Patten, Dabney Coleman. No significant hits.

POP MUSIC CONCERTS ON FILM

Johnny Cash—The Man, His World, His Music Cash performs in concert with Bob Dylan and Carl Perkins.

Monterey Pop Shot in 1967, this was the first major concert film. It highlighted the Monterey Pop Festival and such performers as Otis Redding, Jimi Hendrix, the Jefferson Airplane, Janis Joplin, Big Brother & the Holding Company, Eric Burdon & the Animals, Canned Heat, Hugh Masekela, the Who, the Mamas & the Papas, Scott McKenzie, and Ravi Shankar.

Revolution Focusing on the "San Francisco scene" of the late sixties with performances by the Steve Miller Band, Quicksilver Messenger Service, and Mother Earth.

OTHER POPULAR MOVIES OF 1969

Butch Cassidy and the Sundance Kid
Easy Rider
Hello, Dolly!
Midnight Cowboy
Paint Your Wagon

The Prime of Miss Jean Brodie
The Sterile Cuckoo
They Shoot Horses, Don't They?
True Grit

ACADEMY AWARD WINNERS OF 1969

Best Actor: John Wayne, *True Grit*
Best Actress: Maggie Smith, *The Prime of Miss Jean Brodie*
Best Picture: *Midnight Cowboy*
Best Song: "Raindrops Keep Falling On My Head," *Butch Cassidy and the Sundance Kid* (music by Burt Bacharach, lyrics by Hal David)

TOP TELEVISION SHOWS OF 1969

The Beverly Hillbillies
Bonanza
The Dean Martin Show
A Family Affair
Gomer Pyle, U.S.M.C.

Gunsmoke
Here's Lucy
Julia
Mayberry R.F.D.
Rowan & Martin's Laugh-In

1970

NEWS HIGHLIGHTS OF 1970

⇨ President Nixon sends combat units into Cambodia.

⇨ At Kent State University, National Guardsmen fire into a crowd protesting the Vietnam War, killing four and wounding eight.

⇨ Homosexuals march from New York's Greenwich Village to Central Park demonstrating for gay rights.

⇨ In New York, the nation's most liberal abortion law goes into effect.

⇨ A parade of 10,000 women in New York celebrate the 50th anniversary of the passing of the 19th Amendment.

⇨ FBI agents arrest American Communist Angela Davis at a midtown Manhattan motel.

⇨ Anwar Sadat is elected president of the United Arab Republic (Egypt).

⇨ One million cans of tuna are recalled by the FDA because of mercury contamination.

SPORTS WINNERS

Baseball   The Baltimore Orioles beat the Cincinnati Reds 4 games to 1.

Football   The National and American football leagues merge to form a unified NFL with two divisions, the National Football Conference (NFC) and the American Football Conference (AFC).

NFC: The Dallas Cowboys beat the San Francisco '49ers 17–10 in San Francisco.

AFC: The Baltimore Colts beat the Oakland Raiders 27–17 in Baltimore.

Superbowl V: The Baltimore Colts beat the Dallas Cowboys 16–13 on January 17, 1971, at the Orange Bowl.

Basketball

NBA: The New York Knicks beat the Los Angeles Lakers 4 games to 3.

ABA: The Indiana Pacers beat the Los Angeles Stars 4 games to 2.

Hockey   The Boston Bruins beat the St. Louis Blues 4 games to 0.

MUSIC HIGHLIGHTS OF 1970

⇨ Religious themes start to appear in songs like "Spirit In The Sky" by Norman Greenbaum, "Let It Be" by the Beatles, "My Sweet Lord" by George Harrison, and the play *Jesus Christ Superstar*.

⇨ Rumors begin to circulate that the Beatles will be breaking up because of differences between Paul and John. Paul releases a homemade album titled *McCartney* that goes on to become a number one hit.

⇨ Rod Stewart and Ron Wood leave the disintegrating Jeff Beck Group to join the Small Faces, now simply called the Faces.

Bread (top: Larry Knechtel; bottom l to r: James Griffin, David Gates, Mike Botts)

⇨ Crosby, Stills, Nash & Young record "Ohio" to draw attention to the wasteful killing of four young students by the Ohio National Guard at a Kent State University war protest rally.

⇨ *American Top 40,* a syndicated radio show counting down the Top 40 singles each week as ranked by *Billboard* magazine, debuts. Host Casey Kasem will remain with the show for 18 years.

⇨ On Wednesday, May 20, the Beatles' last film, *Let It Be,* premieres in London at the Palladium.

⇨ The Rolling Stones leave London Records to form their own label, Rolling Stones Records.

1970

DEBUT ARTISTS OF 1970

MAJOR ARTISTS

MAJOR ARTISTS	Debut Single	Label
Lynn Anderson	Rose Garden Ⓖ	Columbia
Badfinger (Peter Ham, Michael Gibbons, Thomas Evans, Ronald Griffiths)	Come And Get It Ⓖ	Apple
Bread (David Gates, James Griffin, Robb Royer, James Gordon)	Make It With You ☆ Ⓖ	Elektra
Eric Burdon & War (Eric Burdon, Howard E. Scott, Lee Oskar, Charles Miller, Lonnie Jordan, Morris "B.B." Dickerson, Thomas "Papa Dee" Allen, Harold Brown)	Spill The Wine Ⓖ	MGM
The Carpenters (Karen and Richard Carpenter)	Ticket To Ride	A & M
The Chairmen of the Board (Norman "General" Johnson, Edward Curtis, Daniel Woods, Harrison Kennedy)	Give Me Just A Little More Time Ⓖ	Invictus
Eric Clapton	After Midnight	Atco
Crosby, Stills, Nash & Young (David Crosby, Stephen Stills, Graham Nash, Neil Young)	Woodstock	Columbia
Mac Davis	Whoever Finds This, I Love You	Columbia
Paul Davis	A Little Bit Of Soap	Bang
Dawn (Tony Orlando, Telma Hopkins, Joyce Vincent)	Candida Ⓖ	Bell
Delaney & Bonnie (Delaney and Bonnie Bramlett)	Coming Home	Atco
Ronnie Dyson	(If You Let Me Make Love To You) Why Can't I Touch You?	Columbia
Fleetwood Mac (Peter Green, John McVie, Jeremy Spencer, Mick Fleetwood, Daniel Kirwan)	Oh Well	Reprise
The Grateful Dead (Jerry Garcia, Bob Weir, Phil Lesh, Bill Kreutzmann, Ron "Pig-Pen" McKernan)	Uncle John's Band	Warner Bros.
George Harrison	My Sweet Lord ☆ Ⓖ	Apple
Luther Ingram	My Honey And Me	Koko
Tommy James	Ball And Chain	Roulette
Elton John	Border Song	Uni
Quincy Jones	Killer Joe	A & M

Dawn (l to r: Joyce Vincent, Tony Orlando, Telma Hopkins)

Gordon Lightfoot	If You Could Read My Mind ⓖ	Reprise
The Main Ingredient (Tony Silvester, Luther Simmons, Jr., Donald McPherson)	You've Been My Inspiration	RCA
Dave Mason	Only You Know And I Know	Blue Thumb
Curtis Mayfield	If There's A Hell Below We're All Going To Go	Curtom
Melanie (Melanie Safka)	Lay Down (Candles In The Rain)	Buddah
Ronnie Milsap	Loving You Is A Natural Thing	Chips
Joni Mitchell	Big Yellow Taxi	Reprise
Anne Murray	Snowbird ⓖ	Capitol
The New Seekers (Eve Graham, Lyn Paul, Peter Doyle, Marty Kristian, Paul Martin Layton)	Look What They've Done To My Song, Ma	Elektra
The Partridge Family (David Cassidy, Shirley Jones)	I Think I Love You ☆ ⓖ	Bell
Freda Payne	Band Of Gold ⓖ	Invictus
Poco (James Messina, Richie Furay, Rusty Young, Randy Meisner, George Grantham)	You'd Better Think Twice	Epic
Rare Earth (Rob Richards, Kenneth James, Gil Bridges, Peter Rivera, Edward Guzman)	Get Ready ⓖ	Rare Earth
Linda Ronstadt	Long Long Time	Capitol
Diana Ross	Reach Out And Touch (Somebody's Hand)	Motown
Todd Rundgren	We Gotta Get You A Woman	Ampex
Ringo Starr	Beaucoups Of Blues	Apple

Stephen Stills	Love The One You're With	Atlantic
James Taylor	Fire And Rain	Warner Bros.
The Whispers (Wallace "Scotty" Scott, Walter Scott, Marcus Hutson, Leaveil Degree, Nicholas Caldwell)	Seems Like I Gotta Do Wrong	Soul Clock
Neil Young	Cinnamon Girl	Reprise

OTHER ARTISTS

Alive & Kicking
The Assembled Multitude
The George Baker Selection
Ginger Baker
Jane Birkin & Serge Gainsbourg
Black Sabbath
Jack Blanchard & Misty Morgan
Bobby Bloom
Blues Image
The Brotherhood of Man
Jim Ed Brown
Christie
Edison Lighthouse
Edward Bear
El Chicano
The Elephant's Memory
Ernie (Jim Henson)
Faith, Hope & Charity
Free
Frijid Pink
Norman Greenbaum
Donny Hathaway
Murray Head
Jake Holmes
Thelma Houston
The Jaggerz
The James Gang
King Floyd
Little Sister

Marmalade
Robin McNamara
Jackie Moore
Mountain
Mungo Jerry
Neighborhood
Michael Nesmith & the First National Band
Laura Nyro
Pacific Gas & Electric
Michael Parks
John Phillips
The Pipkins
The Poppy Family
The Presidents
Gary Puckett
Redbone
Turley Richards
Miguel Rios
David & Jimmy Ruffin
Mavis Staples
The Street People
Sugarloaf
R. Dean Taylor
Teegarden & Van Winkle
The Tee Set
Ten Years After
Wadsworth Mansion
White Plains
Johnny Winter

Eric Clapton in concert (photo: Anastasia Pantsios)

Elton John in concert (photo: Anastasia Pantsios)

ROCK ON ALMANAC

Fleetwood Mac (l to r: Christine McVie, Dave Walker, Bob Welch, Mick Fleetwood, Bob Weston, John McVie; photo: Kriegsmann)

HITS OF 1970

JANUARY

Blowing Away	The 5th Dimension	Soul City
⑥ Didn't I (Blow Your Mind This Time)	The Delfonics	Philly Groove
⑥ Hey There Lonely Girl	Eddie Holman	ABC
Jennifer Tomkins	Street People	Musicor
Johnny B. Goode	Johnny Winter	Columbia
Love Bones	Johnnie Taylor	Stax
Monster	Steppenwolf	Dunhill
Oh Me Oh My (I'm A Fool For You Baby)	Lulu	Atco
Psychedelic Shack	The Temptations	Gordy
⑥ Rainy Night In Georgia	Brook Benton	Cotillion
☆ ⑥ Thank You (Falettin Me Be Mice Elf Agin/Everybody Is A Star	Sly & the Family Stone	Epic
⑥ The Thrill Is Gone	B.B. King	Bluesway
Traces/Memories Medley	The Lettermen	Capitol
Walk A Mile In My Shoes	Joe South	Capitol
Wonderful World, Beautiful People	Jimmy Cliff	A & M

FEBRUARY

⑥ The Bells	The Originals	Soul
☆ ⑥ Bridge Over Troubled Water	Simon & Garfunkel	Columbia
Call Me/Son Of A Preacher Man	Aretha Franklin	Atlantic
⑥ Come And Get It	Badfinger	Apple
⑥ Easy Come, Easy Go	Bobby Sherman	Metromedia
Evil Ways	Santana	Columbia
⑥ Give Me Just A Little More Time	The Chairmen of the Board	Invictus
Honey Come Back	Glen Campbell	Capitol
⑥ House Of The Rising Sun	Frijid Pink	Parrot
⑥ Kentucky Rain	Elvis Presley	RCA Victor
⑥ Love Grows (Where My Rosemary Goes)	Edison Lighthouse	Bell

ⓖ Ma Belle Amie   The Tee Set   Colossus
    Never Had A Dream Come True   Stevie Wonder   Tamla
ⓖ The Rapper   The Jaggerz   Kama Sutra
ⓖ Travelin' Band/Who'll Stop   Creedence Clearwater   Fantasy
    The Rain   Revival

MARCH

☆ ⓖ ABC   The Jackson 5   Motown
☆ ⓖ American Woman/No   The Guess Who   RCA
    Sugar Tonight
    Celebrate   Three Dog Night   Dunhill
    For The Love Of Him   Bobbi Martin   United Artists
ⓖ Get Ready   Rare Earth   Rare Earth
ⓖ Hitchin' A Ride   Vanity Fare   Page One
ⓖ Instant Karma (We All   John Ono Lennon   Apple
    Shine On)
☆ ⓖ Let It Be   The Beatles   Apple
    Love Or Let Me Be Lonely   The Friends of   RCA
      Distinction
ⓖ Reflections Of My Life   Marmalade   London
    Shilo   Neil Diamond   Bang
ⓖ Spirit In The Sky   Norman Greenbaum   Reprise
    Ticket To Ride   The Carpenters   A & M
ⓖ Turn Back The Hands Of Time   Tyrone Davis   Dakar
ⓖ Up The Ladder To The Roof   The Supremes   Motown

APRIL

ⓖ Airport Love Theme   Vincent Bell   Decca
ⓖ Cecilia   Simon & Garfunkel   Columbia
    Come Saturday Morning   The Sandpipers   A & M
☆ ⓖ Everything Is Beautiful   Ray Stevens   Barnaby
    The Letter   Joe Cocker   A & M
    Love Land   Charles Wright & the   Warner Bros.
      Watts 103rd Street
      Rhythm Band

*The Grateful Dead (top l to r: Mickey Hart, Phil Lesh,
Donna Godchaux, Jerry Garcia, Bob Weir, Bill
Kreutzmann; bottom: Keith Godchaux)*

⑥ Love On A Two-Way Street	The Moments	Stang
Make Me Smile	Chicago	Columbia
My Baby Loves Lovin'	White Plains	Deram
Oh Happy Day	Glen Campbell	Capitol
United We Stand	The Brotherhood of Man	Deram
What Is Truth	Johnny Cash	Columbia
⑥ Which Way You Goin' Billy?	The Poppy Family	London
Woodstock	Crosby, Stills, Nash & Young	Atlantic

MAY

⑥ Ball Of Confusion (That's What The World Is Today)	The Temptations	Gordy
⑥ Band Of Gold	Freda Payne	Invictus
Brother Rapp (Part 1)	James Brown	King
Daughter Of Darkness	Tom Jones	Parrot
Gimme Dat Ding	The Pipkins	Capitol
It's All In The Game	The Four Tops	Motown
I Want To Take You Higher	Sly & the Family Stone	Epic
I Want To Take You Higher	Ike & Tina Turner & the Ikettes	Liberty
Lay Down (Candles In The Rain)	Melanie/Edwin Hawkins Singers	Buddah
Question	The Moody Blues	Threshold
Reach Out And Touch (Somebody's Hand)	Diana Ross	Motown
⑥ Ride Captain Ride	Blues Image	Atco
Soolaimon (African Trilogy II)	Neil Diamond	Uni
⑥ Up Around The Bend/Run Through The Jungle	Creedence Clearwater Revival	Fantasy
⑥ The Wonder Of You/Mama Liked The Roses	Elvis Presley	RCA Victor

JUNE

(If You Let Me Make Love To You) Why Can't I Touch You?	Ronnie Dyson	Columbia

Joni Mitchell (photo: Norman Seeff)   **Anne Murray**

I Just Can't Help Believing	B.J. Thomas	Scepter
Lay A Little Lovin' On Me	Robin McNamara	Steed
☆ ⑥ The Long And Winding Road/For You Blue	The Beatles	Apple
☆ ⑥ The Love You Save	The Jackson 5	Motown
☆ ⑥ Make It With You	Bread	Elektra
☆ ⑥ Mama Told Me (Not To Come)	Three Dog Night	Dunhill
Maybe	The Three Degrees	Roulette
⑥ O-o-h Child	The Five Stairsteps	Buddah
A Song Of Joy	Miguel Rios	A & M
⑥ Spill The Wine	Eric Burdon & War	MGM
Teach Your Children	Crosby, Stills, Nash & Young	Atlantic
☆ ⑥ (They Long To Be) Close To You	The Carpenters	A & M
⑥ Tighter, Tighter	Alive & Kicking	Roulette
Westbound #9	Flaming Ember	Hot Wax

JULY

Big Yellow Taxi	The Neighborhood	Big Tree
⑥ Groovy Situation	Gene Chandler	Mercury
Hand Me Down World	The Guess Who	RCA
⑥ In The Summertime	Mungo Jerry	Janus
It's A Shame	The Spinners	V.I.P.
Ohio	Crosby, Stills, Nash & Young	Atlantic
Overture From Tommy	The Assembled Multitude	Atlantic
⑥ Patches	Clarence Carter	Atlantic
⑥ Signed, Sealed, Delivered I'm Yours	Stevie Wonder	Tamla
⑥ Snowbird	Anne Murray	Capitol
Solitary Man	Neil Diamond	Bang
Song From M*A*S*H	Al De Lory	Capitol
Tell It All Brother	Kenny Rogers & the First Edition	Reprise
☆ ⑥ War	Edwin Starr	Gordy
⑥ Yellow River	Christie	Epic

AUGUST

☆ ⑥ Ain't No Mountain High Enough	Diana Ross	Motown
Are You Ready	Pacific Gas & Electric	Columbia
⑥ Candida	Dawn	Bell
☆ ⑥ Cracklin' Rosie	Neil Diamond	Uni
⑥ Don't Play That Song	Aretha Franklin	Atlantic
Green-Eyed Lady	Sugarloaf	Liberty
Hi-De-Ho	Blood, Sweat & Tears	Columbia
(I Know) I'm Losing You	Rare Earth	Rare Earth
I (Who Have Nothing)	Tom Jones	Parrot
Joanne	Michael Nesmith	RCA
⑥ Julie, Do Ya Love Me	Bobby Sherman	Metromedia
Lola	The Kinks	Reprise
⑥ Lookin' Out My Back Door	Creedence Clearwater Revival	Fantasy

231

Only You Know And I Know	Dave Mason	Blue Thumb
25 Or 6 To 4	Chicago	Columbia

SEPTEMBER

El Condor Pasa	Simon & Garfunkel	Columbia
Fire And Rain	James Taylor	Warner Bros.
ⓖ Gypsy Woman	Brian Hyland	Uni
☆ ⓖ I'll Be There	The Jackson 5	Motown
Indiana Wants Me	R. Dean Taylor	Rare Earth
It Don't Matter To Me	Bread	Elektra
Look What They've Done To My Song, Ma	The New Seekers	Elektra
Our House	Crosby, Stills, Nash & Young	Atlantic
Out In The Country	Three Dog Night	Dunhill
Rubber Duckie	Ernie	Columbia
See Me, Feel Me	The Who	Decca
ⓖ Somebody's Been Sleeping	100 Proof Aged in Soul	Hot Wax
Still Water (Love)	The Four Tops	Motown
Uncle John's Band	The Grateful Dead	Warner Bros.
ⓖ We've Only Just Begun	The Carpenters	A & M

OCTOBER

After Midnight	Eric Clapton	Atco
ⓖ Cry Me A River	Joe Cocker	A & M
Deeper And Deeper	Freda Payne	Invictus
Engine Number 9	Wilson Pickett	Atlantic
5-10-15-20 (25-30 Years Of Love)	The Presidents	Sussex
ⓖ Groove Me	King Floyd	Chimneyville
Heaven Help Us All	Stevie Wonder	Tamla
☆ ⓖ I Think I Love You	The Partridge Family	Bell
Lucretia MacEvil	Blood, Sweat & Tears	Columbia
Montego Bay	Bobby Bloom	MGM
ⓖ One Less Bell To Answer	The 5th Dimension	Bell
ⓖ Share The Land	The Guess Who	RCA Victor
Stand By Your Man	Candi Staton	Fame
☆ ⓖ The Tears Of A Clown	Smokey Robinson & the Miracles	Tamla
ⓖ You Don't Have To Say You Love Me/Patch It Up	Elvis Presley	RCA Victor

NOVEMBER

ⓖ Amos Moses	Jerry Reed	RCA Victor
Be My Baby	Andy Kim	Steed
Black Magic Woman	Santana	Columbia
Does Anybody Really Know What Time It Is	Chicago	Columbia
Domino	Van Morrison	Warner Bros.
He Ain't Heavy . . . He's My Brother	Neil Diamond	Uni
Immigration Song	Led Zeppelin	Atlantic
ⓖ It's Impossible	Perry Como	RCA

Linda Ronstadt (photo: *Anastasia Pantsios*)   **Diana Ross** (photo: *Anastasia Pantsios*)

King Of Rock & Roll	Crow	Amaret
☆ ⑥ Knock Three Times	Dawn	Bell
Mr. Bojangles	The Nitty Gritty Dirt Band	Liberty
⑥ No Matter What	Badfinger	Apple
One Man Band	Three Dog Night	Dunhill
⑥ Stoned Love	The Supremes	Motown
Stoney End	Barbra Streisand	Columbia

DECEMBER

⑥ Amazing Grace	Judy Collins	Elektra
Black Night	Deep Purple	Warner Bros.
Born To Wander	Rare Earth	Rare Earth
Bridget The Midget (The Queen Of The Blues)	Ray Stevens	Barnaby
If I Were Your Woman	Gladys Knight & the Pips	Soul
⑥ If You Could Read My Mind	Gordon Lightfoot	Reprise
⑥ Lonely Days	The Bee Gees	Atco
Love The One You're With	Stephen Stills	Atlantic
Maggie	Redbone	Epic
☆ ⑥ My Sweet Lord/Isn't It A Pity	George Harrison	Apple
⑥ Precious, Precious	Jackie Moore	Atlantic
⑥ Rose Garden	Lynn Anderson	Columbia
Stop The War Now	Edwin Starr	Gordy
We Gotta Get You A Woman	Runt	Ampex
Your Song	Elton John	Uni

TOP SINGLES OF 1970

⑥ ABC	The Jackson 5	Motown
⑥ Ain't No Mountain High Enough	Diana Ross	Motown
⑥ American Woman	The Guess Who	RCA
⑥ Bridge Over Troubled Water	Simon & Garfunkel	Columbia
⑥ I'll Be There	The Jackson 5	Motown
⑥ I Think I Love You	The Partridge Family	Bell

Ⓖ The Long And Winding Road	The Beatles	Apple
Ⓖ Raindrops Keep Fallin' On My Head	B.J. Thomas	Scepter
Ⓖ (They Long To Be) Close To You	The Carpenters	A & M
Ⓖ War	Edwin Starr	Motown

TOP ALBUMS OF 1970

Abraxas	Santana	Columbia
Ⓟ Bridge Over Troubled Water	Simon & Garfunkel	Columbia
Ⓖ Chicago II	Chicago	Columbia
Ⓖ Cosmo's Factory	Creedence Clearwater Revival	Fantasy
Ⓖ Deja Vu	Crosby, Stills, Nash & Young	Atlantic
Ⓖ Hey Jude	The Beatles	Apple
Ⓖ Led Zeppelin III	Led Zeppelin	Atlantic
Ⓖ Let It Be	The Beatles	Apple
Ⓖ McCartney	Paul McCartney	Apple
Ⓖ Woodstock	Soundtrack	Cotillion

GRAMMY WINNERS IN 1970

The Grammys were awarded at a new location, the Hollywood Palladium, on Tuesday, March 16, 1971. Gary Owen was the host.

Record of the Year: "Bridge Over Troubled Water," Simon & Garfunkel (Columbia)
Song of the Year: "Bridge Over Troubled Water" (music and lyrics by Paul Simon)
Album of the Year: *Bridge Over Troubled Water,* Simon & Garfunkel (Columbia)
Best Contemporary Vocal Performance, Female: *I'll Never Fall In Love Again,* Dionne Warwick (Scepter)
Best Contemporary Vocal Performance, Male: "Everything Is Beautiful," Ray Stevens (Barnaby)
Best Contemporary Vocal Performance, Group: "(They Long To Be) Close To You," The Carpenters (A & M)
Best New Artist of the Year: The Carpenters
Best Comedy Performance: *The Devil Made Me Buy This Dress,* Flip Wilson (Little David)

Todd Rundgren (photo: *Anastasia Pantsios*)

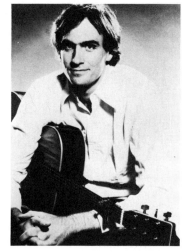

James Taylor

Neil Young (photo: **Anastasia Pantsios**)

1970

Best Soundtrack Album from a Motion Picture or Television: *Let It Be,* The Beatles (Apple).

DEATHS IN 1970

MUSIC PERFORMERS AND MUSIC INDUSTRY NOTABLES WHO DIED IN 1970

Billy Stewart, Saturday, January 17 (car crash; 34)

James "Shep" Sheppard (The Heartbeats), Saturday, January 24 (beating; 34)

Slim Harpo, Saturday, January 31 (heart attack; 46)

Tammi Terrell (Tammi Montgomery), Monday, March 16 (brain tumor; 23)

Earl Grant, Thursday, June 11 (car crash; 39)

Jimi Hendrix, Friday, September 18 (drug overdose; 27)

Janis Joplin, Saturday, October 3 (drug overdose; 27)

OTHERS WHO DIED IN 1970

Charles de Gaulle

Gypsy Rose Lee

Vince Lombardi

Gamal Abdel Nasser

MOVIES OF 1970

POP MUSIC CONCERTS ON FILM

Gimme Shelter   A documentary of the highly publicized Rolling Stones concert at Altamont Raceway in California in 1969, at which a fan was killed by the Hell's Angels. The Jefferson Airplane and Ike & Tina Turner also appear.

Let It Be   This film shows the Beatles rehearsing and later recording the album *Let It Be.* The conclusion of the film features a concert on the roof of the recording studio, their last recording session as a group.

Popcorn   A semidocumentary montage of film clips constituting a 90-minute look at the late sixties. Performers include the Rolling Stones, the Bee Gees, the Beach Boys, Jimi Hendrix, the Vanilla Fudge, Joe Cocker, Otis Redding, the Spencer Davis Group, and the Small Faces.

That's the Way It Is   Documentary on an Elvis Presley concert at the International

235

ROCK ON
ALMANAC

The Carpenters, **Close to You**
album cover

Hotel in Las Vegas, Nevada. The film follows his rehearsals and reaches a thrilling climax with his concert on the hotel's stage.

Woodstock   A rich visual record of the August 1969 music festival that is considered the most important gathering of rock performers and fans in the history of rock 'n' roll. Held in a farmyard at Woodstock, New York, for three days, over 400,000 fans gathered together for peace, love, and music. Performers featured in the film include Joan Baez, the Who, Canned Heat, Sha Na Na, Sly & the Family Stone, Joe Cocker, Richie Havens, John Sebastian, Santana, Jimi Hendrix, Country Joe & the Fish, Ten Years After, and Crosby, Stills, Nash & Young.

OTHER POPULAR MOVIES OF 1970

Airport	Love Story
Catch-22	M*A*S*H
Five Easy Pieces	Patton
Joe	Rio Lobo
Little Big Man	Tora! Tora! Tora!
Lovers and Other Strangers	Women in Love

ACADEMY AWARD WINNERS OF 1970

Best Actor: George C. Scott, *Patton*
Best Actress: Glenda Jackson, *Women in Love*
Best Picture: *Patton*
Best Song: "For All We Know," *Lovers and Other Strangers* (music by Fred Karlin, lyrics by Robb Royer [Robb Wilson] & James Griffin [Arthur James])

TOP TELEVISION SHOWS OF 1970

ABC Movie of the Week	Hawaii Five-O
Bonanza	Here's Lucy
The F.B.I.	Ironside
The Flip Wilson Show	Marcus Welby, M.D.
Gunsmoke	Medical Center

1971

NEWS HIGHLIGHTS OF 1971

⇨ South Dakota's Senator George McGovern opens his campaign for the Democratic presidential nomination.

⇨ Idi Amin and rebels topple the government in Uganda and seize power.

⇨ Rolls-Royce, Ltd., declares bankruptcy after suffering huge losses in developing a new jet engine for Lockheed.

⇨ In New York City's Madison Square Garden, Joe Frazier defeats Muhammad Ali to retain the heavyweight boxing championship.

⇨ The Soviet Union wins the world hockey championship for the ninth consecutive time.

⇨ A cholera epidemic in newly independent but impoverished Bangladesh (East Pakistan) causes worldwide concern.

⇨ Three Soviet cosmonauts are found dead in their spaceship after its return to earth.

⇨ The Apollo 15 astronauts explore the moon's surface riding in a battery-operated vehicle known as the Lunar Rover.

⇨ To combat runaway inflation, President Nixon orders a 90-day freeze on prices and wages.

⇨ After 34 years, *Look* magazine ceases publication.

⇨ The British House of Commons ends a 14-year debate and allows the United Kingdom to join the European Common Market.

⇨ The People's Republic of China is admitted to the United Nations, replacing Taiwan, which is forced to withdraw.

SPORTS WINNERS

Baseball   The Pittsburgh Pirates beat the Baltimore Orioles 4 games to 3.
Football
  NFC: The Dallas Cowboys beat the San Francisco '49ers 14–3 in Dallas.
  AFC: The Miami Dolphins beat the Baltimore Colts 21–0 in Miami.
  Super Bowl VI: The Dallas Cowboys beat the Miami Dolphins 24–3 on January 16, 1972, at Tulane Stadium in New Orleans.
Basketball
  NBA: The Milwaukee Bucks beat the Baltimore Bullets 4 games to 0.
  ABA: The Utah Stars beat the Kentucky Colonels 4 games to 3.
Hockey   The Montreal Canadiens beat the Chicago Black Hawks 4 games to 3.

MUSIC HIGHLIGHTS OF 1971

⇨ On Saturday, January 9, the U.S. Jaycees present an award to Elvis Presley, citing him as one of the 10 outstanding young men in America. This is one of the most important awards Elvis will receive and one that he would forever cherish.

Alice Cooper in concert (photo: Anastasia Pantsios)

Earth, Wind & Fire (top l to r: Phillip Bailey, Maurice White, Andrew Woolfolk; middle l to r: Al McKay, Ralph Johnson; bottom l to r: Johnny Graham, Larry Dunn, Verdine White)

1971

⇨ Alice Cooper emerges as the leading exponent of theatrical "shock rock." Rock 'n' roll begins to fragment into many different styles: "Latin rock," "jazz rock," "progressive rock," "soul rock," and "religious rock," to name a few.

⇨ Producers Kenny Gamble and Leon Huff and arranger Thom Bell develop the "Philly sound" and put Philadelphia on the map as a major rival to Detroit's Motown. Groups like the Intruders, the Stylistics, the Spinners, and later the O'Jays and Harold Melvin & the Bluenotes start turning out a long string of hits.

⇨ The Beatles officially confirm the long-circulating rumor that they are separating permanently to pursue individual careers. The split is attributed to both musical and managerial differences.

⇨ The Rolling Stones release their first single on their new label, Rolling Stones Records, "Brown Sugar." It goes to number one on the charts.

⇨ On Sunday evening, June 27, Bill Graham closes his New York club, the Fillmore East.

⇨ Rod Stewart, after leaving the Faces, has his first major hit single when "Maggie May" rises to number one.

⇨ Michael Jackson, age 13, scores his first solo hit with "Got To Be There."

⇨ On Sunday, August 1, at New York's Madison Square Garden, George Harrison holds his famous Concert for Bangladesh, which generates both a hit album and a hit single. Harrison, Ringo Starr, Eric Clapton, Badfinger, Leon Russell, and others join in to raise money for the starving people of war-torn, cholera-ravaged East Pakistan.

⇨ In November, Don McLean releases the album *American Pie,* whose title single catapults him to worldwide fame. A chronicle of rock history, "American Pie" becomes one of the largest sellers of the seventies and, at more than 8 minutes in length, the longest number one hit in the history of rock 'n' roll.

⇨ Simon & Garfunkel announce that they are separating to pursue individual careers.

DEBUT ARTISTS OF 1971

MAJOR ARTISTS	Debut Single	Label
The Allman Brothers Band (Gregg Allman, Duane Allman, Berry Oakley, Dickey Betts, Jai Johnny "Jaimoe" Johanson, Claude "Butch" Trucks)	Revival (Love Is Everywhere)	Capricorn
Alice Cooper (Vincent Furnier)	Eighteen	Warner Bros.
John Denver	Take Me Home, Country Roads ⑤	RCA

239

The Dramatics (Ron Banks, Willie Lee Ford, Jr., Lawrence Demps, William Howard, Elbert Wilkins)	Whatcha See Is Whatcha Get ⑥	Volt
Earth, Wind & Fire (Maurice White, Verdine White, Phillip Bailey, Larry Dunn, Alan McKay, Ralph Johnson, John Graham, Andrew Woolfolk, Jessica Cleaves)	Love Is Life	Warner Bros.
Yvonne Elliman	I Don't Know How To Love Him	Decca
Roberta Flack (with Donny Hathaway)	You've Got A Friend	Atlantic
J. Geils Band (Peter Wolf, J. Geils, Seth Justman, Magic Dick, Daniel Klein, Stephen Jo Bladd)	Looking For Love	Atlantic
Hamilton, Joe Frank & Reynolds (Dan Hamilton, Joe Frank Carollo, Tom Reynolds)	Don't Pull Your Love ⑥	Dunhill
Michael Jackson	Got To Be There	Motown
Jethro Tull (Ian Anderson, Mick Abrahams, Glenn Cornick, Clive Bunker, John Evan)	Hymn 43	Reprise
Eddie Kendricks	It's So Hard For Me To Say Goodbye	Tamla
Lobo (Kent Lavoie)	Me And You And A Dog Named Boo ⑥	Big Tree
Paul McCartney	Another Day	Apple
Don McLean	American Pie ☆ ⑥	United Artists
New Birth (Charles Hearndon, Leslie Wilson, James Baker, Robert Jackson, Austin Lander, Anthony Churchill, Londie Wiggins, Melvin Wilson, Leroy Taylor, Robin Russell)	It's Impossible	RCA
Olivia Newton-John	If Not For You	Universal
The Ohio Players (Leroy "Sugar" Bonner, Bruce Napier, Marvin "Merve" Pierce, Andrew Noland, Walter Morrison, Ralph Middlebrooks, Marshall "Rock" Jones, Greg Webster)	Pain	Westbound
Donny Osmond	Sweet And Innocent ⑥	MGM
The Osmonds (Alan, Wayne, Merrill, Jay, Donny, Marie, and Jimmy Osmond)	One Bad Apple ☆ ⑥	MGM
Helen Reddy	I Don't Know How To Love Him	Capitol
Boz Scaggs (William Royce Scaggs)	We Were Always Sweethearts	Columbia
Carly Simon	That's The Way I've Always Heard It Should Be	Elektra
Cat Stevens (Stephen Demetri Georgio)	Wild World	A & M
Rod Stewart	Maggie May/Reason To Believe ☆ ⑥	Mercury
The Stylistics (Russell Thompkins, Jr., Herb Murrell, James Dunn, James Smith, Airrion Love)	You're A Big Girl Now	Avco Embassy
Sweet (Brian Connolly, Frank Torpy, Steven Priest, Mick Tucker)	Co-Co	Bell

The Undisputed Truth (Billie Calvin, Brenda Evans, Joe Harris)

Smiling Faces Sometimes — Grody

The Edgar Winter Group (Edgar Winter, Ronnie Montrose, Dan Hartman, Chuck Ruff)

Keep Playing That Rock 'N' Roll — Epic

Bill Withers

Ain't No Sunshine ⓖ — Sussex

Yes (Jon Anderson, Steve Howe, Rick Wakeman, Chris Squire, William Bruford)

Your Move — Atlantic

1971

OTHER ARTISTS

Long John Baldry
Beginning of the End
The Bells
Beverly Bremers
Brewer & Shipley
The Buoys
David Cassidy
C Company featuring Terry Nelson
Tom Clay
Dennis Coffey & the Detroit Guitar Band
The Cornelius Brothers & Sister Rose
Coven
Les Crane
David Crosby
Cymarron
Liz Damon's Orient Express
Kiki Dee
Derek & the Dominos
Daddy Dewdrop
Dusk
Brenda Lee Eager
Dave Edmunds
Jonathan Edwards
The 8th Day
Emerson, Lake & Palmer
The Five Man Electrical Band
The Free Movement
Tom T. Hall
Richie Havens

Hog Heaven
The Hillside Singers
Cissy Houston
Hudson & Landry
Humble Pie
Davy Jones
Mac & Katie Kissoon
Jean Knight
Kris Kristofferson
Denise La Salle
The James Last Band
Lighthouse
Mandrill
Chuck Mangione
Matthews Southern Comfort
Gayle McCormick
Lee Michaels
Graham Nash
The Nite-Liters
Ocean
Carroll O'Connor & Jean Stapleton
Johnny Paycheck
People's Choice
Buffy Sainte-Marie
Joey Scarbury
Sha Na Na
Slade
Sammi Smith
Ronnie Spector

John Denver

Paul McCartney

The Stampeders
Paul Stookey
Livingston Taylor
Think

Tin Tin
Mary Travers
T. Rex

HITS OF 1971

JANUARY

	Bed Of Rose's	The Statler Brothers	Mercury
	D.O.A.	Bloodrock	Capitol
⑥	Don't Let The Green Grass Fool You	Wilson Pickett	Atlantic
	Hang On To Your Life	The Guess Who	RCA
⑥	Help Me Make It Through The Night	Sammi Smith	Mega
	I Don't Know How To Love Him	Helen Reddy	Capitol
⑥	I Hear You Knockin'	Dave Edmunds	MAM
	I Really Don't Want To Know/ There Goes My Everything	Elvis Presley	RCA Victor
	Just Seven Numbers (Can Straighten Out My Life)	The Four Tops	Motown
⑥	Mama's Pearl	The Jackson 5	Motown
☆ ⑥	Me And Bobby McGee	Janis Joplin	Columbia
	Mixed Up Guy	Joey Scarbury	MGM/Lionel
	Mother	John Lennon/Plastic Ono Band	Apple
☆ ⑥	One Bad Apple	The Osmonds	MGM
	Remember Me	Diana Ross	Motown
	Theme From Love Story	Henry Mancini	RCA

FEBRUARY

⑥	Doesn't Somebody Want To Be Wanted	The Partridge Family	Bell
	Eighteen	Alice Cooper	Warner Bros.
⑥	For All We Know	The Carpenters	A & M
	Free	Chicago	Columbia

242

Michael Jackson in concert (photo: *Anastasia Pantsios*)

⑥	Have You Ever Seen The Rain/ Hey Tonight	...dence Clearwater Revival	Fantasy
☆ ⑥	Just My Imagination (Running Away With Me)	The Temptations	Gordy
	1900 Yesterday	Liz Damon's Orient Express	White Whale
	One Toke Over The Line	Brewer & Shipley	Kama Sutra
	Oye Como Va	Santana	Columbia
⑥	Proud Mary	Ike & Tina Turner	Liberty
⑥	She's A Lady	Tom Jones	Parrot
	Sweet Mary	Wadsworth Mansion	Sussex
	Temptation Eyes	The Grass Roots	Dunhill
⑥	What's Going On	Marvin Gaye	Tamla
	Wild World	Cat Stevens	A & M

MARCH

	Angel Baby	Dusk	Bell
⑥	Another Day	Paul McCartney	Apple
	Chairman Of The Board	The Chairmen of the Board	Invictus
	Chick-A-Boom	Daddy Dewdrop	Sunflower
	Cool Aid	Paul Humphrey	Lizard
	Could I Forget You	Tyrone Davis	Dakar
	Friends	Elton John	Uni
⑥	Heavy Makes You Happy	The Staple Singers	Stax
☆ ⑥	Joy To The World	Three Dog Night	Dunhill
	Man In Black	Johnny Cash	Columbia
⑥	Put Your Hand In The Hand	Ocean	Kama Sutra
⑥	Stay Awhile	The Bells	Polydor
	Timothy	The Buoys	Scepter
	What Is Life	George Harrison	Apple
	When There's No You	Engelbert Humperdinck	Parrot

APRIL

⑥	Battle Hymn Of Lt. Calley	C Company featuring Terry Nelson	Plantation
⑥	Don't Knock My Love	Wilson Pickett	Atlantic
	Here Comes The Sun	Richie Havens	Stormy Forest
	I Am . . . I Said	Neil Diamond	Uni
⑥	If	Bread	Elektra
	Layla	Derek & the Dominos	Atco
	Love Her Madly	The Doors	Elektra
⑥	Me And You And A Dog Named Boo	Lobo	Big Tree
⑥	Never Can Say Goodbye	The Jackson 5	Motown
⑥	Power To The People	John Lennon/Plastic Ono Band	Apple
	Right On The Tip Of My Tongue	Brenda & the Tabulations	Top & Bottom
⑥	Sweet And Innocent	Donny Osmond	MGM
	Toast And Marmalade For Tea	Tin Tin	Atco
⑥	Treat Her Like A Lady	The Cornelius Brothers & Sister Rose	United Artists
☆ ⑥	Want Ads	The Honey Cone	Hot Wax

ROCK ON
ALMANAC

Olivia Newton-John

Helen Reddy

MAY

		Albert Flasher	The Guess Who	RCA
☆	⑥	Brown Sugar	The Rolling Stones	Rolling Stones
		Cry Baby	Janis Joplin	Columbia
		Here Comes That Rainy Day Feeling Again	The Fortunes	Capitol
		I Don't Know How To Love Him	Yvonne Elliman	Decca
		I'll Meet You Halfway	The Partridge Family	Bell
☆	⑥	Indian Reservation	The Raiders	Columbia
	⑥	It Don't Come Easy	Ringo Starr	Apple
☆	⑥	It's Too Late	Carole King	Ode
	⑥	Nathan Jones	The Supremes	Motown
	⑥	Rainy Days And Mondays	The Carpenters	A & M
		Reach Out I'll Be There	Diana Ross	Motown
	⑥	She's Not Just Another Woman	The 8th Day	Invictus
	⑥	Signs	The Five Man Electrical Band	Lionel
	⑥	When You're Hot, You're Hot	Jerry Reed	RCA Victor

JUNE

		Ajax Liquor Store	Hudson & Landry	Dore
		Beginnings/Colour My World	Chicago	Columbia
	⑥	Bring The Boys Home	Freda Payne	Invictus
	⑥	Don't Pull Your Love	Hamilton, Joe Frank & Reynolds	Dunhill
		Draggin' The Line	Tommy James	Roulette
☆	⑥	How Can You Mend A Broken Heart	The Bee Gees	Atco
		Moon Shadow	Cat Stevens	A & M
	⑥	Mr. Big Stuff	Jean Knight	Stax
		Puppet Man	Tom Jones	Parrot
		Rings	Cymarron	Entrance
		Smiling Faces Sometimes	The Undisputed Truth	Gordy
		Sooner Or Later	The Grass Roots	Dunhill
		Stop, Look, Listen (To Your Heart)	The Stylistics	Avco Embassy
	⑥	Take Me Home, Country Roads	John Denver	RCA
☆	⑥	You've Got A Friend	James Taylor	Warner Bros.

244

JULY

⑥	Ain't No Sunshine	Bill Withers	Sussex
	He's So Fine	Jody Miller	Epic
	I Just Want To Celebrate	Rare Earth	Rare Earth
	K-Jee	The Nite-Liters	RCA
	Liar	Three Dog Night	Dunhill
⑥	Mercy Mercy Me (The Ecology)	Marvin Gaye	Tamla
	One-Way Ticket	Tyrone Davis	Dakar
	Riders On The Storm	The Doors	Elektra
	Sweet Hitch-Hiker	Creedence Clearwater Revival	Fantasy
	Them Changes	Buddy Miles	Mercury
⑥	Tired Of Being Alone	Al Green	Hi
⑥	Whatcha See Is Whatcha Get	The Dramatics	Volt
	Where You Lead	Barbra Streisand	Columbia
	Wild Horses	The Rolling Stones	Rolling Stone

AUGUST

	Bangla-Desh	George Harrison	Apple
⑥	Easy Loving	Freddie Hart	Capitol
☆ ⑥	Go Away Little Girl	Donny Osmond	MGM
	If You Really Love Me	Stevie Wonder	Tamla
	I Woke Up In Love This Morning	The Partridge Family	Bell
	Make It Funky (Part I)	James Brown	Polydor
⑥	The Night They Drove Old Dixie Down	Joan Baez	Vanguard
	So Far Away	Carole King	Ode
⑥	Spanish Harlem	Aretha Franklin	Atlantic
⑥	Stick-Up	The Honey Cone	Hot Wax
	The Story In Your Eyes	The Moody Blues	Threshold
⑥	Sweet City Woman	The Stampeders	Bell
⑥	Trapped By A Thing Called Love	Denise La Salle	Westbound
☆ ⑥	Uncle Albert/Admiral Halsey	Paul & Linda McCartney	Apple
	Wedding Song (There Is Love)	Paul Stookey	Warner Bros.

SEPTEMBER

Birds Of A Feather	The Raiders	Columbia
Charity Ball	Fanny	Reprise

Carly Simon

245

☆ ⑥ Gypsies, Tramps & Thieves	Cher	Kapp
I Don't Need No Doctor	Humble Pie	A & M
I'm Comin' Home	Tommy James	Roulette
☆ ⑥ Maggie May/Reason To Believe	Rod Stewart	Mercury
Never My Love	The 5th Dimension	Bell
One Fine Morning	Lighthouse	Evolution
One Tin Soldier (The Legend Of Billy Jack)	Coven	Warner Bros.
Only You Know And I Know	Delaney & Bonnie	Atco
Peace Train	Cat Stevens	A & M
Rain Dance	The Guess Who	RCA
⑥ Superstar	The Carpenters	A & M
⑥ Thin Line Between Love And Hate	The Persuaders	Atco
⑥ Yo-Yo	The Osmonds	MGM

OCTOBER

Absolutely Right	The Five Man Electrical Band	Lionel
⑥ All I Ever Need Is You	Sonny & Cher	Kapp
⑥ Baby I'm-A Want You	Bread	Elektra
⑥ Desiderata	Les Crane	Warner Bros.
Everybody's Everything	Santana	Columbia
⑥ Have You Seen Her	The Chi-Lites	Brunswick
⑥ Imagine	John Lennon/Plastic Ono Band	Apple
I'm A Man/Questions 67 & 68	Chicago	Columbia
⑥ Inner City Blues (Make Me Wanna Holler)	Marvin Gaye	Tamla
Life Is A Carnival	The Band	Capitol
Tell Me Why	Matthews Southern Comfort	Decca
☆ ⑥ Theme From Shaft	Isaac Hayes	Enterprise/ MGM
Two Divided By Love	The Grass Roots	Dunhill
Wild Night	Van Morrison	Warner Bros.
You Think You're Hot Stuff	Jean Knight	Stax

Rod Stewart in concert (photo: *Anastasia Pantsios*)

NOVEMBER

☆ ⓖ	American Pie	Don McLean	United Artists
☆ ⓖ	Brand New Key	Melanie	Neighborhood
ⓖ	Cherish	David Cassidy	Bell
ⓖ	Clean Up Woman	Betty Wright	Alston
☆ ⓖ	Family Affair	Sly & the Family Stone	Epic
ⓖ	Got To Be There	Michael Jackson	Motown
	Hallelujah	Sweathog	Columbia
ⓖ	Hey Girl/I Knew You When	Donny Osmond	MGM
	(I Know) I'm Losing You	Rod Stewart	Mercury
ⓖ	An Old Fashioned Love Song	Three Dog Night	Dunhill
	One Monkey Don't Stop No Show	The Honey Cone	Hot Wax
ⓖ	Rock Steady	Aretha Franklin	Atlantic
ⓖ	Scorpio	Dennis Coffey & the Detroit Guitar Band	Sussex
ⓖ	Sunshine	Jonathan Edwards	Capricorn
ⓖ	You Are Everything	The Stylistics	Avco

DECEMBER

ⓖ	Ain't Understanding Mellow	Jerry Butler & Brenda Lee Eager	Mercury
	Anticipation	Carly Simon	Elektra
ⓖ	Day After Day	Badfinger	Apple
ⓖ	Drowning In The Sea Of Love	Joe Simon	Spring
ⓖ	I'd Like To Teach The World To Sing (In Perfect Harmony)	The New Seekers	Elektra
	It's One Of Those Nights (Yes Love)	The Partridge Family	Bell
ⓖ	Kiss An Angel Good Mornin'	Charlie Pride	RCA
	Lay Lady Lay	The Isley Brothers	T-Neck
☆ ⓖ	Let's Stay Together	Al Green	Hi
	Levon	Elton John	Uni
	Lookin' For A Love	The J. Geils Band	Atlantic
	Sugar Daddy	The Jackson 5	Motown
	Truckin'	The Grateful Dead	Warner Bros.
	Turn Your Radio On	Ray Stevens	Barnaby
☆ ⓖ	Without You	Nilsson	RCA

TOP SINGLES OF 1971

ⓖ	Brown Sugar	The Rolling Stones	Rolling Stones
ⓖ	Family Affair	Sly & the Family Stone	Epic
ⓖ	Go Away Little Girl	Donny Osmond	MGM
ⓖ	How Can You Mend A Broken Heart	The Bee Gees	Atco
ⓖ	It's Too Late	Carole King	Ode
ⓖ	Joy To The World	Three Dog Night	Dunhill
ⓖ	Just My Imagination (Running Away With Me)	The Temptations	Gordy
ⓖ	Maggie May	Rod Stewart	Mercury
ⓖ	Me And Bobby McGee	Janis Joplin	Columbia
ⓖ	One Bad Apple	The Osmonds	MGM

Yes (l to r: Rick Wakeman, Jon Anderson, Alan White, Steve Howe, Chris Squire)

TOP ALBUMS OF 1971

ⓖ **All Things Must Pass** — George Harrison — Apple
ⓟ **Chicago III** — Chicago — Columbia
ⓖ **Every Picture Tells A Story** — Rod Stewart — Mercury
ⓖ **Jesus Christ Superstar** — Various Artists — Decca
ⓖ **Love Story** — Soundtrack — Paramount
ⓟ **Mud Slide Slim And The Blue Horizon** — James Taylor — Warner Bros.
ⓟ **Pearl** — Janis Joplin — Columbia
Shaft — Soundtrack — Enterprise
ⓖ **Sticky Fingers** — The Rolling Stones — London
ⓖ **Tapestry** — Carole King — Ode

GRAMMY WINNERS IN 1971

The Grammys were awarded at the Felt Forum in New York on Tuesday, March 14, 1972. They were televised for the first time, on ABC, and Andy Williams was the host.

Record of the Year: "It's Too Late," Carole King (Ode)
Song of the Year: "You've Got A Friend" (music and lyrics by Carole King)
Album of the Year: *Tapestry,* Carole King (Ode)
Best Contemporary Vocal Performance, Female: *Tapestry,* Carole King (Ode)
Best Contemporary Vocal Performance, Male: "You've Got A Friend," James Taylor (Warner Bros.)
Best Contemporary Vocal Performance, Group: *The Carpenters,* The Carpenters (A & M)
Best New Artist of the Year: Carly Simon
Best Comedy Performance: *This Is A Recording,* Lily Tomlin (Polydor)
Best Soundtrack Album from a Motion Picture or Television: *Shaft,* Isaac Hayes (Enterprise)

BIRTHS AND DEATHS IN 1971

MUSIC PERFORMERS BORN IN 1971

Tiffany (Tiffany Renee Darwish), June 2

MUSIC PERFORMERS AND MUSIC INDUSTRY NOTABLES WHO DIED IN 1971

Jim Morrison (The Doors), Saturday, July 3 (heart attack; 27)

Donald McPherson (The Main Ingredient), Sunday, July 4 (leukemia; 29)

Louis Armstrong, Tuesday, July 6 (heart attack; 71)

King Curtis (Curtis Ousley), Friday, August 13 (stabbing; 38)

Gene Vincent (Vincent Eugene Craddock), Tuesday, October 12 (ulcers; 36)

Duane Allman (The Allman Brothers), Friday, October 29 (motorcycle accident; 24)

OTHERS WHO DIED IN 1971

Bennett Cerf
Jeff Chandler
Coco Chanel
Van Heflin
Bobby Jones

Nikita Khrushchev
Sonny Liston
Harold Lloyd
Audie Murphy
J.C. Penney

MOVIES OF 1971

POP MUSIC CONCERTS ON FILM

Celebration at Big Sur   This film of the Big Sur (California) Folk Festival of 1969 features performances by Joan Baez, Joni Mitchell, John Sebastian, and Crosby, Stills, Nash & Young.

Mad Dogs and Englishmen   A filmed record of Joe Cocker's 1970 tour of the United States, with a little help from good friend Leon Russell.

Pink Floyd at Pompeii   A 90-minute presentation of concert footage and interviews with the group, shot at the Roman Amphitheater at Pompeii.

MOVIES FEATURING A POP MUSIC SOUNDTRACK

Shaft   *Stars:* Richard Roundtree, Moses Gunn, Charles Cioffi. Soundtrack by Isaac Hayes. "Theme From Shaft" won the Oscar for Best Song.

OTHER POPULAR MOVIES OF 1971

Bananas
Billy Jack
Carnal Knowledge
A Clockwork Orange
Dirty Harry
Fiddler on the Roof
The French Connection

The Hospital
Klute
The Last Picture Show
Play Misty for Me
Summer of '42
Sunday, Bloody Sunday

Carol King, Tapestry *album cover*

ACADEMY AWARD WINNERS OF 1971

Best Actor: Gene Hackman, *The French Connection*
Best Actress: Jane Fonda, *Klute*
Best Picture: *The French Connection*
Best Song: "Theme From Shaft," *Shaft* (music and lyrics by Isaac Hayes)

TOP TELEVISION SHOWS OF 1971

ABC Movie of the Week
Adam 12
All in the Family
The Flip Wilson Show
Funny Face

Gunsmoke
Mannix
Marcus Welby, M.D.
The Mary Tyler Moore Show
Sanford & Son

1972

ROCK ON ALMANAC

⇨ The Coca-Cola Bottling Company recalls 3 million cans of Coke because some of the aluminum lids are found to be contaminated.

⇨ The Winter Olympics are held in Sapporo, Japan.

⇨ Germany pays $5 million to hijackers of a jumbo jet for the release of passengers held hostage.

⇨ President Nixon becomes the first U.S. president to visit China. He and Chinese leader Chou En-lai sign an accord for increased contacts between their nations.

⇨ The *Pioneer 10* spacecraft takes a 21-month journey to Jupiter, beaming back to earth detailed photos of the planet and its moons.

⇨ President Nixon becomes the first U.S. president to visit Moscow. He spends one week there in talks with Soviet leader Leonid Brezhnev.

⇨ Alabama Governor George Wallace, a controversial presidential candidate because of his white supremacist sympathies, is shot by a sniper and paralyzed from the waist down but plans to continue his quest for the White House.

⇨ Five burglars are charged with breaking into the Washington, D.C., office of the Democratic National Committee, located in the Watergate complex.

⇨ President Nixon orders the biggest ever bombing raid on North Vietnam.

⇨ South Dakota Senator George McGovern chooses Sargent Shriver as his vice-presidential running mate on the Democratic ticket.

⇨ Arabs massacre 11 Israeli athletes at the Summer Olympics in Munich, West Germany. The Olympic flag flies at half mast.

⇨ American swimmer Mark Spitz wins a record seven gold medals at the Munich Olympics.

⇨ President Nixon and Soviet Foreign Minister Andrei Gromyko sign a strategic arms limitation treaty.

⇨ Richard Nixon wins a second term in the White House.

SPORTS WINNERS

Baseball   The Oakland A's beat the Cincinnati Reds 4 games to 3.

Football

NFC: The Washington Redskins beat the Dallas Cowboys 26–3 in Dallas.

AFC: The Miami Dolphins beat the Pittsburgh Steelers 21–17 in Pittsburgh.

Super Bowl VII: The Miami Dolphins beat the Washington Redskins 14–7 on January 14, 1973, at the Memorial Coliseum in Los Angeles.

Basketball

NBA: The Los Angeles Lakers beat the New York Knicks 4 games to 1.

ABA: The Indiana Pacers beat the New York Nets 4 games to 2.

Hockey   The Boston Bruins beat the New York Rangers 4 games to 2.

MUSIC HIGHLIGHTS OF 1972

⇨ The 1950s musical *Grease* opens on Broadway, setting the tone for a nostalgia craze that will sweep the nation.

⇨ In keeping with this, New York radio station WCBS-FM is the first to adopt a "solid gold" format of playing "oldies," a formula that remains especially popular.

⇨ On Friday, June 2, at New York's Madison Square Garden, teen idol Dion reunites with his original group for the Dion & the Belmonts reunion show, their first performance together in years. The show is captured on tape and released as an album on Warner Bros. Records.

⇨ When John Lennon's U.S. immigration visa expires, he begins a long battle to obtain permission to stay permanently in America.

⇨ A 22-year-old singer from Freehold, New Jersey, by the name of Bruce Springsteen

David Bowie **Jackson Browne in concert (photo: Anastasia Pantsios)**

signs with Columbia Records. He then begins work on his debut album for the label, *Greetings From Asbury Park.*

⇨ The musical *Hair* ends its Broadway run after 1742 performances.

⇨ Neil Diamond signs a multimillion-dollar deal to record for Columbia Records, thereby leaving the Uni label.

⇨ Having led the Miracles since 1958, Smokey Robinson leaves the group to go out as a solo performer. His replacement is Bill Griffin.

⇨ One of the biggest summertime concerts is the Pocono Rock Festival in Pennsylvania, which attracts over 240,000 fans to see, among other acts, Emerson, Lake & Palmer and the J. Geils Band.

⇨ Chuck Berry, who first hit the charts in 1955 with "Maybellene," finally lands his first and only national number one hit with "My-Ding-A-Ling."

⇨ James Taylor and Carly Simon get married in New York.

⇨ "Glitter rock" gains notoriety because of groups like the New York Dolls and New York clubs like Max's Kansas City.

⇨ Genesis arrives in America and makes its concert debut.

DEBUT ARTISTS OF 1972

MAJOR ARTISTS

	Debut Single	Label
America (Gerry Beckley, Dewey Bunnell, Dan Peek)	A Horse With No Name ☆ ⑥	Warner Bros.
April Wine (Myles Goodwyn, Gary Moffet, Jim Clench, Richard Henman)	You Could Have Been A Lady	Big Tree
David Bowie	Changes	RCA
Jackson Browne	Doctor My Eyes	Asylum
Brownsville Station (Michael "Cub" Koda, Michael "Sam" Lutz, David Lynn, Anthony Driggins, Bruce Nazarian)	Red Back Spider	Big Tree
Harry Chapin	Taxi	Elektra
Chilliwack (Bill Henderson, Brian MacLeod, Ab Bryant)	Lonesome Mary	A & M
Jim Croce	You Don't Mess Around With Jim	ABC
The Doobie Brothers (Tom Johnston, Patrick R. Simmons, "Little" John Hartman, David Shogren)	Listen To The Music	Warner Bros.

253

ROCK ON
ALMANAC

The Doobie Brothers (top l to r: Keith Knudson, Tiran Porter, Michael McDonald; bottom l to r: Jeff Baxter, John Hartman, Patrick Simmons)

Dr. Hook & the Medicine Show (Ray "Dr. Hook" Sawyer, Dennis Locorriere, George Cummings, William Francis, Jay David, Rik Elswit, Jance Garfat)	Sylvia's Mother Ⓖ	Columbia
The Eagles (Glenn Frey, Don Henley, Randy Meisner, Bernie Leadon)	Take It Easy	Asylum
Donna Fargo	The Happiest Girl In The Whole U.S.A. Ⓖ	Dot
Foghat (Rod Price, Lonesome Dave Peverett, Anthony Stevens, Roger Earl)	I Just Want To Make Love To You	Bearsville
Albert Hammond	Down By The River	Mums
Jermaine Jackson	That's How Love Goes	Motown
Millie Jackson	Ask Me What You Want	Spring
Loggins & Messina (Kenny Loggins, Jim Messina)	Vahevala	Columbia
Harold Melvin & the Blue Notes (Teddy Pendergrass, Harold Melvin, Bernard Wilson, Lawrence Brown, Lloyd Parks)	I Miss You	Philadelphia Int'l
Bette Midler	Do You Want To Dance?	Atlantic
Michael Murphey	Geronimo's Cadillac	A & M
Gilbert O'Sullivan	Alone Again (Naturally) ☆ Ⓖ	MAM
The Raspberries (Eric Carmen, Wally Bryson, David Smalley, Jim Bonfanti)	Don't Want To Say Goodbye	Capitol
Seals & Crofts (Jimmy Seals, Dash Crofts)	Summer Breeze Ⓖ	Warner Bros.
Paul Simon	Mother And Child Reunion	Columbia
Slade (Noddy Holder, Dave Hill, Jim Lea, Don Powell)	Take Me Bak 'Ome	Polydor
Rick Springfield	Speak To The Sky	Capitol
Steely Dan (Don Fagen, Walt Becker, Denny Dias, Jeff Baxter, James Hodder)	Do It Again	ABC
Styx (James Young, John Curulewski, Dennis De Young, Charles Panozzo, John Panozzo)	Best Thing	Wooden Nickel

254

The Sylvers (Olympia-Ann, Leon, Charmaine, James, Edmund, Joseph, and Foster Sylvers)

A Fool's Paradise   Pride

The Tower of Power (Lenny Williams, Bruce Conte, Chester Thompson, Frank "Rocco" Prestina, Brent Byars, Emilio Castillo, Steve Kupka, Lenny Pickett, Greg Adams, Mic Gillette)

You're Still A Young Man   Warner Bros.

Tanya Tucker   Delta Dawn   Columbia

ZZ Top (Billy Gibbons, Dusty Hill, Frank Beard)

Francene   London

OTHER ARTISTS

Apollo 100
Argent
Blue Haze
The Blue Ridge Rangers
Daniel Boone
The Brighter Side of Darkness
Jim Capaldi
Cashman & West
The Chakachas
Climax
Chi Coltrane
Commander Cody & His Lost Planet Airmen
The Delegates
Dr. John
The Faces
The Gallery
Jerry Garcia
Gary Glitter
Godspell
Joey Heatherton
Hot Butter
Jo Jo Gunne
John Kay
King Harvest
Michel Legrand
Lindisfarne

Looking Glass
Love Unlimited
Malo
Manfred Mann's Earth Band
Ian Matthews
Frank Mills
Giorgio Moroder
Mott the Hoople
Mouth & MacNeal
Sam Neely
The New Riders of the Purple Sage
Danny O'Keefe
"Little" Jimmy Osmond
Billy Paul
Austin Roberts
Nino Rota
The Royal Scots Dragoon Guards
Leon Russell
Sailcat
Hurricane Smith
The Stories
Timmy Thomas
The Trammps
Uriah Heep
Paul Williams
Peter Yarrow

Dr. Hook & the Medicine Show (l to r: Jance Garfat, Bill Francis, Rik Elswit, John Wolters, Ray "Dr. Hook" Sawyer, Bob "Willard" Henke, Dennis Locorriere; photo: Tom Hill)

255

HITS OF 1972

JANUARY

	Bang A Gong (Get It On)	T. Rex	Reprise
	Cry	Lynn Anderson	Columbia
⑥	Everything I Own	Bread	Elektra
⑥	Hurting Each Other	The Carpenters	A & M
⑥	I Gotcha	Joe Tex	Dial
	Joy	Apollo 100	Mega
⑥	Jungle Fever	The Chakachas	Polydor
⑥	The Lion Sleeps Tonight	Robert John	Atlantic
	My World	The Bee Gees	Atco
⑥	Precious And Few	Climax	Carousel
⑥	Slippin' Into Darkness	War	United Artists
	Stay With Me	The Faces	Warner Bros.
	Sweet Seasons	Carole King	Ode
	Until It's Time For You To Go	Elvis Presley	RCA Victor
	The Way Of Love	Cher	Kapp

FEBRUARY

⑥	Betcha By Golly, Wow	The Stylistics	Avco
	Brian's Song	Michel Legrand	Bell
	Could It Be Forever	David Cassidy	Bell
	A Cowboy's Work Is Never Done	Sonny & Cher	Kapp
⑥	Down By The Lazy River	The Osmonds	MGM
	Do Your Thing	Isaac Hayes	Enterprise
	Glory Bound	The Grass Roots	Dunhill
☆ ⑥	Heart Of Gold	Neil Young	Reprise
☆ ⑥	A Horse With No Name	America	Warner Bros.
⑥	In The Rain	The Dramatics	Volt
	Mother And Child Reunion	Paul Simon	Columbia
⑥	Nice To Be With You	The Gallery	Sussex
⑥	Puppy Love	Donny Osmond	MGM
	Rock and Roll Lullaby	B.J. Thomas	Scepter
	Taurus	Dennis Coffey & the Detroit Guitar Band	Sussex

MARCH

	Baby Blue	Badfinger	Apple
☆ ⑥	Candy Man	Sammy Davis, Jr.	MGM
⑥	Day Dreaming	Aretha Franklin	Atlantic
	Doctor My Eyes	Jackson Browne	Asylum
	Everyday	John Denver	RCA
	The Family Of Man	Three Dog Night	Dunhill
☆ ⑥	The First Time Ever I Saw Your Face	Roberta Flack	Atlantic
	Give Ireland Back To The Irish	Wings	Apple
	Hot Rod Lincoln	Commander Cody & His Lost Planet Airmen	Paramount
	Rock And Roll	Led Zeppelin	Atlantic
⑥	Rockin' Robin	Michael Jackson	Motown
	Suavecito	Malo	Warner Bros.
	Take A Look Around	The Temptations	Gordy

The Eagles (l to r: Bernie Leadon, Don Henley, Glenn Frey, Don Felder, Randy Meisner; photo: Kriegsmann)

1972

Taxi	Harry Chapin	Elektra
Vincent	Don McLean	United Artists

APRIL

Back Off Boogaloo	Ringo Starr	Apple
⑥ Daddy Don't You Walk So Fast	Wayne Newton	Chelsea
Diary	Bread	Elektra
☆ ⑥ I'll Take You There	The Staple Singers	Stax
⑥ (Last Night) I Didn't Get To Sleep At All	The 5th Dimension	Bell
☆ ⑥ Lean On Me	Bill Withers	Sussex
⑥ Let's Stay Together	Isaac Hayes	Enterprise
Little Bitty Pretty One	The Jackson 5	Motown
⑥ Look What You've Done For Me	Al Green	Hi
Me And Julio Down By The Schoolyard	Paul Simon	Columbia
Morning Has Broken	Cat Stevens	A & M
☆ ⑥ Oh Girl	The Chi-Lites	Brunswick
⑥ Outa-Space	Billy Preston	A & M
⑥ Sylvia's Mother	Dr. Hook & the Medicine Show	Columbia
⑥ Walking In The Rain With The One I Love	Love Unlimited	Uni

MAY

An American Trilogy	Elvis Presley	RCA Victor
Conquistador	Procol Harum	A & M
Day By Day	Godspell	Bell
⑥ The Happiest Girl In The Whole U.S.A.	Donna Fargo	Dot
⑥ How Do You Do?	Mouth & MacNeal	Philips
I Need You	America	Warner Bros.
It's Going To Take Some Time	The Carpenters	A & M
I Wanna Be Where You Are	Michael Jackson	Motown
Layla *(re-entry)*	Derek & the Dominos	Atco
⑥ Rocket Man	Elton John	Uni
Someday Never Comes	Creedence Clearwater Revival	Fantasy

*Seals & Crofts (l to r: **Jimmy Seals, Dash Crofts**)*

☆ ⑥	Song Sung Blue	Neil Diamond	Uni
⑥	Too Late To Turn Back Now	The Cornelius Brothers & Sister Rose	United Artists
⑥	Troglodyte (Cave Man)	The Jimmy Castor Bunch	RCA
	Tumbling Dice	The Rolling Stones	Rolling Stones

JUNE

☆ ⑥	Alone Again (Naturally)	Gilbert O'Sullivan	MAM
⑥	Beautiful Sunday	Daniel Boone	Mercury
⑥	Brandy (You're A Fine Girl)	Looking Glass	Epic
	Coconut	Nilsson	RCA
⑥	Hold Your Head Up	Argent	Epic
	Honky Tonk (Part 1)	James Brown	Polydor
⑥	I Am Woman	Helen Reddy	Capitol
⑥	(If Loving You Is Wrong) I Don't Want To Be Right	Luther Ingram	KoKo
⑥	Long Cool Woman (In A Black Dress)	The Hollies	Epic
	Motorcycle Mama	Sailcat	Elektra
	People Make The World Go Round	The Stylistics	Avco
	School's Out	Alice Cooper	Warner Bros.
	Sealed With A Kiss	Bobby Vinton	Epic
	Take It Easy	The Eagles	Asylum
⑥	Where Is The Love	Roberta Flack & Donny Hathaway	Atlantic

JULY

☆ ⑥	Baby Don't Get Hooked On Me	Mac Davis	Columbia
⑥	Back Stabbers	The O'Jays	Philadelphia Int'l
	The City Of New Orleans	Arlo Guthrie	Reprise
⑥	Everybody Plays The Fool	The Main Ingredient	RCA
⑥	Go All The Way	The Raspberries	Capitol
	Goodbye To Love	The Carpenters	A & M
	The Guitar Man	Bread	Elektra
	Happy	The Rolling Stones	Rolling Stones
	I Miss You	Harold Melvin & the Blue Notes	Philadelphia Int'l

(G) I'm Still In Love With You — Al Green — Hi
(G) Popcorn — Hot Butter — Musicor
(G) Power Of Love — Joe Simon — Spring
(G) Rock And Roll Part 2 — Gary Glitter — Bell
Run To Me — The Bee Gees — Atco
You Don't Mess Around With Jim — Jim Croce — ABC

AUGUST

☆ (G) Ben — Michael Jackson — Motown
☆ (G) Black & White — Three Dog Night — Dunhill
(G) Burning Love — Elvis Presley — RCA Victor
(G) Freddie's Dead — Curtis Mayfield — Curtom
(G) Garden Party — Rick Nelson — Decca
(G) Get On The Good Foot (Part 1) — James Brown — Polydor
(G) Honky Cat — Elton John — Uni
(G) I'll Be Around — The Spinners — Atlantic
☆ (G) My Ding-A-Ling — Chuck Berry — Chess
(G) Nights In White Satin — The Moody Blues — Deram
Rock Me On The Water — Jackson Browne — Asylum
(G) Saturday In The Park — Chicago — Columbia
(G) Use Me — Bill Withers — Sussex
Why/Lonely Boy — Donny Osmond — MGM
You Wear It Well — Rod Stewart — Mercury

SEPTEMBER

All The Young Dudes — Mott the Hoople — Columbia
Don't Ever Be Lonely (A Poor Little Fool Like Me) — The Cornelius Brothers & Sister Rose — United Artists
(G) Good Time Charlie's Got The Blues — Danny O'Keefe — Signpost
☆ (G) I Can See Clearly Now — Johnny Nash — Epic
(G) I'd Love You To Want Me — Lobo — Big Tree
If I Could Reach You — The 5th Dimension — Bell
(G) If You Don't Know Me By Now — Harold Melvin & the Blue Notes — Philadelphia Int'l
Let It Rain — Eric Clapton — Polydor
Listen To The Music — The Doobie Brothers — Warner Bros.
Midnight Rider — Joe Cocker — A & M
Money Back Guarantee — The Five Man Electrical Band — Lion
Rock Me Baby — David Cassidy — Bell
(G) Summer Breeze — Seals & Crofts — Warner Bros.
Witchy Woman — The Eagles — Asylum
With Pen In Hand — Bobby Goldsboro — United Artists

OCTOBER

(G) Clair — Gilbert O'Sullivan — MAM
Convention '72 — The Delegates — Mainstream
Dancing In The Moonlight — King Harvest — Perception
Dialogue — Chicago — Columbia
Elected — Alice Cooper — Warner Bros.

⑥ Funny Face	Donna Fargo	Dot
⑥ I'm Stone In Love With You	The Stylistics	Avco
⑥ It Never Rains In Southern California	Albert Hammond	Mums
Operator (That's Not The Way It Feels)	Jim Croce	ABC/Dunhill
☆ ⑥ Papa Was A Rollin' Stone	The Temptations	Gordy
⑥ Rockin' Pneumonia & The Boogie Woogie Flu	Johnny Rivers	United Artists
Something's Wrong With Me	Austin Roberts	Chelsea
Theme From The Men	Isaac Hayes	Enterprise
Ventura Highway	America	Warner Bros.
⑥ You Ought To Be With Me	Al Green	Hi

NOVEMBER

Been To Canaan	Carole King	Ode
Do It Again	Steely Dan	ABC
I Wanna Be With You	The Raspberries	Capitol
⑥ Keeper Of The Castle	The Four Tops	Dunhill
Living In The Past	Jethro Tull	Chrysalis
☆ ⑥ Me And Mrs. Jones	Billy Paul	Philadelphia Int'l
⑥ Rocky Mountain High	John Denver	RCA
Smoke Gets In Your Eyes	Blue Haze	A & M
⑥ Superfly	Curtis Mayfield	Curtom
☆ ⑥ Superstition	Stevie Wonder	Tamla
Sweet Surrender	Bread	Elektra
Walk On Water	Neil Diamond	Uni
⑥ Why Can't We Live Together	Timmy Thomas	Glades
⑥ The World Is A Ghetto	War	United Artists
⑥ Your Mama Don't Dance	Loggins & Messina	Columbia

DECEMBER

⑥ Could It Be I'm Falling In Love	The Spinners	Atlantic
☆ ⑥ Crocodile Rock	Elton John	MCA
⑥ Daddy's Home	Jermaine Jackson	Motown

Paul Simon in concert (photo: Anastasia Pantsios)

Styx (top l to r: Dennis De Young, James Young, Charles Panozzo, John Panozzo; center: John Curulewski; photo: Kriegsmann)

Don't Expect Me To Be Your Friend	Lobo	Big Tree
Don't Let Me Be Lonely Tonight	James Taylor	Warner Bros.
Do You Want To Dance?	Bette Midler	Atlantic
⑥ **Harry Hippie**	Bobby Womack & Peace	United Artists
☆ ⑥ **I Am Woman**	Helen Reddy	Capitol
⑥ **Last Song**	Edward Bear	Capitol
⑥ **Love Jones**	The Brighter Side of Darkness	20th Century
Oh, Babe, What Would You Say?	Hurricane Smith	Capitol
Peaceful Easy Feeling	The Eagles	Asylum
Separate Ways/Always On My Mind	Elvis Presley	RCA Victor
☆ ⑥ **You're So Vain**	Carly Simon	Elektra

TOP SINGLES OF 1972

⑥ **Alone Again (Naturally)**	Gilbert O'Sullivan	MAM
⑥ **American Pie**	Don McLean	United Artists
⑥ **Baby Don't Get Hooked On Me**	Mac Davis	Columbia
⑥ **Candy Man**	Sammy Davis, Jr.	MGM
⑥ **The First Time Ever I Saw Your Face**	Roberta Flack	Atlantic
⑥ **A Horse With No Name**	America	Warner Bros.
⑥ **I Can See Clearly Now**	Johnny Nash	Epic
⑥ **Lean On Me**	Bill Withers	Sussex
⑥ **My Ding-A-Ling**	Chuck Berry	Chess
⑥ **Without You**	Nilsson	RCA

TOP ALBUMS OF 1972

℗ **America**	America	Warner Bros.
⑥ **American Pie**	Don McLean	United Artists
⑥ **Catch Bull At Four**	Cat Stevens	A & M
℗ **Chicago V**	Chicago	Columbia
⑥ **The Concert for Bangla Desh**	George Harrison & Friends	Apple
⑥ **Exile On Main St.**	The Rolling Stones	Rolling Stones
℗ **Harvest**	Neil Young	Reprise
⑥ **Honky Chateau**	Elton John	Uni

261

ZZ Top in concert (photo: Anastasia Pantsios)

| Ⓖ **Music** | Carole King | Ode |
| Ⓖ **Superfly** | Soundtrack | Curtom |

GRAMMY WINNERS IN 1972

The Grammys were televised from the Tennessee Theater in Nashville on Saturday, March 3, 1973. Andy Williams was the host.

Record of the Year: "The First Time Ever I Saw Your Face," Roberta Flack (Atlantic)

Song of the Year: "The First Time Ever I Saw Your Face" (music and lyrics by Ewan MacColl)

Album of the Year: *The Concert For Bangla Desh,* George Harrison, Ravi Shankar, Bob Dylan, Leon Russell, Ringo Starr, Billy Preston, Eric Clapton, & Klaus Voorman (Apple)

Best Pop Vocal Performance, Female: "I Am Woman," Helen Reddy (Capitol)

Best Pop Vocal Performance, Male: "Without You," Nilsson (RCA)

Best Pop Vocal Performance, Group: "Where Is The Love," Roberta Flack & Donny Hathaway (Atlantic)

Best New Artist of the Year: America

Best Comedy Performance: *FM & AM,* George Carlin (Little David)

Best Soundtrack Album from a Motion Picture or Television: *The Godfather,* Nino Rota (Paramount)

DEATHS IN 1972

MUSIC PERFORMERS AND MUSIC INDUSTRY NOTABLES WHO DIED IN 1972

Maurice Chevalier, Saturday, January 1 (heart attack; 83)

David Seville (Ross Bagdasarian), Sunday, January 16 (unknown causes; 52)

Mahalia Jackson, Wednesday, January 26 (heart failure; 70)

Clyde McPhatter, Monday, March 13 (heart attack; 40)

Linda Jones, Tuesday, March 14 (diabetes; 28)

Brian Cole (The Association), Wednesday, August 2 (drug overdose; 28)

Billy Williams, Thursday, October 12 (diabetes; 62)

Berry Oakley (The Allman Brothers Band), Saturday, November 11 (motorcycle accident; 24)

OTHERS WHO DIED IN 1972

William Boyd (Hopalong Cassidy)
Roberto Clemente
Brian Donlevy
Gil Hodges
Adam Clayton Powell

Jackie Robinson
George Sanders
Harry S Truman
Walter Winchell

MOVIES OF 1972

MOVIES FEATURING POP MUSIC ARTISTS

The Harder They Come   *Stars:* Jimmy Cliff, Janet Barkley, Carl Bradshaw. *Featured songs:* "The Harder They Come," "Many Rivers To Cross," and "You Can Get It If You Really Want" by Jimmy Cliff. This film is filled with great Jamaican reggae music.

POP MUSIC CONCERTS ON FILM

The Concert for Bangla Desh   George Harrison gathered his friends for a concert in 1971 at New York's Madison Square Garden to boost awareness of the plight of the starving people of Bangladesh. The all-star lineup includes Bob Dylan, Eric Clapton, Ringo Starr, Billy Preston, Leon Russell, Ravi Shankar, and Klaus Voorman.

Elvis on Tour   This documentary was Elvis's last film, which won a Golden Globe Award as best documentary. It features a multiple-screen effect for the concert footage, a new technique in presenting Elvis on stage.

Fillmore   This documentary chronicles concert promoter Bill Graham's closing of his landmark Fillmore West in San Francisco. Performers who appear in the film include Santana, the Grateful Dead, the Jefferson Airplane, Hot Tuna, Boz Scaggs, Elvin Bishop, the Quicksilver Messenger Service, and Cold Blood.

Imagine   A film retrospective of John and Yoko Ono Lennon, including TV clips and home movies.

MOVIES FEATURING A POP MUSIC SOUNDTRACK

Superfly   *Stars:* Ron O'Neal, Carl Lee, Sheila Frazier. *Featured song:* "Freddie's Dead" by Curtis Mayfield.

OTHER POPULAR MOVIES OF 1972

Cabaret
The Candidate
Deliverance
The Godfather

Last of the Red Hot Lovers
The Mad Bomber
One Is a Lonely Number
The Poseidon Adventure

America *album cover*

ROCK ON ALMANAC

ACADEMY AWARD WINNERS OF 1972

Best Actor: Marlon Brando, *The Godfather*
Best Actress: Liza Minnelli, *Cabaret*
Best Picture: *The Godfather*
Best Song: "The Morning After," *The Poseidon Adventure* (music and lyrics by Al Kasha and Joel Hirschhorn)

TOP TELEVISION SHOWS OF 1972

All in the Family
Bridget Loves Bernie
Gunsmoke
Hawaii Five-O
Ironside

The Mary Tyler Moore Show
Maude
NBC Sunday Mystery Movie
Sanford and Son
The Wonderful World of Disney

1973

ROCK ON ALMANAC

⇨ An agreement is signed in Paris to stop the fighting in Vietnam.

⇨ G. Gordon Liddy and James W. McCord, Jr., are convicted of plotting to spy on the Democrats in the Watergate break-in.

⇨ The first planeload of POWs return home from the Vietnam War.

⇨ Four top aides to President Nixon quit over the Watergate affair.

⇨ The Pulitzer Prize is awarded to the *Washington Post* for its investigation of the Watergate scandal.

⇨ After more than 300 years of British rule, the Bahamas become independent.

⇨ Vice President Spiro Agnew reveals that he is under scrutiny by the FBI on charges of taking kickbacks from government contractors and resigns. President Nixon nominates Gerald R. Ford to replace him.

⇨ Juan Perón, president of Argentina from 1946 to 1955, is again elected to that post.

⇨ President Nixon agrees to turn over tape recordings of conversations that might have some bearing on the Watergate break-in.

⇨ In retaliation for supporting Israel in the Yom Kippur War, Arab nations place an embargo on oil shipments to the United States. The federal energy director announces a standby gas rationing program.

⇨ O.J. Simpson, pro football player, sets a rushing record of more than 2,000 yards in a season.

SPORTS WINNERS

Baseball   The Oakland A's beat the New York Mets 4 games to 3.
Football
  NFC: The Minnesota Vikings beat the Dallas Cowboys 27–10 in Dallas.
  AFC: The Miami Dolphins beat the Oakland Raiders 27–10 in Miami.
  Super Bowl VIII: The Miami Dolphins beat the Minnesota Vikings 24–7 on January 13, 1974, Rice Stadium in Houston.
Basketball
  NBA: The New York Knicks beat the Los Angeles Lakers 4 games to 1.
  ABA: The Indiana Pacers beat the Kentucky Colonels 4 games to 3.
Hockey   The Montreal Canadiens beat the Chiccago Black Hawks 4 games to 2.

MUSIC HIGHLIGHTS OF 1973

⇨ On Monday, January 8, Elvis Presley's 38th birthday, he sues his wife Priscilla for divorce. One week later is the television event of the year. Elvis returns to the scene of his earlier triumphs, Hawaii, to do a benefit for the battleship *Arizona*. His first TV special in over four years, the show is broadcast worldwide via satellite to over a billion viewers. The entire concert is recorded live at the Honolulu International Center on Sunday, January 14, 12:30 A.M. and beamed live to Japan, New Zealand, Australia, Korea, Thailand, South Vietnam, and the Philippines. Europe sees it the next day, but America has to wait until Wednesday, April 4. This was rock 'n' roll's biggest viewing audience ever.

⇨ Helen Reddy becomes the host of NBC-TV's new late-night Friday night concert series called *Midnight Special*.

⇨ Roberta Flack releases "Killing Me Softly With His Song," based on a Lori Lieberman poem inspired by Lieberman's seeing Don McLean at a singing engagement in Los Angeles.

⇨ In March, Pink Floyd releases the landmark album *Dark Side Of The Moon*. It would remain on *Billboard* magazine's album charts for 741 weeks (15½ years), easily surpassing the previous longevity record of 490 weeks for *Johnny's Greatest Hits* by Johnny Mathis.

⇨ "Country rock" is big, thanks to acts like the Allman Brothers Band, ZZ Top, Lynyrd Skynyrd, and the Marshall Tucker Band.

⇨ Clive Davis, President of Columbia Records, is fired for misappropriating funds.

⇨ After years of singing together as the Everly Brothers, Don and Phil decide to call it quits and go their separate ways.

⇨ A summertime rock festival at Watkins Glen Raceway in New York draws rock's biggest all-time crowd, over 600,000 fans.

⇨ In August, Stevie Wonder, touring the South, is involved in a serious automobile accident that almost claims his life.

⇨ On Thursday, October 11, Elvis and Priscilla Presley's divorce becomes final.

⇨ The government requires that all radios installed in new American cars be capable of receiving both AM and FM.

⇨ After two years of retirement, Frank Sinatra returns to performing under the billing "Ol' Blue Eyes Is Back."

⇨ Thirty-year-old record executive David Geffen launches Asylum Records.

DEBUT ARTISTS OF 1973

MAJOR ARTISTS	Debut Single	Label
Aerosmith (Steve Tyler, Joe Perry, Brad Whitford, Tom Hamilton, Joey Kramer)	Dream On	Columbia
Bachman-Turner Overdrive (Randy, Robin, and Timothy Bachman, Fred "C.F." Turner)	Blue Collar	Mercury
Cheech & Chong (Richard Marin, Tommy Chong)	Basketball Jones Featuring Tyrone Shoelaces	Ode
The Charlie Daniels Band	Uneasy Rider	Kama Sutra
The Electric Light Orchestra (Jeff Lynne, Richard Tandy, Michael Edwards, Colin Walker, Wilf Gibson, Michael Alberquerque, Bev Bevan)	Roll Over Beethoven	United Artists
Art Garfunkel	All I Know	Columbia
David Gates	Clouds	Elektra
Maureen McGovern	The Morning After ☆ ⑥	20th Century
Pink Floyd (David Gilmour, Rick Wright, Roger Waters, Nick Mason)	Money	Harvest
The Pointer Sisters (Ruth, Anita, Bonnie, and June Pointer)	Yes We Can Can	Blue Thumb
Smokey Robinson	Sweet Harmony	Tamla

Aerosmith (top l to r: Joe Perry, Brad Whitford, Tom Hamilton, Joey Kramer; bottom: Steve Tyler)

Jim Stafford	Swamp Witch	MGM
Tavares (Antone "Chubby," Feliciano "Butch," Ralph, Perry "Tiny," Arthur "Pooch," and Vic Tavares)	Check It Out	Capitol
10cc (Lol Creme, Eric Stewart, Graham Gouldman, Kevin Godley)	Rubber Bullets	UK
Joe Walsh	Rocky Mountain Way	Dunhill
Barry White	I'm Gonna Love You Just A Little More Baby ⑥	20th Century

OTHER ARTISTS

Gregg Allman
Black Oak Arkansas
Bloodstone
Roger Daltrey
The DeFranco Family
Deodato
Les Emmerson
David Essex
The First Choice
Focus
Clint Holmes
The Hues Corporation
Vicki Lawrence

The Love Unlimited Orchestra
New York City
Marie Osmond
Lou Reed
Skylark
Stealer's Wheel
B.W. Stevenson
Jud Strunk
Foster Sylvers
Sylvia
Loudon Wainright III
Dottie West
Hank Wilson

HITS OF 1973

JANUARY

Control Of Me	Les Emmerson	Lion
⑥ The Cover Of "Rolling Stone"	Dr. Hook & the Medicine Show	Columbia
Danny's Song	Anne Murray	Capitol
Dead Skunk	Loudon Wainwright III	Columbia
Don't Cross The River	America	Warner Bros.
⑥ Dueling Banjos	Eric Weissberg & Steve Mandel	Warner Bros.
Hummingbird	Seals & Crofts	Warner Bros.
I Got Ants In My Pants	James Brown	Polydor

**Bachman-Turner Overdrive
(l to r: Randy Bachman, Blair
Thornton, Robin Bachman, Fred
Turner)**

Black Oak Arkansas (top l to r: "Little Jimmie" Henderson, Stanley Knight; bottom l to r: Pat Daugherty, Rick Reynolds, Jim Dandy, Tommy Aldridge)

1973

☆ ⑥ Killing Me Softly With His Song	Roberta Flack	Atlantic
⑥ Little Willy	The Sweet	Bell
☆ ⑥ Love Train	The O'Jays	Philadelphia Int'l
⑥ Neither One Of Us (Wants To Be The First To Say Goodbye)	Gladys Knight & the Pips	Soul
Rosalie	Sam Neely	Capitol
Space Oddity	David Bowie	RCA
Today I Started Loving You Again	Bettye Swan	Atlantic

FEBRUARY

⑥ Ain't No Woman (Like The One I've Got)	The Four Tops	Dunhill
Also Sprach Zarathustra (2001)	Deodato	CTI
Aubrey	Bread	Elektra
⑥ Break Up To Make Up	The Stylistics	Avco
⑥ Call Me (Come Back Home)	Al Green	Hi
⑥ Drift Away	Dobie Gray	Decca
⑥ Funky Worm	The Ohio Players	Westbound
I'm Just A Singer (In A Rock And Roll Band)	The Moody Blues	Threshold
Masterpiece	The Temptations	Gordy
☆ ⑥ The Night The Lights Went Out In Georgia	Vicki Lawrence	Bell
Sail On Sailor	The Beach Boys	Reprise
⑥ Sing	The Carpenters	A & M
Stir It Up	Johnny Nash	Epic
☆ ⑥ Tie A Yellow Ribbon Round The Ole Oak Tree	Dawn	Bell
Wildflower	Skylark	Capitol

MARCH

⑥ Cisco Kid	War	United Artists
☆ ⑥ Frankenstein	The Edgar Winter Group	Epic
Hearts Of Stone	The Blue Ridge Rangers	Fantasy
Hocus Pocus	Focus	Sire

269

The Electric Light Orchestra
(top l to r: *Melvyn Gale*, *Hugh McDowell*, *Bev Bevan*, *Jeff Lynne*, *Richard Tandy*, *Kelly Groucutt*;
bottom: *Mik Kaminski*)

	If We Try	Don McLean	United Artists
	Out Of The Question	Gilbert O'Sullivan	MAM
⑥	Pillow Talk	Sylvia	Vibration
⑥	Playground In My Mind	Clint Holmes	Epic
	Reeling In The Years	Steely Dan	ABC
	The Right Thing To Do	Carly Simon	Elektra
⑥	Stuck In The Middle With You	Stealer's Wheel	A & M
	Thinking Of You	Loggins & Messina	Columbia
⑥	The Twelfth Of Never	Donny Osmond	MGM
☆ ⑥	Will It Go Round In Circles	Billy Preston	A & M
☆ ⑥	You Are The Sunshine Of My Life	Stevie Wonder	Tamla

APRIL

	And I Love You So	Perry Como	RCA
☆ ⑥	Bad, Bad Leroy Brown	Jim Croce	ABC
⑥	Behind Closed Doors	Charlie Rich	Epic
⑥	Daniel	Elton John	MCA
	Drinking Wine Spo-Dee O'Dee	Jerry Lee Lewis	Mercury
⑥	Give Your Baby A Standing Ovation	The Dells	Cadet
⑥	Leaving Me	The Independents	Wand
	Long Train Running	The Doobie Brothers	Warner Bros.
☆ ⑥	My Love	Paul McCartney & Wings	Apple
⑥	Natural High	Bloodstone	London
⑥	One Of A Kind (Love Affair)	The Spinners	Atlantic
	Right Place, Wrong Time	Dr. John	Atco
	Steamroller Blues	Elvis Presley	RCA
⑥	Why Me?	Kris Kristofferson	Monument
	You Can't Always Get What You Want	The Rolling Stones	London

MAY

	Boogie Woogie Bugle Boy	Bette Midler	Atlantic
	California Saga (On My Way To Sunny California)	The Beach Boys	Reprise
⑥	Diamond Girl	Seals & Crofts	Warner Bros.
	Dueling Tubas	Martin Mull	Capricorn

☆ ⑥	Give Me Love (Give Me Peace On Earth)	George Harrison	Apple
	Hey You! Get Off My Mountain	The Dramatics	Volt
	Kodachrome	Paul Simon	Columbia
	Money	Pink Floyd	Harvest
⑥	Monster Mash *(re-entry)*	Bobby "Boris" Pickett	Parrot
⑥	Shambala	Three Dog Night	Dunhill
⑥	Smoke On The Water	Deep Purple	Warner Bros.
	Swamp Witch	Jim Stafford	MGM
	What About Me	Anne Murray	Capitol
	With A Child's Heart	Michael Jackson	Motown
	You'll Never Get To Heaven (If You Break My Heart)	The Stylistics	Avco

JUNE

	Are You Man Enough	The Four Tops	Dunhill
☆ ⑥	Brother Louie	The Stories	Kama Sutra
☆ ⑥	Delta Dawn	Helen Reddy	Capitol
⑥	Doin It To Death	Fred Wesley & the J.B.'s	People
	Feelin' Stronger Every Day	Chicago	Columbia
⑥	Get Down	Gilbert O'Sullivan	MAM
	How Can I Tell Her	Lobo	Big Tree
⑥	I Believe In You (You Believe In Me)	Johnnie Taylor	Stax
⑥	If You Want Me To Stay	Sly & the Family Stone	Epic
	I'll Always Love My Mama	The Intruders	Gamble
☆ ⑥	The Morning After	Maureen McGovern	20th Century
	Tequila Sunrise	The Eagles	Asylum
☆ ⑥	Touch Me In The Morning	Diana Ross	Motown
	Watergate	Dickie Goodman	Rainy Wednesday
⑥	Yesterday Once More	The Carpenters	A & M

JULY

	Angel	Aretha Franklin	Atlantic
	Bongo Rock	The Incredible Bongo Band	MGM
	Clouds	David Gates	Elektra
	Didn't I	Sylvia	Vibration
	Gypsy Man	War	United Artists
⑥	Here I Am (Come And Take Me)	Al Green	Hi
☆ ⑥	Let's Get It On	Marvin Gaye	Tamla
⑥	Live And Let Die	Wings	Apple
	A Million To One/Young Love	Donny Osmond	MGM
	My Maria	B.W. Stevenson	RCA
⑥	Say, Has Anybody Seen My Sweet Gypsy Rose?	Dawn	Bell
	Smoke, Smoke, Smoke (That Cigarette)	Commander Cody & His Lost Planet Airmen	Paramount
	Sylvia	Focus	Sire
⑥	That Lady (Part 1)	The Isley Brothers	T-Neck
☆ ⑥	We're An American Band	Grand Funk	Capitol

271

ROCK ON ALMANAC

Lou Reed

AUGUST

	Ashes To Ashes	The 5th Dimension	Bell
	China Grove	The Doobie Brothers	Warner Bros.
	Ghetto Child	The Spinners	Atlantic
☆ ⑥	Half-Breed	Cher	MCA
	Hey Girl (I Like Your Style)	The Temptations	Gordy
	Higher Ground	Stevie Wonder	Tamla
☆ ⑥	Keep On Truckin'	Eddie Kendricks	Tamla
⑥	Loves Me Like A Rock	Paul Simon	Columbia
	Muskrat Love	America	Warner Bros.
	Ramblin' Man	The Allman Brothers Band	Capricorn
⑥	Saturday Night's Alright For Fighting	Elton John	MCA
	Sexy, Sexy, Sexy	James Brown	Polydor
	Twistin' The Night Away	Rod Stewart	Mercury
	You're The Best Thing That Ever Happened To Me	Ray Price	Columbia
	You've Never Been This Far Before	Conway Twitty	MCA

SEPTEMBER

	All I Know	Art Garfunkel	Columbia
☆ ⑥	Angie	The Rolling Stones	Rolling Stones
	Basketball Jones Featuring Tyrone Shoelaces	Cheech & Chong	Ode
⑥	Heartbeat-It's A Lovebeat	The DeFranco Family	20th Century
⑥	Just You And Me	Chicago	Columbia
	Knockin' On Heaven's Door	Bob Dylan	Columbia
⑥	The Love I Lost (Part 1)	Harold Melvin & the Blue Notes	Philadelphia Int'l
☆ ⑥	Midnight Train To Georgia	Gladys Knight & the Pips	Buddah
☆ ⑥	The Most Beautiful Girl	Charlie Rich	Epic
	Outlaw Man	The Eagles	Asylum
⑥	Paper Roses	Marie Osmond	MGM
	Raised On Rock/For Ol' Times Sake	Elvis Presley	RCA
	Rubber Bullets	10cc	UK

272

⑥ Space Race	Billy Preston	A & M
We May Never Pass This Way Again	Seals & Crofts	Warner Bros.

OCTOBER

Cheaper To Keep Her	Johnnie Taylor	Stax
Corazon	Carole King	Ode
Dream On	Aerosmith	Columbia
⑥ Goodbye Yellow Brick Road	Elton John	MCA
Hello, It's Me	Todd Rundgren	Bearsville
⑥ If You're Ready (Come Go With Me)	The Staple Singers	Stax
I Got A Name	Jim Croce	ABC
☆ ⑥ The Joker	Steve Miller	Capitol
⑥ Never, Never Gonna Give Ya Up	Barry White	20th Century
☆ ⑥ Photograph	Ringo Starr	Apple
Rockin' Roll Baby	The Stylistics	Avco
☆ ⑥ Show And Tell	Al Wilson	Rocky Road
⑥ Smokin' In The Boys' Room	Brownsville Station	Big Tree
☆ ⑥ Top Of The World	The Carpenters	A & M
You're A Special Part Of Me	Diana Ross & Marvin Gaye	Motown

NOVEMBER

Come Get To This	Marvin Gaye	Tamla
Frisky	Sly & the Family Stone	Epic
Helen Wheels	Paul McCartney & Wings	Apple
⑥ I've Got To Use My Imagination	Gladys Knight & the Pips	Buddah
⑥ Leave Me Alone (Ruby Red Dress)	Helen Reddy	Capitol
⑥ Let Me Be There	Olivia Newton-John	MCA
Living In The City	Stevie Wonder	Tamla
Mind Games	John Lennon	Apple
⑥ Rock On	David Essex	Columbia
Smarty Pants	First Choice	Philly Groove
⑥ Spiders And Snakes	Jim Stafford	MGM
☆ ⑥ Time In A Bottle	Jim Croce	ABC
⑥ Until You Come Back To Me (That's What I'm Gonna Do)	Aretha Franklin	Atlantic
☆ ⑥ The Way We Were	Barbra Streisand	Columbia
Who's In The Strawberry Patch With Sally	Dawn	Bell

DECEMBER

American Tune	Paul Simon	Columbia
Blue Collar	Bachman-Turner Overdrive	Mercury
A Fool Such As I	Bob Dylan	Columbia
Hangin' Around	The Edgar Winter Group	Epic

273

	I Love	Tom T. Hall	Mercury
	It May Be Winter Outside (But In My Heart It's Spring)	Love Unlimited	20th Century
	Jim Dandy	Black Oak Arkansas	Atco
	Livin' For You	Al Green	Hi
	Love, Reign O'er Me	The Who	MCA
	A Love Song	Anne Murray	Capitol
☆ Ⓖ	Love's Theme	The Love Unlimited Orchestra	20th Century
	Showdown	The Electric Light Orchestra	United Artists
	Stoned To The Bone	James Brown	Polydor
	Will You Love Me Tomorrow	Melanie	Neighborhood
☆ Ⓖ	You're Sixteen	Ringo Starr	Apple

TOP SINGLES OF 1973

Ⓖ	Bad, Bad Leroy Brown	Jim Croce	ABC
Ⓖ	Brother Louie	Stories	Kama Sutra
Ⓖ	Crocodile Rock	Elton John	MCA
Ⓖ	Killing Me Softly With His Song	Roberta Flack	Atlantic
Ⓖ	Let's Get It On	Marvin Gaye	Tamla
Ⓖ	Midnight Train To Georgia	Gladys Knight & the Pips	Buddah
Ⓖ	My Love	Paul McCartney & Wings	Apple
Ⓖ	Tie A Yellow Ribbon Round The Ole Oak Tree	Dawn	Bell
Ⓖ	Top Of The World	The Carpenters	A & M
Ⓖ	You're So Vain	Carly Simon	Elektra

TOP ALBUMS OF 1973

Ⓟ	Aloha From Hawaii Via Satellite	Elvis Presley	RCA
Ⓟ	Billion Dollar Babies	Alice Cooper	Warner Bros.
Ⓖ	Brothers And Sisters	The Allman Brothers Band	Capricorn
Ⓟ	Dark Side Of The Moon	Pink Floyd	Harvest
Ⓖ	Don't Shoot Me I'm Only The Piano Player	Elton John	MCA

Smokey Robinson   **Barry White**

Ⓖ **Goats Head Soup**   The Rolling Stones   Rolling Stones
Ⓖ **Goodbye Yellow Brick Road**   Elton John   MCA
Ⓖ **No Secrets**   Carly Simon   Elektra
Ⓟ **There Goes Rhymin' Simon**   Paul Simon   Columbia
Ⓖ **The World Is A Ghetto**   War   United Artists

1973

GRAMMY WINNERS IN 1973

The Grammys were televised from the Hollywood Palladium in Hollywood on Saturday, March 2, 1974. Andy Williams was the host.

Record of the Year: "Killing Me Softly With His Song," Roberta Flack (Atlantic)
Song of the Year: "Killing Me Softly With His Song" (lyrics by Norman Gimbel and music by Charles Fox)
Album of the Year: *Innervisions,* Stevie Wonder (Tamla)
Best Pop Vocal Performance, Female: "Killing Me Softly With His Song," Roberta Flack (Atlantic)
Best Pop Vocal Performance, Male: "You Are The Sunshine Of My Life," Stevie Wonder (Tamla)
Best Pop Vocal Performance, Group: "Neither One Of Us (Wants To Be The First To Say Goodbye)," Gladys Knight & the Pips (Soul)
Best New Artist of the Year: Bette Midler
Best Comedy Performance: *Los Cochinos,* Cheech & Chong (Ode)
Best Soundtrack Album from a Motion Picture or Television: *Jonathan Livingston Seagull,* Neil Diamond (Columbia)

DEATHS IN 1973

MUSIC PERFORMERS AND MUSIC INDUSTRY NOTABLES WHO DIED IN 1973

Ron "Pig-Pen" McKernan (The Grateful Dead) Thursday, March 8 (liver ailment; 26)
Vaughn Monroe, Monday, May 21 (died in hospital after surgery; 61)
Paul Williams (The Temptations) Friday, August 17 (suicide; 34)
Hugo Winterhalter, Monday, September 17 (cancer; 63)

Jim Croce, Thursday, September 20 (plane crash; 30)
Gene Krupa, Tuesday, October 16 (leukemia; 64)
Allan Sherman, Wednesday, November 21 (respiratory failure; 49)
Bobby Darin, Thursday, December 20 (heart failure; 37)

OTHERS WHO DIED IN 1973

David Ben Gurion
Lon Chaney, Jr.
Noel Coward
John Ford
Betty Grable

Lyndon B. Johnson
Pablo Picasso
Edward G. Robinson
Robert Ryan

MOVIES OF 1973

MOVIES FEATURING POP MUSIC ARTISTS

Godspell *Stars:* Victor Garber, David Haskell, Jerry Sroka. *Featured song:* "Day By Day," sung by the cast.
Jesus Christ, Superstar *Stars:* Ted Neeley, Yvonne Elliman, Carl Anderson, Josh Mostel. *Featured song:* "I Don't Know How To Love Him" by Yvonne Elliman.

275

ROCK ON ALMANAC

10cc (clockwise from top: **Graham Gouldman, Eric Stewart, Kevin Godley, Lol Creme)**

That'll Be the Day   *Stars:* David Essex, Rosemary Leach, Keith Moon, Ringo Starr, Billy Fury. *Featured song:* "Rock On" by David Essex. Also contains many classic American hits from the fifties and early sixties.

POP MUSIC CONCERTS ON FILM

Jimi Hendrix   A full documentary of the life and music of Hendrix, featuring rare clips of many of his shows and interviews over the years.

Let the Good Times Roll   Oldies concert promoter Richard Nader assembled many rock legends for concerts at New York's Madison Square Garden and Long Island's Nassau Coliseum. Among those performing were Chuck Berry, the Shirelles, Bo Diddley, Fats Domino, Danny & the Juniors, Chubby Checker, Little Richard, the Coasters, Bill Haley & His Comets, and the Five Satins.

The London Rock and Roll Show   Filmed at London's Wembley Stadium, the show featured interviews and performances by Bill Haley & His Comets, Chuck Berry, Bo Diddley, Little Richard, and Jerry Lee Lewis.

Save the Children   A concert put together to raise money for Jesse Jackson's PUSH (People United to Save Humanity) campaign in Chicago. Performers included Marvin Gaye, Bill Withers, Jerry Butler, Curtis Mayfield, the Main Ingredient, the Temptations, Gladys Knight & the Pips, Roberta Flack, and the O'Jays.

Wattstax   Richard Pryor hosted this benefit concert for the Los Angeles community of Watts. Stax Records assembled the show, which included Isaac Hayes, Carla Thomas, Rufus Thomas, Kim Weston, the Bar-Kays, the Dramatics, Luther Ingram, Albert King, the Staple Singers, and Jimmy Jones.

Pink Floyd, **The Dark Side Of The Moon** *album cover*

American Graffiti *soundtrack album cover*

MOVIES FEATURING A POP MUSIC SOUNDTRACK

American Graffiti   *Stars:* Richard Dreyfuss, Ron Howard, Paul Le Mat, Charles Martin Smith, Cindy Williams, Candy Clark, Harrison Ford, Suzanne Sommers, MacKenzie Phillips, Wolfman Jack. Features dozens of top oldies from the fifties and early sixties.

Jonathan Livingston Seagull   This film about a seagull from the bird's point of view is enhanced by Neil Diamond's score.

Mean Streets   *Stars:* Robert De Niro, Harvey Keitel, David Proval, Amy Robinson. This film about New York's Little Italy is laced with some of the biggest hits of the fifties and early sixties.

OTHER POPULAR MOVIES OF 1973

Bang the Drum Slowly
The Exorcist
The Last Detail
Last Tango in Paris
Live and Let Die
The Paper Chase
Paper Moon

Save the Tiger
Serpico
Sleeper
The Sting
Walking Tall
The Way We Were

ACADEMY AWARD WINNERS OF 1973

Best Actor: Jack Lemmon, *Save the Tiger*
Best Actress: Glenda Jackson, *A Touch of Class*
Best Picture: *The Sting*
Best Song: "The Way We Were," *The Way We Were* (music by Marvin Hamlisch, lyrics by Alan & Marilyn Bergman)

TOP TELEVISION SHOWS OF 1973

All in the Family
Cannon
Hawaii Five-O
Kojak
The Mary Tyler Moore Show

M*A*S*H
Maude
Sanford and Son
The Sonny and Cher Comedy Hour
The Waltons

1974

NEWS HIGHLIGHTS OF 1974

1974

⇨ Patty Hearst, daughter of multimillionaire publisher Randolph Hearst, is abducted by the so-called Symbionese Liberation Army and held for ransom. None is paid, and weeks later Hearst is seen helping her captors rob a San Francisco bank. She is later captured and sent to jail for the crime.

⇨ The worst disaster in aviation history occurs near Paris when a jumbo jet crashes, killing all 345 passengers and crew.

⇨ *People* magazine debuts with Mia Farrow on the cover and launches the era of celebrity journalism.

⇨ Henry "Hank" Aaron hits his historic 715th home run, breaking the record set by Babe Ruth.

⇨ Streaking—running naked for a few moments in a public place—becomes a fad.

⇨ Golda Meir resigns as premier of Israel.

⇨ Aristocrat Valéry Giscard d'Estaing is elected president of France.

⇨ Leading Soviet ballet dancer Mikhail Baryshnikov defects to the West.

⇨ Faced with impeachment over his role in the Watergate affair, President Nixon resigns, to be succeeded by Vice President Ford.

⇨ With a one-stroke victory over Jack Nicklaus, Lee Trevino captures the Professional Golfers' Association championship.

⇨ President Ford pardons former President Nixon.

⇨ Muhammad Ali knocks out George Foreman and regains his heavyweight title.

⇨ The use of telephone answering machines becomes popular.

SPORTS WINNERS

Baseball   The Oakland A's beat the Los Angeles Dodgers 4 games to 1.

Football

NFC: The Minnesota Vikings beat the Los Angeles Rams 14–10 in Minneapolis.

AFC: The Pittsburgh Steelers beat the Oakland Raiders 24–13 in Oakland.

Super Bowl IX: The Pittsburgh Steelers beat the Minnesota Vikings 16–6 on January 12, 1975, at Tulane Stadium in New Orleans.

Basketball

NBA: The Boston Celtics beat the Milwaukee Bucks 4 games to 3.

ABA: The New York Nets beat the Utah Stars 4 games to 1.

Hockey   The Philadelphia Flyers beat the Boston Bruins 4 games to 2.

MUSIC HIGHLIGHTS OF 1974

⇨ On Wednesday, January 30, Bob Dylan makes his first New York appearance in eight years, at Madison Square Garden.

⇨ On Tuesday, February 12, the New York rock club the Bottom Line opens. This 450-seat night club would become a showplace for the biggest names in rock 'n' roll.

⇨ On Tuesday, February 19, Dick Clark launches the American Music Awards. This 90-minute special, seen on the ABC television network and broadcast from the Aquarius Theater in Hollywood, was hosted by Helen Reddy, Roger Miller, and Smokey Robinson.

⇨ Jefferson Airplane members Marty Balin, Grace Slick, Paul Kantner, and David Freiberg form a new group that they will call the Jefferson Starship.

⇨ Over 200,000 fans flock to see the California Jam Rock Festival, which is taped as a TV special.

⇨ Sly Stone, of Sly & the Family Stone, is married on the stage of Madison Square Garden in New York. The marriage would last only six months.

⇨ Rock 'n' roll's biggest all-time seller, "(We're Gonna) Rock Around The Clock" by Bill Haley & His Comets, is re-released and becomes a major hit all over again.

⇨ The Ramones begin playing popular New York clubs like CBGB. Their brand of rock 'n'

Abba (l to r: Benny Andersson, Annifrid "Frida" Lyngstad Andersson, Agnetha "Anna" Faltskog Ulvaeus, Bjorn Ulvaeus)

roll is pop music with silly lyrics backed by a fast and thunderous wall of power chords. This sound helps set the trend for the "punk" and "new wave" rockers of the seventies and eighties.

⇨ Eric Clapton's number one version of Bob Marley's "I Shot The Sheriff" begins to attract audiences to Marley's Jamaican reggae music.

⇨ Rick Wakeman leaves the highly successful English band Yes to embark on a solo career.

⇨ The Hues Corporation's number one hit "Rock The Boat" and George McCrae's chart-topper "Rock Your Baby" lay the foundation for a new beat that is quickly dubbed "disco." These early recordings generate a new interest in dancing to music, a trend that would really take off several years later.

⇨ J. Geils Band member Peter Wolf and actress Faye Dunaway are married in California.

⇨ George Harrison launches his own label, Dark Horse Records. He also begins touring for the first time in years.

⇨ Gary Wright leaves the band he formed, Spooky Tooth, to launch a successful solo career.

⇨ Mick Taylor leaves the Rolling Stones to join the Jack Bruce Band and is replaced by former Faces member Ron Wood.

⇨ English group Led Zeppelin, along with their manager, Peter Grant, form a new label, Swan Song Records.

DEBUT ARTISTS OF 1974

MAJOR ARTISTS	Debut Single	Label
Abba (Agnetha "Anna" Faltskog, Bjorn Ulvaeus, Benny Andersson, Annifrid "Frida" Lyngstad)	Waterloo ⑥	Atlantic
Ashford & Simpson (Nick Ashford, Valerie Simpson)	Anywhere	Warner Bros.
The Atlanta Rhythm Section (Ronnie Hammond, Barry Bailey, J.R. Cobb, Dean Daughtry, Paul Goddard, Robert Nix)	Doraville	Polydor
The Average White Band (Onnie McIntyre, Michael Rosen, Alan Gorrie, Malcom "Mollie" Duncan, Roger Ball, Steve Ferrone)	Pick Up The Pieces ☆ ⑥	Atlantic
Bad Company (Paul Rodgers, Michael Ralphs, Simon Kirke, Raymond "Boz" Burrell)	Can't Get Enough	Swan Song

The Blackbyrds (Allan Banes, Barney Perry, Kevin Toney, Joseph Hall III, Pericles Jacobs, Jr., Keith Killgo)	Do It, Fluid	Fantasy
B.T. Express (William Risbrook, Louis Risbrook, Richard Thompson, Barbara Joyce Lamas, Orlando "Terrell" Woods, Carlos Ward, Dennis Rowe, Michael Jones)	Do It ('Till You're Satisfied) ⑥	Roadshow
Jimmy Buffet	Come Monday	ABC
The Commodores (Lionel Richie, Walter "Clyde" Orange, Thomas McClary, Ronald La Pread, William King, Milan Williams)	Machine Gun	Motown
Gene Cotton	Sunshine Roses	Myrrh
Gloria Gaynor	Never Can Say Goodbye	MGM
Mickey Gilley	Room Full Of Roses	Playboy
Golden Earring (George Kooymans, Barry Hay, Rinus Gerritsen, Cesar Zuiderwijk)	Radar Love	Track
Hall & Oates (Daryl Hall, John Oates)	She's Gone	Atlantic
Jefferson Starship (Grace Slick, Marty Balin, Paul Kantner, David Freiberg, Pete Sears, Craig Chaquico, John Barbata)	Ride The Tiger	Grunt
Billy Joel	Piano Man	Columbia
Kiss (Ace Frehley, Paul Stanley, Gene Simmons, Peter Criss)	Kissin' Time	Casablanca
Lynyrd Skynyrd (Ronnie Van Zant, Ed King, Allen Collins, Gary Rossington, Leon Wilkeson, William Powell, Robert Burns)	Sweet Home Alabama	MCA
Barry Manilow	Mandy ☆ ⑥	Bell
Dolly Parton	Jolene	RCA
Suzi Quatro	All Shook Up	Bell
Rufus (Paulette McWilliams, Al Ciner, Kevin Murphy, Ron Stocker, Dennis Belfield, Andre Fischer)	Tell Me Something Good ⑥	ABC
Gino Vannelli	People Gotta Move	A & M
Wet Willie (James Hall, Rick Hirsch, John Anthony, Jack Hall, Lewis Ross, Donna Hall, Ella Avery)	Keep On Smilin'	Capricorn

The Average White Band (l to r: Roger Ball, Alan Gorrie, Onnie McIntyre, Steve Ferrone, Malcolm Duncan, Hamish Stuart)

ROCK ON ALMANAC

OTHER ARTISTS

Hoyt Axton
Elvin Bishop
Blue Magic
Blue Swede
Johnny Bristol
Polly Brown
Rick Derringer
William De Vaughn
Disco-Tex & the Sex-o-Lettes
Bo Donaldson & the Heywoods
Carl Douglas
Carol Douglas
Ecstacy, Passion & Pain
Fancy
First Class
Flash Cadillac & the Continental Kids
Graham Central Station
Marvin Hamlisch
Herbie Hancock
The Hudson Brothers
Terry Jacks

Sammy Johns
The Joneses
Dave Loggins
Byron MacGregor
C.W. McCall
George McCrae
Sister Janet Mead
MFSB
Mocedades
Maria Muldaur
Mike Oldfield
The Ozark Mountain Daredevils
Paper Lace
Parliament
Prelude
Reunion
Gordon Sinclair
The Souther-Hillman-Furay Band
Billy Swan
Frank Zappa

HITS OF 1974

JANUARY

⑥ Americans	Byron MacGregor	Westbound
Americans	Gordon Sinclair	Avco
⑥ Boogie Down	Eddie Kendricks	Tamla
Doo Doo Doo Doo Doo (Heartbreaker)	The Rolling Stones	Rolling Stones
Hello It's Me	Todd Rundgren	Bearsville
I Got A Name	Jim Croce	ABC
⑥ Jungle Boogie	Kool & the Gang	De-Lite
Keep Your Head To The Sky	Earth, Wind & Fire	Columbia
Last Time I Saw Him	Diana Ross	Motown
Let Your Hair Down	The Temptations	Gordy
Painted Ladies	Ian Thomas	Janus
This Time I'm Gone For Good	Bobby "Blue" Bland	Dunhill
Walk Like A Man	Grand Funk	Capitol

Jimmy Buffet

The Commodores (l to r: Thomas McClary, Milan Williams, Ronald La Pread, Walter Orange, Lionel Richie, William King; photo: Kriegsmann)

1974

Who's In The Strawberry Patch With Sally	Tony Orlando & Dawn	Bell
W.O.L.D.	Harry Chapin	Elektra

FEBRUARY

☆ ⑥	Bennie And The Jets	Elton John	MCA
⑥	Best Thing That Ever Happened To Me	Gladys Knight & the Pips	Buddah
⑥	Come And Get Your Love	Redbone	Epic
⑥	Dark Lady	Cher	MCA
	Eres Tu (Touch The Wind)	Mocedades	Tara
☆ ⑥	Hooked On A Feeling	Blue Swede	EMI
	Jet	Paul McCartney & Wings	Apple
	Jolene	Dolly Parton	RCA
⑥	Just Don't Want To Be Lonely	The Main Ingredient	RCA
⑥	Lookin' For A Love	Bobby Womack	United Artists
⑥	Mockingbird	Carly Simon & James Taylor	Elektra
☆ ⑥	Seasons In The Sun	Terry Jacks	Bell
	Sexy Mama	The Moments	Stang
☆ ⑥	Sunshine On My Shoulders	John Denver	RCA
	There Won't Be Anymore	Charlie Rich	RCA

MARCH

⑥	Dancing Machine	The Jackson 5	Motown
	I'll Have To Say I Love You In A Song	Jim Croce	ABC
	(I've Been) Searching So Long	Chicago	Columbia
	Keep On Singing	Helen Reddy	Capitol
☆ ⑥	The Loco-Motion	Grand Funk	Capitol
⑥	The Lord's Prayer	Sister Janet Mead	A & M
	Midnight At The Oasis	Maria Muldaur	Reprise
	Mighty Love	The Spinners	Atlantic
	Oh My My	Ringo Starr	Apple
⑥	The Payback (Part I)	James Brown	Polydor
	Piano Man	Billy Joel	Columbia
	She's Gone	Hall & Oates	Atlantic

283

☆ ⑥ TSOP	MFSB	Philadelphia Int'l
⑥ Tubular Bells	Mike Oldfield	Virgin
A Very Special Love Song	Charlie Rich	Epic

APRIL

⑥ The Air That I Breathe	The Hollies	Epic
☆ ⑥ Band On The Run	Paul McCartney & Wings	Capitol
Don't You Worry 'Bout A Thing	Stevie Wonder	Tamla
⑥ The Entertainer	Marvin Hamlisch	MCA
⑥ For The Love Of Money	The O'Jays	Philadelphia Int'l
Help Me	Joni Mitchell	Asylum
⑥ If You Love Me (Let Me Know)	Olivia Newton-John	MCA
I Won't Last A Day Without You	The Carpenters	A & M
Oh Very Young	Cat Stevens	A & M
One Hell Of A Woman	Mac Davis	Columbia
⑥ The Show Must Go On	Three Dog Night	Dunhill
☆ ⑥ The Streak	Ray Stevens	Barnaby
☆ ⑥ Sundown	Gordon Lightfoot	Reprise
⑥ You Make Me Feel Brand New	The Stylistics	Avco
You Won't See Me	Anne Murray	Capitol

MAY

Already Gone	The Eagles	Asylum
⑥ Be Thankful For What You Got	William De Vaughn	Roxbury
☆ ⑥ Billy, Don't Be A Hero	Bo Donaldson & the Heywoods	ABC
Haven't Got Time For The Pain	Carly Simon	Elektra
⑥ Hollywood Swinging	Kool & the Gang	De-Lite
I Don't See Me In Your Eyes Anymore	Charlie Rich	RCA
Kissin' Time	Kiss	Casablanca
⑥ On And On	Gladys Knight & the Pips	Buddah
Rikki, Don't Lose That Number	Steely Dan	ABC
Rock And Roll Heaven	The Righteous Brothers	Haven
☆ ⑥ Rock The Boat	The Hues Corporation	RCA
Save The Last Dance For Me	The De Franco Family	20th Century
⑥ Sideshow	Blue Magic	Atco
Son Of Sagittarius	Eddie Kendricks	Tamla
Teenage Love Affair	Rick Derringer	Blue Sky

JUNE

☆ ⑥ Annie's Song	John Denver	RCA
Call On Me	Chicago	Columbia
⑥ Don't Let The Sun Go Down On Me	Elton John	MCA
☆ ⑥ Feel Like Makin' Love	Roberta Flack	Atlantic
If You Talk In Your Sleep	Elvis Presley	RCA
I'm Coming Home	The Spinners	Atlantic
Machine Gun	The Commodores	Motown

Hall & Oates in concert (l to r: Daryl Hall, John Oates; photo: Anastasia Pantsios)

1974

☆ ⑥ **The Night Chicago Died**	Paper Lace	Mercury
Please Come To Boston	Dave Loggins	Epic
☆ ⑥ **Rock Me Gently**	Andy Kim	Capitol
☆ ⑥ **Rock Your Baby**	George McCrae	TK
Taking Care Of Business	Bachman-Turner Overdrive	Mercury
Train Of Thought	Cher	MCA
⑥ **Waterloo**	Abba	Atlantic
Workin' At The Carwash Blues	Jim Croce	ABC

JULY

Beach Baby	First Class	UK
Clap For The Wolfman	The Guess Who	RCA
Hang On In There Baby	Johnny Bristol	MGM
Happiness Is Just Around The Bend	The Main Ingredient	RCA
☆ ⑥ **I Shot The Sheriff**	Eric Clapton	RSO
Love Is The Message	MFSB	Philadelphia Int'l
Mr. President	Dickie Goodman	Rainy Wednesday
☆ ⑥ **Nothing From Nothing**	Billy Preston	A & M
Secretary	Betty Wright	Alston
Shinin' On	Grand Funk	Capitol
Sure As I'm Sitting Here	Three Dog Night	Dunhill
Time For Livin'	Sly & the Family Stone	Epic
Walk On	Neil Young	Reprise
You And Me Against The World	Helen Reddy	Capitol
☆ ⑥ **(You're) Having My Baby**	Paul Anka	United Artists

AUGUST

Another Saturday Night	Cat Stevens	A & M
Can't Get Enough	Bad Company	Swan Song
☆ ⑥ **Can't Get Enough Of Your Love, Babe**	Barry White	20th Century
Carefree Highway	Gordon Lightfoot	Reprise
☆ ⑥ **I Honestly Love You**	Olivia Newton-John	MCA
⑥ **I'm Leaving It (All) Up To You**	Donny & Marie Osmond	MGM
It's Only Rock 'N Roll	The Rolling Stones	Rolling Stones

285

ROCK ON ALMANAC

Billy Joel in concert (photo: *Anastasia Pantsios*)

Let's Put It All Together	The Stylistics	Avco
Never My Love	Blue Swede	Capitol
Sweet Home Alabama	Lynyrd Skynyrd	MCA
☆ ⑥ Then Came You	Dionne Warwick & the Spinners	Atlantic
Tin Man	America	Warner Bros.
Who Do You Think You Are	Bo Donaldson & the Heywoods	ABC
☆ ⑥ You Haven't Done Nothin'	Stevie Wonder	Tamla
You Little Trustmaker	The Tymes	RCA

SEPTEMBER

Ain't Nothing Like The Real Thing	Aretha Franklin	Atlantic
⑥ Back Home Again	John Denver	RCA
The Bitch Is Back	Elton John	MCA
⑥ Do It Baby	The Miracles	Tamla
⑥ Do It ('Til You're Satisfied)	B.T. Express	Scepter
Everlasting Love	Carl Carlton	Backbeat
☆ ⑥ I Can Help	Billy Swan	Monument
Jazzman	Carole King	Ode
Life Is A Rock (But The Radio Rolled Me)	Reunion	RCA
⑥ Sha-La-La (Makes Me Happy)	Al Green	Hi
⑥ Skin Tight	Ohio Players	Mercury
Steppin' Out (Gonna Boogie Tonight)	Tony Orlando & Dawn	Bell
Stop And Smell The Roses	Mac Davis	Columbia
Whatever Gets You Thru The Night	John Lennon with the Plastic Ono Nuclear Band	Apple
☆ ⑥ You Ain't Seen Nothing Yet	Bachman-Turner Overdrive	Mercury

OCTOBER

☆ ⑥ Angie Baby	Helen Reddy	Capitol
☆ ⑥ Cat's In The Cradle	Harry Chapin	Elektra
Devotion	Earth, Wind & Fire	Columbia

Doraville	The Atlanta Rhythm Section	Polydor
⑥ Honey Honey	Abba	Atlantic
☆ ⑥ Kung Fu Fighting	Carl Douglas	20th Century
Laughter In The Rain	Neil Sedaka	MCA
Longfellow Serenade	Neil Diamond	Columbia
⑥ My Melody Of Love	Bobby Vinton	ABC
Promised Land	Elvis Presley	RCA
Rockin' Soul	The Hues Corporation	RCA
She's Gone	Tavares	Capitol
⑥ When Will I See You Again	The Three Degrees	Philadelphia Int'l
Wishing You Were Here	Chicago	Columbia
You Got The Love	Rufus featuring Chaka Khan	ABC

NOVEMBER

Ain't Too Proud To Beg	The Rolling Stones	Rolling Stones
⑥ Boogie On Reggae Woman	Stevie Wonder	Tamla
Bungle In The Jungle	Jethro Tull	Chrysalis
Junior's Farm	Paul McCartney & Wings	Apple
☆ ⑥ Lucy In The Sky With Diamonds	Elton John	MCA
☆ ⑥ Mandy	Barry Manilow	Bell
Morning Side Of The Mountain	Donny & Marie Osmond	MGM
Must Of Got Lost	The J. Geils Band	Atlantic
Never Can Say Goodbye	Gloria Gaynor	MGM
One Man Woman/One Woman Man	Paul Anka	United Artists
Only You	Ringo Starr	Apple
☆ ⑥ Please Mr. Postman	The Carpenters	A & M
Three Ring Circus	Blue Magic	Atlantic
Willie And The Hand Jive	Eric Clapton	RSO
⑥ You're The First, The Last, My Everything	Barry White	20th Century

DECEMBER

☆ ⑥ Best Of My Love	The Eagles	Asylum
Big Yellow Taxi	Joni Mitchell	Asylum
☆ ⑥ Black Water	The Doobie Brothers	Warner Bros.
Dark Horse	George Harrison	Apple
Doctor's Orders	Carol Douglas	Midland Int'l
The Entertainer	Billy Joel	Columbia
☆ ⑥ Fire	Ohio Players	Mercury
Lady	Styx	Wooden Nickel
Lonely People	America	Warner Bros.
☆ ⑥ My Eyes Adored You	Frankie Valli	Private Stock
#9 Dream	John Lennon	Apple
☆ ⑥ Pick Up The Pieces	The Average White Band	Atlantic
Rock 'N Roll (I Gave You The Best Years Of My Life)	Mac Davis	Columbia
Some Kind Of Wonderful	Grand Funk	Capitol
☆ ⑥ You're No Good	Linda Ronstadt	Capitol

287

*Kiss in concert (photo: **Anastasia Pantsios**)*

TOP SINGLES OF 1974

⑥ Billy, Don't Be A Hero	Bo Donaldson & the Heywoods	ABC
⑥ I Can Help	Billy Swan	Monument
⑥ I Honestly Love You	Olivia Newton-John	MCA
⑥ Kung Fu Fighting	Carl Douglas	20th Century
⑥ The Loco-Motion	Grand Funk	Capitol
⑥ Seasons In The Sun	Terry Jacks	Bell
⑥ The Streak	Ray Stevens	Barnaby
⑥ TSOP	MFSB	Philadelphia Int'l
⑥ The Way We Were	Barbra Streisand	Columbia
⑥ (You're) Having My Baby	Paul Anka	United Artists

TOP ALBUMS OF 1974

⑥ Band On The Run	Paul McCartney & Wings	Apple
⑥ Caribou	Elton John	MCA
⑦ Chicago VII	Chicago	Columbia
⑥ Elton John—Greatest Hits	Elton John	MCA
⑥ 461 Ocean Boulevard	Eric Clapton	RSO

*Lynyrd Skynyrd (l to r: **Ronnie Van Zant, Allen Collins, Gary Rossington, Artemus Pyle, Leon Wilkeson, William Powell**)*

1974

Barry Manilow (photo: Lee Gurst)   **Dolly Parton**

ⓖ **If You Love Me, Let Me Know**   Olivia Newton-John   MCA
ⓖ **I Got A Name**   Jim Croce   ABC
ⓖ **Not Fragile**   Bachman-Turner   Mercury
                             Overdrive
ⓖ **Planet Waves**   Bob Dylan   Columbia
ⓖ **Walls And Bridges**   John Lennon   Apple

GRAMMY WINNERS IN 1974

The Grammys were televised from the Uris Theater in New York on Saturday, March 1, 1975. Andy Williams was the host.

Record of the Year: "I Honestly Love You," Olivia Newton-John (MCA)
Song of the Year: "The Way We Were" (music by Marvin Hamlisch, lyrics by Alan & Marilyn Bergman)
Album of the Year: *Fulfillingness' First Finale,* Stevie Wonder (Tamla)
Best Pop Vocal Performance, Female: "I Honestly Love You," Olivia Newton-John (MCA)
Best Pop Vocal Performance, Male: *Fulfillingness' First Finale,* Stevie Wonder (Tamla)
Best Pop Vocal Performance, Group: "Band On The Run," Paul McCartney & Wings (Apple)
Best New Artist of the Year: Marvin Hamlisch
Best Comedy Performance: *That Nigger's Crazy,* Richard Pryor (Partee)
Best Soundtrack Album from a Motion Picture or Television: *The Way We Were,* Marvin Hamlisch and Alan & Marilyn Bergman (Columbia)

DEATHS IN 1974

MUSIC PERFORMERS AND MUSIC INDUSTRY NOTABLES WHO DIED IN 1974

Tex Ritter, Thursday, January 3 (heart attack; 67)
Cyril Stapleton, Monday, February 25 (natural causes; 60)
Bobby Bloom, Thursday, February 28 (gunshot; 33)
Duke Ellington, Friday, May 24 (lung cancer; 75)

Mama Cass (Elliott), Monday, July 29 (choking; 30)
Robbie McIntosh (The Average White Band), Monday, September 23 (drug overdose; 30)
Ivory Joe Hunter, Friday, November 8 (lung cancer; 63)

ROCK ON ALMANAC

Eric Clapton, 461 Ocean Boulevard *album cover*

OTHERS WHO DIED IN 1974

Bud Abbott
Jack Benny
Walter Brennan
Dizzy Dean
Samuel Goldwyn

Chet Huntley
Sol Hurok
Charles Lindbergh
Juan Perón
Ed Sullivan

MOVIES OF 1974

MOVIES FEATURING POP MUSIC ARTISTS

Phantom of the Paradise   *Stars:* Paul Williams, William Finley, Jessica Harper. Williams score provided no significant hits.
Son of Dracula   *Stars:* Harry Nilsson, Ringo Starr, Rosanna Lee, Freddie Jones. *Featured song:* "Without You" by Nilsson.

OTHER POPULAR MOVIES OF 1974

Airport 1975
Blazing Saddles
Chinatown
Death Wish
The Godfather, Part II
The Great Gatsby
Lenny

Monty Python and the Holy Grail
Murder on the Orient Express
The Texas Chainsaw Massacre
That's Entertainment!
The Towering Inferno
Young Frankenstein

ACADEMY AWARD WINNERS OF 1974

Best Actor: Art Carney, *Harry and Tonto*
Best Actress: Ellen Burstyn, *Alice Doesn't Live Here Anymore*
Best Picture: *The Godfather, Part II*
Best Song: "We May Never Love Like This Again," *The Towering Inferno* (music and lyrics by Al Kasha and Joel Hirschhorn)

TOP TELEVISION SHOWS OF 1974

All in the Family
Chico and the Man
Good Times
Hawaii Five-O
The Jeffersons

M*A*S*H
Maude
Rhoda
Sanford and Son
The Waltons

1975

ROCK ON ALMANAC

NEWS HIGHLIGHTS OF 1975

⇨ Angola gains its independence from Portugal after centuries of foreign rule.

⇨ John N. Mitchell, H.R. Haldeman, and John D. Ehrlichman are sentenced to prison for conspiring to obstruct justice in the Watergate investigation.

⇨ Margaret Thatcher is the first woman elected to lead Britain's Conservative Party.

⇨ King Faisal of Saudi Arabia is assassinated by a crazed nephew.

⇨ The president of South Vietnam, Duong Van Minh, surrenders to the Communists.

⇨ The busing of 21,000 students is ordered in Boston to achieve racial balance in the public schools.

⇨ Egypt reopens the Suez Canal after eight years.

⇨ President Ford escapes assassination twice within 17 days.

⇨ The Supreme Court rules that paddling of unruly students is acceptable under certain circumstances.

⇨ More than $4 million is spent on research by the National Cancer Institute to study the relationship between diet and cancer.

⇨ President Ford meets with Philippine President Ferdinand Marcos in Manila to renew American use of strategic air and naval bases in the Philippines.

SPORTS WINNERS

Baseball   The Cincinnati Reds beat the Boston Red Sox 4 games to 3.

Football

NFC: The Dallas Cowboys beat the Los Angeles Rams 37–7 in Los Angeles.

AFC: The Pittsburgh Steelers beat the Oakland Raiders 16–10 in Pittsburgh.

Super Bowl X: The Pittsburgh Steelers beat the Dallas Cowboys 21–17 on January 18, 1976, at the Orange Bowl in Miami.

Basketball

NBA: Golden State beat the Washington Bullets 4 games to 0.

ABA: The Kentucky Colonels beat the Indiana Pacers 4 games to 1.

Hockey   The Philadelphia Flyers beat the Buffalo Sabres 4 games to 2.

MUSIC HIGHLIGHTS OF 1975

⇨ Linda Ronstadt's album *Heart Like A Wheel* zooms to number one on the national charts. It also produces her first number one hit single, "You're No Good."

⇨ Riding Elton John's wave of popularity, his label, MCA Records, re-releases his first album from 1969, *Empty Sky,* and it becomes a hit.

⇨ New albums carry four established acts to even loftier heights of popularity and respect:

The Bay City Rollers (l to r: Eric Faulkner, Derek Longmuir, Stuart Wood, Leslie McKeown)

292

Bob Dylan's *Blood On The Tracks* and Chicago's *Chicago VIII* on Columbia, John Lennon's *Rock 'N' Roll* on Apple, and Led Zeppelin's *Physical Graffiti* on Swan Song.

⇨ *The Wiz,* a contemporary version of *The Wizard of Oz,* opens on Broadway.

⇨ Producer and songwriter Van McCoy, who wrote songs like "Baby I'm Yours" for Barbara Lewis, "When You're Young And In Love" for Ruby & the Romantics, and "Right On The Tip Of My Tongue" for Brenda & the Tabulations, scores a number one instrumental, "The Hustle." This song sparks one of the biggest dance crazes since the Twist days of the early sixties.

⇨ Elton John's *Captain Fantastic And The Brown Dirt Cowboy* enters the charts at number one and goes on to become his biggest all-time seller.

⇨ Ritchie Blackmore leaves Deep Purple and is replaced by Tommy Bolin, and Peter Gabriel leaves Genesis and is replaced by drummer Phil Collins as the group's new lead singer.

⇨ While on vacation, Robert Plant, lead singer of Led Zeppelin, is involved in a serious auto crash that almost claims his life and those of his family.

⇨ Just prior to the release of the blockbuster album *Born To Run,* Bruce Springsteen and his E Street Band perform at New York's Bottom Line club. Band members Clarence Clemons, "Miami" Steve Van Zandt, Garry Tallent, Max Weinberg, Roy Bittan, and Danny Federici bring down the house with the introduction of such tunes as "Thunder Road," "Tenth Avenue Freeze-Out," "Backstreets," "Jungleland," and "Born To Run."

⇨ Fleetwood Mac's Mick Fleetwood and John and Christine McVie are joined by new members Stevie Nicks and Lindsey Buckingham for the new album for Reprise Records titled *Fleetwood Mac.* It would become the sleeper smash album of the rock era, taking 58 weeks to reach number one on the charts.

⇨ The Captain & Tennille release their album *Love Will Keep Us Together.* The title song, written by Neil Sedaka, becomes the biggest hit single of the year.

⇨ The Bee Gees' first charted album in close to three years is titled *Main Course.* This album produces the number one disco-flavored "Jive Talkin'," a song that would change the whole image and sound of the group, foreshadowing the disco explosion they would launch in late 1977 with the album *Saturday Night Fever.*

⇨ On Thursday, October 9, John Lennon's 35th birthday, John and Yoko's son Sean is born.

⇨ On Saturday, October 11, *Saturday Night Live* premieres on NBC TV. George Carlin is the first host, and Janis Ian and Billy Preston are the first musical guests.

⇨ Rocker Bruce Springsteen appears simultaneously on the covers of both *Newsweek* and *Time* during the same week. He is the first and still the only rock star to have this distinction.

DEBUT ARTISTS OF 1975

MAJOR ARTISTS	Debut Single	Label
Ambrosia (David Pack, Joe Puerta, Burleigh Drummond)	Holdin' On To Yesterday	20th Century
The Bay City Rollers (Eric Faulkner, Leslie McKeown, Stuart Wood, Derek Longmuir, Alan Longmuir)	Saturday Night ☆ ⑥	Arista
The Captain & Tennille (Daryl Dragon, Toni Tennille)	Love Will Keep Us Together ☆ ⑥	A & M
Eric Carmen	All By Myself ⑥	Arista
Natalie Cole	This Will Be	Capitol
Freddy Fender	Before The Next Teardrop Falls ☆ ⑥	Dot
Dan Fogelberg	Part Of The Plan	Epic
John Fogerty	Rockin' All Over The World	Asylum

Hot Chocolate (Errol Brown, Harvey Hinsley, Larry Ferguson, Patrick Olive, Tony Wilson, Tony Connor)	Emma	Big Tree
K.C. & the Sunshine Band (Harry Wayne "K.C." Casey, Rick Finch, Jerome "J" Smith, Fermin Goytisolo, Ronnie Smith, Denvil Liptrot, James Weaver, Charles Williams, Robert "Shotgun" Johnson)	Get Down Tonight ☆ Ⓖ	T.K.
Melissa Manchester	Midnight Blue	Arista
The Manhattan Transfer (Tim Hauser, Janis Siegel, Alan Paul, Laurel Masse)	Operator	Atlantic
The Marshall Tucker Band (Doug Gray, Toy Caldwell, George McCorkle, Jerry Eubanks, Tommy Caldwell, Paul Riddle)	This Ol' Cowboy	Capricorn
Willie Nelson	Blue Eyes Crying In The Rain	Columbia
The Pure Prairie League (George Powell, Billy Hinds, Michael Connor, Michael Reilly, John Call, Larry Goshorn)	Amie	RCA
Queen (Freddie Mercury, Brian May, John Deacon, Roger Taylor)	Killer Queen	Elektra
Leo Sayer	Long Tall Glasses	Warner Bros.
T.G. Sheppard (Bill Browser)	Devil In The Bottle	Melodyland
Sister Sledge (Debbie, Joni, Kim, and Kathy Sledge)	Love Don't You Go Through No Changes On Me	Atco
Bruce Springsteen	Born To Run	Columbia
Donna Summer	Love To Love You Baby Ⓖ	Oasis
Supertramp (Rick Davies, Roger Hodgson, John Anthony Helliwell, Dougie Thomson, Bob C. Benberg)	Bloody Well Right	A & M
John Williams	The Theme From Jaws	MCA

OTHER ARTISTS

Ace	Greg Lake
Morris Albert	Cledus Maggard & the Citizen's Band
Benny Bell	Van McCoy
The Biddu Orchestra	Gwen McCrae
Bimbo Jet	Nazareth
Jessi Colter	Nigel Olsson
Consumer Rapport	Orleans
David Geddes	The Outlaws
Henry Gross	Pilot
Emmylou Harris	Mike Post
Major Harris	Rhythm Heritage
Head East	Minnie Riperton
Loleatta Holloway	The Ritchie Family
Susan Jacks	The Salsoul Orchestra
Jigsaw	Shirley & Company
Kraftwerk	The Silver Convention

The Captain & Tennille (l to r: Daryl "Captain" Dragon, Toni Tennille)

Eric Carmen in concert (photo: Anastasia Pantsios)

Phoebe Snow
The Gary Toms Empire
The Dwight Twilley Band

Grover Washington, Jr.
Roger Whittaker
The Wing & a Prayer Fife & Drum Corps

HITS OF 1975

JANUARY

		Chico And The Man	Jose Feliciano	RCA
		Ding Dong, Ding Dong	George Harrison	Apple
	⑥	Express	B.T. Express	Roadshow
☆	⑥	Have You Never Been Mellow	Olivia Newton-John	MCA
		I Am Love (Parts 1 & 2)	The Jackson 5	Motown
☆	⑥	Lady Marmalade	LaBelle	Epic
		Look In My Eyes Pretty Woman	Tony Orlando & Dawn	Bell
☆	⑥	Lovin' You	Minnie Riperton	Epic
		Movin' On	Bad Company	Swan Song
		Nightingale	Carole King	Ode
		Poetry Man	Phoebe Snow	Shelter
		Roll On Down The Highway	Bachman-Turner Overdrive	Mercury
		Shame, Shame, Shame	Shirley & Company	Vibration
		Up In A Puff Of Smoke	Polly Brown	Epic
		You Are So Beautiful	Joe Cocker	A & M

FEBRUARY

☆	⑥	Before The Next Teardrop Falls	Freddy Fender	ABC/Dot
	⑥	Chevy Van	Sammy Johns	GRC
		Emma	Hot Chocolate	Big Tree
		Good Times, Rock & Roll	Flash Cadillac & the Continental Kids	Private Stock
		Harry Truman	Chicago	Columbia
☆	⑥	(Hey Won't You Play) Another Somebody Done Somebody Wrong Song	B.J. Thomas	ABC

295

ROCK ON ALMANAC

Freddy Fender

Dan Fogelberg (photo: *Kriegsmann*)

		I Fought The Law	Sam Neely	A & M
		I've Been This Way Before	Neil Diamond	Columbia
		Long Tall Glasses	Leo Sayer	Warner Bros.
		Love Corporation	The Hues Corporation	RCA
		No No Song/Snookeroo	Ringo Starr	Apple
		Once You Get Started	Rufus	ABC
		Sally G	Paul McCartney & Wings	Apple
☆	Ⓖ	Shining Star	Earth, Wind & Fire	Columbia
	Ⓖ	Walking In Rhythm	The Blackbyrds	Fantasy

MARCH

		The Bertha Butt Boogie (Part 1)	The Jimmy Castor Bunch	Atlantic
☆	Ⓖ	He Don't Love You (Like I Love You)	Tony Orlando & Dawn	Elektra
		Hijack	Herbie Mann	Atlantic
		I Don't Like To Sleep Alone	Paul Anka	United Artists
		I'm Her Fool	Billy Swan	Monument
		It's A Miracle	Barry Manilow	Arista
		Jackie Blue	The Ozark Mountain Daredevils	A & M
		Leona	Wet Willie	Capricorn
	Ⓖ	L-O-V-E	Al Green	Hi
		Only Yesterday	The Carpenters	A & M
☆	Ⓖ	Philadelphia Freedom	Elton John	MCA
		Stand By Me	John Lennon	Apple
☆	Ⓖ	Thank God I'm A Country Boy	John Denver	RCA
		We're Almost There	Michael Jackson	Motown
		What Am I Gonna Do With You	Barry White	20th Century

APRIL

	Autobahn	Kraftwerk	Vertigo
	Bad Luck (Part 1)	Harold Melvin & the Blue Notes	Philadelphia Int'l
	Bad Time	Grand Funk	Capitol

296

Ease On Down The Road	Consumer Rapport	Wing & a Prayer
How Long	Ace	Anchor
The Immigrant	Neil Sedaka	Rocket
I'm Not Lisa	Jessi Colter	Capitol
I Wanna Dance Wit' Choo (Doo Dat Dance), Part 1	Disco Tex & the Sex-o-Lettes	Chelsea
☆ ⑥ **Love Will Keep Us Together**	The Captain & Tennille	A & M
⑥ **Love Won't Let Me Wait**	Major Harris	Atlantic
⑥ **Magic**	Pilot	EMI
Old Days	Chicago	Columbia
Sail On Sailor *(re-entry)*	The Beach Boys	Reprise/ Brother
☆ ⑥ **Sister Golden Hair**	America	Warner Bros.
When Will I Be Loved	Linda Ronstadt	Capitol

MAY

Attitude Dancing	Carly Simon	Elektra
⑥ **El Bimbo**	Bimbo Jet	Scepter
Hey You	Bachman-Turner Overdrive	Mercury
☆ ⑥ **The Hustle**	Van McCoy & the Soul City Symphony	Avco
I'm Not In Love	10cc	Mercury
Midnight blue	Melissa Manchester	Arista
Misty	Ray Stevens	Barnaby
The Rockford Files	Mike Post	MGM
Rockin' Chair	Gwen McCrae	Cat
Swearin' To God	Frankie Valli	Private Stock
Take Me In Your Arms (Rock Me)	The Doobie Brothers	Warner Bros.
T-R-O-U-B-L-E	Elvis Presley	RCA
The Way We Were/Try To Remember	Gladys Knight & the Pips	Buddah
⑥ **Why Can't We Be Friends?**	War	United Artists
⑥ **Wildfire**	Michael Murphey	Epic

JUNE

At Seventeen	Janis Ian	Columbia
Black Friday	Steely Dan	ABC
☆ ⑥ **Fallin' In Love**	Hamilton, Joe Frank & Reynolds	Playboy
⑥ **Feelings**	Morris Albert	RCA
How Sweet It Is (To Be Loved By You)	James Taylor	Warner Bros.
I'll Do For You Anything You Want Me To	Barry White	20th Century
☆ ⑥ **Jive Talkin'**	The Bee Gees	RSO
⑥ **Listen To What The Man Said**	Wings	Capitol
Mornin' Beautiful	Tony Orlando & Dawn	Elektra
One Of These Nights	The Eagles	Asylum
⑥ **Please Mr. Please**	Olivia Newton-John	MCA
☆ ⑥ **Rhinestone Cowboy**	Glen Campbell	Capitol

297

Saturday Night Special	Lynyrd Skynyrd	MCA
Send In The Clowns	Judy Collins	Elektra
⑥ Wasted Days And Wasted Nights	Freddy Fender	ABC/Dot

JULY

Can't Give You Anything (But My Love)	The Stylistics	Avco
Could It Be Magic	Barry Manilow	Arista
Daisy Jane	America	Warner Bros.
Dance With Me	Orleans	Asylum
☆ ⑥ Fame	David Bowie	RCA
⑥ Fight The Power (Part 1)	The Isley Brothers	T-Neck
Help Me Rhonda	Johnny Rivers	Epic
I Believe There's Nothing Stronger Than Our Love	Paul Anka	United Artists
It Only Takes A Minute	Tavares	Capitol
It's All Down To Goodnight Vienna/Oo-Wee	Ringo Starr	Apple
⑥ Someone Saved My Life Tonight	Elton John	MCA
That's The Way Of The World	Earth, Wind & Fire	Columbia
That's When The Music Takes Me	Neil Sedaka	Rocket
Tush	ZZ Top	London
Two Fine People	Cat Stevens	A & M

AUGUST

Ain't No Way To Treat A Lady	Helen Reddy	Capitol
Brazil	The Ritchie Family	20th Century
⑥ Do It Any Way You Wanna	The People's Choice	TSOP
☆ ⑥ Get Down Tonight	K.C. & the Sunshine Band	TK
Give It What You Got	B.T. Express	Roadshow
☆ ⑥ I'm Sorry/Calypso	John Denver	RCA
I Only Have Eyes For You	Art Garfunkel	Columbia
Miracles	Jefferson Starship	Grunt
Run Joey Run	David Geddes	Big Tree
Solitaire	The Carpenters	A & M

Melissa Manchester   **Leo Sayer**

⑥ SOS	Abba	Atlantic
The Theme From Jaws	John Williams	MCA
⑥ They Just Can't Stop It The (Games People Play)	The Spinners	Atlantic
What A Diff'rence A Day Makes	Esther Phillips	Kudu
Who Loves You	The Four Seasons	Warner Bros.

SEPTEMBER

The Agony And The Ecstasy	Smokey Robinson	Tamla
☆ ⑥ Bad Blood	Neil Sedaka	Rocket
Blue Eyes Crying In The Rain	Willie Nelson	Columbia
Born To Run	Bruce Springsteen	Columbia
Low Rider	War	United Artists
Lyin' Eyes	The Eagles	Asylum
⑥ Mr. Jaws	Dickie Goodman	Cash
Operator	The Manhattan Transfer	Atlantic
Rockin' All Over The World	John Fogerty	Elektra
Salsoul Hustle	The Salsoul Orchestra	Salsoul
Sky High	Jigsaw	Chelsea
Sweet Sticky Thing	Ohio Players	Mercury
This Will Be	Natalie Cole	Capitol
You	George Harrison	Apple
You're All I Need To Get By	Tony Orlando & Dawn	Elektra

OCTOBER

☆ ⑥ Fly, Robin, Fly	The Silver Convention	Midland Int'l
Happy	Eddie Kendricks	Tamla
☆ ⑥ Island Girl	Elton John	MCA
Just A Smile	Pilot	EMI
A Lover's Question	Loggins & Messina	Columbia
Manhattan Spiritual	Mike Post	MGM
Mexico	James Taylor	Warner Bros.
Minstrel In The Gallery	Jethro Tull	Chrysalis
My Little Town	Simon & Garfunkel	Columbia
Nights On Broadway	The Bee Gees	RSO
Our Day Will Come	Frankie Valli	Private Stock
☆ ⑥ Saturday Night	The Bay City Rollers	Arista
Something Better To Do	Olivia Newton-John	MCA
Summer Of '42	The Biddu Orchestra	Epic
⑥ The Way I Want To Touch You	The Captain & Tennille	A & M

NOVEMBER

Baby Face	The Wing & a Prayer Fife & Drum Corps	Wing & a Prayer
Evil Woman	The Electric Light Orchestra	United Artists
⑥ Fox On The Run	The Sweet	Capitol
⑥ I Love Music (Part 1)	The O'Jays	Philadelphia Int'l
☆ ⑥ I Write The Songs	Barry Manilow	Arista
☆ ⑥ Let's Do It Again	The Staple Singers	Curtom
☆ ⑥ Love Machine (Part 1)	The Miracles	Tamla

☆ ⑥ Love Rollercoaster	Ohio Players	Mercury
Over My Head	Fleetwood Mac	Reprise
⑥ Sing A Song	Earth, Wind & Fire	Columbia
☆ ⑥ That's The Way (I Like It)	K.C. & the Sunshine Band	T.K.
☆ ⑥ Theme From Mahogany (Do You Know Where You're Going To)	Diana Ross	Motown
☆ ⑥ Theme From S.W.A.T.	Rhythm Heritage	ABC
Venus And Mars Rock Show	Wings	Capitol
⑥ You Sexy Thing	Hot Chocolate	Big Tree

DECEMBER

⑥ All By Myself	Eric Carmen	Arista
Breaking Up Is Hard To Do	Neil Sedaka	Rocket
☆ ⑥ Convoy	C.W. McCall	MGM
☆ ⑥ December 1963 (Oh, What A Night)	The Four Seasons	Warner Bros.
Fanny (Be Tender With My Love)	The Bee Gees	RSO
☆ ⑥ 50 Ways To Leave Your Lover	Paul Simon	Columbia
Fly Away	John Denver	RCA
The Last Game Of The Season (A Blind Man In The Bleachers)	David Geddes	Tree
Let The Music Play	Barry White	20th Century
⑥ Love Hurts	Nazareth	A & M
⑥ Love To Love You Baby	Donna Summer	Oasis
Paloma Blanca	The George Baker Selection	Warner Bros.
Take It To The Limit	The Eagles	Asylum
Times Of Your Life	Paul Anka	United Artists
Wake Up Everybody (Part 1)	Harold Melvin & the Blue Notes	Philadelphia Int'l

TOP SINGLES OF 1975

⑥ Bad Blood	Neil Sedaka	Rocket
⑥ Fame	David Bowie	RCA
⑥ Fly, Robin, Fly	The Silver Convention	Midland Int'l
⑥ He Don't Love You (Like I Love You)	Tony Orlando & Dawn	Elektra
⑥ Island Girl	Elton John	MCA
⑥ Jive Talkin'	The Bee Gees	RSO
⑥ Love Will Keep Us Together	The Captain & Tennille	A & M
⑥ One Of These Nights	The Eagles	Asylum
⑥ Rhinestone Cowboy	Glen Campbell	Capitol
⑥ Sister Golden Hair	America	Warner Bros.

TOP ALBUMS OF 1975

⑥ Blood On The Tracks	Bob Dylan	Columbia
⑥ Captain Fantastic And The Brown Dirt Cowboy	Elton John	MCA

Queen (l to r: *Freddie Mercury, John Deacon, Brian May, Roger Taylor;* photo: *Christopher Hopper)*

1975

ⓖ **Love Will Keep Us Together**	The Captain & Tennille	A & M
ⓖ **One Of These Nights**	The Eagles	Asylum
ⓖ **Physical Graffiti**	Led Zeppelin	Swan Song
ⓖ **Red Octopus**	The Jefferson Starship	Grunt
ⓟ **That's The Way Of The World**	Earth, Wind & Fire	Columbia
ⓖ **Venus And Mars**	Paul McCartney & Wings	Capitol
ⓖ **Windsong**	John Denver	RCA
ⓟ **Wish You Were Here**	Pink Floyd	Columbia

GRAMMY WINNERS IN 1975

The Grammys were televised from the Hollywood Palladium in Hollywood on Saturday, February 28, 1976. Andy Williams was the host.

Record of the Year: "Love Will Keep Us Together," the Captain & Tennille (A & M)
Song of the Year: "Send In The Clowns" (music and lyrics by Stephen Sondheim)
Album of the Year: *Still Crazy After All These Years,* Paul Simon (Columbia)
Best Pop Vocal Performance, Female: "At Seventeen," Janis Ian (Columbia)
Best Pop Vocal Performance, Male: *Still Crazy After All These Years,* Paul Simon (Columbia)
Best Pop Vocal Performance, Group, "Lyin' Eyes," the Eagles (Asylum)
Best New Artist of the Year: Natalie Cole
Best Comedy Performance: *Is It Something I Said?* Richard Pryor (Reprise)
Best Soundtrack Album from a Motion Picture or Television: *Jaws,* John Williams (MCA)

DEATHS IN 1975

MUSIC PERFORMERS AND MUSIC INDUSTRY NOTABLES WHO DIED IN 1975

Louis Jordan, Tuesday, February 4 (heart attack: 66)

Felicia Sanders, Friday, February 7 (cancer; 53)

Aaron "T-Bone" Walker, Sunday, March 16 (pneumonia; 64)

Peter Ham (Badfinger), Wednesday, April 23 (hanging; 27)

Bob Wills, Tuesday, May 13 (pneumonia; 70)

Leroy Anderson (composer), Sunday, May 18 (lung cancer; 66)

"Moms" Mabley (Loretta Mary Aiken), Friday, May 23 (natural causes; 78)

Ozzie Nelson (bandleader), Tuesday, June 3 (cancer; 69)

Don Robey (record company head), Monday, June 16 (heart attack; 71)

Tim Buckley, Sunday, June 29 (heart attack; 28)

ROCK ON ALMANAC

William "Lefty" Frizzell, Saturday, July 19 (stroke; 47)
Julian "Cannonball" Adderly, Friday, August 8 (stroke; 46)
Thomas Wayne (Perkins), Friday, August 15 (car crash; 31)

Bob Scholl (The Mello-Kings), Wednesday, August 27 (boating accident; 37)
Al Jackson (Booker T & the MG's), Wednesday, October 1 (gunshot; 39)

OTHERS WHO DIED IN 1975

Josephine Baker
Avery Brundage
Ezzard Charles
Chiang Kai-shek
Larry Fine
Susan Hayward
Jimmy Hoffa
Moe Howard

Fredric March
Aristotle Onassis
Rod Serling
Casey Stengel
Arthur Treacher
Richard Tucker
William Wellman
Thornton Wilder

MOVIES OF 1975

MOVIES FEATURING POP MUSIC ARTISTS

Lisztomania *Stars:* Roger Daltrey, Sara Kestelman, Paul Nicholas, Ringo Starr, Fiona Lewis. No significant hits.

The Rocky Horror Picture Show *Stars:* Tim Curry, Susan Sarandon, Barry Bostwick, Meat Loaf, Richard O'Brien, Little Nell (Campbell). The ultimate camp film, a spoof of horror movies that had thousands of slavish fans dressing, speaking, and acting along with the actors at midnight screenings for more than a decade.

Stardust *Stars:* David Essex, Adam Faith, Larry Hagman, Keith Moon, Edd Byrnes. Sequel to Essex's *That'll Be the Day.* Featured songs: Many hits of the sixties, plus performances by David Essex and Dave Edmunds.

That's the Way of the World Later retitled *Shining Star. Stars:* Harvey Keitel, Ed Nelson, Cynthia Bostick, Bert Parks, Jimmy Boyd, Michael Dante, Earth, Wind & Fire. *Featured songs:* "Shining Star," "That's The Way Of The World."

Tommy *Stars:* Roger Daltrey, Ann-Margret, Oliver Reed, Elton John, Keith Moon, Tina Turner, Eric Clapton, Paul Nicholas, Jack Nicholson. The Who's already legendary rock

Bruce Springsteen in concert (photo: Anastasia Pantsios)

302

Donna Summer

1975

opera, brought lavishly to the screen by director Ken Russell. *Featured songs:* "Pinball Wizard" by Elton John, "See Me, Feel Me" by Roger Daltrey.

POP MUSIC CONCERTS ON FILM

Janis   Biography of Janis Joplin featuring interviews and footage from many of her most important concerts.
Ladies and Gentlemen, the Rolling Stones   Filmed account of their 1972 U.S. tour.

OTHER POPULAR MOVIES OF 1975

Barry Lyndon
The Day of the Locust
Dog Day Afternoon
The French Connection II
Jaws

Mahogany
Nashville
One Flew Over the Cuckoo's Nest
Rooster Cogburn
Shampoo

ACADEMY AWARD WINNERS OF 1975

Best Actor: Jack Nicholson , *One Flew Over the Cuckoo's Nest*
Best Actress: Louise Fletcher, *One Flew Over the Cuckoo's Nest*
Best Picture: *One Flew Over the Cuckoo's Nest*
Best Original Song: "I'm Easy," *Nashville* (music and lyrics by Keith Carradine)

TOP TELEVISION SHOWS OF 1975

ABC Monday Night Movie
All in the Family
The Bionic Woman
Laverne and Shirley
Maude

Phyllis
Rhoda
Rich Man, Poor Man
Sanford and Son
The Six Million Dollar Man

1976

NEWS HIGHLIGHTS OF 1976

⇨ Military spending in the world skyrockets to $300 billion a year.

⇨ The Winter Olympics are held in Innsbruck, Austria.

⇨ Barbara Walters is the first broadcaster to be offered a $1-million-per-year contract to cohost the nightly news.

⇨ Racial violence in black townships outside of Johannesburg, South Africa, is the worst in 15 years.

⇨ Jimmy Carter, a "born-again" Baptist from Georgia, is the presidential nominee of the Democratic Party.

⇨ From coast to coast, the United States celebrates its 200th birthday.

⇨ Gymnast Nadia Comaneci of Romania is the darling of the Summer Olympics in Montreal. (Even the theme music played during her performances, released as a single, goes gold.)

⇨ In Philadelphia 28 people die of a mysterious virus dubbed "Legionnaire's disease."

⇨ In a close election, Jimmy Carter is elected president over incumbent Gerald Ford.

⇨ Austrian Kurt Waldheim begins serving his second term as secretary general of the United Nations.

SPORTS WINNERS

Baseball The Cincinnati Reds beat the New York Yankees 4 games to 0.

Football

NFC: The Minnesota Vikings beat the Los Angeles Rams 24–13 in Bloomington.

AFC: The Oakland Raiders beat the Pittsburgh Steelers 24–7 in Oakland.

Super Bowl XI: The Oakland Raiders beat the Minnesota Vikings 32–14 on January 9, 1977, at the Rose Bowl in Pasadena, California.

Basketball

NBA: The Boston Celtics beat the Phoenix Suns 4 games to 2.

ABA: The New York Nets beat the Denver Nuggets 4 games to 2. This was the final ABA season.

Hockey The Montreal Canadiens beat the Philadelphia Flyers 4 games to 2.

MUSIC HIGHLIGHTS OF 1976

⇨ Bernie Leadon, original member of the Eagles since they were organized in 1971, leaves the group and is replaced by Joe Walsh.

⇨ Peter Frampton's album *Frampton Comes Alive!* becomes his biggest hit and one of the top albums of the year. It produces the hit singles "Show Me The Way" and "Baby, I Love Your Way."

⇨ Because of booming record sales in recent years, the Recording Industry Association of America (RIAA) creates a new platinum award. A gold record had been awarded to a

*Boston (l to r: **Sib Hashian, Fran Sheehan, Barry Goudreau, Tom Scholz, Brad Delp**; photo: **Ron Pownall**)*

305

single recording that sold 1 million copies and an album that sold 500,000. The new platinum award would be given to a single that sold in excess of 2 million and an album that sold 1 million units. The first platinum single was awarded to Johnnie Taylor for "Disco Lady," and the first platinum album went to the Eagles for *Eagles/Their Greatest Hits 1971–1975.* Later the RIAA would allow labels to apply for platinum certification of pre-1976 releases.

⇨ The Sex Pistols in England and Blondie in New York are the forerunners of punk rock. Blondie, along with the Ramones, play New York clubs like Max's Kansas City and CBGB, while the Sex Pistols play London's 100 Club.

⇨ *A Chorus Line* opens on Broadway. It would become the longest-running musical in entertainment history.

⇨ Lasers are used in a rock show for the first time, by the Who.

⇨ Genesis begins its first tour of America.

⇨ While working on his new album for Motown, *Songs In The Key Of Life,* Stevie Wonder announces that he has re-signed with the label in a multimillion-dollar deal.

⇨ Bruce Springsteen, while playing Memphis, tries to sneak into Graceland to see his idol Elvis Presley. He is stopped by security guards, who quietly lead him off the grounds, unconcerned that he is a major star.

⇨ Paul McCartney begins his Wings over America tour. Paul, wife Linda, Denny Laine, Jimmy McCulloch, and Joe English perform material that would form the basis of a three-album set called *Wings Over America,* which, when released later in the year, rockets to number one.

⇨ Donna Summer's American debut single in 1975, "Love To Love You Baby," smolders up the charts in 1976 as part of the disco explosion. Such artists as Gloria Gaynor, the Trammps, Tavares, Johnnie Taylor, the Biddu Orchestra, the Salsoul Orchestra, the Sylvers, the Silver Convention, the O'Jays, the Andrea True Connection, K.C. & the Sunshine Band, the Ritchie Family, and Thelma Houston contribute to the craze.

⇨ Prior to the release of the album *No Reason To Cry,* Eric Clapton begins a concert tour of England, his first in years.

⇨ Elton John plays for a week at New York's Madison Square Garden. The summertime concerts smash all attendance records.

DEBUT ARTISTS OF 1976

MAJOR ARTISTS

MAJOR ARTISTS	Debut Single	Label
The Bellamy Brothers (Howard and David Bellamy)	Let Your Love Flow ☆	Warner Bros.
George Benson	This Masquerade	Warner Bros.
Stephen Bishop	Save It For A Rainy Day	ABC
Blue Oyster Cult (Donald "Buck Dharma" Roeser, Eric Bloom, Allen Lanier, Albert Bouchard, Joe Bouchard)	(Don't Fear) The Reaper	Columbia
Boston (Brad Delp, Tom Scholz, Barry Goudreau, Fran Sheehan, Sib Hashian)	More Than A Feeling	Epic
The Brothers Johnson (George and Louis Johnson)	I'll Be Good To You ⑥	A & M
Burton Cummings	Stand Tall ⑥	Portrait
England Dan & John Ford Coley (Dan Seals, John Ford Coley)	I'd Really Love To See You Tonight ⑥	Big Tree
Firefall (Rick Roberts, Larry Burnett, Jock Bartley, Mark Andes, Michael Clarke)	Livin' Ain't Livin'	Atlantic
Peter Frampton	Show Me The Way	A & M
Crystal Gayle	I'll Get Over You	United Artists

England Dan (Seals) & John Ford Coley

Peter Frampton in concert (photo: Anastasia Pantsios)

Heart (Ann Wilson, Nancy Wilson, Roger Fisher, Steve Fossen, Howard Leese, Mike Derosier)	Crazy On You	Mushroom
Dan Hill	Growin' Up	20th Century
Kansas (Robby Steinhardt, Steve Walsh, Kerry Livgren, Rich Williams, Dave Hope, Phil Ehart)	Carry On Wayward Son	Kirshner
The Little River Band (Glenn Shorrock, David Briggs, Beeb Birtles, Graham Goble, George McArdle, Derek Pellicci)	It's A Long Way There	Harvest
L.T.D. (Love, Togetherness & Devotion: Jeffrey Osborne, Johnny McGhee, Henry Davis, Arthur "Lorenzo" Carnegie, Jake Riley, Jr., Carle Vickers, Abraham "Onion" Miller, Jr., Jimmy "J.D." Davis, Melvin Webb, Bill Osborne)	Love Ballad	A & M
Mary MacGregor	Torn Between Two Lovers ☆ Ⓖ	Ariola America
Ted Nugent	Hey Baby	Epic
Billy Ocean	Love Really Hurts Without You	Ariola
Robert Palmer	Man Smart, Woman Smarter	Island
The Alan Parsons Project (Alan Parsons, Eric Woolfson)	(The System Of) Doctor Tarr and Professor Fether	20th Century
Eddie Rabbitt	Rocky Mountain Music	Elektra
Kenny Rogers	Love Lifted Me	United Artists
Rose Royce (Gwen "Rose" Dickey, Michael Moore, Freddie Dunn, Kenji Chiba Brown, Lequeint "Duke" Jobe, Kenny "Captain Gold" Copeland, Mike Nash, Terral "Power-Pack" Santiel, Henry "Hammer" Garner)	Car Wash ☆ Ⓟ	MCA

Crystal Gayle

Starbuck (Bruce Blackman, Jimmy Cobb, Sloan Hayes, Darryl Kutz, David Shaver, Bo Wagner, Ken Crysler)	Moonlight Feels Right	Private Stock
Starz (Michael Lee Smith, Brenden Harkin, Richie Ranno, Peter Sweval, Joe X. Dube)	(She's Just A) Fallen Angel	Capitol
Al Stewart	Year Of The Cat	Janus
John Travolta	Let Her In	Midland Int'l
The Tubes (Fee Waybill, Bill Spooner, Roger Steen, Vince Walnick, Michael Cotten, Rick Anderson, Prairie Prince, Re Styles)	Don't Touch Me There	A & M
Wild Cherry (Bob Parissi, Bryan Bassett, Mark Avsec, Allen Wentz, Ron Beitle)	Play That Funky Music ☆ ℗	Sweet City
Gary Wright	Dream Weaver ⑥	Warner Bros.

OTHER ARTISTS

Terry Bradshaw
Brass Construction
Brick
Keith Carradine
Norman Connors
Rick Dees & His Cast of Idiots
Barry De Vorzon & Perry Botkin, Jr.
Dr. Buzzard's Original Savannah Band
Double Exposure
El Coco
Andrew Gold
Cyndi Greco
Larry Groce
Hamilton, Joe Frank & Dennison
Laverne & Shirley
Bob Marley & the Wailers
Marilyn McCoo & Billy Davis, Jr.

Dorothy Moore
Melba Moore
Walter Murphy & the Big Apple Band
Maxine Nightingale
Kenny Nolan
Pratt & McClain
Vicki Sue Robinson
Roxy Music
Sherbet
Southside Johnny & the Asbury Jukes
The Starland Vocal Band
Thin Lizzy
The Andrea True Connection
Dana Valery
John Paul Young
The Michael Zager Band

HITS OF 1976

JANUARY

⑥ **Bohemian Rhapsody**	Queen	Mercury
Dream On *(re-entry)*	Aerosmith	Columbia

⑤ Dream Weaver	Gary Wright	Warner Bros.
Grow Some Funk Of Your Own/I Feel Like A Bullet (In The Gun Of Robert Ford)	Elton John	MCA
I Could Have Danced All Night/ Jump For Joy	The Biddu Orchestra	Epic
Junk Food Junkie	Larry Groce	Warner Bros./ Curb
☆ Let Your Love Flow	The Bellamy Brothers	Warner Bros./ Curb
⑤ Lonely Night (Angel Face)	The Captain & Tennille	A & M
⑤ Only Sixteen	Dr. Hook	Capitol
⑤ Sweet Thing	Rufus	ABC
Take Me	Grand Funk	Capitol
Tangerine	The Salsoul Orchestra	Salsoul
Tenth Avenue Freeze-Out	Bruce Springsteen	Columbia
This Old Heart Of Mine	Rod Stewart	Warner Bros.
Venus *(disco version)*	Frankie Avalon	De-Lite

FEBRUARY

Action	The Sweet	Capitol
Banapple Gas	Cat Stevens	A & M
☆ ⑤ Boogie Fever	The Sylvers	Capitol
Cupid	Tony Orlando & Dawn	Elektra
☆ ℗ Disco Lady	Johnnie Taylor	Columbia
Hit The Road Jack	The Stampeders	Quality 501
⑤ I Do, I Do, I Do, I Do, I Do	Abba	Atlantic
Money Honey	The Bay City Rollers	Arista
Only Love Is Real	Carole King	Ode
⑤ Right Back Where We Started From	Maxine Nightingale	United Artists
⑤ Sara Smile	Hall & Oates	RCA
⑤ Shannon	Henry Gross	Lifesong
Show Me The Way	Peter Frampton	A & M
There's A Kind Of Hush (All Over The World)	The Carpenters	A & M
You'll Lose A Good Thing	Freddy Fender	ABC/Dot

MARCH

Don't Pull Your Love/Then You Can Tell Me Goodbye	Glen Campbell	Capitol

Heart (top l to r: Mike Derosier, Steve Fossen, Nancy Wilson, Ann Wilson, Roger Fisher; bottom: Howard Leese)

309

Ⓖ Fooled Around And Fell In Love	Elvin Bishop	Capricorn
Ⓖ Get Up And Boogie	The Silver Convention	Midland Int'l
Hurt	Elvis Presley	RCA
I Thought It Took A Little Time (But Today I Fell In Love)	Diana Ross	Motown
Livin' For The Weekend	The O'Jays	Philadelphia Int'l
Looking For Space	John Denver	RCA
Misty Blue	Dorothy Moore	Malaco
Ⓖ More, More, More (Part 1)	The Andrea True Connection	Buddah
Mozambique	Bob Dylan	Columbia
Rhiannon (Will You Ever Win)	Fleetwood Mac	Reprise
Shout It Out Loud	Kiss	Casablanca
Ⓖ Tryin' To Get The Feeling Again	Barry Manilow	Arista
☆ Ⓖ Welcome Back	John Sebastian	Reprise
Young Blood	Bad Company	Swan Song

APRIL

Baretta's Theme (Keep Your Eye On The Sparrow)	Rhythm Heritage	ABC
Crazy On You	Heart	Mushroom
Fool To Cry	The Rolling Stones	Rolling Stones
Get Closer	Seals & Crofts	Warner Bros.
Happy Days	Pratt & McClain	Reprise
I Want You	Marvin Gaye	Tamla
☆ Ⓟ Kiss And Say Goodbye	The Manhattans	Columbia
Lookin' Out For #1	Bachman-Turner Overdrive	Mercury
☆ Ⓖ Love Hangover	Diana Ross	Motown
Love Really Hurts Without You	Billy Ocean	Ariola America
Moonlight Feels Right	Starbuck	Private Stock
☆ Ⓖ Silly Love Songs	Wings	Capitol
Takin' It To The Streets	The Doobie Brothers	Warner Bros.
That's Where The Happy People Go	The Trammps	Atlantic
Turn The Beat Around	Vicki Sue Robinson	RCA

MAY

☆ Ⓖ Afternoon Delight	The Starland Vocal Band	Windsong
The Boys Are Back In Town	Thin Lizzy	Mercury
☆ Ⓖ A Fifth Of Beethoven	Walter Murphy & the Big Apple Band	Private Stock
Ⓖ I'll Be Good To You	The Brothers Johnson	A & M
I'm Easy	Keith Carradine	ABC
Ⓖ "I.O.U."	Jimmy Dean	Casino
Let Her In	John Travolta	Midland Int'l
Making Our Dreams Come True	Cyndi Greco	Private Stock
Never Gonna Fall In Love Again	Eric Carmen	Arista
Rock And Roll Love Letter	The Bay City Rollers	Arista
Ⓖ Shop Around	The Captain & Tennille	A & M
Still Crazy After All These Years	Paul Simon	Columbia

Dan Hill (photo: *Kriegsmann*)

1976

Take The Money And Run	The Steve Miller Band	Capitol
⑥ Tear The Roof Off The Sucker	Parliament	Casablanca
Today's The Day	America	Warner Bros.

JUNE

Another Rainy Day In New York	Chicago	Columbia
Baby, I Love Your Way	Peter Frampton	A & M
Got To Get You Into My Life	The Beatles	Capitol
⑥ Heaven Must Be Missing An Angel (Part 1)	Tavares	Capitol
Hot Stuff/Fool To Cry	The Rolling Stones	Rolling Stones
⑥ I'd Really Love To See You Tonight	England Dan & John Ford Coley	Big Tree
If You Know What I Mean	Neil Diamond	Columbia
I Need To Be In Love	The Carpenters	A & M
Last Child	Aerosmith	Columbia
☆ ℗ Play That Funky Music	Wild Cherry	Epic
Rock And Roll Music	The Beach Boys	Warner/ Reprise
Somebody's Gettin' It	Johnnie Taylor	Columbia
Steppin' Out	Neil Sedaka	Rocket
This Masquerade	George Benson	Warner Bros.
⑥ You'll Never Find Another Love Like Mine	Lou Rawls	Philadelphia Int'l

JULY

⑥ Devil Woman	Cliff Richard	Rocket
☆ ⑥ Don't Go Breaking My Heart	Elton John & Kiki Dee	Rocket
⑥ Getaway	Earth, Wind & Fire	Columbia
⑥ Let 'Em In	Wings	Capitol
⑥ Lowdown	Boz Scaggs	Columbia
Magic Man	Heart	Mushroom
Say You Love Me	Fleetwood Mac	Warner/ Reprise
☆ ⑥ (Shake, Shake, Shake) Shake Your Booty	K.C. & The Sunshine Band	T.K.
She's Gone *(re-entry)*	Hall & Oates	Atlantic
Shower The People	James Taylor	Warner Bros.
Still The One	Orleans	Asylum
⑥ Summer	War	United Artists

311

⑥ Teddy Bear	Red Sovine	Starday
With Your Love	Jefferson Starship	Grunt
☆ ⑥ You Should Be Dancing	The Bee Gees	RSO

AUGUST

The Best Disco In Town	The Ritchie Family	Marlin
☆ ℗ Disco Duck (Part 1)	Rick Dees & His Cast Of Idiots	RSO
Don't Stop Believin'	Olivia Newton-John	MCA
Get The Funk Out Ma Face	The Brothers Johnson	A & M
Get Up Offa That Thing	James Brown	Polydor
I Can't Hear You No More	Helen Reddy	Capitol
☆ ⑥ If You Leave Me Now	Chicago	Columbia
It's O.K.	The Beach Boys	Warner/ Reprise
⑥ Nadia's Theme (The Young And The Restless)	Barry De Vorzon & Perry Botkin, Jr.	A & M
No, No Joe	The Silver Convention	Midland Int'l
☆ Rock'N Me	The Steve Miller Band	Capitol
Wheels Of Fortune	The Doobie Brothers	Warner Bros.
The Wreck Of The Edmund Fitzgerald	Gordon Lightfoot	Reprise
You Are My Starship	Norman Connors	Buddah
You Are The Woman	Firefall	Atlantic

SEPTEMBER

⑥ Beth	Kiss	Casablanca
Don't Think . . . Feel	Neil Diamond	Columbia
Do You Feel Like We Do	Peter Frampton	A & M
⑥ Fernando	Abba	Atlantic
⑥ I Never Cry	Alice Cooper	Warner Bros.
Just To Be Close To You	The Commodores	Motown
Like A Sad Song	John Denver	RCA
⑥ Love So Right	The Bee Gees	RSO
Message In Our Music	The O'Jays	Philadelphia Int'l
More Than A Feeling	Boston	Epic
⑥ Muskrat Love	The Captain & Tennille	A & M
⑥ The Rubberband Man	The Spinners	Atlantic
This One's For You	Barry Manilow	Arista
☆ ⑥ You Don't Have To Be A Star (To Be In My Show)	Marilyn McCoo & Billy Davis, Jr.	ABC

Kansas (l to r: Kerry Livgren, Steve Walsh, Dave Hope, Robby Steinhardt, Phil Ehart, Rich Williams)

The Little River Band (l to r: George McArdle, Derek Pellicci, David Briggs, Glenn Shorrock, Beeb Birtles, Graham Goble; photo: Neil Zlozower/Mirage)

1976

You Gotta Make Your Own Sunshine	Neil Sedaka	Rocket

OCTOBER

ⓖ	After The Lovin'	Engelbert Humperdinck	Epic
	Breezin'	George Benson	Warner Bros.
☆ ⓟ	Car Wash	Rose Royce	MCA
	Dazz	Brick	Bang
	A Dose Of Rock And Roll	Ringo Starr	Atlantic
	Hello Old Friend	Eric Clapton	RSO
ⓖ	Hot Line	The Sylvers	Capitol
	Jump	Aretha Franklin	Atlantic
	Let's Get It Together	El Coco	AVI
	Livin' Thing	The Electric Light Orchestra	United Artists
	Love Ballad	L.T.D.	A & M
	Nights Are Forever Without You	England Dan & John Ford Coley	Big Tree
ⓖ	Stand Tall	Burton Cummings	Portrait
☆ ⓖ	Tonight's The Night (Gonna Be Alright)	Rod Stewart	Warner Bros.
☆ ⓖ	You Make Me Feel Like Dancing	Leo Sayer	Warner Bros.

NOVEMBER

☆ ⓖ	Blinded By The Light	Manfred Mann's Earth Band	Warner Bros.
	Don't Take Away The Music	Tavares	Capitol
ⓖ	Enjoy Yourself	The Jacksons	Epic
	Every Face Tells A Story	Olivia Newton-John	MCA
ⓖ	I Like Dreamin'	Kenny Nolan	20th Century
	It Keeps You Runnin'	The Doobie Brothers	Warner Bros.
	Lost Without Your Love	Bread	Elektra
	Mademoiselle	Styx	A & M
	Ob-La-Di, Ob-La-Da	The Beatles	Capitol
	Saturday Nite	Earth, Wind & Fire	Columbia
	Somebody To Love	Queen	Elektra
ⓖ	Sorry Seems To Be The Hardest Word	Elton John	MCA/Rocket

☆ ⑥ Torn Between Two Lovers	Mary MacGregor	Ariola America
Weekend In New England	Barry Manilow	Arista
Whispering/Cherchez La Femme/Se Si Bon	Dr. Buzzard's Original Savannah Band	RCA

DECEMBER

Baby, You Look Good To Me Tonight	John Denver	RCA
Carry On Wayward Son	Kansas	Kirshner
☆ ⑥ Dancing Queen	Abba	Atlantic
☆ Don't Leave Me This Way	Thelma Houston	Tamla
⑥ Fly Like An Eagle	The Steve Miller Band	Capitol
Hard Luck Woman	Kiss	Casablanca
☆ ⑥ I Wish	Stevie Wonder	Tamla
☆ ⑥ Love Theme From "A Star Is Born" (Evergreen)	Barbra Streisand	Columbia
Moody Blue	Elvis Presley	RCA
☆ ⑥ New Kid In Town	The Eagles	Asylum
Night Moves	Bob Seger	Capitol
Save It For A Rainy Day	Stephen Bishop	ABC
Someone To Lay Down Beside Me	Linda Ronstadt	Asylum
St. Charles	Jefferson Starship	Grunt
⑥ Year Of The Cat	Al Stewart	Janus

TOP SINGLES OF 1976

⑥ Afternoon Delight	The Starland Vocal Band	Windsong
⑥ December 1963 (Oh, What A Night)	The Four Seasons	Warner/Curb
⑰ Disco Lady	Johnnie Taylor	Columbia
⑥ Don't Go Breaking My Heart	Elton John & Kiki Dee	Rocket
⑥ 50 Ways To Leave Your Lover	Paul Simon	Columbia
⑥ If You Leave Me Now	Chicago	Columbia
⑥ Love Hangover	Diana Ross	Motown
⑰ Play That Funky Music	Wild Cherry	Epic
⑥ Silly Love Songs	Wings	Capitol
⑥ Tonight's The Night (Gonna Be Alright)	Rod Stewart	Warner Bros.

TOP ALBUMS OF 1976

⑰ Breezin'	George Benson	Warner Bros.
⑰ Desire	Bob Dylan	Columbia
⑰ Eagles/Their Greatest Hits 1971–1975	The Eagles	Asylum
⑰ Frampton Comes Alive!	Peter Frampton	A & M
⑥ A Night At The Opera	Queen	Elektra
⑰ A Night On The Town	Rod Stewart	Warner Bros.
⑰ Presence	Led Zeppelin	Swan Song
⑰ Silk Degrees	Boz Scaggs	Columbia
⑥ Songs In The Key Of Life	Stevie Wonder	Tamla
⑰ Wings At The Speed Of Sound	Wings	Capitol

Ted Nugent in concert (photo: Anastasia Pantsios)

Marilyn McCoo & Billy Davis, Jr.

GRAMMY WINNERS IN 1976

The Grammys were televised from the Hollywood Palladium in Hollywood on Saturday, February 19, 1977. Andy Williams was the host.

Record of the Year: "This Masquerade," George Benson (Warner Bros.)
Song of the Year: "I Write The Songs" (music and lyrics by Bruce Johnston)
Album of the Year: *Songs In The Key Of Life,* Stevie Wonder (Tamla)
Best Pop Vocal Performance, Female: *Hasten Down The Wind,* Linda Ronstadt (Asylum)
Best Pop Vocal Performance, Male: *Songs In The Key Of Life,* Stevie Wonder (Tamla)
Best Pop Vocal Performance, Group: "If You Leave Me Now," Chicago (Columbia)
Best New Artist of the Year: The Starland Vocal Band
Best Comedy Performance: *Bicentennial Nigger,* Richard Pryor (Warner Bros.)
Best Soundtrack Album from a Motion Picture or Television: *Car Wash,* Norman Whitfield (MCA)

DEATHS IN 1976

MUSIC PERFORMERS AND MUSIC INDUSTRY NOTABLES WHO DIED IN 1976

Chester "Howlin' Wolf" Burnett, Saturday, January 10 (kidney disease; 65)

Chris Kenner, Sunday, January 25 (heart attack; 46)

Rudy Pompelli (Bill Haley & His Comets), Thursday, February 5 (heart attack; 47)

Vince Guaraldi, Friday, February 6 (heart attack; 47)

Percy Faith, Monday, February 9 (cancer; 67)

Sal Mineo, Friday, February 13 (stab wounds; 37)

Lily Pons (opera singer), Friday, February 13 (cancer of the pancreas; 71)

Florence Ballard (The Supremes), Sunday, February 22 (cardiac arrest; 32)

Dave Kapp (record company head), Monday, March 1 (stroke; 72)

Paul Kossoff (Free), Thursday, March 18 (heart attack; 25)

Phil Ochs, Friday, April 9 (hanging; 35)

Keith Relf (Yardbirds), Friday, May 14 (electrocution; 33)

Johnny Mercer (songwriter), Friday, June 25 (brain tumor; 66)

Jimmy Reed, Sunday, August 29 (epilepsy; 50)

Connee Boswell, Sunday, October 10 (stomach cancer; 68)

Tommy Bolin (Deep Purple), Saturday, December 4 (drug overdose; 25)

Freddy King, Tuesday, December 28 (ulcers; 42)

OTHERS WHO DIED IN 1976

Busby Berkeley
Agatha Christie
J. Paul Getty
Howard Hughes
Fritz Lang
Ted Mack

Mao Tse-tung
Paul Robeson
Rosalind Russell
Alastair Sim
Adolph Zukor

MOVIES OF 1976

MOVIES FEATURING POP MUSIC ARTISTS

Pipe Dreams   *Stars:* Gladys Knight, Barry Hankerson, Sherry Bain, Bruce French. No significant hits.
A Star Is Born   *Stars:* Barbra Streisand, Kris Kristofferson, Gary Busey, Paul Mazursky. *Featured song:* "Love Theme From 'A Star Is Born' (Evergreen)" by Barbra Streisand (which won an Oscar).

POP MUSIC CONCERTS ON FILM

The Song Remains the Same   The Led Zeppelin Madison Square Garden concert of 1973, captured on film, showcasing their biggest hits.

MOVIES FEATURING A POP MUSIC SOUNDTRACK

Car Wash   *Stars:* Richard Pryor, Frankie Ajaye, George Carlin, Irwin Corey, Garrett Morris. *Featured song:* "Car Wash" by Rose Roye.

OTHER POPULAR MOVIES OF 1976

All the President's Men
King Kong
Marathon Man
Network
The Omen

Rocky
Silent Movie
Taxi Driver
That's Entertainment, Part 2

ACADEMY AWARD WINNERS OF 1976

Best Actor: Peter Finch, *Network*
Best Actress: Faye Dunaway, *Network*
Best Picture: *Rocky*
Best Original Song: "Love Theme From 'A Star Is Born' (Evergreen)," *A Star Is Born* (music by Barbra Streisand, lyrics by Paul Williams)

TOP TELEVISION SHOWS OF 1976

ABC Monday Night Movie
ABC Sunday Night Movie
Baretta
The Big Event
Charlie's Angels

Happy Days
Laverne and Shirley
M*A*S*H
One Day at a Time
The Six Million Dollar Man

1977

NEWS HIGHLIGHTS OF 1977

⇨ Murderer Gary Gilmore is executed by a firing squad at the Utah State Prison. His is the first execution in the United States in 10 years.

⇨ CB radios in cars and trucks are so popular that they begin interfering with radio and TV signals.

⇨ *Roots,* an ABC miniseries about the family tree of author Alex Haley, attracts 80 million viewers, surpassing *Gone With the Wind* as the highest-rated program ever broadcast.

⇨ The worst aviation diaster in history occurs when two jumbo jets collide in the Canary Islands, killing 574 people.

⇨ An oil well shoots out of control in the North Sea, creating a slick 45 miles long and 30 miles wide.

⇨ For a record fourth time, A.J. Foyt wins the Indianapolis 500 auto race.

⇨ Menachem Begin becomes premier of Israel.

⇨ The $7.7 billion trans-Alaskan pipeline opens, far behind schedule.

⇨ The U.S. State Department urges emergency admission of 10,000 Vietnamese "boat people" as refugees.

⇨ Edward Koch becomes the 105th mayor of New York City.

SPORTS WINNERS

Baseball   The New York Yankees beat the Los Angeles Dodgers 4 games to 2.
Football
   NFC: The Dallas Cowboys beat the Minnesota Vikings 23–6 in Dallas.
   AFC: The Denver Broncos beat the Oakland Raiders 20–17 in Denver.
   Super Bowl XII: The Dallas Cowboys beat the Denver Broncos 27–10 on January 15, 1978, at the Louisiana Superdome in New Orleans.
Basketball   The Portland Trailblazers beat the Philadelphia '76ers 4 games to 2 to take the NBA title.
Hockey   The Montreal Canadiens beat the Boston Bruins 4 games to 0.

MUSIC HIGHLIGHTS OF 1977

⇨ In February, Warner Brothers records releases Fleetwood Mac's *Rumours* album, which would remain on the charts for 3½ years, hold the number one spot for 31 weeks, and sell over 8 million copies. It is the first noncompilation album to produce four Top 10 singles: "Go Your Own Way," "Dreams" (which went to number one), "Don't Stop," and "You Make Lovin' Fun."

⇨ The British-based Clash starts to create an awareness in America of their politicized punk rock sound.

*The Babys (clockwise from top: **Mike Corby, Wally Stocker, John Waite, Tony Brock)***

Debby Boone

Shaun Cassidy

1977

⇨ In April, Steve Rubell and Ian Schrager open Studio 54 in New York, the first big celebrity club to cater to the disco crowd.

⇨ On Thursday, May 26, at the Winter Garden Theater in New York, *Beatlemania* opens. This Beatles simulation starring four performers who look and sound like the originals will perform to capacity crowds for the next several years.

⇨ The musical *Annie* opens on Broadway.

⇨ On Sunday, June 26, as his new single, "Way Down," enters the national charts, Elvis Presley makes what is to be his last live concert appearance at the Market Square Arena in Indianapolis, Indiana.

⇨ On Tuesday, August 16, Elvis, the king of rock 'n' roll, dies of heart failure at his Graceland home in Memphis at the age of 42. The perfect requiem, "My Way," recorded during his June concert tour, is released as a single in November and becomes Elvis's final gold record.

⇨ Steve Hackett quits Genesis, leaving the group to carry on as a trio.

⇨ The movie *Saturday Night Fever* has the entire country dancing to the disco beat.

⇨ Paul Davis scores the most persistent hit of the rock era: "I Go Crazy" stays on the national charts for 40 weeks. It retains this distinction for only five years.

DEBUT ARTISTS OF 1977

MAJOR ARTISTS

MAJOR ARTISTS	Debut Single	Label
The Babys (John Waite, Wally Stocker, Mike Corby, Tony Brock)	If You've Got The Time	Chrysalis
Peter Brown	Do You Wanna Get Funky With Me ⑤	Drive
Shaun Cassidy	Da Doo Ron Ron ☆ ⑤	Warner/Curb
Chic (Norma Jean, Claire Bethe, Nile Rodgers, Bernard Edwards, Kenny Lehman, Andy Schwartz, Tony Thompson)	Dance, Dance, Dance (Yowsah, Yowsah, Yowsah) ⑤	Atlantic
Exile (Jimmy Stokley, J. P. Pennington, Buzz Cornelison, Marlon Hargis, Sonny Lemaire, Steven Goetzman)	Try It On	Atco
Foreigner (Lou Gramm, Mick Jones, Ian McDonald, Ed Gagliardi, Al Greenwood, Dennis Elliott)	Feels Like The First Time	Atlantic
Peter Gabriel	Solsbury Hill	Atco
Leif Garrett	Surfin' USA	Atlantic
Genesis (Phil Collins, Tony Banks, Mike Rutherford, Steve Hackett)	Your Own Special Way	Atco

319

Andy Gibb	I Just Want To Be Your Everything ☆ Ⓖ	RSO
Sammy Hagar	You Make Me Crazy	Capitol
Kenny Loggins	I Believe In Love	Columbia
Meco (Meco Monardo)	Star Wars Theme/ Cantina Band ☆ Ⓟ	Millennium
Pablo Cruise (Cory Lerios, Dave Jenkins, Bud Cockrell, Steve Price)	Whatcha Gonna Do?	A & M
Teddy Pendergrass	I Don't Love You Anymore	Philadelphia Int'l
Tom Petty & the Heartbreakers (Tom Petty, Mike Campbell, Benmont Tench, Ron Blair, Stan Lynch)	Breakdown	Shelter/ABC
Player (Peter Beckett, Wayne Cook, Ronn Moss, John "J.C." Crowley, John Friesen)	Baby Come Back ☆ Ⓖ	RSO
Prism (Ron Tabak, Lindsey Mitchell, Tom Lavin, Ab Bryant, John Hall, Rodney Higgs, Henry Small)	Spaceship Superstar	Ariola America
REO Speedwagon (Kevin Cronin, Gary Richrath, Neal Doughty, Bruce Hall, Alan Gratzer)	Ridin' The Storm Out	Epic
Rush (Alex Lifeson, Geddy Lee, Neil Peart)	Fly By Night/In The Mood	Mercury
Shalamar (Gary Mumford, Jody Watley, Jeffrey Daniel)	Uptown Festival	Soul Train
Jennifer Warnes	Right Time Of The Night	Arista
Bob Welch	Sentimental Lady	Capitol
Deniece Williams	Free	Columbia

OTHER ARTISTS

Angel	Steve Martin
Boney M.	Mass Production
Debby Boone	Maze
The Brooklyn Dreams	Mac McAnally
David Castle	Ronnie McDowell
Cerrone	Frankie Miller
Charlene	Randy Newman
Charlie	Paul Nicholas
The Climax Blues Band	Alan O'Day
Con Funk Shun	Odyssey
Bill Conti	Jane Olivor
Walter Egan	Graham Parker
Enchantment	Bonnie Raitt
Jay Ferguson	The Ramones
Maynard Ferguson	Carole Bayer Sager
The Floaters	The Sanford-Townsend Band
Robert Gordon	Samantha Sang
Heatwave	Santa Esmeralda
Hot	Slave
Grace Jones	David Soul
Lenny LeBlanc	Kate Taylor
LeBlanc & Carr	The T-Connection
Carrie Lucas	Jesse Winchester

Foreigner (l to r: Ian McDonald, Mick Jones, Lou Gramm, Al Greenwood, Ed Gagliardi, Dennis Elliott)

1977

HITS OF 1977

JANUARY

Boogie Child	The Bee Gees	RSO
Crackerbox Palace	George Harrison	Dark Horse
☆ ⓖ Don't Give Up On Us	David Soul	Private Stock
Go Your Own Way	Fleetwood Mac	Warner Bros.
Here Come Those Tears Again	Jackson Browne	Asylum
Hey Baby	Ringo Starr	Atlantic
I Just Can't Say No To You	Parker McGee	Big Tree
ⓖ I've Got Love On My Mind	Natalie Cole	Capitol
Long Time	Boston	Epic
☆ ⓖ Rich Girl	Hall & Oates	RCA
Right Time Of The Night	Jennifer Warnes	Arista
Sam	Olivia Newton-John	MCA
Say You'll Stay Until Tomorrow	Tom Jones	Epic
So In To You	The Atlanta Rhythm Section	Polydor
ⓖ The Things We Do For Love	10cc	Mercury

FEBRUARY

ⓖ Angel In Your Arms	Hot	Big Tree
Bite Your Lip (Get Up And Dance)	Elton John	MCA/Rocket
Couldn't Get It Right	The Climax Blues Band	Sire
The First Cut Is The Deepest	Rod Stewart	Warner Bros.
☆ ⓖ Hotel California	The Eagles	Asylum
☆ ⓖ I'm Your Boogie Man	K.C. & the Sunshine Band	T.K.
I Wanna Get Next To You	Rose Royce	MCA
Love in "C" Minor—Part 1	Cerrone	Cotillion
Maybe I'm Amazed	Wings	Captiol
N.Y., You Got Me Dancing	The Andrea True Connection	Buddah
☆ ⓖ Southern Nights	Glen Campbell	Capitol
Theme From Rocky (Gonna Fly Now)	Rhythm Heritage	ABC
ⓖ Tryin' To Love Two	William Bell	Mercury
☆ ⓖ When I Need You	Leo Sayer	Warner Bros.
Winter Melody	Donna Summer	Casablanca

321

ROCK ON ALMANAC

Andy Gibb in concert (photo: Anastasia Pantsios)

MARCH

Can't Stop Dancing	The Captain & Tennille	A & M
Cherry Baby	Starz	Capitol
Dancing Man	Q	Epic
Disco Inferno	The Trammps	Atlantic
Heard It In A Love Song	The Marshall Tucker Band	Capricorn
Hello Stranger	Yvonne Elliman	RSO
I Think We're Alone Now	The Rubinoos	Beserkley
Lido Shuffle	Boz Scaggs	Columbia
Lonely Boy	Andrew Gold	Asylum
My Sweet Lady	John Denver	RCA
Theme From "Charlie's Angels"	Henry Mancini	RCA
Tie Your Mother Down	Queen	Elektra
Uptown Festival	Shalamar	Soul Train
Your Love	Marilyn McCoo & Billy Davis, Jr.	ABC
Your Own Special Way	Genesis	Atco

APRIL

⑥	Ain't Gonna Bump No More (With No Big Fat Woman)	Joe Tex	Epic
	Cinderella	Firefall	Atlantic
☆ ⑥	Dreams	Fleetwood Mac	Warner Bros.
	Feels Like The First Time	Foreigner	Atlantic
☆ ⑥	Gonna Fly Now (Theme From "Rocky")	Bill Conti	United Artists
☆	Got To Give It Up (Part I)	Marvin Gaye	Tamla
	High School Dance	The Sylvers	Capitol
	I'll Be Standing By	Foghat	Bearsville
⑥	Lucille	Kenny Rogers	United Artists
	Margaritaville	Jimmy Buffett	ABC
	Sing	Tony Orlando & Dawn	Elektra
☆ ⑥	Sir Duke	Stevie Wonder	Tamla
☆ ⑥	Undercover Angel	Alan O'Day	Pacific
	Whodunit	Tavares	Capitol
	You And Me	Alice Cooper	Warner Bros.

322

MAY

All You Get From Love Is A Love Song	The Carpenters	A & M
☆ ⑥ Da Doo Ron Ron	Shaun Cassidy	Warner/Curb
⑥ Do You Wanna Make Love	Peter McCann	20th Century
Hollywood	Rufus featuring Chaka Khan	ABC
☆ ⑥ I Just Want To Be Your Everything	Andy Gibb	RSO
Jet Airliner	The Steve Miller Band	Capitol
⑥ Knowing Me, Knowing You	Abba	Atlantic
Life In The Fast Lane	The Eagles	Asylum
☆ ⑥ Looks Like We Made It	Barry Manilow	Arista
My Heart Belongs To Me	Barbra Streisand	Columbia
On And On	Stephen Bishop	ABC
Peace Of Mind	Boston	Epic
The Pretender	Jackson Browne	Asylum
Solsbury Hill	Peter Gabriel	Atco
⑥ (Your Love Has Lifted Me) Higher And Higher	Rita Coolidge	A & M

JUNE

Barracuda	Heart	Portrait/CBS
☆ ⑥ Best Of My Love	The Emotions	Columbia
Easy	The Commodores	Motown
Give A Little Bit	Supertramp	A & M
Handy Man	James Taylor	Columbia
I'm In You	Peter Frampton	A & M
It Was Almost Like A Song	Ronnie Milsap	RCA
Just A Song Before I Go	Crosby, Stills & Nash	Atlantic
The Killing Of Georgie	Rod Stewart	Warner Bros.
Runaway	Bonnie Raitt	Warner Bros.
Smoke From A Distant Fire	The Sanford-Townsend Band	Warner Bros.
⑥ Telephone Line	The Electric Light Orchestra	United Artists/ Jet
⑥ Telephone Man	Meri Wilson	GRT
⑥ Way Down	Elvis Presley	RCA
You Made Me Believe In Magic	The Bay City Rollers	Arista

Randy Newman

Paul Nicholas

1977

323

JULY

℗ Boogie Nights	Heatwave	Epic
Christine Sixteen	Kiss	Casablanca
Cold As Ice	Foreigner	Atlantic
Don't Worry Baby	B.J. Thomas	MCA
Edge Of The Universe	The Bee Gees	RSO
⑤ Float On	The Floaters	ABC
The Greatest Love Of All	George Benson	Arista
Keep It Comin' Love	K.C. & the Sunshine Band	T.K.
⑤ Nobody Does It Better	Carly Simon	Elektra
O-H-I-O	Ohio Players	Mercury
Sheena Is A Punk Rocker	The Ramones	Sire
Something About You	LeBlanc & Carr	Big Tree
⑤ Strawberry Letter 23	The Brothers Johnson	A & M
⑤ Swayin' To The Music (Slow Dancin')	Johnny Rivers	Big Tree
⑤ That's Rock 'N' Roll	Shaun Cassidy	Warner Bros.

AUGUST

Brickhouse	The Commodores	Motown
Cat Scratch Fever	Ted Nugent	Epic
⑤ Don't It Make My Brown Eyes Blue	Crystal Gayle	United Artists
Help Is On Its Way	The Little River Band	Capitol
⑤ I Feel Love	Donna Summer	Casablanca
I Go Crazy	Paul Davis	Bang
Indian Summer	Poco	ABC
⑤ It's Ecstasy When You Lay Down Next To Me	Barry White	20th Century
Jungle Love	The Steve Miller Band	Capitol
Just Remember I Love You	Firefall	Atlantic
My Cherie Amour	The Soul Train Gang	Soul Train
She Did It	Eric Carmen	Arista
Signed, Sealed, Delivered (I'm Yours)	Peter Frampton	A & M
☆ ℗ Star Wars Theme/Cantina Band	Meco	Millennium
You're The Only One	The J. Geils Band	Atlantic

SEPTEMBER

Baby, What A Big Surprise	Chicago	Columbia
⑤ Blue Bayou	Linda Ronstadt	Asylum
Changes In Latitudes, Changes In Attitudes	Jimmy Buffett	ABC
Come Sail Away	Styx	A & M
Daybreak	Barry Manilow	Arista
⑤ Do You Wanna Get Funky With Me	Peter Brown	Drive
Dusic	Brick	Bang
⑤ Heaven On The 7th Floor	Paul Nicholas	RSO
☆ ⑤ How Deep Is Your Love	The Bee Gees	RSO
I Just Want To Make Love To You	Foghat	Bearsville

324

Pablo Cruise (l to r: Bruce Day, Steve Price, Dave Jenkins, Cory Lerios)

⑥	The King Is Gone	Ronnie McDowell	Scorpion
	Send In The Clowns *(re-entry)*	Judy Collins	Elektra
	We Just Disagree	Dave Mason	Columbia
⑥	We're All Alone	Rita Coolidge	A & M
☆ ⑰	You Light Up My Life	Debby Boone	Warner Bros.

OCTOBER

☆ ⑥	Baby Come Back	Player	RSO
⑥	Dance, Dance, Dance (Yowsah, Yowsah, Yowsah)	Chic	Atlantic
⑥	(Every Time I Turn Around) Back In Love Again	L.T.D.	A & M
	Falling	LeBlanc & Carr	Big Tree
⑥	Here You Come Again	Dolly Parton	RCA
	It's So Easy	Linda Ronstadt	Asylum
	Money, Money, Money	Abba	Atlantic
	Sentimental Lady	Bob Welch	Capitol
	Slip Slidin' Away	Paul Simon	Columbia
	Started Out Dancing, Ended Up Making Love	Alan O'Day	Atlantic
⑰	We Are The Champions/We Will Rock You	Queen	Elektra
	Why Do Lovers (Break Each Other's Heart?)	Hall & Oates	RCA
	You Make Lovin' Fun	Fleetwood Mac	Warner Bros.
⑥	You're In My Heart	Rod Stewart	Warner Bros.
	Your Smiling Face	James Taylor	Columbia

NOVEMBER

	As	Stevie Wonder	Tamla
	Bloat On	Cheech & Chong	ODH
	Don't Let Me Be Misunderstood	Santa Esmeralda	Casablanca
⑰	Emotion	Samantha Sang	Private Stock
⑥	Hey Deanie	Shaun Cassidy	Warner Bros.
⑥	I Honestly Love You	Olivia Newton-John	MCA
⑥	Just The Way You Are	Billy Joel	Columbia
☆ ⑥	Love Is Thicker Than Water	Andy Gibb	RSO
	More Than A Woman	Tavares	Capitol
⑥	My Way	Elvis Presley	RCA

ROCK ON ALMANAC

Player (l to r: Peter Beckett, Wayne Cook, John Freisen, Ronn Moss, John "J.C." Crowley)

Native New Yorker	Odyssey	RCA
Peg	Steely Dan	ABC
⑥ Short People	Randy Newman	Warner Bros.
⑥ Sometimes When We Touch	Dan Hill	20th Century
Turn To Stone	The Electric Light Orchestra	Jet

DECEMBER

Boats Against The Current	Eric Carmen	Arista
Desiree	Neil Diamond	Columbia
Easy To Love	Leo Sayer	Warner Bros.
Ffun	Con Funk Shun	Mercury
Goodbye Girl	David Gates	Elektra
Lovely Day	Bill Withers	Columbia
Mindbender	Stillwater	Capricorn
Rockaway Beach	The Ramones	Sire
☆ ℗ Stayin' Alive	The Bee Gees	RSO
Sweet Music Man	Kenny Rogers	United Artists
Theme From Close Encounters Of The Third Kind	John Williams	Arista
Thunder Island	Jay Ferguson	Asylum
Too Hot To Trot	The Commodores	Motown
Tried To Love	Peter Frampton	A & M
What A Difference You've Made In My Life	Ronnie Milsap	RCA

TOP SINGLES OF 1977

⑥ Best Of My Love	The Emotions	Columbia
⑥ Dancing Queen	Abba	Atlantic
⑥ Love Theme From "A Star Is Born" (Evergreen)	Barbra Streisand	Columbia
⑥ Hotel California	The Eagles	Asylum
⑥ I Just Want To Be Your Everything	Andy Gibb	RSO
⑥ Rich Girl	Hall & Oates	RCA
⑥ Sir Duke	Stevie Wonder	Tamla
℗ Star Wars Theme/Cantina Band	Meco	Casablanca
⑥ Torn Between Two Lovers	Mary MacGregor	Ariola America
℗ You Light Up My Life	Debby Boone	Warner/Curb

TOP ALBUMS OF 1977

℗	Barry Manilow/Live	Barry Manilow	Arista
℗	The Beatles At The Hollywood Bowl	The Beatles	Capitol
℗	Book Of Dreams	The Steve Miller Band	Capitol
℗	Commodores	The Commodores	Motown
℗	Hotel California	The Eagles	Asylum
⑥	Marvin Gaye Live At the London Palladium	Marvin Gaye	Tamla
℗	Point of Know Return	Kansas	Kirshner
℗	Rumours	Fleetwood Mac	Warner Bros.
℗	Simple Dreams	Linda Ronstadt	Asylum
℗	A Star Is Born	Soundtrack	Columbia

GRAMMY WINNERS IN 1977

The Grammys were televised from the Shrine Auditorium In Los Angeles on Thursday, February 23, 1978. John Denver was the host.

Record of the Year: "Hotel California," the Eagles (Asylum)

Song of the Year: "Love Theme From 'A Star Is Born' (Evergreen)" (music by Barbra Steisand, lyrics by Paul Williams); "You Light Up My Life" (music and lyrics by Joe Brooks)

Album of the Year: *Rumours,* Fleetwood Mac (Warner Bros.)

Best Pop Vocal Performance, Female: "Love Theme From 'A Star Is Born' (Evergreen)," Barbra Streisand (Columbia)

Best Pop Vocal Performance, Male: "Handy Man," James Taylor (Warner Bros.)

Best Pop Vocal Performance, Group: "How Deep Is Your Love," the Bee Gees (RSO)

Best New Artist of the Year: Debby Boone

Best Comedy Performance: *Let's Get Small,* Steve Martin (Warner Bros.)

Best Soundtrack Album from a Motion Picture or Television: *Star Wars,* John Williams (20th Century)

DEATHS IN 1977

MUSIC PERFORMERS AND MUSIC INDUSTRY NOTABLES WHO DIED IN 1977

Erroll Garner, Sunday, January 2 (emphysema; 53)

Sherman Garnes (Frankie Lymon & the Teenagers), Saturday, February 26 (heart surgery; 36)

Goddard Lieberson (record company head), Tuesday, March 29 (cancer; 66)

William Powell (The O'Jays), Thursday, May 26 (extended illness; 35)

Paul Desmond, Monday, May 30 (natural causes; 52)

Elvis Presley, Tuesday, August 16 (heart failure; 42)

Leopold Stokowski (conductor), Tuesday, September 13 (coronary attack; 95)

Marc Bolan (T. Rex), Friday, September 16 (car crash; 28)

Maria Callas (opera singer), Friday, September 16 (heart attack; 53)

Mary Ford (Les Paul & Mary Ford), Friday, September 30 (diabetes; 53)

Shirley Brickley (The Orlons), Thursday, October 13 (gunshot; 33)

Bing Crosby, Friday, October 14 (heart attack; 76)

Cassie Gaines, Steve Gaines, Ronald Van Zant (Lynyrd Skynyrd), Thursday, October 20 (plane crash; all 28)

Guy Lombardo, Saturday, November 5 (lung ailment; 75)

OTHERS WHO DIED IN 1977

Eddie "Rochester" Anderson
Stephen Boyd
Charles Chaplin
Joan Crawford
Andy Devine
Peter Finch
Howard Hawks

James Jones
Groucho Marx
Zero Mostel
Freddy Prinze
Adolph Rupp
Ethel Waters

MOVIES OF 1977

POP MUSIC CONCERTS ON FILM

Abba—the Movie   A 90-minute presentation featuring the group's concert tour.
The Movies of the Grateful Dead   A concert appearance in San Francisco, filmed in
1974, that begins with an animated opening.

MOVIES FEATURING A POP MUSIC SOUNDTRACK

Saturday Night Fever   *Stars:* John Travolta, Karen Lynn Gorney, Donna Pescow,
Barry Miller, Joseph Cali. This film's dancing and disco soundtrack helped launch the
disco craze of the seventies. The soundtrack album was the largest-selling album of all
time until displaced by Michael Jackson's *Thriller.*

OTHER POPULAR MOVIES OF 1977

Airport '77
Annie Hall
Black Sunday
Close Encounters of the Third Kind
The Deep
The Eagle Has Landed
Exorcist II: The Heretic
Final Chapter—Walking Tall

The Goodbye Girl
Julia
Looking for Mr. Goodbar
New York, New York
Oh, God!
Pumping Iron
Star Wars
The Turning Point

ACADEMY AWARD WINNERS OF 1977

Best Actor: Richard Dreyfuss, *The Goodbye Girl*
Best Actress: Diane Keaton, *Annie Hall*

*Rush (l to r: Geddy Lee, Neil Peart, Alex
Lifeson)*

1977

Saturday Night Fever
soundtrack album cover

Fleetwood Mac, Rumours
album cover

Best Picture: *Annie Hall*
Best Original Song: "You Light Up My Life," *You Light Up My Life* (music and lyrics by Joe Brooks)

TOP TELEVISION SHOWS OF 1977

Alice
All in the Family
Charlie's Angels
Happy Days
Laverne and Shirley

Little House on the Prairie
M*A*S*H
One Day at a Time
60 Minutes
Three's Company

1978

NEWS HIGHLIGHTS OF 1978

⇨ Leon Spinks takes the world heavyweight boxing championship from Muhammad Ali in Las Vegas.

⇨ In response to threats of a farm strike, President Carter proposes increasing federal aid to the nation's farmers.

⇨ After testifying at his own trial on an obscenity charge, Larry Flint, owner of *Hustler* magazine, is shot by a would-be assassin and critically wounded.

⇨ In a Pennsylvania plant, the first American-made Volkswagen automobile rolls off the assembly line.

⇨ Despite the Vatican's insistence that it is homicide, abortion is legalized in Italy.

⇨ Princess Caroline of Monaco marries French businessman Philippe Junot.

⇨ The Nuclear Regulatory Commission halts the construction of a nuclear power plant at Seabrook, New Hampshire, because of public opposition.

⇨ The first "test-tube baby" is born to a British couple. Fertilization was performed in a glass dish; the fertilized egg was then implanted in the mother.

⇨ The opposition Sandinista Party demands the ouster of dictatorial President Anastasio Somoza Debayle as battling continues in Nicaragua.

⇨ More than 900 American followers of cult leader Jim Jones commit mass suicide at their compound in the jungle of South America.

⇨ George Moscone, mayor of San Francisco, and Harvey Milk, a member of the mayor's board of supervisors, are murdered in their offices by another board member, Dan White.

⇨ The joint winners of the Nobel Peace Prize are Israel's Prime Minister Begin and Egypt's President Sadat.

⇨ The cardinals of the Vatican elect the first non-Italian pope in seven centuries, Karol Wojtyla of Poland, who will serve as Pope John Paul II, a name chosen to honor his predecessor, John Paul I, who died one month after elevation to the papacy.

SPORTS WINNERS

Baseball   The New York Yankees beat the Los Angeles Dodgers 4 games to 2.
Football
   NFC: The Dallas Cowboys beat the Los Angeles Rams 28–0 in Los Angeles.
   AFC: The Pittsburgh Steelers beat the Houston Oilers 34–5 in Pittsburgh.
   Super Bowl XIII: The Pittsburgh Steelers beat the Dallas Cowboys 35–31 on January 21, 1979, at the Orange Bowl in Miami.
Basketball   The Washington Bullets beat the Seattle Supersonics 4 games to 3.
Hockey   The Montreal Canadiens beat the Boston Bruins 4 games to 2.

MUSIC HIGHLIGHTS OF 1978

⇨ The Sex Pistols arrive in America for their first tour.

⇨ Howard Stein's club Xenon opens as an alternative to Studio 54 in New York.

⇨ The Beatles satire *All You Need Is Cash* starring the Rutles (Eric Idle of the Monty Python troupe and Neil Innes of the Bonzo Dog Band) airs on NBC-TV.

⇨ On Friday, June 16, at New York's Beacon Theater, Frankie Lanz, Joe Contorno, and Tony De Lauro stage the first doo-wop oldies show. The Royal New York Doo-Wop Show stars the Skyliners, the Elegants, Jimmy Clanton, the Cleftones, the Mello-Kings, the Earls, and the Chiffons. A few years later, the show would move to New York's Radio City Music Hall, where it is still presented twice a year, featuring the greatest doo-wop groups of the fifties and early sixties.

⇨ The Doobie Brothers, Dave Mason, and Kansas are a few of the acts to perform at Canada's first major rock festival, Canada Jam, held in Ontario.

⇨ Rick James leaves the group the Mynah Birds to go out as a solo performer.

⇨ After three albums as a mostly instrumental progressive rock band, Journey decides to

Karla Bonoff

go for a mainstream sound by adding a vocalist. Steve Perry, discovered via a demo tape, becomes the group's new lead singer.

⇨ Billy Joel's *52nd Street* becomes his first number one album.

⇨ New wave group the Talking Heads enjoys its first hit album with *More Songs About Buildings And Food.*

⇨ The movie soundtrack album *Saturday Night Fever* spends 24 weeks at number one and sells more than 30 million copies, making it the largest-selling album of all time. Michael Jackson's *Thriller* would ultimately beat that sales figure six years later.

⇨ Another big movie soundtrack album, *Grease,* holds the number one spot for 12 weeks.

⇨ On Friday, October 13, Sid Vicious, former bass guitarist for the now defunct Sex Pistols, is arrested in New York and charged with the stabbing murder of his girlfriend, Nancy Spungen.

DEBUT ARTISTS OF 1978

MAJOR ARTISTS	Debut Single	Label
Karla Bonoff	I Can't Hold On	Columbia
The Cars (Ric Ocasek, Benjamin Orr, Elliot Easton, Greg Hawkes, David Robinson)	Just What I Needed	Elektra
Cheap Trick (Robin Zander, Rick Nielsen, Tom Peterson, Bun E. Carlos)	Surrender	Epic
Dan Hartman	Instant Replay ⓖ	Blue Sky
Rupert Holmes	Let's Get Crazy Tonight	Private Stock
Rick James	You And I	Gordy

The Blues Brothers (l to r: Dan Aykroyd, John Belushi)

Journey (Steve Perry, Neal Schon, Gregg Rolie, Ross Valory, Steve Smith)	Wheel In The Sky	Columbia
Evelyn "Champagne" King	Shame ⑥	RCA
Eddie Money	Baby Hold On	Columbia
Juice Newton	It's A Heartache	Capitol
Prince (Prince Rogers Nelson)	Soft And Wet	Warner Bros.
Gerry Rafferty	Baker Street ⑥	United Artists
Raydio (Ray Parker, Jr., Charles Fearing, Arnell Carmichael, Darren Carmichael, Larry Tolbert)	Jack & Jill ⑥	Arista
The Talking Heads (David Byrne, Jerry Harrison, Martina Weymouth, Chris Frantz)	Psycho Killer	Sire
Toto (Bobby Kimball, Steve Lukather, David Paich, Steve Porcaro, David Hungate, Jeff Porcaro)	Hold The Line ⑥	Columbia
Bonnie Tyler	It's A Heartache ⑥	RCA
Van Halen (David Lee Roth, Edward Van Halen, Michael Anthony, Alex Van Halen)	You Really Got Me	Warner Bros.
The Village People (Victor Willis, Randy Jones, David "Scar" Hodo, Felipe Rose, Glenn Hughes, Alexander Briley)	Macho Man ⑥	Casablanca

OTHER ARTISTS

Airwaves
Claudja Barry
Belle Epoque
John Belushi
The Blues Brothers
Bill Brandon
Alicia Bridges
The British Lions
Don Brown
Bobby Caldwell
Cazz
Celebration
Judy Cheeks
City Boy
Allan Clarke

Linda Clifford
Clout
The Continental Miniatures
The Cooper Brothers
John Davis
Teri De Sario
Doucette
George Duke
Eruption
Fotomaker
Foxy
Ace Frehley
Gabriel
Robin Gibb
Nick Gilder

The Cars (l to r: Benjamin Orr, David Robinson, Ric Ocasek, Elliot Easton, Greg Hawkes; photo: E.J. Camp)

Goody Goody
Justin Hayward
Michael Henderson
High Inergy
Jimmy "Bo" Horne
Hotel
Mick Jackson
Michael Johnson
Kayak
Kongas
Bill La Bounty
Cheryl Ladd
Kevin Lamb
Nicolette Larson
Eloise Laws
Louisiana's LeRoux
Love & Kisses
Cheryl Lynn
Barbara Mandrell
The McCrarys
Bob McGilpin
Kristy & Jimmy McNichol
Meat Loaf
Musique
Plastic Bertrand
The Pockets
Bonnie Pointer
The Raes
Genya Ravan
Don Ray

Chris Rea
Demis Roussos
Rubicon
Sea Level
Gene Simmons
Patti Smith
Snail
Spellbound
Spyro Gyra
Paul Stanley
Stargard
Stillwater
Stonebolt
Switch
Sylvester
Gary Tanner
The Tarney/Spencer Band
A Taste of Honey
Toby Beau
Peter Tosh
Joey Travolta
Trooper
Tuxedo Junction
Wendy Waldman
The James Walsh Gypsy Band
Bob Weir
Karen Young
Warren Zevon
Zwol

HITS OF 1978

JANUARY

⑥	**Always And Forever**	Heatwave	Epic
	Crazy On You *(re-entry)*	Heart	Mushroom
⑥	**Dust In The Wind**	Kansas	Kirshner
	Ebony Eyes	Bob Welch	Capitol
☆ ⑥	**If I Can't Have You**	Yvonne Elliman	RSO
⑥	**Jack And Jill**	Raydio	Arista

Cheap Trick (l to r: Bun E. Carlos, Robin Zander, Rick Nielsen, Jon Brant)

334

Lady Love	Lou Rawls	Philadelphia Int'l
⑥ Lay Down Sally	Eric Clapton	RSO
Let It Go, Let It Flow	Dave Mason	Columbia
⑥ Our Love	Natalie Cole	Capitol
So Long	Firefall	Atlantic
Theme From Close Encounters	Meco	Millennium
The Way You Do The Things You Do	Rita Coolidge	A & M
Wonderful World	Art Garfunkel with James Taylor & Paul Simon	Columbia
You Really Got Me	Van Halen	Warner Bros.

FEBRUARY

Baby Hold On	Eddie Money	Columbia
Boogie Shoes	K.C. & the Sunshine Band	T.K.
⑥ Can't Smile Without You	Barry Manilow	Arista
⑥ The Closer I Get To You	Roberta Flack with Donny Hathaway	Atlantic
Disco Inferno	The Trammps	Atlantic
⑥ Flash Light	Parliament	Casablanca
Hot Legs	Rod Stewart	Warner Bros.
Love Is Like Oxygen	The Sweet	Capitol
Mamas Don't Let Your Babies Grow Up To Be Cowboys	Waylon & Willie	RCA
More Than A Woman	Tavares	Capitol
Never Have To Say Goodbye	England Dan & John Ford Coley	Big Tree
☆ ⑫ Night Fever	The Bee Gees	RSO
Runnin' On Empty	Jackson Browne	Asylum
Sweet Talkin' Woman	The Electric Light Orchestra	Jet
Thank You For Being A Friend	Andrew Gold	Asylum

MARCH

Bombs Away	Bob Weir	Arista
Count On Me	Jefferson Starship	RCA
Dance With Me	Peter Brown	Drive
Do You Believe In Magic	Shaun Cassidy	Warner/Curb
Every Kinda People	Robert Palmer	Island
Fantasy	Earth, Wind & Fire	Columbia
Imaginary Lover	The Atlanta Rhythm Section	Polydor
⑥ It's A Heartache	Bonnie Tyler	RCA
Movin' Out (Anthony's Song)	Billy Joel	Columbia
On Broadway	George Benson	Warner Bros.
This Time I'm In It For Love	Player	RSO
Two Doors Down	Dolly Parton	RCA
⑥ Two Out Of Three Ain't Bad	Meat Loaf	Cleveland Int'l
Werewolves Of London	Warren Zevon	Asylum
☆ With A Little Luck	Wings	Capitol

APRIL

Ⓖ	Baker Street	Gerry Rafferty	United Artists
	Because The Night	Patti Smith	Arista
	Bluer Than Blue	Michael Johnson	EMI-America
	Cheeseburger In Paradise	Jimmy Buffett	ABC
	Deacon Blues	Steely Dan	ABC
	Ego	Elton John	MCA
	Everybody Dance	Chic	Atlantic
	Follow You, Follow Me	Genesis	Atlantic
	House Of The Rising Sun	Santa Esmeralda	Casablanca
☆ Ⓟ	Shadow Dancing	Andy Gibb	RSO
Ⓖ	Take A Chance On Me	Abba	Atlantic
☆ Ⓖ	Too Much, Too Little, Too Late	Johnny Mathis & Deniece Williams	Columbia
	Tumbling Dice	Linda Ronstadt	Asylum
	The Wanderer	Leif Garrett	Atlantic
	You Belong To Me	Carly Simon	Elektra
☆ Ⓟ	You're The One That I Want	John Travolta & Olivia Newton-John	RSO

MAY

	Even Now	Barry Manilow	Arista
☆ Ⓟ	Grease	Frankie Valli	RSO
Ⓖ	The Groove Line	Heatwave	Epic
	I Was Only Joking	Rod Stewart	Warner Bros.
Ⓖ	King Tut	Steve Martin	Warner Bros.
Ⓖ	Last Dance	Donna Summer	Casablanca
☆ Ⓖ	Miss You	The Rolling Stones	Rolling Stones
	Only The Good Die Young	Billy Joel	Columbia
	Runaway	Jefferson Starship	Grunt
	Still The Same	Bob Seger	Capitol
	Stone Blue	Foghat	Bearsville
	Take Me Back To Chicago	Chicago	Columbia
	Thank God It's Friday	Love & Kisses	Casablanca
Ⓖ	Use Ta Be My Girl	The O'Jays	Philadelphia Int'l
	Weekend Lover	Odyssey	RCA

JUNE

☆ Ⓟ	Boogie Oogie Oogie	A Taste of Honey	Capitol
Ⓖ	Copacabana	Barry Manilow	Arista
	FM	Steely Dan	MCA
☆ Ⓟ	Hot Child In The City	Nick Gilder	Chrysalis
	Life's Been Good	Joe Walsh	Asylum
	Love Will Find A Way	Pablo Cruise	A & M
Ⓖ	Macho Man	The Village People	Casablanca
Ⓖ	Magnet And Steel	Walter Egan	Columbia
	My Angel Baby	Toby Beau	RCA
	Prove It All Night	Bruce Springsteen	Columbia
Ⓖ	Shame	Evelyn "Champagne" King	RCA
	Songbird	Barbra Streisand	Columbia
	Stay	Jackson Browne	Asylum

Rick James

Eddie Money

1978

This Night Won't Last Forever	Bill La Bounty	Warner/Curb
☆ ⑥ Three Times A Lady	The Commodores	Motown

JULY

⑥ Close The Door	Teddy Pendergrass	Philadelphia Int'l
⑥ An Everlasting Love	Andy Gibb	RSO
Fool If You Think It's Over	Chris Rea	Magnet
Get Off	Foxy	Dash
⑥ Got To Get You Into My Life	Earth, Wind & Fire	Columbia
⑥ Hopelessly Devoted To You	Olivia Newton-John	RSO
⑥ Hot Blooded	Foreigner	Atlantic
⑥ I Love The Night Life (Disco Round)	Alicia Bridges	Polydor
☆ ⑥ Kiss You All Over	Exile	Warner/Curb
Love Is In The Air	John Paul Young	Scotti Bros.
Reminiscing	The Little River Band	Harvest
Whenever I Call You "Friend"	Kenny Loggins	Columbia
You	Rita Coolidge	A & M
You And I	Rick James	Gordy
☆ ⑥ You Needed Me	Anne Murray	Capitol

AUGUST

Back In The U.S.A.	Linda Ronstadt	Asylum
Badlands	Bruce Springsteen	Columbia
Don't Look Back	Boston	Epic
Hollywood Nights	Bob Seger	Capitol
If My Friends Could See Me Now	Linda Clifford	Curtom
Josie	Steely Dan	ABC
Oh Darlin'	Robin Gibb	RSO
Paradise By The Dashboard Light	Meat Loaf	Cleveland Int'l
Right Down The Line	Gerry Rafferty	United Artists
She's Always A Woman	Billy Joel	Columbia
⑥ Summer Nights	John Travolta & Olivia Newton-John	RSO

Sweet Life	Paul Davis	Bang
Who Are You	The Who	MCA
You Never Done It Like That	The Captain & Tennille	A & M
You're All I Need To Get By	Johnny Mathis & Deniece Williams	Columbia

SEPTEMBER

	Beast Of Burden	The Rolling Stones	Rolling Stones
⑥	Double Vision	Foreigner	Atlantic
	Ease On Down The Road	Diana Ross & Michael Jackson	MCA
	Greased Lightnin'	John Travolta	RSO
	Hot Shot	Karen Young	West End
	How Much I Feel	Ambrosia	Warner Bros.
	I Just Wanna Stop	Gino Vannelli	A & M
	Let's Get Crazy Tonight	Rupert Holmes	Private Stock
	London Town	Wings	Capitol
	Louie, Louie	John Belushi	MCA
☆ ⑥	MacArthur Park	Donna Summer	Casablanca
⑥	One Nation Under A Groove (Part 1)	Funkadelic	Warner Bros.
	Ready To Take A Chance Again	Barry Manilow	Arista
⑥	Sharing The Night Together	Dr. Hook	Capitol
	Straight On	Heart	Portrait

OCTOBER

	Alive Again	Chicago	Columbia
	Forever Autumn	Justin Hayward	Columbia
	Get Back	Billy Preston	A & M
	Here Comes The Night	Nick Gilder	Chrysalis
⑥	Hold The Line	Toto	Columbia
	How You Gonna See Me Now	Alice Cooper	Warner Bros.
	I'm Every Woman	Chaka Khan	Warner Bros.
⑥	Instant Replay	Dan Hartman	Blue Sky
	In The Bush	Musique	Prelude
☆ ℗	Le Freak	Chic	Atlantic
⑥	(Our Love) Don't Throw It All Away	Andy Gibb	RSO

Journey (l to r: Jonathan Cain, Steve Smith, Ross Valory, Neal Schon, Steve Perry)

1978

Juice Newton

Prince in concert (photo: Anastasia Pantsios)

Promises	Eric Clapton	RSO
We've Got Tonight	Bob Seger	Capitol
℗ Y.M.C.A.	The Village People	Casablanca
☆ Ⓖ You Don't Bring Me Flowers	Barbra Streisand & Neil Diamond	Columbia

NOVEMBER

Bicycle Race/Fat Bottom Girls	Queen	Elektra
Blame It On The Boogie	The Jacksons	Epic
Don't Cry Out Loud	Melissa Manchester	Arista
Ⓖ Every 1's A Winner	Hot Chocolate	Infinity
Ⓖ Fire	The Pointer Sisters	Planet
The Gambler	Kenny Rogers	United Artists
Ⓖ A Little More Love	Olivia Newton-John	MCA
Lotta Love	Nicolette Larson	Warner Bros.
Ⓖ My Life	Billy Joel	Columbia
Ooh Baby Baby	Linda Ronstadt	Asylum
Part Time Love	Elton John	MCA
Ⓖ September	Earth, Wind & Fire	Arc
Shake It	Ian Matthews	Mushroom
☆ ℗ Too Much Heaven	The Bee Gees	RSO
You Took The Words Right Out Of My Mouth	Meat Loaf	Epic

DECEMBER

Animal House	Stephen Bishop	ABC
Blue Morning, Blue Day	Foreigner	Atlantic
Dancin' Shoes	Nigel Olsson	Bang
☆ ℗ Do Ya Think I'm Sexy	Rod Stewart	Warner Bros.
Gotta Have Lovin'	Don Ray	Polydor
Ⓖ Got To Be Real	Cheryl Lynn	Columbia
☆ ℗ I Will Survive	Gloria Gaynor	Polydor
Lost In Your Love	John Paul Young	Scotti Bros.
No Tell Lover	Chicago	Columbia
Please Come Home For Christmas	The Eagles	Asylum
Radioactive	Gene Simmons	Casablanca
Ⓖ Shake Your Groove Thing	Peaches & Herb	Polydor
Somewhere In The Night	Barry Manilow	Arista

*Toto (top l to r: **Mike
Porcaro, David Paich, Steve
Lukather, Bobby Kimball**;
bottom l to r: **Jeff Porcaro,
Steve Porcaro**)*

| Soul Man | The Blues Brothers | Atlantic |
| This Moment In Time | Engelbert Humperdinck | Epic |

TOP SINGLES OF 1978

Ⓖ Baby Come Back	Player	RSO
Ⓟ Boogie Oogie Oogie	A Taste of Honey	Capitol
Ⓖ Kiss You All Over	Exile	Warner Bros.
Ⓖ Love Is Thicker Than Water	Andy Gibb	RSO
Ⓖ MacArthur Park	Donna Summer	Casablanca
Ⓟ Night Fever	The Bee Gees	RSO
Ⓟ Shadow Dancing	Andy Gibb	RSO
Ⓟ Stayin' Alive	The Bee Gees	RSO
Ⓖ Three Times A Lady	The Commodores	Motown
With A Little Luck	Wings	Capitol

TOP ALBUMS OF 1978

Ⓟ Aja	Steely Dan	ABC
Ⓟ City To City	Gerry Rafferty	United Artists
Ⓟ Even Now	Barry Manilow	Arista
Ⓟ 52nd Street	Billy Joel	Columbia
Ⓟ Grease	Soundtrack	RSO
Ⓟ Live And More	Donna Summer	Casablanca
Ⓟ London Town	Wings	Capitol
Ⓟ Saturday Night Fever	Soundtrack	RSO
Ⓟ Slowhand	Eric Clapton	RSO
Ⓟ Some Girls	The Rolling Stones	Rolling Stones

GRAMMY WINNERS IN 1978

The Grammys were televised from the Shrine Auditorium in Los Angeles on Thursday, February 15, 1979. John Denver was the host.

Record of the Year: "Just The Way You Are," Billy Joel (Columbia)
Song of the Year: "Just The Way You Are" (music and lyrics by Billy Joel)
Album of the Year: *Saturday Night Fever,* the Bee Gees, David Shire, Yvonne Elliman, Tavares, Kool & the Gang, K.C. & the Sunshine Band, MFSB, the Trammps, Walter Murphy, Ralph McDonald (RSO)
Best Pop Vocal Performance, Female: "You Needed Me," Anne Murray (Capitol)

Best Pop Vocal Performance, Male: "Copacabana," Barry Manilow (Arista)
Best Pop Vocal Performance, Group: "Night Fever," the Bee Gees (RSO)
Best New Artist of the Year: A Taste of Honey
Best Comedy Performance: *A Wild And Crazy Guy,* Steve Martin (Warner Bros.)
Best Soundtrack Album from a Motion Picture or Television: *Close Encounters Of The Third Kind,* John Williams (Arista)

1978

DEATHS IN 1978

MUSIC PERFORMERS AND MUSIC INDUSTRY NOTABLES WHO DIED IN 1978

Vic Ames (The Ames Brothers), Monday, January 23 (car crash; 51)

Terry Kath (Chicago), Monday, January 23 (shot himself; 31)

Johnny Bond, Monday, June 12 (stroke; 63)

Enoch Light (bandleader), Monday, July 31 (natural causes; 71)

Louis Prima, Thursday, August 24 (brain tumor; 67)

Joe Negroni (Frankie Lymon & the Teenagers), Tuesday, September 5 (aneurysm of the brain; 37)

Keith Moon (The Who), Thursday, September 7 (drug overdose; 32)

Ralph Marterie (bandleader), Sunday, October 6 (heart attack; 63)

Jacques Brel, Monday, October 9 (blood clot in the lung; 49)

Bob Luman, Wednesday, December 27 (pneumonia; 40)

OTHERS WHO DIED IN 1978

Edgar Bergen
Carl Betz
Charles Boyer
John Cazale
Dan Dailey
Hubert Humphrey
Tim McCoy

Golda Meir
Pope Paul VI (Giovanni Battista Montini)
Pope John Paul I (Albino Luciani)
Norman Rockwell
Gene Tunney
Peggy Wood
Gig Young

MOVIES OF 1978

MOVIES FEATURING POP MUSIC ARTISTS

American Hot Wax *Stars:* Tim McIntire, Jay Leno, Laraine Newman, Fran Drescher, Jeff Altman. Biography of legendary disc jockey Alan Freed features many original hits of the fifties, plus live performances of "Reelin' And Rockin' " and "Sweet Little

Van Halen in concert (photo: Anastasia Pantsios)

341

Grease *soundtrack album cover*

Sixteen" by Chuck Berry, "Whole Lotta Shakin' Goin' On" and "Great Balls Of Fire" by Jerry Lee Lewis and "I Put A Spell On You" by Screamin' Jay Hawkins.

The Buddy Holly Story   *Stars:* Gary Busey, Charles Martin Smith, Don Stroud, Maria Richwine, Conrad Janis, Will Jordan, Fred Travalena, "Stymie" Beard. Buddy Holly's songs were performed by Busey, Smith, and Stroud.

Grease   *Stars:* John Travolta, Olivia Newton-John, Stockard Channing, Jeff Conway, Didi Conn, Eve Arden, Sid Caesar. *Featured songs:* "Hopelessly Devoted To You" by Olivia Newton-John, "Summer Nights" and "You're The One That I Want" by John Travolta & Olivia Newton-John. Frankie Avalon and Sha Na Na also appear and sing in the film; Frankie Valli's number one hit "Grease" is played under the credits.

Renaldo and Clara   *Stars:* Bob Dylan, Sara Dylan, Ronee Blakely, Sam Shepard, Ronnie Hawkins, Harry Dean Stanton, Joni Mitchell, Joan Baez, Bob Neuwirth. This autobiographical look at Dylan and his Rolling Thunder Revue originally ran over four hours but was trimmed down to a more manageable two hours. Features many great performers and songs.

Sgt. Pepper's Lonely Hearts Club Band   *Stars:* Peter Frampton, the Bee Gees, George Burns, Donald Pleasance, Billy Preston, Steve Martin. *Featured song:* "Got To Get You Into My Life" by Earth, Wind & Fire. *Other musical performers:* Aerosmith, Alice Cooper, Paul Nicholas.

Thank God, It's Friday   *Stars:* Donna Summer, Jeff Goldblum, Paul Jabara, Valerie Landsburg, Debra Winger. *Featured songs:* "Last Dance" (Oscar winner) by Donna Summer, "Easy" by the Commodores.

The Wiz   *Stars:* Diana Ross, Michael Jackson, Nipsey Russell, Ted Ross, Lena Horne, Richard Pryor. *Featured song:* "Ease On Down The Road" by Diana Ross & Michael Jackson.

POP MUSIC CONCERTS ON FILM

Bob Marley and the Wailers Live!   Filmed in London in 1977, film captures Marley at his best.

The Last Waltz   Martin Scorsese captures the Band's farewell concert around Thanksgiving 1976 at the Winterland in San Francisco. *Musical performers:* The Band, Rick Danko, Levon Helm, Garth Hudson, Eric Clapton, Neil Diamond, Bob Dylan, Joni Mitchell, Neil Young, Emmylou Harris, Van Morrison, the Staples, Dr. John, Muddy Waters, Paul Butterfield, Ronnie Hawkins, Ringo Starr, Ron Wood.

MOVIES FEATURING A POP MUSIC SOUNDTRACK

FM   *Stars:* Martin Mull, Eileen Brennan, Cleavon Little, Alex Karras. Features great seventies soundtrack, along with live performances by Linda Ronstadt and Jimmy Buffett.

I Wanna Hold Your Hand   *Stars:* Nancy Allen, Marc McClure, Eddie Deezen. Features original Beatles songs on the soundtrack.

National Lampoon's Animal House   *Stars:* John Belushi, Tim Matheson, Tom Hulce,

Kevin Bacon, Donald Sutherland. Soundtrack features hits of the fifties and early sixties.

OTHER POPULAR MOVIES OF 1978

The Cheap Detective
Coming Home
Death on the Nile
The Deer Hunter

Jaws 2
Midnight Express
Oliver's Story
Superman

ACADEMY AWARD WINNERS OF 1978

Best Actor: Jon Voight, *Coming Home*
Best Actress: Jane Fonda, *Coming Home*
Best Picture: *The Deer Hunter*
Best Original Song: "Last Dance," *Thank God, It's Friday* (music and lyrics by Paul Jabara)

TOP TELEVISION SHOWS OF 1978

All in the Family
Angie
Happy Days
Laverne and Shirley
M*A*S*H

Mork and Mindy
The Ropers
60 Minutes
Taxi
Three's Company

1979

NEWS HIGHLIGHTS OF 1979

⇨ The Shah is forced to leave Iran after 37 years on the Peacock Throne. The Ayatollah Khomeini, a Muslim fundamentalist, returns after 15 years of exile to establish a socialist Islamic republic.

⇨ Egypt's President Sadat and Israel's Prime Minister Begin sign a peace agreement at the White House.

⇨ The Three Mile Island nuclear plant in Pennsylvania begins emitting radiation when problems with the cooling system expose part of the core.

⇨ Actor Lee Marvin is sued for "palimony" by a former female companion.

⇨ In Vienna, President Carter and Soviet leader Leonid Brezhnev sign the SALT II agreement limiting strategic weapons. The U.S. Congress would ultimately fail to ratify the treaty, but both sides abide by its terms anyway.

⇨ General Somoza resigns as president of Nicaragua, and the Sandinistas succeed to power.

⇨ Chrysler Corporation asks the federal government for a loan of $1 billion after reporting the largest quarterly loss in its history.

⇨ Pope John Paul II travels to the United States, the first time a pope has set foot on American soil.

⇨ The United States Embassy in Tehran is seized, and 54 American citizens are taken hostage; two are soon released, but the rest are held captive for 444 days.

⇨ Former Governor Ronald Reagan, Senator Edward Kennedy, and President Carter are the leading names for their parties' presidential nominations.

⇨ Mother Teresa, the empress of charity, accepts the Nobel Peace Prize.

⇨ In December, Soviet forces invade Afghanistan.

SPORTS WINNERS

Baseball   The Pittsburgh Pirates beat the Baltimore Orioles 4 games to 3.
Football
   NFC: The Los Angeles Rams beat the Tampa Bay Bucaneers 9–0 in Tampa.
   AFC: The Pittsburgh Steelers beat the Houston Oilers 27–13 in Pittsburgh.
   Super Bowl XIV: The Pittsburgh Steelers beat the Los Angeles Rams 31–19 on January 20, 1980, at the Rose Bowl in Pasadena, California.
Basketball   The Seattle Supersonics beat the Washington Bullets 4 games to 1.
Hockey   The Montreal Canadiens beat the New York Rangers 4 games to 1.

MUSIC HIGHLIGHTS OF 1979

⇨ The Bee Gees, Rod Stewart, Donna Summer, John Denver, and Olivia Newton-John are a few of the performers to take part in a show taped at the United Nations General Assembly. The special, shown on NBC-TV, is to help UNICEF raise money to combat hunger and provide food for the world's children.

AC/DC (l to r: Cliff Williams, Malcolm Young, Simon Wright, Angus Young, Brian Johnson)

⇨ On Saturday, February 3, at the Clear Lake City "Surf Ballroom" in Iowa, Wolfman Jack hosts a tribute show to the memory of the late Buddy Holly, Ritchie Valens, and the Big Bopper. Taped as a cable TV special to honor the 20th anniversary of their deaths, the show stars Del Shannon, Jimmy Clanton, and assorted rock stars of the fifties.

⇨ *Evita,* a musical based on the life of the wife of Argentine dictator Juan Perón, opens on Broadway. Patti LuPone shines in the title role.

⇨ Paul McCartney signs a $20 million recording contract with Columbia Records.

⇨ In Havana, Columbia Records records the first American concert held in Cuba in 20 years, Havana Jam. It stars Billy Joel, Kris Kristofferson, and other recording acts.

⇨ EMI buys United Artists Records, and MCA buys ABC Records.

⇨ A landmark documentary about rock's biggest names debuts on ABC-TV. *The Heroes of Rock 'n' Roll,* starring Jeff Bridges, shows film clips of rock's major performers from the fifties, sixties, and seventies.

⇨ Marty Balin leaves the Jefferson Starship and is replaced by Mickey Thomas.

⇨ Ry Cooder records the first digitally recorded album, *Bop Till You Drop.*

⇨ The Who begins touring with drummer Kenney Jones replacing Keith Moon, who died in 1978.

⇨ At Eric Clapton's wedding to Patti Boyd (the former Mrs. George Harrison), Paul McCartney, Harrison, Ringo Starr, Mick Jagger, and Clapton hold an impromptu jam.

⇨ Chuck Berry enters Lompoc Prison in California to begin a four-month sentence for income tax evasion. He winds up serving only two months.

⇨ At a Who concert in Cincinnati, Ohio, 11 fans are trampled to death as the crowd rushes in for their nonassigned seats.

DEBUT ARTISTS OF 1979

MAJOR ARTISTS	Debut Single	Label
AC/DC (Bon Scott, Angus Young, Malcolm Young, Cliff Williams, Simon Wright)	Highway To Hell	Atlantic
Pat Benatar (Pat Andrzejewski)	Heartbreaker	Chrysalis
Blondie (Debbie Harry, Chris Stein, Jimmy Destri, Nigel Harrison, Clement Burke, Frank Infante)	Heart Of Glass ☆ ⑥	Chrysalis
Kim Carnes	It Hurts So Bad	EMI America
John Cougar (Mellencamp)	I Need A Lover	Riva
Dire Straits (Mark Knopfler, David Knopfler, John Illsley, Pick Withers, Alan Clark)	Sultans Of Swing	Warner Bros.
Joe Jackson	Is She Really Going Out With Him?	A & M
The Knack (Doug Fieger, Berton Averre, Prescott Niles, Burce Gary)	My Sharona ☆ ⑥	Capitol

Pat Benatar in concert (photo: *Anastasia Pantsios*)

Blondie (l to r: Debbie Harry, Clement Burke, Frank Infante, Jimmy Destri, Nigel Harrison, Chris Stein)

1979

Stephanie Mills	What Cha Gonna Do With My Lovin'	20th Century
The Police (Sting [Gordon Sumner], Andy Summers, Stewart Copeland)	Roxanne	A & M
Triumph (Rik "The Rocket" Emmett, Mike Levine, Gil "The Bird" Moore)	Hold On	RCA

OTHER ARTISTS

Arpeggio
The Bama Band
Bandit
Cheryl Barnes
The Barron Knights
The Beckmeier Brothers
Bell & James
Blackfoot
Blackjack
The Blend
Bonnie Boyer
Herman Brood & His Wild Romance
Nancy Brooks
Chuck Brown & the Soul Searchers
Randy Brown
Buckeye
The Buggles
Cindy Bullens
Kate Bush
Chanson
Desmond Child & Rouge
Cherie & Marie Currie
Tim Curry
Steve Dahl
Sarah Dash
Cory Daye
The Delegation
The Euclid Beach Band
The Fabulous Poodles
The Faith Band
The Farragher Brothers
Five Special

Flash & the Pan
The Flying Lizards
Ellen Foley
Steve Forbert
The Funky Communication Committee
Richie Furay
Gary's Gang
The Gibson Brothers
Louise Goffin
Frannie Golde
Ian Gomm
Gonzales
GQ
Grey & Hanks
The Headboys
Keith Herman
Patrick Hernandez
Ian Hunter
Instant Funk
Ironhorse
Tom Johnston
France Joli
The Jones Girls
Rickie Lee Jones
Kermit (Jim Henson)
Fern Kinney
Lazy Racer
Orsa Lia
Liner
Liquid Gold
Ian Lloyd
Nick Lowe

347

M
Machine
Marshall Hain
Moon Martin
Carolyne Mas
Alton McClain & Destiny
McFadden & Whitehead
McGuinn, Clark & Hillman
Mistress
Nature's Divine
David Naughton
New England
Night
Niteflyte
Oak
Pages
Dan Peek
Philly Creme
Pink Lady
Pleasure
The Pousette-Dart Band
Rainbow
The Records
The Rockets
Brenda Russell
Sad Cafe
Saint Tropez
Shoes
Rex Smith

Sniff 'N' the Tears
Errol Sober
Gino Soccio
J.D. Souther
Space
The Sports
Amii Stewart
Glenn Sutton
Taka Boom
The Mark Tanner Band
Bram Tchaikovsky
Third World
Tasha Thomas
Chris Thompson
Billy Thorpe
TMG
Pat Travers
Tycoon
Ultimate
Randy Vanwarmer
Roger Voudouris
Voyage
Narada Michael Walden
Anita Ward
The Wilson Brothers
Witch Queen
The Wonder Band
Lauren Wood
Bill Wray

HITS OF 1979

JANUARY

Crazy Love	Poco	ABC
Every Time I Think Of You	The Babys	Chrysalis
Forever In Blue Jeans	Neil Diamond	Columbia
⑥ **Heaven Knows**	Donna Summer & the Brooklyn Dreams	Casablanca
⑥ **I Don't Know If It's Right**	Evelyn "Champagne" King	RCA

Kim Carnes

John Cougar (Mellencamp) in concert
(photo: *Anastasia Pantsios*)

Dire Straits (l to r: Terry Williams, Alan Clark, Mark Knopfler, Hal Lindes, John Illsley)

1979

I Just Fall In Love Again	Anne Murray	Capitol
☆ Ⓟ Knock On Wood	Amii Stewart	Ariola
Lady	The Little River Band	Capitol
Ⓖ Livin' It Up (Friday Night)	Bell & James	A & M
Maybe I'm A Fool	Eddie Money	Columbia
Ⓖ Music Box Dancer	Frank Mills	Polydor
Song On The Radio	Al Stewart	Arista
Ⓖ Stumblin' In	Suzi Quatro & Chris Norman	RSO
☆ Ⓖ What A Fool Believes	The Doobie Brothers	Warner Bros.
You Stepped Into My Life	Melba Moore	Epic

FEBRUARY

Big Shot	Billy Joel	Columbia
Ⓖ Bustin' Loose, Part I	Chuck Brown & the Soul Searchers	Source
☆ Ⓖ Heart Of Glass	Blondie	Chrysalis
He's The Greatest Dancer	Sister Sledge	Cotillion
Ⓖ I Got My Mind Made Up (You Can Get It Girl)	Instant Funk	Salsoul
It Hurts So Bad	Kim Carnes	EMI-America
Ⓖ I Want Your Love	Chic	Atlantic
Just One Look	Linda Ronstadt	Asylum
Keep On Dancin'	Gary's Gang	Columbia
Love Ballad	George Benson	Warner Bros.
Precious Love	Bob Welch	Capitol
Roxanne	The Police	A & M
Ⓟ Shake Your Body	The Jacksons	Epic
Sultans Of Swing	Dire Straits	Warner Bros.
Ⓖ Take Me Home	Cher	Casablanca

MARCH

Blow Away	George Harrison	Dark Horse
Ⓖ Disco Nights (Rock Freak)	GQ	Arista
Don't You Write Her Off	McGuinn, Clark & Hillman	Capitol
Ⓖ Goodnight Tonight	Wings	Columbia
Ⓖ In The Navy	The Village People	Casablanca
Ⓖ Just When I Needed You Most	Randy Vanwarmer	Bearsville
The Logical Song	Supertramp	A & M
Love Is The Answer	England Dan & John Ford Coley	Big Tree

349

		Love Takes Time	Orleans	Infinity
	Ⓖ	Makin' It	David Naughton	RSO
		Renegade	Styx	A & M
☆	Ⓟ	Reunited	Peaches & Herb	Polydor
		Rock 'N' Roll Fantasy	Bad Company	Swan Song
		Rubber Biscuit	The Blues Brothers	Atlantic
☆	Ⓟ	Tragedy	The Bee Gees	RSO

APRIL

		Ain't Love A Bitch	Rod Stewart	Warner Bros.
		Chuck E's In Love	Rickie Lee Jones	Warner Bros.
		Dance The Night Away	Van Halen	Warner Bros.
		Dancin' Fool	Frank Zappa	Zappa
		Deeper Than The Night	Olivia Newton-John	MCA
		Good Timin'	The Beach Boys	Caribou
		Honesty	Billy Joel	Columbia
☆	Ⓟ	Hot Stuff	Donna Summer	Casablanca
	Ⓖ	I Want You To Want Me	Cheap Trick	Epic
☆	Ⓖ	Love You Inside Out	The Bee Gees	RSO
		Old Time Rock & Roll	Bob Seger	Capitol
	Ⓖ	She Believes In Me	Kenny Rogers	United Artists
	Ⓖ	We Are Family	Sister Sledge	Cotillion
	Ⓖ	When You're In Love With A Beautiful Woman	Dr. Hook	Capitol
	Ⓖ	You Take My Breath Away	Rex Smith	Columbia

MAY

	Ⓟ	Ain't No Stoppin' Us Now	McFadden & Whitehead	P.I.R.
☆	Ⓟ	Bad Girls	Donna Summer	Casablanca
	Ⓖ	Boogie Wonderland	Earth, Wind & Fire with the Emotions	ARC
		Do It Or Die	The Atlanta Rhythm Section	Polydor
		Gold	John Stewart	RSO
		Heart Of The Night	Poco	MCA
	Ⓖ	I Was Made For Lovin' You	Kiss	Casablanca
	Ⓖ	Lead Me On	Maxine Nightingale	Windsong
		Minute By Minute	The Doobie Brothers	Warner Bros.
☆	Ⓖ	Ring My Bell	Anita Ward	T.K.
☆	Ⓖ	Sad Eyes	Robert John	EMI-America
		Shadows In The Moonlight	Anne Murray	Capitol
		Shine A Little Love	The Electric Light Orchestra	Jet
		Weekend	Wet Willie	Epic
		You Can't Change That	Raydio	Arista

JUNE

		Days Gone Down	Gerry Rafferty	United Artists
	Ⓖ	The Devil Went Down To Georgia	The Charlie Daniels Band	Epic
		Getting Closer	Wings	Columbia
☆	Ⓖ	Good Times	Chic	Atlantic

350

1979

Song	Artist	Label
Heaven Must Have Sent You	Bonnie Pointer	Motown
⑥ I'll Never Love This Way Again	Dionne Warwick	Arista
Is She Really Going Out With Him	Joe Jackson	A & M
⑥ The Main Event/Fight	Barbra Streisand	Columbia
⑥ Mama Can't Buy You Love	Elton John	MCA
Morning Dance	Spyro Gyra	Infinity
☆ ⑥ My Sharona	The Knack	Capitol
One Way Or Another	Blondie	Chrysalis
Suspicions	Eddie Rabbitt	Elektra
Up On The Roof	James Taylor	Columbia
⑥ You Gonna Make Me Love Somebody Else	The Jones Girls	Philadelphia Int'l

JULY

Song	Artist	Label
⑥ After The Love Has Gone	Earth, Wind & Fire	Arc
Bad Case Of Loving You (Doctor, Doctor)	Robert Palmer	Island
⑥ Born To Be Alive	Patrick Hernandez	Columbia
The Boss	Diana Ross	Motown
Cruel To Be Kind	Nick Lowe	Columbia
Different Worlds	Maureen McGovern	Warner/Curb
☆ ⑥ Don't Stop 'Til You Get Enough	Michael Jackson	Epic
Driver's Seat	Sniff 'n' the Tears	Atlantic
Girl Of My Dreams	Bram Tchaikovsky	Polydor/Radar
Goodbye Stranger	Supertramp	A & M
Let's Go	The Cars	Elektra
Lonesome Loser	The Little River Band	Capitol
☆ ⑥ Rise	Herb Alpert	A & M
Where Were You When I Was Falling In Love	Lobo	Curb/MCA
Youngblood	Rickie Lee Jones	Warner Bros.

AUGUST

Song	Artist	Label
Ain't That A Shame	Cheap Trick	Epic
Arrow Through Me	Wings	Columbia
Dependin' On You	The Doobie Brothers	Warner Bros.
⑥ Dim All The Lights	Donna Summer	Casablanca
⑥ Don't Bring Me Down	The Electric Light Orchestra	Jet

Joe Jackson

McGuinn, Clark & Hillman (l to r: Chris Hillman, Roger McGuinn, Gene Clark)

351

The Police (l to r: Stewart Copeland, Andy Summers, Sting)

	Found A Cure	Ashford & Simpson	Warner Bros.
	Get It Right Next Time	Gerry Rafferty	United Artists
	Gone, Gone, Gone	Bad Company	Swan Song
☆ ⑥	Please Don't Go	K.C. & the Sunshine Band	T.K.
☆ ⑥	Pop Muzik	M	Sire
	Rolene	Moon Martin	Capitol
	Sail On	The Commodores	Motown
	Then You Can Tell Me Goodbye	Toby Beau	RCA
	This Night Won't Last Forever	Michael Johnson	EMI-America
	The Topical Song	The Barron Knights	Epic

SEPTEMBER

	Broken Hearted Me	Anne Murray	Capitol
	Come To Me	France Joli	Prelude
	Damned If I Do	The Alan Parsons Project	Arista
	Dirty White Boy	Foreigner	Atlantic
	Dreaming	Blondie	Chrysalis
	5:15	The Who	Polydor
	Good Girls Don't	The Knack	Capitol
	Half The Way	Crystal Gayle	Columbia
	Hold On	Ian Gomm	Stiff/Epic
	Rainbow Connection	The Muppets	Atlantic
☆ ⑥	Still	The Commodores	Motown
	Victim Of Love	Elton John	MCA
	Voulez-Vous	Abba	Atlantic
	You Decorated My Life	Kenny Rogers	United Artists
	You're Only Lonely	J.D. Souther	Columbia

OCTOBER

☆ ⑥	Babe	Styx	A & M
	Better Love Next Time	Dr. Hook	Capitol
⑥	Cruisin'	Smokey Robinson	Tamla
☆ ⑥	Escape (The Pina Colada Song)	Rupert Holmes	Infinity
☆ ⑥	Heartache Tonight	The Eagles	Asylum
	Highway To Hell	AC/DC	Atlantic
	I Need A Lover	John Cougar	Riva
	I Want You Tonight	Pablo Cruise	A & M
⑥	Ladies Night	Kool & the Gang	De-Lite

☆ ⑥ No More Tears (Enough Is Enough)	Barbra Streisand & Donna Summer	Columbia (7")/ Casablanca (12")
Ships	Barry Manilow	Arista
Take The Long Way Home	Supertramp	A & M
This Is It	Kenny Loggins	Columbia
Tusk	Fleetwood Mac	Warner Bros.
⑥ We Don't Talk Anymore	Cliff Richard	EMI-America

NOVEMBER

⑥ Coward Of The County	Kenny Rogers	United Artists
Cruel Shoes	Steve Martin	Warner Bros.
Deja Vu	Dionne Warwick	Arista
☆ ⑥ Do That To Me One More Time	The Captain & Tennille	Casablanca
Forever Mine	The O'Jays	P.I.R.
Head Games	Foreigner	Atlantic
⑥ I Wanna Be Your Lover	Prince	Warner Bros.
Jane	Jefferson Starship	Grunt
Lay It On The Line	Triumph	RCA
⑥ Rapper's Delight	The Sugar Hill Gang	Sugar Hill
☆ ⑥ Rock With You	Michael Jackson	Epic
Send One Your Love	Stevie Wonder	Tamla
Third Time Lucky	Foghat	Bearsville
Video Killed The Radio Star	The Buggles	Island
⑥ Yes, I'm Ready	Teri De Sario & K.C.	Casablanca

DECEMBER

An American Dream	The Dirt Band	United Artists
Can We Still Be Friends	Robert Palmer	Island
☆ ⑥ Crazy Little Thing Called Love	Queen	Elektra
Daydream Believer	Anne Murray	Capitol
Fool In The Rain	Led Zeppelin	Swan Song
Heartbreaker	Pat Benatar	Chrysalis
I Can't Help Myself	Bonnie Pointer	Motown
Longer	Dan Fogelberg	Full Moon/Epic
The Long Run	The Eagles	Asylum
Romeo's Tune	Steve Forbert	Nemperor
Sara	Fleetwood Mac	Warner Bros.
⑥ The Second Time Around	Shalamar	Solar
September Morn	Neil Diamond	Columbia
When I Wanted You	Barry Manilow	Arista
⑥ Working My Way Back To You/ Forgive Me, Girl	The Spinners	Atlantic

TOP SINGLES OF 1979

℗ Bad Girls	Donna Summer	Casablanca
℗ Do Ya Think I'm Sexy	Rod Stewart	Warner Bros.
℗ Hot Stuff	Donna Summer	Casablanca
℗ I Will Survive	Gloria Gaynor	Polydor
℗ Le Freak	Chic	Atlantic
⑥ My Sharona	The Knack	Capitol
℗ Reunited	Peaches & Herb	Polydor

Ⓖ Rise   Herb Alpert   A & M
Ⓟ Tragedy   The Bee Gees   RSO
Ⓖ What A Fool Believes   The Doobie Brothers   Warner Bros.

TOP ALBUMS OF 1979

Ⓟ	Blondes Have More Fun	Rod Stewart	Warner Bros.
Ⓟ	Breakfast In America	Supertramp	A & M
Ⓟ	A Briefcase Full Of Blues	The Blues Brothers	Atlantic
Ⓟ	Dire Straits	Dire Straits	Warner Bros.
Ⓟ	Get The Knack	The Knack	Capitol
Ⓟ	In Through The Out Door	Led Zeppelin	Swan Song
Ⓟ	The Long Run	The Eagles	Asylum
Ⓟ	Minute By Minute	The Doobie Brothers	Warner Bros.
Ⓟ	Spirits Having Flown	The Bee Gees	RSO
Ⓟ	Tusk	Fleetwood Mac	Warner Bros.

GRAMMY WINNERS IN 1979

The Grammys were televised from the Shrine Auditorium in Los Angeles on Wednesday, February 27, 1980. Kenny Rogers was the host.

Record of the Year: "What A Fool Believes," the Doobie Brothers (Warner Bros.)
Song of the Year: "What A Fool Believes" (music and lyrics by Kenny Loggins & Michael McDonald)
Album of the Year: *52nd Street,* Billy Joel (Columbia)
Best Vocal Performance, Female: "I'll Never Love This Way Again," Dionne Warwick (Arista)
Best Vocal Performance, Male: *52nd Street,* Billy Joel (Columbia)
Best Vocal Performance, Group: "Minute By Minute," the Doobie Brothers (Warner Bros.)
Best Rock Vocal Performance, Female: "Hot Stuff," Donna Summer (Casablanca)
Best Rock Vocal Performance, Male: "Gotta Serve Somebody," Bob Dylan (Columbia)
Best Rock Vocal Performance, Group: "Heartache Tonight," the Eagles (Asylum)
Best New Artist of the Year: Rickie Lee Jones
Best Comedy Performance: *Reality . . . What A Concept,* Robin Williams (Casablanca)
Best Soundtrack Album from a Motion Picture or Television: *Superman,* John Williams (Warner Bros.)

Triumph (l to r: Rik "The Rocket" Emmett, Mike Levine, Gil "The Bird" Moore)

354

DEATHS IN 1979

MUSIC PERFORMERS AND MUSIC INDUSTRY NOTABLES WHO DIED IN 1979

Charlie Mingus, Friday, January 5 (heart attack; 56)

Donny Hathaway, Saturday, January 13 (suicide jump; 33)

Sid Vicious (The Sex Pistols), Friday, February 2 (drug overdose; 21)

Nino Rota (composer), Tuesday, April 10 (blood clot; 68)

Van McCoy, Friday, July 6 (heart attack; 35)

Arthur Fiedler (conductor), Tuesday, July 10 (natural causes; 83)

Minnie Riperton, Thursday, July 12 (cancer; 30)

Dorsey Burnette, Sunday, August 19 (heart attack; 46)

Stan Kenton (bandleader), Saturday, August 25 (stroke; 67)

James McCulloch (Thunderclap Newman), Monday, September 17 (murdered; 26)

Ray Smith, Thursday, November 29 (gunshot; 41)

Dmitri Tiomkin (composer), Sunday, November 11 (natural causes; 80)

Richard Rodgers (composer), Sunday, December 30 (natural causes; 77)

OTHERS WHO DIED IN 1979

Joan Blondell
Al Capp
Mamie Eisenhower
"Two Ton" Tony Galento
Emmett Kelly
Thurman Munson
Merle Oberon

Mary Pickford
Nelson Rockefeller
Jean Seberg
Bishop Fulton Sheen
Vivian Vance
John Wayne
Darryl F. Zanuck

MOVIES OF 1979

MOVIES FEATURING POP MUSIC ARTISTS

Hair *Stars:* John Savage, Treat Williams, Charlotte Rae, Beverly D'Angelo, performing hits like "Hair," "Easy To Be Hard," "Good Morning Starshine," and "Aquarius" from the original Broadway production.

Rock 'n' Roll High School *Stars:* Vince Van Patten, Clint Howard, Dey Young. *Featured songs:* "Rock 'N' Roll High School" and "Sheena Is A Punk Rocker" by the Ramones, plus hits from the fifties and sixties.

The Rose *Stars:* Bette Midler, Alan Bates, Harry Dean Stanton, David Keith. This film, closely paralleling the life of the late Janis Joplin, features Midler in a brilliant portrayal of a rock singer (for which she was nominated for an Oscar). *Featured songs:* "When A Man Loves A Woman" and "The Rose" by Bette Midler.

POP MUSIC CONCERTS ON FILM

The Kids Are Alright A spectacular look at the music and career of the Who in a film filled with concert footage and interviews.

Rust Never Sleeps The music of Neil Young at a big 1978 concert.

MOVIES FEATURING A POP MUSIC SOUNDTRACK

More American Graffiti *Stars:* Ron Howard, Candy Clark, Paul Le Mat, Mackenzie Phillips, Charles Martin Smith, Cindy Williams, Bo Hopkins. This sequel to the 1973 hit *American Graffiti* features a soundtrack loaded with hits of the sixties.

ROCK ON ALMANAC

Supertramp, Breakfast in America *album cover*

The Wanderers *Stars:* Ken Wahl, Karen Allen, John Friedrich. Features hits of the fifties and sixties.

The Warriors *Stars:* Michael Beck, James Remar, Thomas Waites. Soundtrack features a few songs, mostly originals, recorded for the film.

MADE-FOR-TELEVISION MOVIES ABOUT POP PERFORMERS

Birth of the Beatles *Stars:* Stephan MacKenna, Rod Culbertson, John Altman, Ray Ashcroft. This Dick Clark production illustrates the beginnings of the Fab Four.

Elvis *Stars:* Kurt Russell, Shelley Winters, Pat Hingle, Season Hubley. Another Dick Clark production, this one focuses on the life of the late King of Rock 'n' Roll. Songs for the film were performed by Ronnie McDowell.

OTHER POPULAR MOVIES OF 1979

Alien
All That Jazz
The Amityville Horror
Being There
Breaking Away
The China Syndrome
The Jerk
Kramer vs. Kramer

Manhattan
The Muppet Movie
Norma Rae
Rocky II
Starting Over
Star Trek—The Motion Picture
"10"

ACADEMY AWARD WINNERS OF 1979

Best Actor: Dustin Hoffman, *Kramer vs. Kramer*
Best Actress: Sally Field, *Norma Rae*
Best Picture: *Kramer vs. Kramer*
Best Original Song: "It Goes Like It Goes," *Norma Rae* (music by David Shire, lyrics by Norman Gimbel)

TOP TELEVISION SHOWS OF 1979

Alice
Dallas
The Dukes of Hazzard
Flo
M*A*S*H

One Day at a Time
60 Minutes
That's Incredible
Three's Company

1980

NEWS HIGHLIGHTS OF 1980

⇨ Islamic warriors ask the Soviets to leave Afghanistan.

⇨ American speed skater Eric Heiden wins five gold medals at the Winter Olympics in Lake Placid, New York.

⇨ Dr. Herman Tarnower, author of *The Complete Scarsdale Medical Diet,* is slain by his mistress, Jean Harris.

⇨ Eight American servicemen die in a failed attempt to rescue the Americans being held hostage in Tehran.

⇨ Mount St. Helens, in the state of Washington, erupts, and eight people are found dead.

⇨ Comedian Richard Pryor sets himself afire while freebasing cocaine and nearly dies.

⇨ The United States, West Germany, and Japan boycott the Summer Olympics in Moscow to protest the Soviet Union's military intervention in Afghanistan.

⇨ Republican presidential candidate Ronald Reagan announces that George Bush will be his running mate.

⇨ Senator Edward Kennedy bows out of the presidential race, and President Carter wins the nomination at the Democratic national convention.

⇨ Ronald Wilson Reagan is elected the 40th president of the United States.

SPORTS WINNERS

Baseball   The Philadelphia Phillies beat the Kansas City Royals 4 games to 2.
Football
   NFC: The Philadelphia Eagles beat the Dallas Cowboys 20–7 in Philadelphia.
   AFC: The Oakland Raiders beat the San Diego Chargers 34–27 in San Diego.
   Super Bowl XV: The Oakland Raiders beat the Philadelphia Eagles 27–10 on January 25, 1981, in the Louisiana Superdome in New Orleans.
Basketball   The Los Angeles Lakers beat the Philadelphia '76ers 4 games to 2.
Hockey   The New York Islanders beat the Philadelphia Flyers 4 games to 2.

MUSIC HIGHLIGHTS OF 1980

⇨ The trio Emerson, Lake & Palmer disbands.

⇨ Broadway's longest running show, *Grease,* closes, and *42nd Street* makes its debut. The director of the latter, dancer Gower Champion, dies of a heart attack on opening night, but the cast decides that "the show must go on" and performs brilliantly.

⇨ New York's hottest disco club, Studio 54, shuts down because of tax problems involving its owners.

⇨ Drummer Peter Criss leaves Kiss and is replaced by Eric Carr.

Air Supply in concert (photo: Anastasia Pantsios)

Irene Cara

1980

⇨ Bass player Tom Peterson leaves Cheap Trick and is replaced by Pete Comita.

⇨ Lead singer Bon Scott of AC/DC dies in February and is replaced by Brian Johnson.

⇨ Perry Kimble and Donald Johnson leave the group A Taste of Honey.

⇨ Elton John leaves MCA Records to sign with Geffen Records. This causes a slump in his career that would last until he returns to MCA in 1988.

⇨ After Led Zeppelin's drummer John Bonham dies in September, remaining members Jimmy Page, Robert Plant, and John Paul Jones decide to disband the group.

⇨ The movie *Urban Cowboy* attracts millions of new fans to country music and country-style apparel.

⇨ On Monday, December 8, ex-Beatle John Lennon is shot to death by Mark David Chapman outside Lennon's residence, the Dakota Apartments, in New York.

DEBUT ARTISTS OF 1980

MAJOR ARTISTS

MAJOR ARTISTS	Debut Single	Label
Air Supply (Russell Hitchcock, Graham Russell)	Lost In Love	Arista
Irene Cara	Fame	RSO
The Clash (Joe Strummer [John Mellors], Mick Jones, Paul Simonom, Pete Howard)	Train In Vain	Epic
Christopher Cross (Geppert)	Ride Like The Wind	Warner Bros.
Donnie Iris (Ierace)	Ah! Leah!	MCA/Carousel
Stacy Lattisaw	Let Me Be Your Angel	Cotillion
Teena Marie (Mary Christine Brockert)	I Need Your Lovin'	Gordy
Ray Parker, Jr.	Two Places At The Same Time	Arista
The Pretenders (Chrissie Hynde, James Honeyman-Scott, Pete Farndon, Martin Chambers)	Brass In Pocket	Sire
The Michael Stanley Band (Michael Stanley, Kevin Raleigh, Gary Markasky, Bob Pelander, Rick Bell, Michael Gismondi, Tommy Dobeck)	He Can't Love You	EMI-America
Survivor (David Bickler, Frankie Sullivan, Jim Peterik, Dennis Keith Johnson, R. Gary Smith)	Somewhere In America	Scotti Bros.
38 Special (Donnie Van Zant, Don Barnes, Jeff Carlisi, Larry Junstrom, Steve Brookins, Jack Grondin)	Rockin' Into The Night	A & M
Whitesnake (David Coverdale, Micky Moody, Bernie Marsden, Jon Lord, Neil Murray, Ian Paice)	Fool For Your Loving	Mirage

The Clash in concert (photo: Anastasia Pantsios)

OTHER ARTISTS

Russ Ballard
The B-52's
Jay Black
Kurtis Blow
The Boomtown Rats
Breathless
Gary Burbank with Band McNally
Billy Burnette
Rocky Burnette
Felix Cavaliere
Change
Joyce Cobb
Bruce Cockburn
The Cretones
Rodney Crowell
Cugini
Dandy & the Doolittle Band
Deliverance
Devo
Dollar
Charlie Dore
Robbie Dupree
Dynasty
England Dan Seals
Suzanne Fellini
Festival
The Fools
Charles Fox
Gamma
Larry Graham
Jimmy Hall
Amy Holland
David Hudson
Jim Hurt
The Inmates
The Invisible Man's Band
Debbie Jacobs
The Jags
Jon & Vangelis
Ray Kennedy

The Kingbees
The Kings
Jim Kirk & the TM Singers
Fred Knoblock
The Korgis
Korona (Bruce Blackman)
La Flavour
Robin Lane & the Chartbusters
The Larsen-Feiten Band
Johnny Lee
Marcy Levy
Lipps, Inc.
Benny Mardones
Wayne Massey
Delbert McClinton
Peter McIan
Randy Meisner
Molly Hatchet
The Motors
Nielsen/Pearson
Gary Numan
Off Broadway U.S.A.
Lenore O'Malley
Bernadette Peters
Photoglo
Mike Pinera
Ray, Goodman & Brown
RCR
The Reddings
Red Rider
Burt Reynolds
Rockie Robbins
Rockpile
Dann Rogers
The Romantics
The Rossington Collins Band
Patrice Rushen
707
Shooting Star
The Silencers

Grace Slick
The S.O.S. Band
Spider
Split Enz
Frank Stallone
The Sugarhill Gang
Joe Sun
The Robbin Thompson Band
Ali Thomson
Tierra
Touch

The Tourists
Pete Townshend
Eric Troyer
Twennynine
Utopia
The Vapors
Don Williams
Willis "The Guard" & Vigorish
The Yellow Magic Orchestra
Yipes!
Zapp

HITS OF 1980

JANUARY

☆ ⑥	Another Brick In The Wall (Part II)	Pink Floyd	Columbia
	Desire	Andy Gibb	RSO
	Haven't You Heard	Patrice Rushen	Elektra
	Him	Rupert Holmes	MCA
	I Thank You	ZZ Top	Warner Bros.
	I Wish I Was Eighteen Again	George Burns	Mercury
⑥	On The Radio	Donna Summer	Casablanca
	Refugee	Tom Petty & the Heartbreakers	Backstreet
	Remember	Aerosmith	Columbia
⑥	Special Lady	Ray, Goodman & Brown	Polydor
	Three Times In Love	Tommy James	Millennium
	Too Hot	Kool & the Gang	De-Lite
	Too Late	Journey	Columbia
	When A Man Loves A Woman	Bette Midler	Atlantic
	You Might Need Somebody	Turley Richards	Atlantic

FEBRUARY

⑥	And The Beat Goes On	The Whispers	Solar
☆ ⑥	Call Me	Blondie	Chrysalis
	Cars	Gary Numan	Atco
	Come Back	The J. Geils Band	EMI-America
	Fire In The Morning	Melissa Manchester	Arista
	Fire Lake	Bob Seger	Capitol

Stacy Lattisaw

Teena Marie

361

ROCK ON ALMANAC

Molly Hatchet (l to r: Danny Joe Brown, Duane Roland, John Galvin, Bruce Crump, Riff West, Dave Hlubek)

How Do I Make You	Linda Ronstadt	Asylum
I Can't Tell You Why	The Eagles	Asylum
Lost In Love	Air Supply	Arista
My Heroes Have Always Been Cowboys	Willie Nelson	Columbia
Off The Wall	Michael Jackson	Epic
Pilot Of The Airwaves	Charlie Dore	Island
Ride Like The Wind	Christopher Cross	Warner Bros.
ⓖ Sexy Eyes	Dr. Hook	Capitol
Woman	Foreigner	Atlantic

MARCH

Borrowed Time	Styx	A & M
Breakdown Dead Ahead	Boz Scaggs	Columbia
Don't Cry For Me, Argentina	Festival	RSO
Don't Fall In Love With A Dreamer	Kenny Rogers & Kim Carnes	United Artists
☆ ⓟ Funky Town	Lipps, Inc.	Casablanca
Gee Whiz	Bernadette Peters	MCA
Hold On To My Love	Jimmy Ruffin	RSO
I Can't Help It	Andy Gibb & Olivia Newton-John	RSO
Let Me Be	Korona	United Artists
Let's Get Serious	Jermaine Jackson	Motown
Only A Lonely Heart Sees	Felix Cavaliere	Epic
ⓖ The Rose	Bette Midler	Atlantic
Should've Never Let You Go	Neil Sedaka & Dara Sedaka	Elektra
Think About Me	Fleetwood Mac	Warner Bros.
You May Be Right	Billy Joel	Columbia

APRIL

Biggest Part Of Me	Ambrosia	Warner Bros.
☆ ⓖ Coming Up (Live At Glasgow)	Paul McCartney	Columbia
Fool For A Pretty Face	Humble Pie	Atco
Here Comes My Girl	Tom Petty & the Heartbreakers	Backstreet

362

Hurt So Bad	Linda Ronstadt	Asylum
I Don't Want To Walk Without You	Barry Manilow	Arista
It Takes Time	The Marshall Tucker Band	Warner Bros.
Lady	The Whispers	Solar
Love Stinks	The J. Geils Band	EMI-America
Lucky Me	Anne Murray	Capitol
She's Out Of My Life	Michael Jackson	Epic
⑥ Shining Star	The Manhattans	Columbia
Steal Away	Robbie Dupree	Elektra
Twilight Zone/Twilight Tone	The Manhattan Transfer	Atlantic
White Hot	Red Rider	Capitol

MAY

Against The Wind	Bog Seger & the Silver Bullet Band	Capitol
Cupid/I've Loved You For A Long Time	The Spinners	Atlantic
Gimme Some Lovin'	The Blues Brothers	Atlantic
⑥ I'm Alive	The Electric Light Orchestra	MCA
☆ ⑥ It's Still Rock And Roll To Me	Billy Joel	Columbia
Let Me Love You Tonight	The Pure Prairie League	Casablanca
⑥ Little Jeannie	Elton John	MCA
☆ ⑥ Magic	Olivia Newton-John	MCA
Misunderstanding	Genesis	Atlantic
More Love	Kim Carnes	EMI-America
One Fine Day	Carole King	Capitol
Stand By Me	Mickey Gilley	Asylum
℗ Take Your Time (Do It Right)	The S.O.S. Band	Tabu
Theme From New York, New York	Frank Sinatra	Reprise
Tired Of Toein' The Line	Rocky Burnette	EMI-America

JUNE

⑥ All Out Of Love	Air Supply	Arista
⑥ Drivin' My Life Away	Eddie Rabbitt	Elektra
Fame	Irene Cara	RSO
I Can't Let Go	Linda Ronstadt	Asylum
I'm Happy Just To Dance With You	Anne Murray	Capitol

Ray Parker, Jr.

363

	JoJo	Boz Scaggs	Columbia
	Love The World Away	Kenny Rogers	United Artists
	Make A Little Magic	The Dirt Band	United Artists
	Old-Fashion Love	The Commodores	Motown
⑥	One In A Million You	Larry Graham	Warner Bros.
	Play The Game	Queen	Elektra
☆	Sailing	Christopher Cross	Warner Bros.
	Take A Little Rhythm	Ali Thomson	A & M
	That Lovin' You Feelin' Again	Roy Orbison & Emmylou Harris	Warner Bros.
	Who Shot J.R.?	Gary Burbank with Band McNally	Ovation

JULY

	Boulevard	Jackson Browne	Asylum
	Emotional Rescue	The Rolling Stones	Rolling Stones
	First Time Love	Livingston Taylor	Epic
	Give Me The Night	George Benson	Warner Bros.
⑥	He's So Shy	The Pointer Sisters	Planet
	Hey There Lonely Girl	Robert John	EMI-America
	Hot Rod Hearts	Robbie Dupree	Elektra
	I'm Alright	Kenny Loggins	Columbia
⑥	Lookin' For Love	Johnny Lee	Asylum
	Save Me	Dave Mason	Columbia
☆ ⑥	Upside Down	Diana Ross	Motown
	You Better Run	Pat Benatar	Chrysalis
	You'll Accomp'ny Me	Bob Seger & the Silver Bullet Band	Capitol
	You're The Only Woman	Ambrosia	Warner Bros.

AUGUST

	All Over The World	The Electric Light Orchestra	MCA
☆ ℗	Another One Bites The Dust	Queen	Elektra
⑥	Jesse	Carly Simon	Warner Bros.
	Late In The Evening	Paul Simon	Warner Bros.
	Let Me Be Your Angel	Stacy Lattisaw	Cotillion
	Lola (re-entry)	The Kinks	Arista

The Pretenders (l to r: James Honeyman-Scott, Martin Chambers, Chrissie Hynde, Pete Farndon; photo: Ebet Roberts)

Look What You've Done To Me	Boz Scaggs	Columbia
Midnight Rocks	Al Stewart	Arista
My Guy/My Girl	Amii Stewart & Johnny Bristol	Handshake
ⓖ Never Knew Love Like This Before	Stephanie Mills	20th Century
Out Here On My Own	Irene Cara	RSO
True Love Ways	Mickey Gilley	Epic
ⓖ Whip It	Devo	Warner Bros.
Xanadu	Olivia Newton-John & the Electric Light Orchestra	MCA

SEPTEMBER

ⓖ The Breaks (Part I)	Kurtis Blow	Mercury
Could I Have This Dance	Anne Murray	Capitol
Dreamer	Supertramp	A & M
Dreaming	Cliff Richard	EMI-America
Hold On	Kansas	Kirshner
I'm Happy That Love Has Found You	Jimmy Hall	Epic
Master Blaster (Jammin')	Stevie Wonder	Tamla
ⓖ More Than I Can Say	Leo Sayer	Warner Bros.
On The Road Again	Willie Nelson	Columbia
Real Love	The Doobie Brothers	Warner Bros.
ⓖ Theme From The Dukes Of Hazzard (Good Ol' Boys)	Waylon (Jennings)	RCA
Touch And Go	The Cars	Elektra
ⓖ The Wanderer	Donna Summer	Geffen
☆ ⓖ Woman In Love	Barbra Streisand	Columbia
You've Lost That Lovin' Feeling	Hall & Oates	RCA

OCTOBER

☆ ⓟ Celebration	Kool & the Gang	De-Lite
Cry Like A Baby	Kim Carnes	EMI-America
Deep Inside My Heart	Randy Meisner	Epic
Every Woman In The World	Air Supply	Arista
ⓖ Hit Me With Your Best Shot	Pat Benatar	Chrysalis
☆ ⓖ Lady	Kenny Rogers	Liberty

Let's Be Lovers Again	Eddie Money & Valerie Carter	Columbia
A Little Is Enough	Pete Townshend	Atco
Love X Love	George Benson	Warner Bros.
Never Be The Same	Christopher Cross	Warner Bros.
One Trick Pony	Paul Simon	Warner Bros.
Sherry	Robert John	EMI-America
Sometimes A Fantasy	Billy Joel	Columbia
Suddenly	Olivia Newton-John & Cliff Richard	MCA
When We Get Married	Larry Graham	Warner Bros.

NOVEMBER

Ⓖ Guilty	Barbra Streisand & Barry Gibb	Columbia
Hey Nineteen	Steely Dan	MCA
Hungry Heart	Bruce Springsteen	Columbia
☆ Ⓖ I Love A Rainy Night	Eddie Rabbitt	Elektra
I Made It Through The Rain	Barry Manilow	Arista
☆ Ⓖ (Just Like) Starting Over	John Lennon	Geffen
Love On The Rocks	Neil Diamond	Capitol
☆ Ⓖ 9 To 5	Dolly Parton	RCA
One Step Closer	The Doobie Brothers	Warner Bros.
Passion	Rod Stewart	Warner Bros.
Tell It Like It Is	Heart	Epic
☆ Ⓖ The Tide Is High	Blondie	Chrysalis
Time Is Time	Andy Gibb	RSO
Ⓖ The Winner Takes It All	Abba	Atlantic

DECEMBER

Back In Black	AC/DC	Atlantic
Breakfast In America	Supertramp	A & M
Full Of Fire	Shalamar	Solar
Giving It Up For Your Love	Delbert McClinton	Capitol
Heartbreak Hotel	The Jacksons	Epic
I Can't Stop The Feelin'	The Pure Prairie League	Casablanca
☆ Ⓖ Keep On Loving You	REO Speedwagon	Epic
A Little In Love	Cliff Richard	EMI-America
Merry Christmas In The NFL	Willis "The Guard" & Vigorish	Handshake
Miss Sun	Boz Scaggs	Columbia
Riders In The Sky	The Outlaws	Arista
Same Old Lang Syne	Dan Fogelberg	Full Moon
Set The Night On Fire	Oak	Mercury
Seven Bridges Road	The Eagles	Asylum
Who's Making Love	The Blues Brothers	Atlantic

TOP SINGLES OF 1980

Ⓖ Another Brick In The Wall (Part II)	Pink Floyd	Columbia
Ⓟ Another One Bites The Dust	Queen	Elektra
Ⓖ Call Me	Blondie	Chrysalis
Ⓖ Coming Up (Live At Glasgow)	Paul McCartney	Columbia

Ⓖ Crazy Little Thing Called Love	Queen	Elektra
Ⓟ Funky Town	Lipps, Inc.	Casablanca
Ⓖ Lady	Kenny Rogers	Liberty
Ⓖ Magic	Olivia Newton-John	MCA
Ⓖ Rock With You	Michael Jackson	Epic
Ⓖ Upside Down	Diana Ross	Motown

TOP ALBUMS OF 1980

Ⓟ Against The Wind	Bob Seger & the Silver Bullet Band	Capitol
Ⓟ Emotional Rescue	The Rolling Stones	Rolling Stones
Ⓟ The Game	Queen	Elektra
Ⓟ Glass Houses	Billy Joel	Columbia
Ⓟ Guilty	Barbra Streisand	Columbia
Ⓟ Hold Out	Jackson Browne	Asylum
Ⓟ On The Radio—Greatest Hits, Volumes I & II	Donna Summer	Casablanca
Ⓟ The River	Bruce Springsteen	Columbia
Ⓟ The Wall	Pink Floyd	Columbia
Ⓟ Xanadu	Olivia Newton-John & the Electric Light Orchestra	MCA

GRAMMY WINNERS IN 1980

The Grammys were televised from Radio City Music Hall in New York on Wednesday, February 25, 1981. Paul Simon was the host.

Record of the Year: "Sailing," Christopher Cross (Warner Bros.)
Song of the Year: "Sailing" (music and lyrics by Christopher Cross)
Album of the Year: *Christopher Cross,* Christopher Cross (Warner Bros.)
Best Vocal Performance, Female: "The Rose," Bette Midler (Atlantic)
Best Vocal Performance, Male: "This Is It," Kenny Loggins (Columbia)
Best Vocal Performance, Group: "Guilty," Barbra Streisand & Barry Gibb (Columbia)
Best Rock Vocal Performance, Female: *Crimes Of Passion,* Pat Benatar (Chrysalis)
Best Rock Vocal Performance, Male: *Glass Houses,* Billy Joel (Columbia)
Best Rock Vocal Performance, Group: *Against The Wind,* Bob Seger & the Silver Bullet Band (Capitol)

38 Special (top l to r: Jack Grondin, Larry Junstrom, Jeff Carlisi, Donnie Van Zant, Don Barnes; bottom: Steve Brookins)

ROCK ON
ALMANAC

Pete Townshend in concert (photo: Anastasia Pantsios)

Best New Artist of the Year: Christopher Cross
Best Comedy Performance: *No Respect,* Rodney Dangerfield (Casablanca)
Best Soundtrack Album from a Motion Picture or Television: *The Empire Strikes Back,* John Williams (RSO)

DEATHS IN 1980

MUSIC PERFORMERS AND MUSIC INDUSTRY NOTABLES WHO DIED IN 1980

Larry Williams, Wednesday, January 2 (gunshot; 44)

Amos Milburn, Thursday, January 3 (heart attack; 52)

Carl White (The Rivingtons), Monday, January 7 (47)

Andre Kostelanetz, Sunday, January 13 (heart failure; 78)

Jimmy Durante, Monday, January 28 (pneumonitis; 86)

Bon Scott (AC/DC), Tuesday, February 19 (alcohol poisoning; 33)

Janet Vogel Rapp (The Skyliners), Thursday, February 21 (suicide; 37)

Jon Jon Paulus (The Buckinghams), Wednesday, March 26 (drug overdose; 31)

Dick Haymes, Friday, March 28 (lung cancer; 61)

Mantovani (Annunzio Paulo Mantovani), Saturday, March 29 (extended illness; 74)

Morris Stoloff, Wednesday, April 16 (natural causes; 85)

Tommy Caldwell (The Marshall Tucker Band), Monday, April 28 (car crash; 30)

Bert Kaempfert, Sunday, June 22 (stroke; 56)

Keith Godchaux (The Grateful Dead), Tuesday, July 22 (car crash; 32)

John Bonham (Led Zeppelin), Thursday, September 25 (alcohol; 33)

Bobby Lester (The Moonglows), Wednesday, October 15 (cancer; 50)

Ronnie Goodson (Ronnie & the Hi-Lites), Tuesday, November 4 (brain tumor; 33)

John Lennon, Monday, December 8 (gunshot wounds; 40)

Tim Hardin, Monday, December 29 (unknown causes; 40)

OTHERS WHO DIED IN 1980

Alfred Hitchcock
David Jansen
Steve McQueen
Henry Miller
Jesse Owens

George Raft
Duncan Renaldo (Cisco Kid)
Peter Sellers
Jay Silverheels (Tonto)
Mae West

MOVIES OF 1980

MOVIES FEATURING POP MUSIC ARTISTS

The Blues Brothers   *Stars:* John Belushi, Dan Aykroyd, Cab Calloway, John Candy, Henry Gibson, Carrie Fisher. *Musical performers:* James Brown, Aretha Franklin, Ray Charles. *Featured song:* "Think" by Aretha Franklin.

Coal Miner's Daughter   *Stars:* Sissy Spacek, Tommy Lee Jones, Levon Helm, Beverly D'Angelo. Spacek won an Oscar for her portrayal of country singer Loretta Lynn. Spacek does all her own singing in the film.

Fame   *Stars:* Irene Cara, Anne Meara, Lee Curreri, Eddie Barth. *Featured song:* "Fame" (which won an Oscar) by Irene Cara.

The Idolmaker   *Stars:* Ray Sharkey, Tovah Feldshuh, Peter Gallagher, Paul Land. No significant hits.

The Jazz Singer   *Stars:* Neil Diamond, Laurence Olivier, Lucie Arnaz, Franklin Ajaye, Paul Nicholas. *Featured songs:* "America," "Hello Again," and "Love On The Rocks" by Neil Diamond.

One Trick Pony   *Stars:* Paul Simon, Blair Brown, Rip Torn, Joan Hackett, Lou Reed. *Featured songs:* "One Trick Pony" and "Late In The Evening" by Paul Simon, "Rock Lobster" by the B-52's, "Do You Believe In Magic" by the Lovin' Spoonful, "Soul Man" by Sam & Dave.

Roadie   *Stars:* Meat Loaf, Kaki Hunter, Art Carney, Alice Cooper, Gailard Sartain. *Musical performers:* Blondie, Roy Orbison, Ramblin' Jack Elliot.

Urban Cowboy   *Stars:* John Travolta, Debra Winger, Scott Glenn, Mickey Gilley, the Charlie Daniels Band. *Featured songs:* "Lookin' For Love" by Johnny Lee, "The Devil Went Down To Georgia" by the Charlie Daniels Band, "Look What You've Done To Me" by Boz Scaggs, "Stand By Me" by Mickey Gilley, "Love The World Away" by Kenny Rogers.

Xanadu   *Stars:* Olivia Newton-John, Gene Kelly, Michael Beck, James Sloyan. Cliff Richard and the Electric Light Orchestra are not seen in the film, but their music is heard. *Featured songs:* "All Over The World" by the Electric Light Orchestra, "Xanadu" by Olivia Newton-John & the Electric Light Orchestra, "Suddenly" by Olivia Newton-John & Cliff Richard, "Magic" by Olivia Newton-John.

POP MUSIC CONCERTS ON FILM

Divine Madness   Bette Midler in concert.

No Nukes   Clips of a concert to protest nuclear war held at New York's Madison Square Garden. *Musical performers:* Bruce Springsteen, Jackson Browne, Crosby, Stills & Nash, the Doobie Brothers, Bonnie Raitt, Carly Simon, James Taylor, Jesse Colin Young.

Rockshow   Paul McCartney and Wings on tour.

Christopher Cross
album cover

369

ROCK ON ALMANAC

OTHER POPULAR MOVIES OF 1980

Atlantic City
Dressed to Kill
The Elephant Man
The Empire Strikes Back
The Fog
Friday the 13th
Heaven's Gate

9 to 5
Oh, God! Book II
Popeye
Raging Bull
Stardust Memories
Superman II

ACADEMY AWARD WINNERS OF 1980

Best Actor: Robert De Niro, *Raging Bull*
Best Actress: Sissy Spacek, *Coal Miner's Daughter*
Best Picture: *Ordinary People*
Best Original Song: "Fame," *Fame* (music by Michael Gore, lyrics by Dean Pitchford)

TOP TELEVISION SHOWS OF 1980

Alice
Dallas
The Dukes of Hazzard
The Jeffersons
The Love Boat

M*A*S*H
NBC Tuesday Night Movie
Private Benjamin
60 Minutes
Three's Company

1981

NEWS HIGHLIGHTS OF 1981

⇨ Just moments after Jimmy Carter relinquishes the presidency to Ronald Reagan, 52 American hostages are welcomed home after 444 days in captivity in the American embassy in Tehran.

⇨ Millions of Polish workers go on strike in support of a five-day workweek.

⇨ After addressing a labor convention, President Reagan is shot in the chest by a would-be assassin, John Hinckley. The president recovers rapidly; the gunman is later declared insane and is hospitalized.

⇨ *Columbia,* the world's first reusable spacecraft, dubbed the "space shuttle," completes its first orbital flight.

⇨ Pope John Paul II is shot and wounded in St. Peter's Square by a Turkish terrorist.

⇨ In London, Prince Charles, heir to the British throne, and Lady Diana Spencer are wed at the altar of St. Paul's Cathedral in a ceremony beamed by satellite around the world.

⇨ Sandra Day O'Connor is the first woman appointed to the U.S. Supreme Court.

⇨ Walter Cronkite leaves CBS after 19 years and is replaced as senior news anchor by Dan Rather.

⇨ President Reagan fires 12,000 federal air traffic controllers who have been striking for three days.

⇨ The Polish people demonstrate in support of the nation's first independent union, Solidarity; the Soviet Union speaks out against it.

⇨ At a military parade in Cairo, Egyptian leader Anwar Sadat is assassinated.

⇨ A baffling new disease begins appearing among homosexual men, Haitians, and hemophiliacs in the United States. It is later called acquired immune deficiency syndrome (AIDS) and is found to be widespread in parts of Africa and spreading rapidly in other parts of the world.

⇨ On September 14, "Entertainment Tonight" premieres.

SPORTS WINNERS

Baseball   The Los Angeles Dodgers beat the New York Yankees 4 games to 2.
Football
   NFC: The San Francisco '49ers beat the Dallas Cowboys 28–27 in San Francisco.
   AFC: The Cincinnati Bengals beat the San Diego Chargers 27–7 in Cincinnati.
   Super Bowl XVI: The San Francisco '49ers beat the Cincinnati Bengals 26–21 on January 24, 1982, at the Silverdome in Pontiac, Michigan.
Basketball   The Boston Celtics beat the Houston Rockets 4 games to 2.
Hockey   The New York Islanders beat the Minnesota North Stars 4 games to 1.

Alabama (l to r: Mark Herndon, Jeff Cook, Teddy Gentry, Randy Owen)

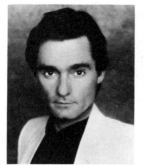

1981

Marty Balin

Phil Collins in concert (photo: Anastasia Pantsios)

MUSIC HIGHLIGHTS OF 1981

⇨ The Sony Walkman pocket stereo becomes popular with millions of music fans on the go.

⇨ Music stars Linda Ronstadt, Rex Smith, Donny Osmond, Debby Boone, and Cher, among others, appear in Broadway shows in New York.

⇨ While touring the United States, Eric Clapton is hospitalized for bleeding ulcers.

⇨ Eddie Van Halen marries actress Valerie Bertinelli, and Ringo Starr weds actress Barbara Bach.

⇨ Yes, Wings, and Steely Dan disband. Laurel Masse leaves the Manhattan Transfer and is replaced by Cheryl Bentyne.

⇨ Bruce Springsteen plays the newly opened Brendan Byrne Arena at East Rutherford, in the Meadowlands of New Jersey.

⇨ On Saturday, August 1, MTV goes on the air with its very first video, the Buggles' "Video Killed The Radio Star." This new way of presenting rock music would change rock 'n' roll forever.

⇨ Diana Ross leaves Motown Records for RCA for a reported $18 million.

⇨ For the first time in years, Paul Simon and Art Garfunkel reunite for a concert in New York's Central Park. The album of the concert would earn them yet another platinum record.

⇨ In the fall, the Rolling Stones do a 10-city tour of the United States.

⇨ Kenny Rogers becomes the top-selling artist of the year.

DEBUT ARTISTS OF 1981

MAJOR ARTISTS	Debut Single	Label
Alabama (Randy Owen, Jeff Cook, Teddy Gentry, Mark Herndon)	Feels So Right	RCA
Patti Austin	Every Home Should Have One	Qwest
Billy & the Beaters (Billy Vera, Jeff "Skunk" Baxter, Bryan Cummings, Jim Elringer, Chuck Fiore, George Marinelli, Jr., Jerry Peterson, Lon Price, Beau Segal, Ron Viola)	I Can Take Care Of Myself	Alfa
Phil Collins	I Missed Again	Atlantic
Sheena Easton	Morning Train ☆ ⑥	EMI-America
The Gap Band (Charlie, Ronnie, and Robert Wilson)	Burn Rubber	Mercury
The Go-Go's (Belinda Carlisle, Charlotte Caffey, Jane Wiedlin, Kathy Valentine, Gina Schock)	Our Lips Are Sealed	I.R.S.

373

James Ingram (with Quincy Jones)	Just Once	A & M
Al Jarreau	We're In This Love Together	Warner Bros.
The Greg Kihn Band (Greg Kihn, Greg Douglas, Gary Phillips, Steven Wright, Larry Lynch)	The Breakup Song (They Don't Write 'Em)	Beserkley
Loverboy (Mike Reno, Paul Dean, Doug Johnson, Scott Smith, Matt Frenette)	Turn Me Loose	Columbia
Stevie Nicks (with Tom Petty & the Heartbreakers)	Stop Draggin' My Heart Around	Modern
The Oak Ridge Boys (Duane Allen, Joe Bonsall, William Lee Golden, Richard Sterban)	Elvira ℗	MCA
Quarterflash (Rindy Ross, Marv Ross, Jack Charles, Rick Di Giallonardo, Rich Gooch, Brian David Willis)	Harden My Heart	Geffen
Lionel Richie (with Diana Ross)	Endless Love ☆ ℗	Motown
Billy Squier	The Stroke	Capitol
Luther Vandross	Never Too Much	Epic
Steve Winwood	While You See A Chance	Island

OTHER ARTISTS

The Afternoon Delights	Eric Hine
Peter Allen	Icehouse
The All Sports Band	Garland Jeffreys
Balance	The Johnny Average Band
Marty Balin	Kano
Lindsey Buckingham	Lakeside
The Cantina Band	Debra Laws
Steve Carlisle	Ronnie Laws
Rosanne Cash	McGuffey Lane
Central Line	Larry John McNally
Champaign	Shamus M'Cool
Bill Champlin	T.S. Monk
The Joe Chemay Band	John O'Banion
Chris Christian	Yoko Ono
Stanley Clarke	Robbie Patton
Michael Damian	Pendulum
Arlan Day	Point Blank
Joel Diamond	Victoria Principal
Diesel	The Producers
The Dillman Band	Leon Redbone
Joe Dolce	The Rings
J.D. Drews	Lee Ritenour
Jackie English	Roger
Don Felder	The Royal Philharmonic Orchestra
Franke & the Knockouts	John Schneider
Gary O.	Eddie Schwartz
Get Wet	Phil Seymour
Terri Gibbs	Sheila B. Devotion
The John Hall Band	The Sherbs
Lani Hall	Shot in the Dark
Debbie Harry	Silverado
The Hawks	Silver Condor
Bertie Higgins	Sky

Sheena Easton

1981

Frankie Smith	Rachel Sweet
Sneaker	Tight Fit
Squeeze	The Tom Tom Club
Stars on 45	Vangelis
The Star Wars Intergalactic Droid Choir & Chorale	Max Werner
Jim Steinman	The West Street Mob
Van Stephenson	Stevie Woods
Shakin' Stevens	Yarbrough & Peoples
Streek	Yutaka

HITS OF 1981

JANUARY

	Ain't Even Done With The Night	John Cougar	Riva
	The Best Of Times	Styx	A & M
	Crying	Don McLean	Millennium
	Flash's Theme a.k.a. Flash	Queen	Elektra
	Fly Away	Peter Allen	A & M
	Guitar Man *(re-entry)*	Elvis Presley	RCA
	Hearts On Fire	Randy Meisner	Epic
	Hello Again	Neil Diamond	Capitol
☆ ⑥	Kiss On My List	Hall & Oates	RCA
☆ ⑥	Rapture	Blondie	Chrysalis
	Somebody's Knockin'	Terri Gibbs	MCA
	Too Tight	Con Funk Shun	Mercury
	Treat Me Right	Pat Benatar	Chrysalis
	What Kind Of Fool	Barbra Streisand & Barry Gibb	Columbia
⑥	Woman	John Lennon	Geffen

FEBRUARY

⑥	Angel Of The Morning	Juice Newton	Capitol
⑥	Being With You	Smokey Robinson	Tamla
	Don't Stand So Close To Me	The Police	A & M
⑥	Don't Stop The Music	Yarbrough & Peoples	Mercury
	Fade Away	Bruce Springsteen	Columbia
	Hold On	Badfinger	Radio
	How 'Bout Us	Champaign	Columbia
	I Can't Stand It	Eric Clapton & His Band	RSO
	I Love You	The Climax Blues Band	Warner Bros.

375

The Go-Go's in concert (photo: Anastasia Pantsios)

Just The Two Of Us	Grover Washington, Jr.	Elektra
Mister Sandman	Emmylou Harris	Warner Bros.
☆ ⑥ Morning Train	Sheena Easton	EMI-America
The Party's Over	Journey	Columbia
Wasn't That A Party	The Rovers	Cleveland Int'l
While You See A Chance	Steve Winwood	Island

MARCH

☆ ⑥ Bette Davis Eyes	Kim Carnes	EMI-America
Her Town Too	James Taylor & J.D. Souther	Columbia
☆ ⑥ Jessie's Girl	Rick Springfield	RCA
Living Inside Myself	Gino Vannelli	Arista
Love You Like I Never Loved Before	John O'Banion	Elektra
Say You'll Be Mine	Christopher Cross	Warner Bros.
⑥ Sukiyaki	A Taste of Honey	Capitol
Sweetheart	Franke & the Knockouts	Millennium
Take It On The Run	REO Speedwagon	Epic
Too Much Time On My Hands	Styx	A & M
Unchained Melody	Heart	Epic
Watching The Wheels	John Lennon	Geffen
What Are We Doin' In Love	Dottie West	Liberty
A Woman Needs Love	Ray Parker, Jr., & Raydio	Arista
You Better You Bet	The Who	Warner Bros.

APRIL

America	Neil Diamond	Capitol
But You Know I Love You	Dolly Parton	RCA
Find Your Way Back	Jefferson Starship	Grunt
I Can Take Care Of Myself	Billy & the Beaters	Alfa
I Don't Need You	Rupert Holmes	MCA
Is It You	Lee Ritenour	Elektra
Just So Lonely	Get Wet	Boardwalk
One Day In Your Life	Michael Jackson	Motown
Seven Year Ache	Rosanne Cash	Columbia
Since I Don't Have You	Don McLean	Millennium
☆ ⑥ Stars On 45	Stars on 45	Radio

This Little Girl	Gary U.S. Bonds	EMI-America
Time	The Alan Parsons Project	Arista
Winning	Santana	Columbia
You Like Me Don't You	Jermaine Jackson	Motown

MAY

	All Those Years Ago	George Harrison	Dark Horse
	Arc Of A Diver	Steve Winwood	Island
	Boy From New York City	The Manhattan Transfer	Atlantic
⑥	Double Dutch Bus	Frankie Smith	WMOT
⑪	Elvira	The Oak Ridge Boys	MCA
	Hearts	Marty Balin	EMI-America
	Modern Girl	Sheena Easton	EMI-America
	Nobody Wins	Elton John	Geffen
☆ ⑥	The One That You Love	Air Supply	Arista
⑥	Queen Of Hearts	Juice Newton	Capitol
	Shaddup You Face	Joe Dolce	MCA
	Sweet Baby	Stanley Clarke/George Duke	Epic
⑥	Theme From "Greatest American Hero" (Believe It Or Not)	Joey Scarbury	Elektra
	The Waiting	Tom Petty & the Heartbreakers	Backstreet
	You Make My Dreams	Hall & Oates	RCA

JUNE

Another Ticket	Eric Clapton & His Band	RSO
Don't Let Him Go	REO Speedwagon	Epic
Don't Want To Wait Anymore	The Tubes	Capitol
Everlasting Love	Rex Smith & Rachel Sweet	Columbia
Fantasy Girl	38 Special	A & M
Gemini Dream	The Moody Blues	Threshold
Hard Times	James Taylor	Columbia
I Don't Need You	Kenny Rogers	Liberty
In The Air Tonight	Phil Collins	Atlantic
It Hurts To Be In Love	Dan Hartman	Blue Sky
Lady	The Commodores	Motown
Love On A Two Way Street	Stacy Lattisaw	Cotillion

Debbie Harry in concert (photo: *Anastasia Pantsios*)

ⓖ **Slow Hand** | The Pointer Sisters | Planet
(There's) No Gettin' Over Me | Ronnie Milsap | RCA
Touch Me When We're Dancing | The Carpenters | A & M

JULY

The Beach Boys Medley | The Beach Boys | Capitol
Cool Love | Pablo Cruise | A & M
Don't Give It Up | Robbie Patton | Liberty
☆ ⓟ **Endless Love** | Diana Ross & Lionel Richie | Motown
Fire And Ice | Pat Benatar | Chrysalis
For Your Eyes Only | Sheena Easton | Liberty
General Hospi-Tale | The Afternoon Delights | MCA
Hold On Tight | The Electric Light Orchestra | Jet
Stars On 45 II | Stars on 45 | Radio
Step By Step | Eddie Rabbitt | Elektra
Stop Draggin' My Heart Around | Steve Nick with Tom Petty & the Heartbreakers | Modern
Summer '81 | The Cantina Band | Millennium
That Old Song | Ray Parker, Jr., & Raydio | Arista
Urgent | Foreigner | Atlantic
Who's Crying Now | Journey | Columbia

AUGUST

All I Have To Do Is Dream | Andy Gibb & Victoria Principal | RSO
☆ ⓖ **Arthur's Theme (Best That You Can Do)** | Christopher Cross | Warner Bros.
Hard To Say | Dan Fogelberg | Full Moon/Epic
In Your Letter | REO Speedwagon | Epic
I've Done Everything For You | Rick Springfield | RCA
Just Once | Quincy Jones featuring James Ingram | A & M
The Night Owl | The Little River Band | Capitol
Our Lips Are Sealed | The Go-Go's | I.R.S.
☆ ⓖ **Private Eyes** | Hall & Oates | RCA
Start Me Up | The Rolling Stones | Rolling Stones

Al Jarreau

Loverboy (l to r: Matt Frenette, Scott Smith, Mike Reno, Doug Johnson, Paul Dean)

1981

Straight From The Heart	The Allman Brothers Band	Arista
Super Freak	Rick James	Gordy
Theme From Hill Street Blues	Mike Post	Elektra
The Voice	The Moody Blues	Threshold
When She Was My Girl	The Four Tops	Casablanca

SEPTEMBER

Atlanta Lady	Marty Balin	EMI-America
Every Little Thing She Does Is Magic	The Police	A & M
Here I Am	Air Supply	Arista
In The Dark	Billy Squier	Capitol
Just Be My Lady	Larry Graham	Warner Bros.
My Girl	Chilliwack	Millennium
No Reply At All	Genesis	Atlantic
Oh No	The Commodores	Motown
Say Goodbye To Hollywood	Billy Joel	Columbia
Share Your Love	Kenny Rogers	Liberty
⑥ She's A Bad Mama Jama (She's Built, She's Stacked)	Carl Carlton	20th Century
Steal The Night	Stevie Woods	Cotillion
Take Me Now	David Gates	Arista
Tryin' To Live My Life Without You	Bob Seger & the Silver Bullet Band	Capitol
Working In The Coal Mine	Devo	Elektra

OCTOBER

Castles In The Air	Don McLean	Millennium
Don't Stop Believin'	Journey	Columbia
Hooked On Classics	The Royal Philharmonic Orchestra	RCA
I Wouldn't Have Missed It For The World	Ronnie Milsap	RCA
Leather And Lace	Stevie Nicks & Don Henley	Modern
⑥ Let's Groove	Earth, Wind & Fire	ABC/Columbia
The Old Songs	Barry Manilow	Arista
☆ ℗ Physical	Olivia Newton-John	MCA
Promises In The Dark	Pat Benatar	Chrysalis

379

ROCK ON ALMANAC

Stevie Nicks in concert (photo: Anastasia Pantsios)

The Sweetest Thing	Juice Newton	Capitol
Take My Heart	Kool & the Gang	De-Lite
Turn Your Love Around	George Benson	Warner Bros.
⑥ Waiting For A Girl Like You	Foreigner	Atlantic
Why Do Fools Fall In Love	Diana Ross	RCA
Young Turks	Rod Stewart	Warner Bros.

NOVEMBER

Anyone Can See	Irene Cara	Network
☆ ⑥ Centerfold	The J. Geils Band	EMI-America
Come Go With Me	The Beach Boys	Caribou
Comin' In And Out Of Your Life	Barbra Streisand	Columbia
Cool Night	Paul Davis	Arista
☆ ⑥ I Can't Go For That (No Can Do)	Hall & Oates	RCA
Key Largo	Bertie Higgins	Kat Family
Leader Of The Band	Dan Fogelberg	Full Moon/Epic
Shake It Up	The Cars	Elektra
She's Got A Way	Billy Joel	Columbia
Someone Could Lose A Heart Tonight	Eddie Rabbitt	Elektra
Under Pressure	Queen & David Bowie	Elektra
WKRP In Cincinnati	Steve Carlisle	MCA/Sweet City
Yesterday's Songs	Neil Diamond	Columbia
You Could Have Been With Me	Sheena Easton	EMI-America

DECEMBER

Abacab	Genesis	Atlantic
All Our Tomorrows	Eddie Schwartz	Atco
Breakin' Away	Al Jarreau	Warner Bros.
Crazy	The John Hall Band	EMI-America
Love Is Like A Rock	Donnie Iris	MCA
One Hundred Ways	Quincy Jones featuring James Ingram	A & M
Sea Of Love	Del Shannon	Network
Somewhere Down The Road	Barry Manilow	Arista
Southern Pacific	Neil Young & Crazy Horse	Reprise

Sweet Dreams	Air Supply	Arista
Take It Easy On Me	The Little River Band	Capitol
Through The Years	Kenny Rogers	Liberty
Waiting On A Friend	The Rolling Stones	Rolling Stones
The Woman In Me	Crystal Gayle	Columbia
A World Without Heroes	Kiss	Casablanca

1981

TOP SINGLES OF 1981

⑥ Arthur's Theme (Best That You Can Do)	Christopher Cross	Warner Bros.
⑥ Bette Davis Eyes	Kim Carnes	EMI-America
⑦ Celebration	Kool & the Gang	De-Lite
⑦ Endless Love	Diana Ross & Lionel Richie	Motown
⑥ Jessie's Girl	Rick Springfield	RCA
⑥ (Just Like) Starting Over	John Lennon	Geffen
⑥ Kiss On My List	Hall & Oates	RCA
⑥ Morning Train	Sheena Easton	EMI-America
⑦ Physical	Olivia Newton-John	MCA
⑥ Rapture	Blondie	Chrysalis

TOP ALBUMS OF 1981

⑦ Bella Donna	Stevie Nicks	Modern
⑦ Double Fantasy	John Lennon/Yoko Ono	Geffen
⑦ Escape	Journey	Columbia
⑦ 4	Foreigner	Atlantic
⑦ Hi Infidelity	REO Speedwagon	Epic
⑦ Long Distance Voyager	The Moody Blues	Threshold
⑦ Mistaken Identity	Kim Carnes	EMI-America
⑦ Paradise Theater	Styx	A & M
⑦ Private Eyes	Hall & Oates	RCA
⑦ Tattoo You	The Rolling Stones	Rolling Stones

GRAMMY WINNERS IN 1981

The Grammys were televised from the Shrine Auditorium in Los Angeles on Wednesday, February 24, 1982. John Denver was the host.

Record of the Year: "Bette Davis Eyes," Kim Carnes (EMI-America)
Song of the Year: "Bette Davis Eyes" (music and lyriccs by Donna Weiss & Jackie De Shannon)
Album of the Year: *Double Fantasy,* John Lennon/Yoko Ono (Geffen)
Best Vocal Performance, Female: *Lena Horne: The Lady And Her Music,* Lena Horne (Qwest)
Best Vocal Performance, Male: *Breakin' Away,* Al Jarreau (Warner Bros.)
Best Vocal Performance, Group: "Boy From New York City," the Manhattan Transfer (Atlantic)
Best Rock Vocal Performance, Female: "Fire And Ice," Pat Benatar (Chrysalis)
Best Rock Vocal Performance, Male: "Jessie's Girl," Rick Springfield (RCA)
Best Rock Vocal Performance, Group: "Don't Stand So Close To Me," the Police (A & M)

Best New Artist of the Year: Sheena Easton
Best Comedy Performance: *Rev. Du Rite,* Richard Pryor (Laff)
Best Soundtrack Album from a Motion Picture or Television: *Raiders Of The Lost Ark,* John Williams (Columbia)

DEATHS IN 1981

MUSIC PERFORMERS AND MUSIC INDUSTRY NOTABLES WHO DIED IN 1981

David Lynch (The Platters), Friday, January 2 (cancer; 51)

Carl Feaster (The Chords), Thursday, January 23 (cancer; 47)

Cozy Cole, Thursday, January 29 (cancer; 71)

Hugo Montenegro, Friday, February 6 (emphysema; 55)

Bill Haley, Monday, February 9 (heart attack; 55)

Bob "The Bear" Hite (Canned Heat), Monday, April 6 (heart attack; 36)

Bob Marley, Monday, May 11 (cancer; 36)

Joan Weber, Wednesday, May 13 (45)

Ernie Freeman, Saturday, May 16 (heart attack; 58)

Roy Brown, Monday, May 25 (heart attack; 56)

Rushton Moreve (Steppenwolf), Wednesday, July 1 (car crash; 35)

Harry Chapin, Thursday, July 16 (car crash; 38)

Tommy Edwards, Friday, July 24 (brain aneurysm; 58)

Vera Ellen, Monday, August 30 (cancer; 61)

Jud Strunk, Monday, October 5 (plane crash; 45)

Sonny Til (Earlington Tilgham) (The Orioles), Wednesday, December 9 (heart attack; 53)

Hoagy Carmichael (songwriter), Sunday, December 27 (heart attack; 82)

OTHERS WHO DIED IN 1981

"Stymie" Beard
Beulah Bondi
Richard Boone
Omar Bradley
Paddy Chayevsky
Melvin Douglas
William Holden

George Jessel
Joe Louis
William Saroyan
Lowell Thomas
Natalie Wood
William Wyler

MOVIES OF 1981

MOVIES FEATURING A POP MUSIC SOUNDTRACK

American Pop   Director Ralph Bakshi's animated film of the history of American music, using some oldies, such as Sam Cooke's "You Send Me."

Lionel Richie

The Oak Ridge Boys (l to r: Joe Bonsall, Duane Allen, William Lee Golden, Richard Sterban)

1981

MADE-FOR-TELEVISION MOVIES ABOUT POP MUSIC PERFORMERS

Elvis and the Beauty Queen   *Stars:* Don Johnson, Stephanie Zimbalist, Rick Lenz. This movie focused on Elvis's relationship with beauty queen Linda Thompson.

OTHER POPULAR MOVIES OF 1981

Absence of Malice
Arthur
Bustin' Loose
Chariots of Fire
Friday the 13th, Part 2
The Gods Must Be Crazy
On Golden Pond

Porky's
The Postman Always Rings Twice
Ragtime
Raiders of the Lost Ark
Reds
S.O.B.
Thief

ACADEMY AWARD WINNERS OF 1981

Best Actor: Henry Fonda, *On Golden Pond*
Best Actress: Katherine Hepburn, *On Golden Pond*
Best Picture: *Chariots of Fire*
Best Original Song: "Arthur's Theme (Best That You Can Do)," *Arthur* (music and lyrics by Burt Bacharach, Carol Bayer Sager, Christopher Cross, and Peter Allen)

TOP TELEVISION SHOWS OF 1981

ABC Monday Night Movie
Alice
Dallas
The Dukes of Hazzard
The Jeffersons

Joanie Loves Chachi
M*A*S*H
60 Minutes
Three's Company
Too Close for Comfort

1982

NEWS HIGHLIGHTS OF 1982

⇨ An Air Florida jet taking off in a snowstorm hits the Potomac Bridge in Washington, killing 78 persons.

⇨ Argentine troops invade the British-held Falkland Islands. Great Britain successfully defends them.

⇨ The last Israeli soldiers leave the Sinai, and the disputed area is returned to Egypt.

⇨ Pope John Paul II is the first Catholic pontiff in over 450 years to visit Britain.

⇨ Israeli forces invade Lebanon.

⇨ More than 80,000 marchers in New York demonstrate against nuclear proliferation.

⇨ The television show *Late Night with David Letterman* debuts.

⇨ During the shooting of the movie *The Twilight Zone,* a helicopter crash kills actor Vic Morrow and two Vietnamese children.

⇨ In eight separate instances, people taking Tylenol capsules die. Before the cause is discovered to be deliberate contamination, the manufacturer withdraws the product from the market. It is later reintroduced and regains its position as the number one pain reliever.

⇨ Barney B. Clark, a retired dentist from Seattle, becomes the first recipient of a permanent artificial heart. He lives over a year, but strokes keep him bedridden.

SPORTS WINNERS

Baseball   The St. Louis Cardinals beat the Milwaukee Brewers 4 games to 3.

Football

NFC: The Washington Redskins beat the Dallas Cowboys 31–17 in Washington, D.C.

AFC: The Miami Dolphins beat the New York Jets 14–0 in Miami.

Super Bowl XVII: The Washington Redskins beat the Miami Dolphins 27–17 on January 30, 1983, at the Rose Bowl in Pasadena, California.

Basketball   The Los Angeles Lakers beat the Philadelphia '76ers 4 games to 2.

Hockey   The New York Islanders beat the Vancouver Canucks 4 games to 0.

MUSIC HIGHLIGHTS OF 1982

⇨ The CD (Compact Disc) is developed jointly by Sony and Philips of the Netherlands. The CD preserves recorded music digitally. Each sound is broken down into tiny fractions of seconds and stored as a digital code on the disc, which the CD player reads and plays back, practically eliminating all extraneous sounds and distortion.

⇨ Synthesizers and computers are used by English "technopop" bands like A Flock of Seagulls and the Human League.

⇨ Blondie, the Eagles, and the Doobie Brothers all break up.

⇨ *Cats* opens on Broadway.

Bryan Adams in concert (photo: Anastasia Pantsios)

385

⇨ On Monday, June 7, Graceland, Elvis Presley's home in Memphis, Tennessee, opens to the public as a tourist attraction.

⇨ Pat Benatar marries her producer, Neil Geraldo, and "Miami" Steve Van Zandt weds longtime girlfrield Maureen Santora.

⇨ On Sunday, July 4, Ozzy Osbourne marries his manager, Sharon Arden.

⇨ Soft Cell's "Tainted Love" becomes the longest-charting single of the rock era, remaining on *Billboard*'s Hot 100 for 43 weeks.

⇨ Tina Turner begins a British tour, her first in that country in four years.

⇨ In a car crash, Teddy Pendergrass, former lead singer of Harold Melvin & the Blue Notes, is paralyzed from the waist down. Shortly thereafter, Billy Joel crashes his motorcycle and spends a month in a Long Island hospital having therapy for his injured hand.

⇨ KTSA radio in San Antonio becomes the first full-time AM stereo station.

⇨ Elton John embarks on his first British tour in three years.

⇨ The Who embarks on a final tour. The legendary group decides to call it quits after nearly 20 years together.

DEBUT ARTISTS OF 1982

MAJOR ARTISTS	Debut Single	Label
Bryan Adams	Lonely Nights	A & M
Atlantic Starr (Wayne Lewis, David Lewiss, Sharon Bryant)	Circles	A & M
Laura Branigan	All Night With Me	Atlantic
Peabo Bryson	Let The Feeling Flow	Capitol
Culture Club (Boy George [George O'Dowd], Roy Hay, Michael Craig, Jon Moss)	Do You Really Want To Hurt Me	Virgin/Epic
Duran Duran (Simon Le Bon, Andy Taylor, Nick Rhodes, John Taylor, Roger Taylor)	Hungry Like The Wolf	Harvest
The Fixx (Cy Curnin, Jamie West-Oram, Adam Woods, Rupert Greenall, Charlie Barrett)	Stand Or Fall	MCA
Glenn Frey	I Found Somebody	Asylum
Don Henley	Johnny Can't Read	Asylum
The Human League (Philip Oakley, Adrian Wright, Joanne Cathedrall, Suzanne Sulley, Ian Burden, Jo Callis)	Don't You Want Me Ⓖ	A & M/Virgin
Billy Idol (William Broad)	Hot In The City	Chrysalis

Boy George of Culture Club in concert (photo: Anastasia Pantsios)

Janet Jackson
Joan Jett & the Blackhearts (Joan Jett, Ricky Byrd, Gary Ryan, Lee Crystal)

Huey Lewis & the News (Huey Lewis [Hugh Anthony Cregg III], Chris Hayes, Johnny Colla, Sean Hopper, Mario Cipollina, Billy Gibson)

Michael McDonald
Men at Work (Colin Hay, Ron Strykert, Greg Ham, John Rees, Jerry Speiser)

Missing Persons (Dale Bozzio, Warren Cuccurullo, Chuck Wild, Patrick O'Hearn, Terry Bozzio)

The Motels (Martha Davis, Guy Perry, Martin Life Jourard, Michael Goodroe, Scott Thurston, Brian Glascock)

Jeffrey Osborne

Steve Perry (with Kenny Loggins)
Robert Plant
The Stray Cats (Brian Setzer, Lee Rocker [Leon Drucker], Slim Jim Phantom MacDonnell)

Kim Wilde

Young Love	A & M
I Love Rock 'N' Roll ☆ ℗	Boardwalk
Do You Believe In Love	Chrysalis
I Keep Forgettin'	Warner Bros.
Who Can It Be Now? ☆	Columbia
Words	Capitol
Only The Lonely	Capitol
I Really Don't Need No Light	A & M
Don't Fight It	Columbia
Burning Down One Side	Swan Song
Rock This Town	EMI-America
Kids In America	EMI-America

1982

OTHER ARTISTS

ABC
Afrika Bambaataa & the Soul Sonic Force
Alessi
Adam Ant
Asia
Christopher Atkins
Aurra
Axe
The Frank Barber Orchestra
Toni Basil
Rick Bowles
Bow Wow Wow
The Boys Band
Buckner & Garcia
Tane Cain
Larry Carlton
Paul Carrack
Cheri
The Clocks
Conductor
Josie Cotton
Marshall Crenshaw
Dayton
The Dazz Band
Duke Jupiter
Larry Elgart & His Manhattan Swing Orchestra
Eye to Eye
Donald Fagen
Joe Fagin

Richard "Dimples" Fields
A Flock of Seagulls
Frida
Gidea Park featuring Adrian Baker
Glass Moon
Grand Master Flash & the Furious Five
Haircut One Hundred
Jennifer Holliday
Judas Priest
Junior
Madleen Kane
David Lasley
Larry Lee
Le Roux
Little Steven & the Disciples of Soul
Bob & Doug McKenzie
The Monroes
Moving Pictures
Musical Youth
Aldo Nova
O'Bryan
One Way
The Henry Paul Band
Leslie Pearl
Rodway
Rough Trade
Saga
Scandal
Timothy B. Schmit

387

The Scorpions
Skyy
Soft Cell
Sparks
Spys
Steel Breeze
Sylvia

Talk Talk
The Time
Toronto
The Waitresses
Yaz
Pia Zadora

HITS OF 1982

JANUARY

☆	**Chariots Of Fire**	Vangelis	Polydor
	Daddy's Home	Cliff Richard	EMI-America
	If Looks Could Kill	Player	RCA
	Mirror, Mirror	Diana Ross	RCA
	My Guy	Sister Sledge	Cotillion
	Open Arms	Journey	Columbia
Ⓖ	**Pac-Man Fever**	Buckner & Garcia	Columbia
	Seasons Of Gold	Gidea Park featuring Adrian Baker	Profile
	Should I Do It	The Pointer Sisters	Planet
	Spirits In The Material World	The Police	A & M
	Tainted Love	Soft Cell	Sire
	That Girl	Stevie Wonder	Tamla
	Tonight I'm Yours	Rod Stewart	Warner Bros.
	Wanna Be With You	Earth, Wind & Fire	Arc/Columbia
Ⓖ	**We Got The Beat**	The Go-Go's	I.R.S.

FEBRUARY

	Baby Makes Her Blue Jeans Talk	Dr. Hook	Casablanca
	Do You Believe In Love	Huey Lewis & the News	Chrysalis
	Edge Of Seventeen	Stevie Nicks	Modern
Ⓖ	**Freeze-Frame**	The J. Geils Band	EMI-America
☆ Ⓟ	**I Love Rock 'N' Roll**	Joan Jett & the Blackhearts	Boardwalk
	Make A Move On Me	Olivia Newton-John	MCA
	Memories Of Days Gone By	Fred Parris & the Five Satins	Elektra
	Memory	Barbra Streisand	Columbia

Glenn Frey

388

Billy Idol in concert (photo: Anastasia Pantsios)

1982

On The Way To The Sky	Neil Diamond	Columbia
Pop Goes The Movies, Part I	Meco	Arista
Pretty Woman	Van Halen	Warner Bros.
Running	Chubby Checker	MCA
'65 Love Affair	Paul Davis	Arista
Sleep Walk	Larry Carlton	Warner Bros.
Theme From Magnum P.I.	Mike Post	Elektra

MARCH

Always On My Mind	Willie Nelson	Columbia
The Beatles Movie Medley	The Beatles	Capitol
Did It In A Minute	Hall & Oates	RCA
Don't Talk To Strangers	Rick Springfield	RCA
☆ ⑥ Don't You Want Me	The Human League	A & M/Virgin
Empty Garden	Elton John	Geffen
I'll Try Something New	A Taste of Honey	Capitol
I've Never Been To Me	Charlene	Motown
Let's Hang On	Barry Manilow	Arista
Lonely Nights	Bryan Adams	A & M
Making Love	Roberta Flack	Atlantic
The Other Woman	Ray Parker, Jr.	Arista
Shanghai Breezes	John Denver	RCA
Since You're Gone	The Cars	Elektra
Stars On 45 III	Stars on 45	Radio

APRIL

Beechwood 4-5789	The Carpenters	A & M
☆ ⑥ Ebony & Ivory	Stevie Wonder with Paul McCartney	Columbia
Friends In Love	Johnny Mathis & Dionne Warwick	Arista
Heat Of The Moment	Asia	Geffen
How Long	Rod Stewart	Warner Bros.
⑥ Hurts So Good	John Cougar	Riva
It's Gonna Take A Miracle	Deniece Williams	Arc/Columbia
Man On Your Mind	The Little River Band	Capitol
Old Fashioned Love	Smokey Robinson	Tamla
Only The Lonely	The Motels	Capitol
Rosanna	Toto	Columbia

*Joan Jett & the Blackhearts
(l to r: Gary Ryan, Lee Crystal,
Joan Jett, Ricky Byrd)*

Run For The Roses	Dan Fogelberg	Full Moon/Epic
Wake Up Little Susie	Simon & Garfunkel	Warner Bros.
When It's Over	Loverboy	Columbia
Work That Body	Diana Ross	RCA

MAY

☆ ⑥	**Abracadabra**	The Steve Miller Band	Capitol
	Any Day Now	Ronnie Milsap	RCA
	Be Mine Tonight	Neil Diamond	Columbia
	Body Language	Queen	Elektra
	Break It Up	Foreigner	Atlantic
	Caught Up In You	38 Special	A & M
	Crimson And Clover	Joan Jett & the Blackhearts	Boardwalk
	Dance Wit' Me	Rick James	Gordy
	Dancing In The Street	Van Halen	Warner Bros.
	Do I Do	Stevie Wonder	Tamla
	I Know What Boys Like	The Waitresses	Polydor
	Island Of Lost Souls	Blondie	Chrysalis
	Love's Been A Little Bit Hard On Me	Juice Newton	Capitol
	Personally	Karla Bonoff	Columbia
	You Should Hear How She Talks About You	Melissa Manchester	Arista

JUNE

	American Music	The Pointer Sisters	Planet
	Even The Nights Are Better	Air Supply	Arista
☆ ℗	**Eye Of The Tiger**	Survivor	Scotti Bros.
	Going To A Go-Go	The Rolling Stones	Rolling Stones
☆ ⑥	**Hard To Say I'm Sorry**	Chicago	Full Moon/ Warner
	Hold Me	Fleetwood Mac	Warner Bros.
	Hooked On Swing	Larry Elgart & His Manhattan Swing Orchestra	RCA
	I Found Somebody	Glenn Frey	Asylum
	If You Want My Love	Cheap Trick	Epic
	Keep The Fire Burnin'	REO Speedwagon	Epic

Route 101	Herb Alpert	A & M
Street Corner	Ashford & Simpson	Capitol
Wasted On The Way	Crosby, Stills & Nash	Atlantic
What Kind Of Fool Am I	Rick Springfield	RCA
Your Imagination	Hall & Oates	RCA

JULY

	Blue Eyes	Elton John	Geffen
	Do You Wanna Touch Me (Oh Yeah)	Joan Jett & the Blackhearts	Boardwalk
	Eye In The Sky	The Alan Parsons Project	Arista
⑥	Gloria	Laura Branigan	Atlantic
	Hot In The City	Billy Idol	Chrysalis
☆ ⑥	Jack And Diane	John Cougar	Riva/Mercury
	Love Will Turn You Around	Kenny Rogers	Liberty
	Oh Julie	Barry Manilow	Arista
⑥	Planet Rock	Afrika Bambaataa & the Soul Sonic Force	Tommy Boy
	Somebody's Baby	Jackson Browne	Asylum
	Take It Away	Paul McCartney	Columbia
	Think I'm In Love	Eddie Money	Columbia
	Vacation	The Go-Go's	I.R.S.
	Valley Girl	Frank Zappa	Barking Pumpkin
	You Can Do Magic	America	Capitol

AUGUST

	Big Fun	Kool & the Gang	De-Lite
	Break It To Me Gently	Juice Newton	Capitol
	Emotions In Motion	Billy Squier	Capitol
	Hold On	Santana	Columbia
	I Keep Forgettin'	Michael McDonald	Warner Bros.
	I Only Want To Be With You	Nicolette Larson	Warner Bros.
	Jump To It	Aretha Franklin	Arista
	Make Believe	Toto	Columbia
⑥	Nobody	Sylvia	RCA
	Should I Stay Or Should I Go?	The Clash	Epic
	Steppin' Out	Joe Jackson	A & M
☆	Up Where We Belong	Joe Cocker & Jennifer Warnes	Island

Huey Lewis in concert (photo: *Anastasia Pantsios*)

You Don't Want Me Anymore	Steel Breeze	RCA
You Dropped A Bomb On Me	The Gap Band	Total Experience
You Keep Runnin' Away	38 Special	A & M

SEPTEMBER

Get Up And Go	The Go-Go's	I.R.S.
Gypsy	Fleetwood Mac	Warner Bros.
Heart Attack	Olivia Newton-John	MCA
Heartlight	Neil Diamond	Columbia
I Get Excited	Rick Springfield	RCA
I'm So Excited	The Pointer Sisters	Planet
The Look Of Love (Part One)	ABC	Mercury
Love Me Tomorrow	Chicago	Full Moon/ Warner
☆ ℗ Mickey	Toni Basil	Chrysalis
On The Wings Of Love	Jeffrey Osborne	A & M
Pressure	Billy Joel	Columbia
Ribbon In The Sky	Stevie Wonder	Tamla
Rock This Town	The Stray Cats	EMI-America
Southern Cross	Crosby, Stills & Nash	Atlantic
What About Me	Moving Pictures	Network

OCTOBER

☆ ⑥ Baby, Come To Me	Patti Austin with James Ingram	Qwest
Be My Lady	Jefferson Starship	Grunt
Cool Magic	Steve Miller	Capitol
⑥ Dirty Laundry	Don Henley	Asylum
Heartbreaker	Dionne Warwick	Arista
I.G.Y. (What A Beautiful World)	Donald Fagen	Warner Bros.
It's Raining Again	Supertramp	A & M
☆ ⑥ Maneater	Hall & Oates	RCA
Missing You	Dan Fogelberg	Full Moon/Epic
Muscles	Diana Ross	RCA
Rock The Casbah	The Clash	Epic
Shadows Of The Night	Pat Benatar	Chrysalis
Shock The Monkey	Peter Gabriel	Geffen
☆ ⑥ Truly	Lionel Richie	Motown
Tug Of War	Paul McCartney	Columbia

NOVEMBER

☆ Africa	Toto	Columbia
☆ ⑥ Down Under	Men at Work	Columbia
⑥ The Girl Is Mine	Michael Jackson/Paul McCartney	Epic
Goody Two Shoes	Adam Ant	Epic
Hand To Hold On To	John Cougar	Riva
I Do	The J. Geils Band	EMI-America
Let's Go Dancin' (Ooh, La, La, La)	Kool & the Gang	De-Lite
Memory	Barry Manilow	Arista
1999	Prince	Warner Bros.

Men at Work (l to r: Greg Ham, John Rees, Colin Hay, Ron Strykert, Jerry Speiser)

1982

The Other Guy	The Little River Band	Capitol
⑥ Sexual Healing	Marvin Gaye	Columbia
Two Less Lonely People In The World	Air Supply	Arista
Valerie	Steve Winwood	Island
You Can't Hurry Love	Phil Collins	Atlantic
You Got Lucky	Tom Petty & the Heartbreakers	Backstreet

DECEMBER

Allentown	Billy Joel	Columbia
All Those Lies	Glenn Frey	Asylum
Bad Boy	Ray Parker, Jr.	Arista
Do You Really Want To Hurt Me	Culture Club	Virgin/Epic
The Elvis Medley	Elvis Presley	RCA
Forever	Little Steven & the Disciples of Soul	EMI-America
Heart Of The Night	Juice Newton	Capitol
Heart To Heart	Kenny Loggins	Columbia
I Knew You When	Linda Ronstadt	Asylum
Love In Store	Fleetwood Mac	Warner Bros.
Shame On The Moon	Bob Seger & the Silver Bullet Band	Capitol
Stray Cat Strut	The Stray Cats	EMI-America
The Woman In Me	Donna Summer	Geffen
Young Love	Janet Jackson	A & M
Your Love Is Driving Me Crazy	Sammy Hagar	Geffen

TOP SINGLES OF 1982

⑥ Abracadabra	The Steve Miller Band	Capitol
⑥ Centerfold	The J. Geils Band	EMI-America
⑥ Don't You Want Me	Human League	A & M/Virgin
⑥ Ebony And Ivory	Paul McCartney with Stevie Wonder	Columbia
℗ Eye Of The Tiger	Survivor	Scotti Bros.
⑥ Hard To Say I'm Sorry	Chicago	Full Moon/ Warner
℗ I Love Rock 'N' Roll	Joan Jett & the Blackhearts	Boardwalk
⑥ Jack And Diane	John Cougar	Riva

393

| ⑥ Truly | Lionel Richie | Motown |
| Up Where We Belong | Joe Cocker & Jennifer Warnes | Island |

TOP ALBUMS OF 1982

⑰ Abracadabra	The Steve Miller Band	Capitol
⑰ American Fool	John Cougar	Riva
⑰ Asia	Asia	Geffen
⑰ Business As Usual	Men at Work	Columbia
⑰ Chicago 16	Chicago	Full Moon/ Warner
⑥ Dare	The Human League	A & M/Virgin
⑰ Freeze-Frame	The J. Geils Band	EMI-America
⑰ Lionel Richie	Lionel Richie	Motown
⑰ Mirage	Fleetwood Mac	Warner Bros.
⑰ Tug Of War	Paul McCartney	Columbia

GRAMMY WINNERS IN 1982

The Grammys were televised from the Shrine Auditorium in Los Angeles on Wednesday, February 23, 1983. John Denver was the host.

Record of the Year: "Rosanna," Toto (Columbia)

Song of the Year: "Always On My Mind" (music and lyrics by Johnny Christopher, Mark James, and Wayne Carson)

Album of the Year: *Toto IV,* Toto (Columbia)

Best Vocal Performance, Female: "You Should Hear How She Talks About You," Melissa Manchester (Arista)

Best Vocal Performance, Male: "Truly," Lionel Richie (Motown)

Best Vocal Performance, Group: "Up Where We Belong," Joe Cocker & Jennifer Warnes (Island)

Best Rock Vocal Performance, Female: "Shadows Of The Night," Pat Benatar (Chrysalis)

Best Rock Vocal Performance, Male: "Hurts So Good," John Cougar (Riva)

Best Rock Vocal Performance, Group: "Eye Of The Tiger," Survivor (Scotti Bros.)

Best New Artist of the Year: Men at Work

Best Comedy Performance: *Live On The Sunset Strip,* Richard Pryor (Warner Bros.)

Best Soundtrack Album from a Motion Picture or Television: *E.T. The Extra-Terrestrial,* John Williams (MCA)

DEATHS IN 1982

MUSIC PERFORMERS AND MUSIC INDUSTRY NOTABLES WHO DIED IN 1982

Tommy Tucker, Sunday, January 17 (poisoning; 48)

Sam "Lightnin' " Hopkins, Saturday, January 30 (natural causes; 69)

Thelonius Monk, Wednesday, February 17 (stroke; 64)

Murray ("The K") Kaufman (disc jockey), Sunday, February 21 (cancer; 60)

John Belushi (The Blues Brothers), Friday, March 5 (drug overdose; 33)

Samuel George, Jr. (The Capitols), Wednesday, March 17 (stabbing; 38)

Cal Tjader, Wednesday, May 5 (heart attack; 56)

Addie "Micky" Harris (The Shirelles), Thursday, June 10 (heart attack; 42)

James Honeyman Scott (The Pretenders), Wednesday, June 16 (drug overdose; 25)

Harry Mills (The Mills Brothers), Monday, June 28 (cancer; 68)

Bill Justis, Friday, July 16 (natural causes; 55)

Sonny Stitt, Thursday, July 22 (cancer; 48)

Joe Tex, Friday, August 13 (heart attack; 49)

Jesse Powell, Tuesday, October 19 (heart attack; 58)

Marty Robbins, Wednesday, December 8 (heart failure; 57)

Arthur Rubenstein, Monday, December 20 (natural causes; 95)

OTHERS WHO DIED IN 1982

Hugh Beaumont
Ingrid Bergman
Leonid Brezhnev
Marty Feldman
Henry Fonda
Dave Garroway
Princess Grace (Kelly)

Paul Lynde
Vic Morrow
Satchel Paige
Lee Strasberg
King Vidor
Jack Webb

MOVIES OF 1982

MOVIES FEATURING POP MUSIC ARTISTS

Grease 2 *Stars:* Maxwell Caulfield, Michelle Pfeiffer, Lorna Luft, Didi Conn, Eve Arden, Tab Hunter, Sid Caesar, Dody Goodman. No new hits.

POP MUSIC CONCERTS ON FILM

Earth, Wind & Fire in Concert   The title says it all.
Let's Spend the Night Together   The Rolling Stones' 1981 concert tour captured on film.

The Motels (l to r: Martin Jourard, Scott Thurston, Brian Glascock, Martha Davis, Michael Goodroe, Guy Perry; photo: Richard E. Aaron/Thunder Thumbs)

395

ROCK ON ALMANAC

*Robert Plant in concert (photo: **Anastasia Pantsios**)*

MOVIES FEATURING A POP MUSIC SOUNDTRACK

Diner *Stars:* Mickey Rourke, Steve Guttenberg, Kevin Bacon, Daniel Stern, Timothy Daly, Ellen Barkin. Features many classic hits of the fifties.

Pink Floyd: The Wall *Stars:* Christine Hargreaves, James Laurenson, Bob Hoskins, and the music of Pink Floyd's album *The Wall*.

OTHER POPULAR MOVIES OF 1982

Annie
The Best Little Whorehouse in Texas
Conan the Barbarian
Creepshow
Deathtrap
Death Wish II
E.T.—The Extra-Terrestrial
48 Hours
Friday the 13th, Part 3

Gandhi
Missing
My Favorite Year
An Officer and a Gentleman
Poltergeist
Rocky III
Star Trek II: The Wrath of Khan
The Thing
Tootsie

ACADEMY AWARD WINNERS OF 1982

Best Actor: Ben Kingsley, *Gandhi*
Best Actress: Meryl Streep, *Sophie's Choice*
Best Picture: *Gandhi*
Best Original Song: "Up Where We Belong," *An Officer and a Gentleman* (music by Jack Nitzsche & Buffy Sainte-Marie, lyrics by Will Hennings)

TOP TELEVISION SHOWS OF 1982

The "A" Team
Dallas
Dynasty
Falcon Crest
The Love Boat

Magnum, P.I.
M*A*S*H
Simon and Simon
60 Minutes
Three's Company

1983

ROCK ON ALMANAC

⇨ Bjorn Borg, Swedish tennis player, retires from competition at the age of 26.

⇨ General Motors and Toyota agree to joint production of a subcompact car in the United States.

⇨ President Reagan proposes the Strategic Defense Initiative, which his critics derogatorily dub "Star Wars."

⇨ Harold Washington is elected the first black mayor of Chicago.

⇨ The West German magazine *Stern* acquires a 60-volume diary supposedly written by Adolf Hitler. It was later exposed as a fraud.

⇨ Peter Jennings becomes ABC's TV anchor, and Tom Brokaw becomes NBC's.

⇨ Sally K. Ride, a 32-year-old physicist, is the first American woman to go into space.

⇨ The Soviet Union "accidentally" downs a Korean 747 jetliner, killing 269 people.

⇨ Israel's leader Menachem Begin resigns.

⇨ In a Beirut bombing on Marine headquarters, 216 Marines are killed.

⇨ More than 1,900 U.S. Marines invade the small Caribbean island of Grenada to prevent its becoming a Soviet puppet state.

⇨ The Palestine Liberation Organization and Israel exchange prisoners.

⇨ Ex-President Gerald Ford appears in a cameo on *Dynasty*.

SPORTS WINNERS

Baseball   The Baltimore Orioles beat the Philadelphia Phillies 4 games to 1.

Football

NFC: The Washington Redskins beat the San Francisco '49ers 24–21 in Washington, D.C.

AFC: The Los Angeles Raiders beat the Seattle Seahawks 30–14 in Los Angeles.

Super Bowl XVIII: The Los Angeles Raiders beat the Washington Redskins 38–9 on January 22, 1984, at Tampa Stadium in Tampa, Florida.

Basketball   The Philadelphia '76ers beat the Los Angeles Lakers 4 games to 0.

Hockey   The New York Islanders beat the Edmonton Oilers 4 games to 0.

MUSIC HIGHLIGHTS OF 1983

⇨ Sony, Philips, and Polygram debut their Compact Disc systems, and CDs begin appearing in retail stores in limited quantities.

⇨ The Rolling Stones leave Atlantic Records to sign with CBS Records for a reported $25 million.

⇨ RCA Records and the late Elvis Presley's manager, Col. Tom Parker, reach an amicable agreement, rather than press a pending lawsuit, over royalty payments.

⇨ The Nashville Network premieres on cable television.

***Bananarama* (photo: *Anastasia Pantsios*)**

Elvis Costello

1983

⇨ On Wednesday, March 23, Motown's 25th anniversary show is taped at the Pasadena City Auditorium in California. This unique show, featuring dozens of original Motown acts plus Michael Jackson's immediately legendary "moon walk" during the first public performance of "Billie Jean," would become a two-hour TV special and later a video offered to the public.

⇨ Marvin Gaye kicks off his first tour in more than seven years with an appearance in San Diego.

⇨ The Everly Brothers reunite for the first time in 10 years on the stage of London's Royal Albert Hall.

⇨ The movie *Eddie and the Cruisers,* featuring a soundtrack by Springsteen sound-alikes John Cafferty & the Beaver Brown Band, opens but doesn't become a hit until one year later, when the movie starts appearing regularly on cable TV.

⇨ Michael Jackson's *Thriller* album generates an astonishing seven Top 10 singles on its way to becoming the biggest-selling album of all time, with 37 million units sold worldwide.

DEBUT ARTISTS OF 1983

MAJOR ARTISTS	Debut Single	Label
Bananarama (Siobhan Fahey, Sarah Dallin, Keren Woodward)	Shy Boy	London
Berlin (Terri Nunn, John Crawford, David Diamond, Rick Olsen, Rob Brill, Matt Reid)	Sex (I'm A . . .)	Geffen
John Cafferty & the Beaver Brown Band (John Cafferty, Gary Gramolini, Robert Cotoia, Pat Lupo, Michael "Tunes" Antunes, Kenny Jo Silva) (as "Eddie & the Cruisers")	On The Dark Side	Scotti Bros.
Tony Carey	I Won't Be Home Tonight	Rocshire
De Barge (Eldra, Bunny, Randy, Mark, and James De Barge)	I Like It	Gordy
Chris De Burgh	Don't Pay The Ferryman	A & M
Def Leppard (Joe Elliott, Steve "Steamin'" Clark, Phil Collen, Rick Savage, Rick Allen)	Photograph	Mercury
Eurythmics (Annie Lennox, David Stewart)	Sweet Dreams (Are Made Of This) ☆ ⓖ	RCA
INXS (Michael Hutchence, Tim Farriss, Kirk Pengilly, Andrew Farriss, Garry Beers, Jon Farriss)	The One Thing	Atco

399

Def Leppard in concert (l to r: Joe Elliott, Steve Clark; photo: Anastasia Pantsios)

Cyndi Lauper	Girls Just Want To Have Fun ⑥	Portrait
Madonna (Madonna Louise Ciccone)	Holiday	Sire
Midnight Star (Reginald Calloway, Vincent Calloway, Jeffrey Cooper, Kenneth Gant, Melvin Gentry, Belinda Lipscomb, William Simmons, Boas "Bo" Watson)	Freak-A-Zoid	Solar
Naked Eyes (Pete Byrne, Rob Fisher)	Always Something There To Remind Me	EMI-America
The New Edition (Ralph Tresvant, Ronald De Voe, Michael Bivins, Bobby Brown, Ricky Bell)	Candy Girl	Streetwise
Night Ranger (Brad Gillis, Jeff Watson, Alan "Fitz" Fitzgerald, Jack Blades, Kelly Keagy)	Don't Tell Me You Love Me	Boardwalk
Quiet Riot (Kevin DuBrow, Carlos Cavazo, Rudy Sarzo, Frankie Banali)	Cum On Feel The Noize ⑥	Pasha
R.E.M. (Michael Stipe, Pete Buck, Mick Mills, Bill Berry)	Radio Free Europe	I.R.S.
Spandau Ballet (Tony Hadley, Gary Kemp, Steve Norman, Martin Kemp, John Keeble)	True	Chrysalis
The Thompson Twins (Tom Bailey, Alannah Currie, Joe Leeway)	Lies	Arista
Tears for Fears (Roland Orzabal, Curt Smith)	Change	Mercury
U2 (Bono Vox [Paul Hewson], The Edge [Dave Evans], Adam Clayton, Larry Mullen)	New Year's Day	Island
Wham! (George Michael, Andrew Ridgeley)	Bad Boys	Columbia
"Weird Al" Yankovic	Ricky	Rock 'n' Roll
Paul Young	Wherever I Lay My Hat (That's My Home)	Columbia

OTHER ARTISTS

After the Fire

Deborah Allen

John Anderson

Joan Armatrading

The Belle Stars

Big Country

Big Ric
Michael Bolton
Martin Briley
The Call
Club House
Elvis Costello
Rodney Dangerfield
F. R. David
Dexy's Midnight Runners
Thomas Dolby
Double Image
Joe "Bean" Esposito
Agnetha Faltskog
Cee Farrow
Felony
Gentle Persuasion
Goanna
Eddy Grant
Lee Greenwood
Haysi Fantayzee
Robert Hazard
Heaven 17
Hughes/Thrall
Industry
The JoBoxers
Jump 'n the Saddle
Kajagoogoo
Kissing the Pink
Klique
Lanier & Company
Madness
Gerard McMahon
Men without Hats
Minor Detail
Modern English
Mtume
Nena

Loz Netto
Ric Ocasek
Robert Ellis Orral
Oxo
Planet P
The Plimsouls
Gary Portnoy
The Psychedelic Furs
Real Life
The Red Rockers
Re-Flex
Roman Holliday
Peter Schilling
Michael Sembello
Shannon
Sheriff
Glenn Shorrock
Patrick Simmons
The Single Bullet Theory
Snuff
The Stompers
Streets
The System
Taco
Total Coelo
Louise Tucker
Twilight 22
Ultravox
Unipop
Vandenberg
Wall of Voodoo
The Weather Girls
Matthew Wilder
Carl Wilson
Bob Wolfer
Zebra

HITS OF 1983

JANUARY

All Right	Christopher Cross	Warner Bros.
☆ Ⓖ **Billie Jean**	Michael Jackson	Epic

Eurythmics (l to r: Annie Lennox, David Stewart)

401

	The Blues	Randy Newman & Paul Simon	Warner Bros.
	Breaking Us In Two	Joe Jackson	A & M
☆	Come On Eileen	Dexy's Midnight Runners	Mercury
	I'm Alive	Neil Diamond	Columbia
	It's Raining Men	The Weather Girls	Columbia
	I've Got A Rock 'N' Roll Heart	Eric Clapton	Warner Bros./ Duck
	Jeopardy	The Greg Kihn Band	Beserkley
	My Kind Of Lady	Supertramp	A & M
	One On One	Hall & Oates	RCA
	Poison Arrow	ABC	Mercury
	We've Got Tonight	Kenny Rogers & Sheena Easton	Liberty
	Winds Of Change	Jefferson Starship	Grunt
	You Are	Lionel Richie	Motown

FEBRUARY

☆ ⑥	Beat It	Michael Jackson	Epic
	Change Of Heart	Tom Petty & the Heartbreakers	Backstreet
	Der Kommissar	After the Fire	Epic
	I Like It	De Barge	Gordy
	Little Red Corvette	Prince	Warner Bros.
	Little Too Late	Pat Benatar	Chrysalis
	Make Love Stay	Dan Fogelberg	Full Moon/Epic
⑥	Mr. Roboto	Styx	A & M
	Nice Girls	Melissa Manchester	Arista
	Separate Ways	Journey	Columbia
	She Blinded Me With Science	Thomas Dolby	Capitol
	Shoppin' From A To Z	Toni Basil	Chrysalis
	Should I Stay Or Should I Go? (re-entry)	The Clash	Epic
	So Close	Diana Ross	RCA
	Take The Short Way Home	Dionne Warwick	Arista

MARCH

	Always Something There To Remind Me	Naked Eyes	EMI-America
	Even Now	Bob Seger & the Silver Bullet Band	Capitol
	Goodnight Saigon	Billy Joel	Columbia
	I Won't Hold Back	Toto	Columbia
	Let Me Go	Heaven 17	Arista
☆ ⑥	Let's Dance	David Bowie	EMI-America
	Love My Way	The Psychedelic Furs	Columbia
	Outstanding	The Gap Band	Total Experience
	Sex (I'm A . . .)	Berlin	Geffen
	Solitaire	Laura Branigan	Atlantic
	Straight From The Heart	Bryan Adams	A & M
⑥	Swingin'	John Anderson	Warner Bros.

Cyndi Lauper in concert (photo: Anastasia Pantsios)

Madonna in concert (photo: Anastasia Pantsios)

1983

Walking In L.A.	Missing Persons	Capitol
Welcome To Heartlight	Kenny Loggins	Columbia

APRIL

Affair Of The Heart	Rick Springfield	RCA
All This Love	De Barge	Gordy
Don't Let It End	Styx	A & M
Ⓖ Electric Avenue	Eddy Grant	Portrait
Faithfully	Journey	Columbia
☆ Ⓖ Flashdance . . . What A Feeling	Irene Cara	Casablanca
Fool Moon Fire	Walter Egan	Backstreet
Gimme All Your Lovin'	ZZ Top	Warner Bros.
Looking For A Stranger	Pat Benatar	Chrysalis
My Love	Lionel Richie	Motown
New Year's Day	U2	Island
Overkill	Men at Work	Columbia
Rio	Duran Duran	Capitol
Time (Clock Of The Heart)	Culture Club	Virgin/Epic
Too Shy	Kajagoogoo	EMI-America

MAY

All My Life	Kenny Rogers	Liberty
Baby Jane	Rod Stewart	Warner Bros.
Come Dancing	The Kinks	Arista
Family Man	Hall & Oates	RCA
How Do You Keep The Music Playing	James Ingram & Patti Austin	Qwest
I'm Still Standing	Elton John	Geffen
No Time For Talk	Christopher Cross	Warner Bros.
Our House	Madness	Geffen
Ricky	"Weird Al" Yankovic	Rock 'n' Roll
Roll Me Away	Bob Seger & the Silver Bullet Band	Capitol
☆ Ⓖ Sweet Dreams (Are Made Of This)	Eurythmics	RCA
Theme From Doctor Detroit	Devo	Backstreet

Quiet Riot (l to r: Frankie Banali, Kevin DuBrow, Carlos Cavazo)

Wanna Be Startin' Something	Michael Jackson	Epic
What Ever Happened To Old Fashioned Love	B.J. Thomas	Cleveland Int'l
White Wedding	Billy Idol	Chrysalis
The Woman In You	The Bee Gees	RSO

JUNE

China Girl	David Bowie	EMI-America
Cuts Like A Knife	Bryan Adams	A & M
☆ ⑥ Every Breath You Take	The Police	A & M
Hot Girls In Love	Loverboy	Columbia
I.O.U.	Lee Greenwood	MCA
Is There Something I Should Know	Duran Duran	Capitol
⑥ Juicy Fruit	Mtume	Epic
(Keep Feeling) Fascination	The Human League	A & M
☆ Maniac	Michael Sembello	Casablanca
Rock 'N' Roll Is King	The Electric Light Orchestra	Jet
Rock Of Ages	Def Leppard	Mercury
She Works Hard For The Money	Donna Summer	Mercury
Stand Back	Stevie Nicks	Modern
Stop In The Name Of Love	The Hollies	Atlantic
Take Me To Heart	Quarterflash	Warner Bros.

JULY

All Time High	Rita Coolidge	A & M
Cold Blooded	Rick James	Gordy
Don't Cry	Asia	Geffen
Far From Over	Frank Stallone	RSO
How Am I Supposed To Live Without You	Laura Branigan	Atlantic
Human Nature	Michael Jackson	Epic
I'll Tumble 4 Ya	Culture Club	Virgin/Epic
It's A Mistake	Men at Work	Columbia
⑥ Making Love Out Of Nothing At All	Air Supply	Arista
Promises, Promises	Naked Eyes	EMI-America
⑥ Puttin' On The Ritz	Taco	RCA
☆ Tell Her About It	Billy Joel	Columbia
Tip Of My Tongue	The Tubes	Capitol

☆ ⑥ **Total Eclipse Of The Heart**	Bonnie Tyler	Columbia
You Belong To Me	The Doobie Brothers	Warner Bros.

1983

AUGUST

Don't Forget To Dance	The Kinks	Arista
High Time	Styx	A & M
☆ ℗ **Islands In The Stream**	Kenny Rogers & Dolly Parton	RCA
King Of Pain	The Police	A & M
Kiss The Bride	Elton John	Geffen
Living On The Edge	Jim Capaldi	Atlantic
One Thing Leads To Another	The Fixx	MCA
(She's) Sexy + 17	The Stray Cats	EMI-America
Ship To Shore	Chris DeBurgh	A & M
Solsbury Hill	Peter Gabriel	Geffen
Someone Belonging To Someone	The Bee Gees	RSO
Telefone (Long Distance Love Affair)	Sheena Easton	EMI-America
Tell Her No	Juice Newton	Capitol
True	Spandau Ballet	Chrysalis
What Am I Gonna Do	Rod Stewart	Warner Bros.

SEPTEMBER

☆ ⑥ **All Night Long (All Night)**	Lionel Richie	Motown
Break My Stride	Matthew Wilder	Private
⑥ **Cum On Feel The Noize**	Quiet Riot	Pasha
Delirious	Prince	Warner Bros.
If Anyone Falls	Stevie Nicks	Modern
Love Is A Battlefield	Pat Benatar	Chrysalis
Modern Love	David Bowie	EMI-America
Old Time Rock & Roll	Bob Seger & the Silver Bullet Band	Capitol
Rockit	Herbie Hancock	Columbia
Sitting At The Wheel	The Moody Blues	Threshold
Suddenly Last Summer	The Motels	Capitol
Tender Is The Night	Jackson Browne	Asylum
This Time	Bryan Adams	A & M
Unconditional Love	Donna Summer	Mercury
⑥ **Uptown Girl**	Billy Joel	Columbia

The Thompson Twins (l to r: Alannah Currie, Tom Bailey, Joe Leeway)

405

ROCK ON ALMANAC

Bono Vox of U2 in concert (photo: Anastasia Pantsios)

OCTOBER

Crumblin' Down	John Cougar Mellencamp	Riva
Holiday	Madonna	Sire
How Many Times Can We Say Goodbye	Dionne Warwick & Luther Vandross	Arista
I Guess That's Why They Call It The Blues	Elton John	Geffen
I Won't Stand In Your Way	The Stray Cats	EMI-America
My Town	The Michael Stanley Band	EMI-America
On The Dark Side	Eddie & the Cruisers (John Cafferty & the Beaver Brown Band)	Scotti Bros.
P.Y.T. (Pretty Young Thing)	Michael Jackson	Epic
Say It Isn't So	Hall & Oates	RCA
☆ ⑥ Say Say Say	Michael Jackson & Paul McCartney	Columbia
The Smile Has Left Your Eyes	Asia	Geffen
Souls	Rick Springfield	RCA
Stop Doggin' Around	Klique	MCA
Take Another Picture	Quarterflash	Geffen
Talking In Your Sleep	The Romantics	Nemperor

NOVEMBER

Gold	Spandau Ballet	Chrysalis
If I'd Been The One	38 Special	A & M
I Still Can't Get Over Loving You	Ray Parker, Jr.	Arista
Joanna	Kool & the Gang	De-Lite
⑥ Let The Music Play	Shannon	Mirage
☆ Owner Of A Lonely Heart	Yes	Atco
Read 'Em And Weep	Barry Manilow	Arista
Running With The Night	Lionel Richie	Motown
The Sign Of Fire	The Fixx	MCA
Synchronicity II	The Police	A & M
That's All	Genesis	Atlantic
Twist Of Fate	Olivia Newton-John	MCA
Undercover Of The Night	The Rolling Stones	Rolling Stones
Union Of The Snake	Duran Duran	Capitol
You Don't Believe	The Alan Parsons Project	Arista

DECEMBER

1983

	The Curly Shuffle	Jump 'n the Saddle	Atlantic
	Ebony Eyes	Rick James featuring Smokey Robinson	Gordy
⑥	Girls Just Want To Have Fun	Cyndi Lauper	Portrait
	Give It Up	K.C.	Meca
	An Innocent Man	Billy Joel	Columbia
☆ ⑥	Karma Chameleon	Culture Club	Virgin/Epic
	Middle Of The Road	The Pretenders	Sire
	Nightbird	Stevie Nicks	Modern
	99 Luftballons	Nena	Epic
	Pink Houses	John Cougar Mellencamp	Riva
	Rappin' Rodney	Rodney Dangerfield	RCA
	Remember The Night	The Motels	Capitol
	So Bad	Paul McCartney	Columbia
	Think Of Laura	Christopher Cross	Warner Bros.
	Yah Mo B There	James Ingram with Michael McDonald	Qwest

TOP SINGLES OF 1983

⑥	All Night Long (All Night)	Lionel Richie	Motown
⑥	Beat It	Michael Jackson	Epic
⑥	Billie Jean	Michael Jackson	Epic
⑥	Down Under	Men at Work	Columbia
⑥	Every Breath You Take	The Police	A & M
⑥	Flashdance . . . What A Feeling	Irene Cara	Casablanca
℗	Islands In The Stream	Kenny Rogers & Dolly Parton	RCA
	Maniac	Michael Sembello	Casablanca
⑥	Say Say Say	Paul McCartney & Michael Jackson	Columbia
⑥	Total Eclipse Of The Heart	Bonnie Tyler	Columbia

TOP ALBUMS OF 1983

℗	Can't Slow Down	Lionel Richie	Motown
℗	Cargo	Men at Work	Columbia
℗	Faster Than The Speed Of Night	Bonnie Tyler	Columbia
℗	Flashdance	Soundtrack	Casablanca
℗	An Innocent Man	Billy Joel	Columbia
℗	Let's Dance	David Bowie	EMI-America
℗	Metal Health	Quiet Riot	Pasha
℗	Synchronicity	The Police	A & M
℗	Thriller	Michael Jackson	Epic
	Too-Rye-Ay	Dexy's Midnight Runners	Mercury

GRAMMY WINNERS IN 1983

The Grammys were televised from the Shrine Auditorium in Los Angeles on Tuesday, February 28, 1984. John Denver was the host.

Record of the Year: "Beat It," Michael Jackson (Epic)

407

Wham! (l to r: Andrew Ridgeley, George Michael)

Song of the Year: "Every Breath You Take" (music and lyrics by Sting)
Album of the Year: *Thriller,* Michael Jackson (Epic)
Best Vocal Performance, Female: "Flashdance . . . What A Feeling," Irene Cara (Casablanca)
Best Vocal Performance, Male: *Thriller,* Michael Jackson (Epic)
Best Vocal Performance, Group: "Every Breath You Take," the Police (A & M)
Best Rock Vocal Performance, Female: "Love Is A Battlefield," Pat Benatar (Chrysalis)
Best Rock Vocal Performance, Male: "Beat It," Michael Jackson (Epic)
Best Rock Vocal Performance, Group: *Synchronicity,* the Police (A & M)
Best New Artist of the Year: Culture Club
Best Comedy Performance: *Eddie Murphy: Comedian,* Eddie Murphy (Columbia)
Best Soundtrack Album from a Motion Picture or Television: *Flashdance,* Various Artists (Casablanca)

DEATHS IN 1983

MUSIC PERFORMERS AND MUSIC INDUSTRY NOTABLES WHO DIED IN 1983

Don Costa, Wednesday, January 19 (heart attack; 57)
Karen Carpenter (The Carpenters), Friday, February 4 (heart failure; 32)
Eubie Blake, Saturday, February 12 (natural causes; 100)
B. Mitchell Reed (disc jockey), Wednesday, March 16 (natural causes; 56)
Danny Rapp (Danny & the Juniors), Monday, April 4 (gunshot; 41)
Pete Farndon (The Pretenders), Thursday, April 14 (29)
Felix Pappalardi, Sunday, April 17 (gunshot; 41)
Earl Fatha Hines, Friday, April 22 (heart attack; 77)

Muddy Waters (McKinley Morganfield), Saturday, April 30 (heart attack; 68)
Clarence E. Quick (The Del Vikings), Thursday, May 5 (heart attack; 46)
Kai Winding, Friday, May 6 (brain tumor; 60)
Bo Gentry (songwriter), Friday, July 1 (pneumonia; 41)
Harry James, Tuesday, July 5 (lymphatic cancer; 67)
Roy Milton (bandleader), Sunday, September 18 (stroke; 76)
James Booker, Tuesday, November 8 (heart attack; 43)
Dennis Wilson (The Beach Boys), Wednesday, December 28 (drowning; 39)

OTHERS WHO DIED IN 1983

Bear Bryant
Terrence Cardinal Cooke
George Cukor
William Demarest
Jack Dempsey
Lynn Fontanne
Arthur Godfrey

George Halas
Raymond Massey
David Niven
Pat O'Brien
Slim Pickens
Gloria Swanson
Tennessee Williams

MOVIES OF 1983

MOVIES FEATURING POP MUSIC ARTISTS

Yentl   *Stars:* Barbra Streisand, Mandy Patinkin, Amy Irving, Nehemiah Persoff, Steven Hill. In addition to starring in the title role, Streisand directed, produced, and co-wrote this film. *Featured songs:* "The Way He Makes Me Feel," "Papa Can You Hear Me?"

MOVIES FEATURING A POP MUSIC SOUNDTRACK

The Big Chill   *Stars:* Glenn Close, Tom Berenger, Jeff Goldblum, William Hurt, JoBeth Williams, Kevin Kline, Meg Tilly, Mary Kay Place. Terrific sixties soundtrack.
Eddie and the Cruisers   *Stars:* Tom Berenger, Michael Paré, Ellen Barkin. *Featured songs:* "On The Dark Side" and "Tender Years" by John Cafferty & the Beaver Brown Band.
Flashdance   *Stars:* Jennifer Beals, Michael Nouri, Lilia Skala, Belinda Bauer, Sunny Johnson. *Featured songs:* "Maniac" by Michael Sembello, "Flashdance . . . What A Feeling" (which won an Oscar) by Irene Cara.
Risky Business   *Stars:* Tom Cruise, Rebecca De Mornay, Bronson Pinchot. *Featured song:* "Old Time Rock & Roll" by Bob Seger & the Silver Bullet Band.
Staying Alive   *Stars:* John Travolta, Cynthia Rhodes, Frank Stallone, Finola Hughes. Sequel to *Saturday Night Fever.* *Featured song:* "Staying Alive" by the Bee Gees.

POP MUSIC CONCERTS ON VIDEO

The Everly Brothers Reunion Concert   Don and Phil Everly reunite on the stage at London's Royal Albert Hall for the first time in 10 years to sing all their biggest hits.
Motown 25: Yesterday, Today, Forever   A TV special becomes a two-hour video celebrating Motown's 25th anniversary with the label's biggest stars: the Commodores, De Barge, the Four Tops, Marvin Gaye, Michael Jackson, the Jacksons, Rick James, the Miracles, Martha Reeves, Lionel Richie, Smokey Robinson, Diana Ross, the Temptations, Mary Wells, Mary Wilson, Stevie Wonder, and others.
The Royal Albert Hall Concert for ARMS   A benefit concert for musician Ronnie Lane, suffering from multiple sclerosis. *Musical performers:* Jeff Beck, Eric Clapton, Jimmy Page, Kenny Jones, Charlie Watts, Bill Wyman, Steve Winwood.

"Weird Al" Yankovic

ROCK ON
ALMANAC

The Police, Synchronicity
album cover

Michael Jackson, Thriller
album cover

OTHER POPULAR MOVIES OF 1983

Breathless
The King of Comedy
Local Hero
The Right Stuff
Rumblefish
Silkwood

Star 80
Superman III
Terms of Endearment
To Be or Not to Be
Trading Places

ACADEMY AWARD WINNERS OF 1983

Best Actor: Robert Duvall, *Tender Mercies*
Best Actress: Shirley MacLaine, *Terms of Endearment*
Best Picture: *Terms of Endearment*
Best Original Song: "Flashdance . . . What A Feeling," *Flashdance* (music by Giorgio
    Moroder, lyrics by Keith Forsey & Irene Cara)

TOP TELEVISION SHOWS OF 1983

The "A" Team
Cagney and Lacey
Dallas
Dynasty
Falcon Crest

Hotel
Kate and Allie
Magnum, P.I.
Simon and Simon
60 Minutes

1984

NEWS HIGHLIGHTS OF 1984

⇨ The Winter Olympics take place in Sarajevo, Yugoslavia, marking the first time they are hosted by a Communist country.

⇨ Pierre Elliott Trudeau, leader of the Liberal Party for 15 years, resigns as prime minister of Canada.

⇨ Yuri Andropov dies in Moscow, and Konstantin Chernenko, 72, becomes the new general secretary.

⇨ President Reagan signs cultural and scientific agreements during a six-day trip to China.

⇨ The Soviets boycott the Summer Olympics in Los Angeles.

⇨ The average price of a new single-family home surpasses $100,000.

⇨ The Motion Picture Association of America introduces the PG-13 rating for movies.

⇨ Walter Mondale chooses as his vice-presidential nominee Geraldine Ferraro, the first woman to be named to a major-party ticket.

⇨ Vanessa Williams, the first black Miss America, relinquishes her title when it is revealed that she posed for nude photos several years earlier. Williams would ride out the scandal and go on to become a successful recording artist in 1988.

⇨ President Reagan is re-elected by a landslide, carrying 49 of the 50 states.

⇨ In Bhopal, India, a toxic gas leak from an insecticide plant kills 2,100 people.

⇨ The Nobel Peace Prize is awarded to Bishop Desmond Tutu of South Africa.

⇨ Bernhard Goetz, the "subway vigilante," shoots four young thugs who accost him on the subway. He is later found guilty only of possessing an unregistered weapon and given a suspended sentence.

SPORTS WINNERS

Baseball   The Detroit Tigers beat the San Diego Padres 4 games to 1.
Football
    NFC: The San Francisco '49ers beat the Chicago Bears 23–0 in San Francisco.
    AFC: The Miami Dolphins beat the Pittsburgh Steelers 45–28 in Miami.
    Super Bowl XIX: The San Francisco '49ers beat the Miami Dolphins 38–16 on January 20, 1985, at Stanford Stadium in Stanford, California.
Basketball   The Boston Celtics beat the Los Angeles Lakers 4 games to 3.
Hockey   The Edmonton Oilers beat the New York Islanders 4 games to 1.

MUSIC HIGHLIGHTS OF 1984

⇨ Michael Jackson's hair catches fire while performing in a soft-drink commercial at the Shrine Auditorium in Los Angeles. He is not badly hurt.

⇨ At the 11th annual American Music Awards television show, Michael Jackson wins seven awards for his *Thriller* album. A month later, at the 26th annual Grammys, he wins a record eight awards for the same album, surpassing Roger Miller's six awards in 1965.

Jon Bon Jovi in concert (photo: Anastasia Pantsios)

Frankie Goes to Hollywood (l to r: Mark O'Toole, Paul Rutherford, Holly Johnson, Peter "Ped" Gill, Brian "Nasher" Nash; photo: Peter Ashworth)

⇨ Duran Duran begins their first American tour.

⇨ Michael Jackson reunites with his brothers for their much acclaimed Victory Tour, which opens in Kansas City on July 6 and ends in Los Angeles on December 9.

⇨ Lionel Richie closes the Olympic festivities in Los Angeles by singing his hit "All Night Long."

⇨ On Saturday, August 4, Phil Collins marries Jill Travelman.

⇨ Herb Alpert begins a limited reunion tour with several original members of the Tijuana Brass.

⇨ On Tuesday, September 14, MTV launches its first video awards show at New York's famed Radio City Music Hall. At the show, hosted by Dan Aykroyd and Bette Midler, Herbie Hancock dominates the awards, with his "Rockit" video winning in five different categories. Performing live were Madonna, Tina Turner, Rod Stewart, and ZZ Top. The show was directed by singers Kevin Godley and Lol Creme of 10cc fame.

⇨ Barbara Mandrell is involved in a near fatal car accident.

⇨ To provide medicine and supplies to the famine victims of Ethiopia, Bob Geldof of the Boomtown Rats organizes members of 15 different rock acts into the group Band Aid to perform the song "Do They Know It's Christmas?" Participating in this historic recording session in England are Geldof, David Bowie, Phil Collins, Paul McCartney, Sting, Jody Watley, George Michael, Paul Young, and members of Culture Club, Duran Duran, Kool & the Gang, and U2, among others. The single, released worldwide, generates millions of dollars in famine aid.

DEBUT ARTISTS OF 1984

MAJOR ARTISTS

	Debut Single	Label
Bon Jovi (Jon Bon Jovi [Bongiovi], Richie Sambora, David Rashbaum, Alec John Such, Tico Torres)	Runaway	Mercury
Frankie Goes to Hollywood (Holly Johnson, Paul Rutherford, Brian "Nasher" Nash, Peter "Ped" Gill, Mark O'Toole)	Relax	Island
Corey Hart	Sunglasses At Night	EMI-America
Howard Jones	New Song	Elektra
Julian Lennon	Valotte	Atlantic
Mötley Crüe (Vince Neil, Mick Mars, Nikki Sixx, Tommy Lee)	Looks That Kill	Elektra
Mr. Mister (Richard Page, Steve Farris, Pat Mastelotto, Steve George)	Hunters Of The Night	RCA

413

ROCK ON ALMANAC

David Gilmour

Julian Lennon

Sheila E. (Sheila Escovedo)	The Glamorous Life	Warner Bros.
Tina Turner	Let's Stay Together	Capitol
John Waite	Missing You ☆	EMI-America
Wang Chung (Jack Hues, Nick Feldman, Darren Costin)	Don't Let Go	Geffen

OTHER ARTISTS

The American Comedy Network	Latoya Jackson
Apollonia 6	Rebbie Jackson
Phillip Bailey	Nik Kershaw
Band Aid	Krokus
J. Blackfoot	Laid Back
Jocelyn Brown	Jeff Lynne
Jenny Burton	Christine McVie
Cameo	Menudo
Cherrelle	Mink De Ville
The Deele	M + M
"D" Train	Newcleus
Dennis De Young	Ollie & Jerry
Dennis Edwards	Orion the Hunter
Face to Face	Billy Rankin
Fire Inc.	Ratt
Andy Fraser	Mike Reno & Ann Wilson
Johnny Gill	Rockwell
David Gilmour	Romeo Void
Michael Gore	Tommy Shaw
Hagar, Schon, Aaronson, Shreive	The Style Council
Sam Harris	The B.E. Taylor Group
The Headpins	Tiggi Clay
Roger Hodgson	Twisted Sister
The Honeydrippers	UB40
Honeymoon Suite	Tracey Ullman
The Icicle Works	Vanity
Julio Iglesias	Peter Wolf

HITS OF 1984

JANUARY

Automatic	The Pointer Sisters	Planet
Bang Your Head (Metal Health)	Quiet Riot	Pasha

☆ ⑥ Footloose	Kenny Loggins	Columbia
Got A Hold On Me	Christine McVie	Warner Bros.
Here Comes The Rain Again	Eurythmics	RCA
I Want A New Drug	Huey Lewis & the News	Chrysalis
I Will Follow	U2	Island
☆ ⑥ Jump	Van Halen	Warner Bros.
Let's Stay Together	Tina Turner	Capitol
New Moon On Monday	Duran Duran	Capitol
New Song	Howard Jones	Elektra
Nobody Told Me	John Lennon	Polydor
⑥ Somebody's Watching Me	Rockwell	Motown
This Woman	Kenny Rogers	RCA
Wrapped Around Your Finger	The Police	A & M

FEBRUARY

Adult Education	Hall & Oates	RCA
☆ ⑥ Against All Odds (Take A Look At Me Now)	Phil Collins	Atlantic
Back Where You Belong	38 Special	A & M
Don't Let Go	Wang Chung	Geffen
Girls	Dwight Twilley	EMI-America
Hold Me Now	The Thompson Twins	Arista
The Language of Love	Dan Fogelberg	Full Moon/Epic
Livin' In Desperate Times	Olivia Newton-John	MCA
Radio Ga-Ga	Queen	Capitol
Rebel Yell	Billy Idol	Chrysalis
Red, Red Wine	UB40	A & M
Tender Years	John Cafferty & the Beaver Brown Band	Scotti Bros.
They Don't Know	Tracy Ullman	MCA
Thriller	Michael Jackson	Epic
Tonight	Kool & the Gang	De-Lite

MARCH

The Authority Song	John Cougar Mellencamp	Riva
Borderline	Madonna	Sire
Eat It	"Weird Al" Yankovic	Rock 'n' Roll
Head Over Heels	The Go-Go's	I.R.S.
☆ ⑥ Hello	Lionel Richie	Motown
Illegal Alien	Genesis	Atlantic

Mötley Crüe (top: Vince Neil; bottom l to r: Tommy Lee, Nikki Sixx, Mick Mars; photo: Barry Levine)

415

	Leave It	Yes	Atco
	The Longest Time	Billy Joel	Columbia
	Love Somebody	Rick Springfield	RCA
	Miss Me Blind	Culture Club	Virgin/Epic
	One In A Million	The Romantics	Nemperor
	Show Me	The Pretenders	Sire
⑥	To All The Girls I've Loved Before	Julio Inglesias & Willie Nelson	Columbia
	Without You	David Bowie	EMI-America
	You Might Think	The Cars	Elektra

APRIL

	Breakdance	Irene Cara	Network/Geffen
	Communication	Spandau Ballet	Chrysalis
	Dance Hall Days	Wang Chung	Geffen
	Give Me Tonight	Shannon	Mirage/Emergency
	The Heart Of Rock 'N' Roll	Huey Lewis & the News	Chrysalis
	I'll Wait	Van Halen	Warner Bros.
	I'm Steppin' Out	John Lennon	Polydor
☆ ⑥	Let's Hear It For The Boy	Deniece Williams	Columbia
	Oh, Sherrie	Steve Perry	Columbia
☆	The Reflex	Duran Duran	Capitol
	Relax	Frankie Goes to Hollywood	Island
	Run, Runaway	Slade	CBS Associated
	Self Control	Laura Branigan	Atlantic
☆	Time After Time	Cyndi Lauper	Portrait
	You Can't Get What You Want	Joe Jackson	A & M

MAY

	Almost Paradise . . . Love Theme From Footloose	Mike Reno & Ann Wilson	Columbia
	Dancing In The Dark	Bruce Springsteen	Columbia
	Doctor! Doctor!	The Thompson Twins	Arista
	Don't Walk Away	Rick Springfield	RCA
	Eyes Without A Face	Billy Idol	Chrysalis

Mr. Mister (l to r: Steve Farris, Richard Page, Steve George, Pat Mastelotto)

Ratt (l to r: Warren DeMartini, Bobby Blotzer, Stephen Pearcy, Robbin Crosby, Juan Croucier)

1984

Infatuation	Rod Stewart	Warner Bros.
It's A Miracle	Culture Club	Virgin/Epic
Jump (For My Love)	The Pointer Sisters	Planet
Legs	ZZ Top	Warner Bros.
Love Will Show You How	Christine McVie	Warner Bros.
Magic	The Cars	Elektra
Stay The Night	Chicago	Full Moon/ Warner
Sunglasses At Night	Corey Hart	EMI-America
☆ ⑥ What's Love Got To Do With It	Tina Turner	Capitol
Who's That Girl	Eurythmics	RCA

JUNE

Black Stations/White Stations	M + M	RCA
Breakin' . . . There's No Stopping Us	Ollie & Jerry	Polydor
☆ ⑥ Ghostbusters	Ray Parker, Jr.	Arista
I'm Free (Heaven Helps The Man)	Kenny Loggins	Columbia
It Can Happen	Yes	Atco
☆ Missing You	John Waite	EMI-America
Panama	Van Halen	Warner Bros.
Sad Songs (Say So Much)	Elton John	Geffen
Sexy Girl	Glenn Frey	MCA
She's Mine	Steve Perry	Columbia
⑥ State Of Shock	The Jacksons	Epic
Stuck On You	Lionel Richie	Motown
Turn To You	The Go-Go's	I.R.S.
The Warrior	Scandal featuring Patty Smyth	Columbia
☆ ⑫ When Doves Cry	Prince	Warner Bros.

JULY

Cruel Summer	Bananarama	London
Dynamite	Jermaine Jackson	Arista
Go Insane	Lindsey Buckingham	Elektra
If This Is It	Huey Lewis & the News	Chrysalis
I Send A Message	INXS	Atco
Leave A Tender Moment Alone	Billy Joel	Columbia

417

ROCK ON ALMANAC

Tracey Ullman

Lights Out	Peter Wolf	EMI-America
My, Oh My	Slade	CBS Associated
Only When You Leave	Spandau Ballet	Chrysalis
Right By Your Side	Eurythmics	RCA
Rock Me Tonite	Billy Squier	Capitol
17	Rick James	Gordy
She Bop	Cyndi Lauper	Portrait
Two Sides Of Love	Sammy Hagar	Geffen
When You Close Your Eyes	Night Ranger	Camel/MCA

AUGUST

	Are We Ourselves?	The Fixx	MCA
	Bop 'Til You Drop	Rick Springfield	RCA
☆ ⑥	Caribbean Queen (No More Love On The Run)	Billy Ocean	Jive/Arista
	Cover Me	Bruce Springsteen	Columbia
	Drive	The Cars	Elektra
	Flesh For Fantasy	Billy Idol	Chrysalis
	Hard Habit To Break	Chicago	Full Moon/Warner
☆ ⑥	I Just Called To Say I Love You	Stevie Wonder	Motown
	I'm So Excited *(re-entry)*	The Pointer Sisters	Planet
☆ ⑥	Let's Go Crazy	Prince & the Revolution	Warner Bros.
	The Lucky One	Laura Branigan	Atlantic
	Lucky Star	Madonna	Sire
	Some Guys Have All The Luck	Rod Stewart	Warner Bros.
	There Goes My Baby	Donna Summer	Geffen
	Torture	The Jacksons	Epic

SEPTEMBER

	Better Be Good To Me	Tina Turner	Capitol
	Blue Jean	David Bowie	EMI-America
⑥	Cool It Now	The New Edition	MCA
	Desert Moon	Dennis De Young	A & M
⑥	I Feel For You	Chaka Khan	Warner Bros.
	It Ain't Enough	Corey Hart	EMI-America
	Left In The Dark	Barbra Streisand	Columbia

418

	On The Wings Of A Nightingale	The Everly Brothers	Mercury
☆	Out Of Touch	Hall & Oates	RCA
	Shine Shine	Barry Gibb	MCA
	Swept Away	Diana Ross	RCA
	Teacher, Teacher	38 Special	Capitol
☆ ⑥	Wake Me Up Before You Go-Go	Wham!	Columbia
	What About Me?	Kenny Rogers, Kim Carnes & James Ingram	RCA
	Who Wears These Shoes?	Elton John	Geffen

1984

OCTOBER

	All Through The Night	Cyndi Lauper	Portrait
	Hot For Teacher	Van Halen	Warner Bros.
	I Need You Tonight	Peter Wolf	EMI-America
	I Wanna Rock	Twisted Sister	Atlantic
	Jungle Love	The Time	Warner Bros.
	Love Songs Are Back Again	Band of Gold	RCA
	No More Lonely Nights	Paul McCartney	Columbia
	Penny Lover	Lionel Richie	Motown
⑥	Purple Rain	Prince & the Revolution	Warner Bros.
	Sea Of Love	The Honeydrippers	Es Paranza
	Two Tribes	Frankie Goes to Hollywood	Island
	Valotte	Julian Lennon	Atlantic
	Walking On A Thin Line	Huey Lewis & the News	Chrysalis
	The War Song	Culture Club	Virgin/Epic
	We Belong	Pat Benatar	Chryslis

NOVEMBER

	Born In The U.S.A.	Bruce Springsteen	Columbia
	The Boys Of Summer	Don Henley	Warner Bros.
	Bruce	Rick Springfield	Mercury
⑥	Easy Lover	Philip Bailey (with Phil Collins)	Columbia
	Foolish Heart	Steve Perry	Columbia
	Heaven (Must Be There)	The Eurogliders	Columbia
	Jamie	Ray Parker, Jr.	Arista
☆ ⑥	Like A Virgin	Madonna	Sire
	Misled	Kool & the Gang	Delight
	Neutron Dance	The Pointer Sisters	Planet
	Run To You	Bryan Adams	A & M
	Solid	Ashford & Simpson	Capitol
	Supernatural Love	Donna Summer	Warner Bros.
	The Wild Boys	Duran Duran	Capitol
	You're The Inspiration	Chicago	Full Moon/Warner

DECEMBER

☆ ⑥	Careless Whisper	Wham! featuring George Michael	Columbia
	Don't Wait For Heroes	Dennis De Young	A & M

419

⑥ Do They Know It's Christmas?	Band Aid	Columbia
The Heat Is On	Glenn Frey	MCA
☆ ⑥ I Want To Know What Love Is	Foreigner	Atlantic
I Would Die 4 U	Prince & the Revolution	Warner Bros.
Love Light In Flight	Stevie Wonder	Motown
Method Of Modern Love	Hall & Oates	RCA
Missing You	Diana Ross	RCA
Mistake No. 3	Culture Club	Virgin/Epic
Money Changes Everything	Cyndi Lauper	Portrait
Mr. Telephone Man	The New Edition	MCA
The Old Man Down The Road	John Fogerty	Warner Bros.
Tonight	David Bowie	EMI-America
20/20	George Benson	Warner Bros.

TOP SINGLES OF 1984

⑥ Against All Odds (Take A Look At Me Now)	Phil Collins	Atlantic
⑥ Caribbean Queen (No More Love On The Run)	Billy Ocean	Jive/Arista
⑥ Footloose	Kenny Loggins	Columbia
⑥ Ghostbusters	Ray Parker, Jr.	Arista
⑥ I Just Called To Say I Love You	Stevie Wonder	Motown
⑥ Jump	Van Halen	Warner Bros.
⑥ Karma Chameleon	Culture Club	Virgin/Epic
⑥ Wake Me Up Before You Go-Go	Wham!	Columbia
⑥ What's Love Got To Do With It	Tina Turner	Capitol
⑫ When Doves Cry	Prince	Warner Bros.

TOP ALBUMS OF 1984

⑫ Born In The U.S.A.	Bruce Springsteen	Columbia
⑫ Colour By Numbers	Culture Club	Virgin/Epic
⑫ Footloose	Soundtrack	Columbia
⑫ Ghostbusters	Soundtrack	Arista
⑫ Make It Big	Wham!	Columbia
⑫ 1984	Van Halen	Warner Bros.
⑫ Private Dancer	Tina Turner	Capitol
⑫ Purple Rain	Prince & the Revolution	Warner Bros.
⑫ Sports	Huey Lewis & the News	Chrysalis
⑫ Suddenly	Billy Ocean	Jive/Arista

Wang Chung (l to r: Nick Feldman, Jack Hues, Darren Costin)

GRAMMY WINNERS IN 1984

The Grammys were televised from the Shrine Auditorium in Los Angeles on Tuesday, February 26, 1985. John Denver was the host.

Record of the Year: "What's Love Got To Do With It," Tina Turner (Capitol)

Song of the Year: "What's Love Got To Do With It" (music and lyrics by Graham Lyle & Terry Britten)

Album of the Year: *Can't Slow Down,* Lionel Richie (Motown)

Best Vocal Performance, Female: "What's Love Got To Do With It," Tina Turner (Capitol)

Best Vocal Performance, Male: "Against All Odds (Take A Look At Me Now)," Phil Collins (Atlantic)

Best Vocal Performance, Group: "Jump (For My Love)," the Pointer Sisters (Planet)

Best Rock Vocal Performance, Female: "Better Be Good To Me," Tina Turner (Capitol)

Best Rock Vocal Performance, Male: "Dancing In The Dark," Bruce Springsteen (Columbia)

Best Rock Vocal Performance, Group: *Purple Rain,* Prince & the Revolution (Warner Bros.)

Best New Artist of the Year: Cyndi Lauper

Best Comedy Performance: "Eat It," "Weird Al" Yankovic (Rock 'n' Roll)

Best Soundtrack Album from a Motion Picture or Television: *Purple Rain,* Prince & the Revolution (Warner Bros.)

DEATHS IN 1984

MUSIC PERFORMERS AND MUSIC INDUSTRY NOTABLES WHO DIED IN 1984

Alexis Korner, Sunday, January 1 (cancer; 55)

Jackie Wilson, Saturday, January 21 (heart attack; 49)

Ethel Merman, Wednesday, February 15 (natural causes; 75)

Joey Vann (The Duprees), Tuesday, February 28 (heart attack; 40)

Marvin Gaye, Sunday, April 1 (gunshot; 44)

Ral Donner, Friday, April 6 (lung cancer; 41)

Mabel Mercer, Friday, April 20 (respiratory ailment; 84)

Count Basie, Thursday, April 26 (cancer; 79)

Gordon Jenkins (conductor), Tuesday, May 1 (Lou Gehrig's disease; 73)

Gordon Sinclair, Thursday, May 17 (heart attack; 83)

Nathaniel Nelson (The Flamingos), Friday, June 1 (heart attack; 52)

Meredith Willson, Friday, June 15 (heart attack; 82)

Phillippe Wynne (The Spinners), Friday, July 13 (heart attack; 43)

Willie Mae Thornton, Wednesday, July 25 (heart attack; 57)

Fred Waring, Sunday, July 29 (stroke; 84)

Esther Phillips, Tuesday, August 7 (complications after long illness; 48)

Percy Mayfield (composer), Saturday, August 11 (heart attack; 64)

Norman Petty (producer), Wednesday, August 15 (natural causes; 57)

Ernest Tubb, Thursday, September 6 (emphysema; 70)

Tasha Thomas, Monday, October 15 (cancer; 34)

Don Addrisi (The Addrisi Brothers), Tuesday, November 13 (cancer; 45)

Jan Peerce, Saturday, December 15 (extended illness; 80)

OTHERS WHO DIED IN 1984

Ansel Adams
Brooks Atkinson

Richard Basehart
Richard Burton

Truman Capote
Jackie Coogan
James F. Fixx
Indira Gandhi
Andy Kaufman
Ray A. Kroc

Peter Lawford
James Mason
Sam Peckinpah
Walter Pidgeon
François Truffaut
Johnny Weismuller

MOVIES OF 1984

MOVIES FEATURING POP MUSIC ARTISTS

Give My Regards to Broad Street   *Stars:* Paul McCartney, Linda McCartney, Ringo Starr, Barbara Bach, Tracy Ullman. *Featured songs:* "No More Lonely Nights," "Ballroom Dancing," "Eleanor Rigby," "Silly Love Songs," "Yesterday," "Good Day Sunshine."

Purple Rain   *Stars:* Prince, Apollonia, Morris Day, Clarence Williams III. *Featured songs:* "When Doves Cry," "Purple Rain," "Darling Nikki," and "I Would Die 4 U" by Prince, "Jungle Love" by Morris Day & the Time.

This Is Spinal Tap   *Stars:* Michael McKean, Christopher Guest, Harry Shearer, Rob Reiner. A parody of a heavy metal band on the road. No significant hits.

MOVIES FEATURING A POP MUSIC SOUNDTRACK

Beverly Hills Cop   *Stars:* Eddie Murphy, Judge Reinhold, Lisa Eilbacher, John Ashton, Ronny Cox. *Featured songs:* "Neutron Dance" by the Pointer Sisters, "The Heat Is On" by Glenn Frey, "Axel F" by Harold Faltermeyer.

Breakdance the Movie   *Stars:* Shabba-Doo (Adolfo Quinones), Lucinda Dickey, Ben Lokey. Film about the art of breakdancing with an appropriate list of danceable hits, including "There's No Stoppin Us" by Ollie & Jerry.

Footloose   *Stars:* Kevin Bacon, Lori Singer, John Lithgow, Christopher Penn. *Featured songs:* "Footloose" by Kenny Loggins, "Almost Paradise" by Mike Reno & Ann Wilson, "Let's Hear It For The Boy" by Deniece Williams.

Ghostbusters   *Stars:* Dan Aykroyd, Bill Murray, Harold Ramis, Sigourney Weaver, Rick Moranis. *Featured song:* "Ghostbusters" by Ray Parker, Jr.

The Woman in Red   *Stars:* Gene Wilder, Kelly Le Brock, Gilda Radner, Joseph Bologna, Charles Grodin. Featured Stevie Wonder's Oscar-winner "I Just Called To Say I Love You."

POP MUSIC ARTISTS ON VIDEO

David Bowie Live   Bowie in concert.

Tina Turner, Private Dancer *album cover*

Madonna, Like A Virgin *album cover*

Prince & the Revolution, Purple Rain *soundtrack album cover*

Neil Diamond: Love at the Greek Recorded at Los Angeles's Greek Theater in 1976, highlighting Diamond at his best.

Elvis: Aloha from Hawaii Elvis's 1973 concerts in Hawaii condensed to a 75-minute video.

Elvis '68 Comeback Special Elvis's 1968 Christmas special released in a 76-minute video.

That Was Rock The 1964 T.A.M.I. and 1965 T.N.T. shows combined in one 90-minute video.

Yoko Ono Then and Now Documentary focusing on the life of Yoko Ono with John Lennon, using many rare photos and family movies.

OTHER POPULAR MOVIES OF 1984

The Bounty
Gremlins
Iceman
Indiana Jones and the Temple of Doom
The Karate Kid
Mass Appeal
Missing in Action

The Muppets Take Manhattan
The Natural
Police Academy
Splash
Star Trek III: The Search for Spock
2010: The Year We Make Contact

ACADEMY AWARD WINNERS OF 1984

Best Actor: F. Murray Abraham, *Amadeus*
Best Actress: Sally Field, *Places in the Heart*
Best Picture: *Amadeus*
Best Original Song: "I Just Called To Say I Love You," *The Woman in Red* (music and lyrics by Stevie Wonder)

TOP TELEVISION SHOWS OF 1984

The "A" Team
The Cosby Show
Dallas
Dynasty
Falcon Crest

Family Ties
Knots Landing
Murder, She Wrote
Simon and Simon
60 Minutes

1985

1985

⇨ General William Westmoreland withdraws his $120 million libel suit against CBS, incited by a 1982 CBS documentary that accused him of lying to his superiors.

⇨ Soviet leader Konstantin Chernenko dies and is succeeded by worldly, reform-minded Mikhail Gorbachev, 54.

⇨ Coca-Cola annnounces a new formula. Mass protests and boycotts force the company to reintroduce the original formulation, now called Coke Classic. It quickly begins outselling new Coke 10 to 1.

⇨ In West Germany, President Reagan visits the Bergen-Belsen concentration camp and attends a memorial ceremony at the Bitburg cemetery.

⇨ The baseball commissioner calls for drug testing for all non-union personnel and players.

⇨ Arab terrorists seize a TWA plane after takeoff from Athens and hold 39 Americans hostage for 17 days.

⇨ The Live Aid concert for African famine relief is held in Philadelphia and London and beamed by satellite around the world. Organizer Bob Geldof, of the Boomtown Rats, is later knighted by Queen Elizabeth for his efforts.

⇨ Media mogul Ted Turner drops his bid to purchase CBS.

⇨ An earthquake measuring 7.8 on the Richter scale kills thousands in Mexico City.

⇨ After 73 years, French and American researchers find the *Titanic* in water 12,000 feet deep south of Newfoundland.

⇨ The Italian cruise ship *Achille Lauro* is hijacked by Palestinian guerrillas.

⇨ President Reagan and Soviet leader Gorbachev meet in Geneva.

⇨ Cincinnati's Pete Rose scores career hit 4,192, beating Ty Cobb's 57-year-old record.

SPORTS WINNERS

Baseball   The Kansas City Royals beat the St. Louis Cardinals 4 games to 3.
Football
   NFC: The Chicago Bears beat the Los Angeles Rams 24–0 in Chicago.
   AFC: The New England Patriots beat the Miami Dolphins 31–14 in Miami.
   Super Bowl XX: The Chicago Bears beat the New England Patriots 46–10 on January 26, 1986, at the Louisiana Superdome in New Orleans.
Basketball   The Los Angeles Lakers beat the Boston Celtics 4 games to 2.
Hockey   The Edmonton Oilers beat the Philadelphia Flyers 4 games to 1.

MUSIC HIGHLIGHTS OF 1985

⇨ On Tuesday, January 1, VH-1 premieres as a 24-hour adult contemporary music video channel with Marvin Gaye's "Star Spangled Banner" video. Don Imus is the first video jock signed to the new music channel.

⇨ On Monday, January 28, in Los Angeles, 43 major stars including Bruce Springsteen, Bob Dylan, Ray Charles, Michael Jackson, Billy Joel, Cyndi Lauper, Diana Ross, Tina Turner, and Lionel Richie gather to record "We Are The World," a song that would become an anthem in the effort to raise funds to fight famine in Africa.

⇨ Wham! becomes the first major rock act to play in China, appearing in both Peking and Canton.

⇨ On Saturday, March 23, Billy Joel marries supermodel Christie Brinkley.

⇨ Capital Cities Communication buys the American Broadcasting Company for $3.5 billion.

⇨ On Monday, May 13, Bruce Springsteen marries actress Juliann Phillips.

⇨ Bruce Springsteen launches his Born in the U.S.A. tour of America.

⇨ On Saturday, July 13, a record 1.6 billion viewers in 156 countries and capacity crowds in Philadelphia's JFK Stadium and London's Wembley arena, watch 40 bands perform for 16 hours in Live Aid. This show, initiated by Bob Geldof and promoters Bill Graham and Larry Magid, helps to raise $40 million to aid African famine relief. Among those perform-

425

ROCK ON ALMANAC

Amy Grant in concert (photo: *Anastasia Pantsios*)

ing were the reunited Who, Led Zeppelin, and Crosby, Stills, Nash & Young, along with U2, David Bowie, Phil Collins, Hall & Oates, Mick Jagger, Tina Turner, Bob Dylan, Madonna, Eric Clapton, Bryan Adams, and Keith Richards.

⇨ Madonna's album *Like A Virgin* becomes the first by a female singer to sell more than 5 million units.

⇨ On Friday, August 16, her 25th birthday, Madonna marries actor Sean Penn in Malibu.

⇨ Michael Jackson buys ATV Music for $40 million, gaining ownership of 250 of John Lennon and Paul McCartney's biggest songs.

⇨ Frank Zappa, Dee Snider of Twisted Sister, and John Denver testify at Senate hearings on explicit lyrics in songs.

⇨ On Sunday, September 22, Willie Nelson, John Cougar Mellencamp, and Neil Young host Farm Aid in Champaign, Illinois, raising $10 million for American farmers.

⇨ After six years at Columbia Records, Paul McCartney returns to Capitol and releases his first single, "Spies Like Us."

⇨ Little Richard is severely injured in an automobile crash in West Hollywod.

⇨ Little Steven (Miami Steve Van Zandt) spearheads a drive to fight apartheid in South Africa with his all-star cast recording "Sun City."

⇨ General Electric buys RCA, owner of NBC, for $6.3 billion.

DEBUT ARTISTS OF 1985

MAJOR ARTISTS	Debut Single	Label
Whitney Houston	You Give Good Love	Arista
Freddie Jackson	Rock Me Tonight	Capitol
Lisa Lisa & Cult Jam (Lisa Velez, Alex Spanador Moseley, Mike Hughes)	I Wonder If I Take You Home	Columbia
Orchestral Manoeuvres in the Dark (Paul Humphreys, Andrew McCluskey, Malcolm Holmes, Martin Cooper)	So In Love	A & M

The Hooters in concert (photo: *Anastasia Pantsios*)

John Parr   Naughty Naughty   Atlantic
David Lee Roth   California Girls   Warner Bros.
Sade (Helen Folasade Adu, Stewart   Smooth Operator   Portrait
    Matthewman, Andrew Hale, Paul
    Denman)
Sting (Gordon Sumner)   If You Love Somebody   A & M
                                  Set Them Free

1985

OTHER ARTISTS

a-ha	The Hooters
Alphaville	John Hunter
Animotion	Paul Hyde & the Payolas
Arcadia	Isley, Jasper, Isley
Steve Arrington	Mick Jagger
Artists United Against Apartheid	Jesse Johnson's Revue
Jon Butcher Axis	Katrina & the Waves
Belouis Some	King
Boy Meets Girl	Klymaxx
Alex Brown	Limahl
Cock Robin	Lone Justice
Al Corley	Loose Ends
Billy Crystal	Los Lobos
Curtie & the Boom Box	Marillion
Morris Day	Eric Martin
Dead or Alive	Marilyn Martin
Depeche Mode	The Mary Jane Girls
Dokken	Kim Mitchell
Eddie & the Tide	Alison Moyet
Harold Faltermeyer	Eddie Murphy
The Family	9.9
Fiona	Oingo Boingo
The Firm	The Power Station
Five Star	Ready for the World
David Foster	Rene & Angela
Robin George	Robey
Giuffria	Nile Rodgers
Godley & Creme	Scritti Politti
Go West	Charlie Sexton
Amy Grant	Jules Shear
Jan Hammer	Simple Minds
Paul Hardcastle	Sly Fox

Freddie Jackson in concert (photo: Anastasia Pantsios)

427

Starpoint
Maureen Steele
Jermaine Stewart
Nolan Thomas
George Thorogood & the Destroyers
'Til Tuesday
Urgent
USA for Africa
UTFO

The Vels
Vitamin Z
Jack Wagner
What Is This
Maurice White
Whodini
Jane Wiedlin
Eugene Wilde
Y&T

HITS OF 1985

JANUARY

	Song	Artist	Label
	California Girls	David Lee Roth	Warner Bros.
☆ ⑤	Can't Fight This Feeling	REO Speedwagon	Epic
	Crazy	Kenny Rogers	RCA
	Gotta Get You Home Tonight	Eugene Wilde	Philly World
	High On You	Survivor	Scotti Bros.
	I Wanna Hear It From Your Lips	Eric Carmen	Geffen
	Keepin' The Faith	Billy Joel	Columbia
	Knocking At Your Back Door	Deep Purple	Mercury
	Nightshift	The Commodores	Motown
	Only The Young	Journey	Geffen
	Ooh Ooh Song	Pat Benatar	Chrysalis
	Private Dancer	Tina Turner	Capitol
	Relax *(re-entry)*	Frankie Goes to Hollywood	Island
	Rockin' At Midnight	The Honeydrippers	Es Paranza
	Too Late For Goodbyes	Julian Lennon	Atlantic

FEBRUARY

	Song	Artist	Label
	All She Wants To Do Is Dance	Don Henley	Geffen
	Along Comes A Woman	Chicago	Full Moon/ Warner
	Baby Come Back To Me	The Manhattan Transfer	Atlantic
☆	Don't You (Forget About Me)	Simple Minds	A & M
	Holyanna	Toto	Columbia
	I'm On Fire	Bruce Springsteen	Columbia
	Just Another Night	Mick Jagger	Columbia
	Material Girl	Madonna	Sire
☆	One More Night	Phil Collins	Atlantic
	One Night In Bangkok	Murray Head	Chess
	Rhythm Of The Night	De Barge	Gordy
	Save A Prayer	Duran Duran	Capitol
	Somebody	Bryan Adams	A & M
	Take Me With U	Prince & the Revolution	Warner Bros.
	This Is Not America	David Bowie/Pat Metheny Group	EMI-America

MARCH

	Song	Artist	Label
☆ ⑤	Crazy For You	Madonna	Geffen
☆	Everybody Wants To Rule The World	Tears for Fears	Mercury

428

☆ Everything She Wants	Wham!	Columbia
Forever Man	Eric Clapton	Warner Bros.
In My House	The Mary Jane Girls	Gordy
Rock And Roll Girls	John Fogerty	Warner Bros.
Roxanne, Roxanne	UTFO	Select
Smooth Operator	Sade	Portrait
Some Like It Hot	The Power Station	Capitol
Some Things Are Better Left Unsaid	Hall & Oates	RCA
Suddenly	Billy Ocean	Jive/Arista
That Was Yesterday	Foreigner	Atlantic
Vox Humana	Kenny Loggins	Columbia
☆ ℗ We Are The World	USA for Africa	Columbia
You Send Me	The Manhattans	Columbia

APRIL

ⓖ Angel	Madonna	Sire
Axel F	Harold Faltermeyer	MCA
Celebrate Youth	Rick Springfield	RCA
Fresh	Kool & the Gang	De-Lite
☆ Heaven	Bryan Adams	A & M
Just A Gigolo/I Ain't Got Nobody	David Lee Roth	Warner Bros.
Lucky In Love	Mick Jagger	Columbia
Say You're Wrong	Julian Lennon	Atlantic
The Search Is Over	Survivor	Scotti Bros.
Show Some Respect	Tina Turner	Capitol
Smuggler's Blues	Glenn Frey	MCA
Voices Carry	'Til Tuesday	Epic
Walking On Sunshine	Katrina & the Waves	Capitol
Welcome To The Pleasuredome	Frankie Goes to Hollywood	Island
Would I Lie To You?	Eurythmics	RCA

MAY

Centerfield	John Fogerty	Warner Bros.
Crazy In The Night (Barking At Airplanes)	Kim Carnes	EMI-America

Jefferson Starship in concert (photo: Anastasia Pantsios)

☆	Dangerous	Natalie Cole	Modern
	Everytime You Go Away	Paul Young	Columbia
	Getcha Back	The Beach Boys	Caribou
	The Goonies 'R' Good Enough	Cyndi Lauper	Portrait
	Little By Little	Robert Plant	Es Paranza
	My Toot Toot	Jean Knight	Mirage
	Raspberry Beret	Prince & the Revolution	Paisley Park
	Sentimental Street	Night Ranger	Camel/MCA
☆	Sussudio	Phil Collins	Atlantic
	Tough All Over	John Cafferty & the Beaver Brown Band	Scotti Bros.
☆	A View To A Kill	Duran Duran	Capitol
	Wake Up (Next To You)	Graham Parker & the Shot	Elektra
	You Give Good Love	Whitney Houston	Arista

JUNE

	Freeway Of Love	Aretha Franklin	Arista
	Get It On (Bang A Gong)	The Power Station	Capitol
	Glory Days	Bruce Springsteen	Columbia
	If You Love Somebody Set Them Free	Sting	A & M
	Never Surrender	Corey Hart	EMI-America
	People Get Ready	Jeff Beck & Rod Stewart	Epic
	Possession Obsession	Hall & Oates	RCA
☆	The Power Of Love	Huey Lewis & the News	Chrysalis
☆ ⑤	Shout	Tears for Fears	Mercury
	State Of The Heart	Rick Springfield	RCA
☆	St. Elmo's Fire (Man In Motion)	John Parr	Atlantic
	Summer Of '69	Bryan Adams	A & M
	Take No Prisoners (In The Game Of Love)	Peabo Bryson	Elektra
	What About Love	Heart	Capitol
	Who's Holding Donna Now	De Barge	Gordy

JULY

	Cherish	Kool & the Gang	De-Lite
	Dare Me	The Pointer Sisters	Planet

Lisa Lisa (photo: Anastasia Pantsios)

David Hidalgo of Los Lobos (photo: Anastasia Pantsios)

1985

	Don't Lose My Number	Phil Collins	Atlantic
	Freedom	Wham!	Columbia
	I Got You Babe	UB40 with Chrissie Hynde	A & M
	Invincible	Pat Benatar	Chrysalis
☆	Money For Nothing	Dire Straits	Warner Bros.
	No Looking Back	Michael McDonald	Warner Bros.
	Pop Life	Prince & the Revolution	Warner Bros.
	Shame	The Motels	Capitol
	Smokin' In The Boys Room	Mötley Crüe	Elektra
☆	Take On Me	a-ha	Warner Bros.
	We Don't Need Another Hero (Thunderdome)	Tina Turner	Capitol
	You Look Marvelous	Billy Crystal	A & M
	You're Only Human (Second Wind)	Billy Joel	Columbia

AUGUST

	And We Danced	The Hooters	Columbia
	C-I-T-Y	John Cafferty & the Beaver Brown Band	Scotti Bros.
	Dancing In The Street	Mick Jagger & David Bowie	EMI-America
	Dress You Up	Madonna	Sire
	Every Step Of The Way	John Waite	EMI-America
	Fortress Around Your Heart	Sting	A & M
	Jessie	Julian Lennon	Atlantic
	Lonely Ol' Night	John Cougar Mellencamp	Riva
	Lovin' Every Minute Of It	Loverboy	Columbia
	A Nite At The Apollo Live! The Way You Do The Things You Do/My Girl	Daryl Hall & John Oates with David Ruffin & Eddie Kendricks	RCA
☆	Oh Sheila	Ready for the World	MCA
☆	Saving All My Love For You	Whitney Houston	Arista
⑥	The Show	Doug E. Fresh & the Get Fresh Crew	Reality
	Sunset Grill	Don Henley	Geffen
	There Must Be An Angel	Eurythmics	RCA

ROCK ON ALMANAC

SEPTEMBER

	Born In East L.A.	Cheech & Chong	MCA
☆	Broken Wings	Mr. Mister	RCA
	Communication	The Power Station	Capitol
	Head Over Heels	Tears for Fears	Mercury
	I'm Goin' Down	Bruce Springsteen	Columbia
	Lay Your Hands On Me	The Thompson Twins	Arista
☆	Miami Vice Theme	Jan Hammer	MCA
	Never	Heart	Capitol
	One Night Love Affair	Bryan Adams	A & M
☆	Part-Time Lover	Stevie Wonder	Tamla
	Screams Of Passion	The Family	Paisley Park
☆ ⑥	We Built This City	Starship	Grunt
	Who's Zoomin' Who	Aretha Franklin	Arista
	You Are My Lady	Freddie Jackson	Capitol
	You Belong To The City	Glenn Frey	MCA

OCTOBER

	Alive & Kicking	Simple Minds	A & M
	America	Prince & the Revolution	Paisley Park
	Do It For Love	Sheena Easton	EMI-America
	Election Day	Arcadia	Capitol
	Emergency	Kool & the Gang	De-Lite
	Girls Are More Fun	Ray Parker, Jr.	Arista
	I'm Gonna Tear Your Playhouse Down	Paul Young	Columbia
	One Of The Living	Tina Turner	Capitol
⑥	Party All The Time	Eddie Murphy	Columbia
☆	Separate Lives	Phil Collins & Marilyn Martin	Atlantic
	Sisters Are Doing It For Themselves	Eurythmics & Aretha Franklin	RCA
	Sleeping Bag	ZZ Top	Warner Bros.
	Soul Kiss	Olivia Newton-John	MCA
	To Live And Die In L.A.	Wang Chung	Geffen
	Wrap Her Up	Elton John	Geffen

NOVEMBER

	Burning Heart	Survivor	Scotti Bros.
	Everyday	James Taylor	Columbia
	I Knew The Bride (When She Used To Rock 'N' Roll)	Nick Lowe	Columbia
	I'm Your Man	Wham!	Columbia
	It's Only Love	Bryan Adams/Tina Turner	A & M
	Love Is The Seventh Wave	Sting	A & M
☆ ⑥	Say You, Say Me	Lionel Richie	Motown
	Small Town	John Cougar Mellencamp	Riva
	Spies Like Us	Paul McCartney	Capitol
	Sun City	Artists United Against Apartheid	Manhattan
	The Sweetest Taboo	Sade	Portrait
	Talk To Me	Stevie Nicks	Modern

432

Sade in concert (photo: Anastasia Pantsios)

1985

☆ ⑥	That's What Friends Are For	Dionne & Friends	Arista
	Tonight She Comes	The Cars	Elektra
	When The Going Gets Tough, The Tough Get Going	Billy Ocean	Jive

DECEMBER

	Beat's So Lonely	Charlie Sexton	MCA
	Day By Day	The Hooters	Columbia
	Go	Asia	Geffen
☆	How Will I Know	Whitney Houston	Arista
☆	Kyrie	Mr. Mister	RCA
	Let Me Down Easy	Roger Daltrey	Atlantic
	Let's Go All The Way	Sly Fox	Capitol
	Living In America	James Brown	Scotti Bros.
	My Hometown	Bruce Springsteen	Columbia
	One Vision	Queen	Capitol
☆	Sara	Starship	Grunt
	Secret	Orchestral Manoeuvres in the Dark	A & M/Virgin
	Secret Lover	Atlantic Starr	A & M
	Somewhere	Barbra Streisand	Columbia
	Stacy	Fortune	Camel/MCA

TOP SINGLES OF 1985

	Broken Wings	Mr. Mister	RCA
⑥	Can't Fight This Feeling	REO Speedwagon	Epic
	Careless Whisper	Wham! featuring George Michael	Columbia
⑥	I Want To Know What Love Is	Foreigner	Atlantic
	Money For Nothing	Dire Straits	Warner Bros.
⑥	The Power Of Love	Huey Lewis & the News	Chrysalis
⑥	Say You, Say Me	Lionel Richie	Motown
⑥	Shout	Tears for Fears	Mercury
℗	We Are The World	USA for Africa	Columbia
⑥	We Built This City	Starship	Grunt

TOP ALBUMS OF 1985

℗	Around The World In A Day	Prince	Paisley Park
℗	Brothers In Arms	Dire Straits	Warner Bros.

433

Sting in concert (photo: Anastasia Pantsios)

℗ **Centerfield**	John Fogerty	Warner Bros.
℗ **Like A Virgin**	Madonna	Sire
℗ **Make It Big**	Wham!	Columbia
℗ **Miami Vice**	TV Soundtrack	MCA
℗ **No Jacket Required**	Phil Collins	Atlantic
℗ **Reckless**	Bryan Adams	A & M
℗ **Songs From The Big Chair**	Tears for Fears	Mercury
℗ **We Are The World**	USA for Africa	Columbia

GRAMMY WINNERS IN 1985

The Grammys were televised from the Shrine Auditorium in Los Angeles on Tuesday, February 25, 1986. Kenny Rogers was the host.

Record of the Year: "We Are The World," USA for Africa (Columbia)
Song of the Year: "We Are The World" (music and lyrics by Michael Jackson & Lionel Richie)
Album of the Year: *No Jacket Required,* Phil Collins (Atlantic)
Best Vocal Performance, Female: "Saving All My Love For You," Whitney Houston (Arista)
Best Vocal Performance, Male: *No Jacket Required,* Phil Collins (Atlantic)
Best Vocal Performance, Group: "We Are The World," USA for Africa (Columbia)
Best Rock Vocal Performance, Female: "One Of The Living," Tina Turner (Capitol)
Best Rock Vocal Performance, Male: "The Boys Of Summer," Don Henley (Geffen)
Best Rock Vocal Performance, Group: "Money For Nothing," Dire Straits (Warner Bros.)
Best New Artist of the Year: Sade
Best Comedy Performance: *Whoopi Goldberg,* Whoopi Goldberg (Geffen)
Best Soundtrack Album from a Motion Picture or Television: *Beverly Hills Cop,* Various Artists (MCA)

DEATHS IN 1985

MUSIC PERFORMERS AND MUSIC INDUSTRY NOTABLES WHO DIED IN 1985

Anton Karas, Thursday, January 10 (natural causes; 78)
Matt Munro, Thursday, February 7 (cancer; 52)

David Byron (Uriah Heep), Thursday, February 28 (cause unknown; 38)
Robert "Bumps" Blackwell (producer), Saturday, March 9 (pneumonia; 66)

Eugene Ormandy (conductor), March 12 (extended illness; 82)

Zoot Sims, Saturday, March 23 (cancer; 59)

Jeanine Deckers (The Singing Nun), Monday, April 1 (drug overdose; 52)

Larry Clinton, Thursday, May 2 (cancer; 75)

Wayne King (bandleader), Tuesday, July 16 (heart attack; 84)

Kay Kyser (bandleader), Tuesday, July 23 (heart attack; 79)

Kyu Sakamoto, Monday, August 12 (plane crash; 44)

Johnny Marks (songwriter), Tuesday, September 3 (natural causes; 75)

J.R. Bailey (The Cadillacs), Friday, September 6 (heart attack; 48)

Johnny Desmond, Friday, September 6 (cancer; 65)

Nelson Riddle, Sunday, October 6 (heart and kidney failure; 64)

Ricky Wilson (The B-52's), Sunday, October 13 (cancer; 32)

Joe Turner, Sunday, November 24 (kidney failure; 74)

Ian Stewart (The Rolling Stones), Thursday, December 12 (heart attack; 47)

Rick Nelson, Tuesday, December 31 (plane crash; 45)

OTHERS WHO DIED IN 1985

Anne Baxter
Yul Brynner
Marc Chagall
Ruth Gordon
Rock Hudson
Henry Cabot Lodge

Lloyd Nolan
Mickey Shaughnessy
Phil Silvers
Sam Spiegel
Orson Welles

MOVIES OF 1985

MOVIES FEATURING POP MUSIC ARTISTS

A Chorus Line *Stars:* Michael Douglas, Terrence Mann, Alyson Reed. *Featured songs:* "One" and "What I Did For Love" by the cast.

Joey *Stars:* Neill Barry, James Quinn, Elisa Heinsohn, Linda Thorson, Ellen Hammill, Dan Grimaldi, Frankie Lanz, Norm N. Nite (briefly). *Featured songs:* "Daddy's Home" by the Limelights, "Boy From New York City" by the Ad-Libs, "Get A Job" by the Silhouettes, "Little Star" by the Elegants, "Unchained Melody" by Vito & His Group, "I Put A Spell On You" by Screamin' Jay Hawkins, "Why Do Fools Fall In Love" by the Teenagers.

MOVIES FEATURING A POP MUSIC SOUNDTRACK

Back to the Future *Stars:* Michael J. Fox, Christopher Lloyd, Crispin Glover. *Featured song:* "Power Of Love" by Huey Lewis & the News

Sweet Dreams *Stars:* Jessica Lange, Ed Harris, Ann Wedgeworth. A look at the life of country great Patsy Cline, using Patsy's original songs for the soundtrack.

POP MUSIC ARTISTS ON VIDEO

British Rock: The First Wave Original clips of sixties greats, including the Beatles, the Rolling Stones, the Kinks, the Animals, Herman's Hermits, the Who, and Gerry & the Pacemakers.

Eric Clapton Live Now Filmed on May 1, 1985, at the Civic Center in Hartford, Connecticut.

John Lennon Live in New York City Lennon's last public concert, filmed on August 30, 1972, at New York's Madison Square Garden with the Plastic Ono Band and Elephant's Memory.

1985

ROCK ON ALMANAC

Whitney Houston *album cover*

Rock and Roll: The Early Days   Original clips of fifties greats, including Elvis, Chuck Berry, Little Richard, Buddy Holly, Jerry Lee Lewis, Fats Domino, and Bill Haley.

Frank Sinatra: Portrait of an Album   Frank Sinatra and Quincy Jones put together an album, with comments from friends.

We Are the World: The Video Event   On January 28, 1985, rock's biggest names gathered in Los Angeles to record a song to help raise money to combat hunger in Africa. Michael Jackson, Lionel Richie, Bruce Springsteen, Bob Dylan, and 40 other stars perform.

OTHER POPULAR MOVIES OF 1985

The Breakfast Club
Cocoon
D.A.R.Y.L.
Death Wish 3
The Jewel of the Nile
King Solomon's Mines

Kiss of the Spider Woman
Out of Africa
Porky's Revenge
Rocky IV
Runaway Train

ACADEMY AWARD WINNERS OF 1985

Best Actor: William Hurt, *Kiss of the Spider Woman*
Best Actress: Geraldine Page, *The Trip to Bountiful*
Best Picture: *Out of Africa*
Best Original Song: "Say You, Say Me," *White Nights* (music and lyrics by Lionel Richie)

TOP TELEVISION SHOWS OF 1985

Cheers
The Cosby Show
Dallas
Dynasty
Family Ties

The Golden Girls
Miami Vice
Murder, She Wrote
60 Minutes
Who's the Boss?

1986

ROCK ON ALMANAC

NEWS HIGHLIGHTS OF 1986

⇨ In retaliation for promoting terrorism, the United States imposes trade sanctions against Libya and freezes Libyan assets.

⇨ The nation watches as the U.S. space shuttle *Challenger* explodes 74 seconds after liftoff, killing all seven crew members.

⇨ Ferdinand Marcos is defeated at the polls, and Corazon Aquino becomes president of the Philippines.

⇨ As punishment for complicity in the fire-bombing of a discotheque in West Germany, American planes bomb Libya.

⇨ An atomic mishap occurs at a nuclear generating plant at Chernobyl in the Ukraine, causing the evacuation of 15,000 residents of the area.

⇨ Despite persistent rumors of an active Nazi past, Kurt Waldheim is elected president of Austria.

⇨ Showered in fireworks, the Statue of Liberty celebrates its 100th birthday.

⇨ Prince Andrew, 26, fourth in line to the British throne, marries Sarah Ferguson in London.

⇨ William Schroeder, the second recipient of a permanent artificial heart, dies 620 days after the implant.

⇨ Sheik Ahmed Zaki Yamani, the man behind OPEC's rise to power, is dismissed as oil minister by King Fahd of Saudi Arabia.

⇨ A summit meeting between President Reagan and Soviet Party Chief Gorbachev in Iceland ends in failure.

⇨ Elie Wiesel, Nazi camp survivor, accepts the Nobel Peace Prize.

⇨ *Voyager,* an experimental airplane flown by Richard C. Rutan and Jeana Yeager, sets records for distance flown without refueling (25,012 miles) and for endurance in its nine-day nonstop flight around the world.

SPORTS WINNERS

Baseball   The New York Mets beat the Boston Red Sox 4 games to 3.

Football

NFC: The New York Giants beat the Washington Redskins 17–0 at Giants Stadium in East Rutherford, New Jersey.

AFC: The Denver Broncos beat the Cleveland Browns 23–20 in overtime at Cleveland.

Super Bowl XXI: The New York Giants beat the Denver Broncos 39–20 on January 25, 1987, at the Rose Bowl in Pasadena, California.

Basketball   The Boston Celtics beat the Houston Rockets 4 games to 2.

Hockey   The Montreal Canadiens beat the Calgary Flyers 4 games to 1.

MUSIC HIGHLIGHTS OF 1986

⇨ Senator Albert Gore (D-Tenn.) launches a full-scale investigation into payola and promotional practices in the record industry.

⇨ On Saturday, February 1, Diana Ross marries Norwegian millionaire Arne Naess in Geneva.

⇨ George Michael announces the official breakup of Wham!

⇨ Joe Leeway leaves the Thompson Twins, who continue to perform as a duo.

⇨ Belinda Carlisle leaves the Go-Go's.

⇨ On Monday, May 5, Rock and Roll Hall of Fame Chairman Ahmet Ertegen announces in New York that Cleveland, Ohio, has been chosen as the city where the Hall of Fame will be built.

⇨ On Saturday, May 10, Tommy Lee of Mötley Crüe marries actress Heather Locklear.

⇨ Hands Across America takes place on Sunday, May 25. Some 5 million participants in 16

Anita Baker in concert (photo: Anastasia Pantsios)

Belinda Carlisle in concert

states, including President Reagan, link hands to raise money for the hungry and the homeless in the United States.

⇨ CDs begin gaining in popularity; sales rise 150 percent in one year, and K mart's 2,000 stores and Waldenbooks' 980 stores agree to start selling them.

⇨ Dolly Parton opens her Dollywood amusement park in Tennessee.

⇨ EMI opens Abbey Road Studios in London, where many of the Beatles' songs were recorded, to the public.

⇨ Boy George, lead singer of Culture Club, is booked in London for heroin possession.

⇨ John Fogerty, former lead voice of Creedence Clearwater Revival, begins a solo tour, his first in 14 years.

⇨ Mickey Dolenz, Peter Tork, and Davy Jones reunite for a Monkees tour. Other original member Michael Nesmith chooses not to join them.

⇨ Andy Taylor leaves Duran Duran.

⇨ On Thursday, October 9, Fox Broadcasting premieres "The Late Show" with Joan Rivers as host. The first guests are Cher, Elton John, David Lee Roth, and Pee-wee Herman; Rivers and Cher join John for a spirited rendition of "The Bitch Is Back."

⇨ Former Supreme Mary Wilson publishes her autobiography, *Dreamgirl: My Life as a Supreme.*

⇨ Dick Clark Productions goes public, raising $14.5 million.

⇨ Bruce Springsteen's five-record boxed set, *Bruce Springsteen & The E Street Band Live/1975–1985,* is released. Containing 40 digitally mixed and mastered songs, it debuts at number one on the *Billboard* magazine album chart, the first package of any size to debut at the top in more than a decade and the first five-album set ever to reach number one.

DEBUT ARTISTS OF 1986

MAJOR ARTISTS

	Debut Single	*Label*
Anita Baker	Sweet Love	Elektra
The Bangles (Vicki Peterson, Debbi Peterson, Michael Steele, Susanna Hoffs)	Manic Monday	Columbia
Bobby Brown	Girlfriend	MCA
Belinda Carlisle	Mad About You	I.R.S.
Peter Cetera	Glory Of Love ☆	Full Moon/Warner
Bruce Hornsby & the Range (Bruce Hornsby, David Mansfield, George Marinelli, Joe Puerta, John Molo)	Every Little Kiss	RCA

439

The Jets (Elizabeth, Kathi, Moana, Rudy, Haini, Eugene, Eddie, and Leroy Wolfgramm)	Crush On You	MCA
Miami Sound Machine (Gloria Estefan, Emilio Estefan, Jr., Enrique Garcia, Raphael Padilla, Jim Trompeter, Clay Oswald, Jorge Casas, John De Farria, Randy Barlow, Teddy Mulet)	Conga	Epic
George Michael	A Different Corner	Columbia
The Pet Shop Boys (Neil Tennant, Chris Lowe)	West End Girls ☆	EMI-America

OTHER ARTISTS

Gregory Abbott
The Alarm
Alisha
The Art of Noise
Baltimora
Jimmy Barnes
The Beastie Boys
Jean Beauvoir
The Blow Monkeys
Bourgeois Tagg
Boys Don't Cry
Luis Cardenas
The Chicago Bears Shufflin' Crew
Gavin Christopher
Clarence Clemons
The Cure
E.G. Daily
David & David
Chico De Barge
El De Barge
The Del Fuegos
Device
The Divinyls
Doctor & the Medics
Double
The Dream Academy
John Eddie
Emerson, Lake & Powell
The Fabulous Thunderbirds
Falco
The Far Corporation
Fine Young Cannibals
The Force M.D.'s
The Georgia Satellites
Glass Tiger
GTR
Gwen Guthrie
Howard Hewett
Isle of Man
Nick Jameson

Jellybean
Don Johnson
Oran "Juice" Jones
The KBC Band
Laban
Level 42
Limited Warranty
Gloria Loring & Carl Anderson
Magazine 60
Mai Tai
Mike + the Mechanics
The Models
Meli'sa Morgan
Phyllis Nelson
Nu Shooz
One to One
Opus
Ozzy Osbourne
The Outfield
David Pack
Platinum Blonde
Regina
Run-D.M.C.
Jennifer Rush
Secret Ties
Feargal Sharkey
Simply Red
Stacey Q
Synch
Ta Mara & the Seen
Andy Taylor
John Taylor
Robert Tepper
Timbuk 3
The Timex Social Club
TKA
Trans-X
The Voices of America
Wax
Wild Blue

HITS OF 1986

JANUARY

Another Night	Aretha Franklin	Arista
Bop	Dan Seals	EMI-America
Just Another Day	Oingo Boingo	MCA
King For A Day	The Thompson Twins	Arista
Manic Monday	The Bangles	Columbia
Night Moves	Marilyn Martin	Atlantic
Nikita	Elton John	Geffen
No Easy Way Out	Robert Tepper	Scotti Bros.
Pleasure And Pain	The Divinyls	Chrysalis
Russians	Sting	A & M
Sanctify Yourself	Simple Minds	A & M/Virgin
Stages	ZZ Top	Warner Bros.
⑥ **Super Bowl Shuffle**	The Chicago Bears Shufflin' Crew	Red Label
☆ **These Dreams**	Heart	Capitol
Your Personal Touch	Evelyn "Champagne" King	RCA

FEBRUARY

☆ ⑥ **Addicted To Love**	Robert Palmer	Island
Goodbye Is Forever	Arcadia	Capitol
I Can't Wait	Stevie Nicks	Modern
I Like You	Phyllis Nelson	Carrere
I'm Not The One	The Cars	Elektra
I Think It's Love	Jermaine Jackson	Arista
☆ ⑥ **Kiss**	Prince & the Revolution	Paisley Park
Le Bel Age (The Best Years)	Pat Benatar	Chrysalis
Needles And Pins	Tom Petty & the Heartbreakers with Stevie Nicks	MCA
Overjoyed	Stevie Wonder	Tamla
☆ **Rock Me Amadeus**	Falco	A & M
R.O.C.K. In The U.S.A.	John Cougar Mellencamp	Riva
Something About You	Level 42	Polydor
Stereotomy	The Alan Parsons Project	Arista
What Have You Done For Me Lately	Janet Jackson	A & M

The Jets (top l to r: Rudy, Kathi, Moana; bottom l to r: Eddie, Elizabeth, Haini, Leroy)

ROCK ON ALMANAC

MARCH

All I Need Is A Miracle	Mike + the Mechanics	Atlantic
American Storm	Bob Seger & the Silver Bullet Band	Capitol
For America	Jackson Browne	Asylum
☆ Greatest Love Of All	Whitney Houston	Arista
Harlem Shuffle	The Rolling Stones	Rolling Stones
Is It Love	Mr. Mister	RCA
Never As Good As The First Time	Sade	Portrait
☆ ⑥ On My Own	Patti LaBelle & Michael McDonald	MCA
Restless	Starpoint	Elektra
Rough Boy	ZZ Top	Warner Bros.
So Far Away	Dire Straits	Warner Bros.
Stick Around	Julian Lennon	Atlantic
Take Me Home	Phil Collins	Atlantic
☆ West End Girls	The Pet Shop Boys	EMI-America
Why Can't This Be Love	Van Halen	Warner Bros.

APRIL

Be Good To Yourself	Journey	Columbia
A Different Corner	George Michael	Columbia
Hands Across America	The Voices of America	EMI-America
☆ Holding Back The Years	Simply Red	Elektra
☆ Live To Tell	Madonna	Sire
Mothers Talk	Tears for Fears	Mercury
Move Away	Culture Club	Virgin/Epic
No One Is To Blame	Howard Jones	Elektra
Nothin' At All	Heart	Capitol
Out Of Mind, Out Of Sight	The Models	Geffen
Rain On The Scarecrow	John Cougar Mellencamp	Riva
☆ There'll Be Sad Songs (To Make You Cry)	Billy Ocean	Jive
Tomorrow Doesn't Matter Tonight	Starship	Grunt
Under The Influence	Vanity	Motown
Vienna Calling	Falco	A & M
Who's Johnny	El De Barge	Gordy

Mark King of Level 42 in concert (photo: Anastasia Pantsios)

Gloria Estefan of Miami Sound Machine in concert (photo: Anastasia Pantsios)

MAY

Digging Your Scene	The Blow Monkeys	RCA
Dreams	Van Halen	Warner Bros.
Has Anyone Ever Written Anything For You	Stevie Nicks	Modern
If She Knew What She Wants	The Bangles	Columbia
Like A Rock	Bob Seger & the Silver Bullet Band	Capitol
Like No Other Night	38 Special	A & M
Love Touch (From Legal Eagles)	Rod Stewart	Warner Bros.
Mountains	Prince & the Revolution	Paisley Park
Nasty	Janet Jackson	A & M
One Hit (To The Body)	The Rolling Stones	Columbia
Opportunities (Let's Make Lots Of Money)	The Pet Shop Boys	EMI-America
Peter Gunn	The Art of Noise	China
Secret Separation	The Fixx	MCA
☆ Sledgehammer	Peter Gabriel	Geffen
When The Heart Rules The Mind	GTR	Arista

JUNE

All The Love In The World	The Outfield	Columbia
☆ Glory Of Love	Peter Cetera	Full Moon/ Warner
☆ Higher Love	Steve Winwood	Island
Hyperactive	Robert Palmer	Island
Modern Woman	Billy Joel	Columbia
☆ Papa Don't Preach	Madonna	Sire
Rock 'N' Roll To The Rescue	The Beach Boys	Capitol
Rumbleseat	John Cougar Mellencamp	Riva
Rumors	The Timex Social Club	Jay
Suzanne	Journey	Columbia
Sweet Freedom	Michael McDonald	MCA
☆ Take My Breath Away	Berlin	Columbia
Taken In	Mike + the Mechanics	Atlantic
Venus	Bananarama	London
Words Get In The Way	The Miami Sound Machine	Epic

JULY

Dancing On The Ceiling	Lionel Richie	Motown
The Edge Of Heaven	Wham!	Columbia
Every Little Kiss	Bruce Hornsby & the Range	RCA
Friends And Lovers	Gloria Loring & Carl Anderson	Carrere
If Looks Could Kill	Heart	Capitol
Love Of A Lifetime	Chaka Khan	Warner Bros.
Love Zone	Billy Ocean	Jive
Man Size Love	Klymaxx	MCA
Money$ Too Tight (To Mention)	Simply Red	Elektra
Somebody Like You	38 Special	A & M
That Was Then, This Is Now	The Monkees	Arista

443

Two Of Hearts	Stacey Q	Atlantic
Velcro Fly	ZZ Top	Warner Bros.
Walk Like A Man	The Mary Jane Girls	Motown
Yankee Rose	David Lee Roth	Warner Bros.

AUGUST

	Dreamtime	Daryl Hall	RCA
	Earth Angel	The New Edition	MCA
	Girl Can't Help It	Journey	Columbia
	Heartbeat	Don Johnson	Epic
	Heaven In Your Eyes	Loverboy	Columbia
	A Matter Of Trust	Billy Joel	Columbia
	Paranoimia	The Art of Noise	China
	Press	Paul McCartney	Capitol
☆	Stuck With You	Huey Lewis & the News	Chrysalis
	Sweet Love	Anita Baker	Elektra
	Take Me Home Tonight	Eddie Money	Columbia
	Throwing It All Away	Genesis	Atlantic
☆	True Colors	Cyndi Lauper	Portrait
	Typical Male	Tina Turner	Capitol
☆	When I Think Of You	Janet Jackson	A & M

SEPTEMBER

	Amanda	Boston	MCA
☆			
	California Dreamin'	The Beach Boys	Capitol
	Can't Wait Another Minute	Five Star	RCA
	Emotion In Motion	Ric Ocasek	Geffen
	Freedom Overspill	Steve Winwood	Island
	Goin' Crazy	Davie Lee Roth	Warner Bros.
☆	Human	The Human League	A & M
	I Am By Your Side	Corey Hart	EMI-America
☆	The Next Time I Fall	Peter Cetera with Amy Grant	Warner Bros.
☆	Walk Like An Egyptian	The Bangles	Columbia
☆	The Way It Is	Bruce Hornsby & the Range	RCA
	What About Love	'Til Tuesday	Epic
	Word Up	Cameo	Atlanta Artists
☆	You Give Love A Bad Name	Bon Jovi	Mercury

OCTOBER

	Don't Stand So Close To Me '86	The Police	A & M
	Everybody Have Fun Tonight	Wang Chung	Geffen
	Foolish Pride	Daryl Hall	RCA
	Heartache All Over The World	Elton John	Geffen
	Hip To Be Square	Huey Lewis & the News	Chrysalis
	Is This Love	Survivor	Scotti Bros.
	Lady Soul	The Temptations	Gordy
	Love Is Forever	Billy Ocean	Jive
	Love Will Conquer All	Lionel Richie	Motown
☆	Shake You Down	Gregory Abbott	Columbia
	Stand By Me (re-entry)	Ben E. King	Atlantic

To Be A Lover	Billy Idol	Chrysalis
True Blue	Madonna	Sire
Where Did Your Heart Go?	Wham!	Columbia
You Know I Love You . . . Don't You?	Howard Jones	Elektra

NOVEMBER

☆ At This Moment *(re-entry)*	Billy Vera & the Beaters	Rhino
Change Of Heart	Cyndi Lauper	Portrait
Control	Janet Jackson	A & M
Every Beat Of My Heart	Rod Stewart	Warner Bros.
Heartache Away	Don Johnson	Epic
Keep Your Hands To Yourself	The Georgia Satellites	Elektra
Land Of Confusion	Genesis	Atlantic
Love You Down	Ready for the World	MCA
Notorious	Duran Duran	Capitol
Talk To Me	Chico De Barge	Motown
That's Life	David Lee Roth	Warner Bros.
This Is The Time	Billy Joel	Columbia
Two People	Tina Turner	Capitol
War	Bruce Springsteen	Columbia
Will You Still Love Me?	Chicago	Warner Bros.

DECEMBER

Ballerina Girl	Lionel Richie	Motown
Candy	Cameo	Atlanta Artists
Can't Help Falling In Love	Corey Hart	EMI-America
Don't Leave Me This Way	The Communards	MCA
Girlfriend	Bobby Brown	MCA
Graceland	Paul Simon	Warner Bros.
I'll Be Alright Without You	Journey	Columbia
I Wanna Go Back	Eddie Money	Columbia
☆ Livin' On A Prayer	Bon Jovi	Mercury
☆ Open Your Heart	Madonna	Sire
Somewhere Out There	Linda Ronstadt & James Ingram	MCA
True To You	Ric Ocasek	Geffen
We're Ready	Boston	MCA
Without Your Love	Toto	Columbia
(You Gotta) Fight For Your Right (To Party!)	The Beastie Boys	Def Jam

ROCK ON ALMANAC

TOP SINGLES OF 1986

Ⓖ	Addicted To Love	Robert Palmer	Island
	Greatest Love Of All	Whitney Houston	Arista
	How Will I Know	Whitney Houston	Arista
Ⓖ	Kiss	Prince & the Revolution	Paisley Park
	Kyrie	Mr. Mister	RCA
Ⓖ	On My Own	Patti LaBelle & Michael McDonald	MCA
	Rock Me Amadeus	Falco	A & M
	Sara	Starship	Grunt
Ⓖ	That's What Friends Are For	Dionne & Friends	Arista
	West End Girls	The Pet Shop Boys	EMI-America

TOP ALBUMS OF 1986

Ⓟ	Bruce Springsteen & The E Street Band Live/1975–1985	Bruce Springsteen	Columbia
Ⓟ	Dancing On The Ceiling	Lionel Richie	Motown
Ⓟ	5150	Van Halen	Warner Bros.
Ⓟ	Fore!	Huey Lewis & the News	Chrysalis
Ⓟ	Promise	Sade	Portrait
Ⓟ	Slippery When Wet	Bon Jovi	Mercury
Ⓟ	Third Stage	Boston	MCA
Ⓟ	Top Gun	Soundtrack	Columbia
Ⓟ	True Blue	Madonna	Sire
Ⓟ	Whitney Houston	Whitney Houston	Arista

GRAMMY WINNERS IN 1986

The Grammys were televised from the Shrine Auditorium in Los Angeles on Tuesday, February 24, 1987. Billy Crystal was the host.

Record of the Year: "Higher Love," Steve Winwood (Island)
Song of the Year: "That's What Friends Are For" (music and lyrics by Burt Bacharach & Carol Bayer Sager)

Ozzy Osbourne in concert (photo: Anastasia Pantsios)

Album of the Year: *Graceland,* Paul Simon (Warner Bros.)
Best Vocal Performance, Female: *The Broadway Album,* Barbra Streisand (Columbia)
Best Vocal Performance, Male: "Higher Love," Steve Winwood (Island)
Best Vocal Performance, Group: "That's What Friends Are For," Dionne & Friends (Stevie Wonder, Elton John, Gladys Knight) (Arista)
Best Rock Vocal Performance, Female: *Break Every Rule,* Tina Turner (Capitol)
Best Rock Vocal Performance, Male: "Addicted To Love," Robert Palmer (Island)
Best Rock Vocal Performance, Group: "Missionary Man," Eurythmics (RCA)
Best New Artist of the Year: Bruce Hornsby & the Range
Best Comedy Performance: *Those Of You Without Children, You'll Understand,* Bill Cosby (Geffen)
Best Soundtrack Album from a Motion Picture or Television: *Beverly Hills Cop,* Various Artists (MCA)

ROCK AND ROLL HALL OF FAME INDUCTEES

The first annual induction ceremony was held on Thursday, January 23, 1986, at the Waldorf Astoria hotel in New York City. The first award was presented to Chuck Berry by Keith Richards.

PERFORMERS

Inductee (Born and Died)	Debut Single (Year)	Label
Chuck Berry (October 18, 1926–)	Maybellene (1955)	Chess
James Brown (May 3, 1928–)	Please, Please, Please (1956)	Federal
Ray Charles (September 23, 1930–)	Babe Let Me Hold Your Hand (1951)	Swing Time
Sam Cooke (January 22, 1935–December 11, 1964)	You Send Me (1957)	Keen
Fats Domino (February 26, 1928–)	The Fat Man (1950)	Imperial
The Everly Brothers (Don: February 1, 1937– ; Phil: January 19, 1939–)	Bye, Bye Love (1957)	Cadence
Buddy Holly (September 7, 1936–February 3, 1959)	That'll Be The Day (1957)	Brunswick
Jerry Lee Lewis (September 29, 1935–)	Whole Lot Of Shakin' Going On (1957)	Sun
Little Richard (Penniman) (December 5, 1932–)	Tutti-Frutti (1955)	Specialty
Elvis Presley (January 8, 1935–August 16, 1977)	That's All Right (Mama) (1954)	Sun

NONPERFORMERS

Alan Freed (December 15, 1921–January 20, 1965)   Disc jockey and the "Father of Rock 'n' Roll," credited with popularizing the phrase "rock 'n' roll"
Sam Phillips (January 5, 1923–)   Founder of Sun Records in Memphis, Tennessee

EARLY INFLUENCES

Robert Johnson (May 8, 1911–August 16, 1938)   Father of folk blues
Jimmie Rodgers (September 8, 1897–May 26, 1933)   Country music pioneer
Jimmy Yancey (February 20, 1898–September 17, 1951)   Boogie woogie piano player

ROCK ON ALMANAC

DEATHS IN 1986

MUSIC PERFORMERS AND INDUSTRY NOTABLES WHO DIED IN 1986

Phil Lynott (Thin Lizzy), Saturday, January 4 (drug overdose; 36)

Gordon MacRae, Friday, January 24 (cancer; 54)

Howard Greenfield, Tuesday, March 4 (brief illness; 47)

Richard Manuel (The Band), Tuesday, March 4 (hanging; 41)

Mark Dinning, Saturday, March 22 (heart failure; 52)

O'Kelly Isley (The Isley Brothers), Monday, March 31 (cerebral hemorrhage; 49)

Linda Creed, Thursday, April 10 (cancer; 37)

Harold Arlen (composer), Wednesday, April 23 (natural causes; 81)

Hugo Peretti (Hugo & Luigi), Thursday, May 1 (natural causes; 68)

Ralph Garone (Bob Knight Four), Monday, May 5 (cancer; 46)

Benny Goodman, Friday, June 13 (heart attack; 77)

Alan Jay Lerner, Saturday, June 14 (lung cancer; 67)

Teddy Wilson, Thursday, July 31 (intestinal illness; 73)

Lee Dorsey, Tuesday, December 2 (emphysema; 59)

OTHERS WHO DIED IN 1986

Desi Arnaz
Herschel Bernardi
James Cagney
Myron Cohen
Broderick Crawford
Cary Grant
Sterling Hayden

Jacob Javits
Elsa Lanchester
Harold Macmillan
Ray Milland
Vincent Minnelli
Otto Preminger
Donna Reed

MOVIES OF 1986

MOVIES FEATURING POP MUSIC ARTISTS

Under the Cherry Moon   *Stars:* Prince, Jerome Benton, Kristin Scott-Thomas, Steven Berkoff, Francesca Annis, Emmanuelle Sallet, Alexandria Stewart, Victor Spinetti. *Featured songs:* "Kiss," "Mountains."

MOVIES FEATURING A POP MUSIC SOUNDTRACK

Crossroads   *Stars:* Ralph Macchio, Joe Seneca. Features the music of Robert Johnson.

Stand by Me   *Stars:* Wil Wheaton, River Phoenix, Corey Feldman, Jerry O'Connell, Keifer Sutherland, Richard Dreyfuss. Features hits of the fifties and early sixties.

Andy Taylor in concert (photo: Anastasia Pantsios)

Van Halen, 5150 album cover

1986

Top Gun *Stars:* Tom Cruise, Kelly McGillis, Val Kilmer, Anthony Edwards, Tom Skerritt. *Featured songs:* "Take My Breath Away" by Berlin, "Danger Zone" by Kenny Loggins.

POP MUSIC ARTISTS ON VIDEO

Blue Suede Shoes: A Rockabilly Session with Carl Perkins and Friends Hall of Famer Carl Perkins jams with Eric Clapton, George Harrison, Ringo Starr, Dave Edmunds, Rosanne Cash, Slim Jim Phantom, and Lee Rocker.

Dick Clark's Best of Bandstand Original clips from *American Bandstand*'s early years include Bill Haley & His Comets, Buddy Holly, Jerry Lee Lewis, the Big Bopper, the Everly Brothers, Chubby Checker, the Silhouettes, and Dion & the Belmonts.

The Prince's Trust All-Star Rock Concert The Prince of Wales asked Britain's biggest rockers to perform for his favorite charity. Performers included Elton John, Phil Collins, Tina Turner, Eric Clapton, Sting, Rod Stewart, Bryan Adams, George Michael, and Paul McCartney.

OTHER POPULAR MOVIES OF 1986

Aliens
Brighton Beach Memoirs
Children of a Lesser God
Extremities
F/X
Howard the Duck
The Karate Kid, Part II
Legal Eagles
The Mission
The Money Pit

9½ Weeks
Peggy Sue Got Married
Platoon
Poltergeist II
Psycho III
Ruthless People
She's Gotta Have It
Soul Man
Star Trek IV: The Voyage Home
Three Amigos!

ACADEMY AWARD WINNERS OF 1986

Best Actor: Paul Newman, *The Color of Money*
Best Actress: Marlee Matlin, *Children of a Lesser God*
Best Picture: *Platoon*
Best Original Song: "Take My Breath Away," *Top Gun* (music by Giorgio Moroder, lyrics by Tim Whitlock)

TOP TELEVISION SHOWS OF 1986

Cheers
The Cosby Show
Family Ties
The Golden Girls
Growing Pains

Moonlighting
Murder, She Wrote
Night Court
60 Minutes
Who's the Boss?

449

1987

NEWS HIGHLIGHTS OF 1987

- ⇨ Saudi Arabia contributes $20 million in aid to the *contra* rebels in Nicaragua.
- ⇨ A presidential commission criticizes President Reagan for failing to control a secret arms deal with Iran.
- ⇨ Fawn Hall, 27-year-old personal secretary to Lieut. Col. Oliver North, admits to helping Col. North destroy national security documents related to the Iran-*contra* fund-diversion affair.
- ⇨ Eastman Kodak and Fuji both market a disposable camera.
- ⇨ Rev. Jim Bakker resigns his TV ministry in the face of charges of sexual misconduct.
- ⇨ Gary Hart drops out of the race for the presidential nomination after being linked to Donna Rice, a part-time actress and model.
- ⇨ In the Persian Gulf, the U.S.S. *Stark* is struck by an Iraqi missile, killing 37 American sailors.
- ⇨ A 19-year-old German pilot lands a single-engine plane in Moscow's Red Square.
- ⇨ Late-night TV talk show host Johnny Carson, 61, weds for the fourth time.
- ⇨ The Sunday night TV newsmagazine *60 Minutes* starts its 20th season on CBS.
- ⇨ The Dow Jones industrial average plunges a record 508 points in a single day.
- ⇨ Stockbroker Ivan Boesky is sentenced to three years in prison for insider trading (using privileged information to guide his investments).

SPORTS WINNERS

Baseball   The Minnesota Twins beat the St. Louis Cardinals 4 games to 3.
Football
   NFC: The Washington Redskins beat the Minnesota Vikings 17–10 in Washington.
   AFC: The Denver Broncos beat the Cleveland Browns 38–33 in Denver.
   Super Bowl XXII: The Washington Redskins beat the Denver Broncos 42–10 on January 31, 1988, in San Diego, California.
Basketball   The Los Angeles Lakers beat the Detroit Pistons 4 games to 3.
Hockey   The Edmonton Oilers sweep the Boston Bruins 4 games to 0.

MUSIC HIGHLIGHTS 1987

- ⇨ Capitol Records releases the first four albums by the Beatles on CD.
- ⇨ The Doobie Brothers re-form after a five-year hiatus.
- ⇨ Sony starts testing the 3-inch CD.
- ⇨ George Michael's single "I Want Your Sex" is banned by many U.S. radio stations.

Beastie Boys in concert (photo: Anastasia Pantsios)

⇨ Super VHS video, which produces an extremely sharp picture, debuts.

⇨ Whitney Houston becomes the first female artist in the history of the *Billboard* magazine pop album charts to debut at number one, which she does with her second album, *Whitney*.

⇨ Michael Jackson invites top retailers to his California home to preview his new album, *Bad*. In September he starts a world tour in Tokyo.

⇨ On June 19 and 20, Dion makes a comeback to rock 'n' roll at New York's Radio City Music Hall for the first time in over a decade, singing all his old hits. The show is sponsored by local radio station WCBS-FM, which is celebrating 15 years as New York's oldies station.

⇨ CBS sells CBS Records Group to Sony of Japan for $2 billion.

⇨ MTV debuts in 14 countries in Europe.

⇨ *Rolling Stone* magazine celebrates 20 years of publication.

⇨ On Saturday, September 5, *American Bandstand* is broadcast for the last time before going into syndication.

⇨ ABC-TV premieres *Dolly*, a variety show starring Dolly Parton.

⇨ Terence Trent D'Arby makes his U.S. debut at the Roxy Theater in Los Angeles.

⇨ Andy Gibb files for bankruptcy.

⇨ Billy Joel performs at concerts in the USSR that are taped for broadcast back home on HBO.

⇨ The National Music Foundation was founded on October 21 by Joey Dee, Lois Lee, Allen Haimes, and Judith Richardson-Haimes.

DEBUT ARTISTS OF 1987

Donna Allen	Elisa Fiorillo
Amazulu	4 by Four
Ana	Samantha Fox
Jon Astley	Frozen Ghost
Rick Astley	Bob Geldof
Beau Coup	Debbie Gibson
Regina Belle	Lou Gramm
Big Trouble	Great White
Boy George	David Hallyday
The Breakfast Club	Colin James Hay
Glen Burtnick	Nona Hendryx
Jonathan Butler	Hipsway
Cinderella	Glenn Jones
Club Nouveau	Rob Jungklas
Company B	The Kane Gang
Julian Cope	Kenny G.
The Cover Girls	Tom Kimmel
The Robert Cray Band	K.T.P.
Crowded House	Paul Lekakis
Curiosity Killed the Cat	LeVert
The Cutting Crew	Living in a Box
Terence Trent D'Arby	L.L. Cool J
Jimmy Davis & Junction	Jeff Lorber
Martha Davis	M/A/R/R/S
Taylor Dayne	Nancy Martinez
Kool Moe Dee	Richard Marx
Deja	Glenn Medeiros
Eight Seconds	Mel & Kim
Europe	Millions Like Us
Exposé	Mondo Rock
The Fat Boys	Shirley Murdock

1987

Robert Cray in concert (photo: Anastasia Pantsios)

Terence Trent D'Arby in concert (photo: Anastasia Pantsios)

Robbie Nevil
The Newcity Rockers
New Order
Nocera
Noel
The Nylons
Alexander O'Neal
Benjamin Orr
The Other Ones
The Partland Brothers
Pepsi & Shirlie
Buster Poindexter & His Banshees of Blue
Poison
Powersource
Pretty Poison
Pseudo Echo
Restless Heart
Rock & Hyde
Ron & the D.C. Crew
Salt-n-Pepa
Taja Sevelle
Simon F.
Patty Smyth
The Stabilizers

Stryper
Surface
Patrick Swayze
Sweet Sensation
Swing Out Sister
Tony Terry
Tesla
Tia
Tiffany
T'Pau
The Truth
Uptown
Suzanne Vega
the Venetians
Jody Watley
Wa Wa Nee
Wendy & Lisa
Bruce Willis
Will to Power
Danny Wilson
Shanice Wilson
World Party
Yello

HITS OF 1987

JANUARY

	Come Go With Me	Exposé	Arista
	Coming Up Close	'Til Tuesday	Epic
	Cry Wolf	a-ha	Warner Bros.
	Don't Dream It's Over	Crowded House	Capitol
	Don't Need A Gun	Billy Idol	Chrysalis
	Fire	Bruce Springsteen	Columbia
☆	**Jacob's Ladder**	Huey Lewis & the News	Chrysalis
	Let's Go	Wang Chung	Geffen
	Let's Wait Awhile	Janet Jackson	A & M
	Mandolin Rain	Bruce Hornsby & the Range	RCA
	Midnight Blue	Lou Gramm	Atlantic
☆ ⑥	**Nothing's Gonna Stop Us Now**	Starship	Grunt

453

The Cutting Crew in concert
(photo: Anastasia Pantsios)

Respect Yourself	Bruce Willis	Motown
Shelter	Lone Justice	Geffen
That Ain't Love	REO Speedwagon	Epic

FEBRUARY

Come As You Are	Peter Wolf	EMI-America
Hold Me	Sheila E.	Paisley Park
How Much Love	Survivor	Scotti Bros.
I Got The Feelin' (It's Over)	Gregory Abbott	Columbia
☆ I Knew You Were Waiting (For Me)	Aretha Franklin & George Michael	Arista
I Will Be There	Glass Tiger	Manhattan
The Lady In Red	Chris De Burgh	A & M
☆ ⑥ Lean On Me	Club Nouveau	Warner Bros.
Light Of Day	The Barbusters (Joan Jett & the Blackhearts and Michael J. Fox)	CBS Associated
Nothing's Gonna Change My Love For You	Glenn Medeiros	Amherst
The Right Thing	Simply Red	Elektra
Show Me	The Cover Girls	Fever
Tonight, Tonight, Tonight	Genesis	Atlantic
What You Get Is What You See	Tina Turner	Capitol
Winner Takes It All	Sammy Hagar	Columbia

MARCH

☆ Always	Atlantic Starr	Warner Bros.
Big Love	Fleetwood Mac	Warner Bros.
Boom Boom (Let's Go Back To My Room)	Paul Lekakis	ZYX
Brass Monkey	The Beastie Boys	Def Jam
Heat Of The Night	Bryan Adams	A & M
☆ (I Just) Died In Your Arms	The Cutting Crew	Virgin
La Isla Bonita	Madonna	Sire
Looking For A New Love	Jody Watley	MCA
Right On Track	The Breakfast Club	MCA
Se La	Lionel Richie	Motown
Sign 'O' The Times	Prince	Paisley Park
Talk Dirty To Me	Poison	Capitol
What's Going On	Cyndi Lauper	Portrait

☆　With Or Without You　　　　U2　　　　　　　　　Island
☆　You Keep Me Hangin' On　　Kim Wilde　　　　　　MCA

APRIL

Day-In Day-Out　　　　　　David Bowie　　　　　　EMI-America
Don't Give Up　　　　　　　Peter Gabriel & Kate　Geffen
　　　　　　　　　　　　　　　Bush

Endless Nights　　　　　　　Eddie Money　　　　　　Columbia
☆ ⑥ Head To Toe　　　　　　Lisa Lisa & Cult Jam　Columbia
I Know What I Like　　　　Huey Lewis & the News　Chrysalis
In Too Deep　　　　　　　　Genesis　　　　　　　　Atlantic
Lessons In Love　　　　　　Level 42　　　　　　　　Polydor
Meet El Presidente　　　　　Duran Duran　　　　　　Capitol
Rock The Night　　　　　　Europe　　　　　　　　　Epic
Shy Girl　　　　　　　　　　Stacey Q　　　　　　　　On The Spot
Soul City　　　　　　　　　The Partland Brothers　Manhattan
Wanted Dead Or Alive　　　Bon Jovi　　　　　　　　Mercury
We Are What We Are　　　　The Other Ones　　　　　Virgin
Wild Horses　　　　　　　　Gino Vannelli　　　　　CBS Asso-
　　　　　　　　　　　　　　　　　　　　　　　　　　　ciated

Young Blood　　　　　　　Bruce Willis　　　　　　Motown

MAY

☆　Alone　　　　　　　　　　Heart　　　　　　　　　Capitol
Back In The High Life Again　Steve Winwood　　　　Island
Break Every Rule　　　　　Tina Turner　　　　　　Capitol
Flames Of Paradise　　　　　Jennifer Rush & Elton　Epic
　　　　　　　　　　　　　　　John
Funkytown　　　　　　　　　Pseudo Echo　　　　　　RCA
Girls, Girls, Girls　　　　　Mötley Crüe　　　　　　Elektra
If I Was Your Girlfriend　　Prince　　　　　　　　Paisley Park
☆ ⓟ I Wanna Dance With Somebody　Whitney Houston　Arista
　　(Who Loves Me)
Kiss Him Goodbye　　　　　The Nylons　　　　　　Open Air
The Pleasure Principle　　　Janet Jackson　　　　　A & M
Point Of No Return　　　　　Exposé　　　　　　　　Arista
The Rhythm Is Gonna Get You　The Miami Sound　Epic
　　　　　　　　　　　　　　　Machine
☆　Shakedown　　　　　　　　Bob Seger & the Silver　MCA
　　　　　　　　　　　　　　　Bullet Band

The Fat Boys

| Weatherman Says | Jack Wagner | Qwest |
| Wot's It To Ya | Robbie Nevil | Manhattan |

JUNE

Breakout	Swing Out Sister	Mercury
Cross My Broken Heart	The Jets	MCA
Dreamin'	Will to Power	Epic
Give To Live	Sammy Hagar	Geffen
Hearts On Fire	Bryan Adams	A & M
☆ I Still Haven't Found What I'm Looking For	U2	Island
It's Not over ('Til It's Over)	Starship	Grunt
I Want Your Sex	George Michael	Columbia
Jam Tonight	Freddie Jackson	Capitol
☆ La Bamba	Los Lobos	Slash
Lies	Jonathan Butler	Jive
One For The Mockingbird	The Cutting Crew	Virgin
Rock Steady	The Whispers	Solar
Seven Wonders	Fleetwood Mac	Warner Bros.
Since You've Been Gone	The Outfield	Columbia

JULY

Back To Paradise	38 Special	A & M
Doing It All For My Baby	Huey Lewis & the News	Chrysalis
☆ Here I Go Again	Whitesnake	Geffen
I Heard A Rumour	Bananarama	London
In Love With Love	Debbie Harry	Geffen
In My Dreams	REO Speedwagon	Epic
Love Power	Dionne Warwick & Jeffrey Osborne	Arista
Luka	Suzanne Vega	A & M
Shattered Glass	Laura Branigan	Atlantic
Touch Of Grey	Grateful Dead	Arista
Twistin' The Night Away	Rod Stewart	Geffen
When Smokey Sings	ABC	Mercury
Who Found Who	Jellybean featuring Elisa Fiorillo	Chrysalis
☆ Who's That Girl	Madonna	Sire
Wipe Out	The Fat Boys with the Beach Boys	Tin Pan Apple

AUGUST

Be There	The Pointer Sisters	MCA
☆ Didn't We Almost Have It All	Whitney Houston	Arista
☆ ⑥ I Just Can't Stop Loving You	Michael Jackson with Siedah Garrett	Epic
I Need Love	L.L. Cool J	Def Jam
☆ I Think We're Alone Now	Tiffany	MCA
Let Me Be The One	Exposé	Arista
Little Lies	Fleetwood Mac	Warner Bros.
☆ Lost In Emotion	Lisa Lisa & Cult Jam	Columbia
Paper In Fire	John Cougar Mellencamp	Mercury

1987

Something Real (Inside Me/ Inside You)	Mr. Mister	RCA
That's What Love Is All About	Michael Bolton	Columbia
U Got The Look	Prince	Paisley Park
Victim Of Love	Bryan Adams	A & M
Who Will You Run To	Heart	Capitol
You Are The Girl	The Cars	Elektra

SEPTEMBER

☆	Bad	Michael Jackson	Epic
	Causing A Commotion	Madonna	Sire
	Come On, Let's Go	Los Lobos	Slash
	Heart And Soul	The Monkees	Rhino
☆	Heaven Is A Place On Earth	Belinda Carlisle	MCA
	Hourglass	Squeeze	A & M
	It's A Sin	The Pet Shop Boys	EMI-America
	I've Been In Love Before	The Cutting Crew	Virgin
☆ ⑥	(I've Had) The Time Of My Life	Bill Medley & Jennifer Warnes	RCA
	Let's Work	Mick Jagger	Columbia
	Love Is Contagious	Taja Sevelle	Paisley Park
☆	Mony Mony	Billy Idol	Chrysalis
	Should've Known Better	Richard Marx	EMI-Manhattan
	Waterfall	Wendy & Lisa	Columbia
	Where The Streets Have No Name	U2	Island

OCTOBER

	Animal	Def Leppard	Mercury
	Brilliant Disguise	Bruce Springsteen	Columbia
	Cherry Bomb	John Cougar Mellencamp	Mercury
	Don't You Want Me?	Jody Watley	MCA
☆ ⑥	Faith	George Michael	Columbia
☆	Got My Mind Set On You	George Harrison	Dark Horse
	I Do You	The Jets	MCA
	Is This Love	Whitesnake	Geffen
	Love Will Find A Way	Yes	Atco
	Pop Goes The World	Men without Hats	Mercury
	Reservations For Two	Dionne Warwick & Kashif	Arista

	Skeletons	Stevie Wonder	Motown
☆	So Emotional	Whitney Houston	Arista
	Valerie *(re-entry)*	Steve Winwood	Island
	We'll Be Together	Sting	A & M

NOVEMBER

	Candle In The Wind	Elton John	MCA
	Can't Stay Away From You	Gloria Estefan & the Miami Sound Machine	Epic
☆	Could've Been	Tiffany	MCA
	Don't Shed A Tear	Paul Carrack	Chrysalis
	Dude (Looks Like A Lady)	Aerosmith	Geffen
	Everywhere	Fleetwood Mac	Warner Bros.
	Hazy Shade Of Winter	The Bangles	Def Jam
	I Can't Help It	Bananarama	London
	I Could Never Take The Place Of Your Man	Prince	Paisley Park
	I Found Someone	Cher	Geffen
☆	Need You Tonight	INXS	Atlantic
Ⓖ	Pump Up The Volume	M/A/R/R/S	4th & Broadway
Ⓟ	Push It	Salt-n-Pepa	Next Plateau
☆	Seasons Change	Exposé	Arista
☆	The Way You Make Me Feel	Michael Jackson	Epic

DECEMBER

	853-5937	Squeeze	A & M
	Hungry Eyes	Eric Carmen	RCA
	I Need A Man	Eurythmics	RCA
	In God's Country	U2	Island
	Live My Life	Boy George	Virgin
	Lonely Won't Leave Me Alone	Glenn Medeiros	Amherst
	Lover's Lane	Giorgio	Motown
☆ Ⓖ	Never Gonna Give You Up	Rick Astley	RCA
	Never Thought (That I Could Love)	Dan Hill	Columbia
	Rhythm Of Love	Yes	Atco

Poison in concert (l to r: C.C. Deville, Bret Michaels; photo: Anastasia Pantsios)

458

Say You Will	Foreigner	Atlantic	**1987**
She's Like The Wind	Patrick Swayze (featuring Wendy Frazer)	RCA	
Tunnel Of Love	Bruce Springsteen	Columbia	
Twilight World	Swing Out Sister	Mercury	
What Have I Done To Deserve This?	The Pet Shop Boys & Dusty Springfield	EMI-Manhattan	

TOP SINGLES OF 1987

	Alone	Heart	Capitol
⑥	Head To Toe	Lisa Lisa & Cult Jam	Columbia
	Here I Go Again	Whitesnake	Geffen
	I Think We're Alone Now	Tiffany	MCA
⑫	I Wanna Dance With Somebody (Who Loves Me)	Whitney Houston	Arista
	La Bamba	Los Lobos	Slash
	Livin' On A Prayer	Bon Jovi	Mercury
⑥	Nothing's Gonna Stop Us Now	Starship	Grunt
	Shakedown	Bob Seger & the Silver Bullet Band	MCA
	With Or Without You	U2	Island

TOP ALBUMS OF 1987

⑫	Bad	Michael Jackson	Epic
⑫	Dirty Dancing	Soundtrack	RCA
⑫	The Joshua Tree	U2	Island
⑫	La Bamba	Soundtrack	Slash
⑫	Licensed To Ill	The Beastie Boys	Columbia
⑫	A Momentary Lapse Of Reason	Pink Floyd	Columbia
⑫	Tango In The Night	Fleetwood Mac	Warner Bros.
⑫	Tunnel Of Love	Bruce Springsteen	Columbia
⑫	Whitesnake	Whitesnake	Geffen
⑫	Whitney	Whitney Houston	Arista

GRAMMY WINNERS IN 1987

The Grammys were televised from Radio City Music Hall in New York on Wednesday, March 2, 1988. Billy Crystal was the host.

Record of the Year: "Graceland," Paul Simon (Warner Bros.)
Song of the Year: "Somewhere Out There" (music and lyrics by James Horner, Barry Mann, and Cynthia Weil)
Album of the Year: *The Joshua Tree,* U2 (Island)
Best Pop Vocal Performance, Female: "I Wanna Dance With Somebody (Who Loves Me)," Whitney Houston (Arista)
Best Pop Vocal Performance, Male: *Bring On The Night,* Sting (A & M)
Best Pop Vocal Performance, Group: "(I've Had) The Time Of My Life," Bill Medley & Jennifer Warnes (RCA)
Best Pop Instrumental: "Minute By Minute," Larry Carlton (MCA)
Best Rock Vocal Performance, Male or Female: "Tunnel Of Love," Bruce Springsteen (Columbia)

459

Best Rock Vocal Performance, Duo or Group: *The Joshua Tree,* U2 (Island)
Best Rock Instrumental: "Jazz From Hell," Frank Zappa (Barking Pumpkin)
Best R&B Performance, Female: *Aretha,* Aretha Franklin (Arista)
Best R&B Performance, Male: "Just To See Her," Smokey Robinson (Motown)
Best R&B Vocal, Duo or Group: "I Knew You Were Waiting (For Me)," Aretha Franklin & George Michael (Arista)
Best R&B Instrumental: "Chicago Song," David Sanborn (Warner Bros.)
Best R&B Song: "Lean On Me" (music and lyrics by Bill Withers)
Best New Artist of the Year: Jody Watley
Best Comedy Performance: *A Night At The Met,* Robin Williams (Columbia)
Best Soundtrack Album from a Motion Picture or Television: *The Untouchables,* Ennio Morricone (A & M)

ROCK AND ROLL HALL OF FAME INDUCTEES

The second induction ceremony was held on Wednesday, January 21, 1987, at the Waldorf Astoria hotel in New York City.

PERFORMERS

Inductee (Born and Died)	Debut Single (Year)	Label
The Coasters (Carl Gardner: April 29, 1928– ; Billy Guy: June 20, 1936– ; Leon Hughes, replaced by Young Jessie, Cornell Gunther (Died February 26, 1990), and Earl "Speedo" Carroll; Bobby Nunn (Died November 5, 1987) replaced by Will "Dub" Jones and Ronnie Bright; Adolf Jacobs)	Down In Mexico (1956)	Atco
Eddie Cochran (October 3, 1938–April 17, 1960)	Sittin' In The Balcony (1957)	Liberty
Bo Diddley (Ellas McDaniel) (December 30, 1928–)	Bo Diddley (1955)	Checker
Aretha Franklin (March 25, 1942–)	Won't Be Long (1961)	Columbia
Marvin Gaye (April 2, 1939–April 1, 1984)	Stubborn Kind Of Fellow (1962)	Tamla
Bill Haley (July 6, 1925–February 9, 1981)	Rocket 88 (1951)	Holiday
B.B. King (Riley "Blues Boy" King) (September 16, 1925–)	3 O'Clock Blues (1951)	RPM
Clyde McPhatter (November 15, 1931–June 13, 1972)	Seven Days (1955)	Atlantic
Rick Nelson (May 8, 1940–December 31, 1985)	I'm Walking/A Teenager's Romance (1957)	Verve
Roy Orbison (April 23, 1936–December 6, 1988)	Ooby Dooby (1956)	Sun
Carl Perkins (April 9, 1932–)	Blue Suede Shoes (1956)	Sun
Smokey Robinson (William Robinson) (February 19, 1940–)	Got A Job (1958)	End
Big Joe Turner (May 18, 1911–November 24, 1985)	Still In The Dark (1950)	Freedom
Muddy Waters (McKinley Morganfield) (April 4, 1915–April 30, 1983)	Louisiana Blues (1951)	Chess
Jackie Wilson (June 9, 1934–January 21, 1984)	Reet Petite (1957)	Brunswick

Tiffany

Jody Watley

1987

NONPERFORMERS

Leonard Chess (March 12, 1917–October 16, 1969)   Founder of Chess Records
Ahmet Ertegun (July 31, 1923–   )   Founder of Atlantic Records and chairman of the
Rock and Roll Hall of Fame Foundation
Leiber & Stoller (Jerry Leiber: April 25, 1933–   ; Mike Stoller: March 13, 1933–
)   Songwriters responsible for some of the biggest hits of all time ("Hound Dog,"
"Poison Ivy," "Jailhouse Rock," "Searchin'," "Yakety Yak")
Jerry Wexler (January 10, 1917–   )   Writer, producer, arranger

EARLY INFLUENCES

Louis Jordan (July 8, 1908–February 4, 1975)   Alto sax player
T-Bone Walker (Aaron Thibeaux Walker) (May 28, 1910–March 16, 1975)   Electric
blues guitar player
Hank Williams (September 17, 1923–January 1, 1953)   Country singer-songwriter

DEATHS IN 1987

MUSIC PERFORMERS AND MUSIC INDUSTRY NOTABLES WHO DIED IN 1987

Liberace, Wednesday, February 4 (AIDS;
67)
Buddy Rich, Thursday, April 2 (brain
tumor; 69)
Paul Butterfield, Monday, May 4 (drug
overdose; 44)
Sammy Kaye, Wednesday, June 3 (cancer;
77)
Andrés Segovia, Wednesday, June 3 (heart
attack; 94)
Kate Smith, Tuesday, June 17 (natural
causes; 79)
Leroy Holmes, Sunday, July 27 (heart
attack; 72)

William B. Williams, Sunday, August 3
(respiratory failure; 62)
Lorne Greene, Friday, September 11
(heart attack; 72)
Peter Tosh, Friday, September 11
(gunshot; 42)
Woody Herman, Thursday, October 29
(congestive heart failure; 74)
Eddie "Lockjaw" Davis, Monday,
November 3 (kidney failure; 65)
Bobby Nunn (The Coasters), Wednesday,
November 5 (heart attack; 61)
Horace Heidt, Monday, December 1
(pneumonia; 85)

OTHERS WHO DIED IN 1987

Fred Astaire
Mary Astor

Michael Bennett
Ray Bolger

461

Bob Fosse
Hermione Gingold
Jackie Gleason
Woody Hayes
Rita Hayworth
John Huston
Danny Kaye
Joseph E. Levine
Lee Marvin

Geraldine Page
Robert Preston
Dan Rowan
Randolph Scott
Dick Shawn
David Susskind
Andy Warhol
Earl Wilson

MOVIES OF 1987

MOVIES FEATURING POP MUSIC ARTISTS

Hail! Hail! Rock 'n' Roll   This Taylor Hackford film depicts the life and music of rock legend Chuck Berry. Performing in the film with Berry are Keith Richards, Eric Clapton, Robert Cray, Etta James, Julian Lennon, and Linda Ronstadt. Berry songs featured in the film include "Maybellene," "Johnny B. Goode," "Rock And Roll Music," and "Sweet Little Sixteen."

La Bamba   *Stars:* Lou Diamond Phillips, Esai Morales, Rosana De Soto, Rick Dees, Marshall Crenshaw, Brian Setzer. The life and music of rocker Ritchie Valens, with his tunes recorded by Los Lobos. *Featured songs:* "Come On, Let's Go," "Donna," and "La Bamba" by Los Lobos, with Phillips lip-synching.

Light of Day   *Stars:* Michael J. Fox, Gena Rowlands, Joan Jett, Michael McKean. *Featured song:* "Light Of Day."

MOVIES FEATURING A POP MUSIC SOUNDTRACK

Beverly Hills Cop II   *Stars:* Eddie Murphy, Judge Reinhold, Brigitte Nielson, John Ashton, Ronny Cox. *Featured song:* "Shakedown" by Bob Seger.

Dirty Dancing   *Stars:* Patrick Swayze, Jennifer Grey, Cynthia Rhodes. *Featured songs:* "(I've Had) The Time Of My Life" by Bill Medley and Jennifer Warnes (won Oscar as best song), "Hungry Eyes" by Eric Carmen, "Love Is Strange" by Mickey & Sylvia, "Do You Love Me" by the Contours. Soundtrack sold an incredible 10 million units and went platinum.

POP MUSIC ARTISTS ON VIDEO

Dick Clark's Best of Bandstand: The Superstars   Original *Bandstand* clips of the Supremes, the Jackson 5, the Beach Boys, Roy Orbison, the Four Seasons, Danny & the Juniors, Jackie Wilson, Sam Cooke, Connie Francis, and Annette Funicello.

Dirty Dancing *soundtrack
album cover*

George Michael, Faith
album cover

OTHER POPULAR MOVIES OF 1987

Angel Heart
Black Widow
Blue Velvet
Creepshow 2
Dragnet
Gardens of Stone
Hoosiers
Ishtar
Jaws: The Revenge
Lethal Weapon
Outrageous Fortune

Planes, Trains, and Automobiles
Police Academy 4
Predator
Project X
Radio Days
Raising Arizona
Superman IV: The Quest for Peace
Tin Men
The Untouchables
The Witches of Eastwick

ACADEMY AWARD WINNERS OF 1987

Best Actor: Michael Douglas, *Wall Street*
Best Actress: Cher, *Moonstruck*
Best Picture: *The Last Emperor*
Best Original Song: "(I've Had) The Time Of My Life," *Dirty Dancing* (music by Franke Previte, John DeNicola, and Donald Markowitz, lyrics by Franke Previte)

TOP TELEVISION SHOWS OF 1987

Alf
Cheers
The Cosby Show
A Different World
The Golden Girls

Growing Pains
Murder, She Wrote
Night Court
60 Minutes
Who's the Boss?

1988

⇨ The nation endures a record-shattering heat wave and drought during the summer.

⇨ U.S. warship *Vincennes,* under assault by Iranian gunboats in the Persian Gulf, mistakes a civilian airliner on a routine flight for an attacking Iranian fighter plane and shoots it down, killing all 290 people aboard the Iranian plane.

⇨ After eight years of fighting in which close to two million people were killed or wounded, a cease-fire is announced in the war between Iran and Iraq and peace talks begin.

⇨ Vice President George Bush beats Massachusetts Governor Michael Dukakis in a presidential race that creates little national enthusiasm.

⇨ Hurricane Gilbert, the worst of the century, ravages Cancun, Mexico.

⇨ Three stranded whales in Point Barrow, Alaska, attract international attention when both Soviet and American teams try to free them. One of the whales perishes in the process.

⇨ Soviet leader Mikhail Gorbachev flies to New York for three days to address the United Nations on a proposed Soviet troop and arms reduction. His visit is cut short by one day because of an earthquake in Armenia that kills tens of thousands of people.

⇨ Yasser Arafat, the head of the Palestine Liberation Organization, accepts the existence of Israel and renounces all forms of terrorism.

⇨ A bomb explodes on a Pan Am 747 jumbo jet over Lockerbie, Scotland, on a flight from London to New York, killing all 259 people aboard and a dozen on the ground.

SPORTS WINNERS

Baseball   The Los Angeles Dodgers beat the Oakland A's 4 games to 1.

Football

NFC: The San Francisco '49ers beat the Chicago Bears 28–3 in Chicago.

AFC: The Cincinnati Bengals beat the Buffalo Bills 21–10 in Cincinnati.

Super Bowl XXIII: The San Francisco '49ers beat the Cincinnati Bengals 20–16 on January 22, 1989, in Miami, Florida.

Basketball   The Detroit Pistons beat the Los Angeles Lakers 4 games to 0.

Hockey   The Calgary Flames beat the Montreal Canadiens 4 games to 2.

MUSIC HIGHLIGHTS 1988

⇨ Michael Jackson launches the North American leg of his first-ever solo tour in Kansas City, Missouri, while Bruce Springsteen launches his Tunnel of Love tour at Worcester, Massachusetts.

⇨ Louis Armstrong's "What A Wonderful World," heard in the movie *Good Morning Vietnam,* becomes a Top 40 hit, making his career the longest in chart history (52 years).

⇨ After 18 years as host of *American Top 40,* the highly successful syndicated radio show,

*Crowded House in concert (*l to r: *Neil Finn, Nicholas Seymour;* photo: *Anastasia Pantsios)*

465

Casey Kasem leaves to host a similar show for the Westwood One Radio Network. His replacement is Shadoe Stevens of TV's *Hollywood Squares.*

⇨ Michael Jackson makes his first live television appearance in five years when he performs in New York at the Grammys' 30th annual awards show.

⇨ Michael Jackson's *Bad* album is the first by one artist to yield five number one pop hits: "I Just Can't Stop Loving You," "Bad," "The Way You Make Me Feel," "Man In The Mirror," and "Dirty Diana."

⇨ Twenty-four-year old Whitney Houston becomes the first artist on *Billboard* magazine's charts to score seven consecutive number one hits. The Beatles held the old record with six straight number one singles in 1966, a record that was tied by the Bee Gees in 1979. Houston's toppers were "Saving All My Love For You," "How Will I Know," "Greatest Love Of All," "I Wanna Dance With Somebody (Who Loves Me)," "Didn't We Almost Have It All," "So Emotional," and "Where Do Broken Hearts Go."

⇨ Daryl Hall and John Oates release *Ooh Yeah!,* their first studio album in three years.

⇨ In White Plains, New York, Mick Jagger is found not guilty of infringing on the copyright of musician Patrick Alley and his tune "Just Another Night."

⇨ Some retailers deem Prince's *Lovesexy* album cover too sexy to display.

⇨ Polydor Records releases Eric Clapton's boxed-set career retrospective, *Crossroads.*

⇨ Atlantic Records celebrates its 40th anniversary with a star-studded gala at New York's Madison Square Garden on Saturday, May 14. The televised cable show features reunions of Led Zeppelin, the Bee Gees, the Rascals, Genesis, and Crosby, Stills & Nash and appearances by Wilson Pickett, the Coasters, Foreigner, Yes, and others.

⇨ The Monsters of Rock Heavy Metal show is launched with Van Halen, the Scorpions, Metallica, Dokken, and Kingdom Come.

⇨ On Saturday, June 11, some 70,000 fans gather at London's Wembley Stadium for Freedom Fest, a concert in honor of the 70th birthday of Nelson Mandela, leader of the African National Congress imprisoned in South Africa since 1962. Performing were Sting, George Michael, Stevie Wonder, Whitney Houston, Phil Collins, Dire Straits, and others.

⇨ Motown Records is sold to MCA Records and an investment firm from Boston for $61 million.

⇨ On Friday, September 2, the Amnesty International tour begins at London's Wembley Stadium starring Bruce Springsteen, Sting, Peter Gabriel, Tracy Chapman, and Youssou N'Dour. The Human Rights Now tour travels to 15 countries before ending in Buenos Aires on October 15.

⇨ Bobby McFerrin's "Don't Worry, Be Happy" becomes the first a cappella single to reach number one.

⇨ Albert Goldman's controversial biography *The Lives of John Lennon* is released.

⇨ On Sunday, October 3, Elvis Presley's 20-year-old daughter, Lisa Marie, marries musician Danny Keough in Los Angeles.

W. Axl Rose of Guns N' Roses in concert (photo: Anastasia Pantsios)

⇨ Bob Dylan, George Harrison, Jeff Lynne, Roy Orbison, and Tom Petty record an album under the name the Traveling Wilburys.

⇨ In recognition of the decline of singles sales in recent years, the Recording Industry Association of America will halve its gold and platinum certification requirements for singles. A single selling 500,000 units will be certified gold, and sales of 1 million units will earn the platinum certification. This goes into effect January 1, 1989.

⇨ Whitney Houston's debut album, *Whitney Houston,* tops the 9 million sales mark, making it the best-selling debut album ever. The previous mark was set by Boston's album *Boston,* in 1976.

⇨ WTG Records, Columbia's new West Coast label, debuts with its first single, Michael Rodgers's "I Like It Like That," and Eighth Wonder's album *Fearless.*

⇨ Soul singer and Hall of Fame inductee James Brown enters prison in Columbia, South Carolina, to begin a six-year term for trying to run down a police officer.

DEBUT ARTISTS OF 1988

Paula Abdul	Good Question
The Adventures	Guns N' Roses
Al B. Sure!	Ice-T
Bardeux	Information Society
Rob Base & D.J. E-Z Rock	J.J. Fad
Basia	Johnny Hates Jazz
Big Pig	Johnny Kemp
Blue Mercedes	Kingdom Come
Book of Love	Kings of the Sun
The Boys	Holly Knight
Boys Club	Denise Lopez
Breathe	L'Trimm
Edie Brickell & the New Bohemians	Ziggy Marley & the Melody Makers
Bros.	Bobby McFerrin
The California Raisins	Midnight Oil
Candi	Kylie Minogue
Cellarful of Noise	Ivan Neville
Tracy Chapman	New Kids on the Block
Toni Childs	Pebbles
The Church	Nia Peeples
Merry Clayton	Maxi Priest
Gardner Cole	Cheryl "Pepsi" Riley
Dan Reed Network	Romeo's Daughter
Dino	Roxanne
D.J. Jazzy Jeff & the Fresh Prince	Sa-Fire
Eighth Wonder	Scarlett & Black
Erasure	S-Express
The Escape	Michelle Shocked
The Escape Club	Siouxsie & the Banshees
E.U.	The Smithereens
Eria Fachin	So
Bryan Ferry	Judson Spence
Elisa Fiorillo	Tracie Spencer
Climie Fisher	Brenda K. Starr
Lita Ford	Stevie B
Britny Fox	Suave
Siedah Garrett	Henry Lee Summer
Gene Loves Jezebel	Keith Sweat
Giant Steps	Tami Show

467

Bruce Hornsby & the Range

10,000 Maniacs
3 Man Island
Times Two
Tone Loc
Tony! Toni! Tone!
Transvision Vamp
The Traveling Wilburys
Underworld

Vixen
Was (Not Was)
Wet Wet Wet
When In Rome
Karyn White
White Lion
Vanessa Williams
World Class Wreckin Cru

HITS OF 1988

JANUARY

Be Still My Beating Heart	Sting	A & M
Endless Summer Nights	Richard Marx	EMI-Manhattan
☆ Father Figure	George Michael	Columbia
Girlfriend	Peebles	MCA
Hysteria	Def Leppard	Mercury
I Get Weak	Belinda Carlisle	MCA
⑥ I Want Her	Keith Sweat	Vintertainment
Just Like Paradise	David Lee Roth	Warner Bros.
Love Overboard	Gladys Knight & the Pips	MCA
Never Can Say Goodbye	The Communards	MCA
Out Of The Blue	Debbie Gibson	Atlantic
Rocket 2 U	The Jets	MCA
(Sittin' On) The Dock Of The Bay	Michael Bolton	Columbia
Some Kind Of Lover	Jody Watley	MCA
☆ ⑥ Wishing Well	Terence Trent D'Arby	Columbia

FEBRUARY

Angel	Aerosmith	Geffen
Check It Out	John Cougar Mellencamp	Mercury
Devil Inside	INXS	Atlantic
Electric Blue	Icehouse	Chrysalis
☆ Get Outta My Dreams, Get Into My Car	Billy Ocean	Jive
I Saw Him Standing There	Tiffany	MCA
I Want You So Bad	Heart	Capitol
I Wish I Had A Girl	Henry Lee Summer	CBS Associated

☆	Man In The Mirror	Michael Jackson	Epic
	One Step Up	Bruce Springsteen	Columbia
	Prove Your Love	Taylor Dayne	Arista
	Rock Of Life	Rick Springfield	RCA
	What A Wonderful World	Louis Armstrong	A & M
	When We Was Fab	George Harrison	Dark Horse
☆	Where Do Broken Hearts Go	Whitney Houston	Arista

MARCH

	Always On My Mind	The Pet Shop Boys	EMI
☆ ⑥	Anything For You	Gloria Estefan & the Miami Sound Machine	Epic
	Beds Are Burning	Midnight Oil	Columbia
	Dreaming	Orchestral Manoeuvres in the Dark	A & M
	I Don't Want To Live Without You	Foreigner	Atlantic
	I Want To Be Your Property	Blue Mercedes	MCA
	Love In The First Degree	Bananarama	London
	Naughty Girls (Need Love Too)	Samantha Fox	Jive
	One Good Reason	Paul Carrack	Chrysalis
	Pink Cadillac	Natalie Cole	EMI-Manhattan
	Promise Me	The Cover Girls	Fever
	Ritual	The Dan Reed Network	Mercury
	Say It Again	Jermaine Stewart	Arista
	Shattered Dreams	Johnny Hates Jazz	Virgin
	Strange But True	Times Two	Reprise

APRIL

	Alphabet St.	Prince	Paisley Park
	Circle In The Sand	Belinda Carlisle	MCA
	Everything Your Heart Desires	Daryl Hall & John Oates	Arista
☆	The Flame	Cheap Trick	Epic
☆	Foolish Beat	Debbie Gibson	Atlantic
	Heart Of Mine	Boz Scaggs	Columbia
	I'm Still Searching	Glass Tiger	EMI-Manhattan
	I Still Believe	Brenda K. Starr	MCA
	Kiss Me Deadly	Lita Ford	RCA
	Make It Real	The Jets	MCA
	Nothin' But A Good Time	Poison	Enigma
☆ ⑥	One More Try	George Michael	Columbia
	Supersonic	J.J. Fad	Ruthless
☆	Together Forever	Rick Astley	RCA
	The Valley Road	Bruce Hornsby & the Range	RCA

MAY

| | Black And Blue | Van Halen | Warner Bros. |
| | The Colour Of Love | Billy Ocean | Jive |

469

	Darlin' Danielle Don't	Henry Lee Summer	CBS Association
☆	Dirty Diana	Michael Jackson	Epic
☆	Hold On To The Nights	Richard Marx	EMI-Manhattan
	I Should Be So Lucky	Kylie Minogue	Geffen
	Lost In You	Rod Stewart	Warner Bros.
	Make Me Lose Control	Eric Carmen	Arista
	Mercedes Boy	Pebbles	MCA
	New Sensation	INXS	Atlantic
⑥	Parents Just Don't Understand	D.J. Jazzy Jeff & the Fresh Prince	Jive
	Sign Your Name	Terence Trent D'Arby	Columbia
	Tomorrow People	Ziggy Marley & the Melody Makers	Virgin
	Trouble	Nia Peeples	Mercury
	Wishing I Was Lucky	Wet Wet Wet	UNI

JUNE

	Do You Love Me *(re-entry)*	The Contours	Motown
⑥	Do You Love Me *(re-entry)*	The Contours	Motown
	Fast Car	Tracy Chapman	Elektra
	Here With Me	REO Speedwagon	Epic
	I Don't Wanna Go On With You Like That	Elton John	MCA
	I Don't Wanna Live Without Your Love	Chicago	Reprise
	I Hate Myself For Loving You	Joan Jett & the Blackhearts	Blackheart
⑥	I'll Always Love You	Taylor Dayne	Arista
	In Your Soul	Corey Hart	EMI-Manhattan
	1-2-3	Gloria Estefan & the Miami Sound Machine	Epic
	Rag Doll	Aerosmith	Geffen
	Rhythm Of Love	The Scorpions	Mercury
☆	Roll With It	Steve Winwood	Virgin
	Say It's Gonna Rain	Will to Power	Epic
☆ ⑥	Sweet Child O' Mine	Guns N' Roses	Geffen
	The Twist	The Fat Boys	Tin Pan Apple

JULY

	All Fired Up	Pat Benatar	Chrysalis
	Another Part Of Me	Michael Jackson	Epic
	Better Be Home Soon	Crowded House	Capitol
	Hole In My Heart (All The Way To China)	Cyndi Lauper	Epic
	It Would Take A Strong, Strong Man	Rick Astley	RCA
	Look Out Any Window	Bruce Hornsby & the Range	RCA
	Love Will Save The Day	Whitney Houston	Arista
	Missed Opportunity	Daryl Hall & John Oates	Arista
☆	Monkey	George Michael	Columbia

1988

	Nobody's Fool	Kenny Loggins	Columbia
	One Good Woman	Peter Cetera	Full Moon
	Perfect World	Huey Lewis & the News	Chrysalis
	Simply Irresistible	Robert Palmer	EMI-Manhattan
⑥	What's On Your Mind (Pure Energy)	The Information Society	Tommy Boy
	When It's Love	Van Halen	Warner Bros.

AUGUST

	Another Lover	Giant Steps	A & M
	Chains Of Love	Erasure	Sire
	Don't Be Cruel	Cheap Trick	Epic
☆ ⑥	Don't Worry, Be Happy	Bobby McFerrin	EMI-Manhattan
	Don't You Know What The Night Can Do?	Steve Winwood	Virgin
	Fallen Angel	Poison	Enigma
	Forever Young	Rod Stewart	Warner Bros.
	The Loco-Motion	Kylie Minogue	Geffen
☆	Love Bites	Def Leppard	Mercury
	Never Tear Us Apart	INXS	Atlantic
	A Nightmare On My Street	D.J. Jazzy Jeff & the Fresh Prince	Jive
☆ ⑥	Red, Red Wine *(re-entry)*	UB40	A & M
	Staying Together	Debbie Gibson	Atlantic
	True Love	Glenn Frey	MCA
☆ ⑥	Wild Wild West	The Escape Club	Atlantic

SEPTEMBER

☆ ⑥	Baby, I Love Your Way/Freebird Medley	Will to Power	Epic
☆	Bad Medicine	Bon Jovi	Mercury
	Dance Little Sister	Terence Trent D'Arby	Columbia
	Don't Know What You Got (Till It's Gone)	Cinderella	Mercury
	Edge Of A Broken Heart	Vixen	EMI-Manhattan
	Giving You Best That I Got	Anita Baker	Elektra
☆ ⑥	Groovy Kind Of Love	Phil Collins	Atlantic

471

	How Can I Fall?	Breathe	A & M
☆ Ⓟ	Kokomo	The Beach Boys	Elektra
☆ Ⓖ	Look Away	Chicago	Reprise
	One Moment In Time	Whitney Houston	Arista
	The Promise	When in Rome	Virgin
	Waiting For A Star To Fall	Boy Meets Girl	RCA
	A Word In Spanish	Elton John	MCA
	You Came	Kim Wilde	MCA

OCTOBER

Ⓖ	Desire	U2	Island
	Domino Dancing	The Pet Shop Boys	EMI-Manhattan
	Downtown Life	Daryl Hall & John Oates	Arista
	Early In The Morning	Robert Palmer	EMI
☆ Ⓖ	Every Rose Has Its Thorn	Poison	Enigma
	Finish What Ya Started	Van Halen	Warner Bros.
	I Don't Want Your Love	Duran Duran	Capitol
	In Your Room	The Bangles	Columbia
	Kissing A Fool	George Michael	Columbia
☆ Ⓖ	My Prerogative	Bobby Brown	MCA
	Silhouette	Kenny G	Arista
	Small World	Huey Lewis & the News	Chrysalis
	Till I Loved You	Barbra Streisand & Don Johnson	Columbia
	Walk On Water	Eddie Money	Columbia
	Welcome To The Jungle	Guns N' Roses	Geffen

NOVEMBER

Armageddon It	Def Leppard	Mercury
Baby Can I Hold You	Tracy Chapman	Elektra
Back On Holiday	Robbie Nevil	EMI
Born To Be My Baby	Bon Jovi	Mercury
Cross My Heart	Eighth Wonder	WTG
Don't Rush Me	Taylor Dayne	Arista
Forever Young	Alphaville	Atlantic
Handle With Care	The Traveling Wilburys	Wilbury
Holding On	Steve Winwood	Virgin
(It's Just) The Way That You Love Me	Paula Abdul	Virgin

Keith Richards in concert (photo: Anastasia Pantsios)

⑤ I Wanna Have Some Fun	Samantha Fox	Jive
Killing Me Softly	Al B. Sure!	Warner Bros.
Smooth Criminal	Michael Jackson	Epic
☆ Two Hearts	Phil Collins	Atlantic
Walking Away	The Information Society	Tommy Boy

DECEMBER

All She Wants Is	Duran Duran	Capitol
Angel Of Harlem	U2	Island
As Long As You Follow	Fleetwood Mac	Warner Bros.
Dial My Heart	The Boys	Motown
Ghost Town	Cheap Trick	Epic
It's No Secret	Kylie Minogue	Geffen
Kiss	The Art of Noise, featuring Tom Jones	China
A Little Respect	Erasure	Sire
New Day For You	Basia	Epic
Put A Little Love In Your Heart	Annie Lennox & Al Green	A & M
Shake For The Sheik	The Escape Club	Atlantic
She Wants To Dance With Me	Rick Astley	RCA
☆ ⑫ Straight Up	Paula Abdul	Virgin
Surrender To Me	Ann Wilson and Robin Zander	Capitol
☆ ⑤ When I'm With You	Sheriff	Capitol

TOP SINGLES OF 1988

Could've Been	Tiffany	MCA
⑤ Faith	George Michael	Columbia
Got My Mind Set On You	George Harrison	Dark Horse
Heaven Is A Place On Earth	Belinda Carlisle	MCA
⑤ Never Gonna Give You Up	Rick Astley	RCA
⑤ One More Try	George Michael	Columbia
Roll With It	Steve Winwood	Virgin
So Emotional	Whitney Houston	Arista
⑤ Sweet Child O' Mine	Guns N' Roses	Geffen
⑤ Wishing Well	Terence Trent D'Arby	Columbia

TOP ALBUMS OF 1988

⑫ Appetite For Destruction	Guns N' Roses	Geffen
⑫ Cocktail Soundtrack	Various Artists	Elektra
⑫ Faith	George Michael	Columbia
⑫ Hysteria	Def Leppard	Mercury
⑫ New Jersey	Bon Jovi	Mercury
⑫ OU812	Van Halen	Warner Bros.
⑫ Rattle And Hum	U2	Island
⑫ Roll With It	Steve Winwood	Virgin
⑫ Tiffany	Tiffany	MCA
⑫ Tracy Chapman	Tracy Chapman	Elektra

1988

473

ROCK ON ALMANAC

GRAMMY WINNERS IN 1988

The Grammys were televised from the Shrine Auditorium in Los Angeles, California, on Wednesday, February 22, 1989. Billy Crystal was the host.

Record of the Year: "Don't Worry, Be Happy," Bobby McFerrin (EMI-Manhattan)

Song of the Year: "Don't Worry, Be Happy" (music and lyrics by Bobby McFerrin)

Album of the Year: *Faith,* George Michael (Columbia)

Best Pop Vocal Performance, Female: "Fast Car," Tracy Chapman (Elektra)

Best Pop Vocal Performance, Male: "Don't Worry, Be Happy," Bobby McFerrin (EMI-Manhattan)

Best Pop Vocal Performance, Duo or Group: "Brazil," Manhattan Transfer (Atlantic)

Best Pop Instrumental: "Close Up," David Sanborn (Reprise)

Best Rock Vocal Performance, Female: *Tina Live In Europe,* Tina Turner (Capitol)

Best Rock Vocal Performance, Male: *Simply Irresistable,* Robert Palmer (EMI-Manhattan)

Best Rock Vocal Performance, Duo or Group: "Desire," U2 (Island)

Best Rock Instrumental: "Blues For Salvador," Carlos Santana (Columbia)

Best New Artist: Tracy Chapman

Best R&B Performance, Female: "Giving You The Best That I Got," Anita Baker (Elektra)

Best R&B Performance, Male: *Introducing The Hardline According To Terence Trent D'Arby,* Terence Trent D'Arby (Columbia)

Best R&B Performance, Duo or Group: "Love Overboard," Gladys Knight & the Pips (MCA)

Best R&B Instrumental: *Light Years,* Chick Corea (GRP)

Best R&B Song: "Giving You The Best That I Got," Anita Baker (Elektra)

Best Hard Rock–Metal Vocal or Instrumental: *Crest Of A Knave,* Jethro Tull (Chrysalis)

Best Performance, Rap: "Parents Just Don't Understand," D. J. Jazzy Jeff & the Fresh Prince (Jive)

Best Comedy Performance: *Good Morning Vietnam,* Robin Williams (A & M)

Best Song Written for a Motion Picture or Television: "Two Hearts" (from movie *Buster*), written by Phil Collins and Lamont Dozier (Atlantic)

Best New Age: *Folksongs For A Nuclear Village,* Shadowfax (Capitol)

Best Music Video: *Where The Streets Have No Name,* U2 (Island)

ROCK AND ROLL HALL OF FAME INDUCTEES

The third induction ceremony was held on Wednesday, January 20, 1988, at the Waldorf Astoria hotel in New York City.

PERFORMERS

Inductee (Born and Died)	Debut Single (Year)	Label
The Beach Boys (Brian Wilson: June 20, 1942– ; Carl Wilson: December 21, 1946– ; Dennis Wilson: December 4, 1944–December 28, 1983; Mike Love: March 15, 1941– ; Al Jardine: September 3, 1942–)	Surfin (1962)	Candix
The Beatles (John Lennon: October 9, 1940–December 8, 1980; Paul McCartney: June 18, 1942– ; George Harrison: February 25, 1943– ; Ringo Starr [Richard Starkey, Jr.]: July 7, 1940–)	Love Me Do (1962)	Parlophone

The Drifters (Clyde McPhatter: November 15, 1931–June 13, 1972; Johnny Moore: December 14, 1934– ; Ben E. King [Benjamin Nelson]: September 28, 1938– ; Rudy Lewis: August 23, 1936–1964; Charlie Thomas: April 7, 1937– ; Bill Pinkney: August 15, 1925– ; Other members: Gerhart Thrasher, Andrew Thrasher, Bobby Hendricks, David Baughan, Charlie Hughes, Tommy Evans, Doc Green: Died March 10, 1989 and Elsberry Hobbs)	Money Honey (1953)	Atlantic
Bob Dylan (Robert Zimmerman) (May 24, 1941–)	Song To Woody (1962)	Columbia
The Supremes (Diana Ross: March 26, 1944– ; Mary Wilson: March 6, 1944– ; Florence Ballard: June 30, 1943–February 22, 1976)	Your Heart Belongs To Me (1962)	Motown

NONPERFORMERS

Berry Gordy, Jr. (November 28, 1929–   ) Founder of Motown Records

EARLY INFLUENCES

Woody Guthrie (July 14, 1912–October 3, 1967) Folksinger and songwriter
Leadbelly (Huddie Ledbetter) (1885–December 6, 1949) Folk and blues songwriter and singer
Les Paul (Lester William Polfus) (June 9, 1915–   ) Inventor of multitrack recording and the solid-body guitar

DEATHS IN 1988

MUSIC PERFORMERS AND MUSIC INDUSTRY NOTABLES WHO DIED IN 1988

Frederick Loewe (composer), Sunday, February 14 (83)
Memphis Slim (Peter Chatman), Wednesday, February 24 (kidney failure; 72)
Andy Gibb, Thursday, March 10 (heart ailment; 30)
Brook Benton (Benjamin Franklin Peay), Saturday, April 9 (spinal meningitis; 56)
Dave Prater (Sam & Dave), Saturday, April 9 (car crash; 50)
Sy Oliver, Friday, May 27 (cancer; 77)
Dennis Day, Wednesday, June 22 (Lou Gehrig's disease; 72)
Jimmy Soul (James McLeese), Saturday, June 25 (heart attack; 45)

Roy Buchanan, Sunday, August 14 (hanging; 48)
Billy Daniels, Friday, October 7 (cancer; 73)
Johnnie Richardson (Johnnie & Joe), Tuesday, October 25 (tuberculosis; 49)
Janet Ertel (The Chordettes), Thursday, November 24 (cancer; 57)
Roy Orbison, Tuesday, December 6 (heart attack; 52)
Bill Harris (The Clovers), Saturday, December 10 (pancreatic cancer; 63)
Sylvester, Friday, December 16 (AIDS; 40)

OTHERS WHO DIED IN 1988

Alan Ameche
Milton Caniff
John Carradine
Richard Castellano
Gabe Dell

Divine (Harry Glenn Milstead)
John Houseman
Trevor Howard
Jim Jordan (Fibber McGee)
Ted Kluzewski

Harvey Kuenn
Louis L'Amour
Joshua Logan
"Pistol" Pete Maravich
Christina Onassis

Heather O'Rourke
Jackie Presser
Anne Ramsey
Art Rooney

MOVIES OF 1988

MOVIES FEATURING POP MUSIC ARTISTS

Imagine   Never-seen-before film clips supplied by Yoko Ono are intermingled in a 2-hour documentary about the life and music of the late John Lennon.

U2 Rattle and Hum   Concert footage detailing U2's 1987 tour of the United States.

MOVIES FEATURING A POP MUSIC SOUNDTRACK

Cocktail   *Stars:* Tom Cruise, Bryan Brown, Elizabeth Shue. *Featured songs:* "Don't Worry, Be Happy" by Bobby McFerrin, "Kokomo" by the Beach Boys, "Hippy Hippy Shake" by the Georgia Satellites, "Rave On" by John Cougar Mellencamp.

Coming to America   *Stars:* Eddie Murphy, Arsenio Hall, James Earl Jones. *Featured songs:* "Addicted To You" by Levert, "To Be Loved" by Jackie Wilson.

Good Morning Vietnam   *Star:* Robin Williams. *Featured songs:* "Nowhere To Run" by Martha & the Vandellas, "I Get Around" by the Beach Boys, "Game Of Love" by Wayne Fontana & the Mindbenders, "Liar, Liar" by the Castaways, "I Got You (I Feel Good)" by James Brown, "What A Wonderful World" by Louis Armstrong.

Hairspray   *Stars:* Sonny Bono, Ruth Brown, Divine, Debbie Harry, Ricki Lake, Jerry Stiller. *Featured songs:* "The Madison Time" by the Ray Bryant Combo, "Mama Didn't Lie" by Jan Bradley, "Foot Stomping" by the Flares, "I'm Blue (The Gong-Gong Song)" by the Ikettes, "You'll Lose A Good Thing" by Barbara Lynn.

Heartbreak Hotel   *Stars:* David Keith, Tuesday Weld, Charlie Schlatter. Elvis songs featured in the film included "Heartbreak Hotel," "One Night," "Burning Love," "Love Me," "If I Can Dream," and "Can't Help Falling In Love."

Oliver & Company   An animated film from Walt Disney. *Featured songs:* "Why Should I Worry?" by Billy Joel, "Once Upon A Time In New York City" by Huey Lewis, "Perfect Isn't Easy" by Bette Midler, "Streets Of Gold" by Ruth Pointer.

Scrooged   *Stars:* Bill Murray, Karen Allen, Bobcat Goldthwait, John Forsythe, Carol Kane, Robert Mitchum. *Featured songs:* "Put A Little Love In Your Heart" by Annie Lennox and Al Green, "Brown-eyed Girl" by Buster Poindexter, "The Christmas Song" by Natalie Cole.

Steve Winwood in concert (photo: Anastasia Pantsios)

OTHER POPULAR MOVIES OF 1988

The Accused
Alien Nation
Betrayed
Big
Big Top Pee-Wee
Bull Durham
Clara's Heart
Clean and Sober
Colors
Crocodile Dundee II
Die Hard
Eight Men Out

A Fish Called Wanda
Gorillas in the Mist
Halloween 4
The Last Temptation of Christ
Rambo III
Red Heat
Shoot to Kill
Tucker
Who Framed Roger Rabbit
Willow
Young Guns

1988

ACADEMY AWARD WINNERS OF 1988

Best Actor: Dustin Hoffman, *Rain Man*
Best Actress: Jodie Foster, *The Accused*
Best Picture: *Rain Man*
Best Original Song: "Let the River Run," *Working Girl* (music and lyrics by Carly Simon)

TOP TELEVISION SHOWS OF 1988

Cheers
The Cosby Show
A Different World
The Golden Girls
Growing Pains

Murder, She Wrote
Night Court
60 Minutes
Who's the Boss?
The Wonder Years

1989

➡ Lieut. Col. Oliver L. North goes on trial for the Iran-*contra* coverup.

➡ On Tuesday, January 3, "The Arsenio Hall Show" premieres.

➡ In Tiananmen Square, Chinese Communist troops kill 2,000 students who were demonstrating for democracy.

➡ Fifty-two-year-old Colin L. Powell becomes the youngest man and first black to serve as Chairman of the Joint Chiefs of Staff.

➡ Baseball great Pete Rose is permanently banned from the game of baseball by Commissioner A. Bartlett Giamatti.

➡ Chris Evert retires from tennis; Kareem Abdul-Jabbar retires from basketball.

➡ Art Shell becomes coach of the Los Angeles Raiders; he is the first black coach in the National Football League since the 1920s.

➡ Germans begin dismantling the Berlin Wall, starting a process that will end in the unification of East and West Germany.

➡ 24,000 U.S. troops invade Panama in an attempt to oust General Manuel Noriega from power.

➡ The worst oil spill in U.S. history occurs when the tanker *Exxon Valdez* hits a submerged reef in Prince William Sound, Alaska, spilling 240,000 barrels of oil into the sound.

➡ On October 17, an earthquake measuring 6.9 on the Richter Scale rocks the San Francisco Bay area causing 3,000 injuries and $2 billion in damage.

SPORTS WINNERS

Baseball The Oakland A's beat the San Francisco Giants 4 games to 0.

Football

NFC: The San Francisco '49ers beat the Los Angeles Rams 30–3 in San Francisco.

AFC: The Denver Broncos beat the Cleveland Browns 37–21 in Denver.

Super Bowl XXIV: The San Francisco '49ers beat the Denver Broncos 55–10 on January 28, 1990, in New Orleans, Louisiana.

Basketball The Detroit Pistons beat the Portland Trailblazers 4 games to 1.

Hockey The Edmonton Oilers beat the Boston Bruins 4 games to 1.

MUSIC HIGHLIGHTS OF 1989

➡ The records of Cat Stevens, who is now a devout Muslim, are banned by some radio stations for his support of the Ayatollah Khomeini's call for the murder of *Satanic Verses* author Salman Rushdie.

➡ As part of a multimillion-dollar deal with Pepsi-Cola, Madonna endorses the soft drink with a worldwide television debut of her new single in a video commercial. Shortly thereafter, an Italian Catholic group in Rome, Italy, questions the video, *Like a Prayer,* and its Christian imagery.

➡ After a year of negotiations, Grace Slick, Paul Kantner, Jorma Kaukonen, and Jack Casady re-form the Jefferson Airplane.

➡ After five years together, Michael Jackson and his personal manager, Frank DiLeo, part company.

➡ After eight years with RCA Records, Diana Ross returns to her original label, Motown Records.

➡ Prince is asked to contribute several songs to a new Batman movie.

➡ Michael Jackson concludes his Bad tour at the Los Angeles Sports Arena. The sixteen-month tour saw Jackson do 123 concerts in 15 countries and on 3 continents. The tour grossed $125 million and was seen by 4.4 million fans.

➡ After 33 years, Dick Clark steps down as host of *American Bandstand* and turns the show over to 26-year-old David Hirsch, who will host the show on cable on USA Network.

ROCK ON ALMANAC

⇨ Major record stores begin to phase out the former staple of the music industry, the black vinyl LP and single, due to the rising popularity of cassette tapes and Compact Discs.

⇨ Nearly seven years after disbanding, Roger Daltrey, Pete Townshend, and John Entwistle of the Who reunite for a 25-city North American summer concert tour.

⇨ After having disbanded in 1982, the Doobie Brothers' original lead singer Tom Johnston and former band mates Patrick Simmons, John Hartman, Tiran Porter, and Michael Hossack re-form the band and sign a contract with Capitol Records.

⇨ Jon Anderson, Steve Howe, Rick Wakeman, and William Bruford, original members of Yes from the early seventies, reunite as the group Anderson, Bruford, Wakeman & Howe.

⇨ After 12 years, New York City's Lone Star Cafe closes its doors.

⇨ On August 31, the Rolling Stones begin their Steel Wheels tour in Philadelphia.

⇨ On October 24, in Cleveland, Ohio, for the first time, the Rock and Roll Hall of Fame begins announcing its selection of New Inductees for the induction in January 1990.

⇨ Rap music starts moving into the mainstream of popularity among young people.

⇨ Donny Osmond makes a major comeback with "Soldier of Love" single, while Bette Midler does it with single "Wind Beneath My Wings," from the film *Beaches*.

⇨ Nostalgia is big business with great ticket sales being generated by acts like the Who, the Rolling Stones, the Bee Gees, the Doobie Brothers, Jefferson Airplane, Elton John, Ringo Starr, Paul McCartney, Dion, Diana Ross, the Kinks, and the Grateful Dead.

DEBUT ARTISTS OF 1989

Abstrac	Indigo Girls
After 7	Inner City
Marc Almond	Jaya
Babyface	Jive Bunny and the Mastermixers
Bad English	Holly Johnson
Adrian Belew	Kiara
Big Noise	Kix
Bonham	Lil Louis
Chuckii Booker	Living Colour
Sam Brown	Love and Money
Sharon Bryant	Love and Rockets
Neneh Cherry	Martika
Choirboys	Christopher Max
Chunky A	Metallica
The Cult	Michel'Le
De La Soul	Milli Vanilli
Diving for Pearls	Michael Morales
D-Mob	1927
Easterhouse	One 2 Many
Enuff Z'Nuff	Tommy Page
Enya	Kevin Paige
Deon Estus	Pajama Party
Melissa Etheridge	Mica Paris
Figures on a Beach	The Pasadenas
Giant	Q-Feel
Gina Go-Go	Kevin Raleigh
The Graces	The Replacements
Marcia Griffiths	Roachford
Guy	Roxette
Jeff Healey Band	Saraya
House of Lords	Seduction
Grayson Hugh	Paul Shaffer

Metallica (l to r: Lars Ulrich, Kirk Hammett, James Hetfield; photo: Anastasia Pantsios)

1989

Shana	Tora Tora
Sinitta	2 Live Crew
Sir Mix-a-Lot	Midge Ure
Skid Row	Warrant
Soulsister	Waterfront
Soul II Soul	Whistle
Stage Dolls	Christopher Williams
Sybil	Vesta Williams
Tangier	Winger
Technotronic	XTC
Texas	Young MC

HITS OF 1989

JANUARY

	Don't Tell Me Lies	Breathe	A & M
	Feels So Good	Van Halen	Warner Bros.
℗	Girl You Know It's True	Milli Vanilli	Arista
	Give Me The Keys (And I'll Drive You Crazy)	Huey Lewis & the News	Chrysalis
	The Great Commandment	Camouflage	Atlantic
	Just Because	Anita Baker	Elektra
☆	The Living Years	Mike + the Mechanics	Atlantic
☆ Ⓖ	Lost In Your Eyes	Debbie Gibson	Atlantic
	The Love In Your Eyes	Eddie Money	Columbia
	Paradise City	Guns N' Roses	Geffen
	Roni	Bobby Brown	MCA
	She Won't Talk To Me	Luther Vandross	Epic
	Walk The Dinosaur	Was (Not Was)	Chrysalis
	You Got It	Roy Orbison	Virgin
	You're Not Alone	Chicago	Reprise

FEBRUARY

Can You Stand The Rain	New Edition	MCA
Driven Out	The Fixx	RCA
End Of The Line	The Traveling Wilburys	Wilbury

481

ROCK ON ALMANAC

☆ ⑥ Eternal Flame	The Bangles	Columbia
Heaven Help Me	Deon Estus	Mika
It's Only Love	Simply Red	Elektra
☆ ⑥ The Look	Roxette	EMI
Never Had A Lot To Lose	Cheap Trick	Epic
⑥ One	Metallica	Elektra
Room To Move	Animotion	Polydor
Second Chance	38 Special	A & M
Seventeen	Winger	Atlantic
☆ ⑥ She Drives Me Crazy	Fine Young Cannibals	I.R.S.
Tell Her	Kenny Loggins	Columbia
Thinking Of You	Sa-Fire	Cutting
Your Mama Don't Dance	Poison	Capitol

MARCH

⑥ After All	Cher & Peter Cetera	Geffen
⑥ Close My Eyes Forever	Lita Ford (with Ozzy Osbourne)	RCA
Cult Of Personality	Living Colour	Epic
Everlasting Love	Howard Jones	Elektra
⑥ Every Little Step	Bobby Brown	MCA
☆ ⑥ Forever Your Girl	Paula Abdul	Virgin
⑫ Funky Cold Medina	Tone Loc	Delicious Vinyl
Iko Iko	The Belle Stars	Capitol
☆ I'll Be There For You	Bon Jovi	Mercury
☆ ⑫ Like A Prayer	Madonna	Sire
⑥ Real Love	Jody Watley	MCA
Rocket	Def Leppard	Mercury
☆ ⑥ Rock On	Michael Damian	Cypress
Soldier Of Love	Donny Osmond	Capitol
Somebody Like You	Robbie Nevil	EMI

APRIL

⑥ Buffalo Stance	Neneh Cherry	Virgin
Circle	Edie Brickell & the New Bohemians	Geffen
Cry	Waterfront	Polydor

The Cult (l to r: Ian Astbury, Billy Duffy; photo: Anastasia Pantsios)

Ⓖ	Electric Youth	Debbie Gibson	Atlantic
	Giving Up On Love	Rick Astley	RCA
☆ Ⓖ	I'll Be Loving You (Forever)	New Kids on the Block	Columbia
	Let Me In	Eddie Money	Columbia
	Little Jackie Wants To Be A Star	Lisa Lisa & Cult Jam	Columbia
	Miss You Like Crazy	Natalie Cole	EMI
Ⓖ	Patience	Guns N' Roses	Geffen
	Seeing Is Believing	Mike + the Mechanics	Atlantic
Ⓖ	This Time I Know It's For Real	Donna Summer	Atlantic
	Through The Storm	Aretha Franklin & Elton John	Arista
	Veronica	Elvis Costello	Warner Bros.
	When Love Comes To Town	U2 with B. B. King	Island

MAY

☆ Ⓖ	Baby Don't Forget My Number	Milli Vanilli	Arista
	Be With You	The Bangles	Columbia
	Crazy About You	Rod Stewart	Warner Bros.
	The Doctor	The Doobie Brothers	Capitol
	Down Boys	Warrant	Columbia
☆	Good Thing	Fine Young Cannibals	I.R.S.
	I Drove All Night	Cyndi Lauper	Epic
☆ Ⓖ	If You Don't Know Me By Now	Simply Red	Elektra
	I Won't Back Down	Tom Petty	MCA
	My Brave Face	Paul McCartney	Capitol
	Pop Singer	John Cougar Mellencamp	Mercury
	Rooms On Fire	Stevie Nicks	Modern
☆	Satisfied	Richard Marx	EMI
	Send Me An Angel '89	Real Life	Curb
Ⓖ	What You Don't Know	Exposé	Arista

JUNE

☆ Ⓟ	Batdance	Prince	Warner Bros.
	Calling It Love	Animotion	Polygram
Ⓖ	Cold Hearted	Paula Abdul	Virgin
	Cover Of Love	Michael Damian	Cypress
Ⓖ	Express Yourself	Madonna	Sire
	Friends	Jody Watley with Eric B. & Rakim	MCA
	Lay Your Hands On Me	Bon Jovi	Polygram
	Me Myself and I	De La Soul	Tommy Boy
	My Brave Face	Paul McCartney	Capitol
	No More Rhyme	Debbie Gibson	Atlantic
Ⓟ	On Your Own	Bobby Brown	MCA
	Sacred Emotion	Donny Osmond	Capitol
	Secret Rendezvous	Karyn White	Warner Bros.
	The End Of The Innocence	Don Henley	Geffen
☆ Ⓖ	Toy Soldiers	Martika	Columbia

JULY

Ⓟ	Bust A Move	Young M.C.	Delicious Vinyl
	Closer To Fine	Indigo Girls	Epic

ROCK ON ALMANAC

Melissa Etheridge (photo: Anastasia Pantsios)

☆ ⑥	**Don't Wanna Lose You**	Gloria Estefan	Epic
☆ ⑫	**Hangin' Tough**	New Kids on the Block	Columbia
⑥	**Heaven**	Warrant	Columbia
⑥	**If I Could Turn Back Time**	Cher	Geffen
	It Isn't, It Wasn't, It Ain't Never Gonna Be	A. Franklin/W. Houston	Arista
	Jackie Brown	John Cougar Mellencamp	Polygram
	Kisses On The Wind	Neneh Cherry	Virgin
	One	Bee Gees	Warner Bros.
	Pride & Passion	John Cafferty & the Beaver Brown Band	Scotti Bros.
☆ ⑫	**Right Here Waiting**	Richard Marx	EMI
⑥	**Shower Me With Your Love**	Surface	Columbia
	Soul Provider	Michael Bolton	Columbia
	The Prisoner	Howard Jones	Elektra

AUGUST

	Ain't Too Proud To Beg	Rick Astley	RCA
	And The Night Stood Still	Dion	Arista
	Cherish	Madonna	Sire
	Don't Look Back	Fine Young Cannibals	I.R.S.
☆ ⑥	**Girl I'm Gonna Miss You**	Milli Vanilli	Arista
	Healing Hands	Elton John	MCA
	Hey Ladies	Beastie Boys	Capitol
	It's No Crime	Babyface	Solar
	It's Not Enough	Starship	RCA
☆	**Listen To Your Heart**	Roxette	EMI
	Love Song	The Cure	Elektra
⑥	**Partyman**	Prince	Warner Bros.
⑥	**Rock Wit'cha**	Bobby Brown	MCA
	Still Cruisin'	The Beach Boys	Capitol
	When I Looked At Him	Exposé	Arista

SEPTEMBER

⑫	**Back To Life**	Soul II Soul (Featuring Caron Wheeler)	Virgin
⑥	**Cover Girl**	New Kids on the Block	Columbia

484

⑥ Didn't I (Blow Your Mind)	New Kids on the Block	Columbia
Don't Know Much	Linda Ronstadt (Featuring Aaron Neville)	Elektra
⑥ Dr. Feelgood	Mötley Crüe	Elektra
Get On Your Feet	Gloria Estefan	Epic
I Feel The Earth Move	Martika	Columbia
Leave A Light On	Belinda Carlisle	MCA
⑥ Love In An Elevator	Aerosmith	Geffen
☆ ℗ Miss You Much	Janet Jackson	A & M
Mixed Emotions	The Rolling Stones	Columbia
⑥ Poison	Alice Cooper	Epic
Sowing The Seeds Of Love	Tears for Fears	Fontana
The Best	Tina Turner	Capitol
☆ ⑥ When I See You Smile	Bad English	Epic

OCTOBER

Angelia	Richard Marx	EMI
Baby Come To Me	Regina Belle	Columbia
☆ ℗ Blame It On The Rain	Milli Vanilli	Arista
☆ How Am I Supposed To Live Without You	Michael Bolton	Columbia
I Live By The Groove	Paul Carrack	Chrysalis
Just Between You And Me	Lou Gramm	Atlantic
Just Like Jesse James	Cher	Geffen
License To Chill	Billy Ocean	Jive
Living In Sin	Bon Jovi	Mercury
The Arms of Orion	Prince (with Sheena Easton)	Warner Bros.
The Last Worthless Evening	Don Henley	Geffen
Was It Nothing At All	Michael Damian	Cypress
☆ ⑥ We Didn't Start The Fire	Billy Joel	Columbia
When The Night Comes	Joe Cocker	Capitol
With Every Beat Of My Heart	Taylor Dayne	Arista

NOVEMBER

☆ ⑥ Another Day In Paradise	Phil Collins	Atlantic
Downtown Train	Rod Stewart	Warner Bros.
Fool For Your Loving	Whitesnake	Geffen

Vernon Reid of Living Colour (photo: *Anastasia Pantsios*)

485

Free Fallin'	Tom Petty	MCA
I Remember You	Skid Row	Atlantic
Janie's Got A Gun	Aerosmith	Geffen
Oh Father	Madonna	Sire
Pretending	Eric Clapton	Duck
⑥ Rhythm Nation	Janet Jackson	A & M
Rock And A Hard Place	The Rolling Stones	Columbia
Steamy Windows	Tina Turner	Capitol
Tender Lover	Babyface	Solar
⑥ This One's For The Children	New Kids on the Block	Columbia
Touch Me Tonight	Shooting Star	Enigma
⑥ Two To Make It Right	Seduction	Vendetta

DECEMBER

A Girl Like You	The Smithereens	Enigma
Dangerous	Roxette	EMI
Don't Take It Personal	Jermaine Jackson	Arista
Electric Boogie	Marcia Griffiths	Mango
Foolish Heart	Sharon Bryant	Wing
Here We Are	Gloria Estefan	Epic
I Don't Know	Michael Morales	Polydor
I Will Survive	Sa-Fire	Mercury
Lullaby	The Cure	Elektra
Nothin' To Hide	Poco	RCA
☆ ⑥ Opposites Attract	Paula Abdul (Duet with the Wild Pair)	Virgin
Peace In Our Time	Eddie Money	Columbia
Tell Me Why	Exposé	Arista
We Can't Go Wrong	The Cover Girls	Capitol
Woman In Chains	Tears for Fears	Fontana

TOP SINGLES OF 1989

⑥ Baby, I Love Your Way/Freebird Medley	Will to Power	Epic
⑥ Cold Hearted	Paula Abdul	Virgin
⑥ Every Rose Has Its Thorn	Poison	Enigma
℗ Girl You Know It's True	Milli Vanilli	Arista
Giving You The Best That I Got	Anita Baker	Elektra
⑥ Look Away	Chicago	Reprise
℗ Miss You Much	Janet Jackson	A & M
⑥ My Prerogative	Bobby Brown	MCA
℗ Straight Up	Paula Abdul	Virgin
℗ Wind Beneath My Wings	Bette Midler	Atlantic

TOP ALBUMS OF 1989

℗ Appetite For Destruction	Guns N' Roses	Geffen
℗ Don't Be Cruel	Bobby Brown	MCA
℗ Forever Your Girl	Paula Abdul	Virgin
℗ G N' R Lies	Guns N' Roses	Geffen
℗ Girl You Know It's True	Milli Vanilli	Arista

486

Sebastian Bach of Skid Row (photo: Anastasia Pantsios)

1989

℗ **Hangin' Tough**	New Kids on the Block	Columbia
℗ **Hysteria**	Def Leppard	Mercury
℗ **New Jersey**	Bon Jovi	Mercury
℗ **The Raw & The Cooked**	Fine Young Cannibals	I.R.S.
℗ **The Traveling Wilburys Vol. 1**	The Traveling Wilburys	Wilbury

GRAMMY WINNERS IN 1989

The Grammys were televised by CBS from the Shrine Auditorium in Los Angeles, California, on Wednesday, February 21, 1990. Gary Shandling was the host.

Record of the Year: "Wind Beneath My Wings," Bette Midler (Atlantic)

Song of the Year: "Wind Beneath My Wings," Bette Midler (music and lyrics by Larry Henley & Jeff Silbar)

Album of the Year: *Nick Of Time,* Bonnie Raitt (Capitol)

Best Pop Vocal Performance, Female: "Nick Of Time," Bonnie Raitt (Capitol)

Best Pop Vocal Performance, Male: "How Am I Supposed To Live Without You," Michael Bolton (Columbia)

Best Pop Vocal Performance, Duo or Group: "Don't Know Much," Linda Ronstadt & Aaron Neville (Elektra)

Best Pop Instrumental: "Healling Chant," Neville Brothers (A & M)

Best Rock Vocal Performance, Female: "Nick Of Time," Bonnie Raitt (Capitol)

Best Rock Vocal Performance, Male: "End Of The Innocence," Don Henley (Geffen)

Best Rock Vocal Performance, Duo or Group: "Traveling Wilburys, Vol. I," The Traveling Wilburys (Wilbury/Warner Bros.)

Best Rock Instrumental: "Jeff Beck's Guitar Shop With Terry Bozzio And Tony Hymas," Jeff Beck with Terry Bozzio And Tony Hymas (Epic)

Best New Artist: Milli Vanilli (later revoked)

Best R & B Performance, Female: "Giving You The Best That I Got," Anita Baker (Elektra)

Best R & B Performance, Male: "Every Little Step," Bobby Brown (MCA)

Best R & B Performance, Duo or Group: "Back To Life," Soul II Soul (Virgin)

Best R & B Instrumental: "African Dance," Soul II Soul (Virgin)

Best R & B Song: "If You Don't Know Me By Now," Simply Red (Elektra) (music and lyrics by Kenny Gamble & Leon Huff)

Best Hard Rock Vocal or Instrumental: "Cult of Personality," Living Colour (Epic)

Best Metal Vocal or Instrumental: "One," Metallica (Elektra)

Best Performance, Rap: "Bust A Move," Young M.C. (Delicious Vinyl)

Best Comedy Performance: "P.D.Q. Bach 1712 Overture & Other Musical Assaults," Professor Peter Schickele: The Greater Hoople Area Off-Season Philharmonic (Telarc)

Best Song Written for a Motion Picture or Television: "Let The River Run" (from the movie *Working Girl*), written by Carly Simon (Arista)

Best New Age: "Passion-Music From *The Last Temptation of Christ*," Peter Gabriel (Geffen)

Best Music Video, Short Form: *Leave Me Alone,* Michael Jackson (Epic)

Best Music Video, Long Form: *Rhythm Nation,* Janet Jackson (A & M)

ROCK AND ROLL HALL OF FAME INDUCTEES

The fourth induction ceremony was held on Wednesday, January 18, 1989, at the Waldorf Astoria hotel in New York City.

PERFORMERS

Inductee (Born and Died)	Debut Single (Year)	Label
Dion (DiMucci) (July 18, 1939–)	I Wonder Why (1958) (with the Belmonts)	Laurie
Otis Redding (September 9, 1941–December 10, 1967)	These Arms of Mine (1963)	Volt
The Rolling Stones (Mick Jagger: July 26, 1943– ; Keith Richards: December 18, 1943– ; Brian Jones: February 28, 1942–July 3, 1969; Mick Taylor: January 17, 1948– ; Ron Wood: June 1, 1947– ; Bill Wyman: October 24, 1936– ; Charlie Watts; June 2, 1941–)	Not Fade Away (1964)	London
The Temptations (David Ruffin: January 18, 1941–June 1, 1991; Eddie Kendricks: December 17, 1939– ; Otis Williams: October 30, 1939– ; Melvin Franklin: October 12, 1942– ; Paul Williams: July 2, 1939–August 17, 1973; Dennis Edwards: February 3, 1943–)	The Way You Do The Things You Do (1964)	Gordy
Stevie Wonder (May 13, 1950–)	Fingertips—Part 2 (1963)	Tamla

Jani Lane of Warrant (photo: *Anastasia Pantsios*)

NONPERFORMERS

Phil Spector (December 26, 1940–   )   Legendary record producer and label founder (Philles Records) who created the "wall of sound" effect (overdubbed and layered "sound on sound") on recordings of the Crystals, the Ronettes, singer Darlene Love, and others

EARLY INFLUENCES

The Ink Spots   Forerunners of the R&B group singing style
Bessie Smith (April 15, 1894–September 26, 1937)   Blues singer
The Soul Stirrers   Creators of the gospel quartet style, who reshaped traditional gospel material into a more soulful sound

DEATHS IN 1989

MUSIC PERFORMERS AND MUSIC INDUSTRY NOTABLES WHO DIED IN 1989

Eddie Heywood, Monday, January 2 (extended illness; 73)

Patti McCabe Barnes (The Poni-Tails), Tuesday, January 17 (cancer; 48)

Steve Wahrer (The Trashmen), Saturday, January 21 (throat cancer; 47)

Herman "Sonny" Chaney (Jaguars), Sunday, January 29 (diabetes; 50)

Paul Robi (The Platters), Tuesday, January 31 (pancreatic cancer; 57)

Kenneth "Jethro" Burns (Homer & Jethro), Saturday, February 4 (cancer; 69)

Frank "Killer Joe" Piro, Tuesday, February 7 (kidney disease; 68)

Roy Eldridge, Sunday, February 26 (undisclosed illness; 78)

Stuart Hamblen, Tuesday, February 28 (brain tumor; 80)

Lloyd "Tiny" Grimes, Saturday, March 4 (meningitis; 72)

Doc Green (The Drifters), Friday, March 10 (cancer; 54)

Al Bennett (Liberty Records), Wednesday, March 15 (extended illness; 62)

Archie Bleyer (record industry mogul), Monday, March 20 (extended illness; 79)

Herbert Mills (The Mills Brothers), Wednesday, April 12 (viral meningitis; 77)

Nesuhi Ertegun (record industry mogul), Saturday, July 15 (cancer; 71)

Steve Rubell (founder, Studio 54 in New York City), Tuesday, July 25 (hepatitis; 45)

Benjamin "Bull Moose" Jackson, Monday, July 31 (brain tumor; 71)

Damaso Perez Prado, Thursday, September 14 (stroke; 72)

Irving Berlin, Friday, September 22 (natural causes; 101)

Carmen Cavallaro, Thursday, October 12 (cancer; 76)

Vladimir Horowitz, Sunday, November 5 (heart attack; 85)

Barry Sadler, Sunday, November 5 (gunshot wound to head; 49)

Dickie Goodman (Buchanan and Goodman), Monday, November 6 (self-inflicted gunshot; 55)

Alvin Ailey (Black Dance School Head), Friday, December 1 (dyscrasia; 58)

Sammy Fain (songwriter), Wednesday, December 6 (heart attack; 87)

OTHERS WHO DIED IN 1989

Fran Allison
Jim Backus
Lucille Ball
Frances Bavier
Amanda Blake
Mel Blanc
John Cassavetes
Salvador Dali

Bette Davis
Carl Furillo
Hy Gardner
A. Bartlett Giamatti
Vernon (Lefty) Gomez
Andrei Gromyko
Emperor Hirohito
Abbie Hoffman

ROCK ON ALMANAC

Kip Winger of Winger (photo: Anastasia Pantsios)

Christine Jorgensen
Ayatollah Khomeini
Beatrice Lillie
Ferdinand Marcos
Billy Martin
John Matuszak
Huey P. Newton
Laurence Olivier

Claude Pepper
Anthony Quayle
Gilda Radner
Sugar Ray Robinson
Lee Van Cleef
Cornel Wilde
Guy Williams (Zorro)

MOVIES OF 1989

MOVIES FEATURING A POP MUSIC SOUNDTRACK

Always   *Stars:* Richard Dreyfus, Holly Hunter, John Goodman. The Platters' "Smoke Gets In Your Eyes" is a featured song.

Eddie & the Cruisers II—Eddie Lives   *Stars:* Michael Paré, Marina Orsini, Bernie Coulson. Cameos by Bo Diddley, Martha Quinn, and Larry King. Music by John Cafferty and the Beaver Brown Band. Produced by Kenny Vance.

Great Balls of Fire   *Stars:* Dennis Quaid, Winona Ryder. The life of Hall of Fame inductee Jerry Lee Lewis, featuring his best-known music.

Lean on Me   *Stars:* Morgan Freeman, Beverly Todd, Robert Guillaume. Features Bill Withers' 1972 number-one hit, "Lean On Me."

Lethal Weapon 2   *Stars:* Mel Gibson, Danny Glover, Joe Pesci. Music by Michael Kamen, Eric Clapton, and David Sandborn, with many tunes by the Skyliners.

Shag   *Stars:* Phoebe Cates, Scott Coffey, Bridget Fonda, Annabeth Gish, Tyrone Power, Jr. A film about Southern youths in 1963, with period songs, including Lloyd Price's "Stagger Lee."

When Harry Met Sally . . .   *Stars:* Billy Crystal, Meg Ryan, Carrie Fisher, Bruno Kirby. Harry Connick, Jr. does the soundtrack, which includes "It Had To Be You."

OTHER POPULAR MOVIES OF 1989

The Accidental Tourist
Back to the Future II
Batman, the Movie
Crimes and Misdemeanors
Dirty Rotten Scoundrels

Do the Right Thing
Dream Team
Friday the 13th, Part VIII—
    Jason Takes Manhattan
Ghostbusters II

Indiana Jones and the Last Crusade
The Karate Kid, Part III
License to Kill
Major League
Mississippi Burning
New York Stories
Pet Sematary
Pink Cadillac

Rain Man
Say Anything
Sex, Lies, and Videotape
Skin Deep
Star Trek V—The Final Frontier
True Believers
Working Girl

1989

ACADEMY AWARD WINNERS OF 1989

Best Actor: Daniel Day-Lewis, *My Left Foot*
Best Actress: Jessica Tandy, *Driving Miss Daisy*
Best Picture: *Driving Miss Daisy*
Best Original Song: "Under The Sea," *The Little Mermaid* (music by Alan Menken and lyrics by Howard Ashman)

TOP TELEVISION SHOWS OF 1989

A Different World
America's Funniest Home Videos
Cheers
The Cosby Show
Empty Nest

The Golden Girls
NFL Monday Night Football
Roseanne
60 Minutes
The Wonder Years

491

1990

1990

⇨ Washington, D.C., Mayor Marion Barry, 53, is arrested for smoking "crack."

⇨ Soviet Union gets its first McDonald's restaurant.

⇨ Explicit posters to promote safer sex start appearing to help educate young people in the battle against AIDS.

⇨ Nelson Mandela leaves prison near Cape Town, a free man for the first time in 27 years.

⇨ Mikhail Gorbachev becomes first elected President of the Soviet Union.

⇨ Lithuania declares its independence from the Soviet Union.

⇨ Seventy-nine-year-old Mother Teresa of Calcutta, a Nobel Peace Prize–winner, retires as head of her Missionaries of Charity Order.

⇨ U.S. hostages Robert Polhill and Frank Reed, held captive by the pro-Iranian Islamic Jihad since 1986, are freed into Syrian custody.

⇨ Boris Yeltsin becomes President of the Russian Republic.

⇨ Nelson Mandela arrives in New York City for a ticker-tape parade and later addresses the U.N.

⇨ On August 2, Iraqi forces invade and seize control of Kuwait.

⇨ By a vote of 51–35, the International Olympic Committee awards the 1996 summer games to Atlanta, Georgia.

⇨ After 45 years, Germany unites as one nation again.

⇨ John Major becomes Britain's new Prime Minister, succeeding Margaret Thatcher in the election. At 47, he becomes Britain's youngest Prime Minister of this century.

SPORTS WINNERS

Baseball   The Cincinnati Reds beat the Oakland A's 4 games to 0.

Football

NFC: The New York Giants beat the San Francisco '49ers 15–13 in San Francisco.

AFC: The Buffalo Bills beat the Los Angeles Raiders 51–3 in Buffalo.

Super Bowl XXV: The New York Giants beat the Buffalo Bills 20–19 on January 27, 1991, in Tampa, Florida.

Basketball   The Chicago Bulls beat the Los Angeles Lakers 4 games to 1.

Hockey   The Pittsburgh Penguins beat the Minnesota North Stars 4 games to 2.

MUSIC HIGHLIGHTS IN 1990

⇨ On January 2, Paul McCartney performs in Birmingham, England, for the first time on a British stage in 13 years.

⇨ BMI (Broadcast Music Incorporate) celebrates its 50th anniversary.

⇨ The Rolling Stones' home video, "25 × 5," a definitive history of the band, is released in February.

⇨ Janet Jackson's Rhythm Nation World Tour, presented by MTV, begins March 1, in Miami, Florida.

⇨ Tommy Hammond, the first U.S. retailer indicted on obscenity charges for selling 2 Live Crew's *Move Somethin'*, was cleared of the charge by an Alabama jury.

⇨ Other record retail chains, in various parts of the country, refuse to stock 2 Live Crew's controversial album *As Nasty As They Wanna Be.*

⇨ Arista Records celebrates its 15th anniversary with a star-studded benefit concert, "That's What Friends Are For," on March 17, at Radio City Music Hall in New York, with proceeds going to help fight AIDS.

⇨ On March 20, Gloria Estefan of the Miami Sound Machine, injures her back in a serious bus accident near Tobyhanna, Pennsylvania, while on an East Coast tour.

⇨ On April 28, after 6,137 performances during a 15-year run, "A Chorus Line" closes in New York.

⇨ After 18 years, WCBS-FM, New York, becomes the market's new no. 1 radio station with a 5.1 share, 12-plus in the latest Arbitron Ratings. It is the first time an oldies station dominates the New York market.

⇨ The historic Chess Records Studio at 2120 S. Michigan Ave. in Chicago is designated a City Landmark. Willie Dixon, Muddy Waters, Chuck Berry, Bo Diddley, and others recorded there.

⇨ Legendary stars of the sixties Crosby, Stills and Nash release their first new album in years, *Live It Up,* for their old label, Atlantic Records.

⇨ David Bowie draws millions of fans to his sold-out "Sound & Vision" tour.

⇨ Singer Curtis Mayfield is injured on August 13, after stepping out on stage at Brooklyn, New York's Wingate Field, when a gust of wind knocks over a light rack, which falls on the singer's neck. The accident leaves him paralyzed from the neck down.

⇨ Sinead O'Connor causes a stir when she refuses to let The Garden State Arts Center in New Jersey play "The Star-Spangled Banner" before her August 24 concert.

⇨ German producer Frank Farian, who produced Milli Vanilli's hits, claims the duo, Rob Pilatus and Fabrice Morvan, did not sing on the group's smash debut album *Girl You Know It's True,* and lip-synched the vocals for their videos. Farian says German singers Brad Howell and Johnny Davis are the real voices behind Milli Vanilli.

⇨ On November 3, the Righteous Brothers, due to the popularity of the movie *Ghost,* have two versions of their hit "Unchained Melody" on *Billboard* magazine's Top 100 listing, both in the top 20: the original version on Verve Records and the remake on Curb Records.

⇨ Mick Jagger and longtime girlfriend Jerry Hall are wed on November 21, on the Island of Bali in Indonesia.

⇨ Reprise Records releases a four-CD, 44-track musical biography of the late Jimi Hendrix, *The Jimi Hendrix Story.*

DEBUT ARTISTS OF 1990

Oleta Adams	The Brat Pack
Adventures of Stevie V	Brother Beyond
Alias	C + C Music Factory/Freedom Williams
Anything Box	Calloway
Bang	Tevin Campbell
Beats International	Candyman
Bell Biv Devoe	Mariah Carey
Betty Boo	Jane Child
Biscuit	The Chimes
Biz Markie	Jude Cole
Black Box	Tyler Collins
The Black Crowes	Concrete Blonde
Brent Bourgeois	Cynthia & Johnny 'O'

Nelson (l to r: Matthew, Gunnar; photo: Anastasia Pantsios)

Damn Yankees
Danger Danger
Deee-Lite
del Amitri
Digital Underground
Celine Dion
Doc Box & B. Fresh
Electric Boys
Electronic
Entouch
En Vogue
Faith No More
John Farnham
Faster Pussycat
Favorite Angel
Tricia Leigh Fisher
49er's
The 4 of Us
Gorky Park
Hi Tek 3 (featuring Ya Kid K)
Indecent Obsession
Joyce "Fenderella" Irby
Kaoma
Joey Kid
Kid Frost
Lenny Kravitz
Kyper
L.A. Guns
George LaMond
Leila K with Rob 'N' Raz
The Lightning Seeds
Little Caesar
The London Quireboys
A'me Lorain
Louie Louie
Mantronix (featuring Wondress)
McAuley Schenker Group
M. C. Hammer

Mellow Man Ace
Ms. Adventures
Peter Murphy
Alannah Myles
Nelson
Nikki
Notorious
Sinead O'Connor
Partners in Kryme
The Party
Pat & Mick
Michael Penn
Perfect Gentlemen
Andrew Ridgeley
Jimmy Ryser
St. Paul
Seiko and Donnie Wahlberg
Snap!
Soho
Jimmy Somerville
The Soup Dragons
Special Generation
Lisa Stansfield
Tiana
Timmy T
Troop
2 in a Room
2 NU
The U-Krew
Vanilla Ice
The Vaughan Brothers
The West Coast Rap All-Stars
Caron Wheeler
Wilson Phillips
XYMOX
Young & Restless
Sydney Youngblood
Yvonne

HITS OF 1990

JANUARY

All Or Nothing	Milli Vanilli	Arista
☆ ⑥ **Black Velvet**	Allanah Myles	Atlantic
Dirty Deeds	Joan Jett	Blackheart
☆ ⑥ **Escapade**	Janet Jackson	A & M
⑥ **Get Up! (Before The Night Is Over)**	Technotronic	SBK
Going Home	Kenny G	Arista
I Go To Extremes	Billy Joel	Columbia
⑫ **Just A Friend**	Biz Markie	Cold Chillin'
☆ ⑥ **Love Will Lead You Back**	Taylor Dayne	Arista
No Myth	Michael Penn	RCA
Sometimes She Cries	Warrant	Columbia

The Deeper The Love	Whitesnake	Geffen
To Late To Say Goodbye	Richard Marx	EMI
Walk On By	Sybil	Next Plateau
Whole Wide World	A'me Lorain	RCA

FEBRUARY

℗ All Around The World	Lisa Stansfield	Arista
All My Life	Linda Ronstadt (featuring Aaron Neville)	Elektra
Almost Hear You Sigh	The Rolling Stones	Columbia
Blue Sky Mine	Midnight Oil	Columbia
⑥ Don't Wanna Fall In Love	Jane Child	Warner Bros.
Forever	Kiss	Mercury
Heart Beat	Seduction	Vendetta
House of Pain	Faster Pussycat	Elektra
I'll Be There	Joyce "Fenderella" Irby	Motown
☆ ⑥ I'll Be Your Everything	Tommy Page	Sire
I Wish It Would Rain Down	Phil Collins	Atlantic
⑥ Keep It Together	Madonna	Sire
Love Me For Life	Stevie B	LMR
Wild Women Do	Natalie Cole	EMI
Without You	Mötley Crüe	Elektra

MARCH

A Face In The Crowd	Tom Petty	MCA
⑥ All I Wanna Do Is Make Love To You	Heart	Capitol
Getting Away With It	Electronic	Warner Bros.
☆ ⑥ Hold On	Wilson Phillips	SBK
How Can We Be Lovers	Michael Bolton	Columbia
Hurting Kind (I've Got My Eyes On You)	Robert Plant	Esparanza
Lambada	Kaoma	Epic
Love Child	Sweet Sensation	Atco
☆ ℗ Nothing Compares 2 U	Sinead O'Connor	Ensign
Room At The Top	Adam Ant	MCA
⑥ The Secret Garden	Quincy Jones	Q West
This Old Heart Of Mine	Rod Stewart (with Ronald Isley)	Warner Bros.
Time After Time	Timmy T	Jam City
What It Takes	Aerosmith	Geffen
Your Baby Never Looked Good In Blue	Exposé	Arista

APRIL

⑥ Alright	Janet Jackson	A & M
Baby It's Tonight	Jude Cole	Reprise
Children Of The Night	Richard Marx	EMI
Coming Of Age	Damn Yankees	Warner Bros.
Deadbeat Club	The B-52's	Reprise
Do You Remember?	Phil Collins	Atlantic

1990

	Heaven Is A 4 Letter Word	Bad English	Epic
☆ ⑥	It Must Have Been Love	Roxette	EMI
	Notice Me	Nikki	Geffen
	Ooh La La (I Can't Get Over You)	Perfect Gentlemen	Columbia
⑫	Poison	Bell Biv Devoe	MCA
	Save Me	Fleetwood Mac	Warner Bros.
⑥	Turtle Power	Partners In Kryme	SBK
	U Can't Touch This	M. C. Hammer	Capitol
☆ ⑫	Vogue	Madonna	Sire

MAY

	Bad Of The Heart	George LaMond	Columbia
⑥	Cradle Of Love	Billy Idol	Chrysalis
	Doubleback	ZZ Top	Warner Bros.
⑫	Hold On	En Vogue	Atlantic
	I'll Be Your Shelter	Taylor Dayne	Arista
	Kiss This Thing Goodbye	del Amitri	A & M
⑥	Rub You The Right Way	Johnny Gill	Motown
	Shake	Andrew Ridgeley	Columbia
☆ ⑥	She Ain't Worth It	Glenn Medeiros (featuring Bobby Brown)	MCA
	Show Me	Howard Hewett	Elektra
☆ ⑫	Step By Step	New Kids on the Block	Columbia
	The Downeaster "Alexa"	Billy Joel	Columbia
⑫	The Power	Snap!	Arista
	When I'm Back On My Feet Again	Michael Bolton	Columbia
	You Can't Deny It	Lisa Stansfield	Arista

JUNE

	Across The River	Bruce Hornsby & the Range	RCA
	Could This Be Love	Seduction	A & M
	Don't Go Away Mad (Just Go Away)	Mötley Crüe	Elektra
⑥	Hanky Panky	Madonna	Sire
⑥	Have You Seen Her	M. C. Hammer	Capitol

	I Didn't Want To Need You	Heart	Capitol
☆	If Wishes Came True	Sweet Sensation	Atco
⑥	Jerk Out	The Time	Paisley Park
	Love And Emotion	Stevie B	LMR
	My Kinda Girl	Babyface	Solar
☆ ⑥	Release Me	Wilson Phillips	SBK
	Rise To It	Kiss	Mercury
	The Blues	Tony! Toni! Tone!	Wing
	The Girl I Used To Know	Brother Beyond	EMI
☆ ⑥	Vision Of Love	Mariah Carey	Columbia

JULY

	All I Do Is Think Of You	Troop	Atlantic
	All The Way	Calloway	Solar
⑥	Banned In The USA	Luke Featuring The 2 Live Crew	Luke
☆ ℗	Blaze Of Glory	Jon Bon Jovi	Mercury
⑥	Can't Stop	After 7	Virgin
	Can't Stop Falling Into Love	Cheap Trick	Epic
	Come Back To Me	Janet Jackson	A & M
	Don't You Come Cryin'	Linear	Atlantic
⑥	Epic	Faith No More	Slash
	Hearts In Trouble	Chicago	DGC
	La Raza	Kid Frost	Virgin
	Oh Girl	Paul Young	Columbia
	Stranger To Love	St. Paul	Atlantic
	Tell Me Something	Indecent Obsession	MCA
⑥	Unskinny Bop	Poison	Enigma

AUGUST

	All I'm Missing Is You	Glenn Medeiros (featuring Ray Parker, Jr.)	MCA
	Crazy	The Boys	Motown
	Georgia On My Mind	Michael Bolton	Columbia
	Giving You The Benefit	Pebbles	MCA
	Heart Of Stone	Taylor Dayne	Arista
	I Won't Give Up On You	TKA	Tommy Boy
	Lies	En Vogue	Atlantic
	My, My, My	Johnny Gill	Motown
	Policy Of Truth	Depeche Mode	Sire
	Romeo	Dino	Island
	Say A Prayer	Breathe	A & M
	Something Happened On The Way To Heaven	Phil Collins	Atlantic
⑥	Thieves In The Temple	Prince	Paisley Park
	This Is The Right Time	Lisa Stansfield	Arista
	Tonight	New Kids on the Block	Columbia

SEPTEMBER

☆ ⑥	Black Cat	Janet Jackson	A & M
⑥	Feels Good	Tony! Toni! Tone!	Wing

⑥ High Enough	Damn Yankees	Warner Bros.
☆ ⑫ Ice Ice Baby	Vanilla Ice	SBK
☆ ⑥ Love Takes Time	Mariah Carey	Columbia
More Than Words Can Say	Alias	EMI
⑥ Pray	M. C. Hammer	Capitol
☆ Praying For Time	George Michael	Columbia
Same Ol' Situation (S.O.S.)	Mötley Crüe	Elektra
So Close	Daryl Hall & John Oates	Arista
Stranded	Heart	Capitol
⑥ Suicide Blonde	INXS	Atlantic
The Boomin' System	L. L. Cool J	Def Jam
⑫ Unchained Melody	The Righteous Brothers	Curb
Violence Of Summer (Love's Taking Over)	Duran Duran	Capitol

OCTOBER

And So It Goes	Billy Joel	Columbia
☆ ⑥ Because I Love You (The Postman Song)	Stevie B	LMR
Biscuit's In The House	Biscuit	Columbia
Each And Every Time	Sweet Sensation	Atco
Fairweather Friend	Johnny Gill	Motown
⑥ Freedom	George Michael	Columbia
⑫ From A Distance	Bette Midler	Atlantic
Impulsive	Wilson Phillips	SBK
☆ ⑥ I'm Your Baby Tonight	Whitney Houston	Arista
Love Is A Rock	REO Speedwagon	Epic
Miracle	Jon Bon Jovi	Mercury
Misunderstanding	Al B. Sure!	Warner Bros.
My Love Is A Fire	Donny Osmond	Capitol
⑥ Something To Believe In	Poison	Enigma
Unchained Melody	The Righteous Brothers	Verve

NOVEMBER

Anything Is Possible	Debbie Gibson	Atlantic
For You	The Outfield	MCA
Gentle	Dino	Island
☆ ⑫ Gonna Make You Sweat	C & C Music Factory (featuring Freedom Williams)	Columbia
Hang In Long Enough	Phil Collins	Atlantic
I'm Not In Love	Will to Power	Epic
I Wanna Get With U	Guy	MCA
☆ ⑫ Justify My Love	Madonna	Sire
☆ ⑥ Love Will Never Do (Without You)	Janet Jackson	A & M
New Power Generation	Prince	Paisley Park
New York Minute	Don Henley	Geffen
One And Only Man	Steve Winwood	Virgin
⑥ Sensitivity	Ralph Tresvant	MCA
The Shoop Shoop Song (It's In His Kiss)	Cher	Geffen
World In My Eyes	Depeche Mode	Sire

499

Little Caesar (photo: *Anastasia Pantsios*)

DECEMBER

☆ ⑥ All The Man That I Need	Whitney Houston	Arista
⑥ Around The Way Girl	L. L. Cool J	Def Jam
Get Here	Oleta Adams	Fontana
House Full Of Reasons	Jude Cole	Reprise
I'll Give All My Love To You	Keith Sweat	Vintertainment
I Saw Red	Warrant	Columbia
It Never Rains (In Southern California)	Tony! Toni! Tone!	Wing
Moneytalks	AC/DC	Atco
⑥ Play That Funky Music	Vanilla Ice	SBK
⑥ Round And Round	Tevin Campbell	Paisley Park
The Swalk	Notorious	DGC
This House	Tracie Spencer	Capitol
This Is Ponderous	2NU	Atlantic
Use It Up And Wear It Out	Pat & Mick	Charisma
Where Does My Heart Beat Now	Celine Dion	Epic

TOP SINGLES OF 1990

⑥ Another Day In Paradise	Phil Collins	Atlantic
℗ Blaze Of Glory	Jon Bon Jovi	Mercury
⑥ Cradle Of Love	Billy Idol	Chrysalis
℗ Hold On	En Vogue	Atlantic
⑥ Hold On	Wilson Phillips	SBK
⑥ It Must Have Been Love	Roxette	EMI
℗ Nothing Compares 2 U	Sinead O'Connor	Ensign
℗ Poison	Bell Biv Devoe	MCA
⑥ Vision Of Love	Mariah Carey	Columbia
℗ Vogue	Madonna	Sire

TOP ALBUMS OF 1990

℗ . . . But Seriously	Phil Collins	Atlantic
℗ Cosmic Thing	The B-52's	Reprise
℗ Dr. Feelgood	Mötley Crüe	Elektra
℗ The End Of Innocence	Don Henley	Geffen
℗ Forever Your Girl	Paula Abdul	Virgin
℗ Janet Jackson's Rhythm Nation 1814	Janet Jackson	A & M
℗ Please Hammer Don't Hurt 'Em	M. C. Hammer	Capitol

℗ **Pump**	Aerosmith	Geffen
℗ **Soul Provider**	Michael Bolton	Columbia
℗ **Storm Front**	Billy Joel	Columbia

GRAMMY WINNERS IN 1990

The Grammys were televised by CBS from Radio City Music Hall in New York City, on Wednesday, February 20, 1991. Gary Shandling was the host.

Record of the Year: "Another Day In Paradise," Phil Collins (Atlantic)
Song of the Year: "From A Distance," Bette Midler (music and lyrics by Julie Gold)
Album of the Year: *Back On The Block,* Quincy Jones (Qwest)
Best Pop Vocal Performance, Female: "Vision Of Love," Mariah Carey (Columbia)
Best Pop Vocal Performance, Male: "Oh, Pretty Woman," Roy Orbison (Virgin)
Best Pop Vocal Performance, Duo or Group: "All My Life," Linda Ronstadt & Aaron Neville (Elektra)
Best Pop Instrumental: "Twin Peaks Theme," Angelo Badalamenti (Warner Bros.)
Best Rock Vocal Performance, Female: "Black Velvet," Alannah Myles (Atlantic)
Best Rock Vocal Performance, Male: "Bad Love," Eric Clapton (Duck)
Best Rock Vocal Performance, Duo or Group: "Janie's Got A Gun," Aerosmith (Geffen)
Best Rock Instrumental: "D/FW," The Vaughan Brothers (Epic)
Best New Artist: Mariah Carey
Best R & B Performance, Female: "Compositions," Anita Baker (Elektra)
Best R & B Performance, Male: "Here And Now," Luther Vandross (Epic)
Best R & B Performance, Duo or Group: "I'll Be Good To You," Ray Charles & Chaka Khan (Qwest)
Best R & B Song: "U Can't Touch This," Rick James, Alonzo Miller, and M. C. Hammer (Capitol)
Best Hard Rock Vocal or Instrumental: "Time's Up," Living Colour (Epic)
Best Metal Vocal or Instrumental: "Stone Cold Crazy," Metallica (Elektra)
Best Rap Solo Performance: "U Can't Touch This," M. C. Hammer (Capitol)
Best Rap Performance, Duo or Group: "Back On The Block," Ice-T, Melle Mel, Big Daddy Kane, and Kool Moe Dee, Quincy D. III, and Quincy Jones (Qwest)
Best Comedy Performance: "P.D.Q. Bach: Oedipus Tex & Other Choral Calamities," Professor Peter Schickele (Telarc)
Best Song Written for a Motion Picture or Television: "Under The Sea" (from the movie, *The Little Mermaid*), music by Alan Menken and lyrics by Howard Ashman (Virgin)
Best New Age: *Mark Ishman,* Mark Ishman (Virgin)
Best Music Video, Short Form: *Opposites Attract,* Paula Abdul (Virgin)
Best Music Video, Long Form: *Please Hammer Don't Hurt 'Em—The Movie,* M. C. Hammer (Capitol)

ROCK AND ROLL HALL OF FAME INDUCTEES

The fifth induction ceremony was held on Wednesday, January 17, 1990, at the Waldorf Astoria Hotel in New York City.

PERFORMERS

Inductee (Born and Died)	Debut Single (Year)	Label
Hank Ballard (November 18, 1936–)	Get It (1953) (with The Royals)	Federal

Bobby Darin (Walden Robert Cassotto) (May 14, 1936–December 20, 1973)	Splish Splash (1958)	Atco
The Four Seasons (Frankie Valli [Francis Castelluccio]: May 3, 1937– ; Nick Massi [Nicholas Macioci]: September 19, 1935– ; Tommy DeVito: June 19, 1936– ; Bob Gaudio: November 17, 1942–)	Sherry (1962)	Vee-Jay
The Four Tops (Levi Stubbs: June 6, 1936– ; Abdul "Duke" Fakir: December 26, 1935– ; Renaldo "Obie" Benson: June 14, 1936– ; Lawrence Payton: March 2, 1938–)	Baby I Need Your Loving (1964)	Motown
The Kinks (Raymond Douglas Davies: June 21, 1944– ; David Russel Davies: February 3, 1947– ; Peter Quaife: December 27, 1943– ; Mick Avory: February 15, 1944–)	You Really Got Me (1964)	Reprise
The Platters (Tony Williams: April 5, 1928–August 14, 1992; Zola Taylor: March 17, 1938– ; David Lynch: July 3, 1929–January 2, 1981; Paul Robi: August 20, 1931–January 31, 1989; Herb Reed: August 7, 1938–)	Only You (1955)	Mercury
Simon & Garfunkel (Paul Simon: November 5, 1941– ; Arthur Garfunkel: October 13, 1942–)	The Sounds of Silence (1965)	Columbia
The Who (Roger Daltry: March 1, 1944– ; Peter Townshend: May 19, 1945– ; John Entwistle: September 10, 1944– ; Keith Moon: August 23, 1946–September 7, 1978)	I Can't Explain (1965)	Decca

NONPERFORMERS

Gerry Goffin & Carole King (Gerry Goffin: February 11, 1939–   ; Carole King: February 9, 1941–   ) Husband and wife song writing team who, during their peak years, 1961–1963, wrote hundreds of hits, including "Chains," "Hey Girl," "The Loco-Motion," "Take Good Care Of My Baby," "Will You Love Me Tomorrow," "Go Away Little Girl," and "One Fine Day."

Holland-Dozier-Holland (Brian Holland: February 15, 1941–   ; Lamont Dozier: June 16, 1941–   ; Eddie Holland: October 30, 1939–   ) The song writing team of the Motown sound who wrote "Stop! In The Name Of Love," "Heat Wave," "Reach Out I'll Be There," "How Sweet It Is," "Baby Love," "I Can't Help Myself," and hundreds more.

EARLY INFLUENCES

Louis Armstrong (August 4, 1900–July 6, 1971) Born in the "Cradle of Jazz," New Orleans, this legendary trumpeter became America's "Jazz Ambassador."

Charlie Christian (July 29, 1916–March 2, 1942) The man who pioneered the amplified guitar in the late 1930s and used this instrument to pave the way for rock 'n' roll.

Ma Rainey (April 26, 1886–December 22, 1939) Ma Rainey (Gertrude Pridgett) was the Queen of blues singers.

DEATHS IN 1990

MUSIC PERFORMERS AND MUSIC INDUSTRY NOTABLES WHO DIED IN 1990

Jimmy Van Heusen (songwriter), Tuesday, February 6 (extended illness; 77)

Del Shannon, Thursday, February 8 (self-inflicted gunshot wound; 50)

Johnnie Ray, Saturday, February 24 (liver failure; 63)

Cornell Gunther (The Coasters), Monday, February 26 (gunshot wound; 53)

"Big" Al Sears (saxophonist), Friday, March 23 (cancer; 80)

Sarah Vaughan, Tuesday, April 3 (lung cancer; 66)

Thurston Harris, Saturday, April 14 (heart attack; 58)

Dexter Gordon (saxophonist), Wednesday, April 25 (kidney failure; 67)

Wesley Rose (country music giant), Thursday, April 26 (long illness; 72)

Sergio Franchi, Tuesday, May 1 (cancer; 57)

Sammy Davis, Jr., Wednesday, May 16 (throat cancer; 64)

Morris Levy, Monday, May 21 (cancer; 62)

Stiv Bators (The Dead Boys), Monday, June 4 (hit by car; 40)

Clyde McCoy, Monday, June 11 (Alzheimer's disease; 86)

June Christy, Thursday, June 21 (kidney failure; 64)

Corinthian "Kripp" Johnson (The Del Vikings), Friday, June 22 (prostate cancer; 57)

Snooky Lanson (Roy Landman), Monday, July 2 (lung cancer; 76)

Bobby Day (Robert Byrd), Sunday, July 15 (cancer; 60)

Brent Mydland (The Grateful Dead), Thursday, July 26 (unknown causes; 38)

Lew Dewitt (The Statler Brothers), Wednesday, August 15 (long-term illness; 52)

Pearl Bailey, Friday, August 17 (heart failure; 72)

David Rose, Thursday, August 23 (heart disease; 80)

Stevie Ray Vaughan, Monday, August 27 (helicopter crash; 35)

Tom Fogerty, Thursday, September 6 (respiratory failure; 48)

Leonard Bernstein, Sunday, October 14 (emphysema; 72)

Art Blakey (drummer), Tuesday, October 16 (lung cancer; 71)

Xavier Cugat, Friday, October 26 (heart attack; 90)

Mary Martin, Saturday, November 3 (cancer; 76)

Ronnie Dyson, Saturday, November 10 (heart failure; 40)

Aaron Copland, Sunday, December 2 (respiratory failure; 90)

Dee Clark, Friday, December 7 (heart attack; 52)

OTHERS WHO DIED IN 1990

Rev. Ralph Abernathy
George Allen
Eve Arden
Joan Bennett
Capucine
Tony Conigliaro
Bill Cullen
Bob Cummings
Howard Duff
Irene Dunne
Douglas Edwards
Rene Enriquez
Charles Farrell
Malcolm Forbes
Frederick of Hollywood (Mellinger)
Greta Garbo
Ava Gardner

Jack Gilford
Paulette Goddard
Ray Goulding
Rocky Graziano
Alan Hale, Jr.
Halston (Roy Frowick)
Rusty Hamer
Tom Harmon
Rex Harrison
Jim Henson
Jill Ireland
Arthur Kennedy
Mike Mazurki
Gary Merrill
Bronco Nagurski
William Paley
David Rappaport

Martin Ritt
Barbara Stanwyck
Vic Tayback

Terry-Thomas
Irving Wallace
Ryan White

MOVIES OF 1990

MOVIES FEATURING A POP MUSIC SOUNDTRACK

Cry Baby   *Stars:* Johnny Depp, Amy Locane, Polly Bergen, Iggy Pop, Ricki Lake, Traci Lords, Troy Donahue, Joey Heatherton, David Nelson, Patricia Hearst, Willem Dafoe. Features '50s tunes like "Gee" by the Crows, "I'm So Young" by the Students, and "Mr. Sandman" by the Chordettes.

Ghost   *Stars:* Patrick Swayze, Demi Moore, Whoopi Goldberg, Tony Goldwyn, Rick Aviles. Features "Unchained Melody" by the Righteous Brothers, which becomes a '90s classic for younger people.

Goodfellas   *Stars:* Robert DeNiro, Ray Liotta, Joe Pesci, Lorraine Bracco, Paul Sorvino, Frank DiLeo. Henny Youngman, Jerry Vale, and Bobby Vinton's son do cameos. Songs include "Speedo" by the Cadillacs, "Can't We Be Sweethearts" by the Cleftones, "Rags To Riches" by Tony Bennett, "Stardust" by Billy Ward and the Dominoes, "Life Is But A Dream" by the Harptones, "Unchained Melody" by Vito & the Salutations, and "Layla" by Derek and the Dominoes.

Home Alone   *Stars:* Macaulay Culkin, Joe Pesci, Daniel Stern, John Heard, John Candy, Catherine O'Hara. Features Christmas classics like "White Christmas" by the Drifters, "Rocking Around The Christmas Tree" by Brenda Lee, and "Run Rudolph Run" by Chuck Berry.

Mo' Better Blues   *Stars:* Denzel Washington, Spike Lee, Wesley Snipes, Giancarlo Esposito, John Turturro, Ruben Blades, Abbey Lincoln. Branford Marsalis quartet provides the music for the soundtrack.

My Blue Heaven   *Stars:* Steve Martin, Rick Moranis, Joan Cusack, Carol Kane, William Hickey, Daniel Stern. Fats Domino's "My Blue Heaven" is title song of film.

Mystery Train   *Stars:* Masatoshi Nagase, Youki Kudoh, Rick Aviles, Cinque Lee, Screamin' Jay Hawkins. Joe Strummer and Rufus Thomas in cameos. Songs by Elvis Presley include "Mystery Train" and "Blue Moon."

Vanilla Ice (photo: *Anastasia Pantsios*)

Pretty Woman *Stars:* Richard Gere, Julia Roberts, Ralph Bellamy, Jason Alexander, Hector Elizondo. Songs by Roxette and Go West, along with Roy Orbison's "Oh, Pretty Woman."

OTHER POPULAR MOVIES OF 1990

Another 48 Hours
Arachnophobia
Avalon
Bad Influence
Betsy's Wedding
Blaze
Cadillac Man
Coupe De Ville
Dances with Wolves
Days of Thunder
Delta Force 5
Dick Tracy
Die Hard 2
Fire Birds
Flatliners
The Freshman
Glory
Godfather III
Hard to Kill
Havana
Heart Condition
The Hunt for Red October
Internal Affairs
Joe Versus the Volcano
Marked for Death

Memphis Belle
Miami Blues
Miller's Crossing
Misery
Mr. Destiny
Narrow Margin
Pacific Heights
Predator 2
Presumed Innocent
Q & A
Quick Change
Quigley Down Under
Revenge
Reversal of Fortune
Robo Cop 2
Rocky V
The Rookie
The Russia House
Sibling Rivalry
Taking Care of Business
Tango and Cash
The Two Jakes
Total Recall
White Palace

ACADEMY AWARD WINNERS OF 1990

Best Actor: Jeremy Irons, *Reversal of Fortune*
Best Actress: Kathy Bates, *Misery*
Best Picture: *Dances with Wolves*
Best Original Song: "Sooner or Later (I Always Get My Man)," *Dick Tracy* (music and lyrics by Stephen Sondheim)

ROCK ON ALMANAC

TOP TELEVISION SHOWS OF 1990

A Different World
America's Funniest Home Videos
Cheers
The Cosby Show
Empty Nest

The Golden Girls
Murphy Brown
NFL Monday Night Football
Roseanne
60 Minutes

1991

ROCK ON ALMANAC

NEWS HIGHLIGHTS OF 1991

⇨ On January 16, the outbreak of war in the Persian Gulf begins with "Operation Desert Storm," as U.S.-led air units launch a devastating series of air attacks against Iraq's command and control facilities. The U.S. emerges as the leader of a 28-nation coalition, backed by the United Nations, that forces Iraq out of Kuwait.

⇨ Pan American World Airways files for bankruptcy.

⇨ Soviet President Mikhail Gorbachev is asked by the President of the Russian Federation, Boris Yeltsin, to resign.

⇨ Congress approves a $78-billion package to help bail out insolvent savings and loan associations.

⇨ In Los Angeles, Rodney Glenn King is stopped by police and asked to get out of his car and lie on the pavement, where he is repeatedly beaten by them with nightsticks. The entire two-minute ordeal is captured on video tape.

⇨ On April 4, a helicopter and a chartered plane collide over a suburb of Philadelphia, killing all five aboard including Senator John Heinz of Pennsylvania. The next day, former U.S. Senator John Tower of Texas is among 23 people killed in a commercial plane crash in Brunswick, Georgia.

⇨ Thurgood Marshall, the only black on the U.S. Supreme Court, announces his retirement.

⇨ Boris Yeltsin, with about 60 percent of the vote, is elected President of Russia.

⇨ President George Bush lifts economic sanctions imposed on South Africa by Congress in 1986.

⇨ Charges against Oliver North in the Iran-*contra* affair, which began in 1986, are finally dropped.

⇨ A fire at a chicken processing plant in Hamlet, North Carolina, kills 25 and injures 55.

⇨ The Senate begins hearings on 43-year-old Judge Clarence Thomas to serve on the U.S. Supreme Court. Judge Thomas is accused of sexual harassment on the job by 35-year-old Anita Hill, a professor of law at the University of Oklahoma. Thomas is eventually confirmed by the Senate 52–48.

SPORTS WINNERS

Baseball   The Minnesota Twins beat the Atlanta Braves 4 games to 3.

Football
NFC: The Washington Redskins beat the Detroit Lions 41–10 in Washington, D.C.
AFC: The Buffalo Bills beat the Denver Broncos 10–7 in Buffalo.
Super Bowl XXVI: The Washington Redskins beat the Buffalo Bills 37–24 on January 26, 1992, in Minneapolis, Minnesota.

Basketball   The Chicago Bulls win the NBA Championship for a second year in a row, beating the Portland Trailblazers 4 games to 2.

Hockey   The Pittsburgh Penguins win the Stanley Cup for a second year in a row, beating the Chicago Black Hawks 4 games to 0.

MUSIC HIGHLIGHTS 1991

⇨ From January 18–26, more than 360,000 fans attend the "Rock in Rio II" Music Festival in Rio De Janeiro. Performing are George Michael, Guns N' Roses, Prince, A-Ha, Santana, Judas Priest, Lisa Stansfield, Queensryche, Megadeth, and Deee-Lite.

⇨ Rock 'N' Roll Hall of Famer James Brown is granted parole on February 27 in South Carolina after serving two and a half years of a six-year sentence for assault.

⇨ With the release of the new album *Union*, Jon Anderson, Bill Bruford, Rick Wakeman, Stephen Howe, Tony Kaye, Trevor Rabin, Chris Squire, and Alan White, reunite as "Yes" for this Arista album and world-wide tour, ending a two-year fight over the group's name.

⇨ On March 20 rock legend Eric Clapton loses his 4-year-old son, Connor, when the child falls to his death from an apartment window in New York City.

⇨ Atlantic Records releases a nine-CD collection called *The Complete Stax-Volt Singles, 1959–1968,* containing a complete catalog of hits from these legendary soul labels.

⇨ Bob Dylan turns 50 on May 24th, and the music world remembers with birthday wishes in the media.

⇨ Dick Clark releases a home video, *The Rock & Roll Collection,* of Golden Greats containing four tapes with 55 original full-length performances spanning four decades of rock's greatest memories.

⇨ On June 8, Bruce Springsteen marries his long-time girlfriend Patti Scialfa in Los Angeles.

⇨ Rapper Joseph Simmons of Run-D.M.C. is charged with the rape of a 22-year-old woman after a concert in Cleveland, Ohio.

⇨ On August 3, at New York City's Madison Square Garden, 10,000 fans hear the world premiere of Metallica's new album, *Metallica,* during a two-hour event where they listened to the band's album in its entirety, along with video interviews and other Metallica footage.

⇨ On August 15, Paul Simon performs in front of 750,000 fans at a free concert in New York's Central Park. It is televised by HBO, with proceeds going to help maintain Central Park.

⇨ September sees the release of Guns N' Roses blockbuster two albums, *Use Your Illusion I & II* and Garth Brooks' *Ropin' the Wind.*

⇨ Columbia Records releases a deluxe boxed set of four compact discs with 90 songs, a chronological retrospective on Barbra Streisand called *Just for the Record.*

⇨ AC/DC, Metallica, the Black Crowes, and Pantera perform on September 28 at a free, open-air concert at the Tushino Air Field in Moscow along with Russian rock groups.

⇨ On October 24, by mayoral proclamation, "Fats Domino Day" is established in New Orleans, coinciding with the release of a four-CD boxed set of his musical career called *They Call Me The Fat Man—Antoine 'Fats' Domino, the Legendary Imperial Recordings.*

⇨ On November 3, at the Polo Fields in San Francisco's Golden Gate State Park, 350,000 fans gather in "Laughter, Love & Music," a tribute to concert promoter Bill Graham, who was killed in a helicopter crash on October 25. Performing are the Grateful Dead, Santana, John Fogerty, Crosby, Stills, Nash & Young, Jackson Browne, Joan Baez, and Los Lobos.

⇨ The boxed set, *Phil Spector—Back to Mono (1958–1969),* a four-CD, 73-song retrospective, is released.

⇨ *The Beatles—The First U.S. Visit,* a video of their February 1964 visit to the U.S., is released.

⇨ Michael Jackson's new album, *Dangerous,* and the new video and single from the album, "Black And White," are released.

DEBUT ARTISTS OF 1991

Aftershock	Brandon
A Lighter Shade of Brown (featuring Teardrop & Shiro)	Cartouche
Angelica	Shawn Christopher
Another Bad Creation	Chubb Rock
B Angie B	Marc Cohn
B.G. the Prince of Rap	Color Me Badd
Big Audio Dynamite II	The Commitments
Bingo Boys	Corina
Blue Train	Coro
Boyz II Men	Crash Test Dummies
Daryl Braithwaite	Cut 'N' Move
The Brand New Heavies (featuring N' Dea Davenport)	Damian Dame

ROCK ON ALMANAC

Daisey Dee	Laissez Faire
Cathy Dennis	The LA's
DJ Quik	The Latin Alliance (featuring War)
D'Zyre	Latour
Stacy Earl	Londonbeat
EMF	Marky Mark & the Funky Bunch
Enigma	M.C. Breed & D.F.C.
Ex-Girlfriend	MC Skat Kat & the Stray Mob
Extreme	Lisette Melendez
Billy Falcon	Monie Love
The Farm	Gary Moore
Father M.C.	Natural Selection
Firehouse	Naughty by Nature
Lisa Fischer	Troy Newman
Gerardo	Nirvana
Geto Boys	Oaktown's 3.5.7
Lonnie Gordon	Or-N-More (featuring Father M.C.)
Grandmaster Slice	PC Quest
Jasmine Guy	The Peace Choir
Guys Next Door	Cece Peniston
Happy Mondays	P.M. Dawn
Chesney Hawkes	Pretty in Pink
Heavy D. & the Boyz	Public Enemy
Hi-C	Queensryche
Hi-Five	Shabba Ranks (featuring Maxi Priest)
Susanna Hoffs	The Rebel Pebbles
Icy Blu	Red Hot Chili Peppers
Russ Irwin	The Rembrandts
Jesse Jaymes	Riff
Jellyfish	Right Said Fred
Jesus Jones	Kane Roberts
Jinny	RTZ
Jodeci	Rude Boys
Jomanda	Rythm Syndicate
Keedy	Richie Sambora
Tara Kemp	Sandee
Kid 'N Play	Fred Scheider
King of the Hill	Seal
The KLF	The Shamen
K.M.C. KRU	Shanice

The Simpson's (featuring Bart & Homer)
Kym Sims
Michael W. Smith
Steelheart
Stereo MC's
David A. Stewart Introducing Candy Dulfer
Curtis Stigers
The Storm
Tesla
3rd Bass
Thunder

Titiyo
Ralph Tresvant
Triology
The Triplets
Trixter
Voices of the Beehive
Voices That Care
Keith Washington
Crystal Waters
Yasmin
Yo-Yo (featuring Ice Cube)

1991

HITS OF 1991

JANUARY

	All This Time	Sting	A & M
	Chasin' The Wind	Chicago	Reprise
☆	Coming Out Of The Dark	Gloria Estefan	Epic
	Here Comes The Hammer	M.C. Hammer	Capitol
⑥	Hold You Tight	Tara Kemp	Giant
⑥	Iesha	Another Bad Creation	Motown
⑥	I'll Do 4 You	Father M.C.	Uptown
	I've Been Waiting For You	Guys Next Door	SBK
	Night And Day	Bette Midler	Atlantic
	Remember My Name	House of Lords	Simmons
	Signs	Tesla	Geffen
☆ ⑥	Someday	Mariah Carey	Columbia
	Something In My Heart	Michel'Le	Ruthless
	Waiting For Love	Alias	EMI
	Waiting For That Day	George Michael	Columbia

FEBRUARY

	Another Sleepless Night	Shawn Christopher	Arista
☆	Baby Baby	Amy Grant	A & M
	Call It Poison	The Escape Club	Atlantic
	Cry For Help	Rick Astley	RCA
	Easy Come Easy Go	Winger	Atlantic
	How To Dance	Bingo Boys	Atlantic
	I'll Be By Your Side	Stevie B	LMR
☆ ⑥	I've Been Thinking About You	Londonbeat	Radioactive
	Just The Way It Is Baby	The Rembrandts	Atco
	Let's Chill	Guy	Uptown
	Mercy Mercy Me (The Ecology)/I Want You	Robert Palmer	EMI
	Mother's Pride	George Michael	Columbia
	Stone Cold Gentleman	Ralph Tresvant	MCA
	Who Said I Would	Phil Collins	Atlantic
☆	You're In Love	Wilson Phillips	SBK

MARCH

	Another Like My Lover	Jasmine Guy	Warner Bros.
	Give Peace A Chance	The Peace Choir	Virgin

511

⑥ Here We Go	C & C Music Factory/ Freedom Williams/ Zelma Davis	Columbia
I Touch Myself	Divinyls	Virgin
It's A Shame (My Sister)	Monie Love	Warner Bros.
☆ Joyride	Roxette	EMI
☆ ⑥ More Than Words	Extreme	A & M
Rescue Me	Madonna	Sire
Rhythm Of My Heart	Rod Stewart	Warner Bros.
Silent Lucidity	Queensryche	EMI
⑥ The Star Spangled Banner	Whitney Houston	Arista
Touch Me (All Night Long)	Cathy Dennis	Polydor
⑥ Voices That Care	Voices That Care	Giant
Written All Over Your Face	Rude Boys	Atlantic
You Don't Have To Go Home Tonight	The Triplets	Mercury

APRIL

Bitter Tears	INXS	Atlantic
Come Again	Damn Yankees	Warner Bros.
Couple Days Off	Huey Lewis & the News	EMI
How Much Is Enough	The Fixx	Impact
☆ I Don't Wanna Cry	Mariah Carey	Columbia
⑥ Losing My Religion	R.E.M.	Warner Bros.
Love Is A Wonderful Thing	Michael Bolton	Columbia
⑥ Mama Said Knock You Out	L. L. Cool J	Def Jam
Miracle	Whitney Houston	Arista
New Jack Hustler (Nino's Theme)	Ice-T	Giant
Playground	Another Bad Creation	Motown
Power Of Love/Love Power	Luther Vandross	Epic
Seal Our Fate	Gloria Estefan	Epic
What Comes Naturally	Sheena Easton	MCA
Whatever You Want	Tony!Toni!Tone!	Wing

MAY

A Better Love	Londonbeat	Radioactive
⑥ Gypsy Woman (She's Homeless)	Crystal Waters	Mercury
⑥ I'll Be There	The Escape Club	Atlantic
Kissing You	Keith Washington	Q West
Nights Like This	After 7	Virgin
Over And Over	Timmy T	Quality
Part Of Me, Part Of You	Glenn Frey	MCA
Piece Of My Heart	Tara Kemp	Giant
Place In This World	Michael W. Smith	Reunion
☆ ⑥ Rush Rush	Paula Abdul	Virgin
See The Lights	Simple Minds	A & M
This Time Make It Funky	Tracie Spencer	Capitol
We Want The Funk	Gerardo	Interscope
Where The Streets Have No Name	Pet Shop Boys	EMI
You Can't Play With My Yo-Yo	Yo-Yo (featuring Ice Cube)	East West

Richie Sambora (photo: Anastasia Pantsios)

1991

JUNE

Crazy	Seal	Sire
Every Heartbeat	Amy Grant	A & M
☆ ℗ (Everything I Do) I Do It For You	Bryan Adams	A & M
Fading Like A Flower (Every Time You Leave)	Roxette	EMI
Forever Amo'r	D'Zyre	Atlantic
☆ ⑥ Good Vibrations	Marky Mark & the Funky Bunch/ Loleatta Holloway	Interscope
I Can't Wait Another Minute	Hi-Five	Jive
It Ain't Over Til It's Over	Lenny Kravitz	Virgin
Love And Understanding	Cher	Geffen
⑥ Love Of A Lifetime	Firehouse	Epic
℗ Motownphilly	Boyz II Men	Motown
My Body Says Yes	Titiyo	Arista
P.A.S.S.I.O.N.	Rythm Syndicate	Impact
℗ Summertime	D.J. Jazzy Jeff & the Fresh Prince	Jive
The Dream Is Still Alive	Wilson Phillips	SBK

JULY

☆ ⑥ I Adore Mi Amor	Color Me Badd	Giant
I Don't Wanna See You	Michael Morales	Wing
It Hit Me Like A Hammer	Huey Lewis & the News	EMI
Just Like You	Robbie Nevil	EMI
My Name Is Not Susan	Whitney Houston	Arista
⑥ Pop Goes The Weasel	3rd Bass	Def Jam
Pump It (Nice An' Hard)	Icy Blu	Giant
Shiny Happy People	R.E.M.	Warner Bros.
The Motown Song	Rod Stewart	Warner Bros.
☆ The Promise Of A New Day	Paula Abdul	Captive
⑥ Things That Make You Go HMMMM . . .	C & C Music Factory/ F. Williams	Columbia
Time, Love And Tenderness	Michael Bolton	Columbia
Too Many Walls	Cathy Dennis	Polydor
⑥ Unforgettable	Natalie Cole	Elektra
⑥ You Could Be Mine	Guns N' Roses	Geffen

ROCK ON ALMANAC

AUGUST

	Do Anything	Natural Selection	East West
☆ ⑥	Emotions	Mariah Carey	Columbia
⑥	Enter Sandman	Metallica	Elektra
⑥	Gett Off	Prince and the New Power Generation	Paisley Park
	Hole Hearted	Extreme	A & M
	Kiss Them For Me	Siouxsie & the Banshees	Geffen
	Love . . . Thy Will Be Done	Martika	Columbia
	Real Real Real	Jesus Jones	SBK
☆	Romantic	Karyn White	Warner Bros.
	Running Back To You	Vanessa Williams	Wing
	Straight To Your Heart	Bad English	Epic
	The One And Only	Chesney Hawkes	Chrysalis
	The Real Love	Bob Seger & the Silver Bullet Band	Capitol
	The Truth	Tami Show	RCA
	Walk Through Fire	Bad Company	Atco

SEPTEMBER

	Ain't No Future In Yo Fronting	M.C. Breed & D.F.C.	S.D.E.G.
⑥	Can't Stop This Thing We Started	Bryan Adams	A & M
☆ ⑥	Cream	Prince and the New Power Generation	Paisley Park
⑥	Don't Cry	Guns N' Roses	Geffen
	Heaven In The Back Seat	Eddie Money	Columbia
	Hey Donna	Rythm Syndicate	Impact
⑥	It's So Hard To Say Goodbye To Yesterday	Boys II Men	Motown
	Lies	EMF	EMI
℗	O.P.P.	Naughty by Nature	Tommy Boy
	Primal Scream	Mötley Crüe	Elektra
	Save Me	Lisa Fischer	Elektra
	Set The Night To Music	Roberta Flack (with Maxi Priest)	Atlantic
	Something Got Me Started	Simply Red	East West
	Sometimes (It's A Bitch)	Stevie Nicks	Modern
	That's What Love Is For	Amy Grant	A & M

OCTOBER

	Angel Baby	Angelica	Quality
	Blowing Kisses In The Wind	Paula Abdul	Captive
⑥	Can't Truss It	Public Enemy	Def Jam
	Forever My Lady	Jodeci	Uptown
	Get A Leg Up	John Mellencamp	Mercury
	Housecall	Shabba Ranks (featuring Maxi Priest)	Epic
	Live For Loving You	Gloria Estefan	Epic
⑥	Mind Playing Tricks On Me	Geto Boys	Rap-A-Lot
⑥	Ring My Bell	D.J. Jazzy Jeff & the Fresh Prince	Jive
☆ ⑥	Set Adrift On Memory Bliss	P.M. Dawn	Island

Street Of Dreams	Nia Peeples	Charisma
Superman's Song	Crash Test Dummies	Arista
Top Of The World	Van Halen	Warner Bros.
Try A Little Tenderness	The Commitments	MCA
☆ When A Man Loves A Woman	Michael Bolton	Columbia

NOVEMBER

☆ ⓖ All 4 Love	Color Me Badd	Giant
☆ ⓟ Black Or White	Michael Jackson	Epic
Can't Let Go	Mariah Carey	Columbia
Home Sweet Home	Mötley Crüe	Elektra
Keep Coming Back	Richard Marx	Capitol
Keep It Comin'	Keith Sweat	Elektra
ⓖ Kiss You Back	Digital Underground	Tommy Boy
Mysterious Ways	U2	Island
No Son Of Mine	Genesis	Atlantic
Pop That Coochie	2 Live Crew	Luke
Shot Of Poison	Lita Ford	RCA
The Fly	U2	Island
Too Blind To See It	Kym Sims	I.D.
ⓟ 2 Legit 2 Quit	Hammer	Capitol
ⓖ Wildside	Marky Mark & the Funky Bunch	Interscope

DECEMBER

ⓖ Addams Groove	Hammer	Capitol
All Through The Night	Tone-Loc	Delicious Vinyl
Diamonds And Pearls	Prince & the New Power Generation	Paisley Park
☆ ⓖ Don't Let The Sun Go Down On Me	George Michael (with Elton John)	Columbia
Every Road Leads Back To You	Bette Midler	Atlantic
Give It Away	Red Hot Chili Peppers	Warner Bros.
Hearts Don't Think (They Feel)	Natural Selection	East West
I'll Get By	Eddie Money	Columbia

Queensryche (l to r: Geoff Tate, Chris DeGarmo; photo: Anastasia Pantsios)

☆ ℗ I'm Too Sexy	Right Said Fred	Charisma
Live And Let Die	Guns N' Roses	Geffen
℗ Smells Like Teen Spirit	Nirvana	DGC
There Will Never Be Another Tonite	Bryan Adams	A & M
The Unforgiven	Metallica	Elektra
☆ ⑥ To Be With You	Mr. Big	Atlantic
Uhh Ahh	Boyz II Men	Motown

TOP SINGLES OF 1991

Baby Baby	Amy Grant	A & M
℗ (Everything I Do) I Do It For You	Bryan Adams	A & M
℗ Gonna Make You Sweat	C & C Music Factory	Columbia
⑥ I Like The Way (The Kissing Game)	Hi-Five	Jive
℗ I Wanna Sex You Up	Color Me Badd	Giant
⑥ More Than Words	Extreme	A & M
℗ One More Try	Timmy T.	Quality
⑥ Rush Rush	Paula Abdul	Captive
⑥ The First Time	Surface	Columbia
⑥ Unbelievable	EMF	EMI

TOP ALBUMS OF 1991

℗ Mariah Carey	Mariah Carey	Columbia
℗ Empire	Queensryche	EMI
℗ Gonna Make You Sweat	C & C Music Factory	Columbia
℗ The Immaculate Collection	Madonna	Sire
℗ I'm Your Baby Tonight	Whitney Houston	Arista
℗ No Fences	Garth Brooks	Capitol
℗ Please Hammer Don't Hurt 'Em	M.C. Hammer	Capitol
℗ Shake Your Money Maker	The Black Crowes	Def American
℗ To The Extreme	Vanilla Ice	SBK
℗ Wilson Phillips	Wilson Phillips	SBK

GRAMMY WINNERS IN 1991

The Grammys were televised by CBS from Radio City Music Hall in New York on Tuesday, February 25, 1992. Whoopi Goldberg was the host.

Record of the Year: "Unforgettable," Natalie Cole (with Nat "King" Cole) (Elektra)
Song of the Year: "Unforgettable," (music and lyrics by Irving Gordon)
Album of the Year: *Unforgettable,* Natalie Cole (Elektra)
Best Pop Vocal Performance, Female: "Something To Talk About," Bonnie Raitt (Capitol)
Best Pop Vocal Performance, Male: "When A Man Loves A Woman," Michael Bolton (Columbia)
Best Pop Vocal Performance, Duo or Group: "Losing My Religion," R.E.M. (Warner Bros.)
Best Pop Instrumental: "Robin Hood—Prince of Thieves," Michael Kamen, conductor, Greater Los Angeles Orchestra (Morgan Creek)
Best Rock Vocal Performance, Solo: "Luck Of The Draw," Bonnie Raitt (Capitol)

Peter Loran of Trixter (photo: *Anastasia Pantsios*)

Best Rock Vocal Performance, Duo or Group: "Good Man, Good Woman," Bonnie Raitt & Delbert McClinton (Capitol)

Best Rock Instrumental: "Cliffs of Dover," Eric Johnson (Capitol)

Best Rock Song: "Soul Cages," Sting (A & M)

Best New Artist: Marc Cohn

Best R & B Performance, Female: *Burnin',* Pattie LaBelle (album, MCA); "How Can I Ease The Pain," Lisa Fischer (single, Elektra)

Best R & B Performance, Male: *Power of Love,* Luther Vandross (album, Epic)

Best R & B Performance, Duo or Group: *Cooley High Harmony,* Boyz II Men (album, Motown)

Best R & B Song: "Power Of Love/Love Power," Luther Vandross, Marcus Miller, and Teddy Vann (Epic)

Best Hard Rock Performance, Vocal: "For Unlawful Carnal Knowledge," Van Halen (single, Warner Bros.)

Best Metal Performance, Vocal: *Metallica,* Metallica (album, Elektra)

Best Rap Solo Performance: "Mama Said Knock You Out," L. L. Cool J. (Def Jam)

Best Rap Performance, Duo or Group: "Summertime," D.J. Jazzy Jeff & the Fresh Prince (Jive)

Best Comedy Performance: "P.D.Q. Bach: WTWP Classical Talkity-Talk Radio," Professor Peter Schickele (Telarc)

Best Song Written for a Motion Picture or Television: "(Everything I Do) I Do It For You" (from the movie *Robin Hood—Prince of Thieves*), songwriters Bryan Adams, Robert John "Mutt" Lange, and Michael Kamen (A & M)

Best New Age: *Fresh Aire 7,* Mannheim Steam Roller (American Gramaphone)

Best Music Video, Short Form: *Losing My Religion,* R.E.M. (Warner Bros.)

Best Music Video, Long Form: *Madonna—Blonde Ambition World Tour Live,* Madonna (Sire)

ROCK AND ROLL HALL OF FAME INDUCTEES

The sixth induction ceremony was held on Wednesday, January 16, 1991, at the Waldorf Astoria hotel in New York City.

PERFORMERS

Inductee (Born and Died)	Debut Single (Year)	Label	
La Vern Baker (November 11, 1929–)	Tweedle Dee (1954)	Atlantic	517

The Byrds (James Joseph "Roger" McGuinn III: July 13, 1942– ; David Van Cortland Crosby: August 14, 1941– ; Harold Eugene Clark: November 17, 1944–May 24, 1991; Christopher Hillman: December 4, 1942– ; Michael Clark: June 3, 1944–)	Mr. Tambourine Man (1965)	Columbia
John Lee Hooker (August 22, 1920–)	Boogie Chillen' (1948)	Modern
The Impressions (Jerry Butler: December 8, 1939– ; Curtis Mayfield: June 3, 1942– ; Fred Cash: October 8, 1940– ; Sam Gooden: September 2, 1939– ; Richard Brooks: May 13, 1940– ; Arthur Brooks: November 4, 1933–)	For Your Precious Love (1958)	Falcon
Wilson Pickett (March 18, 1941–)	If You Need Me (1963)	Double-L
Jimmy Reed (September 6, 1925–August 29, 1976)	You Don't Have To Go (1955)	Vee-Jay
Ike & Tina Turner (Ike Turner [Izear Luster Turner]: November 5, 1931– ; Tina Turner [Anna Mae Bullock]: November 26, 1939–)	A Fool In Love (1960)	Sue

NONPERFORMERS

Ralph Bass (May 1, 1911–   ) Founded Federal Records in 1951, and worked with the Dominoes, Hank Ballard and the Midnighters, and James Brown. Was the artists and repertoire man at Chess Records from 1958–1976, working with Etta James, Howlin' Wolf, and others. Began his career with Savoy Records in 1948.

Dave Bartholomew (December 24, 1920–   ) Writer, arranger, bandleader,

Jeff Keith of Tesla (photo: *Anastasia Pantsios*)

trumpeter, and vocalist from New Orleans, who wrote many hit songs with Fats Domino and also worked with Lloyd Price, Shirley & Lee, and the Spiders.

Nesuhi Ertegun (November 26, 1917–July 15, 1989)   Recording executive with Atlantic Records who was responsible for many hits and careers over the years.

EARLY INFLUENCES

Howlin' Wolf (Chester Arthur Burnett) (June 10, 1910–January 10, 1976)   Premier Blues Singer, guitarist, and harmonica player of the 1930s.

DEATHS IN 1991

MUSIC PERFORMERS AND MUSIC INDUSTRY NOTABLES WHO DIED IN 1991

Steve Clark (Def Leppard), Tuesday, January 8 (respiratory failure; 30)

Webb Pierce, Sunday, February 24 (pancreatic cancer; 69)

Doc Pomus (Jerome E. Felder, songwriter), Thursday, March 14 (lung cancer; 65)

Clarence "Leo" Fender, Thursday, March 21 (Parkinson's Disease; 82)

Dave Guard (Kingston Trio), Friday, March 22 (lymphoma; 56)

Paul Gayten, Tuesday, March 26 (bleeding ulcers; 71)

Henry Glover (songwriter), Sunday, April 7 (heart attack; 69)

Steve Marriott (Small Faces), Saturday, April 20 (house fire; 44)

Johnny Thunders (John Anthony Genzale, N.Y. Dolls), Tuesday, April 23 (undetermined causes; 38)

Harold Eugene "Gene" Clark (The Byrds), Friday, May 24 (natural causes; 46)

David Ruffin (The Temptations), Saturday, June 1 (drug overdose; 50)

Stan Getz, Thursday, June 6 (cancer; 64)

Richard "Groove" Holmes, Saturday, June 29 (prostate cancer; 60)

Bert Convy (The Cheers), Monday, July 15 (brain tumor; 56)

Jeri Southern (Genevieve Hering), Sunday, August 4 (pneumonia; 64)

Richard Maltby, Monday, August 19 (long illness; 77)

Charlie Barnet, Wednesday, September 4 (pneumonia; 77)

Dottie West, Wednesday, September 4 (auto crash; 58)

Alex North (songwriter), Sunday, September 8 (pancreatic cancer; 81)

Billy Vaughn, Friday, September 27 (natural causes; 72)

Miles Davis, Saturday, September 28 (pneumonia and respiratory failure; 65)

J. Frank Wilson, Friday, October 4 (long illness; 48)

"Tennessee" Ernie Ford, Thursday, October 17 (liver ailment; 72)

Bill Graham (Wolfgang Grajonca, concert promoter) Friday, October 25 (helicopter crash; 60)

Margo Sylvia (The Tune Weavers), Friday, October 25 (heart attack; 55)

Jim Reese (The Bobby Fuller Four), Saturday, October 26 (heart attack; 49)

Mort Shuman (songwriter), Monday, November 4 (heart attack; 52)

Carter Cornelius (Cornelius Brothers and Sister Rose), Saturday, November 9 (heart attack; 43)

Jacques Morali (writer/producer), Friday, November 15 (AIDS; 44)

Freddie Mercury (Queen), Sunday, November 24 (AIDS; 45)

Eric Carr (Kiss), Sunday, November 24 (cancer; 41)

Richard Blandon (The Dubs), Monday, December 30 (cancer; 57)

OTHERS WHO DIED IN 1991

Irwin Allen
Luke Appling
Jean Arthur

Pete Axthelm
Ralph Bellamy
Paul Brown

519

Frank Capra
Joan Caulfield
Ken Curtis
John Daly
Brad Davis
Colleen Dewhurst
Leo Durocher
Margot Fonteyn
Redd Foxx
James Franciscus
Theodore Geisl (Dr. Seuss)
George Gobel
Sam Goody
Martha Graham
Harold "Red" Grange
Dean Jagger
Ken Keltner

Douglas Kiker
Jerzy Kosinski
Michael Landon
David Lean
Keye Luke
Fred MacMurray
Yves Montand
Arthur Murray
Joseph Papp
Joe Pasternak
Aldo Ray
Harry Reasoner
Lee Remick
Gene Roddenberry
Danny Thomas
Gene Tierney
Tom Tryon

MOVIES OF 1991

MOVIES FEATURING A POP MUSIC SOUNDTRACK

Boyz N the Hood   *Stars:* Cuba Gooding, Jr., Ice Cube, Larry Fishburne, Nia Long, Morris Chestnut. Features music of Ice Cube, Tevin Campbell, Yo-Yo, 2 Live Crew, and Tony!Toni!Tone!

The Commitments   *Stars:* Andrew Strong, Robert Arkins, Kenneth McCluskey, Michael Aherne, Angeline Ball. Songs include "Try A Little Tenderness" and "Mustang Sally."

The Doors   *Stars:* Val Kilmer, Frank Whaley, Kevin Dillon, Meg Ryan, Kyle McLachlan, Billy Idol, John Densmore, Will Jordan, Mimi Rogers, Paul Williams, Bill Graham, Billy Vera, William Kunstler, Dennis Burkley. Movie features actual songs of Jim Morrison and the Doors.

The Five Heartbeats   *Stars:* Robert Townsend, Michael Wright, Harry J. Lennix, Tico Wells, Leon, Diahann Carroll, John Canada Terrell, Harold Nicholas. Music by Stanley Clarke.

Juice   *Stars:* Omar Epps, Jermaine Hopkins, Khalil Kain, Tupac Shakus. Music by Eric B. & Rakim, Naughty by Nature, Big Daddy Kane, EPMD, Short, Cypress Hill Crew, and Salt N' Pepa.

My Girl   *Stars:* Macaulay Culkin, Jamie Lee Curtis, Dan Aykroyd, Anna Chlimsky. Features songs like "My Girl" by the Temptations, "Hot Fun In The Summertime" by Sly & the Family Stone, "Do Wah Diddy Diddy" by Manfred Mann, "Good Lovin' " by the Young Rascals, "Bad Moon Rising" by Creedence Clearwater Revival, "I Only Have Eyes For You" by the Flamingos, and "Saturday In The Park" by Chicago.

New Jack City   *Stars:* Wesley Snipes, Ice T, Mario Van Peebles, Judd Nelson, Vanessa Williams, Nik Ashford, Allen Payne, Chris Rock. Music by Ice T, Keith Sweat, Johnny Gill, 2 Live Crew, Color Me Badd, and Guy.

OTHER POPULAR MOVIES OF 1991

The Addams Family
A Kiss Before Dying
Backdraft
Beauty and the Beast
Billy Bathgate
Black Robe

Bonfire of the Vanities
Bugsy
Cape Fear
Career Opportunities
City Slickers
Class Action

Dead Again
Deceived
Defending Your Life
Doc Hollywood
Dutch
Father of the Bride
The Field
The Fisher King
For the Boys
Frankie and Johnny
FX 2
Green Card
The Grifters
Guilty by Suspicion
The Hard Way
Harley Davidson and the Marlboro Man
He Said, She Said
Hook
Hudson Hawk
JFK
Jungle Fever
L.A. Story
Life Stinks
The Marrying Man
Mobsters
Mortal Thoughts

Naked Gun 2½
Once Around
One Good Cop
Only the Lonely
Oscar
Other People's Money
Out for Justice
Perfect Weapon
Point Break
The Prince Of Tides
Pure Luck
Robin Hood—Prince of Thieves
The Rocketeer
Scenes from a Mall
Shattered
Silence of the Lambs
Sleeping with the Enemy
Soap Dish
Star Trek VI
The Super
Terminator 2—Judgment Day
Thelma and Louise
Toy Soldiers
29th Street
What About Bob?
White Fang

ACADEMY AWARD WINNERS OF 1991

Best Actor: Anthony Hopkins, *Silence of the Lambs*
Best Actress: Jodie Foster, *Silence of the Lambs*
Best Picture: *Silence of the Lambs*
Best Original Song: "Beauty and the Beast," *Beauty and the Beast* (music by Alan Menken and lyrics by Howard Ashman)

TOP TELEVISION SHOWS OF 1991

Cheers
Coach
Designing Women
Full House
Home Improvement

Major Dad
Murder, She Wrote
Murphy Brown
Roseanne
60 Minutes

1992

NEWS HIGHLIGHTS OF 1992

⇨ The Winter Olympics begin on February 8, in Albertville, France.

⇨ On February 10, heavyweight champ Mike Tyson is convicted of raping Desiree Washington, a Miss Black America contestant, in Indianapolis, and is sentenced to six years in prison.

⇨ Many Congressmen are cited for abusing their over-draft privileges as elected officials.

⇨ After 208 episodes since the first show in 1984, "The Cosby Show" becomes a part of TV history, ending its successful run at a taping on March 6, aired April 30.

⇨ On Sunday, March 22, 27 lives are lost at La Guardia Airport in New York, when USAir Flight 405 crashes into Flushing Bay on takeoff.

⇨ "Mighty Mo," the USS *Missouri*, the ship where Japan formally surrendered in 1945, is decommissioned because of defense cuts, and is the last active battleship to be retired to Bremerton, Washington.

⇨ On April 2, John Gotti, reputed head of the nation's most powerful Mafia family, is convicted in New York of murder and racketeering.

⇨ After 34 years of marriage, Nelson and Winnie Mandela separate.

⇨ On April 29, the four police officers in the March 3, 1991 Rodney King beating in Los Angeles, are acquitted, touching off riots in South Central Los Angeles.

⇨ On May 22, after being host of the "Tonight Show" for 30 years, Johnny Carson retires as Mr. Late Night Television. Jay Leno becomes the new host.

⇨ The Summer Olympics begin on July 25, from Barcelona, Spain.

MUSIC HIGHLIGHTS 1992

⇨ *Better Days,* the new album from Southside Johnny & the Asbury Jukes, on Impact Records, reunites Johnny Lyon with pal Steven Van Zandt, who produced the album. The two of them, along with Bruce Springsteen, team up on the single "It's Been A Long Time."

⇨ The public votes on which of two designs for an Elvis Presley stamp, selected by a Citizens Advisory Board of the U.S. Postal Commission, will be used as part of a 14-part Legends of American Music series due to be released by the Postal Service between 1993 and 1995.

⇨ Twenty-seven-year-old rap star Joseph Simmons of Run D.M.C. is acquitted of rape charges in Cleveland.

⇨ U2 begins its 31-city Zoo TV tour in Lakeland, Florida. It is the group's first U.S. tour since 1987.

⇨ On March 14, Willie Nelson hosts "Farm Aid V" in Irving, Texas. The 12-hour show, featuring 50 other country and rock stars, draws 50,000 fans, raising money to help rural farmers. Among those performing are Paul Simon, John Mellencamp, Richard Marx, Tracy Chapman, Kris Kristofferson, Joe Walsh, Arlo Guthrie, Waylon Jennings, the Kentucky Head Hunters, Roseanne Arnold, Steve Allen, and others.

⇨ On March 21, exactly 40 years after legendary disc jockey Alan Freed hosted the first rock n' roll show billed as the "Moondog Coronation Ball" at Cleveland, Ohio's Cleveland Arena, local Cleveland radio station WMJI-Magic 105.7 and Canterburry Productions host an anniversary special called the "Moondog Coronation Ball '92," at Cleveland's Public Hall. Ten thousand fans celebrate the 40 year anniversary of rock n' roll's first concert by watching performers like Len Barry, the Tokens, the Drifters, Jerry Butler, Clarence "Frogman" Henry, Ronnie Spector, all four original Diamonds, and Little Anthony reuniting with the original Imperials. The four-hour show pays tribute to the late Alan Freed and the birth of rock n' roll. Paul Williams, bandleader at the original show, flew in from New York City for a rare appearance. David Freed, Alan's brother, also was in attendance.

⇨ Dionne Warwick, Burt Bacharach, and Hal David reunite for the first time in 20 years for

Dionne's new album for Arista Records. Bacharach and David write the song "Sunny Weather Lover" for the album.

⇨ Hammer begins his 135-city Too Legit To Quit tour on April 1, two days after his thirtieth birthday, in Hampton, Virginia.

⇨ On April 2, Wynonna Judd goes out as a solo performer in Midland, Texas, after years performing with her mom, Naomi, as The Judds. Her solo album is called *Wynonna*, featuring the single "She's His Only Need."

⇨ After five years, Bruce Springsteen releases two new albums, *Human Touch* and *Lucky Town*, with the singles "Human Touch" and "Better Days" coming from each album. He also does a seven-minute "Human Touch" video, filmed on location in New Orleans. The two albums, his 10th and 11th, are his first since his *Tunnel of Love* LP in 1987.

⇨ David Bowie (45) marries fashion model Iman (36) in Lausanne, Switzerland on April 24.

⇨ Guitar great Eric Clapton begins a 20-city U.S. tour on April 25 in Dallas, Texas.

⇨ On June 4 Priscilla Presley announces at Graceland that by a vote of nearly three to one the public has chosen the youthful-looking Elvis stamp, which will be issued by the Post Office on January 8, 1993.

⇨ Capitol records celebrates its 50th anniversary this year. This Hollywood based label was founded by Johnny Mercer, Glenn Wallichs and Buddy DeSylva on June 4, 1942.

⇨ Since *Billboard* magazine's album charts for stereo and mono rankings were combined as one chart in 1963, Billy Ray Cyrus' *Some Gave All* album becomes the first debut album to reach number one on the charts in just two weeks.

⇨ Newcomers Kris Kross' single "Jump," becomes the first debut single on *Billboard* magazine's singles chart to maintain eight straight weeks at number one since 1977, when Debby Boone's "You Light Up My Life" logged ten weeks at number one.

Debut Artists of 1992

A.L.T. and The Lost Civilization	Jade
Arrested Development	Joe Public
Arthur Baker Featuring Nikeeta	R. Kelly & Public Announcement
A Tribe Called Quest	Kris Kross
Black Sheep	K.W.S.
Mary J. Blige	L.A. Style
Blur	Gerald Levert
Brotherhood Creed	Lil Suzy
Cause & Effect	Luke
Charm	Mitch Malloy
Clivilles & Cole	M. C. Brains
Clubland	MC Lyte
Tom Cochrane	Midi Maxi & Efti
The College Boyz	Mint Condition
Colourhaus	Mocca Soul
Erin Cruise	Nice & Smooth
Chris Cuevas	The Northern Pikes
Cypress Hill	N2Deep
Billy Ray Cyrus	NYASIA
DAS EFX	One 2 One
Degrees of Motion	Pet Rock & C.L. Smooth
Laura Enea	Redhead Kingpin & the F.B.I.
Giggles	Rozalla
Good 2Go	St. Etienne
Aaron Hall	John Secada
Sophie B. Hawkins	2nd II None
House of Pain	Shakespear's Sister

Tag
Toad The Wet Sprocket
Tony Terry
TKA
TLC
Lidell Townsell
Kathy Troccoli

2 Hyped Brothers & a Dog
Chris Walker
Geoffrey Williams
The Williams Brothers
Ugly Kid Joe
Z Unlimited

1992

HITS OF 1992

JANUARY

Be True To Yourself	2nd II None	Profile
Blinded By Love	Rythm Syndicate	Impact
Breakin' My Heart (Pretty Brown Eyes)	Mint Condition	Perspective
Cold Shower	Erin Cruise	Purple Heart
Good For Me	Amy Grant	A & M
Missing You Now	Michael Bolton	Columbia
Paper Doll	P.M. Dawn	Gee Street
Pride (In The Name Of Love)	Clivilles & Cole	Fever
Ⓖ **Remember The Time**	Michael Jackson	Epic
Stars	Simply Red	Atco EastWest
Stay	Jodeci	Uptown
There's No Other Way	Blur	SBK
The Rush	Luther Vandross	Epic
Vibeology	Paula Abdul	Captive
Wasted Time	Skid Row	Atlantic

FEBRUARY

Again Tonight	John Mellencamp	Mercury
Caribbean Blue	Enya	Reprise
Church Of Your Heart	Roxette	EMI
Everything Changes	Kathy Troccoli	Reunion
Hazard	Richard Marx	Capitol
I Can't Dance	Genesis	Atlantic
If You Go Away	NKOTB	Columbia
Justified And Ancient	The KLF (featuring Tammy Wynette)	Arista
Masterpiece	Atlantic Starr	Reprise
Nu Nu	Lidell Townsell	Mercury
☆ Ⓖ **Save The Best For Last**	Vanessa Williams	Mercury
Ⓟ **Tears In Heaven**	Eric Clapton	Reprise
Thinkin' Back	Color Me Badd	Giant
What Becomes Of The Brokenhearted	Paul Young	MCA
You Showed Me	Salt-N-Pepa	Next Plateau

MARCH

Ⓟ **Ain't 2 Proud 2 Beg**	TLC	LaFace
All Woman	Lisa Stansfield	Arista
Bohemian Rhapsody	Queen	Hollywood
Come As You Are	Nirvana	DGC

525

Do Not Pass Me By	Hammer	Capitol
Human Touch/Better Days	Bruce Springsteen	Columbia
I'm The One You Need	Jody Watley	MCA
I Wanna Rock	Luke	Luke
Live And Learn	Joe Public	Columbia
Love Me	Tracie Spencer	Capitol
ⓖ My Lovin' (You're Never Gonna Get It)	En Vogue	Atco EastWest
Nothing Else Matters	Metallica	Elektra
One	U2	Island
Poor Georgie	MC Lyte	Priority
Take Time	Chris Walker	Pendulum

APRIL

☆ ⓟ Baby Got Back	Sir Mix-a-Lot	Def American
Damn I Wish I Was Your Lover	Sophie B. Hawkins	Columbia
Don't Talk Just Kiss	Right Said Fred	Charisma
Everything About You	Ugly Kid Joe	Stardog
High	The Cure	Elektra
If You Asked Me To	Celine Dion	Epic
ⓖ In The Closet	Michael Jackson	Epic
☆ ⓟ Jump	Kris Kross	Ruffhouse
Just Take My Heart	Mr. Big	Atlantic
Let's Get Rocked	Def Leppard	Mercury
Not The Only One	Bonnie Raitt	Capitol
Silent Prayer	Shanice	Motown
ⓖ Tennessee	Arrested Development	Chrysalis
ⓖ Under The Bridge	Red Hot Chili Peppers	Warner Bros.
Will You Marry Me?	Paula Abdul	Captive

MAY

ⓟ Achy Breaky Heart	Billy Ray Cyrus	Mercury
Anything At All	Mitch Malloy	Interscope
The Best Things In Life Are Free	Luther Vandross and Janet Jackson	Perspective
Do It To Me	Lionel Richie	Motown
Hold On My Heart	Genesis	Atlantic
☆ I'll Be There	Mariah Carey	Columbia
Innocent Child	Colourhaus	Interscope
Just For Tonight	Vanessa Williams	Wing
Life Is A Highway	Tom Cochrane	Capitol
Slow Motion	Color Me Badd	Giant
ⓖ They Want EFX	DAS EFX	Atco EastWest
This Is The Way We Roll	Hammer	Capitol
T.L.C.	Linear	Atlantic
Wishing On A Star	The Cover Girls	Epic
You Won't See Me Cry	Wilson Phillips	SBK

JUNE

Baby-Baby-Baby	TLC	Laface
Everybody's Free (To Feel Good)	Rozalla	Epic

57 Channels (And Nothin' On)	Bruce Springsteen	Columbia
Friday I'm In Love	The Cure	Fiction
Giving Him Something He Can Feel	En Vogue	Atco EastWest
Good Stuff	The B-52's	Reprise
Make Love Like A Man	Def Leppard	Mercury
Mr. Loverman	Shabba Ranks	Epic
November Rain	Guns N' Roses	Geffen
The One	Elton John	MCA
Remedy	The Black Crowes	American
Scenario	A Tribed Called Quest	Jive
Sleeping With The Lights On	Curtis Stigers	Arista
Strawberry Letter 23	Tevin Campbell	Qwest
Take This Heart	Richard Marx	Capitol
⑥ **Too Funky**	George Michael	Columbia
⑥ **Warm It Up**	Kris Kross	Columbia
Whatever It Takes (To Make You Stay)	Troop	Atlantic
You Remind Me	Mary J. Blige	Uptown

JULY

All I Want	Toad The Wet Sprocket	Columbia
Back To The Hotel	N2Deep	Profile
Brainstorming	M. C. Brains	Motown
☆ **End Of The Road**	Boyz II Men	Motown
Even Better Than The Real Thing	U2	Island
I Miss You	Joe Public	Columbia
Jam	Michael Jackson	Epic
Jump Around	House of Pain	Tommy Boy
Money Can't Buy You Love	Ralph Tresvant	Perspective
Reach For The Sky	Firehouse	Epic
Stay	Shakespear's Sister	London
The Way I Feel	Tag	Scotti Bros.
They Reminisce Over You (T.R.O.Y)	Pet Rock & C. L. Smooth	Elektra
☆ **This Used To Be My Playground**	Madonna	Sire
Wherever I May Roam	Metallica	Elektra

ROCK AND ROLL HALL OF FAME INDUCTEES

The seventh induction ceremony was held on Wednesday, January 15, 1992, at the Waldorf Astoria hotel in New York City.

PERFORMERS

Inductee (Born and Died)	Debut Single (Year)	Label
Bobby "Blue" Bland (Robert Calvin Bland: January 27, 1930–)	Farther Up The Road (1957)	Duke

Booker T. and the MG's (Booker T. Jones: December 11, 1944– ; Steve Cropper: October 21, 1942– ; Donald "Duck" Dunn: November 24, 1941– ; Al Jackson, Jr.: November 27, 1934–October 1, 1975; Lewis Steinberg: September 13, 1933–)	Green Onions (1962)	Stax
Johnny Cash (February 26, 1932–)	Cry! Cry! Cry! (1955)	Sun
The Jimi Hendrix Experience (James Marshall "Jimi" Hendrix: November 27, 1942–September 18, 1970; Noel Redding: December 25, 1945– ; John "Mitch" Mitchell: July 9, 1947–)	Purple Haze (1967)	Reprise
The Isley Brothers (Ronald: June 21, 1941– ; Rudolph: July 1, 1939– ; O'Kelly, Jr.: December 25, 1937–March 31, 1986; Marvin: August 18, 1953– ; Ernie: March 7, 1952–)	An Angel Cried (1956)	Teenage
Sam and Dave (Samuel David Moore: October 12, 1935– ; David Prater, Jr.: May 9, 1937–April 9, 1988)	You Don't Know Like I Know (1965)	Stax
The Yardbirds (Keith Relf: March 22, 1943–May 14, 1976; Eric Clapton: March 30, 1945– ; Chris Dreja: November 11, 1946– ; Paul Samwell-Smith: May 8, 1943– ; Jim McCarty: July 25, 1943– ; Jeff Beck: June 24, 1944– ; Jimmy Page: January 9, 1944–)	For Your Love (1965)	Epic

NONPERFORMERS

Clarence "Leo" Fender (August 10, 1908–March 21, 1991) Designed and marketed the Fender Telecaster and Stratocaster guitars in the early fifties and invented the electric bass in 1950, the Fender Precision, and produced some of the world's best amplifiers

Bill Graham (Wolfgang Grajonca: January 8, 1931–October 25, 1991) Concert promoter who also began The Fillmore West and Fillmore East Clubs in the late 1960s. Also put together the benefit concerts "Live Aid" and "Amnesty International" in the late 1980s

Doc Pomus (Jerome Felder: June 27, 1925–March 14, 1991) Songwriter who, with his partner Mort Shuman, wrote rock classics like "This Magic Moment" and "Save The Last Dance For Me" for the Drifters, "A Teenager In Love" for Dion & the Belmonts, "Hushabye" for the Mystics, "Little Sister," "His Latest Flame," and "Viva Las Vegas" for Elvis Presley, and hundreds of others

EARLY INFLUENCES

Elmore James (January 27, 1918–March 24, 1963) Blues singer and guitar player whose signature was his powerful full-octave slide guitar opening on his classic song, "Dust My Broom," a song written by blues giant Robert Johnson. James's style influenced hundreds of slide guitar players ever since

Professor Longhair (Henry Roeland Byrd: December 19, 1918–January 30, 1980) The cornerstone of New Orleans rhythm and blues piano playing and singing

528

DEATHS IN 1992

MUSIC PERFORMERS AND MUSIC INDUSTRY NOTABLES WHO DIED IN 1992

Jerry Nolan (N.Y. Dolls), Tuesday, January 14 (stroke; 45)

Charlie Ventura (saxophonist), Friday, January 17 (lung cancer; 75)

"Champion" Jack Dupree (blues pianist), Tuesday, January 21 (cancer; 82)

Ken Darby (composer), Friday, January 24 (heart attack; 82)

Willie Dixon (bluesman), Wednesday, January 29 (deteriorating health; 76)

Al Silver (founder of Herald and Ember Records), Wednesday, March 4 (undisclosed illness; 78)

Andy Russell (Andres Robago), Thursday, April 16 (stroke; 72)

Milton Kellum (songwriter), Friday, April 17 (natural causes; 81)

Sylvia Syms, Sunday, May 10 (heart attack; 73)

Lawrence Welk, Sunday, May 17 (pneumonia; 89)

Peter Allen, Thursday, June 18 (AIDS; 48)

Allan Jones, Saturday, June 27 (lung cancer; 84)

Herb Kenny (Inkspots), Saturday, July 11 (cancer)

Mary Wells (of Motown fame), Sunday, July 26 (throat cancer; 49)

Jeff Porcaro (Toto), Wednesday, August 5 (heart attack; 38)

John Cage (composer), Wednesday, August 12 (stroke; 79)

Tony Williams (The Platters), Friday, August 14 (diabetes; 64)

OTHERS WHO DIED IN 1992

Lyle Alzado
Dame Judith Anderson
Isaac Asimov
Freddie Bartholomew
Menachem Begin
Neville Brand
Richard Brooks
Mae Clark
Sandy Dennis
Marlene Dietrich
Jose Ferrer
William Gaines
Alex Haley
Paul Henreid
Benny Hill

John Ireland
Sam Kinison
John Lund
Robert Morley
George Murphy
Bert Parks
Robert Reed
Jilly Rizzo
Lee Salk
Earl Scheib
Eric Sevareid
Rick Sklar
Nancy Walker
Sam Walton
Dick York

MOVIES OF 1992

MOVIES FEATURING A POP MUSIC SOUNDTRACK

The Mambo Kings *Stars:* Armand Assante, Antonio Banderas, Cathy Moriarty, Desi Arnaz, Jr., Marushka Detmers. Music provided by mambo legend Tito Puente.

Wayne's World *Stars:* Mike Myers (Wayne), Dana Carvey (Garth), Rob Lowe, Alice Cooper, Tia Carere, Frank DiLeo. Music features "Bohemian Rhapsody" by Queen, "Time Machine" by Black Sabbath, "Hot And Bothered" by Cinderella, "Dream Weaver" by Gary Wright, along with songs by the Bullet Boys, Eric Clapton, Alice Cooper, the Red Hot Chili Peppers, and Jimi Hendrix.

OTHER POPULAR MOVIES OF 1992

A League of Their Own
Alien 3
American Me

Article 99
At Play in the Fields of the Lord
The Babe

ROCK ON ALMANAC

Batman Returns
Basic Instinct
Beethoven
Buffy, the Vampire Slayer
Cool World
The Cutting Edge
Death Becomes Her
Encino Man
Far and Away
Fern Gully
Fried Green Tomatoes
Gladiator
Grand Canyon
The Hand That Rocks the Cradle
Hear My Song
Honey, I Blew Up the Kid
The Housesitter
Ladybugs
The Last Boy Scout
The Last of the Mohicans
The Lawnmower Man

Lethal Weapon 3
Love Crimes
Medicine Man
Memoirs of an Invisible Man
My Cousin Vinny
Newsies
Passed Away
The Player
The Power of One
Raising Cain
Rock-a-Doodle
Ruby
Sister Act
Sleepwalkers
Straight Talk
Thunderheart
Unforgiven
Unlawful Entry
White Men Can't Jump
White Sands

GLOSSARY

A&R Artists and repertoire; the person in charge of A&R for a record label seeks out new talent and finds material for acts signed to the label to record.

Acid rock Heavy, loud music of the late 1960s and early 1970s that was supposedly drug-inspired.

Album A 12-inch circular piece of vinyl, with a micro-groove that plays at 33⅓ revolutions per minute (rpm) and usually contains five or more different musical selections.

AOR Adult-oriented rock.

A side The side of the single recording that is hoped to be the hit side; the side that is promoted.

Ballad A love song with a slow tempo.

Blues Music that is generally associated with black performers.

Boogie To party.

Bootleg Unofficial reproduction of recorded product or concert.

Bop A dance that has no other name.

Bridge A musical connection between the last verse and the chorus.

B side The "flip" side of a recording; the side that is not usually promoted.

Bubblegum Music aimed at a preteen audience.

Bullet A marking, usually a star, circle, or arrow, showing the fastest-rising songs on a music popularity chart.

C&W Country and western music.

CD Compact Disc.

Charts Weekly listings that show the most popular current hits, based on sales and radio station airplay. Hits are listed numerically, the one at number one being the most popular.

Comp Complimentary tickets to a show.

Concept album An album with a unifying theme.

Country rock The combining of country and rock music.

Cover record A new recording by a different artist of a song already recorded. The term was first applied to white performers' remakes of black performers' hits in the mid-fifties.

Crossover A record whose popularity "spills over" from one field, such as country, to another, such as Top 40.

Cut A specific song or selection on an album; also, to record.

Deleted No longer part of the original catalog of recordings.

Demo A demonstration record used by music publishers to show an artist how a song will sound; also, any recording that new artists submit to a recording company to demonstrate their skill or sound in the hope of obtaining a record deal.

Disc jockey A radio personality who plays records on the air.

Disco Derived from the French term *discothèque* (meaning "record library"), applied in the sixties to nightclubs that played recorded music; in the seventies, it described the dance music played in nightclubs.

Doo-wop Barbershop harmonies with a beat, often associated with black singing groups of the fifties.

Dub To make a copy of an original recording; also, to add background vocals or music to an already recorded song.

Easy listening Light music that has a wide range of appeal, especially for adults.

EP A 7-inch or 12-inch disc that is played at 45 rpm, with usually two songs on each side.

Feedback A loud, distorted sound produced when a microphone gets near a loudspeaker, causing current to reverse ("feed back" from output to input).

Fender Brand of guitar designed by Leo Fender.

GLOSSARY

Festival A concert performed outdoors, usually drawing huge crowds.

Flip side B side.

Folk music Traditional music sung in group harmonies to the accompaniment of guitars and banjos.

Folk rock Electronically amplified folk music.

45 A 7-inch-diameter vinyl disc of recorded music that revolves at 45 rpm; also known as a disc, single, or platter.

Funk Music, of primarily black performers, with heavy rhythms and a throbbing beat.

Fuzz A sound distortion created with an electric guitar by overloading the amplification circuit.

Glitter rock Driving rhythms made popular by Gary Glitter in England in 1972 and copied by other groups, most of whom dressed in glittery costumes and makeup; also called glam rock.

Go-go Early name for a disco; also applied to the danceable music played in such clubs in the sixties.

Gold disc An award given to a single that sells 1 million copies (500,000 copies after January 1, 1989) and an album that sells 500,000 copies.

Gospel Fervent religious music combining aspects of folk music and blues.

Groupie An obsessively devoted female fan of a male rock star.

Hard rock Heavy, loud, and powerful music.

Heavy metal A term first used in the late sixties to describe the music of groups that wore long hair, tight-fitting clothes, chains, and leather jewelry and played extremely loud hard rock.

Hit A recording that garners a lot of airplay and consequent sales.

Hook A very catchy melody or lyric that sticks in a listener's mind.

Hype Advance promotion of a record or an artist; from *hyperbole,* "exaggeration."

Improvise To perform without any advance planning.

Instrumental Music without any vocal accompaniment.

Jam session A spontaneous musical performance.

Jazz rock A brassy jazz sound combined with rock.

Jesus rock Music with a religious theme.

Lick A short musical passage played on a guitar.

Light show Strobe and laser lights used to create an effect at concerts.

Liner notes Text on an album sleeve about the music or the performer.

Live Performed before an audience.

LP A long-playing record, usually on 12-inch-diameter vinyl and played at 33⅓ revolutions per minute.

Lyricist The person who wrote the words for a song. The composer writes the music.

Lyrics Words to a song.

Mix To blend, amplify, and otherwise modify the various tracks of a recording to obtain a final product for release or club play; also, the version of a song that results from such manipulation.

Moog The first synthesizer, developed by Robert Moog.

MOR Middle-of-the-road; popular music with the greatest appeal to the masses.

Multitracking Combining music tracks.

Muzak Bland background music that is heard in elevators, offices, restaurants, and super-markets.

New age Electronically produced or enhanced meditative instrumental music with jazz and progressive pop influences.

New wave Anti-establishment music performed by outlandishly dressed rockers.

Outtake A cut unavailable on an album or as a single.

Overdub To add voices and instruments to an already recorded song.

Platinum disc Awarded to a single that sells in excess of 2 million copies (1 million copies after January 1, 1989) and an album that sells in excess of 1 million copies.

Pop Generally pleasant music with broad appeal, aimed at an adult audience.

Progressive   Contemporary sound characterized by musical experimentation.

Protest music   Folk music that expressed the ills of society, sung by performers like Bob Dylan, Joan Baez, and Peter, Paul & Mary.

Psychedelic rock   Music of the mid-sixties focused on or inspired by experiences people had under the influence of various hallucinatory drugs.

Punk rock   Rebellious music of the mid-seventies intended to be anti-establishment. The Ramones, the Sex Pistols, Blondie, and the Clash played this form of loud, beat-heavy rock 'n' roll.

Race music   Black music of the early fifties, the forerunner of rock 'n' roll; also called sepia music.

R&B   Rhythm and blues; formerly called race music or sepia music.

Rap   Commentary chanted in phrases that rhyme over a pulsating beat and usually with little or no musical accompaniment.

Record sleeve   The cardboard cover in which a record is packaged.

Reggae   Music of the Rastafarian culture of Jamaica, an outgrowth of ska, a lilting beat inspired by Chubby Checker's "Limbo Rock." Bob Marley popularized reggae in the United States in the mid-seventies.

Release   The time when a new product is offered to the public.

Rhythm guitar   Guitar part that supplies the rhythm and melody of a song.

Roadie   A member of the group of technicians that travels with a rock act and is usually in charge of setting up the equipment.

Rock   Rock 'n' roll; rock 'n' roll simply became known as rock during the seventies.

Rockabilly   The combination of country and rock 'n' roll music originally played by performers like Elvis Presley, Carl Perkins, Johnny Burnette, Jerry Lee Lewis, Johnny Cash, and Eddie Cochran and later revived by Billy Swan, the Stray Cats, and Dave Edmunds.

Rock 'n' roll   Contemporary music with a throbbing beat, originally inspired by R&B. Cleveland, Ohio, disc jockey Alan Freed is credited with popularizing the expression, which was used by black musicians in the thirties and forties as a euphemism for lovemaking.

Sepia music   Race music.

Session musician   A musician hired for a recording session.

Singer-songwriter   A performer who writes and records his or her own music; early examples were Chuck Berry, Fats Domino, and Little Richard.

Single   A 45.

Skiffle   Mid-fifties sound from England that was a cross between folk and Dixieland music. Lonnie Donegan popularized it; Mungo Jerry revived it in 1970.

Solo   (1) A performer who leaves a group to begin a career as an individual performer. (2) In a recording, a voice or instrument that is featured at one point during the performance.

Soul   A combination of gospel and R&B music, sung with great intensity and feeling.

Surf music   California sound, with lyrics about beaches, girls, and cars, made popular in the early sixties by the Beach Boys and Jan & Dean.

Swamp rock   Southern bayou music of Louisiana and Mississippi, popularized by Creedence Clearwater Revival in the late sixties.

Synthesizer   An instrument that can create every imaginable musical sound electronically.

Take   One recorded performance at a recording session.

Teenybopper   A young teenage music fan.

Tex-Mex   A sound from the Texas-Mexican border area, popularized by Freddy Fender.

Tin Pan Alley   The part of New York City in and around the Brill Building, where many music publishers had offices in the early part of this century.

Top 40   A listing of the 40 most popular records nationally for a given week, on the basis of radio station playlists and retail sales of singles.

Tour   A series of concerts in various cities.

Track   (1) A cut. (2) A separate channel of recorded sound; as many as 64 tracks can be combined to form a recording.

Wall of sound   The lush, multitracked sound Phil Spector created as producer of hits for such acts as the Crystals, the Ronettes, and the Righteous Brothers.

INDEX OF PERFORMERS

In this index, dates show where a performer's name appears in the hit lists. References to a performer in other sections of the book are identified in the index by page numbers, which appear in *italic type* after the dates. Names of musical groups that are formed from a person's name are alphabetized under the person's surname (for example, "Geils, J., Band, The").

Champs, The: Mar. 1958, Jan. 1962; *64, 72*

Chandler, Chas: *170*

Chandler, Gene: Jan. 1962, July 1970; *115, 123*

Chaney, Herman "Sonny": *489*

Change: *360*

Channel, Bruce: Feb. 1962; *117, 123*

Channels, The: July 1956; *39*

Chanson: *347*

Chantays, The: Mar. 1963; *129*

Chantels, The: Sep. 1957, Jan. 1958, May 1958, July 1958, Sep. 1961; *51*

Chanters: The: *65*

Chapin, Harry: Mar. 1972, Jan. 1974, Oct. 1974; *253, 382*

Chapman, Tracy: *466, 467, 473, 474, 523*

Charlene: Mar. 1982; *320*

Charles, Jimmy: Aug. 1960; *90, 97*

Charles, Ray: May 1954, Jan. 1955, Aug. 1955, Dec. 1955, July 1959, Oct. 1960, Jan. 1961, Mar. 1961, Sep. 1961, Dec. 1961, May 1962, Aug. 1962, Apr. 1963, Sep. 1963, Dec. 1963, Jan. 1965, Dec. 1965; *5, 6, 123, 124, 135, 180, 369, 425, 447*

Charles, Ray and Chaka Khan: *501*

Charles, Ray, Singers, The: May 1964; *142*

Charles, Sonny, & the Checkmates Ltd.: May 1969; *213*

Charlie: *320*

Charm: *524*

Charms, The: Sep. 1954, Feb. 1955, Mar. 1955; *16, 38*

Charts, The: July 1957; *52*

Cheap Trick: Apr. 1979, Aug. 1979, June 1982, Apr. 1988, Feb. 1989, July 1990; *332, 334, 359*

Checker, Chubby: Aug. 1960, Oct. 1960, Jan. 1961, Mar. 1961, July 1961, Oct. 1961, Nov. 1961, Mar. 1962, July 1962, Sep. 1962, Mar. 1963, Nov. 1963, Dec. 1963, Apr. 1964, Feb. 1982; *64, 77, 96, 100, 110, 111, 114, 124, 125, 276, 449*

Checker, Chubby, & Dee Dee Sharp: *124*

Cheech & Chong: Sep. 1973, Nov. 1977, Sep. 1985; *267*

Cheeks, Judy: *333*

Cheers, The: Nov. 1954, Sep. 1955, Feb. 1956; *16, 519*

Chemay, Joe, Band, The: *374*

Cher: Mar. 1966, Nov. 1967, Sep. 1971, Jan. 1972, Aug. 1973, Feb. 1974, June 1974, Feb. 1979, Nov. 1987, July 1989, Oct. 1989, Nov. 1990, June 1991; *162, 193, 373, 439*

Cher & Peter Cetera: Mar. 1989

Cheri: *387*

Cherrelle: *414*

Cherry, Don: Sep. 1955; *3*

Cherry, Neneh: Apr. 1989, July 1989; *480*

Chevalier, Maurice: *262*

Chic: Oct. 1977, Apr. 1978, Oct. 1978, Feb. 1979, June 1979; *319, 353*

Chicago: Apr. 1970, Aug. 1970, Nov. 1970, Feb. 1971, June 1971, Oct. 1971, Aug. 1972, Oct. 1972, June 1973, Sep. 1973, Mar. 1974, June 1974, Oct. 1974, Feb. 1975, Apr. 1975, June 1976, Aug. 1976, Sep. 1977, May 1978, Oct. 1978, Dec. 1978, June 1982, Sep. 1982, May 1984, Aug. 1984, Nov. 1984, Feb. 1985, Nov. 1986, June 1988, Sep. 1988, Jan. 1989, July 1990, Jan. 1991; *212, 213, 234, 248, 261, 288, 293, 314, 315, 341, 393, 394, 486, 520*

Chicago Bears Shufflin' Crew, The: Jan. 1986; *440*

Chiffons, The: Mar. 1963, June 1963, Dec. 1963, May 1966; *89, 135, 331*

Child, Desmond, & Rouge: *347*

Child, Jane: Feb. 1990; *494*

Childs, Toni: *467*

Chi-Lites, The: Oct. 1971, Apr. 1972; *212*

Chilliwack: Sep. 1981; *253*

Chimes, The: Dec. 1960; *90, 494*

Chipmunks, The: Dec. 1958; *64, 73*

Choir, The: *185*

Choirboys: *480*

Chordettes, The: Oct. 1954, Dec. 1955, July 1956, Sep. 1957, Mar. 1958; *15, 18, 22, 475, 504*

Chords, The: May 1954, Sep. 1954; *14, 16, 382*

Christian, Charlie: *502*

Christian, Chris: *374*

Christie: July 1970; *227*

Christie, Lou: Feb. 1963, Apr. 1963, Jan. 1966, Apr. 1966, Sep. 1969; *128*

Christopher, Gavin: *440*

Christopher, Shawn: Feb. 1991; *509*

Christy, June: *503*

Chubb Rock: *509*

Chuckles, The: Nov. 1954

Chunky A: *480*

Church, The: *467*

Church, Eugene, & the Fellows: Mar. 1959; *65*

Cinderella: Sep. 1988; *452, 529*

Cirino & the Bowties: *48*

City Boy: *333*

Clanton, Jimmy: July 1958, Dec. 1959, May 1960, Sep. 1962; *64, 74, 211, 331, 346*

Clapton, Eric: Oct. 1970, Sep. 1972, July 1974, Nov. 1974, Oct. 1976, Jan. 1978, Oct. 1978, Jan. 1983, Mar. 1985, Nov. 1989, Feb. 1992; *154, 197, 211, 225, 227, 239, 262, 263, 280, 288, 290, 302, 306, 340, 342, 346, 373, 409, 426, 435, 449, 462, 466, 490, 501, 509, 524, 528, 529*

Clapton, Eric, & His Band: Feb. 1981, June 1981

Clark, Claudine: July 1962; *114, 117*

Clark, Dave, Five, The: Mar. 1964, Apr. 1964, May 1964, June 1964, Aug. 1964, Oct. 1964, Mar. 1965, July 1965, Aug. 1965, Nov. 1965, Apr. 1967, Jan. 1968; *142, 151*

Clark, Dee: May 1959, Sep. 1959, Jan. 1960, May 1961; *64, 503*

Clark, Dick: *v, 46, 50–51, 77, 98, 110, 127, 140, 279, 356, 439, 449, 462, 479, 509*

Clark, Harold Eugene: *518, 519*

Clark, Mike: *196, 518*

Clark, Petula: Dec. 1964, Mar. 1965, Jan. 1966, Apr. 1966, July 1966, Jan. 1967, Mar. 1967, June 1967, Dec. 1967, Mar. 1968; *142, 151*

Clark, Roy: July 1969; *212*

Clark, Sanford: July 1956; *40*

Clark, Steve: *519*

Clarke, Allan: *333*

Clarke, Stanley: *374, 520*

Clarke, Stanley/George Duke: May 1981

Clash, The: Oct. 1982, Feb. 1983; *318, 359, 360*

Classics, The: July 1963; *129*

Classics IV, The: Dec. 1967, Nov. 1968, Feb. 1969, May 1969; *183*

Clay, Tom: *241*

Clayton, Merry: *467*

Cleftones, The: Jan. 1956, Apr. 1956, June 1956, June 1961, Sep. 1961; *38, 39, 101, 331, 504*

Clemons, Clarence: *440*

Cliburn, Van: *73*

Cliff, Jimmy: Jan. 1970; *213, 263*

Clifford, Buzz: Jan. 1961

Clifford, Linda: Aug. 1978; *333*

Clifford, Mike: Oct. 1962; *117*

Climax: Jan. 1972; *255*

Climax Blues Band, The: Feb. 1977, Feb. 1981; *320*

Cline, Patsy: Mar. 1957, May 1961, Nov. 1961, Feb. 1962, May 1963; *51, 114, 136, 435*

Clinton, Larry: *435*

Clique, The: *213*

Cliques, The: Apr. 1956; *40*

Clivilles & Cole: Jan. 1992; *524*

Clocks, The: *387*

Clooney, Rosemary: 1951, 1952, July 1954, Oct. 1954, Aug. 1955, May 1956; *5, 22*

Clout: *333*

Clovers, The: 1952, Feb. 1954, July 1954, Feb. 1955, Aug. 1955, Dec. 1955, June 1956, Oct. 1956, Oct. 1959; *5, 26, 475*

Club House, The: *401*

Clubland: *524*

Club Nouveau: Feb. 1987; *452*

Coasters, The: Mar. 1956, Apr. 1957, May 1957, June 1958, Feb. 1959, June 1959, Aug. 1959, Mar. 1961; *38, 39, 211, 276, 460, 461, 466, 503*

Cobb, Danny: *2*

Cobb, Joyce: *360*

Cochran, Eddie: Feb. 1957, Aug. 1958, Dec. 1958, Sep. 1959; *48, 51, 74, 88, 98, 460*

Cochrane, Tom: May 1992; *524*

Cockburn, Bruce: *360*

Cocker, Joe: Apr. 1970, Oct. 1970, Sep. 1972, Jan. 1975, Oct. 1989; *198, 211, 235, 236, 249*

Cocker, Joe, & Jennifer Warnes: Aug. 1982; *394*

Cock Robin: *427*

Coffey, Dennis, & the Detroit Guitar Band: Nov. 1971, Feb. 1972; *241*

Cohn, Marc: *509, 510, 517*

Cold Blood: *263*

Cole, Cozy: Sep. 1958; *65, 382*

Cole, Gardner: *467*

Cole, Jude: Apr. 1990, Dec. 1990; *494*

Cole, Natalie: Sep. 1975, Jan. 1977, Jan. 1978, May 1985, Mar. 1988, Apr. 1989, Feb. 1990, July 1991; *293, 301, 476, 516*

Cole, Nat "King": 1950, 1951, 1953, Jan. 1954, Aug. 1954, Nov. 1954, Jan. 1955, Feb. 1955, Mar. 1955, Apr. 1955, June 1955, Aug. 1955, Mar. 1956, July 1956, Dec. 1956, May 1957, Apr. 1958, Oct. 1958, Jan. 1961, Aug. 1962, Nov. 1962, May 1963, Sep. 1963; *23, 47, 59, 165, 516*

College Boyz, The: *524*

Collins, Judy: Nov. 1968, Dec. 1970, June 1975, Sep. 1977; *170, 172, 193*

Collins, Phil: June 1981, Nov. 1982, Feb. 1984, Feb. 1985, May 1985, July 1985, Mar. 1986, Sep. 1988, Nov. 1989, Feb. 1990, Apr. 1990, Aug. 1990, Nov. 1990, Feb. 1991; *293, 373, 413, 420, 421, 426, 434, 449, 466, 500, 501. See also* Bailey, Philip (with Phil Collins)

Collins, Phil, & Lamont Dozier: *474*

Collins, Phil, & Marilyn Martin: Oct. 1985

Collins, Tyler: *494*

Color Me Badd: July 1991, Nov. 1991, Feb. 1992, May 1992; *509, 516, 520*

Colourhaus: May 1992; *524*

Colter, Jessi: Apr. 1975; *294*

Coltrane, Chi: *255*

Coltrane, John: *192*

Colts, The: Oct. 1955; *28*

Comita, Pete: *359*

Commander Cody & His Lost Planet Airmen: Mar. 1972, July 1973; *255*

Commitments, The: Oct. 1991; *509, 520*

Commodores, The: June 1974, Sep. 1976, June 1977, Aug. 1977, Dec. 1977, June 1978, Aug. 1979, Sep. 1979, June 1980, June 1981, Sep. 1981, Jan. 1985; *281, 283, 327, 340, 342, 409*

Communards, The: Dec. 1986, Jan. 1988

Como, Perry: 1951, 1952, 1953, Feb. 1954, July 1954, Sep. 1954, Nov. 1954, Feb. 1955, July 1955, Mar. 1956, May 1956, Aug. 1956, Mar. 1957, Dec. 1957, Jan. 1958, Feb. 1958, June 1958, Nov. 1958, Apr. 1973; *22, 26, 26, 34, 73*

Como, Perry, & Jaye P. Morgan: June 1955

Company B: *452*

Comstock, Bobby: *78*

Concrete Blonde: *494*

Conductor: *387*

Con Funk Shun: Dec. 1977, Jan. 1981; *320*

Conley, Arthur: Mar. 1967; *184*

Connick, Harry, Jr.: *490*

Conniff, Ray: *52, 64*

Conniff, Ray, & the Singers: June 1966

Conniff, Ray, Singers, The: *144*

Connor, Chris: Dec. 1956; *40*

Connors, Norman: Aug. 1976; *308*

Consumer Rapport: Apr. 1975; *294*

Conti, Bill: Apr. 1977; *320*

Continental Miniatures, The: *333*

Contours, The: Oct. 1962; *115, 462*

Convy, Bert: *519*

Cooder, Ry: *346*

Cooke, Sam: Oct. 1957, Nov. 1957, Jan. 1958, Sep. 1958, Dec. 1958, Mar. 1959, June 1959, Mar. 1960, May 1960, Sep. 1960, Dec. 1960, June 1961, Feb. 1962, June 1962, Feb. 1963, Apr. 1963, Feb. 1964, July 1964, Jan. 1965; *51, 59, 115, 151, 382, 447, 462*

Cookies, The: Nov. 1962; *114, 117*

Cooley, Eddie, & the Dimples: Oct. 1956; *40*

Coolidge, Rita: May 1977, Sep. 1977, Jan. 1978, July 1978, July 1983; *212*

Cooper, Alice: Feb. 1971, June 1972, Oct. 1972, Sep. 1976, Apr. 1977, Oct. 1978, Sep. 1989; *238, 239, 274, 342, 369, 529*

Cooper, Les: Nov. 1962; *117*

Cooper Brothers, The: *333*

Cope, Julian: *85, 452*

Corea, Chick: *474*

Corey, Jill: Aug. 1957; *40*

Corina: *509*

Corley, Al: *427*

Cornelius, Carter: *519*

Cornelius Brothers, The, & Sister Rose: Apr. 1971, May 1972, Sep. 1972; *241, 519*

Cornell, Don: Aug. 1954, May 1955, Aug. 1955, Dec. 1955; *7*

Coro: *509*

Corsairs, The: Jan. 1962; *103*

Cortez, Dave "Baby": Mar. 1959, July 1959, Aug. 1962; *77*

Cosby, Bill: Sep. 1967

Costa, Don: *78, 408*

Costello, Elvis: Apr. 1989; *34, 399, 401*

Cotton, Gene: *281*

Cotton, Josie: *387*

Cougar, John: Oct. 1979, Jan. 1981, Apr. 1982, July 1982, Nov. 1982; *346, 393, 394. See also* Mellencamp, John Cougar; Mellencamp, John

Count Basie: *421*

Count Five, The: Sep. 1966; *172*

Country Joe & the Fish: *185, 236*

Covay, Don, & the Goodtimers: *103*

Coven: Sep. 1971, July 1973; *241*

Cover Girls, The: Feb. 1987, Mar. 1988, Dec. 1989, May 1992; *452*

Cowboy Church Sunday School: Jan. 1955; *28*

Cowsills, The: Oct. 1967, Jan. 1968, June 1968, Apr. 1969; *184*

Cramer, Floyd: Oct. 1960, Mar. 1961; *64*

Crane, Les: Oct. 1971; *241*

Crash Test Dummies: Oct. 1991; *509*

Crawford, Johnny: *101*

Cray, Robert: *452, 453, 462*

Crazy Elephant: Mar. 1969; *213*

Crazy Otto: *33*

Crazy World of Arthur Brown, The: Sep. 1968; *199*

Cream: Feb. 1968, July 1968, Oct. 1968, Feb. 1969; *183, 197, 198, 206, 220*

Creed, Linda: *448*

Creedence Clearwater Revival: Sep. 1968, Feb. 1969, May 1969, Aug. 1969, Nov. 1969, Feb. 1970, May 1970, Aug. 1970, Feb. 1971, July 1971, May 1972; *198, 220, 224, 234, 439, 520*

Creme, Lol: *413*

Crenshaw, Marshall: *387*

Crescendos, The: Dec. 1957; *52*

Crests, The: July 1957, Nov. 1957, Dec. 1958, Aug. 1959, Dec. 1959, Mar. 1960, July 1960; *51*

Cretones, The: *360*

Crew Cuts, The: May 1954, June 1954, Sep. 1954, Jan. 1955, Mar. 1955, June 1955, July 1955, Jan. 1956; *14, 15, 19, 22*

Crewe, Bob: Feb. 1956; *40*

Crewe, Bob, Generation, The: Jan. 1967; *172*

Crickets, The: July 1957, Nov. 1957, Apr. 1958, Aug. 1958; *51, 52, 137, 166*

Criss, Peter: *358*

Critters, The: June 1966, Aug. 1966; *172*

Croce, Jim: July 1972, Oct. 1972, Apr. 1973, Oct. 1973, Nov. 1973, Jan. 1974, Mar. 1974, June 1974; *253, 274, 275, 289*

Crosby, Bing: Mar. 1954; *34, 327*

Crosby, Bing, & Grace Kelly: Sep. 1956

Crosby, David: *196, 208, 215, 241, 518*

Crosby, Stills & Nash: Aug. 1969, Oct. 1969, June 1977, June 1982, Sep. 1982; *197, 212, 215, 221, 249, 369, 466, 494*

Crosby, Stills, Nash & Young: Apr. 1970, June 1970, July 1970, Sep. 1970; *225, 234, 236, 426, 509*

Cross, Christopher: Feb. 1980, June 1980, Oct. 1980, Mar. 1981, Aug. 1981, Jan. 1983, May 1983, Dec. 1983; *359, 367, 368, 369, 381*

Crow: Nov. 1970; *213*

Crowded House: Jan. 1987, July 1988; *452, 465*

Crowell, Rodney: *360*

Crows, The: Mar. 1954, May 1954, Aug. 1954, Jan. 1955; *15, 160*

Cruddup, Arthur "Big Boy": 1945; *15*

Cruise, Erin: Jan. 1992; *524*

Crusaders, The: *172*

Cryan' Shames, The: *172*

Crystal, Billy: July 1985; *427, 446, 459*

Crystals, The: Nov. 1961, Apr. 1962, Oct. 1962, Jan. 1963, May 1963, Aug. 1963; *100, 101, 114, 489*

Cuevas, Chris: *524*

Cuff Links, The: Oct. 1969; *213*

Cugini: *360*

Cult, The: *480, 482*

Culture Club: Dec. 1982, Apr. 1983, July 1983, Dec. 1983, Mar. 1984, May 1984, Oct. 1984, Dec. 1984, Apr. 1986; *111, 386, 408, 413, 420, 439*

Cummings, Burton: Oct. 1976; *306*

Cure, The: Aug. 1989, Dec. 1989, Apr. 1992, June 1992; *440*

Curiosity Killed the Cat: *452*

Currie, Cherie & Marie: *347*

Curry, Tim: *347*

Curtie & the Boom Box: *427*

Curtis, King: Apr. 1962; *115, 249*

Curtola, Bobby: *117*

Cut 'N' Move: *509*

Cutting Crew, The: Mar. 1987, June 1987, Sep. 1987; *452, 454*

Cymarron: June 1971; *241*

Cymbal, Johnny: Mar. 1963; *129*

Cynthia & Johnny 'O': *494*

Cypress Hill: *520, 524*

Cyrkle, The: May 1966, Aug. 1966; *170*

Cyrus, Billy Ray: May 1992; *524*

Dahl, Steve: *347*

Daily, E.G.: *440*

Daisey Dee: *510*

Dale, Allen: *47, 48*

Dale, Dick, & the Deltones: *137, 152*

Dale & Grace: Oct. 1963, Feb. 1964; *129*

Daltrey, Roger: Dec. 1985; *268, 303, 480*

Damian, Michael: Mar. 1989, June 1989, Oct. 1989; *374*

Damian Dame: *509*

Damita Jo: Nov. 1960

Damn Yankees: Apr. 1990, Sep. 1990, Apr. 1991; *495*

Damone, Vic: Feb. 1954, Apr. 1956, Sep. 1957

Damon's, Liz, Orient Express: Feb. 1971; *241*

Dana, Vic: Dec. 1961; *101, 124*

Dancer, Prancer & Nervous: Dec. 1959

Dandy & the Doolittle Band: *360*

Danger Danger: *495*

Dangerfield, Rodney: Dec. 1983; *401*

Daniels, Billy: *475*

Daniels, Charlie, Band, The: June 1979; *267, 369*

Danko, Rick: *342*

Danleers, The: July 1958; *65*

Danny & the Juniors: Nov. 1957, Mar. 1958, Oct. 1960; *51, 72, 74, 276, 408, 462*

Dante, Ron: *197*

Dante & the Evergreens: *90*

D'Arby, Terence Trent: Jan. 1988, May 1988, Sep. 1988; *452, 453, 473, 474*

Darensbourg, Joe, & His Dixie Flyers: Feb. 1958; *65*

Darin, Bobby: July 1958, Oct. 1958, Feb. 1959, May 1959, Sep. 1959, Feb. 1960, Mar. 1960, May 1960, Oct. 1960, Dec. 1960, Feb. 1961, Sep. 1961, Dec. 1961, Feb. 1963, May 1963, Oct. 1966; *64, 65, 84, 85, 89, 127, 275, 502*

Darren, James: Oct. 1961, Feb. 1962; *77, 152*

Dartells, The: Apr. 1963; *129*

DAS EFX: May 1992; *524*

Dash, Sarah: *347*

David, F.R.: *401*

David, Hal: *523*

David & David: *440*

David & Jonathan: *172*

Davie, Hutch: *65*

Davis, Billy, Jr. *See* McCoo, Marilyn, & Billy Davis, Jr.

Davis, Eddie "Locksaw": *461*

Davis, Jimmy, & Junction: *452*

Davis, John: *333*

Davis, Mac: May 1970, July 1972, Apr. 1974, Sep. 1974, Dec. 1974; *225, 261*

Davis, Martha: *452*

Davis, Miles: *519*

Davis, Paul: Aug. 1977, Aug. 1978, Nov. 1981, Feb. 1982; *225, 319*

Davis, Sammy, Jr.: July 1954, June

1955, Jan. 1969, Mar. 1972; *15, 34, 88, 261, 503*

Davis, Skeeter: Feb. 1963, Sep. 1963; *89, 92*

Davis, Spencer, Group, The: Jan. 1967, Apr. 1967; *167, 172, 183, 235*

Davis, Tyrone: Dec. 1968, Mar. 1970, Mar. 1971, July 1971; *198, 199*

Dawn: Aug. 1970, Nov. 1970, Feb. 1973, July 1973, Nov. 1973; *225, 226, 274*

Day, Arlan: *374*

Day, Bobby: Aug. 1958; *51, 503*

Day, Dennis: *475*

Day, Doris: 1952, Feb. 1954, June 1955, June 1956, Aug. 1958; *22*

Day, Doris, & Howard Keel: *22*

Day, Morris: *427*

Day, Morris, & the Time: *422*

Daye, Cory: *347*

Dayne, Taylor: Feb. 1988, June 1988, Oct. 1989, Jan. 1990, May 1990, Aug. 1990; *452*

Dayton: *387*

Dazz Band, The: *387*

Dead Boys, The: *503*

Dead or Alive: *427*

Deal, Bill, & the Rhondels: Feb. 1969, Sep. 1969; *213*

Dean, Jimmy: Oct. 1961, Jan. 1962, Feb. 1962, Apr. 1962, May 1976; *51, 110*

Dean & Jean: Dec. 1963; *129*

De Barge: Feb. 1983, Apr. 1983, Feb. 1985, June 1985; *339, 409*

De Barge, Chico: Nov. 1986; *440*

De Barge, El: Apr. 1986; *111, 440*

De Burgh, Chris: Aug. 1983, Feb. 1987; *399*

De Castro Sisters, The: Oct. 1954, Mar. 1955; *15*

Dee, Jimmie: Jan. 1958; *53*

Dee, Joey: *452*

Dee, Joey, & the Starliters: Nov. 1961, Feb. 1962; *100, 101, 111, 123*

Dee, Johnny: *53*

Dee, Kiki: *241. See also* John, Elton, & Kiki Dee

Dee, Kool Moe: *452, 501*

Dee, Lenny: Jan. 1955; *28*

Dee, Tommy: *78*

Deee-Lite: *495, 508*

Deele, The: *414*

Deep Purple: Aug. 1968, Dec. 1970, May 1973, Jan. 1985; *196, 198, 200, 293, 315*

Dees, Rick, & His Cast of Idiots: Aug. 1976; *308*

Def Leppard: June 1983, Oct. 1987, Jan. 1988, Aug. 1988, Mar. 1989, Apr. 1992, June 1992; *98, 399, 400, 473, 487, 519*

DeFranco Family, The: Sep. 1973, May 1974; *85, 268*

Degrees of Motion: *524*

Deja: *452*

DeJohn Sisters, The: Jan. 1955; *16*

Dekker, Desmond, & the Aces: May 1969; *213*

del Amitri: May 1990; *495*

Delaney & Bonnie: Sep. 1971; *225*

De La Soul: June 1989; *480*

Delegates, The: Oct. 1972; *255*

Delegation, The: *347*

Delfonics, The: Feb. 1968, Dec. 1968, Jan. 1970; *198*

Del Fuegos, The: *440*

Deliverance: *360*

Dells, The: Mar. 1955, Aug. 1956, Feb. 1968, July 1968, Jan. 1969, Aug. 1969, Apr. 1973; *27*

DeLory, Al: July 1970

Del Shannon: *110, 125, 128, 346*

Del Vikings, The: Jan. 1957, June 1957, July 1957; *51, 53, 60, 408, 503*

Demensions, The: Aug. 1960; *90*

Dennis, Cathy: Mar. 1991, July 1991; *510*

Denny, Martin: Apr. 1959; *78, 84*

Denver, John: June 1971, Mar. 1972, Nov. 1972, Feb. 1974, June 1974, Sep. 1974, Mar. 1975, Aug. 1975, Dec. 1975, Mar. 1976, Sep. 1976, Dec. 1976, Mar. 1977, Mar. 1982; *239, 241, 301, 340, 345, 381, 394, 407, 421, 426*

Deodato: Feb. 1973; *268*

Depeche Mode: Aug. 1990, Nov. 1990; *11, 427*

Derek: Nov. 1968; *199*

Derek & the Dominos: Apr. 1971, May 1972; *241, 504*

Derringer, Rick: May 1974; *282*

De Sario, Teri, & K.C.: Nov. 1979; *333*

DeShannon, Jackie: June 1965, July 1969; *152, 193*

Desmond, Johnny: Feb. 1954, Apr. 1955; *435*

Desmond, Paul: *327*

Detergents, The: Dec. 1964; *144*

Detroit Emeralds, The: *198*

De Vaughn, William: May 1974; *282*

Device: *440*

Devo: Aug. 1980, Sep. 1981, May 1983; *360*

De Vorzon, Barry, & Perry Botkin, Jr.: Aug. 1976; *308*

Devotions, The: Mar. 1964; *144*

Dewdrop, Daddy: Mar. 1971; *241*

Dewitt, Lew: *503*

Dexy's Midnight Runners: Jan. 1983; *401, 407*

DeYoung, Dennis: Sep. 1984, Dec. 1984; *414*

Diablos, The: June 1954; *16*

Diamond, Joel: *374*

Diamond, Neil: Sep. 1966, Feb. 1967, Apr. 1967, July 1967, Oct. 1967, Apr. 1968, Mar. 1969, July 1969, Nov. 1969, Mar. 1970, May 1970, July 1970, Aug. 1970, Nov. 1970, Apr. 1971, May 1972, Nov. 1972, Oct. 1974, Feb. 1975, June 1976, Sep. 1976, Dec. 1977, Jan. 1979, Dec. 1979, Nov. 1980, Jan. 1981, Apr. 1981, Nov. 1981, Feb. 1982, May 1982, Sep. 1982, Jan. 1983; *170, 172, 211, 253, 275, 277, 342, 369, 423. See also* Streisand, Barbra, & Neil Diamond

Diamonds, The: May 1956, Feb. 1957, Aug. 1957, Dec. 1957, Nov. 1958, Feb. 1959; *39, 41, 60, 523*

Dick & DeeDee: Aug. 1961, Apr. 1962, Apr. 1963; *101, 180*

Dickens, "Little" Jimmy: Nov. 1965; *158*

Dickey Doo & the Don'ts: Feb. 1958; *65*

Diddley, Bo. *See* Bo Diddley

Diesel: *374*

Digital Underground: Nov. 1991; *495*

Dillard, Varetta: *2*

Dillman Band, The: *374*

Dinning, Mark: Dec. 1959; *78, 448*

Dino: Aug. 1990, Nov. 1990; *467*

Dino, Kenny: *103*

Dino, Paul: *103*

Dino, Desi & Billy: *156*

Dion: Dec. 1960, Jan. 1961, Oct. 1961, Dec. 1961, Apr. 1962, July 1962, Nov. 1962, Feb. 1963, Mar. 1963, Sep. 1963, Nov. 1963, Oct. 1968, Aug. 1989; *64, 66, 89, 100, 110, 111, 252, 452, 480, 488*

Dion, Celine: Dec. 1990, Apr. 1992; *495*

Dion & the Belmonts: May 1958, Sep. 1958, Jan. 1959, Apr. 1959, Jan. 1960, May 1960; *64, 66, 89, 97, 252, 449, 528*

Dionne & Friends: Nov. 1985

Gayten, Paul: Nov. 1957; *52, 519*
G-Clefs, The: June 1956, Oct. 1961; *40*
Geddes, David: Aug. 1975, Dec. 1975; *294*
Geils, J., Band, The: Dec. 1971, Nov. 1974, Aug. 1977, Feb. 1980, Apr. 1980, Nov. 1981, Feb. 1982, Nov. 1982; *240, 253, 280, 393*
Geldof, Bob: *23, 413, 425, 452*
Gene & Debbe: Mar. 1968; *185*
Gene & Eunice: Dec. 1954, Mar. 1955; *16*
Gene Loves Jezebel: *467*
Genesis: Mar. 1977, Apr. 1978, May 1980, Sep. 1981, Dec. 1981, Nov. 1983, Mar. 1984, Aug. 1986, Nov. 1986, Feb. 1987, Apr. 1987, Nov. 1991, Feb. 1992, May 1992; *253, 293, 306, 319, 466*
Genies, The: *78*
Gentle Persuasion: *401*
Gentry, Bobbie: Aug. 1967; *184, 191, 192, 408*
Gentrys, The: Sep. 1965; *156, 193, 211*
George, Barbara: Jan. 1962; *103, 114*
George, Boy: *439*
George, Robin: *427*
Georgia Satellites, The: Nov. 1986; *440, 476*
Georgio: Dec. 1987
Gerardo: May 1991; *510*
Gerry & the Pacemakers: June 1964, July 1964, Nov. 1964, Jan. 1965, Apr. 1965; *142, 152, 166, 435*
Geto Boys: Oct. 1991; *510*
Get Wet: Apr. 1981; *374*
Getz, Stan: *519*
Getz, Stan, & Charlie Byrd: Nov. 1962; *117*
Getz, Stan, & Astrud Gilberto: *144, 151*
Getz, Stan, & João Gilberto: *151*
Getz/Gilberto: June 1964
Giant: *480*
Giant Steps: Aug. 1988; *467*
Gibb, Andy: May 1977, Nov. 1977, Apr. 1978, July 1978, Oct. 1978, Jan. 1980, Nov. 1980; *73, 320, 322, 326, 340, 452, 475*
Gibb, Andy, & Olivia Newton-John: Mar. 1980
Gibb, Andy, & Victoria Principal: Aug. 1981
Gibb, Barry: Sep. 1984. *See also* Streisand, Barbra, & Barry Gibb
Gibb, Robin: Aug. 1978; *333*
Gibbs, Georgia: 1952, Jan. 1955, Feb. 1955, Oct. 1958; *3, 14*
Gibbs, Terri: Jan. 1981; *23, 374*
Gibson, Debbie: Jan. 1988, Apr. 1988, Aug. 1988, Jan. 1989, Apr. 1989, June 1989, Nov. 1990; *452*
Gibson, Don: Mar. 1958; *65*
Gibson Brothers, The: *347*
Gidea Park featuring Adrian Baker: Jan. 1982; *387*
Giggles: *524*
Gilder, Nick: June 1978, Oct. 1978; *333*
Gilkyson, Terry, & the Easy Riders: Jan. 1957; *52*
Gill, Johnny: May 1990, Aug. 1990, Oct. 1990; *414, 520*
Gilley, Mickey: May 1980, Aug. 1980; *281, 369*
Gilmer, Jimmy, & the Fireballs: Sep. 1963, Dec. 1963; *129, 135*
Gilmour, David: *414*
Gina Go-Go: *480*
Giuffria: *427*
Gladiolas, The: *52*
Glass Moon: *387*
Glass Tiger: Feb. 1987, Apr. 1988; *440*
Glazer, Tom, & the Children's Choir: June 1963; *129*
Gleason, Jackie: *22, 34*
Glencoves, The: *129*

Glitter, Gary: July 1972; *255*
Glover, Henry: *519*
Goanna: *401*
Godley, Kevin: *413*
Godley & Creme: *427*
Godspell: May 1972; *255*
Goffin, Louise: *347*
Go-Go's, The: Aug. 1981, Jan. 1982, July 1982, Sep. 1982, Mar. 1984, June 1984; *373, 376, 438*
Gold, Andrew: Mar. 1977, Feb. 1978; *308*
Gold, Ernest: *97*
Golde, Frannie: *347*
Golden Earring, The: *281*
Goldsboro, Bobby: Mar. 1965, Mar. 1966, Sep. 1966, Mar. 1968, July 1968, Nov. 1968, Sep. 1969, Sep. 1972; *116, 206*
Gomm, Ian: Sep. 1979; *347*
Gone All Stars, The: Mar. 1958; *66*
Gonzales: *347*
Gooden, Sam: *518*
Goodman, Benny: *448*
Goodman, Dickie: June 1973, July 1974, Sep. 1975; *101, 489*
Good Question: *467*
Good 2 Go: *524*
Goodwin, Ron: Aug. 1957; *52*
Goody & Goody: *334*
Gordon, Barry: Dec. 1955; *28, 48*
Gordon, Dexter: *503*
Gordon, Lonnie: *510*
Gordon, Robert: *320*
Gore, Lesley: May 1963, July 1963, Oct. 1963, Jan. 1964, Apr. 1964, Aug. 1964, July 1965, Feb. 1967; *128, 129, 152, 166*
Gore, Michael: *414*
Gorky Park: *495*
Gorme, Eydie: Feb. 1963; *39, 179*
Goulet, Robert: Dec. 1964; *117, 124*
Go West: *427, 505*
GQ: Mar. 1979; *347*
Graces, The: *480*
Gracie, Charlie: Feb. 1957, Apr. 1957; *52, 60*
Graham, Bill: *519*
Graham, Larry: June 1980, Oct. 1980, Sep. 1981; *360*
Graham Central Station: *282*
Gramm, Lou: Jan. 1987, Oct. 1989; *452*
Grammer, Billy: Dec. 1958; *66*
Granahan, Gerry: *66*
Granata, Rocco: *78*
Grand Funk: July 1973, Jan. 1974, Mar. 1974, July 1974, Dec. 1974, Apr. 1975, Jan. 1976; *212, 288*
Grand Master Flash & the Furious Five: *387*
Grandmaster Slice: *510*
Grant, Amy: Feb. 1991, June 1991, Sep. 1991, Jan. 1992; *426, 427, 516. See also* Cetera, Peter, with Amy Grant
Grant, Earl: Sep. 1958; *65, 235*
Grant, Earl, Trio, The: *86*
Grant, Eddy: Apr. 1983; *401*
Grant, Gogi: Apr. 1956; *28, 47, 60*
Grant, Janie: *103*
Grass Roots, The: May 1967, Sep. 1968, July 1969, Nov. 1969, Feb. 1971, June 1971, Oct. 1971, Feb. 1972; *170*
Grateful Dead, The: Sep. 1970, Dec. 1971, July 1987; *211, 225, 229, 263, 275, 328, 368, 480, 503, 509*
Graves, Billy: *78*
Gray, Dobie: Jan. 1965, Feb. 1973; *128, 180*
Grean, Charles Randolph, Sound, The: *213*
Great White: *452*
Greaves, R.B.: Oct. 1969; *213*
Greco, Buddy: *117*
Greco, Cyndi: May 1976; *308*
Green, Al: July 1971, Dec. 1971, Apr.

1972, July 1972, Oct. 1972, Feb. 1973, July 1973, Dec. 1973, Sep. 1974, Mar. 1975; *184*
Green, Doc: *489*
Greenbaum, Norman: Mar. 1970; *224, 227*
Greene, Lorne: Nov. 1964; *144, 461*
Greenfield, Howard: *448*
Greenwood, Lee: June 1983; *401*
Gregg, Bobby, & His Friends: *117*
Grey & Hanks: *347*
Griffin, Bill: *253*
Griffith, Andy: Jan. 1954
Griffiths, Marcia: Dec. 1989; *480*
Grimes, Lloyd "Tiny": *2, 489*
Groce, Larry: Jan. 1976; *308*
Gross, Henry: June 1976; *294*
Groves, Big Boy: May 1955
GTR: May 1986; *440*
Guaraldi, Vince: *315*
Guaraldi, Vince, Trio: Jan. 1963; *117*
Guard, Dave: *519*
Guess Who, The: May 1965, Apr. 1969, July 1969, Nov. 1969, Mar. 1970, July 1970, Oct. 1970, Jan. 1971, May 1971, Sep. 1971, July 1974; *156, 158, 233*
Guitar, Bonnie: Apr. 1957; *52*
Guitar Slim: Feb. 1954
Guns N' Roses: June 1988, Oct. 1988, Jan. 1989, Apr. 1989, July 1991, Sep. 1991, Dec. 1991, June 1992; *466, 467, 473, 486, 508, 509*
Gunther, Cornell: *503*
Guthrie, Arlo: July 1972; *213, 221*
Guy: Nov. 1990, Feb. 1991; *480, 520*
Guy, Jasmine: Mar. 1991; *510*
Guys Next Door: Jan. 1991; *510*
Guthrie, Arlo: *523*
Guthrie, Gwen: *440*
Guthrie, Woody: *192, 196, 475*

Hackett, Steve: *319*
Hagar, Sammy: Dec. 1982, July 1984, Feb. 1987, June 1987; *320*
Hagar, Schon, Aaronson, Shreive: *414*
Haggard, Merle: *212*
Hain, Marshall: *348*
Haircut One Hundred: *387*
Haley, Bill: *382, 436, 460*
Haley, Bill, & His Comets: June 1954, July 1954, Nov. 1954, Feb. 1955, Mar. 1955, May 1955, June 1955, Oct. 1955, Nov. 1955, Feb. 1956, Mar. 1956, May 1956, Oct. 1956, Apr. 1958; *2, 5, 6, 14, 26, 27, 33, 35, 47, 48, 276, 279, 315, 449*
Hall, Aaron: *524*
Hall, Daryl: Aug. 1986, Oct. 1986
Hall, Daryl, & John Oates: Apr. 1988, July 1988, Oct. 1988, Sep. 1990; *281, 285, 326, 381, 426, 466*
Hall, Daryl, & John Oates with David Ruffin & Eddie Kendricks: Aug. 1985
Hall, Jimmy: Sep. 1980; *360*
Hall, John, Band, The: Dec. 1981; *374*
Hall, Lani: *374*
Hall, Larry: Dec. 1959; *78*
Hall, Tom T.: Dec. 1973; *241*
Hall & Oates: Mar. 1974, Feb. 1976, July 1976, Jan. 1977, Oct. 1977, Sep. 1980, Jan. 1981, May 1981, Aug. 1981, Nov. 1981, Mar. 1982, June 1982, Oct. 1982, Jan. 1983, May 1983, Oct. 1983, Feb. 1984, Sep. 1984, Dec. 1984, Mar. 1985, June 1985. *See also* Hall, Daryl, & John Oates
Hallyday, David: *452*
Halos, The: July 1961; *103*
Hamblen, Stuart: *489*
Hamilton, George, IV: Nov. 1956, Dec. 1957, July 1963; *39*
Hamilton, Joe Frank & Dennison: *308*
Hamilton, Joe Frank & Reynolds: June 1971, June 1975; *240*

Hamilton, Roy: Mar. 1954, May 1954, Oct. 1954, Apr. 1955, Feb. 1961; *15, 16, 74, 221*
Hamilton, Russ: June 1957; *52*
Hamlisch, Marvin: Apr. 1974; *282, 289*
Hammer: Nov. 1991, Dec. 1991, Mar. 1992, May 1992; *524. See also* Hammer, M.C.
Hammer, Jan: Sep. 1985; *427*
Hammer, M.C.: Apr. 1990, June 1990, Sep. 1990, Jan. 1991; *124, 495, 500, 501, 516. See also* Hammer.
Hammerstein, Oscar, II: *98*
Hammond, Albert: Oct. 1972; *254*
Hampton, Lionel, & His Band: *60*
Hancock, Herbie: Sep. 1983; *282, 413*
Handy, W.C.: *73*
Happenings, The: July 1966, Oct. 1966, Apr. 1967, July 1967; *171*
Happy Mondays: *510*
Hardcastle, Paul: *427*
Hardin, Tim: *368*
Harnell, Joe: Jan. 1963; *117*
Harpers Bizarre: Mar. 1967; *185, 208*
Harpo, Slim: Feb. 1966; *103, 235*
Harptones, The: Mar. 1954, Apr. 1954, July 1955, Aug. 1956; *10, 11, 26, 504*
Harris, Eddie: Mar. 1961; *103*
Harris, Emmylou: Feb. 1981; *294, 342. See also* Orbison, Roy, & Emmylou Harris
Harris, Major: Apr. 1975; *294*
Harris, Phil: 1950; *3*
Harris, Richard: Mar 1968; *199*
Harris, Rolf: June 1963; *129*
Harris, Sam: *414*
Harris, Thurston: Sep. 1957, Dec. 1957, Jan. 1958; *52, 503*
Harris, Wynonie: 1948
Harrison, George: Dec. 1970, Mar. 1971, Aug. 1971, May 1973, Dec. 1974, Jan. 1975, Sep. 1975, Jan. 1977, Mar. 1979, May 1981, Nov. 1982, Oct. 1987, Feb. 1988; *169, 224, 225, 239, 248, 262, 263, 280, 346, 449, 467, 473*
Harrison, George, & Friends: *261*
Harrison, Noel: *158*
Harrison, Wilbert: Apr. 1959; *78, 84*
Harry, Bobby. *See* Boyce, Tommy, & Bobby Hart
Harry, Debbie: July 1987; *374, 377*
Hart, Corey: May 1984, Sep. 1984, June 1985, Sep. 1986, Dec. 1986, June 1988; *413*
Hart, Freddie: Aug. 1971
Hartman, Dan: Oct. 1978, June 1981; *332*
Harvey & the Moonglows: Sep. 1958
Hathaway, Donny: *227, 355. See also* Flack, Roberta, with Donny Hathaway
Havens, Richie: Apr. 1971; *236, 241*
Hawkes, Chesney: Aug. 1991; *510*
Hawkins, Dale: May 1957; *52*
Hawkins, Edwin, Singers, The: May 1969; *213. See also* Melanie/Edwin Hawkins Singers
Hawkins, Erskine: 1945
Hawkins, Ronnie: June 1959; *78, 342*
Hawkins, Screamin' Jay: Nov. 1956; *40, 342, 435*
Hawkins, Sophie B.: Apr. 1992; *524*
Hawks, The: *374*
Hawley, Dean: *90*
Hay, Colin James: *452*
Hayes, Bill: Feb. 1955; *26, 28, 33*
Hayes, Isaac: Oct. 1971, Feb. 1972, Apr. 1972, Oct. 1972; *212, 276*
Hayman, Richard: *10*
Haynes, Dick: *368*
Haysi Fantayzee: *401*
Hayward, Justin: Oct. 1978; *334*
Haywood, Leon: *156*
Hazard, Robert: *401*

McCartney, Paul, & Michael Jackson: *407*

McCartney, Paul, & Stevie Wonder: *393*

McCartney, Paul, & Wings: Apr. 1973, Nov. 1973, Feb. 1974, Apr. 1974, Nov. 1974, Feb. 1975; *274, 288, 289, 301, 369, 393, 407*

McClain, Alton, & Destiny: *348*

McClinton, Delbert: Dec. 1980; *360*

McCoo, Marilyn, & Billy Davis, Jr.: Sep. 1976, Mar. 1977; *308, 315*

McCormick, Gayle: *241*

McCoy, Clyde: *503*

McCoy, Van: *293, 294, 355*

McCoy, Van, & Soul City Symphony: May 1975

McCoys, The: Sep. 1965, Nov. 1965; *156*

McCracklin, Jimmy: Mar. 1958; *66*

McCrae, George: June 1974; *280, 282*

McCrae, Gwen: May 1975; *294*

McCrarys, The: *334*

McDaniels, Gene: Mar. 1961, July 1961, Oct. 1961, Feb. 1962, Aug. 1962; *102, 125*

McDonald, Michael: Aug. 1982, July 1985, June 1986; *354, 387, 446. See also* Ingram, James, with Michael McDonald; Labelle, Patti, & Michael McDonald

McDonald, Ralph: *340*

McDowell, Ronnie: Sep. 1977; *320, 356*

McFadden & Whitehead: May 1979; *348*

McFerrin, Bobby: Aug. 1988; *466, 467, 474, 476*

McGee, Parker: Jan. 1977

McGhee, Stick: 1949

McGill, Rollie: Sep. 1955

McGilpin, Bob: *334*

McGovern, Maureen: June 1973, July 1979; *267*

MacGregor, Byron: Jan. 1974; *282*

MacGregor, Mary: Nov. 1976; *307, 326*

McGuinn, Clark & Hillman: Mar. 1979; *348, 351*

McGuinn, James Joseph "Roger", III: *518*

McGuire, Barry: Aug. 1965; *155, 158, 208*

McGuire Sisters, The: July 1954, Sep. 1954, Dec. 1954, Feb. 1955, Mar. 1955, May 1955, May 1956, Jan. 1958, Jan. 1959; *14, 16, 19, 33*

Machine: *348*

Mack, Lonnie: June 1963; *129*

McKenzie, Bob & Doug: *387*

MacKenzie, Gisele: Aug. 1955

McKenzie, Scott: June 1967; *183, 185, 222*

McLain, Tommy: July 1966; *172*

Mclan, Peter: *360*

McLean, Don: Nov. 1971, Mar. 1972, Mar. 1973, Jan. 1981, Apr. 1981, Oct. 1981; *77, 239, 240, 261, 266*

McLean, Phil: *103*

McLollie, Oscar: Nov. 1955

McMahon, Gerard: *401*

McNally, Larry John: *374*

McNamara, Robin: June 1970; *227*

McNeely, Big Jay: 1949; *78*

McNichol, Kristy: *136*

McNichol, Kristy & Jimmy: *334*

McPhatter, Clyde: Dec. 1955, Apr. 1956, Dec. 1956, Nov. 1958, Mar. 1962; *15, 27, 31, 60, 262, 460*

MacRae, Gordon: *448*

McVie, Christine: Jan. 1984, May 1984; *414*

Maddox, Johnny: Jan. 1955

Madigan, Betty: June 1954

Madness: May 1983; *401*

Madonna: Oct. 1983, Mar. 1984, Aug. 1984, Nov. 1984, Feb. 1985, Mar. 1985, Apr. 1985, Aug. 1985, Apr. 1986, June 1986, Oct. 1986, Dec. 1986, Mar. 1987, Sep. 1987, Mar. 1989, June 1989, Aug. 1989, Nov. 1989, Feb. 1990, Apr. 1990, June 1990, Nov. 1990, Mar. 1991, July 1992; *98, 400, 403, 413, 422, 426, 434, 446, 479, 500, 516, 517*

Maestro, Johnnie: *103*

Magazine 60: *440*

Maggard, Cledus, & the Citizen's Band: *294*

Magic Lanterns, The: Nov. 1968; *199*

Magnificents, The: July 1956; *40*

Main Ingredient, The: July 1972, Feb. 1974, July 1974; *249, 276*

Mai Tai: *440*

Majors, The: Sep. 1962; *117*

Makeba, Miriam: Oct. 1967; *185*

Malloy, Mitch: May 1992; *524*

Malo: Mar. 1972; *23, 255*

Maltby, Richard: *16, 519*

Mama Cass: July 1969; *198, 202, 289*

Mamas, The, & the Papas: Feb. 1966, Apr. 1966, July 1966, Dec. 1966, Mar. 1967, May 1967, July 1968; *171, 178, 179, 222*

Manchester, Melissa: May 1975, Nov. 1978, Feb. 1980, May 1982, Feb. 1983; *294, 298, 394*

Mancini, Henry: Apr. 1960, May 1962, Mar. 1963, May 1969, Jan. 1971; *73, 85, 90, 95, 97, 110, 111, 112, 123, 136*

Mancini, Henry, & Orchestra: Mar. 1977

Mandel, Steve. *See* Weissberg, Eric, & Steve Mandel

Mandrell, Barbara: *334, 413*

Mandrill: *241*

Mangione, Chuck: *241*

Manhattan Brothers, The: Nov. 1955; *40*

Manhattans, The: Apr. 1976, Apr. 1980, Mar. 1985; *156*

Manhattan Transfer, The: Sep. 1975, Apr. 1980, May 1981, Feb. 1985; *294, 373, 381, 474*

Manilow, Barry: Nov. 1974, Mar. 1975, July 1975, Nov. 1975, Mar. 1976, Sep. 1976, Nov. 1976, May 1977, Sep. 1977, Feb. 1978, May 1978, June 1978, Sep. 1978, Dec. 1978, Oct. 1979, Dec. 1979, Apr. 1980, Nov. 1980, Oct. 1981, Dec. 1981, Mar. 1982, July 1982, Nov. 1982, Nov. 1983; *281, 289, 327, 340, 341*

Mann, Barry: Aug. 1961; *103*

Mann, Gloria: Mar. 1955, Jan. 1956; *28*

Mann, Herbie: Mar. 1975; *171*

Mann, Manfred: Sep. 1964, Nov. 1964, Mar. 1968; *143, 155, 520*

Mannheim Steam Roller: *517*

Mann's, Manfred, Earth Band: Nov. 1976

Mantovani: *5, 368*

Mantovani & His Orchestra: 1951

Mantronix (featuring Wondress): *495*

Marathons, The: Mar. 1961; *103*

Marcels, The: Mar. 1961, June 1961, Oct. 1961; *101, 103, 110, 111*

March, Little Peggy: Mar. 1963; *129, 130, 135*

Marchan, Bobby: *90*

Mardones, Benny: *360*

Maresca, Ernie: Apr. 1962; *117*

Marillion: *427*

Marketts, The: Jan. 1964, Feb. 1966; *117*

Mar-Keys, The: July 1961; *103*

Mark IV, The: Feb. 1959; *66*

Markham, Pigmeat: *199*

Marks, Johnny: *435*

Marky Mark & the Funky Bunch: Nov. 1991; *510*

Marky Mark & the Funky Bunch/Loleatta Holloway: June 1991

Marley, Bob: *280, 382*

Marley, Bob, & the Wailers: *308, 342*

Marley, Ziggy, & the Melody Makers: May 1988; *467*

Marmalade: Mar. 1970; *227*

Marriott, Steve: *519*

M/A/R/R/S: Nov. 1987; *10, 341, 452*

Marsalis, Branford, quartet: *504*

Marterie, Ralph: Aug. 1954

Martha & the Vandellas: Aug. 1963, Jan. 1964, Sep. 1964, Mar. 1965, Nov. 1966, Mar. 1967; *128, 132, 476*

Martika: June 1989, Sep. 1989, Aug. 1991; *480*

Martin, Bobbi: Mar. 1970; *144*

Martin, Dean: 1953, June 1954, Nov. 1955, Apr. 1956, Apr. 1958, July 1964, Oct. 1964, June 1965, Aug. 1965, July 1967; *3, 4, 46, 150*

Martin, Eric: *519*

Martin, Marilyn: Jan. 1986; *427. See also* Collins, Phil, & Marilyn Martin

Martin, Moon: Aug. 1979; *348*

Martin, Steve: May 1978, Nov. 1979; *320*

Martin, Tony: Mar. 1954, June 1956

Martin, Vince, with the Tarriers: Sep. 1956; *40*

Martindale, Wink: Sep. 1959; *78*

Martinez, Nancy: *452*

Martinez, Tony: *48*

Martino, Al: *7*

Marvelettes, The: Sep. 1961, Feb. 1962, May 1962, Sep. 1962, Dec. 1964, Jan. 1966, Mar. 1967, Dec. 1967; *102, 114*

Marvelows, The: June 1965; *158*

Marvin & Johnny: July 1954; *16*

Marx, Richard: Sep. 1987, Jan. 1988, May 1988, May 1989, July 1989, Oct. 1989, Jan. 1990, Apr. 1990, Nov. 1991, Feb. 1992, June 1992; *452, 523*

Mary Jane Girls, The: Mar. 1985, July 1986; *427*

Mas, Carolyne: *348*

Masekela, Hugh: June 1968; *185, 222*

Mason, Barbara: June 1965; *156*

Mason, Dave: Aug. 1970, Sep. 1977, Jan. 1978, July 1980; *226, 331*

Masse, Laurel: *373*

Massey, Wayne: *360*

Mass Production: *320*

Mathis, Johnny: Jan. 1957, Mar. 1957, Aug. 1957, Dec. 1957, July 1958, Oct. 1958, July 1959, Oct. 1959, Dec. 1961, Oct. 1962, Feb. 1963; *52, 73, 85, 97, 110, 266*

Mathis, Johnny, & Dionne Warwick: Apr. 1982

Mathis, Johnny, & Deniece Williams: Apr. 1978, Aug. 1978

Matthews, Ian: Nov. 1978; *255*

Matthews Southern Comfort: Oct. 1971; *241*

Matys Brothers, The: *129*

Mauriat, Paul: Jan. 1968; *199, 206*

Mauriat, Paul, & His Orchestra: *206*

Max, Christopher: *480*

Maxwell, Robert: Apr. 1964; *7, 144*

May, Billy: Feb. 1956; *40*

Mayall, John: *214*

Mayer, Nathaniel: May 1962; *117*

Mayfield, Curtis: Aug. 1972, Nov. 1972; *226, 263, 276, 494, 518*

Mayfield, Percy: *421*

Maze: *320*

M.C. Brains: July 1992; *524*

M.C. Breed & D.F.C.: Sep. 1991; *510*

MC Lyte: Mar. 1992; *524*

M'Cool, Shamus: *374*

MC Skat Kat & the Stray Mob: *510*

Mead, Sister Janet: Mar. 1974; *282*

Meat Loaf: Mar. 1978, Aug. 1978, Nov. 1978; *302, 334, 369*

Meco: Aug. 1977, Jan. 1978, Feb. 1982; *320, 326*

Medallions, The: Nov. 1954; *16*

Medeiros, Glenn: Dec. 1987; *452*

Medeiros, Glenn (featuring Bobby Brown): May 1990

Medeiros, Glenn (featuring Ray Parker Jr.): Aug. 1990

Medley, Bill: *198*

Medley, Bill, & Jennifer Warnes: Sep. 1987; *459, 462*

Megadeth: *508*

Megatrons, The: *78*

Meisner, Randy: Oct. 1980, Jan. 1981; *360*

Melanie: Nov. 1971, Dec. 1973; *226*

Melanie/Edwin Hawkins Singers: May 1970

Melendez, Lisette: *510*

Mel & Kim: *452*

Melle Mel: *501*

Mellencamp, John: Oct. 1991, Feb. 1992; *523. See also* Cougar, John; Mellencamp, John Cougar

Mellencamp, John Cougar: Oct. 1983, Dec. 1983, Mar. 1984, Aug. 1985, Nov. 1985, Feb. 1986, Apr. 1986, June 1986, Aug. 1987, Oct. 1987, Feb. 1988, May 1989, July 1989; *426, 476. See also* Cougar, John; Mellencamp, John

Mello-Kings, The: June 1957; *52, 302, 331*

Mello-Tones, The: Apr. 1957; *52*

Mellow Man Ace: *495*

Mel & Tim: Oct. 1969; *214*

Melvin, Harold, & the Blue Notes: July 1972, Sep. 1972, Sep. 1973, Apr. 1975, Dec. 1975; *239, 254, 386*

Memphis Slim: *475*

Mendes, Sergio, & Brasil '66: Oct. 1966, May 1968, Aug. 1968; *171*

Men without Hats: Oct. 1987; *401*

Menudo: *414*

Men At Work: Nov. 1982, Apr. 1983, July 1983; *387, 393, 394, 407*

Mercer, Johnny: *112, 315, 524*

Mercer, Mabel: *421*

Mercury, Freddie: *519*

Mercy: Apr. 1969; *214*

Merman, Ethel: *421*

Metallica: Feb. 1989, Aug. 1991, Dec. 1991, Mar. 1992, July 1992; *466, 480, 481, 487, 501, 509, 517*

Meters, The: *213*

Metheny, Pat, Group. *See* Bowie, David/Pat Metheny Group

MFSB: Mar. 1974, July 1974; *282, 288, 340*

Miami Sound Machine, The: June 1986, May 1987, Nov. 1987; *440, 493. See also* Estefan, Gloria, & the Miami Sound Machine

Michael, George: Apr. 1986, June 1987, Oct. 1987, Jan. 1988, Apr. 1988, July 1988, Oct. 1988, Sep. 1990, Oct. 1990, Jan. 1991, Feb. 1991, June 1991; *136, 413, 433, 438, 440, 449, 451, 462, 466, 473, 474, 508. See also* Franklin, Aretha, & George Michael; Wham! featuring George Michael

Michael, George, (with Elton John): Dec. 1991

Michaels, Lee: *241*

Michel'Le: Jan. 1991; *480*

Mickey Mozart Quintet, The: *78*

Mickey & Sylvia: Nov. 1956, Jan. 1957; *40, 462*

Midi Maxi & Efti: *524*

Midler, Bette: Dec. 1972, May 1973, Jan. 1980, Mar. 1980, Oct. 1990, Jan. 1991, Dec. 1991; *254, 275, 355, 367, 369, 413, 476, 480, 486, 487, 501*

Midnighters, The: Apr. 1954, June 1954, Aug. 1954, Oct. 1954; *16, 20.*

Midnighters, The (cont.)
See also Ballard, Hank, & the Midnighters
Midnight Oil: Aug. 1988, Feb. 1990; *467*
Midnight Star: *400*
Mike + the Mechanics: Mar. 1986, June 1986, Jan. 1989, Apr. 1989; *440*
Milburn, Amos: 1949; *368*
Miles, Buddy: July 1971; *213*
Miles, Gary: *90*
Miller, Alonzo: *501*
Miller, Chuck: May 1955; *28*
Miller, Frankie: *320*
Miller, Glenn, & His Orchestra: *22*
Miller, Jody: May 1965, July 1971; *143*
Miller, Marcus: *517*
Miller, Mitch: June 1955, Sep. 1956, Jan. 1958; *3, 4, 33, 73*
Miller, Mrs.: *172*
Miller, Ned: Jan. 1963; *117*
Miller, Roger: June 1964, Oct. 1964, Feb. 1965, May 1965, Nov. 1965; *143, 165, 279, 412*
Miller, Steve: Oct. 1973, Oct. 1982; *202*
Miller, Steve, Band, The: May 1976, Aug. 1976, Dec. 1976, May 1977, Aug. 1977, May 1982; *198, 222, 327, 343, 394*
Millinder, Lucky: 1949
Millions Like Us: *452*
Milli Vanilli: Jan. 1989, May 1989, Aug. 1989, Oct. 1989, Jan. 1990; *480, 486, 487, 494*
Mills, Frank: Jan. 1979; *255*
Mills, Garry: July 1960; *90*
Mills, Hayley: Sep. 1961; *103*
Mills, Herbert: *489*
Mills, Stephanie: Aug. 1980; *59, 347*
Mills Brothers, The: 1952, Jan. 1954, Mar. 1968; *60, 395, 489*
Milsap, Ronnie: June 1977, Dec. 1977, June 1981, Oct. 1981, May 1982; *226*
Milton, Roy: 1946, 1947; *408*
Mimms, Garnet, & the Enchanters: Sep. 1963; *128*
Mindbenders, The: Apr. 1966; *172*
Mineo, Sal: Apr. 1957; *52, 315*
Mink De Ville: *414*
Minogue, Kylie: May 1988, Aug. 1988; *467*
Minor Detail: *401*
Mint Condition: Jan. 1992; *524*
Miracles, The: Dec. 1960, Jan. 1963, Aug. 1963, Apr. 1965, July 1965, Oct. 1965, Jan. 1966, Sep. 1974, Nov. 1975; *65, 69, 89, 253, 409*
Missing Persons: Mar. 1983; *34, 387, 394*
Mistress: *348*
Mitchell, Chad, Trio, The: Dec. 1963; *117*
Mitchell, Guy: 1951, Feb. 1956, Oct. 1956, Mar. 1957, Oct. 1959; *3, 5, 47, 84*
Mitchell, Joni: Apr. 1974, Dec. 1974; *226, 230, 249, 342*
Mitchell, Kim: *427*
Mitchell, Willie: *143*
Mitchum, Robert: *66*
M + M: June 1984: *414*
Mocca Soul: *524*
Mocedades: Feb. 1974; *282*
Models, The: Apr. 1986; *440*
Modern English: *59, 401*
Modugno, Domenico: Aug. 1958; *66, 72, 73*
Molly Hatchet: *360, 362*
Moments, The: Apr. 1970, Feb. 1974; *198*
Monarchs, The: *144*
Mondo Rock: *452*
Money, Eddie: Feb. 1978, Jan. 1979, July 1982, Aug. 1986, Dec. 1986, Apr. 1987, Oct. 1988, Jan. 1989, Apr. 1989, Dec. 1989, Sep. 1991, Dec. 1991; *333, 337*

Money, Eddie, & Valerie Carter: Oct. 1980
Monie Love: Mar. 1991; *510*
Monk, Thelonius: *395*
Monk, T.S.: *374*
Monkees, The: Sep. 1966, Dec. 1966, Apr. 1967, July 1967, Nov. 1967, Mar. 1968, June 1968, July 1986, Sep. 1987; *170, 171, 173, 179, 191, 192, 207, 439*
Monotones, The: Apr. 1958; *66*
Monro, Matt: June 1961
Monroe, Vaughn: Aug. 1954; *275*
Monroes, The: *387*
Monte, Lou: Feb. 1954, Dec. 1962; *16*
Montenegro, Hugo: *199, 382*
Montez, Chris: Sep. 1962, June 1966, Sep. 1966; *116*
Moody Blues, The: Mar. 1965, Aug. 1968, Oct. 1968, May 1970, Aug. 1971, Aug. 1972, Feb. 1973, June 1981, Aug. 1981, Sep. 1983; *157, 381*
Moon, Keith: *197, 346, 502*
Mooney, Art: Apr. 1955
Moonglows, The: Apr. 1954, Oct. 1954, Apr. 1955, Dec. 1955, June 1956, Sep. 1956; *10, 11, 14, 26, 48, 60, 368*
Moore, Bob: *103*
Moore, Dorothy: Mar. 1976; *308*
Moore, Gary: *510*
Moore, Jackie: Dec. 1970; *227*
Moore, Johnny: 1947
Moore, Melba: Jan. 1979; *308*
Moore, Scotty: *15*
Morales, Michael: Dec. 1989, July 1991; *480*
Morali, Jacques: *519*
Morgan, Jane: Aug. 1957, Oct. 1958; *40*
Morgan, Jaye P.: Sep. 1954, Sep. 1955; *16. See also* Como, Perry, & Jaye P. Morgan
Morgan, Meli'sa: *440*
Morisette, Johnnie: *117*
Moroder, Giorgio: *255*
Morrison, Dorothy: *214*
Morrison, Jim: *211, 520*
Morrison, Van: Aug. 1967, Nov. 1970, Oct. 1971; *184, 186, 342*
Motels, The: Apr. 1982, Sep. 1983, Dec. 1983, July 1985; *387, 395*
Mother Earth: *222*
Motherlode: Aug. 1969; *214*
Mötley Crüe: July 1985, May 1987, Sep. 1989, Feb. 1990, June 1990, Sep. 1990, Sep. 1991, Nov. 1991; *111, 413, 415, 438, 500*
Motors, The: *360*
Mott the Hoople: Sep. 1972; *255*
Mountain: *227*
Mouth & MacNeal: May 1972; *255*
Moving Pictures: Sep. 1982; *387*
Moyet, Alison: *427*
Mr. Big: Dec. 1991, Apr. 1992
Mr. Mister: Sep. 1985, Dec. 1985, Mar. 1986, Aug. 1987; *413, 416, 433, 446*
Ms. Adventures: *495*
Mtume: June 1983; *401*
Muddy Waters: June 1954; *5, 342, 408, 460, 494*
Muldaur, Maria: Mar. 1974; *282*
Mull, Martin: May 1973
Mungo Jerry: July 1970; *227*
Munro, Matt: *434*
Muppets, The: Sep. 1979
Murdock, Shirley: *452*
Murmaids, The: Dec. 1963; *129*
Murphey, Michael: May 1975; *254*
Murphy, Eddie: Oct. 1985; *v, 111, 427*
Murphy, Peter: *495*
Murphy, Walter: *340*
Murphy, Walter, & the Big Apple Band: May 1976; *308*
Murray, Anne: July 1970, Jan. 1973, May 1973, Dec. 1973, Apr. 1974, July

1978, Jan. 1979, May 1979, Sep. 1979, Dec. 1979, Apr. 1980, June 1980, Sep. 1980; *226, 230, 340*
Musical Youth: *387*
Music Explosion, The: May 1967; *185*
Music Machine, The: *172*
Musique: Oct. 1978; *334*
Mydland, Brent: *503*
Myles, Billy: Oct. 1957; *52*
Myles, Alannah: Jan. 1990; *495, 501*
Mynah Birds, The: *331*
Mystics, The: May 1959; *78, 528*

Naked Eyes: Mar. 1983, July 1983; *400*
Napoleon XIV: July 1966; *170, 172*
Nash, Graham: *215, 241*
Nash, Johnny: Sep. 1968, Sep. 1972, Feb. 1973; *52, 261*
Nashville Teens, The: Oct. 1964; *144, 167*
Natural Selection: Aug. 1991, Dec. 1991; *510*
Nature's Divine: *348*
Naughton, David: Mar. 1979; *348*
Naughty by Nature: Sep. 1991; *510, 520*
Nazareth: Dec. 1975; *294*
Nazz, The: *214*
N'Dour, Youssou: *466*
Neely, Sam: Jan. 1973, Feb. 1975; *255*
Neighborhood, The: July 1970; *227*
Nelson: *494, 495*
Nelson, Ozzie: *301*
Nelson, Phyllis: Feb. 1986; *440*
Nelson, Ricky: May 1957, Aug. 1957, Sep. 1957, Dec. 1957, Apr. 1958, July 1958, Oct. 1958, Mar. 1959, July 1959, Dec. 1959, May 1960, Mar. 1961, Oct. 1961, Mar. 1962, Aug. 1962, Dec. 1962, June 1963, Sep. 1963, Jan. 1964, May 1964, Aug. 1972; *51, 52, 58, 72, 435, 460*
Nelson, Sandy: Sep. 1959, Nov. 1961; *78*
Nelson, Terry. *See* C Company featuring Terry Nelson
Nelson, Willie: Sep. 1975, Feb. 1980, Sep. 1980, Mar. 1982; *294, 426, 523. See also* Iglesias, Julio, & Willie Nelson
Nena: Dec. 1983; *401*
Neon Philharmonic, The: May 1969; *214*
Nero, Peter: *111*
Nervous Norvus: June 1956; *40*
Nesmith, Michael: Aug. 1970
Nesmith, Michael, & the First National Band: *227*
Netto, Loz: *401*
Nevil, Robbie: May 1987, Mar. 1989, July 1991; *453*
Neville, Aaron: Dec. 1966; *172*
Neville, Ivan: *467*
Neville Brothers: *487*
Newbeats, The: Aug. 1964, Oct. 1965; *143*
New Birth: *240*
New Christy Minstrels, The: July 1963, May 1964; *116, 155, 183*
Newcity Rockers, The: *453*
Newcleus: *414*
New Colony Six, The: Apr. 1968, Jan. 1969; *171*
New Edition, The: Sep. 1984, Dec. 1984, Aug. 1986, Feb. 1989; *400*
New England: *348*
New Kids on the Block: Apr. 1989, July 1989, Sep. 1989, Nov. 1989, May 1990, Aug. 1990; *467, 487*
Newman, Randy: Nov. 1977; *320, 323*
Newman, Randy, & Paul Simon: Jan. 1983
Newman, Thunderclap: Oct. 1969
Newman, Troy: *510*
New Order: Apr. 1988; *453*

New Riders of the Purple Sage, The: *255*
New Seekers, The: Sep. 1970, Dec. 1971; *226*
Newton, Juice: Feb. 1981, May 1981, Oct. 1981, May 1982, Aug. 1982, Dec. 1982, Aug. 1983; *333, 339*
Newton, Wayne: Apr. 1972; *128*
Newton-John, Olivia: Nov. 1973, Apr. 1974, Aug. 1974, Jan. 1975, June 1975, Oct. 1975, Aug. 1976, Nov. 1976, Jan. 1977, Nov. 1977, July 1978, Nov. 1978, Apr. 1979, May 1980, Oct. 1981, Feb. 1982, Sep. 1982, Nov. 1983, Feb. 1984, Oct. 1985; *240, 244, 288, 289, 342, 345, 367, 381. See also* Gibb, Andy, & Olivia Newton-John: Travolta, John, & Olivia Newton-John
Newton-John, Olivia, & The Electric Light Orchestra: Aug. 1980; *367, 369*
Newton-John, Olivia, & Cliff Richard: Oct. 1980; *369*
New Vaudeville Band, The: Nov. 1966; *172, 178, 179*
New Yardbirds, The: *196*
New York City: *268*
New York Dolls, The: *253, 519, 529*
Nice & Smooth: *524*
Nicholas, Paul: Sep. 1977; *302, 320, 323, 342, 369*
Nichols, Mike, & Elaine May: *111*
Nicks, Stevie: Feb. 1982, June 1983, Sep. 1983, Dec. 1983, Nov. 1985, Feb. 1986, May 1986, May 1989, Sep. 1991; *293, 374, 380, 381. See also* Petty, Tom, & the Heartbreakers with Stevie Nicks
Nicks, Stevie, & Don Henley: Oct. 1981
Nicks, Stevie, with Tom Petty & the Heartbreakers: June 1981
Nielsen/Pearson: *360*
Night: *348*
Nightingale, Maxine: Feb. 1976, May 1979; *308*
Night Ranger: July 1984, May 1985; *59, 400*
Nikki: Apr. 1990; *495*
Nilsson: Sep. 1969, Nov. 1969, Dec. 1971, June 1972; *213, 221, 261, 262, 290*
9.9: *427*
1910 Fruitgum Company, The: Feb. 1968, Aug. 1968, Feb. 1969; *197, 198*
1927: *480*
Nino & the Ebb Tides: Sep. 1961; *40*
Nirvana: Dec. 1991, Mar. 1992; *510*
Niteflyte: *348*
Nite-Liters, The: July 1971; *241*
Nitty Gritty Dirt Band, The: Nov. 1970; *184, 189*
Nitzsche, Jack: *129*
NKOTB: Feb. 1992; xxx
Noble, Nick: July 1955
Nobles, Cliff, & Co.: June 1968; *199*
Nocera: *453*
Noel: *453*
Nolan, Kenny: Nov. 1976; *308*
Norman, Chris. *See* Quatro, Suzi, & Chris Norman
North, Alex: *519*
Northern Pikes, The: *524*
Notorious: Dec. 1990; *495*
Nova, Aldo: *387*
N2Deep: July 1992; *524*
Nugent, Ted: Aug. 1977; *307, 315*
Numan, Gary: Feb. 1980; *73, 360*
Nu Shooz: *440*
Nutmegs, The: May 1955; *28*
Nu Tornados: Dec. 1958; *66*
Nutty Squirrels, The: Dec. 1959; *78*
NYASIA: *524*
Nylons, The: May 1987; *453*
Nyro: *227*

Oak: Dec. 1980; *348*
Oak Ridge Boys, The: May 1981; *374, 383*
Oaktown's 3.5.7: *510*
Oates, John, *See* Hall, Daryl, & John Oates
O'Banion, John: Mar, 1981; *374*
O'Bryan: *387*
Ocasek, Ric: Sep. 1986, Dec. 1986; *401*
Ocean: Mar. 1971; *241*
Ocean, Billy: Apr. 1976, Aug. 1984, Mar. 1985, Nov. 1985, Apr. 1986, July 1986, Oct. 1986, Feb. 1988, May 1988, Oct. 1989; *307, 420*
O'Connor, Carroll, & Jean Stapleton: *241*
O'Connor, Sinead: Mar. 1990; *494, 495, 500*
O'Day, Alan: Apr. 1977, Oct. 1977; *320*
O'Dell, Kenny: *185*
Odyssey: Nov. 1977, May 1978; *320*
Off Broadway U.S.A.: *360*
Ohio Express, The: May 1968, Oct. 1968; *184, 197*
Ohio Players, The: Feb. 1973, Sep. 1974, Dec. 1974, Sep. 1975, Nov. 1975, July 1977; *240*
Oingo Boingo: Jan. 1986; *427*
O'Jays, The: July 1972, Jan. 1973, Apr. 1974, Nov. 1975, Mar. 1976, Sep. 1976, May 1978, Nov. 1979; *128, 239, 276, 306, 327*
O'Kaysions, The: Sep. 1968; *199*
O'Keefe, Danny: Sep. 1972; *255*
Oldfield, Mike: Mar. 1974; *282*
Oliver: June 1969, Sep. 1969; *214*
Oliver, Sy: *475*
Olivor, Jane: *320*
Ollie & Jerry: June 1984; *414, 422*
Olsson, Nigel: Dec. 1978; *294*
Olympics, The: July 1958, Sep. 1960; *65*
O'Malley, Lenore: *360*
O'Neal, Alexander: *453*
100 Proof Aged in Soul: Sep. 1970; *214*
One to One: *440*
One 2 Many: *480*
One 2 One: *524*
One Way: *387*
Ono, Yoko: *170, 211, 293, 374, 423, 476*
Opus: *440*
Orbison, Roy: June 1956, July 1960, Oct. 1960, Mar. 1961, Aug. 1961, Mar. 1962, Feb. 1963, June 1963, Sep. 1963, Apr. 1964, Sep. 1964, Jan. 1989; *40, 43, 150, 369, 460, 462, 467, 475, 501, 505*
Orbison, Roy, & Emmylou Harris: June 1980
Orchestral Manoeuvres in the Dark: Dec. 1985, Mar. 1988; *426*
Original Caste, The: Dec. 1969
Originals, The: Oct. 1969, Feb. 1970; *214*
Orioles, The: 1953, Aug. 1954; *382*
Orion the Hunter: *414*
Orlando, Tony: May 1961, Aug. 1961; *102, 226*
Orlando, Tony, & Dawn: Jan. 1974, Sep. 1974, Jan. 1975, Mar. 1975, June 1975, Sep. 1975, Feb. 1976, Apr. 1977; *300*
Orleans: July 1975, July 1976, Mar. 1979; *294*
Orlons, The: June 1962, Oct. 1962, Mar. 1963, July 1963, Oct. 1963; *114, 116, 119, 327*
Ormandy, Eugene: *435*
Or-N-More (featuring Father M.C.): *510*
Orpheus: *214*
Orr, Benjamin: *453*
Orral, Robert Ellis: *401*
Osborne, Jeffrey: Sep. 1982; *387. See also* Warwick, Dionne, & Jeffrey Osborne

Osbourne, Ozzy: *386, 440, 446. See also* Ford, Lita (with Ozzy Osbourne)
Osmond, Donny: Apr. 1971, Aug. 1971, Nov. 1971, Feb. 1972, Aug. 1972, Mar. 1973, July 1973, Mar. 1989, June 1989, Oct. 1990; *59, 240, 247, 373, 480*
Osmond, Donny & Marie: Aug. 1974, Nov. 1974
Osmond, "Little" Jimmy: *136, 255*
Osmond, Marie: Sep. 1973; *85, 268*
Osmonds, The: Jan. 1971, Sep. 1971, Feb. 1972; *240, 247*
O'Sullivan, Gilbert: June 1972, Oct. 1972, Mar. 1973, June 1973; *254, 261*
Other Ones, The: Apr. 1987; *453*
Otis, Johnny: *86*
Otis, Johnny, Little Esther & Mel Walker: 1950
Otis, Johnny, Show, The: July 1958
Outfield, The: June 1986, June 1987, Nov. 1990; *440*
Outlaws, The: Dec. 1980; *294*
Outsiders, The: Mar. 1966, Aug. 1966; *172*
Overbea, Danny: *26*
Owen, Reg: Jan. 1959; *66*
Owens, Donnie: Oct. 1958; *66*
Oxo: *401*
Ozark Mountain Daredevils, The: Mar. 1975; *282*

Pablo Cruise: June 1978, Oct. 1979, June 1981; *320, 325*
Pacific Gas & Electric: Aug. 1970; *227*
Pack, David: *440*
Page, Jimmy: *196, 409, 528*
Page, Patti: 1950, 1951, 1952, 1953, Jan. 1954, Feb. 1954, May 1954, Aug. 1954, Oct. 1954, Dec. 1954, Nov. 1955, Jan. 1956, May 1956, Sep. 1956, June 1957, Jan. 1962, May 1965
Page, Tommy: Feb. 1990; *480*
Pages: *348*
Paige, Kevin: *480*
Pajama Party: *480*
Palmer, Robert: Mar. 1978, July 1979, Dec. 1979, Feb. 1986, June 1986, July 1988, Oct. 1988, Feb. 1991; *307, 446, 447, 474*
Pantera: *509*
Paper Lace: June 1974; *282*
Pappalardi, Felix: *408*
Paradons, The: Sep. 1960; *90*
Paragons, The: May 1957; *52*
Paris, Mica: *480*
Paris Sisters, The: Sep. 1961; *103*
Parker, Charlie "Bird": *34*
Parker, Fess: Apr. 1955; *28*
Parker, Graham: *320*
Parker, Graham, & the Shot: May 1985
Parker, Little Junior: *52*
Parker, Ray, Jr.: Mar. 1982, Dec. 1982, Nov. 1983, June 1984, Nov. 1984, Oct. 1985; *23, 359, 363, 420, 422*
Parker, Ray, Jr., & Raydio: Mar. 1981, June 1981
Parker, Robert: May 1966; *172*
Parks, Michael: *227*
Parliament: May 1976, Feb. 1978; *282*
Parliaments, The: July 1967; *185*
Parr, John: June 1985; *427*
Parris, Fred, & Five Satins: Feb. 1982
Parsons, Alan, Project, The: Sep. 1979, Apr. 1981, July 1982, Nov. 1983, Feb. 1986; *307*
Parsons, Bill: Jan. 1959; *66*
Parsons, Gram: *196, 197*
Partland Brothers, The: Apr. 1987; *453*
Partners in Kryme: Apr. 1990; *495*
Parton, Dolly: Feb. 1974, Oct. 1977, Mar. 1978, Nov. 1980, Apr. 1981;

281, 289, 439, 452. See also Rogers, Kenny, & Dolly Parton
Partridge Family, The: Oct. 1970, Feb. 1971, May 1971, Aug. 1971, Dec. 1971; *226, 233*
Party, The: *495*
Pasadenas, The: *480*
Passions, The: *78*
Pastels, The: Mar. 1958; *66*
Pastel 6, The: *117*
Patience & Prudence: Aug. 1956, Oct. 1956; *40*
Pat & Mick: Dec. 1990; *495*
Pat & the Satellites: *78*
Patton, Robbie: June 1981; *374*
Patty & the Emblems: Aug. 1964; *144*
Paul, Billy: Nov. 1972; *255*
Paul, Henry, Band, The: *387*
Paul, Les, & Mary Ford: 1951, 1953, Apr. 1954, July 1954, Oct. 1954, July 1955; *3, 5, 327*
Paul & Paula: Jan. 1963, Apr. 1963; *135*
Paycheck, Johnny: *241*
Payne, Freda: May 1970, Oct. 1970, June 1971; *226*
PC Quest: *510*
Peace Choir, The: Mar. 1991; *510*
Peaches & Herb: Feb. 1967, Apr. 1967, July 1967, Dec. 1978, Mar. 1979; *171, 353*
Pearcy, Steven: *85*
Pearl, Leslie: *387*
Pebbles: May 1988, Aug. 1990; *467*
Pedicin, Mike: *40*
Pedicin, Mike, Quintet: Feb. 1958
Peebles: Jan. 1988
Peek, Dan: *348*
Peeples, Nia: May 1988, Oct. 1991; *467*
Peerce, Jan: *421*
Pendergrass, Teddy: July 1978; *320, 386*
Pendulum: *374*
Penguins, The: Oct. 1954, Jan. 1955; *16, 21, 26*
Peniston, Cece: *510*
Penn, Michael: Jan. 1990; *495*
Pentagons, The: Feb. 1961; *103*
People, The: *199*
People's Choice, The: Aug. 1975; *241*
Peppermint, Danny, & the Jumping Jacks: Dec. 1961
Peppermint Rainbow, The: July 1969; *214*
Pepsi & Shirlie: *453*
Pericoli, Emilio: June 1962; *117*
Perfect Gentlemen: Apr. 1990; *495*
Perkins, Carl: Mar. 1956, June 1956, Mar. 1957; *40, 43, 60, 222, 449, 460*
Perry, Steve: Apr. 1984, June 1984, Nov. 1984; *332, 387*
Perry, Steve, & Kenny Loggins: *387*
Persuaders, The: Sep. 1971
Peter & Gordon: May 1964, July 1964, Jan. 1965, May 1965, Feb. 1966, Nov. 1966, Jan. 1967; *143, 167*
Peter, Paul & Mary: June 1962, Sep. 1962, Mar. 1963, July 1963, Sep. 1963, Dec. 1963, Nov. 1969; *115, 116, 124, 125, 135, 136, 150*
Peters, Bernadette: Mar. 1980; *360*
Petersen, Paul: Apr. 1962, Dec. 1962; *116*
Peterson, Ray: May 1959, July 1960, Dec. 1960; *78, 80*
Peterson, Tom: *359*
Pet Rock & C.L. Smooth: July 1992; *524*
Pets, The: *66*
Pet Shop Boys: Mar. 1986, May 1986, Sep. 1987, Mar. 1988, Oct. 1988, May 1991; *85, 440, 446*
Pet Shop Boys, The, & Dusty Springfield: Dec. 1987
Petty, Norman, Trio, The: Nov. 1954
Petty, Tom: May 1989, Nov. 1989, Mar. 1990; *467*

Petty, Tom, & the Heartbreakers: Jan. 1980, Apr. 1980, May 1981, Nov. 1982, Feb. 1983; *320. See also* Nicks, Stevie, with Tom Petty & the Heartbreakers
Petty, Tom, & the Heartbreakers with Stevie Nicks: Feb. 1986
Phantom, Slim Jim: *449*
Phillips, Esther: Nov. 1962, Aug. 1975; *3, 421*
Phillips, John: *227*
Phillips, Phil: July 1959; *78*
Philly Creme: *348*
Photoglo: *360*
Pickett, Bobby "Boris": Oct. 1962, May 1973; *117*
Pickett, Wilson: Aug. 1965, Feb. 1966, Aug. 1966, Nov. 1966, Aug. 1967, May 1968, Dec. 1968, Oct. 1970, Jan. 1971, Apr. 1971; *128, 133, 466, 518*
Pierce, Webb: Nov. 1954, Sep. 1959; *52, 519*
Pilot: Apr. 1975, Oct. 1975; *294*
Pinera, Mike: *360*
Pink Floyd: May 1973, Jan. 1980; *183, 249, 266, 267, 274, 276, 301, 366, 367, 396, 459*
Pink Lady: *348*
Pipkins, The: May 1970; *227*
Piro, Frank "Killer Joe": *489*
Pitney, Gene: Feb. 1961, Nov. 1961, May 1962, Oct. 1962, Dec. 1962, Apr. 1963, Nov. 1963, June 1964, Nov. 1964, May 1965, June 1968; *102, 108*
Planet P: *401*
Plant, Robert: May 1985, Aug. 1988, Mar. 1990; *293, 387, 396*
Plastic Bertrand: *334*
Plastic Ono Band: Aug. 1969; *211, 213, 435. See also* Lennon, John/Plastic Ono Band
Platinum Blonde: *98, 440*
Platt, Eddie: *66*
Platters, The: Aug. 1954, July 1955, Jan. 1956, Mar. 1956, June 1956, Sep. 1956, Dec. 1956, Feb. 1957, Apr. 1958, Nov. 1958, July 1959, Feb. 1960, June 1960, July 1960, June 1966, Mar. 1967; *16, 23, 38, 46, 47, 48, 60, 84, 86, 88, 211, 382, 489, 490, 502*
Playboys, The: *66*
Player: Oct. 1977, Mar. 1978, Jan. 1982; *320, 326, 340*
Playmates, The: Dec. 1957, June 1958, Nov. 1958, July 1959, Nov. 1960; *65*
Pleasure: *348*
Plimsouls, The: *401*
P.M. Dawn: Oct. 1991, Jan. 1992; *510*
Pockets, The: *334*
Poco: Aug. 1977, Jan. 1979, May 1979, Dec. 1989; *226*
Poindexter, Buster (David Johansen): *457, 476*
Poindexter, Buster, & His Banshees of Blue: *453*
Point Blank: *374*
Pointer, Bonnie: June 1979, Dec. 1979; *334*
Pointer, Ruth: *476*
Pointer Sisters, The: Nov. 1978, July 1980, June 1981, Jan. 1982, June 1982, Sep. 1982, Jan. 1984, May 1984, Aug. 1984, Nov. 1984, July 1985, Aug. 1987; *267, 421, 422*
Poison: Mar. 1987, Apr. 1988, Aug. 1988, Oct. 1988, Feb. 1989, July 1990, Oct. 1990; *453, 458, 486*
Police, The: Feb. 1979, Feb. 1981, Sep. 1981, Jan. 1982, June 1983, Aug. 1983, Nov. 1983, Jan. 1984, Oct. 1986; *347, 352, 381, 407, 408, 410*
Pomus, Doc: *519*
Poni-Tails, The: July 1958; *66, 489*
Pons, Lily: *315*

Rockpile: *360, 365*
Rockwell: Jan. 1984; *151, 414*
Rocky Fellers, The: *129*
Rodgers, Eileen: *40*
Rodgers, Jimmie: Aug. 1957, Nov.
  1957, Feb. 1958, May 1958, Nov.
  1958, Apr. 1960; *52, 447*
Rodgers, Michael: *467*
Rodgers, Nile: *427*
Rodgers, Richard: *355*
Rodway: *387*
Roe, Tommy: Aug. 1962, Oct. 1963,
  June 1966, Oct. 1966, Feb. 1969,
  Dec. 1969; *116, 123, 220*
Roger: *374*
Rogers, Dann: *360*
Rogers, Julie: Dec. 1964; *144*
Rogers, Kenny: Apr. 1977, Dec. 1977,
  Nov. 1978, Apr. 1979, Sep. 1979,
  Nov. 1979, June 1980, Oct. 1980,
  June 1981, Sep. 1981, Dec. 1981,
  July 1982, May 1983, Jan. 1984, Jan.
  1985; *183, 307, 354, 367, 369, 373,
  434*
Rogers, Kenny, & Kim Carnes: Mar.
  1980
Rogers, Kenny, Kim Carnes & James
  Ingram: Sep. 1984
Rogers, Kenny, & Sheena Easton: Jan.
  1983
Rogers, Kenny, & the First Edition:
  July 1969, Oct. 1969, July 1970
Rogers, Kenny, & Dolly Parton: Aug.
  1983; *407*
Rogers, Timmie: Sep. 1957; *52*
Rolling Stones, The: Aug. 1964, Nov.
  1964, Jan. 1965, Apr. 1965, June
  1965, Oct. 1965, Jan. 1966, Feb.
  1966, May 1966, July 1966, Oct.
  1966, Feb. 1967, Sep. 1967, June
  1968, Aug. 1969, May 1971, July
  1971, May 1972, July 1972, Apr.
  1973, Sep. 1973, Jan. 1974, Aug.
  1974, Nov. 1974, Apr. 1976, June
  1976, May 1978, Sep. 1978, July
  1980, Aug. 1981, Dec. 1981, June
  1982, Nov. 1983, Mar. 1986, May
  1986, Sep. 1989, Nov. 1989, Feb.
  1990; *114, 127, 141, 143, 147, 152,
  164, 165, 178, 179, 192, 211, 220,
  221, 225, 235, 239, 247, 248, 261,
  275, 280, 303, 340, 367, 373, 381,
  395, 398, 435, 480, 488, 493*
Roman Holliday: *401*
Romantics, The: Oct. 1983, Mar. 1984;
  360
Romeo's Daughter: *467*
Romeo Void: *23, 414*
Ron & the D.C. Crew: *453*
Rondo, Don: Oct. 1956, Aug. 1957; *40*
Ronettes, The: Sep. 1963, Jan. 1964,
  July 1964, Nov. 1964; *101, 128, 136,
  180, 489*
Ronnie & the Hi-Lites: Apr. 1962; *117,
  368*
Ronny & the Daytonas: Aug. 1964; *144*
Ronstadt, Linda: Dec. 1974, Apr. 1975,
  Dec. 1976, Sep. 1977, Oct. 1977, Apr.
  1978, Aug. 1978, Nov. 1978, Feb.
  1979, Feb. 1980, Apr. 1980, June
  1980, Dec. 1982; *226, 233, 292, 315,
  327, 342, 373, 462*
Ronstadt, Linda, & James Ingram:
  Dec. 1986
Ronstadt, Linda, & Aaron Neville: *487,
  501*
Ronstadt, Linda (featuring Aaron
  Neville): Sep. 1989, Feb. 1990
Rooftop Singers, The: Jan. 1963; *129*
Roommates, The: Mar. 1961
Rose, David: June 1962; *124, 503*
Rose Garden, The: Dec. 1967; *185*
Rose Royce: Oct. 1976, Feb. 1977; *307,
  316*
Rosie & the Originals: Dec. 1960, Jan.
  1961; *90*

Ross, Diana: May 1970, Aug. 1970, Jan.
  1971, May 1971, June 1973, Jan.
  1974, Nov. 1975, Mar. 1976, Apr.
  1976, July 1979, July 1980, Oct.
  1981, Jan. 1982, Apr. 1982, Oct.
  1982, Feb. 1983, Sep. 1984, Dec.
  1984; *226, 233, 314, 342, 367, 373,
  409, 425, 438, 479, 480*
Ross, Diana, & Marvin Gaye: Oct.
  1973
Ross, Diana, & Michael Jackson: Sep.
  1978; *342*
Ross, Diana, & Lionel Richie: June
  1981; *381*
Ross, Diana, & the Supremes: Aug.
  1967, Nov. 1967, June 1968, Oct.
  1968, Dec. 1968, Feb. 1969, Nov.
  1969
Ross, Jackie: Aug. 1964; *144*
Ross, Spencer: Jan. 1960; *90*
Rossington Collins Band, The: *360*
Rota, Nino: *255, 355*
Roth, David Lee: Jan. 1985, Apr. 1985,
  July 1986, Sep. 1986, Nov. 1986, Jan.
  1988; *34, 427, 431, 439*
Rough Trade: *387*
Roussos, Demis: *334*
Routers, The: Nov. 1962; *117, 152*
Rover Boys, The: May 1956; *40*
Rovers, The: Feb. 1981
Roxanne: *467*
Roxette: Feb. 1989, Aug. 1989, Dec.
  1989, Apr. 1990, Mar. 1991, June
  1991, Feb. 1992; *480, 500, 505*
Roxy Music: *308*
Royal, Billy Joe: July 1965, Oct. 1965,
  Oct. 1969; *157, 196*
Royalettes, The: Aug. 1965; *158*
Royal Guardsmen, The: Dec. 1966;
  171
Royal Philharmonic Orchestra, The:
  Oct. 1981; *374*
Royal Scots Dragoon Guards: *255*
Royal Teens, The: Feb. 1958, Nov.
  1959; *63, 66, 74*
Royaltones, The: Oct. 1958; *66*
Rozalla: June 1992; *524*
RTZ: *510*
Rubenstein, Arthur: *395*
Rubicon: *334*
Rubinoos, The: Mar. 1977
Ruby & the Romantics: Feb. 1963;
  129, 293
Rude Boys: Mar. 1991; *510*
Ruffin, David: Feb. 1969; *213, 220,
  488, 519. See also* Hall, Daryl, &
  John Oates with David Ruffin &
  Eddie Kendricks
Ruffin, David & Jimmy: *227*
Ruffin, Jimmy: Sep. 1966, Dec. 1966,
  Mar. 1980; *171*
Rufus: Feb. 1975, Jan. 1976; *281*
Rundgren, Todd: Oct. 1973, Jan. 1974;
  226, 234
Run-D.M.C.: *440, 445, 509, 523*
Runt: Dec. 1970
Rush: *320, 328*
Rush, Jennifer: *440*
Rush, Jennifer, & Elton John: May 1987
Rush, Merrilee: *211*
Rush, Merrilee, & the Turnabouts:
  May 1968; *199*
Rushen, Patrice: Jan. 1980; *23, 360*
Russell, Andy: *529*
Russell, Brenda: *348*
Russell, Leon: *239, 249, 255, 262, 263*
Rutles, The: *331*
Ryan, Charlie: *90*
Rydell, Bobby: Oct. 1959, Feb. 1960,
  May 1960, July 1960, Nov. 1960, Jan.
  1961, May 1961, Mar. 1962, June
  1962, Oct. 1962, May 1963, Nov.
  1963; *51, 78, 80, 98*
Ryder, Mitch, & the Detroit Wheels:
  Dec. 1965, Oct. 1966, Feb. 1967; *157*

Ryser, Jimmy: *495*
Rythm Syndicate: June 1991, Sep.
  1991, Jan. 1992; *510*

Sad Cafe: *348*
Sade: Mar. 1985, Nov. 1985, Mar.
  1986; *426, 433, 434, 446*
Sadler, SSgt. Barry: Feb. 1966; *172,
  178, 179, 489*
Safaris, The: June 1960; *90*
Sa-Fire: Feb. 1989, Dec. 1989; *467*
Saga: *387*
Sager, Carole Bayer: *320*
Sailcat: June 1972; *255*
St. Etienne: *480*
Saint-Marie, Buffy: *193, 241*
St. Paul: July 1990; *495*
St. Peters, Crispian: June 1966; *172*
Saint Tropez: *348*
Sakamoto, Kyu: May 1963; *127, 129,
  135, 435*
Salsoul Orchestra, The: Sep. 1975, Jan.
  1976; *294, 306*
Salt-N-Pepa: Nov. 1987, Feb. 1992;
  453, 520
Sambora, Richie: *510, 513*
Sam & Dave: May 1966, Sep. 1967,
  Feb. 1968; *171, 173, 369, 475, 528*
Sam the Sham & the Pharoahs: Apr.
  1965, June 1966; *157, 164*
Sanborn, David: *460, 474*
Sandborn, David: *490*
Sandee: *510*
Sanders, Felicia: *301*
Sandpipers, The: Aug. 1966, Apr. 1970;
  172
Sands, Jodie: *52*
Sands, Tommy: Feb. 1957; *52, 60, 74*
Sanford-Townsend Band, The: June
  1977; *320*
Sang, Samantha: Nov. 1977; *320*
San Remo Golden Strings, The: *158*
Santa Esmeralda: Nov. 1977, Apr.
  1978; *320*
Santamaria, Mongo: *129*
Santana: Feb. 1970, Nov. 1970, Feb.
  1971, Oct. 1971, Apr. 1981, Aug.
  1982; *211, 213, 234, 236, 263, 474,
  508, 509*
Santo & Johnny: Aug. 1959, Dec. 1959,
  Dec. 1960; *78*
Sapphires, The: Feb. 1964; *129*
Saraya: *480*
Saridis, Saverio: *117*
Saville, Jimmy: *166*
Savoy Brown: *214*
Sayer, Leo: Feb. 1975, Oct. 1976, Feb.
  1977, Dec. 1977, Sep. 1980; *294, 298*
Scaggs, Boz: July 1976, Mar. 1977,
  Mar. 1980, June 1980, Aug. 1980,
  Dec. 1980, Apr. 1988; *240, 263, 314,
  369*
Scandal: *387*
Scandal featuring Patty Smyth: June
  1984; *59*
Scarbury, Joey: Jan. 1971, May 1981;
  34, 241
Scarlett & Black: *467*
Scheider, Fred: *510*
Schickele, Peter: *488, 501, 517*
Schifrin, Lalo: *185*
Schilling, Peter: *47, 401*
Schmit, Timothy B.: *387*
Schneider, John: *34, 374*
Schoolboys, The: Mar. 1957; *40*
Schwartz, Eddie: Dec. 1981; *374*
Scorpions, The: June 1988; *388, 466*
Scott, Bobby: Feb. 1956; *28*
Scott, Bon: *359*
Scott, Freddie: Aug. 1963; *129*
Scott, Jack: July 1958, Dec. 1958, Jan.
  1959, Feb. 1960; *65*
Scott, Linda: Mar. 1961, July 1961;
  102, 124
Scott, Mabel: *1948*
Scritti Politti: *427*

Seal: June 1991; *510*
Sea Level: *334*
Seals, Dan: Jan. 1986; *360*
Seals & Crofts: Sep. 1972, Jan. 1973,
  May 1973, Sep. 1973, Apr. 1976;
  254, 258
Searchers, The: Mar. 1964, June 1964,
  Dec. 1964; *143*
Sears, "Big" Al: *503*
Sebastian, John: Mar. 1976; *197, 214,
  236, 249*
Secada, John: *524*
2nd II None: Jan. 1992; *524*
Secrets, The: Dec. 1963; *129*
Secret Ties: *440*
Sedaka, Neil: Dec. 1958, Oct. 1959,
  Apr. 1960, Aug. 1960, Dec. 1960,
  May 1961, Nov. 1961, July 1962, Oct.
  1962, Oct. 1974, Apr. 1975, July
  1975, Sep. 1975, Dec. 1975, Apr.
  1976, June 1976, Sep. 1976; *65, 70,
  293, 300*
Sedaka, Neil, & Dara Sedaka: Mar.
  1980
Seduction: Nov. 1989, Feb. 1990, June
  1990; *480*
Seeds, The: *172, 208*
Seekers, The: Apr. 1965, June 1965,
  Dec. 1966; *158*
Seger, Bob: Dec. 1976, May 1978, Aug.
  1978, Oct. 1978, Apr. 1979, Feb.
  1980; *205, 462*
Seger, Bob, & the Silver Bullet Band:
  May 1980, July 1980, Sep. 1981, Dec.
  1982, Mar. 1983, May 1983, Sep.
  1983, Mar. 1986, May 1986, May
  1987, Aug. 1991; *367, 459*
Seger, Bob, System, The: Jan. 1969;
  198
Segovia, Andres: *461*
Seiko and Donnie Wahlberg: *495*
Sembello, Michael: June 1983; *401,
  407, 409*
Senator Bobby: Jan. 1967; *185*
Sensations, The: Nov. 1955, Jan. 1962;
  28
Serendipity Singers, The: Mar. 1964,
  June 1964; *144*
Sevelle, Taja: Sep. 1987; *453*
707: *360*
Seville, David: Apr. 1958; *40, 262*
Seville, David, & the Chipmunks: Mar.
  1959, July 1959
Sevilles, The: *103*
Sex Pistols, The: *306, 331, 332, 355*
S-Express: *467*
Sexton, Charlie: Dec. 1985; *427*
Seymour, Phil: *374*
Shades of Blue, The: May 1966; *172*
Shadowfax: *474*
Shadows of Knight, The: Apr. 1966;
  172
Shaffer, Paul: *480*
Shakespear's Sister: July 1992; *524*
Shalamar: Mar. 1977, Dec. 1979, Dec.
  1980; *59, 320*
Shamen, The: *510*
Shana: *481*
Sha Na Na: *211, 236, 241, 342*
Shangri-Las, The: Sep. 1964, Oct. 1964,
  Jan. 1965; *172*
Shanice: Apr. 1992; *510*
Shankar, Ravi: *222, 262, 263*
Shannon: Nov. 1983, Apr. 1984; *401*
Shannon, Del: Mar. 1961, June 1961,
  Jan. 1963, Dec. 1964, Dec. 1981;
  102, 108, 503
Sharkey, Feargal: *440*
Sharp, Dee Dee: Mar. 1962, June 1962,
  Oct. 1962, Mar. 1963; *114, 116*
Sharpe, Ray: Aug. 1959; *78*
Shaw, Georgie: Apr. 1954
Shaw, Sandie: *144*
Shaw, Tommy: *414*
Shawn, Christopher
Shear: *427*

Stevens, Ray: July 1962, June 1963, Aug. 1968, Apr. 1969, Apr. 1970, Dec. 1970, Dec. 1971, Apr. 1974, May 1975; *102, 234, 288*

Stevens, Shadoe: *466*

Stevens, Shakin': *375*

Stevenson, B.W.: July 1973; *268*

Stevie B: Feb. 1990, June 1990, Oct. 1990, Feb. 1991; *467*

Stewart, Al: Dec. 1976, Jan. 1979, Aug. 1980; *307*

Stewart, Amii: Jan. 1979; *348*

Stewart, Amii, & Johnny Bristol: Aug. 1980

Stewart, Billy: Apr. 1965, Aug. 1966; *40, 235*

Stewart, David A., Introducing Candy Dulfer: *511*

Stewart, Jermaine: Mar. 1988; *428*

Stewart, John: May 1979; *214*

Stewart, Rod: Sep. 1971, Nov. 1971, Aug. 1972, Aug. 1973, Jan. 1976, Oct. 1976, Feb. 1977, June 1977, Oct. 1977, Feb. 1978, May 1978, Dec. 1978, Apr. 1979, Nov. 1980, Oct. 1981, Jan. 1982, Apr. 1982, May 1983, Aug. 1983, May 1984, Aug. 1984, May 1986, Nov. 1986, July 1987, May 1988, May 1989, Nov. 1989, Mar. 1991, July 1991; *224, 239, 240, 246, 247, 248, 314, 345, 353, 354, 413, 449. See also* Beck, Jeff, & Rod Stewart

Stewart, Rod (with Ronald Isley): Mar. 1990

Stewart, Sandy: Jan. 1963; *74, 117*

Stigers, Curtis: *511*

Stills, Stephen: Dec. 1970; *215, 227*

Stillwater: Dec. 1977; *334*

Sting: June 1985, Aug. 1985, Nov. 1985, Jan. 1986, Oct. 1987, Jan. 1988, Jan. 1991; *408, 413, 427, 434, 449, 459, 466, 517*

Stites, Gary: *79*

Stitt, Sonny: *395*

Stokowski, Leopold: *327*

Stoloff, Morris: Apr. 1956; *40, 368*

Stompers, The: *401*

Stone, Sly: *206, 279*

Stonebolt: *334*

Stone Poneys, The: Nov. 1967; *185*

Stookey, Paul: Aug. 1971; *242*

Stories, The: June 1973; *255, 274*

Storm, The: *511*

Storm, Billy: *79*

Storm, Gale: Sep. 1955, Dec. 1955, Sep. 1956; *26, 27, 32*

Storm, Rory, & the Hurricanes: *114*

Strangeloves, The: July 1965; *158*

Strawberry Alarm Clock, The: Oct. 1967; *185, 208*

Stray Cats, The: Sep. 1982, Dec. 1982, Aug. 1983, Oct. 1983; *97, 387*

Streek: *375*

Street People, The: Jan. 1970; *227*

Streets: *401*

Streisand, Barbra: May 1964, Nov. 1970, July 1971, Nov. 1973, Dec. 1976, May 1977, June 1978, June 1979, Sep. 1980, Nov. 1981, Feb. 1982, Sep. 1984, Dec. 1985; *136, 143, 150, 151, 165, 288, 316, 326, 327, 367, 409, 447, 509*

Streisand, Barbra, & Neil Diamond: Oct. 1978

Streisand, Barbra, & Barry Gibb: Nov. 1980, Jan. 1981; *367*

Streisand, Barbra, & Don Johnson: Oct. 1988

Streisand, Barbra, & Donna Summer: Oct. 1979

String-A-Longs, The: Jan. 1961; *103*

Strong, Barrett: Feb. 1960; *89, 90*

Strunk, Jud: *268, 382*

Stryper: *453*

Students, The: *504*

Style Council, The: *414*

Stylistics, The: June 1971, Nov. 1971, Feb. 1972, June 1972, Oct. 1972, Feb. 1973, May 1973, Oct. 1973, Apr. 1974, Aug. 1974, July 1975; *239, 240*

Styx: Dec. 1974, Nov. 1976, Sep. 1977, Mar. 1979, Oct. 1979, Mar. 1980, Jan. 1981, Mar. 1981, Feb. 1983, Apr. 1983, Aug. 1983; *254, 261, 381*

Suave: *467*

Sugar Hill Gang, The: Nov. 1979; *361*

Sugarloaf: Aug. 1970; *227*

Summer, Donna: Dec. 1975, Feb. 1977, Aug. 1977, May 1978, Sep. 1978, Apr. 1979, May 1979, Aug. 1979, Jan. 1980, Sep. 1980, Dec. 1982, June 1983, Sep. 1983, Aug. 1984, Nov. 1984, Apr. 1989; *294, 303, 306, 340, 342, 345, 353, 354, 367. See also* Streisand Barbra, & Donna Summer

Summer, Donna, & the Brooklyn Dreams: Jan. 1979

Summer, Henry Lee: May 1988, Sep. 1988; *467*

Sun, Joe: *361*

Sunnysiders, The: May 1955

Sunny & the Sunglows: Sep. 1963; *129*

Sunshine Company, The: *185*

Supertramp: June 1977, Mar. 1979, July 1979, Sep. 1980, Dec. 1980, Oct. 1982, Jan. 1983; *294, 354, 356*

Supremes, The: Dec. 1963, July 1964, Oct. 1964, Nov. 1964, Feb. 1965, May 1965, Aug. 1965, Nov. 1965, Jan. 1966, Apr. 1966, Aug. 1966, Nov. 1966, Feb. 1967, Apr. 1967, Mar. 1970, Nov. 1970, May 1971; *116, 122, 150, 152, 164, 165, 178, 315, 439, 462, 475. See also* Ross, Diana, & the Supremes

Supremes, The, & the Temptations: Mar. 1969

Surface: July 1989; *453, 516*

Surfaris, The: July 1963; *129, 152*

Survivor: June 1982, Jan. 1985, Apr. 1985, Nov. 1985, Oct. 1986, Feb. 1987; *359, 393, 394*

Sutcliffe, Stuart: *114*

Sutton, Glenn: *348*

Swallows, The: *5*

Swan, Bettye: Mar. 1969, Jan. 1973

Swan, Billy: Sep. 1974, Mar. 1975; *282, 288*

Swayze, Patrick: *453*

Swayze, Patrick (featuring Wendy Frazer): Dec. 1987

Sweat, Keith: Jan. 1988, Dec. 1990, Nov. 1991; *467, 520*

Sweathog: Nov. 1971

Sweet, The: Jan. 1973, Nov. 1975, Feb. 1976, Feb. 1978; *240*

Sweet, Rachel: *375. See also* Smith, Rex, & Rachel Sweet

Sweet Inspirations, The: *185*

Sweet Sensation: Sep. 1988, Mar. 1990, June 1990, Oct. 1990; *453*

Swinging Blue Jeans, The: Apr. 1964; *144*

Swingin' Medallions, The: May 1966; *172*

Swingle Singers, The: *136*

Swing Out Sister: June 1987, Dec. 1987; *453*

Switch: *334*

Sybil: Jan. 1990; *481*

Sylers, Foster: *268*

Sylvers, The: Feb. 1976, Oct. 1976, Apr. 1977; *124, 255, 306*

Sylvester: *334, 475*

Sylvia: Mar. 1973, Aug. 1982; *268, 388*

Sylvia, Margo: *519*

Syms, Sylvia: *40, 529*

Synch: *440*

Syndicate of Sound, The: June 1966; *172*

System, The: *401*

Taco: July 1983; *34, 401*

Tag: July 1992; *525*

Taka Boom: *348*

Talking Heads, The: *332, 333*

Talk Talk: *388*

Ta Mara & the Seen: *440*

Tami Show: Aug. 1991; *467*

Tams, The: *116*

Tanega, Norma: *172*

Tangier: *481*

Tanner, Gary: *334*

Tanner, Mark, Band, The: *348*

Tarney/Spencer Band, The: *334*

Tarriers, The: Jan. 1957

Taste of Honey, A: June 1978, Mar. 1981, Mar. 1982; *334, 340, 359*

Tavares: Oct. 1974, July 1975, June 1976, Nov. 1976, Apr. 1977, Nov. 1977, Feb. 1978; *268, 306, 340*

Taylor, Andy: *111, 439, 440, 448*

Taylor, B.E., Group, The: *414*

Taylor, Bobby, & the Vancouvers: *199*

Taylor, James: Sep. 1970, June 1971, Dec. 1972, June 1975, Oct. 1975, July 1976, June 1977, Oct. 1977, June 1979, June 1981, Nov. 1985; *226, 227, 235, 248, 253, 327, 369. See also* Garfunkel, Art, with James Taylor & Paul Simon; Simon, Carly, & James Taylor

Taylor, James, & J.D. Souther: Mar. 1981

Taylor, John: *97, 440*

Taylor, Johnnie: Oct. 1968, Jan. 1970, June 1973, Oct. 1973, Feb. 1976, June 1976; *185, 193, 306, 314*

Taylor, Kate: *320*

Taylor, Koko: *158*

Taylor, Livingston: July 1980; *242*

Taylor, Mick: *211, 280, 488*

Taylor, R. Dean: Sep. 1970; *227*

T-Bones, The: Dec. 1965; *158*

T-Connection: *320*

Tchaikovsky, Bram: July 1979; *348*

Tears for Fears: Mar. 1985, June 1985, Sep. 1985, Apr. 1986, Sep. 1989, Dec. 1989; *400, 433, 434*

Technotronic: Jan. 1990; *481*

Teddy Bears, The: Oct. 1958; *66, 72*

Teegarden & Van Winkle: *227*

Teenagers: *435*

Teena Marie: Mar. 1988; *59, 359, 361*

Teen Queens, The: Feb. 1956; *40*

Tee Set, The: Feb. 1970; *227*

Tempo, Nino, & April Stevens: Sep. 1963, Jan. 1964; *117, 136, 196*

Tempos, The: *79*

Temptations, The: May 1960, Mar. 1964, Sep. 1964, Jan. 1965, July 1965, Nov. 1965, Mar. 1966, June 1966, Sep. 1966, Nov. 1966, May 1967, Aug. 1967, Jan. 1968, May 1968, Nov. 1968, Feb. 1969, May 1969, Sep. 1969, Jan. 1970, May 1970, Feb. 1971, Mar. 1972, Oct. 1972, Feb. 1973, Aug. 1973, Jan. 1974, Oct. 1986; *90, 143, 220, 247, 275, 276, 409, 488, 519, 520. See also* Supremes, The, & the Temptations

10cc: Sep. 1973, May 1975, Jan. 1977; *268, 276, 413*

Tennille, Toni. *See* Captain, The, & Tennille

10,000 Maniacs: *468*

Ten Years After: *227, 236*

Tepper, Robert: Jan. 1986; *440*

Terrell, Tammi: *172, 235. See also* Gaye, Marvin, & Tammi Terrell

Terry, Tony: June 1988; *453*

Tesla: Jan. 1991; *453, 511, 518*

Tex, Joe: Jan. 1965, Nov. 1967, Jan. 1972, Apr. 1977; *143, 149, 395*

Texas: *481*

Them: June 1965; *158*

Think: *242*

Thin Lizzy: May 1976; *308, 448*

3rd Bass: July 1991; *511*

Third World: *348*

38 Special: June 1981, May 1982, Aug. 1982, Nov. 1983, Feb. 1984, Sep. 1984, May 1986, July 1986, July 1987, Feb. 1989; *359, 367*

Thomas, B.J.: Aug. 1968, Dec. 1968, Nov. 1969, June 1970, Dec. 1970, Feb. 1972, Feb. 1975, July 1977, May 1983; *172, 174, 234*

Thomas, B.J., & the Triumphs: Mar. 1966

Thomas, Carla: Feb. 1961, Sep. 1966; *102, 155, 276*

Thomas, Ian: Jan. 1974

Thomas, Irma: May 1964; *144*

Thomas, Mickey: *346*

Thomas, Nolan: *428*

Thomas, Rufus: Oct. 1963; *129, 276*

Thomas, Tasha: *348, 421*

Thomas, Timmy: Nov. 1972; *255*

Thompson, Chris: *348*

Thompson, Robbin, Band, The: *361*

Thompson, Sue: Sep. 1961, Dec. 1961; *102, 114*

Thompson Twins, The: Feb. 1984, May 1984, Sep. 1985, Jan. 1986; *47, 400, 405, 438*

Thomson, Ali: June 1980; *361*

Thornton, Willie Mae: 1953; *10, 421*

Thorogood, George, & the Destroyers, *428*

Thorpe, Billy: *348*

Three Chuckles, The: *48*

Three Degrees, The: June 1970, Oct. 1974; *157*

Three Dog Night: Feb. 1969, Apr. 1969, May 1969, Aug. 1969, Nov. 1969, Mar. 1970, June 1970, Sep. 1970, Nov. 1970, Mar. 1971, July 1971, Nov. 1971, Mar. 1972, Aug. 1972, May 1973, Apr. 1974, July 1974; *213, 221, 247*

Three Friends, The: June 1956; *40*

Three Man Island: *468*

Thunder: *511*

Thunder, Johnny: Jan. 1963; *117*

Thunderclap Newman: *214, 355*

Thunders, Johnny: *519*

Tia: *453*

Tiana: *495*

Tico & the Triumphs: *103*

Tierra: *361*

Tiffany: Aug. 1987, Nov. 1987, Feb. 1988; *248, 453, 459, 461, 473*

Tiggi Clay: *414*

Tight Fit: *375*

Tijuana Brass, The: Nov. 1962; *413. See also* Alpert, Herb, & the Tijuana Brass

Tillotson, Johnny: Oct. 1960, Aug. 1961, May 1962, Sep. 1962, Dec. 1963; *65, 137*

'Til Tuesday: Apr. 1985, Sep. 1986, Jan. 1987; *428*

Timbuk 3: *440*

Time, The: Oct. 1984, June 1990; *388*

Times Two: Mar. 1988; *468*

Time-Tones, The: *103*

Timex Social Club, The: June 1986; *440*

Timmy T: Mar. 1990, May 1991; *495, 516*

Tin Tin: Apr. 1971; *242*

Tiny Tim: June 1968; *199, 207, 208*

Tiomkin, Dmitri: *355*

Titiyo: June 1991; *511*

Tjader, Cal: *395*

TKA: Aug. 1990; *440, 525*

TLC: Mar. 1992, June 1992; *525*

TMG: *348*

Toad the Wet Sprocket: July 1992; *525*

Toby Beau: *334*

Todd, Art & Dotty: Apr. 1958; *66*

Todd, Nick: *52*

Tokens, The: Mar. 1961, Nov. 1961;

102, 110, 523
Tom & Jerry: Nov. 1957; 52
Toms, Gary, Empire, The: 295
Tom Tom Club, The: 375
Tone Loc: Mar. 1989, Dec. 1991; 468
Tony Terry: 525
Tony! Toni! Tone!: June 1990, Sep. 1990, Dec. 1990, Apr. 1991; 468, 520
Tora Tora: 481
Tornadoes, The: Nov. 1962; 114, 117
Toronto: 388
Tosh, Peter: 334, 461
Total Coelo: 401
Toto: Oct. 1978, Apr. 1982, Aug. 1982, Nov. 1982, Mar. 1983, Feb. 1985, Dec. 1986; 23, 333, 340, 394, 529
Touch: 361
Tourists, The: 361
Tower of Power, The: 255
Townsell, Lidell: Feb. 1992; 525
Townsend, Ed: Apr. 1958; 66
Townshend, Pete: Oct. 1980; 361, 368, 480, 502
Toys, The: Sep. 1965, Jan. 1966; 158, 193
T'Pau: 453
Trade Winds, The: Feb. 1965; 158
Traffic: 183, 185
Trammps, The: Apr. 1976, Mar. 1977, Feb. 1978; 255, 306, 340
Transvision Vamp: 468
Trans-X: 440
Trashmen, The: Dec. 1963; 129, 489
Traveling Wilburys, The: Feb. 1989; 467, 468, 487
Travers, Mary: 242
Travers, Pat: 23, 348
Travis & Bob: Mar. 1959; 79
Travolta, Joey: 334
Travolta, John: May 1976, Sep. 1978; 23, 308
Travolta, John, & Olivia Newton-John: Apr. 1978, Aug. 1978; 342
Tremeloes, The: Apr. 1967, July 1967; 137, 185
Treniers, The: 48, 86
Tresvant, Ralph: Nov. 1990, Feb. 1991, July 1992; 207, 511
T. Rex: Jan. 1972; 242, 327
Triology: 511
Triplets, The: Mar. 1991; 511
Triumph: Nov. 1979; 347, 354
Trixter: 511, 517
Troccoli, Kathy: Feb. 1992; 525
Troggs, The: July 1966, Mar. 1968; 172, 177, 178
Troop: July 1990; 495
Trooper: 334
Troy, Doris: June 1963; 129
Troyer, Eric: 361
True, Andrea, Connection, The: Mar. 1976, Feb. 1977; 306, 308
Truth, The: 453
Tubb, Ernest: 421
Tubes, The: June 1981, July 1983; 308
Tucker, Louise: 401
Tucker, Marshall, Band, The: Mar. 1977, Apr. 1980; 266, 294, 368
Tucker, Sophie: 179
Tucker, Tanya: 73, 255
Tucker, Tommy: Feb. 1964; 144, 395
Tull, Jethro. See Jethro Tull
Tune Rockers, The: Sep. 1958; 66
Tune Weavers, The: Aug. 1957; 52, 519
Turbans, The: July 1955; 27, 33
Turner, Ike & Tina: Sep. 1960, Aug. 1961, Feb. 1971; 90, 180, 235, 518
Turner, Joe: 1951, Mar. 1954, Apr. 1954, Feb. 1955, Dec. 1955, Apr. 1956, Jan. 1960; 3, 5, 14, 26, 48, 435, 460
Turner, Sammy: June 1959, Nov. 1959; 79
Turner, Sonny: 88
Turner, Spyder: Dec. 1966; 172

Turner, Tina: Jan. 1984, May 1984, Sep. 1984, Jan. 1985, Apr. 1985, July 1985, Oct. 1985, Aug. 1986, Nov. 1986, Feb. 1987, May 1987, Sep. 1989, Nov. 1989; 302, 386, 413, 414, 420, 421, 422, 425, 426, 434, 447, 449, 474. See also Adams, Bryan/Tina Turner; Turner, Ike & Tina
Turner, Titus: 103
Turtles, The: Aug. 1965, Feb. 1966, Feb. 1967, May 1967, Aug. 1967, Nov. 1967, Sep. 1968, Jan. 1969; 157, 180, 191
Tuxedo Junction: 334
Twennynine: 361
Twilight 22: 401
Twilley, Dwight: Feb. 1984
Twilley, Dwight, Band, The: 295
Twisted Sister: Oct. 1984; 34, 414, 426
Twitty, Conway: Sep. 1958, Aug. 1959, Oct. 1959, Aug. 1973; 52
2 Hyped Brothers & a Dog: 525
2 Live Crew: Nov. 1991; 481, 493, 520
2NU: Dec. 1990; 495
2 in a Room: 495
Tycoon: 348
Tyler, Bonnie: Mar. 1978, July 1983; 333, 407
Tymes, The: June 1963, Aug. 1963, Dec. 1963, Aug. 1974; 129

UB40: Feb. 1984, July 1985, Aug. 1988; 414
Ugly Kid Joe: Apr. 1992; 525
U-Krew, The: 495
Ullman, Tracey: Feb. 1984; 85, 414, 418, 422
Ultimate: 348
Ultravox: 401
Underworld: 468
Undisputed Truth, The: June 1971; 241
Unifics, The: Jan. 1969
Unipop: 401
Unit Four Plus Two: May 1965; 158
Upchurch, Phil, Combo, The: June 1961; 103
Uptown: 453
Ure, Midge: 481
Urgent: 428
Uriah Heep: 255
USA for Africa: Mar. 1985; 428, 433, 434
UTFO: Mar. 1985; 428
Utopia: 361
U2: Apr. 1983, Jan. 1984, Mar. 1987, June 1987, Sep. 1987, Dec. 1987, Oct. 1988, Nov. 1991, Nov. 1991, Mar. 1992, July 1992; 97, 400, 406, 413, 426, 459, 460, 473, 474, 476, 523
U2 with B.B. King: Apr. 1989

Vale, Jerry: July 1956, Oct. 1957; 40
Valens, Ritchie: Nov. 1958, Dec. 1958; 65, 76, 86, 88, 346, 462
Valente, Caterina: Apr. 1955
Valentines, The: Nov. 1955; 28
Valentino, Mark: 117
Valentinos, The: 117
Valery, Dana: 308
Valiants, The: Nov. 1957; 52
Valino, Joe: Oct. 1956; 40
Valjean: 117
Valli, Frankie: June 1967, Dec. 1974, May 1975, Oct. 1975, May 1978; 74, 172, 174, 342, 502
Valli, June: May 1955; 10
Vandenberg: 401
Vandenberg, Adrian: 23
Vandross, Luther: Jan. 1989, Apr. 1991, Jan. 1992; 374, 501, 517. See also Warwick, Dionne, & Luther Vandross
Vandross, Luther, and Janet Jackson: May 1992

Van Dyke, Leroy: Nov. 1956, Nov. 1961; 40
Vangelis: Jan. 1982; 375
Van Halen: Jan. 1978, Apr. 1979, Feb. 1982, May 1982, Jan. 1984, Apr. 1984, June 1984, Oct. 1984, Mar. 1986, May 1986, May 1988, July 1988, Jan. 1989, Oct. 1991; 333, 341, 373, 420, 446, 449, 466, 473, 517
Van Heusen, Jimmy: 503
Vanilla Ice: Sep. 1990, Dec. 1990; 495, 504, 516
Vanilla Fudge: July 1968; 185, 235
Vanity: Apr. 1986; 414
Vanity Fare, The: Dec. 1969, Mar. 1970; 214
Vann, Teddy: 517
Vannelli, Gino: Sep. 1978, Mar. 1981, Apr. 1987; 281
Vanwarmer, Randy: Mar. 1979; 34, 348
Van Zandt, "Miami" Steve: 386, 523. See also Little Steven
Vapors: 361
Vaughan, Sarah: Dec. 1954, Apr. 1955, Apr. 1956, Aug. 1959; 503
Vaughan, Stevie Ray: 503
Vaughan Brothers, The: 495, 501
Vaughn, Billy: Jan. 1955, Jan. 1958, Aug. 1962; 16, 97, 519
Vaughn, Billy, Orchestra: Sep. 1955
Vee, Bobby: Aug. 1960, Dec. 1960, Aug. 1961, Nov. 1961, Mar. 1962, June 1962, Dec. 1962; 78, 84, 110, 137, 193
Vee, Bobby, & the Strangers: Aug. 1967
Vega, Suzanne: July 1987; 453
Velours, The: June 1957; 52
Vels, The: 428
Velvets, The: June 1961; 103
Venetians: 453
Ventures, The: Aug. 1960, Nov. 1960, Aug. 1964, Apr. 1969; 90
Venus, Vik: 214
Vera, Billy: July 1968
Vera, Billy, & the Beaters: Nov. 1986
Vera, Billy, & Judy Clay: 185
Vibrations, The: 103
Vicious, Sid: 332, 355
Village People, The: June 1978, Oct. 1978, Mar. 1978; 333
Village Stompers, The: Oct. 1963; 129
Vincent, Gene: 125, 349
Vincent, Gene, & His Blue Caps: May 1956, July 1957, Dec. 1957; 40, 45, 48, 74
Vinton, Bobby: June 1962, May 1963, Aug. 1963, Jan. 1964, Mar. 1964, June 1964, Nov. 1964, Oct. 1967, Jan. 1968, Nov. 1968, June 1972, Oct. 1974; 117, 123, 135, 150, 151
Virtues, The: Mar. 1959; 79
Viscounts, The: 90
Vitamin Z: 428
Vito & His Group: 435
Vito & the Salutations: 117, 504
Vixen: 468
Vogues, The: Oct. 1965, Dec. 1965, Mar. 1966, June 1968, Sep. 1968; 157, 164
Voices of America: Apr. 1986; 440
Voices of the Beehive: 511
Voices that Care: Mar. 1991; 511
Volumes, The: May 1962; 117
Voorman, Klaus: 211, 262, 263
Voudouris, Roger: 348
Voxpoppers, The: 66
Voyage: 348

Wade, Adam: Apr. 1960, May 1961; 90, 96
Wadsworth Mansion: Feb. 1971; 227
Wagner, Jack: May 1987; 85, 428
Wahrer, Steve: 489

Wailers, The: May 1959; 79
Wainwright, Loudon, III: Jan. 1973; 268
Waite, John: June 1984, Aug. 1985; 34, 414
Waitresses, The: May 1982; 388
Wakeman, Rick: 280, 480, 508
Walden, Narada Michael: 348
Waldman, Wendy: 334
Walker, Aaron "T-bone": 301, 461
Walker, Chris: Mar. 1992; 525
Walker, Jerry Jeff: 199
Walker, Jr., & the All Stars: Feb. 1965, June 1969; 157
Walker Brothers, The: Nov. 1965, Apr. 1966; 158, 166
Wallace, Jerry: Sep. 1958, Sep. 1959, Dec. 1960, Jan. 1961, Jan. 1963, Aug. 1964; 65
Wall of Voodoo: 401
Walsh, James, Gypsy Band, The: 334
Walsh, Joe: June 1978; 268, 305, 523
Wanderley, Walter: 172
Wang Chung: Feb. 1984, Apr. 1984, Oct. 1985, Oct. 1986, Jan. 1987; 414, 420
War: Jan. 1972, Nov. 1972, Mar. 1973, July 1973, May 1975, Sep. 1975, July 1976; 275
Ward, Anita: May 1979; 348
Ward, Billy, & His Dominoes: May 1957, Oct. 1957; 504
Ward, Robin: Nov. 1963; 129
Waring, Fred: 421
Warnes, Jennifer: Jan. 1977; 320. See also Cocker, Joe, & Jennifer Warnes; Medley, Bill, & Jennifer Warnes
Warrant: May 1989, July 1989, Jan. 1990, Dec. 1990; 481, 488
Warwick, Dionne: Dec. 1962, Dec. 1963, May 1964, Nov. 1964, Apr. 1966, July 1966, Oct. 1967, Feb. 1968, Apr. 1968, Nov. 1968, Feb. 1969, June 1969, Dec. 1969, June 1979, Nov. 1979, Oct. 1982, Feb. 1983; 117, 123, 207, 234, 354, 523. See also Mathis, Johnny, & Dionne Warwick
Warwick, Dionne, & Friends: 446, 447
Warwick, Dionne, & Kashif: Oct. 1987
Warwick, Dionne, & Jeffrey Osborne: July 1987
Warwick, Dionne, & the Spinners: Aug. 1974
Warwick, Dionne, & Luther Vandross: Oct. 1983
Washington, Baby: 78
Washington, Dinah: Dec. 1954, May 1955, May 1959, Oct. 1959, July 1960, Oct. 1961; 136
Washington, Dinah, & Brook Benton: Feb. 1960, May 1960
Washington, Grover, Jr.: Feb. 1981; 295
Washington, Keith: May 1991; 511
Was (Not Was): Jan. 1989; 468
Waterfront: Apr. 1989; 481
Waters, Crystal: May 1991; 511
Waters, Muddy: See Muddy Waters
Watley, Jody: Mar. 1987, Oct. 1987, Jan. 1988, Mar. 1989, Mar. 1992; 413, 453, 460, 461
Watley, Jody with Eric B. & Rakim: June 1989
Watts, Charlie: 409, 488
Watts, Noble "Thin Man": Nov. 1957; 52
Watts 103rd St. Rhythm Band, The: 185
Wa Wa Nee: 453
Wax: 440
Waylon (Jennings): Sep. 1980
Waylon & Willie: Feb. 1978
Wayne, Thomas: Feb. 1959; 79, 302
Weather Girls, The: Jan. 1983; 401

INDEX OF SONG TITLES

In this index, a date shows where a song title appears in the hit lists. References to a song in other sections of the book are identified in the index by page numbers, which appear in *italic type* after the date.

Blues, The: Jan. 1983, June 1990
Blues For Salvador: *474*
Blue Suede Shoes: Mar. 1956, Apr. 1956; *38, 40, 460*
Blue Tango: 1952
Blue Velvet: Feb. 1955, Aug. 1963; *135*
Boats Against The Current: Dec. 1977
Bobby's Girl: Oct. 1962
Bobby Sox Blues: 1947
Bobby Sox To Stockings: June 1959
Bo Diddley: Apr. 1955; *460*
Body Language: May 1982
Bohemian Rhapsody: Jan. 1976, Mar. 1992; *529*
Boll Weevil Song, The: May 1961
Bombs Away: Mar. 1978
Bongo Rock: May 1959, July 1973
Bongo Stomp: July 1962
Bony Moronie: Oct. 1957
Boogaloo Down Broadway: Oct. 1967
Boogie At Midnight: 1949
Boogie Child: Jan. 1977
Boogie Children: 1949
Boogie Chillen': *518*
Boogie Down: Jan. 1974
Boogie Fever: Feb. 1976
Boogie Nights: July 1977
Boogie On Reggae Woman: Nov. 1974
Boogie Oogie Oogie: June 1978; *340*
Boogie Shoes: Feb. 1978
Boogie Wonderland: May 1979
Boogie Woogie Bugle Boy: May 1973
Book Of Love: Apr. 1958
Boom Boom Boomerang: Mar. 1955
Boom Boom (Let's Go Back To My Room): Mar. 1987
Boomin' System, The: Sep. 1990
Bop: Jan. 1986
Boppin' The Blues: June 1956
Bop 'Til You Drop: Aug. 1984
Bop Ting-A-Ling: Mar. 1955
Borderline: Mar. 1984
Border Song: *225*
Born A Woman: Aug. 1966
Born Free: Oct. 1966
Born In East L.A.: Sep. 1985
Born In The U.S.A.: Nov. 1984
Born To Be Alive: July 1979
Born To Be My Baby: Nov. 1988
Born To Be Wild: July 1968; *199*
Born To Be With You: July 1956
Born Too Late: July 1958
Born To Run: Sep. 1975; *293, 294*
Born To Wander: Dec. 1970
Borrowed Time: Mar. 1980
Boss, The: July 1979
Bossa Nova. *See* Fly Me To The Moon
Bossa Nova Baby: Oct. 1963; *137*
Boss Guitar: Jan. 1963
Both Sides Now: Nov. 1968
Bottle Of Wine: Jan. 1968
Boulevard: July 1980
Bo Weevil: Feb. 1956
Boxer, The: Apr. 1969
Boy From New York City: May 1981; *381, 435*
Boy From New York City, The: Feb. 1965
Boy I'm Gonna Marry, The. *See* (Today I Met) The Boy I'm Gonna Marry
Boy Named Sue, A: Aug. 1969
Boy Next Door, The: Dec. 1963
Boys Are Back In Town, The: May 1976
Boys Of Summer, The: Nov. 1984; *434*
Brainstorming: July 1992
Brand New Key: Nov. 1971
Brandy (You're A Fine Girl): June 1972
Brass In Pocket: *359*
Brass Monkey: Mar. 1987
Brazil: Aug. 1975; *474*
Bread And Butter: Aug. 1964; *143*
Breakdance: Apr. 1984
Breakdown: *320*

Breakdown Dead Ahead: Mar. 1980
Break Every Rule: May 1987
Breakfast In America: Dec. 1980
Breakin' Away: Dec. 1981
Breaking My Heart (Pretty Brown Eyes): Jan. 1992
Breaking Up Is Hard To Do: July 1962, Dec. 1975
Breaking Us In Two: Jan. 1983
Breakin' In A Brand New Broken Heart: Apr. 1961
Breakin' My Heart (Pretty Brown Eyes): Jan. 1992
Breakin' … There's No Stopping Us: June 1984
Break It To Me Gently: Jan. 1962, Aug. 1982
Break It Up: May 1982
Break My Stride: Sep. 1983
Breakout: June 1987
Breaks, The (Part I): Sep. 1980
Breakup Song, The (They Don't Write 'Em): *374*
Break Up To Make Up: Feb. 1973
Breathless: Mar. 1958
Breeze And I, The: Feb. 1954, Apr. 1955
Breezin': Oct. 1976
Brian's Song: Feb. 1972
Brickhouse: Aug. 1977
Bridge Over Troubled Water: Feb. 1970; *233, 234*
Bridget The Midget (The Queen Of The Blues): Dec. 1970
Brilliant Disguise: Oct. 1987
Bring The Boys Home: June 1971
Bristol Stomp: Sep. 1961; *100, 101, 124*
Bristol Twistin' Annie: June 1962
Broken Hearted Me: Sep. 1979
Broken-Hearted Melody: Aug. 1959
Broken Wings: Sep. 1985; *433*
Brother Louie: June 1973; *274*
Brother Love's Travelling Salvation Show: Mar. 1969
Brother Rapp (Part 1): May 1970
Brown Eyed Girl: Aug. 1967; *184*
Brown-eyed Girl: *476*
Brown Eyed Handsome Man: Oct. 1956
Brown Sugar: May 1971; *239, 247*
Bruce: Nov. 1984
Buchanan And Goodman On Trial: Nov. 1956
Buffalo Stance: Apr. 1989
Build Me Up, Buttercup: Jan. 1969
Bulldog: Jan. 1960
Bumble Boogie: Mar. 1961
Bungle In The Jungle: Nov. 1974
Burning Down One Side: *387*
Burning Heart: Nov. 1985
Burning Love: Aug. 1972; *476*
Burn Rubber: *373*
Burn The Candle: Nov. 1955
Bus Stop: Aug. 1966
Bus Stop Song, The (A Paper Of Pins): Sep. 1956
Bust A Move: July 1989; *487*
Busted: Sep. 1963
Bustin' Loose, Part 1: Feb. 1979
But I Do: Feb. 1961
But It's Alright: Nov. 1966
But Not For Me: *85*
Butterfly: Feb. 1957
But You Know I Love You: Feb. 1969, Apr. 1981
Buy For Me The Rain: *184*
Buzz-Buzz-Buzz: Oct. 1957
Buzz Me: 1946
Bye Bye Baby: Feb. 1965; *102*
Bye Bye Baby Blues: 1948
Bye, Bye Love: May 1957; *52, 447*
By The Time I Get To Phoenix: Nov. 1967; *192*

Cab Driver: Mar. 1968
Cajun Queen: Feb. 1962
Calcutta: Dec. 1960
Caldonia: 1945
Calendar Girl: Dec. 1960
California Dreamin': Feb. 1966, Sep. 1986; *171*
California Girls: July 1965, Jan. 1985; *427*
California Nights: Feb. 1967
California Saga (On My Way To Sunny California): May 1973
California Soul: Jan. 1969
California Sun: Apr. 1961, Feb. 1964
Calling It Love: June 1989
Call It Poison: Feb. 1991
Call Me: Oct. 1958, Feb. 1970, Feb. 1980; *366*
Call Me (Come Back Home): Feb. 1973
Call On Me: June 1974
Calypso: Aug. 1975
Canadian Sunset: Aug. 1956, Sep. 1956
Candida: Aug. 1970; *225*
Candle In The Wind: Nov. 1987
Candles In The Rain. *See* Lay Down
Candy: Dec. 1986
Candy Girl: July 1963; *400*
Candy Man: Aug. 1961, Mar. 1972; *261*
Can I Change My Mind: Dec. 1968; *198*
Can I Come Over Tonight: June 1957
Can I Get A Witness: Nov. 1963
Cannonball: Nov. 1958
Can't Buy Me Love: Mar. 1964; *140, 150, 151*
Can't Fight This Feeling: Jan. 1985; *433*
Can't Get Enough: Aug. 1974; *280*
Can't Get Enough Of Your Love, Babe: Aug. 1974
Can't Get Used To Losing You: Mar. 1963
Can't Give You Anything (But My Love): July 1975
Can't Help Falling In Love: Dec. 1961, Dec. 1986; *111, 476*
Can't Hide From Love. *See* Ready Or Not Here I Come
Cantina Band: Aug. 1977; *320, 326*
Can't Let Go: Nov. 1991
Can't Smile Without You: Feb. 1978
Can't Stay Away From You: Nov. 1987
Can't Stop: July 1990
Can't Stop Falling Into Love: July 1990
Can't Stop Dancing: Mar. 1977
Can't Stop This Thing We Started: Sep. 1991
Can't Take My Eyes Off You: June 1967, Dec. 1967
Can't Truss It: Oct. 1991
Can't Wait Another Minute: Sep. 1986
Can't We Be Sweethearts: June 1956; *504*
Can't You Hear My Heartbeat: Feb. 1965
Can't You See That She's Mine: June 1964
Can We Still Be Friends: Dec. 1979
Can You Find It In Your Heart: June 1956
Can You Stand The Rain: Feb. 1989
Cara Mia: July 1954, June 1965
Carefree Highway: Aug. 1974
Careless Whisper: Dec. 1984; *433*
Caribbean Blue: Feb. 1992
Caribbean Queen (No More Love On The Run): Aug. 1984; *420*
Carol: Sep. 1958
Carrie Ann: July 1967
Carry On Wayward Son: Dec. 1976; *307*
Cars: Feb. 1980
Car Wash: Oct. 1976; *307, 316*
Castles In The Air: Oct. 1981
Cast Your Fate To The Wind: Jan.

1963, Mar. 1965
Casual Look, A: July 1956
Catch A Falling Star: Feb. 1958; *73*
Catch The Wind: June 1965; *156*
Catch Us If You Can: Aug. 1965
Cathy's Clown: May 1960; *96*
Cat Scratch Fever: Aug. 1977
Cat's In The Cradle: Oct. 1974
Cattle Call: July 1955
Caught Up In You: May 1982
Causing A Commotion: Sep. 1987
Cave Man. *See* Troglodyte
C.C. Rider: Mar. 1957
Cecilia: Apr. 1970
Celebrate: Mar. 1970
Celebrate Youth: Apr. 1985
Celebration: Oct. 1980; *381*
Centerfield: May 1985
Centerfold: Nov. 1981; *393*
Certain Smile, A: July 1958
Cha-Cha-Cha, The: Oct. 1962
Chained: Oct. 1968
Chain Gang: Feb. 1956, Sep. 1960
Chain Of Fools: Dec. 1967
Chains: Nov. 1962; *502*
Chains Of Love: 1951, Aug. 1988
Chairman Of The Board: Mar. 1971
Chances Are: Aug. 1957
Change: *400*
Change Of Heart: Feb. 1983, Nov. 1986
Changes: *253*
Changes In Latitudes, Changes In Attitudes: Sep. 1977
Changing Partners: Jan. 1954
Chanson D'Amour: Apr. 1958
Chantez Chantez: Mar. 1957
Chantilly Lace: Aug. 1958
Chapel Of Love: May 1964; *142, 150*
Chariots Of Fire: Jan. 1982
Charity Ball: Sep. 1971
Charlie Brown: Feb. 1959
Charlie's Angels theme. *See* Theme From "Charlie's Angels"
Charmaine: 1951, Jan. 1956
Chasin' The Wind: Jan. 1991
Chattanooga Shoe Shine Boy: 1950, Mar. 1960
Cheaper To Keep Her: Oct. 1973
Cheater, The: Feb. 1966
Check It Out: Feb. 1988; *268*
Chee Chee Oo Chee: June 1955
Cheeseburger In Paradise: Apr. 1978
Cherchez La Femme/Se Si Bon: Nov. 1976
Cherish: Sep. 1966, Nov. 1971, July 1985, Aug. 1989; *178*
Cherry Baby: Mar. 1977
Cherry Bomb: Oct. 1987
Cherry, Cherry: Sep. 1966
Cherry Hill Park: Oct. 1969
Cherry Pie: July 1954, Apr. 1960
Cherry Pink And Apple Blossom White: Jan. 1955; *26, 33*
Chevy Van: Feb. 1975
Chewy Chewy: Oct. 1968
Chicago: Sep. 1957
Chicago Song: *460*
Chick-A-Boom: Mar. 1971
Chicken: Feb. 1956
Chicken An' The Hawk: Dec. 1955
Chico And The Man: Jan. 1975
Children Of The Night: Apr. 1990
Children's Marching Song, The: Feb. 1959
China Girl: June 1983
China Grove: Aug. 1973
Chip Chip: Feb. 1962
Chipmunk Song, The: Dec. 1958; *64, 73*
Chokin' Kind, The: Mar. 1969
Christine Sixteen: July 1977
Christmas Auld Lang Syne: Dec. 1960
Christmas Song, The: *476*
Chuck E's In Love: Apr. 1979
Chug-A-Lug: Oct. 1964

Each And Every Time: Oct. 1990
Early In The Morning: Aug. 1958, Dec. 1969, Oct. 1988
Earth Angel: Oct. 1954, Mar. 1955, Aug. 1986
Ease On Down The Road: Apr. 1975, Sep. 1978; *342*
Easier Said Than Done: June 1963
Easy: June 1977; *342*
Easy Come Easy Go: Feb. 1991
Easy Come, Easy Go: Feb. 1970
Easy Lover: Nov. 1984
Easy Loving: Aug. 1971
Easy To Be Hard: Aug. 1969; *355*
Easy To Love: Dec. 1977
Eating Goober Peas: June 1955
Eat It: Mar. 1984; *421*
Ebb Tide: 1953, Jan. 1954, June 1960, Dec. 1965
Ebony & Ivory: Apr. 1982; *393*
Ebony Eyes: Feb. 1961, Jan. 1978, Dec. 1983
Eddie My Love: Feb. 1956
Edge Of A Broken Heart: Sep. 1988
Edge Of Heaven, The: July 1986
Edge Of Seventeen: Feb. 1982
Edge Of The Universe: July 1977
Ego: Apr. 1978
Eh Cumpari: 1953
Eight Days A Week: Feb. 1965
Eighteen: Feb. 1971; *239*
18 Yellow Roses: May 1963 853-5937: Dec. 1987
Eight Miles High: Apr. 1966 81, The: Jan. 1965
El Bimbo: May 1975
El Condor Pasa: Sep. 1970
Eleanor Rigby: Aug. 1966, Nov. 1969; *208, 422*
Elected: Oct. 1972
Election Day: Oct. 1985
Electric Avenue: Apr. 1983
Electric Blue: Feb. 1988
Electric Boogie: Dec. 1989
Electric Youth: Apr. 1989
Elenore: Sep. 1968
Eli's Coming: Nov. 1969
Elevator Boogie: 1948
El Paso: Jan. 1960
Elusive Butterfly: Feb. 1966
Elvira: May 1981; *374*
Elvis Medley, The: Dec. 1982
El Watusi: May 1963
Emergency: Oct. 1985
Emma: Feb. 1975; *292*
Emotion: Nov. 1977
Emotional Rescue: July 1980
Emotion In Motion: Sep. 1986
Emotions: Jan. 1961, Aug. 1991
Emotions In Motion: Aug. 1982
Empty Arm Blues: 1949
Empty Arms: Apr. 1957
Empty Garden: Mar. 1982
End, The: Sep. 1958; *65*
Endless Love: June 1981; *374, 381*
Endlessly: May 1959
Endless Nights: Apr. 1987
Endless Sleep: May 1958
Endless Summer Nights: Jan. 1988
End Of The Innocence, The: June 1989; *487*
End Of The Line: Feb. 1989
End Of The Road: July 1992
End Of The World, The: Feb. 1963
Engine, Engine #9: May 1965
Engine Number 9: Oct. 1970
England Swings: Nov. 1965
Enjoy Yourself: Nov. 1976
Enough Is Enough: *See* No More Tears
Enter Sandman: Aug. 1991
Entertainer, The: Apr. 1974, Dec. 1974
Epic: July 1990
Epistle To Dippy: Mar. 1967
Eres Tu (Touch The Wind): Feb. 1974
Escapade: Jan. 1990

Escape (The Pina Colada Song): Oct. 1979
Eso Beso: Nov. 1962
Eternal Flame: Feb. 1989
Even Better Than The Real Thing: July 1992
Even Now: May 1978, Mar. 1983
Even The Nights Are Better: June 1982
Eve Of Destruction: Aug. 1965; *155*
Evergreen. *See* Love Theme From "A Star Is Born"
Everlasting Love: Oct. 1967, Sep. 1974, June 1981, Mar. 1989
Everlasting Love, An: July 1978
Everlovin': Oct. 1961
Every Beat Of My Heart: May 1961, Nov. 1986; *101*
Everybody: Oct. 1963
Everybody Dance: Apr, 1978
Everybody Have Fun Tonight: Oct. 1986
Everybody Is A Star: Jan. 1970
Everybody Knows: Oct. 1964, Jan. 1968
Everybody Likes To Cha Cha Cha: Mar. 1959
Everybody Loves A Clown: Oct. 1965
Everybody Loves A Lover: Aug. 1958, Dec. 1962
Everybody Loves Somebody: July 1964
Everybody Plays The Fool: July 1972
Everybody's Everything: Oct. 1971
Everybody's Free (To Feel Good): June 1992
Everybody's Somebody's Fool: May 1960
Everybody's Talkin': Sep. 1969; *213, 221*
Everybody Wants To Rule The World: Mar. 1985
Every Breath You Take: June 1983; *407, 408*
Everyday: Oct. 1957, Mar. 1972, Nov. 1985; *52*
Every Day I Have The Blues: Mar. 1955
Every Day I Have To Cry: Feb. 1963
Everyday People: Dec. 1968; *220*
Everyday With You Girl: May 1969
Every Face Tells A Story: Nov. 1976
Every Heartbeat: June 1991
Every Home Should Have One: *373*
Every Kinda People: Mar. 1978
Every Little Bit Hurts: May 1964; *142*
Every Little Kiss: July 1986; *439*
Every Little Step: Mar. 1989; *487*
Every Little Thing She Does Is Magic: Sep. 1981
Every Night: May 1958
Every 1's A Winner: Nov. 1978
Everyone's Gone To The Moon: Oct. 1965
Everyone's Laughing: May 1957
Every Road Leads Back To You: Dec. 1991
Every Rose Has Its Thorn: Oct. 1988; *486*
Every Step Of The Way: Aug. 1985
Everything About You: Apr. 1992
Everything Changes: Feb. 1992
(Everything I Do) I Do It For You: June 1991; *516, 517*
Everything I Own: Jan. 1972
Everything Is Beautiful: Apr. 1970; *234*
Everything's Alright. *See* Uptight
Everything She Wants: Mar. 1985
Everything That Touches You: Feb. 1968
Everything Your Heart Desires: Apr. 1988
Every Time I Think Of You: Jan. 1979
(Every Time I Turn Around) Back In Love Again: Oct. 1977
Everytime You Go Away: May 1985
Everywhere: Nov. 1987

Every Woman In The World: Oct. 1980
Evil Ways: Feb. 1970
Evil Woman: Nov. 1975
Exodus: Nov. 1960
Exodus (In Jazz): Apr. 1961
Exordium & Terminus. *See* In The Year 2525
Express: Jan. 1975
Expressway To Your Heart: Sep. 1967
Express Yourself: June 1989
Eye In The Sky: July 1982
Eye Of The Tiger: June 1982; *393, 394*
Eyes Of A New York Woman, The: Aug. 1968
Eyes Without A Face: May 1984

Face In The Crowd, A: Mar. 1990
Fade Away: Feb. 1981
Faded Love: *128*
Fading Like A Flower (Every Time You Leave): June 1991
Fa-Fa-Fa-Fa-Fa (Sad Song): Oct. 1966
Fairweather Friend: Oct. 1990
Faith: Oct. 1987; *473*
Faithfully: Apr. 1983
Fakin' It: Aug. 1967
Fallen Angel: Aug. 1988
Fallen Star, A: July 1957
Fallin': Nov. 1958
Falling: June 1963, Oct. 1977
Fallin' In Love: June 1975
Fame: July 1975, June 1980; *300, 359, 369, 370*
Fame And Fortune: Apr. 1960; *88*
Family Affair: Nov. 1971; *247*
Family Man: May 1983
Family Of Man, The: Mar. 1972
Fanny (Be Tender With My Love): Dec. 1975
Fantasy: Mar. 1978
Fantasy Girl: June 1981
Far From Over: July 1983
Farther Up The Road: July 1957; *51, 527*
Fascination: Aug. 1957. *See also* (Keep Feeling) Fascination
Fast Car: June 1988; *474*
Fat Bottom Girls: Nov. 1978
Father Figure: Jan. 1988
Fat Man, The: *447*
Feelin' Groovy. *See* 59th Street Bridge Song, The
Feelings: June 1975
Feelin' Stronger Every Day: June 1973
Feel Like Makin' Love: June 1974
Feels Good: Sep. 1990
Feels So Fine: July 1960
Feel So Good: June 1955
Feels So Good: Jan. 1989
Feels So Right: *373*
Fernando: Sep. 1976
Ferry Cross The Mersey: *166*
Fever: July 1956, July 1958, Nov. 1965
Ffun: Dec. 1977
Fifth Of Beethoven, A: May 1976 59th Street Bridge Song, The (Feelin' Groovy): Mar. 1967
57 Channels (And Nothin' On): June 1992
50 Ways To Leave Your Lover: Dec. 1975; *314*
Fight: June 1979
Fight For Your Right (To Party!). *See* (You Gotta) Fight For Your Right (To Party!)
Fight The Power (Part 1): July 1975
Find Your Way Back: Apr. 1981
Finger Poppin' Time: July 1960
Fingertips—Part 2: July 1963; *129, 135, 151, 488*
Finish What Ya Started: Oct. 1988
Fire: Sep. 1968, Dec. 1974, Nov. 1978, Jan. 1987
Fire And Ice: June 1981; *381*

Fire And Rain: Sep. 1970: *227*
Firefly: Oct. 1958
Fire In The Morning: Feb. 1980
Fire Lake: Feb. 1980
First Cut Is The Deepest, The: Feb. 1977
First Hymn From Grand Terrace: *213*
First Taste Of Love: Jan. 1961; *101*
First Time Ever I Saw Your Face, The: Mar. 1972; *261, 262*
First Time Love: July 1980 5:15: Sep. 1979
500 Miles Away From Home: Oct. 1963
Five O'Clock World: Dec. 1965
5-10-15-20 (25–30 Years Of Love): Oct. 1970
Flame, The: Apr. 1988
Flames Of Paradise: May 1987
Flaming Star: Apr. 1961; *98*
Flashdance … What A Feeling: Apr. 1983; *407, 408, 409, 410*
Flash Light: Feb. 1978
Flash's Theme a.k.a. Flash: Jan. 1981
Flesh For Fantasy: Aug. 1984
Flip, Flop And Bop: *64*
Flip, Flop And Fly: Feb. 1955; *38*
Float On: July 1977
Florence: May 1957
Flowers On The Wall: Dec. 1965
Fly, The: Oct. 1961, Nov. 1991; *100, 124*
Fly Away: Dec. 1975, Jan. 1981
Fly By Night: *320*
Flying Saucer: Aug. 1956
Flying Saucer The 2nd: June 1957
Fly Like An Eagle: Dec. 1976
Fly Me To The Moon (Bossa Nova): Jan. 1963; *199*
Fly, Robin, Fly: Oct. 1975; *300*
FM: June 1978
Follow That Dream: May 1962; *124*
Follow The Boys: *124*
Follow You, Follow Me: Apr. 1978
Folsom Prison Blues: June 1968
Fool, The: July 1956
Fooled Around And Fell In Love: Mar. 1976
Fool For A Pretty Face: Apr. 1980
Fool For You, A: Aug. 1955
Fool For Your Loving: Nov. 1989; *359*
Fool If You Think It's Over: July 1978
Fool In Love, A: Sep. 1960; *90*
Fool In The Rain: Dec. 1979
Foolish Beat: Apr. 1988
Foolish Heart: Nov. 1984, Dec. 1989
Foolish Little Girl: Apr. 1963
Foolish Pride: Oct. 1986
Fool Moon Fire: Apr. 1983
Fool Never Learns, A: Jan. 1964
Fool On The Hill, The: Aug. 1968; *193*
Fools Fall In Love: Feb. 1957
Fool's Paradise, A: *255*
Fools Rush In: Nov. 1960, Sep. 1963
Fool Such As I, A: Mar. 1959, Dec. 1973
Fool To Cry: Apr. 1976, June 1976
Footloose: Jan. 1984; *420, 422*
Footloose theme. *See* Almost Paradise
Footsteps: Mar. 1960
Foot Stomping: *476*
For All We Know: Feb. 1971; *236*
For America: Mar. 1986
Forever: Feb. 1960, Dec. 1982, Feb. 1990
Forever Afternoon. *See* Tuesday Afternoon
Forever Amo'r: June 1991
Forever Autumn: Oct. 1978
Forever In Blue Jeans: Jan. 1979
Forever My Lady: Oct. 1991
Forever Man: Mar. 1985
Forever Mine: Nov. 1979
Forever Young: Aug. 1988, Nov. 1988
Forever Your Girl: Mar. 1989

Forget Him: Nov. 1963
Forget Me Not: Oct. 1958
Forgive Me, Girl: Dec. 1979
Forgive My Heart: Aug. 1955
For Ol' Times Sake: Sep. 1973
For Once In My Life: Nov. 1968
For Sentimental Reasons. *See* (I Love You) For Sentimental Reasons
For The Love Of Him: Mar. 1970
For The Love Of Money: Apr. 1974
Fortress Around Your Heart: Aug. 1985
Forty Days: June 1959
Forty Miles Of Bad Road: June 1959
For Unlawful Carnal Knowledge: *517*
For What It's Worth: Feb. 1967; *183*
For You: Jan. 1964, Nov. 1990
For You Blue: June 1970
For Your Eyes Only: June 1981
For Your Love: Apr. 1958, May 1965, July 1967; *154, 157, 528*
For Your Precious Love: June 1958; *518*
Found A Cure: Aug. 1979 409: Sep. 1962
Four Walls: Apr. 1957
Fox On The Run: Nov. 1975
Francene: *255*
Frankenstein: Mar. 1973
Frankie: May 1959
Frankie And Johnny: *180*
Fraulein: *52*
Freak-A-Zoid: *400*
Freddie's Dead: Aug. 1972; *263*
Free: Feb. 1971; *320*
Freebird Medley: Sep. 1988
Freedom: July 1985, Oct. 1990
Freedom Overspill: Sep. 1986
Free Fallin': Nov. 1989
Freeway Of Love: June 1985
Freeze-Frame: Feb. 1982
Freight Train: Apr. 1957
Fresh: Apr. 1985
Friday I'm In Love: June 1992
Friday Night. *See* Livin' It Up
Friday On My Mind: Apr. 1967
Friendly Persuasion (Thee I Love): Aug. 1956
Friends: Mar. 1971, June 1989
Friends And Lovers: July 1986
Friends In Love: Apr. 1982
Frisky: Nov. 1973
From A Distance: Oct. 1990; *501*
From A Jack To A King: Jan. 1963
From Me To You: Feb. 1964; *127*
From The Bottom Of My Heart: Oct. 1956
From The Vine Came The Grape: Feb. 1954
Full Of Fire: Dec. 1980
Fun, Fun, Fun: Mar. 1964
Funky Broadway: Aug. 1967
Funky Cold Medina: Mar. 1989
Funky Town: Mar. 1980; *367*
Funkytown: May 1987
Funky Worm: Feb. 1973
Funny: Mar. 1961, Sep. 1964
Funny Face: Oct. 1972
Funny Way Of Laughin': Apr. 1962

Gallant Men: Jan. 1967
Galveston: Mar. 1969
Gambler, The: Nov. 1978
Game Of Love: Mar. 1965; *476*
Games People Play: Jan. 1969; *220*. *See also* They Just Can't Stop It The Gang That Sang "Heart Of My Heart", The: Feb. 1954
Garden Of Eden: Oct. 1956
Garden Party: Aug. 1972
Gee: Mar. 1954; *504*
Gee Baby: *157*
Gee Whittakers: Nov. 1955
Gee Whiz: Mar. 1980
Gee Whiz (Look At His Eyes): Feb. 1961; *102*

Gemini Dream: June 1981
General Hospi-Tale: June 1981
Gentle: Nov. 1990
Georgia On My Mind: Oct. 1960, Aug. 1990; *97*
Georgy Girl: Dec. 1966
Geronimo's Cadillac: *254*
Get A Job: Jan. 1958
Get A Leg Up: Oct. 1991
Getaway: July 1976
Get Back: May 1969, Oct. 1978; *220*
Getcha Back: May 1985
Get Closer: Apr. 1976
Get Down: June 1973
Get Down Tonight: Aug. 1975; *294*
Get Here: Dec. 1990
Get It: *501*
Get It On (Bang A Gong): June 1985. *See also* Bang A Gong
Get It Right Next Time: Aug. 1979
Get Off: July 1978
Get Off Of My Cloud: Oct. 1965; *164*
Get On The Good Foot (Part 1): Aug. 1972
Get On Up: Sep. 1967
Get On Your Feet: Sep. 1989
Get Outta My Dreams, Get Into My Car: Feb. 1988
Get Ready: Mar. 1966, Mar. 1970; *226*
Get The Funk Out Ma Face: Aug. 1976
Getting Away With It: Mar. 1990
Getting Closer: June 1979
Gettin' Together: Sep. 1967
Gett Off: Aug. 1991
Get Together: July 1969
Get Up! (Before The Night Is Over): Jan. 1990
Get Up And Boogie: Mar. 1976
Get Up And Dance. *See* Bite Your Lip
Get Up And Go: Sep. 1982
Get Up Offa That Thing: Aug. 1976
Ghetto Child: Aug. 1973
Ghostbusters: June 1984; *420, 422*
Ghost Town: Dec. 1988
G.I. Blues: *98*
Gidget: *77*
Gilly, Gilly, Ossenfeffer. Katzenellen Bogen By The Sea: July 1954
Gimme All Your Lovin': Apr. 1983
Gimme Dat Ding: May 1970
Gimme Gimme Good Lovin': Mar. 1969
Gimme Little Sign: Aug. 1967
Gimme Some Lovin': Jan. 1967, May 1980
Gina: Oct. 1962
Ginger Bread: July 1958
Girl, A Girl, A: Mar. 1954
Girl Can't Help It: Aug. 1986
Girl Can't Help It, The: Jan. 1957; *48*
Girlfriend: Dec. 1986, Jan. 1988; *439*
Girl From Ipanema, The: June 1964; *151*
Girl I Knew Somewhere, The: Apr. 1967
Girl I'm Gonna Miss You: Aug. 1989
Girl Is Mine, The: Nov. 1982
Girl I Used To Know, The: June 1990
Girl Like You, A: July 1967, Dec. 1989
Girl Of My Best Friend: Apr. 1961; *101*
Girl Of My Dreams: Apr. 1956, July 1979
Girls: Feb. 1984
Girls Are More Fun: Oct. 1985
Girls Can't Do What The Guys Do: *199*
Girls, Girls, Girls: May 1987
(Girls, Girls, Girls) Were Made To Love: July 1962
Girls Just Want To Have Fun: Dec. 1983; *400*
Girl Watcher: Sep. 1968
Girl (Why You Wanna Make Me Blue): Sep. 1964
Girl You Know It's True: Jan. 1989; *486*

Girl, You'll Be A Woman Soon: Apr. 1967
Gitarzan: Apr. 1969
Give A Little Bit: June 1977
Give Him A Great Big Kiss: Jan. 1965
Give Ireland Back To The Irish: Mar. 1972
Give It Away: Dec. 1991; *212*
Give It Up: Dec. 1983
Give It What You Got: Aug. 1975
Give Me Just A Little More Time: Feb. 1970; *225*
Give Me Love (Give Me Peace On Earth): May 1973
Give Me Peace On Earth. *See* Give Me Love
Give Me The Keys (And I'll Drive You Crazy): Jan. 1989
Give Me The Night: July 1980
Give Me Tonight: Apr. 1984
Give Peace A Chance: Aug. 1969, Mar. 1991; *211, 213*
Give To Live: June 1987
Give Your Baby A Standing Ovation: Apr. 1973
Giving Him Something He Can Feel: June 1992
Giving It Up For Your Love: Dec. 1980
Giving Up On Love: Apr. 1989
Giving You The Benefit: Aug. 1990
Giving You The Best That I Got: Sep. 1988; *474, 486, 487*
Glad All Over: Mar. 1964; *142*
Glamorous Life, The: *414*
Glendora: May 1956
Gloria: June 1954, Apr. 1966, July 1982
Glory Bound: Feb. 1972
Glory Days: June 1985
Glory Of Love: 1951, Apr. 1961, June 1986; *439*
Glow Worm, The: 1952
Go: Dec. 1985
Go All The Way: July 1972
Go Away. *See* Dawn
Go Away Little Girl: Nov. 1962, Aug. 1971; *247, 502*
Go Away, Little Girl: Oct. 1966
God Only Knows: Aug. 1966
Goin' Crazy: Sep. 1986
Going Home: Jan. 1990
Going In Circles: Sep. 1969
Going To A Go-Go: Jan. 1966, June 1982
Going Up The Country: Dec. 1968
Goin' Home: 1952
Goin' Out Of My Head: Nov. 1964, Dec. 1967
Go Insane: July 1984
Go, Jimmy, Go: Dec. 1959
Gold: May 1979, Nov. 1983
Goldfinger: Feb. 1965
Gone: Jan. 1957
Gone, Gone, Gone: Aug. 1979
Gong-Gong Song, The. *See* I'm Blue
Gonna Boogie Tonight. *See* Steppin' Out
Gonna Find Me A Bluebird: Apr. 1957
Gonna Fly Now. *See* Gonna Fly Now; Theme From Rocky
Gonna Fly Now (Theme From "Rocky"): Apr. 1977
Gonna Get Along Without Ya Now: Oct. 1956
Gonna Make You Sweat: Nov. 1990; *516*
Go Now: Mar. 1965; *157*
Goodbye: May 1969
Goodbye Baby: Dec. 1958, Jan. 1959
Goodbye Cruel World: Oct. 1961
Goodbye Girl: Dec. 1977
Goodbye Is Forever: Feb. 1986
Goodbye, Jimmy, Goodbye: May 1959
Goodbye Stranger: July 1979
Goodbye To Love: July 1972
Goodbye Yellow Brick Road: Oct. 1973
Good Day Sunshine: *422*

Good For Me: Jan. 1992
Good Girls Don't: Sep. 1979
Good Golly Miss Molly: Feb. 1958
Good Life, The: May 1963
Good Lovin': *520*
Good Luck Charm: Mar. 1962; *123*
Good Man, Good Woman: *517*
Good Morning Starshine: June 1969; *355*
Good News: Feb. 1964
Goodnight Irene: 1950; *116*
Goodnight My Love: Jan. 1969
Goodnight Saigon: Mar. 1983
Goodnight Sweetheart, Goodnight: Mar. 1954, July 1954; *14*
Goodnight Tonight: Mar. 1979
Good Ol' Boys. *See* Theme From The Dukes Of Hazzard
Good Old Rock 'N Roll: July 1969
Good Rockin' Tonight: 1948, Oct. 1954
Good Stuff: June 1992
Good Thing: Jan. 1967, May 1989
Good Time Baby: Jan. 1961
Good Time Charlie's Got The Blues: Sep. 1972
Good Times: July 1964, June 1979
Good Times, Bad Times: *212*
Good Times Never Seemed So Good. *See* Sweet Caroline
Good Times, Rock & Roll: Feb. 1975
Good Timin': Apr. 1960, Apr. 1979
Good Vibrations: Nov. 1966, June 1991
Goody Goody: June 1957
Goody Two Shoes: Nov. 1982
Go On Home: Jan. 1962
Goonies 'R' Good Enough, The: May 1985
Go On With The Wedding: Jan. 1956
Got A Hold On Me: Jan. 1984
Got A Job: *65, 460*
Got A Lot O' Livin' To Do: *60*
Got My Mind Set On You: Oct. 1987; *473*
Gotta Get You Home Tonight: Jan. 1985
Gotta Have Lovin': Dec. 1978
Gotta Serve Somebody: *354*
Gotta Travel On: Dec. 1958
Got The Feeling: Sep. 1959
Got To Be Real: Dec. 1978
Got To Be There: Nov. 1971; *239, 240*
Got To Get You Into My Life: June 1976, July 1978; *342*
Got To Give It Up (Part I): Apr. 1977
Go Where You Wanna Go: Feb. 1967; *184*
Go Your Own Way: Jan. 1977; *318*
Graceland: Dec. 1986; *459*
Graduation Day: May 1956
Grass Is Greener, The: Oct. 1963
Gravy: June 1962
Grazing In The Grass: June 1968, May 1969; *212*
Grease: May 1978; *342*
Greased Lightnin': Sep. 1978
Great Balls Of Fire: Nov. 1957; *60, 63, 342*
Great Commandment, The: Jan. 1989
Greatest American Hero theme. *See* Theme From "Greatest American Hero"
Greatest Hurt, The: Jan. 1962
Greatest Love Of All: Mar. 1986; *446, 466*
Greatest Love Of All, The: July 1977
Great Pretender, The: Jan. 1956; *48, 88*
Greenback Dollar: Feb. 1963
Green Chritma: Dec. 1958
Green Door, The: Oct. 1956
Green-Eyed Lady: Aug. 1970
Greenfields: Mar. 1960; *89*
Green Grass: May 1966
Green, Green: July 1963
Green, Green Grass Of Home: Jan. 1967

Holding Back The Years: Apr. 1986
Holding On: Nov. 1988
Holdin' On To Yesterday: *293*
Hold Me: June 1982, Feb. 1987
Hold Me Now: Feb. 1984
Hold Me, Thrill Me, Kiss Me: July 1965
Hold Me Tight: Sep. 1968
Hold My Hand: Aug. 1954
Hold On: Sep. 1979, Sep. 1980, Feb. 1981, Aug. 1982, Mar. 1990, May 1990; *347, 500*
Hold On! I'm Comin': May 1966
Hold On My Heart: May 1992
Hold On Tight: June 1981
Hold On To My Love: Mar. 1980
Hold On To The Nights: May 1988
Hold The Line: Oct. 1978; *333*
Hold What You've Got: Jan. 1965; *143*
Hold Your Head Up: June 1972
Hold You Tight: Jan. 1991
Hole Hearted: Aug. 1991
Hole In My Heart (All The Way To China): July 1988
Holiday: Oct. 1967, Oct. 1983; *400*
Holly Holy: Nov. 1969
Hollywood: May 1977
Hollywood Nights: Aug. 1978
Hollywood Swinging: May 1974
Holyanna: Feb. 1985
Home For The Holidays: Nov. 1954
Homesick Blues: 1949
Home Sweet Home: Nov. 1991
Homeward Bound: Feb. 1966
Honesty: Apr. 1979
Honey: Mar. 1968: *206*
Honey Babe: Apr. 1955
Honey Chile: Nov. 1967; *48*
Honeycomb: Aug. 1957; *52*
Honey Come Back: Feb. 1970
Honey Honey: Oct. 1974
Honey Hush: Mar. 1954, Jan. 1960
Honey Love: May 1954
Honky Cat: Aug. 1972
Honky Tonk: Aug. 1956; *39*
Honky Tonk (Part 1): June 1972
Honky Tonk Women: Aug. 1969; *220*
Hooka Tooka: Nov. 1963
Hooked On A Feeling: Dec. 1968, Feb. 1974
Hooked On Classics: Oct. 1981
Hooked On Swing: June 1982
Hooray For Hazel: Oct. 1966
Hopeless: July 1963
Hopelessly Devoted To You: July 1978; *342*
Horse, The: June 1968
Horse With No Name, A: Feb. 1972; *253, 261*
Hot And Bothered: *529*
Hot Blooded: July 1978
Hot Child In The City: June 1978
Hot Diggity: Mar. 1956
Hot Dog Buddy Buddy: May 1956; *47*
Hotel California: Feb. 1977; *326, 327*
Hot For Teacher: Oct. 1984
Hot Fun In The Summertime: Aug. 1969; *520*
Hot Girls In Love: June 1983
Hot In The City: July 1982; *386*
Hot Legs: Feb. 1978
Hot Line: Oct. 1976
Hot Pastrami: Apr. 1963
Hot Rod Hearts: July 1980
Hot Rod Lincoln: Aug. 1960, Mar. 1972
Hot Shot: Sep. 1978
Hot Smoke And Sassafras: Feb. 1969
Hot Stuff: June 1976, Apr. 1979; *353, 354*
Hound Dog: 1953, July 1956; *38, 39, 46, 50, 461*
Hound Dog Man: Nov. 1959; *86*
Hourglass: Sep. 1987
Housecall: Oct. 1991
House Full Of Reasons: Dec. 1990
House Of Blue Lights, The: May 1955

House Of Pain: Feb. 1990
House Of The Rising Sun, The: Aug. 1964, Feb. 1970, Apr. 1978; *141, 150*
House That Jack Built, The: Aug. 1968
Houston: Aug. 1965
How About That: Jan. 1960
How Am I Supposed To Live Without You: July 1983, Oct. 1989; *487*
How 'Bout Us: Feb. 1981
How Can I Be Sure: Sep. 1967
How Can I Ease The Pain: *517*
How Can I Fall?: Sep. 1988
How Can I Tell Her: June 1973
How Can We Be Lovers: Mar. 1990
How Can You Mend A Broken Heart: June 1971; *247*
How Deep Is Your Love: Sep. 1977; *327*
How Does That Grab You, Darlin'?: Apr. 1966
How Do I Make You: Feb. 1980
How Do You Do?: May 1972
How Do You Do It?: July 1964
How Do You Keep The Music Playing: May 1983
How'd We Ever Get This Way: May 1968; *198*
How Glad I Am. *See* (You Don't Know) How Glad I Am
How High The Moon: 1951
How Important Can It Be?: Jan. 1955
How Little We Know: May 1956
How Long: Apr. 1975, Apr. 1982
How Many Times Can We Say Goodbye: Oct. 1983
How Much I Feel: Sep. 1978
How Much Is Enough: Apr. 1991
How Much Love: Feb. 1987
How Sweet It Is: Dec. 1964; *502*
How Sweet It Is (To Be Loved By You): June 1975
How The Time Flies: Sep. 1958; *65*
How To Dance: Feb. 1991
How Will I Know: Dec. 1985; *446, 466*
How You Gonna See Me Now: Oct. 1978
Hucklebuck, The: Oct. 1960
Hula Hoop Song, The: Oct. 1958
Hula Love: Aug. 1957; *60*
Hully Gully Baby: Sep. 1962
Human: Sep. 1986
Human Nature: July 1983
Human Touch/Better Days: Mar. 1992; *524*
Hummingbird: Jan. 1973
Hummingbird Song: July 1955
Hundred Pounds Of Clay, A: Mar. 1961; *102*
Hungry Eyes: Dec. 1987; *462*
Hungry Heart: Nov. 1980
Hungry Like The Wolf: *386*
Hunter Gets Captured By The Game, The: Mar. 1967
Hunters Of The Night: *413*
Hurdy Gurdy Man: July 1968
Hurt: Oct. 1954, Aug. 1961, Mar. 1976; *102*
Hurting Each Other: Jan. 1972
Hurting Kind (I've Got My Eyes On You): Mar. 1990
Hurt So Bad: Aug. 1969, Apr. 1980
Hurts So Bad: Feb. 1965
Hurts So Good: Apr. 1982; *394*
Hurt Yourself: *172*
Hush: Aug. 1968; *196, 198*
Hushabye: May 1959, June 1969; *528*
Hush, Hush Sweet Charlotte: May 1965
Hustle, The: May 1975; *293*
Hymn 43: *240*
Hyperactive: June 1986
Hysteria: Jan. 1988

I Adore Mi Amor: July 1991
I Ain't Gonna Eat Out My Heart Anymore: *158*

I Ain't Never: Sep. 1959
I Almost Lost My Mind: 1950, May 1956
I Am A Rock: May 1966
I Am By Your Side: Sep. 1986
I Am ... I Said: Apr. 1971
I Am Love (Parts 1 & 2): Jan. 1975
I Am The Walrus: Dec. 1967; *193*
I Am Woman: June 1972, Dec. 1972; *262*
I Beg Of You: Feb. 1958; *72*
I Believe In Love: *320*
I Believe In You (You Believe In Me): June 1973
I Believe There's Nothing Stronger Than Our Love: July 1975
I Can Dream, Can't I: 1950
I Can Hear Music: Mar. 1969
I Can Help: Sep. 1974; *288*
I Can See Clearly Now: Sep. 1972; *261*
I Can See For Miles: Oct. 1967
I Can Take Care Of Myself: Apr. 1981; *373*
I Can't Dance: Feb. 1992
I Can't Explain: *154, 157, 502*
I Can't Get Next To You: Sep. 1969; *220*
(I Can't Get No) Satisfaction: June 1965; *164*
I Can't Go For That (No Can Do): Nov. 1981
I Can't Hear You No More: Aug. 1976
I Can't Help It: Mar. 1980, Nov. 1987
(I Can't Help You) I'm Falling Too: *89*
I Can't Help Myself: May 1965, Dec. 1979; *502*
I Can't Hold On: *332*
I Can't Let Go: June 1980
I Can't Make It Alone: *198*
I Can't Say Goodbye: Jan. 1960
I Can't Stand It: Feb. 1981
I Can't Stay Mad At You: Sep. 1963
I Can't Stop Dancing: Aug. 1968
I Can't Stop Loving You: May 1962; *123*
I Can't Stop The Feelin': Dec. 1980
I Can't Tell You Why: Feb. 1980
I Can't Wait: Feb. 1986
I Can't Wait Another Minute: June 1991
Ice Ice Baby: Sep. 1990
I Confess: *171*
I Could Have Danced All Night: May 1956, Jan. 1976
I Could Never Love Another (After Loving You): May 1968
I Could Never Take The Place Of Your Man: Nov. 1987
I Couldn't Live Without Your Love: July 1966
I Count The Tears: Dec. 1960
I Cried: Aug. 1954
I Cried A Tear: Dec. 1958
I Didn't Get To Sleep At All. *See* (Last Night) I Didn't Get To Sleep At All
I Didn't Want To Need You: June 1990
I'd Like To Teach The World To Sing (In Perfect Harmony): Dec. 1971
I'd Love You To Want Me: Sep. 1972
I Do: June 1965, Nov. 1982
I Do, I Do, I Do, I Do, I Do: Feb. 1976
I Do Love You: Apr. 1965
Idol With The Golden Head: Dec. 1957
I Don't Hurt Anymore: July 1954
I Don't Know: Dec. 1989
I Don't Know How To Love Him: Jan. 1971, May 1971; *240, 275*
I Don't Know If It's Right: Jan. 1979
I Don't Know What It Is: *77*
I Don't Like To Sleep Alone: Mar. 1975
I Don't Love You Anymore: *320*
I Don't Need No Doctor: Sep. 1971
I Don't Need Your Love: Apr. 1981, June 1981
I Don't See Me In Your Eyes Anymore: May 1974
I Don't Wanna Cry: Apr. 1991

I Don't Wanna Go On With You Like That: June 1988
I Don't Wanna Live Without Your Love: June 1988
I Don't Wanna See You: July 1991
I Don't Want To Be Right. *See* (If Loving You Is Wrong) I Don't Want To Be Right
I Don't Want To Cry: Feb. 1961; *101*
I Don't Want To Live Without You: Mar. 1988
I Don't Want To Spoil The Party: Feb. 1965
I Don't Want To Walk Without You: Apr. 1980
I Don't Want Your Love: Oct. 1988
I Do You: Oct. 1987
I'd Rather Be An Old Man's Sweetheart: *213*
I'd Really Love To See You Tonight: June 1976; *306*
I Dreamed: Dec. 1956
I Drove All Night: May 1989
I'd Wait A Million Years: July 1969
Iesha: Jan. 1991
If: 1951, Apr. 1971
I Fall To Pieces: May 1961
If Anyone Falls: Sep. 1983
I Feel Fine: Dec. 1964
I Feel For You: Sep. 1984
I Feel Good: Nov. 1956. *See also* I Got You
I Feel Like A Bullet (In The Gun Of Robert Ford): Jan. 1976
I Feel Love: Aug. 1977
I Feel So Bad: May 1961
I Feel The Earth Move: Sep. 1989
If I Can Dream: Dec. 1968; *197, 476*
If I Can't Have You: Jan. 1978
If I Could Build My Whole World Around You: Dec. 1967
If I Could Reach You: Sep. 1972
If I Could Turn Back Time: July 1989
I'd Been The One: Nov. 1983
If I Didn't Care: Aug. 1954
If I Fell: *151*
If I Give My Heart To You: Oct. 1959
If I Had A Girl: Jan. 1960
If I Had A Hammer: Sep. 1962, Aug. 1963; *124, 128*
If I Had You. *See* La La La
If I Knew: Jan. 1961
If I Knew You Were Comin': 1950
If I Loved You: May 1954
If I May: Apr. 1955
If It's The Last Thing I Do: May 1955
If I Was Your Girlfriend: May 1987
If I Were A Carpenter: Oct. 1966, May 1968
If I Were Your Woman: Dec. 1970
If Looks Could Kill: Jan. 1982, July 1986
(If Loving You Is Wrong) I Don't Want To Be Right: June 1972
If My Friends Could See Me Now: Aug. 1978
If Not For You: *240*
I Fought The Law: Feb. 1966, Feb. 1975
I Found Somebody: June 1982; *386*
I Found Someone: Nov. 1987
If She Knew What She Wants: May 1986
If There's A Hell Below We're All Going To Go: *226*
If This Is It: July 1984
If We Try: Mar. 1973
If Wishes Came True: June 1990
If You Asked Me To: Apr. 1992
If You Can Dream: Feb. 1956
If You Could Read My Mind: Dec. 1970; *226*
If You Don't Know Me By Now: Sep. 1972, May 1989; *487*
If You Don't Want My Love: *198*
If You Go Away: Feb. 1992

If You Know What I Mean: June 1976
If You Leave Me Now: Aug. 1976; *314, 315*
(If You Let Me Make Love To You) Why Can't I Touch You?: June 1970; *225*
If You Love Me (Let Me Know): Apr. 1974
If You Love Me (Really Love Me): Apr. 1954, July 1954
If You Love Somebody Set Them Free: June 1985; *427*
If You Need Me: *128, 518*
If You Really Love Me: Aug. 1971
If You're Ready (Come Go With Me): Oct. 1973
If You Talk In Your Sleep: June 1974
If You've Got The Time: *319*
If You Wanna Be Happy: Apr. 1963
If You Want Me To Stay: June 1973
If You Want My Love: June 1982
I Get Around: June 1964; *150, 476*
I Get Excited: Sep. 1982
I Get So Lonely (When I Dream About You): Feb. 1954
I Get Weak: Jan. 1988
I Go Crazy: Aug. 1977; *319*
I Got A Feeling: Oct. 1958
I Got A Name: Oct. 1973, Jan. 1974
I Got Ants In My Pants: Jan. 1973
I Got A Wife: Feb. 1959
I Got A Woman: *38*
I Gotcha: Jan. 1972
I Got My Mind Made Up (You Can Get It Girl): Feb. 1979
I Go To Extremes: Jan. 1990
I Go To Pieces: Jan. 1965
I Got Rhythm: Apr. 1967
I Got Stung: Nov. 1958
I Gotta Know: Nov. 1960
I Gotta New Car: May 1955
I Got The Feelin': Mar. 1968
I Got The Feelin' (It's Over): Feb. 1987
I Got You Babe: July 1965, July 1985; *157, 164, 193*
I Got You (I Feel Good): Nov. 1965; *166, 476*
I Guess That's Why They Call It The Blues: Oct. 1983
I Guess The Lord Must Be In New York City: Nov. 1969
I.G.Y. (What A Beautiful World): Oct. 1982
I Had Too Much To Dream (Last Night): Dec. 1966
I Hate Myself For Loving You: June 1988
I Have A Boyfriend: Dec. 1963
I Hear A Symphony: Nov. 1965
I Heard A Rumour: July 1987
I Heard It Through The Grapevine: Oct. 1967, Nov. 1968; *206*
I Hear You Knockin': Jan. 1971
I Hear You Knocking: Sep. 1955
I Honestly Love You: Aug. 1974, Nov. 1977; *288, 289*
I Just Called To Say I Love You: Aug. 1984; *420, 422, 423*
I Just Can't Help Believing: June 1970
I Just Can't Say No To You: Jan. 1977
I Just Can't Stop Loving You: Aug. 1987; *466*
(I Just) Died In Your Arms: Mar. 1987
I Just Fall In Love Again: Jan. 1979
I Just Wanna Stop: Sep. 1978
I Just Want To Be Your Everything: May 1977; *320, 326*
I Just Want To Celebrate: July 1971
I Just Want To Make Love To You: Sep. 1977; *254*
I Keep Forgettin': Aug. 1982; *387*
I Kissed You. *See* ('Til) I Kissed You
I Knew The Bride (When She Used To Rock 'N' Roll): Nov. 1985
I Knew You Were Waiting (For Me): Feb. 1987; *460*

I Knew You When: Oct. 1965, Nov. 1971, Dec. 1982
I Know: Jan. 1962
I Know A Place: Mar. 1965
(I Know) I'm Losing You: Nov. 1966, Aug. 1970, Nov. 1971
I Know What Boys Like: May 1982
I Know What I Like: Apr. 1987
Iko Iko: Apr. 1965, Mar. 1989
I Left My Heart In San Francisco: Aug. 1962; *124*
I Like Dreamin': Nov. 1976
I Like It: Nov. 1964, Feb. 1983; *399*
I Like It Like That: June 1961, July 1965; *467*
I Like The Way: July 1967
I Like The Way (The Kissing Game): *516*
I Like You: Feb. 1986
I Like Your Kind Of Love: May 1957
I Live By The Groove: Oct. 1989
I'll Always Love My Mama: June 1973
I'll Always Love You: June 1988
I'll Be Alright Without You: Dec. 1986
I'll Be Around: Aug. 1972
I'll Be By Your Side: Feb. 1991
I'll Be Doggone: Mar. 1965
I'll Be Good To You: May 1976; *306, 501*
I'll Be Home: Jan. 1956
I'll Be Loving You (Forever): Apr. 1989
I'll Be Satisfied: June 1959
I'll Be Standing By: Apr. 1977
I'll Be There: Jan. 1965, Sep. 1970, Feb. 1990, May 1991, May 1992; *233*
I'll Be There For You: Mar. 1989
I'll Be Your Everything: Feb. 1990
I'll Bet You: *212*
I'll Be Your Shelter: May 1990
I'll Come Running Back To You: Nov. 1957
I'll Cry Instead: *151*
I'll Do For You Anything You Want Me To: June 1975
I'll Do 4 You: Jan. 1991
Illegal Alien: Mar. 1984
I'll Get By: Dec. 1991
I'll Get Over You: *306*
I'll Give All My Love To You: Dec. 1990
I'll Have To Say I Love You In A Song: Mar. 1974
I'll Meet You Halfway: May 1971
I'll Never Dance Again: June 1962
I'll Never Fall In Love Again: Aug. 1969, Dec. 1969
I'll Never Find Another You: Apr. 1965
I'll Never Love This Way Again: June 1979; *354*
I'll Never Smile Again: *2*
I'll Never Stop Loving You: June 1955
I'll Save The Last Dance For You: Nov. 1960
I'll Take You There: Apr. 1972
I'll Try Something New: Mar. 1969, Mar. 1982
I'll Tumble 4 Ya: July 1983
I'll Wait: Apr. 1984; *39*
I'll Wait For You: Nov. 1958
I Love: Dec. 1973
I Love A Rainy Night: Nov. 1980
I Love How You Love Me: Sep. 1961, Nov. 1968
I Love Music (Part 1): Nov. 1975
I Love Rock 'N' Roll: Feb. 1982; *387, 393*
I Love The Night Life (Disco Round): July 1978
I Love The Way You Love: Mar. 1960
I Love You: May 1962, Feb. 1981
(I Love You) For Sentimental Reasons: Jan. 1958, Sep. 1961
I Love You Madly: Dec. 1954
I Love You 1,000 Times: June 1966
I Love You So: July 1958
I Love You, Yes I Do: 1947

I'm A Believer: Dec. 1966; *191*
I Made It Through The Rain: Nov. 1980
I'm A Fool: *156*
I'm A Fool For You Baby. *See* Oh Me Oh My
I'm A Fool To Care: July 1954, Apr. 1961
Image Of A Girl: June 1960
Imaginary Lover: Mar. 1978
Imagine: Oct. 1971
I'm A Happy Man: Sep. 1965
I'm Alive: May 1980, Jan. 1983
I'm Alright: July 1980
I'm A Man: Jan. 1959, Nov. 1965, Apr. 1967, Oct. 1971; *77*
I'm Available: Oct. 1957
I'm Blue (The Gong-Gong Song): Jan. 1962; *476*
I'm Coming Home: June 1974
I'm Comin' Home: Sep. 1971
I'm Easy: May 1976; *303*
I Met Him On A Sunday: May 1958; *65*
I'm Every Woman: Oct. 1978
I'm Free (Heaven Helps The Man): June 1984
I'm Goin' Down: Sep. 1985
I'm Gonna Be A Wheel Someday: Aug. 1959
I'm Gonna Be Strong: Nov. 1964
I'm Gonna Get Married: Aug. 1959
I'm Gonna Love You Just A Little More Baby: *268*
I'm Gonna Make You Love Me: Feb. 1968, Dec. 1968
I'm Gonna Make You Mine: Sep. 1969
I'm Gonna Sit Right Down And Write Myself A Letter: May 1957; *51*
I'm Gonna Tear Your Playhouse Down: Oct. 1985
I'm Happy Just To Dance With You: June 1980; *151*
I'm Happy That Love Has Found You: Sep. 1980
I'm Henry VIII, I Am: July 1965
I'm Her Fool: Mar. 1975
I'm In Love Again: Apr. 1956; *48*
I'm Into Something Good: Oct. 1964; *142*
I'm In You: June 1977
I Missed Again: *373*
I Miss You: July 1972, July 1992; *254*
I Miss You So: Dec. 1956, Apr. 1959
I'm Just A Singer (In A Rock And Roll Band): Feb. 1973
I'm Just Your Fool: Jan. 1954
I'm Leaving It (All) Up To You: Aug. 1974
I'm Leaving It Up To You: Oct. 1963
I'm Livin' In Shame: Feb. 1969
I'm Losing You. *See* (I Know) I'm Losing You
Immigrant, The: Apr. 1975
Immigration Song: Nov. 1970
I'm Not A Juvenile Delinquent: Dec. 1956; *48*
I'm Not In Love: May 1975, Nov. 1990
I'm Not Lisa: Apr. 1975
I'm Not The One: Feb. 1986
(I'm Not Your) Steppin' Stone: Dec. 1966
I'm On Fire: Feb. 1985
I'm On The Outside (Looking In): Sep. 1964
Impossible: *101*
Impossible Dream, The: June 1966
Impulsive: Oct. 1990
I'm Ready: June 1959
I'm Ready For Love: Nov. 1966
I'm So Excited: Sep. 1982, Aug. 1984
I'm So Lonesome I Could Cry: Mar. 1966; *172*
I'm Sorry: Feb. 1957, June 1960, Aug. 1975; *60, 96*
I'm So Young: *504*
I'm Steppin' Out: Apr. 1984

I'm Sticking With You: Feb. 1957
I'm Still In Love With You: July 1972
I'm Still Searching: Apr. 1988
I'm Still Standing: May 1983
I'm Stone In Love With You: Oct. 1972
I'm Telling You Now: Mar. 1965
I'm The One Who Loves You. *See* (Remember Me) I'm The One Who Loves You
I'm The One You Need: Mar. 1992
I'm Too Sexy: Dec. 1991
I'm Walkin': Feb. 1957, May 1957; *60*
I'm Walking: *51, 52, 460*
I'm Walking Behind You: 1953
I'm Wondering: Oct. 1967
I'm Your Baby Tonight: Oct. 1990
I'm Your Boogie Man: Feb. 1977
I'm Your Man: Nov. 1985
I'm Your Puppet: Oct. 1966; *171*
I'm Yours: Oct. 1965. *See also* Signed, Sealed, Delivered
In-A-Gadda-Da-Vida: Oct. 1968
In And Out Of Love: Nov. 1967
In A Shanty In Old Shanty Town: Aug. 1956
Incense And Peppermints: Oct. 1967; *208*
"In" Crowd, The: Jan. 1965, Aug. 1965
Indescribably Blue: Jan. 1967
Indiana Wants Me: Sep. 1970
Indian Giver: Feb. 1969
Indian Lake: June 1968
Indian Reservation: May 1971
Indian Summer: Aug. 1977
In Dreams: Feb. 1963
I Need A Lover: Oct. 1979; *346*
I Need A Man: Dec. 1987
I Need Love: Aug. 1987
I Need To Be In Love: June 1976
I Need You: May 1972; *166*
I Need You Now: Sep. 1954
I Need Your Love Tonight: Mar. 1959
I Need Your Lovin': *359. See also* (Bazoom) I Need Your Lovin'
I Need Your Loving: July 1962; *52*
I Need You Tonight: Oct. 1984
I Never Cry: Sep. 1976
I Never Loved A Man The Way I Love You: Apr. 1967
Infatuation: May 1984
In God's Country: Dec. 1987
In Love With Love: July 1987
In My Diary: Dec. 1955
In My Dreams: July 1987
In My House: Mar. 1985
In My Little Corner Of The World: July 1960
In My Room: Nov. 1963
Innamorata: Apr. 1956; *40*
Inner City Blues (Make Me Wanna Holler): Oct. 1971
Innocent Child: May 1992
Innocent Man, An: Dec. 1983
Inside Me/Inside You. *See* Something Real
Instant Karma (We All Shine On): Mar. 1970
Instant Replay: Oct. 1978; *332*
In The Air Tonight: June 1981
In The Bush: Oct. 1978
In The Chapel In The Moonlight: June 1954, Aug. 1954, July 1967
In The Closet: Apr. 1992
In The Dark: Sep. 1981
In The Ghetto: May 1969; *211*
In The Middle Of An Island: Aug. 1957
In The Midnight Hour: Aug. 1965
In The Misty Moonlight: Aug. 1964
In The Mood: Oct. 1959; *320*
In The Navy: Mar. 1979
In The Rain: Feb. 1972
In The Still Of The Night: July 1956; *39*
In The Summertime: July 1970
In The Year 2525 (Exordium & Terminus): July 1969; *220*

In Too Deep: Apr. 1987
Invincible: July 1985
In Your Letter: Aug. 1981
In Your Room: Oct. 1988
In Your Soul: June 1988
I Only Have Eyes For You: June 1959, Aug. 1975; *520*
I Only Know I Love You: Aug. 1956
I Only Want To Be With You: Feb. 1964, Aug. 1982; *143*
I.O.U.: June 1983
"I.O.U.": May 1976
I Promise To Remember: July 1956
I Put A Spell On You: Nov. 1956; *342, 435*
I Ran All The Way Home. *See* Sorry
I Really Don't Need No Light: *387*
I Really Don't Want To Know: Apr. 1954, Jan. 1971
I Really Love You: Oct. 1961
I Remember You: Oct. 1962, Nov. 1989
Irresistible You: Dec. 1961
I Saw Esau: Nov. 1956
I Saw Her Again: July 1966
I Saw Her Standing There: Jan. 1964
I Saw Him Standing There: Feb. 1988
I Saw Linda Yesterday: Dec. 1962
I Saw Mommy Kissing Santa Claus: 1952
I Saw Red: Dec. 1990
I Say A Little Prayer: Oct. 1967, Aug. 1968
I Second That Emotion: Nov. 1967
I See The Light: *170*
I Send A Message: July 1984
I Shot Mr. Lee: Aug. 1960
I Shot The Sheriff: July 1974; *280*
I Should Be So Lucky: May 1988
I Should Have Known Better: July 1964; *151*
Is It Love: Mar. 1986
Is It You: Apr. 1981
Island Girl: Oct. 1975; *300*
Island Of Lost Souls: May 1982
Islands In The Stream: Aug. 1983; *407*
Isle Of Capri: Apr. 1954
Isn't It A Pity: Dec. 1970
Israelites, The: May 1969
Is She Really Going Out With Him: June 1979; *346*
I Started A Joke: Dec. 1968
Is That All There Is: Oct. 1969; *221*
Is There Something I Should Know: June 1983
Is This Love: Oct. 1986, Oct. 1987
I Still Believe: Apr. 1988
I Still Can't Get Over Loving You: Nov. 1983
I Still Haven't Found What I'm Looking For: June 1987
It Ain't Enough: Sep. 1984
It Ain't Me Babe: Aug. 1965; *157*
It Ain't Over Til It's Over: June 1991
It Can Happen: June 1984
Itchycoo Park: Dec. 1967
Itchy Twitchy Feeling: Aug. 1958
It Doesn't Matter Anymore: Mar. 1959
It Don't Come Easy: May 1971
It Don't Matter To Me: Sep. 1970
I Thank The Lord For The Night Time: July 1967
I Thank You: Feb. 1968, Jan. 1980
It Happened Today: Nov. 1959
I Think I Love You: Oct. 1970; *226, 233*
I Think It's Love: Feb. 1986
I Think We're Alone Now: Mar. 1967, Mar. 1977, Aug. 1987; *459*
It Hit Me Like A Hammer: July 1991
I Thought It Took A Little Time (But Today I Fell In Love): Mar. 1976
It Had To Be You: *490*
It Hurts Me: Sep. 1966
It Hurts So Bad: Feb. 1979; *346*
It Hurts To Be In Love: Aug. 1964, June 1981

It Isn't, It Wasn't, It Ain't Never Gonna Be: July 1989
It Isn't Right: Sep. 1956
It Keeps Right On A-Hurtin': May 1962
It Keeps You Runnin': Nov. 1976
It May Be Winter Outside (But In My Heart It's Spring): Dec. 1973
It May Sound Silly: Mar. 1955
It Might As Well Rain Until September: *116*
It Must Be Him: Sep. 1967; *183*
It Must Have Been Love: Apr. 1990; *500*
It Never Rains In Southern California: Oct. 1972
It Never Rains (In Southern California): Dec. 1990
It Only Hurts For A Little While: May 1956
It Only Takes A Minute: July 1975
I Touch Myself: Mar. 1991
It's A Heartache: Mar. 1978; *333*
It's All Down To Goodnight Vienna: July 1975
It's All In The Game: Aug. 1958, May 1970; *64, 72*
It's All Right: Oct. 1963
It's Almost Tomorrow: Oct. 1955
It's A Long Way There: *307*
It's A Man's, Man's, Man's World: June 1966
It's A Miracle: Mar. 1975, May 1984
It's A Mistake: July 1983
It's A Shame: July 1970
It's A Shame (My Sister): Mar. 1991
It's A Sin: Sep. 1987
It's A Sin To Tell A Lie: Feb. 1955
It's A Woman's World: Sep. 1954
It's Been A Long Time: *523*
It's Ecstasy When You Lay Down Next To Me: Aug. 1977
It's Getting Better: July 1969
It's Going To Take Some Time: May 1972
It's Gonna Be Alright: Apr. 1965; *166*
It's Gonna Take A Miracle: Aug. 1965, Apr. 1982
It's Gonna Work Out Fine: Aug. 1961
It Should've Been Me: May 1954
It's Impossible: Nov. 1970; *240*
It's In His Kiss. *See* Shoop Shoop Song, The
It's Just A Matter Of Time: Mar. 1959
(It's Just) The Way That You Love Me: Nov. 1988
It's Late: Mar. 1959
It's Love, Baby: Aug. 1955
It's Midnight: 1949
It's My Life: Nov. 1965
It's My Party: May 1963; *128*
It's Nice To Be With You: June 1968
It's No Crime: Aug. 1989
It's No Secret: Dec. 1988
It's Not Enough: Aug. 1989
It's Not For Me To Say: Mar. 1957
It's Not Over ('Til It's Over): June 1987
It's Not Unusual: Apr. 1965; *156*
It's Now Or Never: July 1960; *96*
It's O.K.: Aug. 1976
It's One Of Those Nights (Yes Love): Dec. 1971
It's Only Love: Nov. 1985, Feb. 1989
It's Only Make Believe: Sep. 1958
It's Only Rock 'N Roll: Aug. 1974
It's Over: Apr. 1964
It's Raining Again: Oct. 1982
It's Raining Men: Jan. 1983
It's So Easy: Oct. 1977
It's So Hard For Me To Say Goodbye: *240*
It's So Hard To Say Goodbye To Yesterday: Sep. 1991
It's Still Rock And Roll To Me: May 1980
It's The Same Old Song: Aug. 1965
It's Time To Cry: Nov. 1959

It's Too Late: June 1956, Mar. 1966, May 1971; *247, 248*
It's Too Soon To Know: Feb. 1958
It's Up To You: Dec. 1962
It's Wonderful: Dec. 1967
Itsy Bitsy Teenie Weenie Yellow Polka Dot Bikini: July 1960; *89*
It's You I Love: May 1957
It's Your Thing: Mar. 1969
It Takes Time: Apr. 1980
It Takes Two: Jan. 1967
It Was Almost Like A Song: June 1977
It Was A Very Good Year: Jan. 1966; *165*
It Was I: July 1959
It Will Stand: Nov. 1961
It Would Take A Strong Strong Man: July 1988
I Understand Just How You Feel: May 1954
I Understand (Just How You Feel): Oct. 1961
I've Been In Love Before: Sep. 1987
I've Been Lonely Too Long: Feb. 1967
(I've Been) Searching So Long: Mar. 1974
I've Been Thinking About You: Feb. 1991
I've Been This Way Before: Feb. 1975
I've Been Waiting For You: Jan. 1991
I've Done Everything For You: Aug. 1981
I've Got A Right To Cry: 1946
I've Got A Rock 'N' Roll Heart: Jan. 1983
I've Got A Woman: Jan. 1955
I've Got Bonnie: Mar. 1962
I've Got Love On My Mind: Jan. 1977
I've Gotta Be Me: Jan. 1969
I've Gotta Get A Message To You: Sep. 1968
I've Got To Use My Imagination: Nov. 1973
I've Got You Under My Skin: Sep. 1966
I've Had It: Feb. 1959
(I've Had) The Time Of My Life: Sep. 1987; *459, 462, 463*
I've Loved You For A Long Time: May 1980
I've Never Been To Me: Mar. 1982
I've Passed This Way Before: Dec. 1966
I've Told Every Little Star: Mar. 1961; *102*
Ivory Tower: Mar. 1956
I Walk The Line: Sep. 1956; *39*
I Wanna Be: *156*
I Wanna Be Around: Feb. 1963
I Wanna Be Loved: Dec. 1959
I Wanna Be Where You Are: May 1972
I Wanna Be With You: Nov. 1972
I Wanna Be Your Lover: Nov. 1979
I Wanna Dance Wit' Choo (Doo Dat Dance), Part 1: Apr. 1975
I Wanna Dance With Somebody (Who Loves Me): May 1987; *459, 466*
I Wanna Get Next To You: Feb. 1977
I Wanna Get With You: Nov. 1990
I Wanna Go Back: Dec. 1986
I Wanna Have Some Fun: Nov. 1988
I Wanna Hear It From Your Lips: Jan. 1985
I Wanna Love Him So Bad: July 1964
(I Wanna) Love My Life Away: Feb. 1961; *102*
I Wanna Rock: Oct. 1984, Mar. 1992
I Wanna Sex You Up: *516*
(I Wanna) Testify: July 1967
I Want A New Drug: Jan. 1984
I Want Candy: July 1965
I Want Her: Jan. 1988
I Want To Be Wanted: Sep. 1960
I Want To Be Your Property: Mar. 1988
I Want To Hold Your Hand: Jan. 1964; *127, 141, 142, 150*

I Want To Know What Love Is: Dec. 1984; *433*
I Want To Take You Higher: May 1970
I Want You: July 1966, Apr. 1976
I Want You All To Myself: Sep. 1954
I Want You Back: Dec. 1969; *212*
I Want You, I Need You, I Love You: May 1956; *38, 46*
I Want Your Love: Feb. 1979
I Want Your Sex: June 1987; *451*
I Want You So Bad: Feb. 1988
I Want You To Be My Baby: Sep. 1955
I Want You To Be My Girl: Apr. 1956
I Want You To Know: Dec. 1957
I Want You Tonight: Oct. 1979
I Want You To Want Me: Apr. 1979
I Was Kaiser Bill's Batman: May 1967
I Was Made For Lovin' You: May 1979
I Was Made To Love Her: June 1967
I Was Only Joking: May 1978
I Was The One: Mar. 1956; *38*
I Went To Your Wedding: 1952
I (Who Have Nothing): July 1963, Aug. 1970
I Will Always Think About You: Apr. 1968
I Will Be There: Feb. 1987
I Will Follow: Jan. 1984
I Will Follow Him: Mar. 1963; *135*
I Will Survive: Dec. 1978, Dec. 1989; *353*
I Wish: Dec. 1976
I Wish I Had A Girl: Feb. 1988
I Wish It Would Rain: Jan. 1968
I Wish It Would Rain Down: Feb. 1990
I Wish I Was Eighteen Again: Jan. 1980
I Wish That We Were Married: Apr. 1962
I Woke Up In Love This Morning: Aug. 1971
I Wonder If I Take You Home: *426*
I Wonder What She's Doing Tonight: Oct. 1963, Jan. 1968
I Wonder Why: May 1958; *64, 488*
I Won't Back Down: May 1989
I Won't Be Home Tonight: *399*
I Won't Give Up On You: Aug. 1990
I Won't Hold Back: Mar. 1983
I Won't Last A Day Without You: Apr. 1974
I Won't Stand In Your Way: Oct. 1983
I Would Die 4 U: Dec. 1984; *422*
I Wouldn't Have Missed It For The World: Oct. 1981
I Write The Songs: Nov. 1975; *315*

Jack And Diane: July 1982; *393*
Jack And Jill: Jan. 1978; *333*
Jackie Blue: Mar. 1975
Jackie Brown: July 1989
Jackson: July 1967
Jacob's Ladder: Jan. 1987
Jailhouse Rock: Sep. 1957; *59, 60, 461*
Jam: July 1992
Jamaica Farewell: Oct. 1956; *39*
Jambalaya: Dec. 1961
Jamie: Nov. 1984
Jammin'. *See* Master Blaster
Jam Tonight: June 1987
Jam Up Jelly Tight: Dec. 1969
Jane: Nov. 1979
Janie's Got A Gun: Nov. 1989; *501*
Java: Jan. 1964; *142*
Jaws theme. *See* Theme From Jaws, The
Jay Walker: *74*
Jazz From Hell: *460*
Jazzman: Sep. 1974
Jean: Sep. 1969
Jeff Beck's Guitar Shop With Terry Bozzio And Tony Hymas: *487*
Jennie Lee: May 1958
Jennifer Juniper: Mar. 1968
Jennifer Tomkins: Jan. 1970
Jenny, Jenny: June 1957

Jenny Take A Ride: Dec. 1965; *157*
Jeopardy: Jan. 1983
Jeremiah Peabody's Poly Unsaturated Quick Dissolving Fast Acting Pleasant Tasting Green and Purple Pills: *102*
Jerk, The: Nov. 1964
Jerk Out: June 1990
Jesse: Aug. 1980
Jessie: Aug. 1985
Jessie's Girl: Mar. 1981; *381*
Jet: Feb. 1974
Jet Airliner: May 1977
Jilted: Mar. 1954
Jim Dandy: Jan. 1957, Dec. 1973
Jim Dandy Got Married: May 1957
Jimmy Mack: Mar. 1967
Jingle Bell Rock: Dec. 1957
Jingle Bells: Dec. 1957
Jingle Jangle: Dec. 1969
Jingo: *213*
Jive Talkin': June 1975; *293, 300*
Jo-Ann: Jan. 1958; *65*
Joanna: Nov. 1983
Joanne: Aug. 1970
Joey: June 1954
Johnny Angel: Mar. 1962
Johnny B. Goode: May 1958, Jan. 1970; *74, 462*
Johnny Can't Read: *386*
JoJo: June 1980
Joker, The: Oct. 1957, Oct. 1973
Jolene: Feb. 1974; *281*
Jolly Green Giant, The: Feb. 1965
Jones Boy, The: Jan. 1954
Josephine: July 1960
Josie: Aug. 1978
Journey To The Center Of Your Mind: July 1968
Joy: Jan. 1972
Joyride: Mar. 1991
Joy To The World: Mar. 1971; *247*
Judy In Disguise (With Glasses): Dec. 1967; *206*
Judy's Turn To Cry: July 1963
Juicy Fruit: June 1983
Juke Box Saturday Night: Sep. 1961
Julie, Do Ya Love Me: Aug. 1970
Jump: Oct. 1976, Jan. 1984, Apr. 1992; *420, 524*
Jump Around: July 1992
Jump For Joy: Jan. 1976
Jump (For My Love): May 1984; *421*
Jumpin' Jack Flash: June 1968
Jump Over: May 1960
Jump To It: Aug. 1982
Jungle Boogie: Jan. 1974
Jungle Fever: Jan. 1972
Jungleland: *293*
Jungle Love: Aug. 1977, Oct. 1984; *422*
Junior's Farm: Nov. 1974
Junk Food Junkie: Jan. 1976
Just A Closer Walk With Thee: Apr. 1960
Just A Dream: July 1958; *64*
Just A Friend: Jan. 1990
Just A Gigolo/I Ain't Got Nobody: Apr. 1985
Just A Little: Sep. 1960, Apr. 1965
Just A Little Bit Better: Sep. 1965
Just A Little Too Much: July 1959
Just Another Day: Jan. 1986
Just Another Night: Feb. 1985; *466*
Just Ask Your Heart: Aug. 1959
Just A Smile: Oct. 1975
Just As Much As Ever: Jan. 1968
Just A Song Before I Go: June 1977
Just Because: Feb. 1957, Jan. 1989
Just Be My Lady: Sep. 1981
Just Between You And Me: Sep. 1957, Oct. 1989
Just Don't Want To Be Lonely: Feb. 1974
Just Dropped In (To See What Condition My Condition Was In): Feb. 1968; *198*

Just For Tonight: May 1992
Justified And Ancient: Feb. 1992
Justify My Love: Nov. 1990
Just In Time: Oct. 1956
Just Keep It Up: May 1959
Just Like A Woman: Sep. 1966
Just Like Jesse James: Oct. 1989
Just Like Paradise: Jan. 1988
(Just Like) Romeo And Juliet: Apr. 1964
(Just Like) Starting Over: Nov. 1980; *381*
Just Like You: July 1991
Just Make Love To Me: June 1954
Just My Imagination (Running Away With Me): Feb. 1971; *247*
Just Once: Aug. 1981; *374*
Just Once In My Life: Apr. 1965
Just One Look: June 1963, Feb. 1979; *142*
Just Out Of Reach: *101*
Just Remember I Love You: Aug. 1977
Just Seven Numbers (Can Straighten Out My Life): Jan. 1971
Just So Lonely: Apr. 1981
Just Take My Heart: Apr. 1992
Just The Two Of Us: Feb. 1981
Just The Way It Is Baby: Feb. 1991
Just The Way You Are: Nov. 1977; *340*
Just To Be Close To You: Sep. 1976
Just To See Her: *460*
Just Walking In The Rain: Sep. 1956
Just What I Needed: *332*
Just When I Needed You Most: Mar. 1979
Just You And Me: Sep. 1973

Ka-Ding-Dong: June 1956
Kansas City: Apr. 1959; *84*
Karma Chameleon: Dec. 1983; *420*
Kaw-Liga: 1953
Keem-O-Sabe: Aug. 1969
Keep A Knockin': Sep. 1957; *60*
Keep Coming Back: Nov. 1991
Keeper Of The Castle: Nov. 1972
(Keep Feeling) Fascination: June 1983
Keepin' The Faith: Jan. 1985
Keep It Comin': Nov. 1991
Keep It Comin' Love: July 1977
Keep It Together: Feb. 1990
Keep On Dancin': Feb. 1979
Keep On Dancing: Sep. 1965; *156*
Keep On Loving You: Dec. 1980
Keep On Pushing: July 1964
Keep On Singing: Mar. 1974
Keep On Smilin': *281*
Keep On Truckin': Aug. 1973
Keep Playing That Rock 'N' Roll: *241*
Keep Searchin': Dec. 1964
Keep The Ball Rollin': Nov. 1967
Keep The Fire Burnin': June 1982
Keep Your Eye On The Sparrow. See Baretta's Theme
Keep Your Hands Off My Baby: Nov. 1962
Keep Your Hands To Yourself: Nov. 1986
Keep Your Head To The Sky: Jan. 1974
Kentuckian Song, The: Oct. 1955
Kentucky Rain: Feb. 1970
Kentucky Woman: Oct. 1967
Kewpie Doll: June 1958
Key Largo: Nov. 1981
Kicks: Mar. 1966
Kiddio: Aug. 1960
Kids In America: *387*
Kid's Last Fight: May 1954
Killer Joe: Apr. 1963; *225*
Killer Queen: *294*
Killing Me Softly: Nov. 1988
Killing Me Softly With His Song: Jan. 1973; *266, 274, 275*
Killing Of Georgie, The: June 1977
Kind Of A Drag: Jan. 1967; *183*

Kind Of Boy You Can't Forget, The: Aug. 1963
King Creole: *74*
King For A Day: Jan. 1986
King Is Gone, The: Sep. 1977
King Of Pain: Aug. 1983
King Of Rock & Roll: Nov. 1970
King Of The Road: Feb. 1965; *165*
King Of The Whole Wide World: *125*
King Tut: May 1978
Kiss: Feb. 1986, Dec. 1988; *446, 448*
Kiss An Angel Good Mornin': Dec. 1971
Kiss And Say Goodbye: Apr. 1976
Kisses On The Wind: July 1989
Kisses Sweeter Than Wine: Nov. 1957
Kiss From Your Lips, A: Mar. 1956
Kiss Him Goodbye: May 1987
Kissin' Cousins: Feb. 1964; *152*
Kissing A Fool: Oct. 1988
Kissing You: May 1991
Kissin' Time: May 1974; *78, 281*
Kiss Me Deadly: Apr. 1988
Kiss Me Goodbye: Mar. 1968
Kiss Of Fire: 1952
Kiss On My List: Jan 1981; *381*
Kiss The Bride: Aug. 1983
Kiss Them For Me: Aug. 1991
Kiss This Thing Goodbye: May 1990
Kiss You All Over: July 1978; *340*
Kiss You Back: Nov. 1991
K-Jee: July 1971
Knight In Rusty Armour: Jan. 1967
Knocking At Your Back Door: Jan. 1985
Knockin' On Heaven's Door: Sep. 1973
Knock On Wood: Jan. 1979; *170*
Knock Three Times: Nov. 1970
Knock Yourself Out: *See* Shout! Shout!
Knowing Me, Knowing You: May 1977
Kodachrome: May 1973
Ko Ko Mo: Dec. 1954, Jan. 1955, Feb. 1955
Kokomo: Sep. 1988; *476*
Kookie, Kookie (Lend Me Your Comb): Apr. 1959
Kool & The Gang: *212*
Kozmic Blues: *212*
Kung Fu Fighting: Oct. 1974; *288*
Kyrie: Dec. 1985; *446*

La Bamba: Dec. 1958, June 1987; *459, 462*
La Dee Dah: Dec. 1957
Ladies Night: Oct. 1979
Lady: Dec. 1974, Jan. 1979, Apr. 1980, Oct. 1980, June 1981; *367*
Lady Godiva: Nov. 1966
Lady In Red, The: Feb. 1987
Lady Jane: July 1966
Lady Love: Jan. 1978
Lady Luck: Feb. 1960
Lady Madonna: Mar. 1968
Lady Marmalade: Jan. 1975
Lady Soul: Oct. 1986
Lady Willpower: June 1968
La Isla Bonita: Mar. 1987
La La La (If I Had You): Dec. 1969
La-La Means I Love You: Feb. 1968; *198*
Lambada: Mar. 1990
Land Of Confusion: Nov. 1986
Land Of 1000 Dances: Mar. 1965, Aug. 1966
Language Of Love, The: Feb. 1984
La Raza: July 1990
L'Armour Est Bleu. *See* Love Is Blue
Last Chance To Turn Around: May 1965
Last Child: June 1976
Last Dance: May 1978; *342, 343*
Last Date: Oct. 1960
Last Game Of The Season, The (A Blind Man In The Bleachers): Dec. 1975
Last Kiss: Sep. 1964

Last Night: July 1961
(Last Night) I Didn't Get To Sleep At All: Apr. 1972
Last Song: Dec. 1972
Last Time, The: Apr. 1965
Last Time I Saw Him: Jan. 1974
Last Train To Clarksville: Sep. 1966; *171*
Last Worthless Evening, The: Oct. 1989
Late In The Evening: Aug. 1980; *369*
Laugh At Me: Sep. 1965
Laughing: July 1969
Laugh, Laugh: Feb. 1965; *156*
Laughter In The Rain: Oct. 1974
Laurie: June 1965
Lavender Blue: June 1959
Lawdy, Miss Clawdy: 1952
Lay A Little Lovin' On Me: June 1970
Lay Down (Candles In The Rain): May 1970; *226*
Lay Down Sally: Jan. 1978
Lay It On The Line: Nov. 1979
Layla: Apr. 1971, May 1972; *504*
Lay Lady Lay: Aug. 1969, Dec. 1971
Lay Your Hands On Me: Sep. 1985, June 1989
Lazy Day: Oct. 1967
Lazy River: Feb. 1961
Lazy Summer Night: Sep. 1958
Leader Of The Band: Nov. 1981
Leader Of The Laundromat: Dec. 1964
Leader Of The Pack: Oct. 1964
Lead Me On: May 1979
Leaning On The Lamp Post: Apr. 1966; *180*
Lean On Me: Apr. 1972, Feb. 1987; *261, 460, 490*
Learnin' The Blues: May 1955
Leather And Lace: Oct. 1981
Leave A Light On: Sep. 1989
Leave A Tender Moment Alone: July 1984
Leave It: Mar. 1984
Leave Me Alone (Ruby Red Dress): Nov. 1973
Leaving Me: Apr. 1973
Leaving On A Jet Plane: Nov. 1969
Le Bel Age (The Best Years): Feb. 1986
Le Freak: Oct. 1978; *353*
Left In The Dark: Sep. 1984
Legal Eagles theme. *See* Love Touch
Legend Of Billy Jack, The. *See* One Tin Soldier
Legs: May 1984
Lemon Tree: June 1962; *116*
Lend Me Your Comb. *See* Kookie, Kookie
Leona: Mar. 1975
Leroy: July 1958; *65*
Les Bicyclettes De Belsize: Nov. 1968
Lessons In Love: Apr. 1987
Let 'Em In: July 1976
Let Her In: May 1976; *308*
Let It All Hang Out. *See* Let It Out
Let It Be: Mar. 1970; *224*
Let It Be Me: Jan. 1960, Sep. 1964
Let It Go, Let It Flow: Jan. 1978
Let It Out (Let It All Hang Out): Sep. 1967
Let It Rain: Sep. 1972
Let Me: June 1969
Let Me Be: Mar. 1980
Let Me Be The One: Aug. 1987
Let Me Be There: Nov. 1973
Let Me Be Your Angel: Aug. 1980; *359*
(Let Me Be Your) Teddy Bear: July 1957; *59, 60*
Let Me Down Easy: Dec. 1985
Let Me Go: Mar. 1983
Let Me Go, Lover: Dec. 1954; *14, 33*
Let Me In: Jan. 1962, Apr. 1989
Let Me Love You Tonight: May 1980
Let's Be Lovers Again: Oct. 1980
Let's Chill: Feb. 1991

Let's Dance: Sep. 1962, Mar. 1983; *116*
Let's Do It Again: Nov. 1975
Let's Fall In Love: Feb. 1967; *171*
Let's Get Crazy Tonight: Sep. 1978; *332*
Let's Get It On: July 1973; *274*
Let's Get It Together: Oct. 1976
Let's Get Rocked: Apr. 1992
Let's Get Serious: Mar. 1980
Let's Get Together: Sep. 1961
Let's Go: Nov. 1962, July 1979, Jan. 1987
Let's Go All The Way: Dec. 1985
Let's Go Back To My Room. *See* Boom Boom
Let's Go Crazy: Aug. 1984
Let's Go Dancin' (Ooh La, La, La): Nov. 1982
Let's Go, Let's Go, Let's Go: Oct. 1960
Let's Groove: Oct. 1981
Let's Hang On: Oct. 1965, Mar. 1982
Let's Have A Party: Sep. 1960
Let's Hear It For The Boy: Apr. 1984; *422*
Let's Limbo Some More: Mar. 1963
Let's Live For Today: May 1967
Let's Lock The Door (And Throw Away The Key): Jan. 1965
Let's Make Lots Of Money. *See* Opportunities
Let's Put It All Together: Aug. 1974
Let's Spend The Night Together: Feb. 1967
Let's Stay Together: Dec. 1971, Apr. 1972, Jan. 1984; *414*
Let's Think About Livin': Oct. 1960
Let's Twist Again: July 1961; *111*
Let's Wait Awhile: Jan. 1987
Let's Work: Sep. 1987
Letter, The: Nov. 1954, Aug. 1967, Apr. 1970; *183, 191*
Let The Feeling Flow: *386*
Let The Four Winds Blow: Aug. 1961
Let The Good Times Roll: 1946, Sep. 1956
Let The Music Play: Dec. 1975, Nov. 1983
Let There Be Drums: Nov. 1961
Let The River Run: *477, 488*
Let The Sunshine In: Mar. 1969; *220, 221*
Let Your Hair Down: Jan. 1974
Let Your Love Flow: Jan. 1976; *306*
Let Yourself Go: *208*
Levon: Dec. 1971
Liar: July 1971
Liar, Liar: Jul. 1965; *476*
License To Chill: Oct. 1989
Licking Stick: June 1968
Lido Shuffle: Mar. 1977
Lies: Dec. 1965, June 1987, Aug. 1990, Sep. 1991; *400*
Life In The Fast Lane: May 1977
Life Is A Carnival: Oct. 1971
Life Is A Highway: May 1992
Life Is A Rock (But The Radio Rolled Me): Sep. 1974
Life Is But A Dream: Mar. 1954, July 1955; *101, 504*
Life's Been Good: June 1978
Light My Fire: June 1967, Aug. 1968; *184, 191, 198, 207*
Lightnin' Strikes: Jan. 1966
Light Of Day: Feb. 1987; *462*
Lights Out: July 1984
(The Lights Went Out In) Massachusetts: Nov. 1967
Like A Baby: Jan. 1966
Like A Prayer: Mar. 1989
Like A Rock: May 1986
Like A Rolling Stone: Aug. 1965; *154–55*
Like A Sad Song: Sep. 1976
Like A Virgin: Nov. 1984
Like Long Hair: *102*
Like No Other Night: May 1986

Like To Get To Know You: Apr. 1968
Lil' Red Riding Hood: June 1966
Lily Maebelle: Nov. 1955
Limbo Rock: Sep. 1962
Linda: Apr. 1963
Linda Lu: Aug. 1959
Ling, Ting, Tong: Oct. 1954, Feb. 1955
Lion Sleeps Tonight, The: Nov. 1961, Jan. 1972; *110*
Lipstick On Your Collar: May 1959
Lipstick, Powder And Paint: *48*
Lip Sync: *155*
Lisbon Antigua: Jan. 1956; *46*
Listen People: Feb. 1966
Listen To The Music: Sep. 1972; *253*
Listen To What The Man Said: June 1975
Listen To Your Heart: Aug. 1989
Little Altar Boy: Dec. 1961; *101, 124*
Little Arrows: Oct. 1968
Little Bit Of Heaven, A: June 1965
Little Bit Of Soap, A: Aug. 1961; *225*
Little Bit O' Soul: May 1967
Little Bitty Girl: Feb. 1960
Little Bitty Pretty One: Sep. 1957, Aug. 1960, Apr. 1972; *51*
Little Bitty Tear, A: Dec. 1961, Jan. 1962
Little Bit You, A Little Bit Me, A: Apr. 1967
Little Boy Sad: Feb. 1961
Little By Little: May 1985
Little Children: May 1964; *142*
Little Darlin': Feb. 1957; *60*
Little Deuce Coupe: Aug. 1963; *127*
Little Devil: May 1961
Little Diane: July 1962
Little Drummer Boy, The: Dec. 1958
Little Egypt: Apr. 1961; *152*
Little Girl: June 1966
Little Girl I Once Knew, The: Dec. 1965
Little Girl Of Mine: Apr. 1956
Little Green Apples: Aug. 1968; *206*
Little Honda: Oct. 1964
Little In Love, A: Dec. 1980
Little Is Enough, A: Oct. 1980
Little Jackie Wants To Be A Star: Apr. 1989
Little Jeannie: May 1980
Little Latin Lupe Lu: *128*
Little Less Conversation, A: *208*
Little Lies: Aug. 1987
Little More Love, A: Nov. 1978
Little Old Lady (From Pasadena), The: July 1964
Little Ole Man (Uptight—Everything's Alright): Sep. 1967; *184*
Little Queenie: *74*
Little Red Corvette: Feb. 1983
Little Respect, A: Dec. 1988
Little Shoemaker, The: June 1954
Little Sister: Aug. 1961; *528*
Little Star: July 1958; *435*
Little Things: Mar. 1965
Little Things Mean A Lot: Mar. 1954, Aug. 1954; *14*
Little Too Late: Feb. 1983
Little Town Flirt: Jan. 1963
Little Willy: Jan. 1973
Little Woman: Sep. 1969; *213*
Live And Learn: Mar. 1992
Live And Let Die: July 1973, Dec. 1991
Live At Glasgow. *See* Coming Up
Live For Loving You: Oct. 1991
Live My Life: Dec. 1987
Live To Tell: Apr. 1986
Livin' Ain't Livin': *306*
Livin' For The Weekend: Mar. 1976
Livin' For You: Dec. 1973
Living Doll: *78*
Living In America: Dec. 1985
Living Inside Myself: Mar. 1981
Living In Sin: Oct. 1989
Living In The City: Nov. 1973
Living In The Past: Nov. 1972

Living In The U.S.A.: *198*
Living On The Edge: Aug. 1983
Living Years, The: Jan. 1989
Livin' In Desperate Times: Feb. 1984
Livin' It Up (Friday Night): Jan. 1979
Livin' On A Prayer: Dec. 1986; *459*
Livin' Thing: Oct. 1976
Loco-Motion, The: July 1962, Mar. 1974, Aug. 1988; *288, 502*
Loddy Lo: Nov. 1963
Logical Song, The: Mar. 1979
Lola: Aug. 1970, Aug. 1980
Lollipop: Mar. 1958
Lollipops And Roses: *110, 116*
London Town: July 1978
Lonely Boy: June 1959, Aug. 1972, Mar. 1977; *84, 86*
Lonely Bull, The: Nov. 1962; *115*
Lonely Days: Dec. 1970
Lonely Drifter, The: *128*
Lonely Guitar: July 1959
Lonely Man: Feb. 1961; *111*
Lonely Night (Angel Face): Jan. 1976
Lonely Nights: Mar. 1955, Mar. 1982; *386*
Lonely Ol' Night: Aug. 1985
Lonely One, The: Feb. 1959
Lonely People: Dec. 1974
Lonely Street: Sep. 1959
Lonely Teardrops: Dec. 1958
Lonely Teenager: Nov. 1960; *89*
Lonely Weekends: Apr. 1960; *90*
Lonely Won't Leave Me Alone: Dec. 1987
Lonesome Loser: July 1979
Lonesome Mary: *253*
Lonesome Town: Oct. 1958
Long And Winding Road, The: June 1970; *234*
Long Cool Woman (In A Black Dress): June 1972
Long Distance Love Affair. *See* Telefone
Longer: Dec. 1979
Longest Time, The: Mar. 1984
Longest Walk, The: Sep. 1955
Longfellow Serenade: Oct. 1974
Long Lonely Nights: May 1957
Long Long Time: *226*
Long Run, The: Dec. 1979
Long Tall Glasses: Feb. 1975; *294*
Long Tall Sally: Mar. 1956; *48, 169*
Long Time: Jan. 1977
Long Train Running: Apr. 1973
Look, The: Feb. 1989
Look At His Eyes. *See* Gee Whiz
Look At Me: *128*
Look Away: Sep. 1988; *486*
Look For A Star: July 1960
Look Homeward Angel: Mar. 1956
Lookin' For A Love: Dec. 1971, Feb. 1974
Lookin' For Love: July 1980; *369*
Looking Back: Apr. 1958
Looking For A New Love: Mar. 1987
Looking For A Stranger: Apr. 1983
Looking For Love: *240*
Looking For Space: Mar. 1976
Look In My Eyes: Sep. 1961
Look In My Eyes Pretty Woman: Jan. 1975
Lookin' Out For #1: Apr. 1976
Lookin' Out My Back Door: Aug. 1970
Look Of Love, The: May 1968
Look Of Love, The (Part One): Sep. 1982
Look Out Any Window: July 1988
Looks Like A Lady. *See* Dude
Looks Like We Made It: May 1977
Looks That Kill: *413*
Look What They've Done To My Song, Ma: Sep. 1970; *226*
Look What You've Done For Me: Apr. 1972
Look What You've Done To Me: Aug. 1980; *369*

Loop De Loop: Jan. 1963
Lord's Prayer, The: Mar. 1974
Losing My Religion: Apr. 1991; *516*
Losing You: Apr. 1963
Lost In Emotion: Aug. 1987
Lost In Love: Feb. 1980; *359*
Lost In You: May 1988
Lost In Your Eyes: Jan. 1989
Lost In Your Love: Dec. 1978
Lost Without Your Love: Nov. 1976
Lotta Love: Nov. 1978
Lotta Lovin': July 1957
Louie Louie: Nov. 1963; *128*
Louie, Louie: Sep. 1978
Louisiana Blues: *460*
Love. *See* Still Water
L-O-V-E: Mar. 1975
Love And Emotion: June 1990
Love And Marriage: Oct. 1955
Love And Understanding: June 1991
Love Ballad: Oct. 1976, Feb. 1979; *307*
Love Bites: Aug. 1988
Love Bones: Jan. 1970
Love Came To Me: Nov. 1962
Love (Can Make You Happy): Apr. 1969
Love Child: Oct. 1968, Mar. 1990
Love Corporation: Feb. 1975
Love Don't Go Through No Changes On Me: *294*
Love Grows (Where My Rosemary Goes): Feb. 1970
Love Hangover: Apr. 1976; *314*
Love Her Madly: Apr. 1971
Love Hurts: Dec. 1975
Love I Lost, The (Part 1): Sep. 1973
Love In An Elevator: Sep. 1989
Love In "C" Minor—Part 1: Feb. 1977
Love In Store: Dec. 1982
Love In The First Degree: Mar. 1988
Love In Your Eyes, The: Jan. 1989
Love Is A Battlefield: Sep. 1983; *408*
Love Is A Hurtin' Thing: Oct. 1966
Love Is All Around: Mar. 1968
Love Is All We Need: Nov. 1958, Feb. 1966
Love Is A Many Splendored Thing: Aug. 1955; *33*
Love Is A Rock: Oct. 1990
Love Is A Wonderful Thing: Apr. 1991
Love Is Blue (L'Amour Est Bleu): Jan. 1968; *206*
Love Is Contagious: Sep. 1987
Love Is Forever: Oct. 1986
Love Is Here And Now You're Gone: Feb. 1967
Love Is In The Air: July 1978
Love Is Life: *240*
Love Is Like An Itching In My Heart: Apr. 1966
Love Is Like A Rock: Dec. 1981
Love Is Like Oxygen: Feb. 1978
Love Is Strange: Nov. 1956, Jan. 1957; *462*
Love Is The Answer: Mar. 1979
Love Is The Message: July 1974
Love Is The Seventh Wave: Nov. 1985
(Love Is) The Tender Trap: Feb. 1956
Love Is Thicker Than Water: Nov. 1977; *340*
Love Jones: Dec. 1972
Love Land: Apr. 1970
Love Letters: Mar. 1962, July 1966
Love Letters In The Sand: May 1957; *59*
Love Lifted Me: *307*
Love Light In Flight: Dec. 1984
Love, Love, Love: June 1956
Lovely Day: Dec. 1977
Lovely Lies: Nov. 1955
Love Machine (Part 1): Nov. 1975
Love Me: Nov. 1956, Mar. 1992; *476*
Love Me Do: May 1964; *115, 127, 474*
Love Me Forever: Sep. 1957
Love Me For Life: Feb. 1990
Love Me Or Leave Me: July 1955

Love Me Tender: Oct. 1956; *39, 46, 48, 50*
Love Me Tomorrow: Sep. 1982
Love Me Tonight: May 1969
Love Me To Pieces: Aug. 1957
Love Me Warm And Tender: Mar. 1962
Love Me With All Your Heart: May 1964; *142*
Love My Life Away. *See* (I Wanna) Love My Life Away
Love My Way: Mar. 1983
Love No One But You: *52*
Love Of A Lifetime: July 1986, June 1991
Love On A Two-Way Street: Apr. 1970
Love On A Two Way Street: June 1981
Love On The Rocks: Nov. 1980; *369*
Love Or Let Me Be Lonely: Mar. 1970
Love Overboard: Jan. 1988; *474*
Love Potion No. 9: Oct. 1959
Love Potion Number Nine: Dec. 1964
Love Power: July 1987
Love Really Hurts Without You: Apr. 1976; *307*
Love, Reign O'er Me: Dec. 1973
Love Rollercoaster: Nov. 1975
Lover, Please: Mar. 1962
Lover's Concerto, A: Sep. 1965
Lover's Island: Aug. 1961
Lover's Lane: Dec. 1987
Lovers Never Say Goodbye: Feb. 1959
Lover's Question, A: Nov. 1958, Oct. 1975
Lovers Who Wander: Apr. 1962
Love's Been A Little Bit Hard On Me: May 1982
Loves Me Like A Rock: Aug. 1973
Love Somebody: Mar. 1984
Love Song: Aug. 1989
Love Song, A: Dec. 1973
Love Songs Are Back Again: Oct. 1984
Love So Right: Sep. 1976
Love's Theme: Dec. 1973
Love Stinks: Apr. 1980
Love Story theme. *See* Theme From Love Story
Love Takes Time: Mar. 1979, Sep. 1990
Love Theme From "A Star Is Born" (Evergreen): Dec. 1976; *316, 326, 327*
Love Theme From Romeo & Juliet: May 1969
Love The One You're With: Dec. 1970; *227*
Love The World Away: June 1980; *369*
Love … Thy Will Be Done: Aug. 1991
Love To Love You Baby: Dec. 1975; *294, 306*
Love Touch (From Legal Eagles): May 1986
Love Train: Jan. 1973
Love Will Conquer All: Oct. 1986
Love Will Find A Way: June 1978. Oct. 1987
Love Will Keep Us Together: Apr. 1975; *293, 300, 301*
Love Will Lead You Back: Jan. 1990
Love Will Never Do (Without You): Nov. 1990
Love Will Save The Day: July 1988
Love Will Show You How: May 1984
Love Will Turn You Around: July 1982
Love Won't Let Me Wait: Apr. 1975
Love X Love: Oct. 1980
Lovey Dovey: Feb. 1954
Love You Down: Nov. 1986
Love You Inside Out: Apr. 1979
Love You Like I Never Loved Before: Mar. 1981
Love You Most Of All: Dec. 1958
Love You Save, The: June 1970
Love You So: Apr. 1960
Love Zone: July 1986
Lovin' Every Minute Of It: Aug. 1985

Loving You: July 1957; *60*
Loving You Is A Natural Thing: *226*
Lovin' You: Jan. 1975
Lowdown: July 1976
Low Rider: Sep. 1975
Lucille: Mar. 1957, Sep. 1960, Apr. 1977; *60*
Luck Of The Draw: *516*
Lucky In Love: Apr. 1985
Lucky Ladybug: Jan. 1959
Lucky Lips: Feb. 1957
Lucky Me: Apr. 1980
Lucky One, The: Aug. 1984
Lucky Star: Aug. 1984
Lucretia MacEvil: Oct. 1970
Lucy In The Sky With Diamonds: Nov. 1974; *208*
Luka: July 1987
Lullaby: Dec. 1989
Lyin' Eyes: Sep. 1975; *301*

Ma Belle Amie: Feb. 1970
MacArthur Park: May 1968, Sep. 1978; *212, 340*
Machine Gun: June 1974; *281*
Macho Man: June 1978; *333*
Mack The Knife: Sep. 1959; *84, 85, 97*
Mad About You: *439*
Mademoiselle: Nov. 1976
Madison, The: Apr. 1960
Madison Time, The: *476*
Maggie: Dec. 1970
Maggie May: Sep. 1971; *239, 240, 247*
Magic: Apr. 1975, May 1980, May 1984; *367, 369*
Magical Mystery Tour: *193*
Magic Bus: Aug. 1968
Magic Carpet Ride: Oct. 1968
Magic Man: July 1976
Magic Moments: Jan. 1958
Magic Touch, The. *See* (You've Got) The Magic Touch
Magic Town: Mar. 1966
Magnet And Steel: June 1978
Magnificent Seven, The: Dec. 1960
Magnum P.I. theme. *See* Theme From Magnum P.I.
Mahogany theme. *See* Theme From Mahogany
Main Event, The: June 1979
Main Title (Theme From *The Man With The Golden Arm*): Feb. 1956; *39*
Main Title And Molly-O: *39*
Majestic, The: Dec. 1961; *100, 111*
Make A Little Magic: June 1980
Make A Move On Me: Feb. 1982
Make Believe: Aug. 1982
Make It Easy On Yourself: Aug. 1962, Nov. 1965
Make It Funky (Part I): Aug. 1971
Make It Real: Apr. 1988
Make It With You: June 1970; *225*
Make Love Like A Man: June 1992
Make Love Stay: Feb. 1983
Make Love To Me!: Feb. 1954
Make Me Lose Control: May 1988
Make Me Smile: Apr. 1970
Make Me Your Baby: Sep. 1965
Make The World Go Away: Nov. 1965
Make Yourself Comfortable: Dec. 1954
Making Every Minute Count: Sep. 1967
Making Love: Mar. 1982
Making Love Out Of Nothing At All: July 1983
Making Our Dreams Come True: May 1976
Makin' It: Mar. 1979
Makin' Love: Aug. 1959
Mama: Mar. 1960
Mama Can't Buy You Love: June 1979
Mama Didn't Lie: Jan. 1963; *476*
Mama Doll Song, The: Oct. 1954
Mama From The Train: Sep. 1956

(Mama) He Treats Your Daughter Mean: 1953
Mama Liked The Roses: May 1970
Mama Look-A Booboo: Apr. 1957
Mama Said: Apr. 1961
Mama Said Knock You Out: Apr. 1991; *517*
Mama's Pearl: Jan. 1971
Mama Told Me (Not To Come): June 1970
Mambo Baby: Dec. 1954
Mambo Italiano: Oct. 1954
Mambo Rock: Feb. 1955; *48*
Mammas Don't Let Your Babies Grow Up To Be Cowboys: Feb. 1978
Man Chases A Girl, A: Dec. 1954
Mandolin Rain: Jan. 1987
Mandy: Nov. 1974; *281*
Maneater: Oct. 1982
Manhattan Spiritual: Jan. 1959, Oct. 1975
Maniac: June 1983; *407*
Manic Monday: Jan. 1986; *439*
Man In Black: Mar. 1971
Man In Motion. *See* St. Elmo's Fire
Man In The Mirror: Feb. 1988; *466*
Man On Your Mind: Apr. 1982
Man Size Love: July 1986
Man Smart, Woman Smarter: *307*
Man Upstairs: May 1954
Man Who Shot Liberty Valance, The: May 1962
Man Without Love, A (Quando M'Innamora): May 1968
Man With The Banjo: Mar. 1954
Man With The Golden Arm, The, theme. *See* Main Title
Many Rivers To Cross: *263*
Many Tears Ago: Nov. 1960
March From The River Kwai And Colonel Bogey: Jan. 1958
Margaritaville: Apr. 1977
Maria: Dec. 1961
Marianne: Jan. 1957
(Marie's The Name) His Latest Flame: Aug. 1961; *528*
Marlena: July 1963
Marrakesh Express: Aug. 1969; *212*
Marvelous Toy, The: Dec. 1963
Mary's Boy Child: Dec. 1956
Mashed Potatoes: *115*
Mashed Potato Time: Mar. 1962; *116, 124*
Mas Que Nada: Oct. 1966; *171*
Massachusetts. *See* (The Lights Went Out In) Massachusetts
Master Blaster (Jammin'): Sep. 1980
Master Jack: May 1968
Masterpiece: Feb. 1973, Feb. 1992
Matador, The: Apr. 1964
Matchbox: Mar. 1957
Material Girl: Feb. 1985
Matter Of Trust, A: Aug. 1986
Maybe: Jan. 1958, June 1970
Maybe Baby: Apr. 1958
Maybe I Know: Aug. 1964
Maybe I'm A Fool: Jan. 1979
Maybe I'm Amazed: Feb. 1977
Maybellene: July 1955; *447, 462*
May I: Feb. 1969
May The Bird Of Paradise Fly Up Your Nose: Nov. 1965
May You Always: Jan. 1959
Me And Bobby McGee: Jan. 1971; *247*
Me And Julio Down By The Schoolyard: Apr. 1972
Me And Mrs. Jones: Nov. 1972
Me And You And A Dog Named Boo: Apr. 1971; *240*
Mean Woman Blues: *60*
Mecca: Apr. 1963
Meet El Presidente: Apr. 1987
Mellow Yellow: Nov. 1966
Melodie D'Amour: Sep. 1957
Melody Of Love: Dec. 1954, Jan. 1955
Memories: Apr. 1969

Memories Are Made Of This: Nov. 1955; *46*
Memories Medley: Jan. 1970
Memories Of Days Gone By: Feb. 1982
Memories Of You: Jan. 1956
Memory: Feb. 1982, Nov. 1982
Memphis: June 1963, June 1964; *74, 143*
Memphis Train: *213*
Me Myself and I: June 1989
Men, The, theme. *See* Theme From The Men
Men In My Little Girl's Life, The: Jan. 1966
Mercedes Boy: May 1988
Mercy, Mercy, Mercy: Jan. 1967, June 1967
Mercy Mercy Me (The Ecology): July 1971
Mercy Mercy Me (The Ecology)/I Want You: Feb. 1991
Merry Christmas In The NFL: Dec. 1980
Message In Our Music: Sep. 1976
Message To Michael: Apr. 1966
Mess Around. *See* (Dance The) Mess Around
Mess Of Blues, A: July 1960
Metal Health. *See* Bang Your Head
Method Of Modern Love: Dec. 1984
Mexican Hat Dance: Oct. 1958
Mexico: Oct. 1975
Miami Vice Theme: Sep. 1985
Michael: July 1961; *110*
Michelle: *179*
Mickey: Sep. 1982
Mickey's Monkey: Aug. 1963
Middle Of The Road: Dec. 1983
Midnight At The Oasis: Mar. 1974
Midnight Blue: May 1975, Jan. 1987; *294*
Midnight Confessions: Sep. 1968
Midnight Cowboy; Nov. 1969
Midnight In Moscow: Feb. 1962
Midnight Mary: Nov. 1963
Midnight Rider: Sep. 1972
Midnight Rocks: Aug. 1980
Midnight Special: Feb. 1960
Midnight Special, Part I: *116*
Midnight Train To Georgia: Sep. 1973; *274*
Mighty Love: Mar. 1974
Mighty Quinn (Quinn The Eskimo): Mar. 1968
Million Miles From Nowhere, A: *64*
Million To One, A: Aug. 1960, July 1973
Mindbender: Dec. 1977
Mind Games: Nov. 1973
Mind Playing Tricks On Me: Oct. 1991
Minstrel In The Gallery: Oct. 1975
Minute By Minute: May 1979; *354, 459*
Miracle: Oct. 1990, Apr. 1991
Miracles: Aug. 1975; *40*
Mirage: May 1967
Mirror, Mirror: Jan. 1982
Misled: Nov. 1984
Miss Ann: June 1957
Missed Opportunity: July 1988
Missing You: Oct. 1982, June 1984, Dec. 1984; *414*
Missing You Now: Jan. 1992
Missionary Man: *447*
Miss Me Blind: Mar. 1984
Miss Sun: Dec. 1980
Miss You: May 1978
Miss You Like Crazy: Apr. 1989
Miss You Much: Sep. 1989; *486*
Mistake No. 3: Dec. 1984
Mr. Bass Man: Mar. 1963
Mr. Big Stuff: June 1971
Mr. Blue: Sep. 1959
Mr. Bojangles: Nov. 1970
Mr. Businessman: Aug. 1968

Mr. Custer: Sep. 1960
Mr. Dieingly Sad: Aug. 1966
Mr. Jaws: Sep. 1975
Mr. Lee: July 1957
Mr. Lonely: Nov. 1964
Mr. Loverman: June 1992
Mr. Lucky: Apr. 1960; *90*
Mr. President: July 1974
Mr. Roboto: Feb. 1983
Mr. Sandman: Oct. 1954; *504*
Mister Sandman: Feb. 1981
Mr. Tambourine Man: June 1965; *154, 156, 518*
Mr. Telephone Man: Dec. 1984
Mr. Wonderful: Apr. 1956
Misty: Oct. 1959, May 1975
Misty Blue: Mar. 1976
Misunderstanding: May 1980, Oct. 1990
Mixed Emotions: Sep. 1989
Mixed Up Guy: Jan. 1971
Mixed-Up, Shook-Up Girl: Aug. 1964
Mockin' Bird Hill: 1951
Mockingbird: Aug. 1963, Feb. 1974
Modern Girl: May 1981
Modern Love: Sep. 1983
Modern Woman: June 1986
Mohair Sam: Sep. 1965
Molly: *116*
Moments To Remember: June 1955
Mona Lisa: 1950, Aug. 1959
Monday, Monday: Apr. 1966; *178*
Money: Feb. 1960, Apr. 1964, May 1973; *89, 267*
Money Back Guarantee: Sep. 1972
Money Can't Buy You Love: July 1992
Money Changes Everything: Dec. 1984
Money For Nothing: July 1985; *433, 434*
Money Honey: Feb. 1976; *38, 475*
Money, Money, Money: Oct. 1977
Money$ Too Tight (To Mention): July 1986
Moneytalks: Dec. 1990
Monkey: July 1988
Monkey Time, The: Aug. 1963; *128*
Monster: Jan. 1970
Monster Mash: Oct. 1962, May 1973
Montego Bay: Oct. 1970
Monterey: Jan. 1968
Mony Mony: Apr. 1968, Sep. 1987
Mood Indigo: Nov. 1954
Moody Blue: Dec. 1976
Moody River: May 1961
Moody Woman: June 1969
Moonglow And Theme From Picnic: Apr. 1956
Moonlight Feels Right: Apr. 1976; *308*
Moonlight Gambler: Dec. 1956
Moon River: Oct. 1961, May 1962; *110, 112*
Moon Shadow: June 1971
Moovin' N' Groovin': *64*
More: July 1963
More And More: Nov. 1954
More I See You, The: June 1966
More Love: June 1967, May 1980
More, More, More (Part 1): Mar. 1976
More Than A Feeling: Sep. 1976; *306*
More Than A Woman: Nov. 1977, Feb. 1978
More Than I Can Say: Sep. 1980
More Than Words: Mar. 1991; *516*
More Than Words Can Say: Sep. 1990
More Today Than Yesterday: Apr. 1969
Morgen: Aug. 1959
Mornin' Beautiful: June 1975
Morning After, The: June 1973; *264, 267*
Morning Dance: June 1979
Morning Girl: May 1969
Morning Has Broken: Apr. 1972
Morning Side Of The Mountain: Nov. 1974

Morning Train: Feb. 1981; *373, 381*
Most Beautiful Girl, The: Sep. 1973
Most Of All: Apr. 1955, May 1955
Mother: Jan. 1971
Mother And Child Reunion: Feb. 1972; *254*
Mother-In-Law: Mar. 1961
Mother's Little Helper: July 1966
Mother's Pride: Feb. 1991
Mothers Talk: Apr. 1986
Motorcycle Mama: June 1972
Motown Song, The: July 1991
Mountain Of Love: Apr. 1960, Nov. 1964
Mountains: May 1986; *448*
Mountain's High, The: Aug. 1961; *101*
Move Away: Apr. 1986
Move Two Mountains: Sep. 1960
Movin' On: Jan. 1975
Movin' Out (Anthony's Song): Mar. 1978
Mowtownphilly: June 1991
Mozambique: Mar. 1976
Mrs. Brown, You've Got A Lovely Daughter: Apr. 1965; *164, 208*
Mrs. Robinson: Apr. 1968; *194, 206, 207*
M.T.A.: June 1959
Muddy Mississippi Line: Sep. 1969
Mule Skinner Blues: June 1960
Multiplication: Dec. 1961
Muscles: Oct. 1982
Music Box Dancer: Jan. 1979
Music! Music! Music!: 1950
Music To Watch Girls By: Jan. 1967
Muskrat Love: Aug. 1973, Sep. 1976
Muskrat Ramble: Sep. 1954
Mustang Sally: Nov. 1966; *520*
Must Of Got Lost: Nov. 1974
Must To Avoid, A: Dec. 1965; *180*
My Angel Baby: June 1978
My Baby: Nov. 1965
My Baby Left Me: May 1956
My Baby Loves Lovin': Apr. 1970
My Baby Must Be A Magician: Dec. 1967
My Blue Heaven: Apr. 1956; *504*
My Body Says Yes: June 1991
My Bonnie: Mar. 1964
My Bonnie Lassie: Aug. 1955
My Boomerang Won't Come Back: Feb. 1962
My Boy Flat-Top: Sep. 1955
My Boyfriend's Back: Aug. 1963; *135*
My Boy Lollipop: June 1964
My Brave Face: May 1989, June 1989
My Cherie Amour: June 1969, Aug. 1977
My Coloring Book: Jan. 1963
My Cup Runneth Over: Feb. 1967
My Dad: Dec. 1962
My Ding-A-Ling: Aug. 1972; *253, 261*
My Empty Arms: Feb. 1961
My Eyes Adored You: Dec. 1974
My Girl: Jan. 1965, Aug. 1980, Sep. 1981, Aug. 1985; *520*
My Girl Friend: Mar. 1957
My Girl Has Gone: Oct. 1965
My Girl Josephine: Nov. 1960, May 1967
My Guy: Apr. 1964, Aug. 1980, Jan. 1982
My Happiness: Jan. 1959
My Heart Belongs To Me: May 1977
My Heart Belongs To Only You: Mar. 1964
My Heart Has A Mind Of Its Own: *96*
My Heart Sings. *See* (All Of A Sudden) My Heart Sings
My Heart's Symphony: Aug. 1966
My Heroes Have Always Been Cowboys: Feb. 1980
My Home Town: June 1960
My Hometown: Dec. 1985
My Honey And Me: *225*
My Juanita: Nov. 1957
My Kinda Girl: June 1990

My Kind Of Girl: June 1961
My Kind Of Lady: Jan. 1983
My Life: Nov. 1978
My Little Town: Oct. 1975
My Love: Jan. 1966, Apr. 1973, Apr. 1983; *274*
My Love Forgive Me (Amore, Scusami): Dec. 1964
My Love Is A Fire: Oct. 1990
My Lovin' (You're Never Gonna Get It): Mar. 1992
My Mammy: July 1967
My Maria: July 1973
My Melody Of Love: Oct. 1974
My Memories Of You: Apr. 1954
My Name Is Not Susan: July 1991
My, My, My: Aug. 1990
My One Sin: June 1955
My Own True Love: Nov. 1962
My Pledge Of Love: July 1969
My Prayer: June 1956; *46, 88*
My Prerogative: Oct. 1988; *486*
My Sharona: June 1979; *346, 353*
My Shoes Keep Walking Back To You: *52*
My Song: Nov. 1968
My Special Angel: Sep. 1957, Sep. 1968
Mysterious Ways: Nov. 1991
Mystery Train: Aug. 1955; *504*
My Sweet Lady: Mar. 1977
My Sweet Lord: Dec. 1970; *224, 225*
My Toot Toot: May 1985
My Town: Oct. 1983
My True Love: July 1958; *65*
My True Story: July 1961
My Truly, Truly Fair: 1951
My Way: Apr. 1969, Nov. 1977; *319*
My Whole World Ended (The Moment You Left Me): Feb. 1969; *213*
My Whole World Is Falling Down: May 1963
My Wish Came True: July 1959
My World: Jan. 1972
My World Is Empty Without You: Jan. 1966

Nadia's Theme (The Young And The Restless): Aug. 1976
Nadine: Apr. 1964
Nag: July 1961
Na Na Hey Hey Kiss Him Goodbye: Nov. 1969; *220*
Nashville Cats: Dec. 1966
Nasty: May 1986
Nathan Jones: May 1971
National City: June 1960
Native New Yorker: Nov. 1977
Natural High: Apr. 1973
Natural Woman, A: Oct. 1967
Naughty Girls (Need Love Too): Mar. 1988
Naughty Lady Of Shady Lane, The: Nov. 1954
Naughty Naughty: *427*
Navy Blue: Feb. 1964
Near You: Sep. 1958
Needles And Pins: Mar. 1964, Feb. 1986; *143*
Need You: Oct. 1958
Need You Tonight: Nov. 1987
Neither One Of Us (Wants To Be The First To Say Goodbye): Jan. 1973; *275*
Nel Blu Dipinto Di Blu. *See* Volare
Neon Rainbow: Nov. 1967
Nervous Boogie: Nov. 1957
Neutron Dance: Nov. 1984; *422*
Never: Sep. 1985
Never As Good As The First Time: Mar. 1986
Never Be Anyone Else But You: Mar. 1959
Never Be The Same: Oct. 1980
Never Can Say Goodbye: Apr. 1971, Nov. 1974, Jan. 1988; *281*

Never Give You Up: May 1968
Never Gonna Fall In Love Again: May 1976
Never Gonna Give You Up: Dec. 1987; *473*
Never Had A Dream Come True: Feb. 1970
Never Had A Lot To Lose: Feb. 1989
Never Have To Say Goodbye: Feb. 1978
Never Knew Love Like This Before: Aug. 1980
Never My Love: Sep. 1967. Sep. 1971, Aug. 1974
Never, Never Gonna Give Ya Up: Oct. 1973
Never Surrender: June 1985
Never Tear Us Apart: Aug. 1988
Never Thought (That I Could Love): Dec. 1987
Never Too Much: *374*
New Day For You: Dec. 1988
New Jack Hustler (Nino's Theme): Apr. 1991
New Kid In Town: Dec. 1976
New Moon On Monday: Jan. 1984
New Orleans: Oct. 1960; *89*
New Power Generation: Nov. 1990
New Sensation: May 1988
New Song: Jan. 1984; *413*
New Year's Day: Apr. 1983; *400*
New York Mining Disaster 1941: June 1967; *182–83*
New York Minute: Nov. 1990
New York, New York theme. *See* Theme From New York, New York
New York's A Lonely Town: Feb. 1965
N.Y., You Got Me Dancing: Feb. 1977
Next Door To An Angel: Oct. 1962
Next Plane To London: Dec. 1967
Next Time I Fall, The: Sep. 1986
Next Time You See Me: *52*
Nice Girls: Feb. 1983
Nice 'N' Easy: Sep. 1960
Nice To Be With You: Feb. 1972
Nick Of Time: *487*
Night: Mar. 1960
Night And Day: Jan. 1991
Night Before, The: *166*
Nightbird: Dec. 1983
Night Chicago Died, The: June 1974
Night Fever: Feb. 1978; *340, 341*
Night Has A Thousand Eyes, The: Dec. 1962; *137*
Nightingale: Jan. 1975
Night Lights: Dec. 1956
Nightmare On My Street, A: Aug. 1988
Night Moves: Dec. 1976, Jan. 1986
Night Owl, The: Aug. 1981
Nights Are Forever Without You: Oct. 1976
Nightshift: Jan. 1985
Nights In White Satin: Aug. 1972
Nights Like This: May 1991
Nights On Broadway: Oct. 1975
Night The Lights Went Out In Georgia, The: Feb. 1973
Night They Drove Old Dixie Down, The: Aug. 1971
Night Train: 1952
Nikita: Jan. 1986
9 Dream: Dec. 1974
1900 Yesterday: Feb. 1971
1999: Nov. 1982
19th Nervous Breakdown: Feb. 1966
9 To 5: Nov. 1980
98.6: Dec. 1966
99 Luftballons: Dec. 1983
Ninety-Nine Ways: Apr. 1957
Ninety-Nine Years: Feb. 1956
96 Tears: Sep. 1966
Nip Sip: Aug. 1955
Nite At The Apollo Live, A! The Way You Do The Things You Do: Aug. 1985
Nite Owl: Oct. 1955

tion of Christ: 488
Pata Pata: Oct. 1967
Patches: Sep. 1962, July 1970; *116*
Patch It Up: Oct. 1970
Patience: Apr. 1989
Patricia: June 1958
Payback, The (Part I): Mar. 1974
P.D.Q. Bach: Oedipus Tex & Other
    Choral Calamaties: *501*
P.D.Q. Bach 1712 Overture & Other
    Musical Assaults: *488*
P.D.Q. Bach: WTWP Classical Talkity-
    Talk Radio: *517*
Peaceful Easy Feeling: Dec. 1972
Peace In Our Time: Dec. 1989
Peace In The Valley: Apr. 1957; *50*
Peace Of Mind: May 1977
Peace Train: Sep. 1971
Peanut Butter: Apr. 1961
Peanuts: Sep. 1957
Peek-A-Boo: Dec. 1958
Peg: Nov. 1977
Peggy Sue: Oct. 1957; *52*
Pennies From Heaven: June 1960
Penny Lane: Mar. 1967; *193*
Penny Lover: Oct. 1984
Penny Nickel Dime Quarter (On A
    Teenage Date): Feb. 1956
People: May 1964; *143, 151*
People Are Strange: Sep. 1967
People Get Ready: Mar. 1965, June
    1985
People Gotta Move: *281*
People Got To Be Free: July 1968; *206*
People Make The World Go Round:
    June 1972
People Say: Aug. 1964
Pepino The Italian Mouse: Dec. 1962
Peppermint Twist: Nov. 1961, Dec.
    1961; *100, 101, 111, 123*
Percolator (Twist): Feb. 1962
Perfect Isn't Easy: *476*
Perfect World: July 1988
Perfidia: Nov. 1960
Personality: May 1959
Personally: May 1982
Pete Kelly's Blues: Sep. 1955
Peter Cottontail: 1950
Peter Gunn: May 1986
Peter Gunn Theme: Jan. 1959
Petite Fleur: Feb. 1959
Pet Me, Poppa: Aug. 1955
Philadelphia Freedom: Mar. 1975
Philadelphia U.S.A.: Dec. 1958
Philly Dog: *171*
Photograph: Oct. 1973; *399*
Physical: Oct. 1981; *381*
Piano Man: Mar. 1974; *281*
Pick Up The Pieces: Dec. 1974; *280*
Picnic: May 1956
Piece Of My Heart: May 1991
Pied Piper, The: June 1966
Pillow Talk: Mar. 1973
Pilot Of The Airwaves: Feb. 1980
Pina Colada Song, The. *See* Escape
Pinball Wizard: Apr. 1969; *302*
Pineapple Princess: Aug. 1960
Pink Cadillac: Mar. 1988
Pink Champagne: 1950, Sep. 1954
Pink Houses: Dec. 1983
Pink Shoelaces: Mar. 1959
Pipeline: Mar. 1963
Plain Jane: Feb. 1959
Place In This World: May 1991
Planet Rock: July 1982
Plantation Boogie: Jan. 1955
Playboy: May 1962, Mar. 1968
Playground: Apr. 1991
Playground In My Mind: Mar. 1973
Playing For Keeps: Jan. 1957
Play It Fair: Dec. 1955
Play Me Hearts And Flowers: Apr.
    1955
Play That Funky Music: June 1976,
    Dec. 1990; *308, 314*
Play The Game: June 1980

Plea, The: Mar. 1958
Pleasant Valley Sunday: July 1967
Please Come Home For Christmas:
    Dec. 1978
Please Come To Boston: June 1974
Please Don't Ask About Barbara: Mar.
    1962
Please Don't Go: Aug. 1979
Please Forgive Me: July 1954
Please Help Me, I'm Falling: June 1960
Please Love Me Forever: Feb. 1961,
    Oct. 1967
Please Mr. Johnson: *74*
Please Mr. Please: June 1975
Please Mr. Postman: Sep. 1961, Nov.
    1974; *102*
Please Mr. Sun: Mar. 1959
Please Please Me: Feb. 1964; *127, 141*
Please, Please, Please: Apr. 1956; *39,
    447*
Please Stay: June 1961
Pleasing You (As Long As You Live):
    1948
Pleasure And Pain: Jan. 1986
Pleasure Principle, The: May 1987
Pledging My Love: Dec. 1954, Feb.
    1955; *15*
Pocketful Of Miracles: Dec. 1961
Poetry In Motion: Oct. 1960
Poetry Man: Jan. 1975
Point Of No Return: Aug. 1962, May
    1987
Point Of Order: May 1954
Poison: Sep. 1989, Apr. 1990; *500*
Poison Arrow: Jan. 1983
Poison Ivy: Aug. 1959; *461*
Policy Of Truth: Aug. 1990
Polk Salad Annie: July 1969
Pony Time: Jan. 1961; *100, 110*
Poor Boy: Dec. 1956, Oct. 1958; *48*
Poor Butterfly: Apr. 1954
Poor Georgie: Mar. 1992
Poor Little Fool: July 1958; *72*
Poor Little Fool Like Me, A. *See* Don't
    Ever Be Lonely
Poor People Of Paris, The: Jan. 1956;
    46
Poor Side Of Town: Oct. 1966
Popcorn: July 1972
Popcorn, The: June 1969
Popeye The Hitchhiker: Sep. 1962
Pop Goes The Movies, Part I: Feb.
    1982
Pop Goes The Weasel: July 1991
Pop Goes The World: Oct. 1987
Pop Life: July 1985
Pop Muzik: Aug. 1979
Popsicle: June 1966
Popsicles And Icicles: Dec. 1963
Pop Singer: May 1989
Pop That Coochie: Nov. 1991
Portrait Of My Love: Mar. 1961
Portuguese Washerwoman: Aug. 1956
Positively 4th Street: Oct. 1965
Possession Obsession: June 1985
Pot Likker: 1949
Power, The: May 1990
Power Of Love: July 1972
Power Of Love, The: June 1985; *433,
    435*
Power Of Love/Love Power: Apr.
    1991; *517*
Power To The People: Apr. 1971
Pray: Sep. 1990
Praying For Time: Sep. 1990
Precious And Few: Jan. 1972
Precious Love: Feb. 1979
Precious, Precious: Dec. 1970
Press: Aug. 1986
Pressure: Sep. 1982
Pretend: 1953
Pretender, The: May 1977
Pretending: Nov. 1989
Pretend You Don't See Her: Oct. 1957
Pretty Ballerina: Jan. 1967
Pretty Blue Eyes: Nov. 1959

Pretty Girls Everywhere: Mar. 1959
Pretty Little Angel Eyes: July 1961
Pretty Paper: Dec. 1963
Pretty Woman: Feb. 1982
Pretty Young Thing. *See* P.Y.T.
Pride And Joy: June 1963
Pride & Passion: July 1989
Pride (In The Name Of Love): Jan.
    1992
Primal Scream: Sep. 1991
Primrose Lane: Sep. 1959
Priscilla: Oct. 1956
Prisoner, The: July 1989
Private Dancer: Jan. 1985
Private Eyes: Aug. 1981
Problems: Nov. 1958
Promise, The: Sep. 1988
Promised Land: Oct. 1974
Promise Me: Mar. 1988
Promise Of A New Day, The: July 1991
Promises: Oct. 1978
Promises In The Dark: Oct. 1981
Promises, Promises: Nov. 1968, July
    1983
Proud Mary: Feb. 1969, Feb. 1971
Proud Ones. The, theme. *See* Theme
    From The Proud Ones
Prove It All Night: June 1978
Prove Your Love: Feb. 1988
P.S. I Love You: 1953, May 1964
Psychedelic Shack: Jan. 1970
Psycho Killer: *333*
Psychic Reaction: Sep. 1966
P.T. 109: Apr. 1962
Puff The Magic Dragon: Mar. 1963
Pump It (Nice An' Hard): July 1991
Pump Up The Volume: Nov. 1987
Puppet Man: June 1971
Puppet On A String: Dec. 1965; *166*
Puppy Love: Feb. 1960, Feb. 1972
Pure Energy. *See* What's On Your
    Mind
Purple Haze: *184, 528*
Purple People Eater, The: June 1958;
    72
Purple People Eater Meets The Witch
    Doctor, The: *65*
Purple Rain: Oct. 1984; *422*
Pushin' Too Hard: *208*
Push It: Nov. 1987
Put A Light In The Window: Nov.
    1957, Jan. 1958
Put A Little Love In Your Heart: July
    1969, Dec. 1988; *476*
Puttin' On The Ritz: July 1983
Put Your Hand In The Hand: Mar.
    1971
Put Your Head On My Shoulder: Sep.
    1959
P.Y.T. (Pretty Young Thing): Oct.
    1983

Quando M'Innamora. *See* Man
Without Love, A
Quarter To Three: June 1961
Queen Of Hearts: May 1981
Queen Of The Blues, The. *See* Bridget
    The Midget
Queen Of The Hop: Oct. 1958
Queen Of The House: May 1965
Que Sera, Sera. *See* Whatever Will Be,
    Will Be
Question: July 1960, May 1970
Questions 67 & 68: Oct. 1971; *212*
Quick Joey Small (Run Joey Run): Oct.
    1968
Quicksand: Jan. 1964
Quiet Three, The: June 1959
Quiet Village: Apr. 1959
Quinn The Eskimo. *See* Mighty Quinn

Radar Love: *281*
Radioactive: Dec. 1978
Radio Free Europe: *400*
Radio Ga-Ga: Feb. 1984
Rag Doll: June 1964, June 1988; *150*

Rag Mop: 1950
Rags To Riches: 1953; *504*
Ragtime Cowboy Joe: July 1959
Rain: June 1966
Rainbow: June 1957
Rainbow Connection: Sep. 1979
Rain Dance: Sep. 1971
Raindrops: May 1961
Raindrops Keep Fallin' On My Head:
    Nov. 1969; *222, 234*
Raining In My Heart: Mar. 1959
Rain On The Roof: Nov. 1966
Rain On The Scarecrow: Apr. 1986
Rain, Rain, Rain: Dec. 1954
Rain, The Park And Other Things,
    The: Oct. 1967; *184*
Rainy Days And Mondays: May 1971
Rainy Day Women #12 & 35: Apr. 1966
Rainy Night In Georgia: Jan. 1970
Raised On Rock: Sep. 1973
Ramblin' Gamblin' Man: Jan. 1969; *198*
Ramblin' Man: Aug. 1973
Ramblin' Rose: Aug. 1962
Rang Tang Ding Dong: May 1957
Rapper, The: Feb. 1970
Rapper's Delight: Nov. 1979
Rappin' Rodney: Dec. 1983
Rapture: Jan. 1981; *381*
Raspberry Beret: May 1985
Raunchy: Oct. 1957
Rave On: June 1958; *476*
Razzle Dazzle: June 1955; *48*
Reach For The Sky: May 1978
Reach Out And Touch (Somebody's
    Hand): May 1970; *226*
Reach Out For Me: Nov. 1964
Reach Out I'll Be There: Sep. 1966,
    May 1971; *502*
Reach Out Of The Darkness: May
    1968
Read 'Em And Weep: Nov. 1983
Ready Or Not Here I Come (Can't
    Hide From Love): Dec. 1968
Ready Teddy: July 1956; *39, 48*
Ready To Take A Chance Again: Sep.
    1978
Real Love: Sep. 1980, Mar. 1989
Real Love, The: Aug. 1991
Real Real Real: Aug. 1991
Reason To Believe: Sep. 1971; *240*
Rebel Rouser: July 1958
Rebel Yell: Feb. 1984
Red Back Spider: *253*
Red Red Wine: Apr. 1968
Red, Red Wine: Feb. 1984, Aug. 1988
Red River Rock: Aug. 1959
Red Roses For A Blue Lady: Feb. 1965
Red Rubber Ball: May 1966; *170*
Red Sails In The Sunset: July
    1960
Reelin' And Rockin': *341*
Reeling In The Years: Mar. 1973
Reet Petite: Oct. 1957; *52, 460*
Reflections: Aug. 1967
Reflections Of My Life: Mar. 1970
Reflex, The: Apr. 1984
Refugee: Jan. 1980
Relax: Apr. 1984, Jan. 1985; *413*
Release Me: Nov. 1962, June 1990
Release Me (And Let Me Love Again):
    Apr. 1967; *184*
Remedy: June 1992
Remember: Jan. 1980
Remember Me: Jan. 1971
(Remember Me) I'm The One Who
    Loves You: June 1965
Remember My Name: Jan. 1991
Remember Then: Dec. 1962
Remember The Night: Dec. 1983
Remember The Time: Jan. 1992
Remember (Walkin' In The Sand):
    Sep. 1964; *143*
Remember When: July 1959; *60*
Remember You're Mine: July 1957
Reminiscing: July 1978
Renegade: Mar. 1979

Rescue Me: Oct. 1965, Mar. 1991
Reservations For Two: Oct. 1987
Respect: May 1967
Respectable: Aug. 1966
Respect Yourself: Jan. 1987
Restless: Mar. 1986
Return To Me: Apr. 1958
Return To Sender: Oct. 1962; *125*
Reunited: Mar. 1979; *353*
Reveille Rock: Nov. 1959
Reverend Mr. Black: Apr. 1963
Revival (Love Is Everywhere): *239*
Revolution: Sep. 1968
Rhapsody In The Rain: Apr. 1966
Rhiannon (Will You Ever Win): Mar. 1976
Rhinestone Cowboy: June 1975; *300*
Rhythm Is Gonna Get You, The: May 1987
Rhythm Nation: Nov. 1989
Rhythm Of Love: Dec. 1987, June 1988
Rhythm Of My Heart: Mar. 1991
Rhythm Of The Night: Feb. 1985
Rhythm Of The Rain: Jan. 1963
Ribbon In The Sky: Sep. 1982
Rich Girl: Jan. 1977; *326*
Ricky: May 1983; *400*
Ricochet: Jan. 1954
Ride!: Oct. 1962
Ride Captain Ride: May 1970
Ride Like The Wind: Feb. 1980; *359*
Ride My See-Saw: Oct. 1968
Riders In The Sky: Dec. 1980
Riders On The Storm: July 1971
Ride The Tiger: *281*
Ride The Wild Surf: Oct. 1964
Ridin' The Storm Out: *320*
Right Back Where We Started From: Feb. 1976
Right By Your Side: July 1984
Right Down The Line: Aug. 1978
Right Here Waiting: July 1989
Right Now, Right Now: May 1956; *48*
Right On The Tip Of My Tongue: Apr. 1971
Right On Track: Mar. 1987
Right Or Wrong: Nov. 1964
Right Place, Wrong Time: Apr. 1973
Right Thing, The: Feb. 1987
Right Thing To Do, The: Mar. 1973
Right Time Of The Night: Jan. 1977; *320*
Rikki, Don't Lose That Number: May 1974
Ring My Bell: May 1979, Oct. 1991
Ringo: Nov. 1964
Ring Of Fire: June 1963
Ringo's Theme (This Boy): *151*
Rings: June 1971
Rinky Dink: Aug. 1962
Rio: Apr. 1983
Rip It Up: July 1956
Rip Van Winkle: Mar. 1964
Rise: July 1979: *354*
Rise To It: June 1990
Ritual: Mar. 1988
R.M. Blues: 1946
Robin Hood—Prince Of Thieves: *516*
R-O-C-K: Mar. 1956; *48*
Rock-A-Beatin' Boogie: Dec. 1954, Oct. 1955; *48*
Rock-A-Billy: Mar. 1957
Rock-A-Bye Your Baby: Nov. 1956
Rock-A-Hula Baby: Dec. 1961; *111*
Rock And A Hard Place: Nov. 1989
Rock And Roll: Mar. 1972
Rock And Roll Girls: Mar. 1985
Rock And Roll Heaven: May 1974
Rock And Roll Is Here To Stay: Mar. 1958
Rock And Roll Love Letter: May 1976
Rock And Roll Lullaby: Feb. 1972
Rock And Roll Music: Oct. 1957, June 1976; *462*
Rock And Roll Part 2: July 1972
Rock And Roll Waltz: Jan. 1956

Rock Around The Clock. *See* (We're Gonna) Rock Around The Clock
Rockaway Beach: Dec. 1977
Rocket: Mar. 1989
Rocket 88: 1951: *460*
Rocket Man: May 1972
Rocket 2 U: Jan. 1988
Rockford Files, The: May 1975
Rock Freak, *See* Disco Nights
Rockin' All Over The World: Sep. 1975; *293*
Rockin' Around The Christmas Tree: Dec. 1960; *504*
Rockin' At Midnight: Jan. 1985
Rockin' Chair: May 1975
Rockin' Good Way, A: May 1960
Rocking Pneumonia And The Boogie Woogie Flu: July 1957
Rockin' Into The Night: *359*
Rockin' Little Angel: Feb. 1960
Rockin' Pneumonia & The Boogie Woogie Flu: Oct. 1972
Rockin' Robin: Aug. 1958, Mar. 1972
Rockin' Roll Baby: Oct. 1973
Rockin' Soul: Oct. 1974
R.O.C.K. In The U.S.A.: Feb. 1986
Rock Island Line: Feb. 1956
Rockit: Sep. 1983
Rock Lobster: *369*
Rock Love: Feb. 1955
Rock Me: Mar. 1969
Rock Me. *See* Take Me In Your Arms
Rock Me Amadeus: Feb. 1986; *446*
Rock Me Baby: May 1964, Sep. 1972
Rock Me Gently: June 1974
Rock Me Mama: 1945
Rock Me On The Water: Aug. 1972
Rock Me Tonight: *426*
Rock Me Tonite: July 1984
Rock'N Me: Aug. 1976
Rock 'N' Roll Fantasy: Mar. 1979
Rock 'N' Roll High School: *355*
Rock 'N' Roll (I Gave You The Best Years Of My Life): Dec. 1974
Rock 'N' Roll Is King: June 1983
Rock 'N' Roll Party: Feb. 1956
Rock 'N' Roll To The Rescue: June 1986
Rock Of Ages: June 1983
Rock Of Life: Feb. 1988
Rock On: Nov. 1973, Mar. 1989: *276*
Rock Steady: Nov. 1971, June 1987
Rock The Boat: May 1974; *280*
Rock The Casbah: Oct. 1982
Rock The Night: Apr. 1987
Rock This Town: Sep. 1982; *387*
Rock Wit'cha: Aug. 1989
Rock With You: Nov. 1979; *367*
Rocky Mountain High: Nov. 1972
Rocky Mountain Music: *307*
Rocky Mountain Way: *268*
Rock Your Baby: June 1974; *280*
Rocky theme. *See* Gonna Fly Now: Theme From Rocky
Rolene: Aug. 1979
Rollin' Stone: June 1955
Roll Me Away: May 1983
Roll On Down The Highway: Jan. 1975
Roll Over Beethoven: June 1956; *267*
Roll With It: June 1988; *473*
Romantic: Aug. 1991
Romeo: Aug. 1990
Romeo And Juliet. *See* (Just Like) Romeo And Juliet
Romeo & Juliet theme. *See* Love Theme From Romeo & Juliet
Romeo's Tune: Dec. 1979
Roni: Jan. 1989
Ronnie: Apr. 1964
Room At The Top: Mar. 1990
Room Full Of Roses: *281*
Rooms On Fire: May 1989
Room To Move: Feb. 1989
Rosalie: Jan. 1973
Rosanna: Apr. 1982; *394*
Rose, The: Mar. 1980; *355, 367*

Rose And A Baby Ruth, A: Nov. 1956; *39*
Rose Garden: Dec. 1970; *225*
Rose-Marie: Apr. 1954
Roses Are Red: June 1962; *117, 123*
Rosie Lee: Apr. 1957
Rough Boy: Mar. 1986
Round And Round: Mar. 1957, Dec. 1990
Route 101: June 1982
Route 66 Theme: July 1962
Roxanne: Feb. 1979; *347*
Roxanne, Roxanne: Mar. 1985
Rubber Ball: Dec. 1960
Rubberband Man, The: Sep. 1976
Rubber Biscuit: Mar. 1979
Rubber Bullets: Sep. 1973; *268*
Rubber Duckie: Sep. 1970
Rubberneckin': Dec. 1969; *211, 222*
Ruben James: Oct. 1969
Ruby: Apr. 1960, Jan. 1961
Ruby Baby: May 1956, Feb. 1963
Ruby, Don't Take Your Love To Town: July 1969
Rub You The Right Way: May 1990
Ruby Red Dress. *See* Leave Me Alone
Ruby's Rock: Oct. 1956; *48*
Ruby Tuesday: Feb. 1967
Rumble: May 1958
Rumbleseat: June 1986
Rumors: June 1986
Runaround: Nov. 1954, July 1961
Runaround Sue: Oct. 1961; *110, 111*
Runaway: Mar. 1961, June 1977, May 1978; *101, 110, 413*
Run Away Child, Running Wild: Feb. 1969
Run, Baby, Run: Oct. 1965
Run For The Roses: Apr. 1982
Run Joey Run: Aug. 1975. *See also* Quick Joey Small
Running: Feb. 1982
Running Back To You: Aug. 1991
Running Bear: Dec. 1959
Running Scared: Apr. 1961
Running With The Night: Nov. 1983
Runnin' On Empty: Feb. 1978
Run Rudolph Run: *504*
Run, Runaway: Apr. 1984
Run Through The Jungle: May 1970
Run To Him: Nov. 1961
Run To Me: July 1972
Run To You: Nov. 1984
Rush, The: Jan. 1992
Rush Rush: May 1991; *516*
Russians: Jan. 1986

Sacred: June 1961
Sacred Emotion: June 1989
Sad Eyes: May 1979
Sad Mood: Dec. 1960
Sad Movies (Make Me Cry): Sep. 1961: *102*
Sad Song. *See* Fa-Fa-Fa-Fa-Fa
Sad Songs (Say So Much): June 1984
Sail Along Silvery Moon: Jan. 1958
Sailing: June 1980; *367*
Sail On: Aug. 1979
Sail On Sailor: Feb. 1973, Apr. 1975
Sailor (Your Home Is The Sea): Nov. 1960
St. Charles: Dec. 1976
St. Elmo's Fire (Man In Motion): June 1985
St. George And The Dragonet: 1953
Sally G: Feb. 1975
Sally Go 'Round The Roses: Sep. 1963
Salsoul Hustle: Sep. 1975
Sam: Jan. 1977
Same Old Lang Syne: Dec. 1980
Same Ole Saturday Night: Nov. 1955
Same Ol'Situation (S.O.S): Sep. 1990
Sanctify Yourself: Jan. 1986
Sand And The Sea, The: Feb. 1955
Sandy: Dec. 1959, Mar. 1963
San Franciscan Nights: Aug. 1967

San Francisco (Be Sure To Wear Some Flowers In Your Hair): June 1967; *183*
Santa & The Satellite: Dec. 1957
Santa Baby: Jan. 1954
Santa Claus Is Coming To Town: Dec. 1962
Santo Natale: Dec. 1954
Sara: Dec. 1979, Dec. 1985; *446*
Sara Smile: Feb. 1976
Sgt. Pepper's Lonely Hearts Club Band: *208*
Satisfaction. *See* (I Can't Get No) Satisfaction
Satisfied: May 1989
Saturday In The Park: Aug. 1972; *520*
Saturday Night: Oct. 1975; *293*
Saturday Night At The Movies: Dec. 1964
Saturday Night Fish Fry: 1949
Saturday Night's Alright For Fighting: Aug. 1973
Saturday Night Special: June 1975
Saturday Nite: Nov. 1976
Save A Prayer: Feb. 1985
Save It For A Rainy Day: Dec. 1976; *306*
Save It For Me: Sep. 1964
Save Me: July 1980, Apr. 1990, Sep. 1991
Save The Best For Last: Feb. 1992
Save The Last Dance For Me: Sep. 1960, May 1974; *89, 96, 528*
Save Your Heart For Me: July 1965
Saving All My Love For You: Aug. 1985; *434, 466*
Saving My Love For You: Jan. 1954
Say A Prayer: Aug. 1990
Say Goodbye To Hollywood: Sep. 1981
Say, Has Anybody Seen My Sweet Gypsy Rose?: July 1973
Say It Again: July 1988
Say It Isn't So: Oct. 1983
Say It's Gonna Rain: June 1988
Say Man: Oct. 1959
Say Say Say: Oct. 1983; *407*
Say You: *142*
Say You'll Be Mine: Mar. 1981
Say You'll Stay Until Tomorrow: Jan. 1977
Say You Love Me: July 1976
Say You're Wrong: Apr. 1985
Say You, Say Me: Nov. 1985; *433, 436*
Say You Will: Dec. 1987
Scarborough Fair: Mar. 1968; *194*
School Day: Mar. 1957
School Is In: Nov. 1961
School Is Out: July 1961
School's Out: June 1972
Scorpio: Nov. 1971
Screams Of Passion: Sep. 1985
Sea Cruise: Mar. 1959
Sealed With A Kiss: June 1962, June 1972
Seal Our Fate: Apr. 1991
Sea Of Love: July 1959, Dec. 1981, Oct. 1984
Searchin': May 1957; *461*
Searching So Long. *See* (I've Been) Searching So Long
Search Is Over, The: Apr. 1985
Seasons Change: Nov. 1987
Seasons In The Sun: Feb. 1974; *288*
Seasons Of Gold: Jan. 1982
Second Chance: Feb. 1989
Second Fiddle: May 1956
Second Time Around, The: Dec. 1979; *100*
Second Wind. *See* You're Only Human
Secret: Dec. 1985
Secret Agent Man: Mar. 1966
Secretary: July 1974
Secret Garden, The: Mar. 1990
Secret Love: Feb. 1954, Apr. 1954
Secret Lover: Dec. 1985
Secretly: May 1958

There's A Moon Out Tonight: Feb. 1961; *101*
There's A Place: Mar. 1964
(There's Gonna Be A) Showdown: Dec. 1968
There She Goes: Dec. 1960, Jan. 1961
(There's) No Gettin' Over Me: June 1981
There's No Other (Like My Baby): Nov. 1961; *101*
There's No Other Way: Jan. 1992
There's No Stoppin Us: *422*
There Will Never Be Another Tonite: Dec. 1991
There Will Never Be Another You: Sep. 1966
There Won't Be Anymore: Feb. 1974
These Arms Of Mine: *128, 488*
These Boots Are Made For Walkin': Jan. 1966
These Dreams: Jan. 1986
These Eyes: Apr. 1969
(The System Of) Doctor Tarr And Professor Fether: *307*
The Truth: Aug. 1991
The Way I Feel: July 1992
They Don't Know: Feb. 1984
They Just Can't Stop It The (Games People Play): Aug. 1975
(They Long To Be) Close To You: June 1970; *234*
The Young And The Restless. *See* Nadia's Theme
They're Coming To Take Me Away, Ha-Haaa!: July 1966; *169–70*
They Reminisce Over You (T.R.O.Y.): July 1992
They're Playing Our Song. *See* Hey Baby
They Want EFX: May 1992
They Were Doing The Mambo: Aug. 1954
Thieves In The Temple: Aug. 1990
Thing, The: 1950
Things I'd Like To Say: Jan. 1969
Things I Love, The: June 1958
Things That I Used To Do, The: Feb. 1954
Things That Make You Go HMMMM …: July 1991
Things We Do For Love, The: Jan. 1977
Think: May 1960, May 1968; *369*
Think About Me: Mar. 1980
Think I'm In Love: July 1982
Thinkin' Back: Feb. 1992
Thinking Of You: Mar. 1973, Feb. 1989
Think It Over: Aug. 1958
Think Of Laura: Dec. 1983
Thin Line Between Love And Hate: Sep. 1971
Third Man Theme: 1950, Oct. 1965
Third Time Lucky: Nov. 1979
Thirty Days: Oct. 1955
This Bitter Earth: July 1960
This Diamond Ring: Jan. 1965; *156*
This Door Swings Both Ways: July 1966
This Friendly World: Nov. 1959; *86*
This Girl Is A Woman Now: Sep. 1969
This Girl's In Love With You: Feb. 1969
This Guy's In Love With You: May 1968; *197, 206*
This House: Dec. 1990
This Is It: Oct. 1979; *367*
This Is My Song: Mar. 1967
This Is My Story: Mar. 1955
This Is Not America: Feb. 1985
This Is Ponderous: Dec. 1990
This Is The Night: Nov. 1957
This Is The Right Time: Aug. 1990
This Is The Time: Nov. 1986
This Is The Way We Roll: May 1992
This Land Is Your Land: *116*
This Little Girl: Apr. 1981

This Little Girl's Gone Rockin': Oct. 1958
This Magic Moment: Feb. 1960, Jan. 1969; *528*
This Masquerade: June 1976; *306, 315*
This Moment In Time: Dec. 1978
This Night Won't Last Forever: June 1978, Aug. 1979
This Ol' Cowboy: *294*
This Old Heart Of Mine: Jan. 1976, Mar. 1990
This Old Heart Of Mine (Is Weak For You): Mar. 1966
This Ole House: July 1954
This One's For The Children: Nov. 1989
This One's For You: Sep. 1976
This Time: Oct. 1961, Sep. 1983
This Time I Know It's For Real: Apr. 1989
This Time I'm Gone For Good: Jan. 1974
This Time I'm In It For Love: Mar. 1978
This Time Make It Funky: May 1991
This Used To Be My Playground: July 1992
This Will Be: Sep. 1975; *293*
This Woman: Jan. 1984
Those Lazy-Hazy-Crazy Days Of Summer: May 1963
Those Oldies But Goodies: May 1961; *101*
Those Were The Days: Oct. 1968; *198*
Thousand Miles Away, A: Nov. 1956
Thousand Stars, A: Nov. 1960
Thread The Needle: *183*
Three Bells, The: Aug. 1959; *77, 84*
Three Coins In The Fountain: May 1954; *7*
Three Nights A Week: Sep. 1960
3 O'Clock Blues: *460*
Three O'Clock In The Morning: *157*
Three Ring Circus: Nov. 1974
Three Times A Lady: June 1978; *340*
Three Times In Love: Jan. 1980
Thriller: Feb. 1984
Thrill Is Gone, The: Jan. 1970
Through The Storm: Apr. 1989
Through The Years: Dec. 1981
Throwing It All Away: Aug. 1986
Thunderdome. *See* We Don't Need Another Hero
Thunder Island: Dec. 1977
Thunder Road: *293*
Ticket To Ride: Apr. 1965, Mar. 1970; *166, 225*
Tide Is High, The: Nov. 1980
Tie A Yellow Ribbon Round The Ole Oak Tree: Feb. 1973; *274*
Tie Me Kangaroo Down, Sport: June 1963
Ties That Bind, The: Apr. 1960
Tie Your Mother Down: Mar. 1977
Tiger: June 1959
Tighten Up: Apr. 1968; *197*
Tighter, Tighter: June 1970
'Til: Oct. 1961; *101*
('Til) I Kissed You: Aug. 1959
Till I Loved You: Oct. 1988
Till I Waltz Again With You: 1952
Till Then: Feb. 1954, July 1963
Till There Was You: *77*
Till We Two Are One: Apr. 1954
Time: Apr. 1981; *78, 171*
Time After Time: Apr. 1984, Mar. 1990
Time (Clock Of The Heart): Apr. 1983
Time For Livin': May 1968, July 1974
Time Has Come Today: Sep. 1968
Time Is On My Side: Nov. 1964
Time Is Tight: Apr. 1969; *208*
Time Is Time: Nov. 1980
Time, Love And Tenderness: July 1991
Time Machine: *212, 529*
Time Of My Life, The. *See* (I've Had) The Time Of My Life

Time Of The Season: Feb. 1969
Times Of Your Life: Dec. 1975
Time's Up: *501*
Time Was: July 1961
Time Won't Let Me: Mar. 1966
Timothy: Mar. 1971
Tina Marie: July 1955
Tin Man: Aug. 1974
Tip Of My Tongue: July 1983
Tip-Toe Thru The Tulips With Me: June 1968
Tired Of Being Alone: July 1971
Tired Of Toein' The Line: May 1980
Tired Of Waiting For You: Mar. 1965
T.L.C.: May 1992
To All The Girls I've Loved Before: Mar. 1984
Toast And Marmalade For Tea: Apr. 1971
Tobacco Road: Oct. 1964
To Be A Lover: Oct. 1986
To Be Loved: Apr. 1958; *476*
To Be Loved (Forever): Feb. 1961
To Be With You: Dec. 1991
Today: May 1964
(Today I Met) The Boy I'm Gonna Marry: Apr. 1963
Today I Started Loving You Again: Jan. 1973
Today's The Day: May 1976
Together Forever: Apr. 1988
To Know Him Is To Love Him: Oct. 1958; *72*
To Live And Die In L.A.: Oct. 1985
To Love Somebody: July 1967
Tom Dooley: Nov. 1958; *64, 65*
Tomorrow Doesn't Matter Tonight: Apr. 1986
Tomorrow People: May 1988
Tonight: Oct. 1961, Feb. 1984, Dec. 1984, Aug. 1990
Tonight (Could Be The Night): June 1961
Tonight I Fell In Love: Mar. 1961; *102*
Tonight I'm Yours: Jan. 1982
Tonight She Comes: Nov. 1985
Tonight's The Night: Oct. 1960; *89*
Tonight's The Night (Gonna Be Alright): Oct. 1976; *314*
Tonight, Tonight, Tonight: Feb. 1987
Tonight You Belong To Me: Aug. 1956
Tonite, Tonite: June 1957
Too Blind To See It: Nov. 1991
Too Busy Thinking About My Baby: May 1969
Too Close For Comfort: *39*
Too Funky: June 1992
Too Hot: Jan. 1980
Too Hot To Trot: Dec. 1977
Too Late: Jan. 1980
Too Late For Goodbyes: Jan. 1985
Too Late To Say Goodbye: Jan. 1990
Too Late To Turn Back Now: May 1972
Too Many Fish In The Sea: Dec. 1964
Too Many Walls: July 1991
Too Much: Jan. 1957; *50, 59*
Too Much Heaven: Nov. 1978
Too Much Monkey Business: Oct. 1956
Too Much Talk: Jan. 1968
Too Much Time On My Hands: Mar. 1981
Too Much, Too Little, Too Late: Apr. 1978
Too Shy: Apr. 1983
Too Tight: Jan. 1981
Too Weak To Fight: Nov. 1968
Too Young: 1951
Too Young To Go Steady: Mar. 1956
Topical Song, The: Aug. 1979
Top Of The World: Oct. 1973, Oct. 1991; *274*
Topsy II: Sep. 1958
Torn Between Two Lovers: Nov. 1976; *307, 326*

Torquay: *78*
Torture: Aug. 1984
To Sir With Love: Sep. 1967; *191*
Tossin' And Turnin': Apr. 1961; *110*
Total Eclipse Of The Heart: July 1983; *407*
To The Aisle: July 1957
Touchables, The: *101*
Touch And Go: Sep. 1980
Touch Me: Jan. 1969
Touch Me (All Night Long): Mar. 1991
Touch Me In The Morning: June 1973
Touch Me Tonight: Nov. 1989
Touch Me When We're Dancing: June 1981
Touch Of Grey: July 1987
Touch The Wind. *See* Eres Tu
Tough All Over: May 1985
Tower Of Strength: Oct. 1961
Town Without Pity: Nov. 1961
Toy Soldiers: June 1989
Traces: Feb. 1969, Jan. 1970
Tracks Of My Tears: July 1965
Tracks Of My Tears, The: June 1967
Tracy: Oct. 1969
Tracy's Theme: Jan. 1960
Tragedy: Feb. 1959, Apr. 1961, Mar. 1979; *354*
Train In Vain: *359*
Train Of Thought: June 1974
Trains And Boats And Planes: July 1966
Tra La La: *48*
Tra La La La Suzy: Dec. 1963
Transfusion: June 1956
Trapped By A Thing Called Love: Aug. 1971
Travelin' Band: Feb. 1970
Traveling Wilburys, Vol. I: *487*
Travelin' Man: Apr. 1961
Treasure Of Love: Apr. 1956
Treat Her Like A Lady: Apr. 1971
Treat Her Right: Sep. 1965; *156*
Treat Me Nice: Sep. 1957; *60*
Treat Me Right: Jan. 1981
Tried To Love: Dec. 1977
Troglodyte (Cave Man): May 1972
T-R-O-U-B-L-E: May 1975
Trouble: May 1988; *74*
Trouble In Paradise: July 1960
Truckin': Dec. 1971
True: Aug. 1983; *400*
True Blue: Oct. 1986
True Blues: 1947
True Colors: Aug. 1986
True Love: Sep. 1956, Aug. 1988
True Love Ways: May 1965, Aug. 1980
True To You: Dec. 1986
Truly: Oct. 1982; *394*
Try A Little Tenderness: Feb. 1969, Apr. 1969, Oct. 1991; *213, 520*
Tryin' To Get The Feeling Again: Mar. 1976
Tryin' To Live My Life Without You: Sep. 1981
Tryin' To Love Two: Feb. 1977
Try It On: *319*
Try Me: Feb. 1959
Try The Impossible: June 1958
Try To Remember: May 1975; *155*
TSOP: Mar. 1974; *288*
Tubular Bells: Mar. 1974
Tuesday Afternoon (Forever Afternoon): Aug. 1968
Tuff: Jan. 1962
Tug Of War: Oct. 1982
Tumbling Dice: May 1972, Apr. 1978
Tumbling Tumbleweeds: Sep. 1956
Tunnel Of Love: Dec. 1987; *459*
Turn Around And Love You: *212*
Turn Around, Look At Me: June 1968; *101*
Turn Back The Hands Of Time: Mar. 1970
Turn Down Day: Aug. 1966
Turn Me Loose: Apr. 1959; *374*

You Talk Too Much: Sep. 1960
You Think You're Hot Stuff: Oct. 1971
You Took The Words Right Out Of My Mouth: Nov. 1978
You Turn Me On: June 1965
You Upset Me Baby: Sep. 1954
You've Been My Inspiration: *226*
You've Got A Friend: June 1971; *240, 248*
(You've Got) The Magic Touch: Mar. 1956

You've Got To Hide Your Love Away: Oct. 1965; *166*
You've Got Your Troubles: Sep. 1965; *156*
You've Lost That Lovin' Feelin': Jan. 1965
You've Lost That Lovin' Feeling: Sep. 1980
You've Made Me So Very Happy: Mar. 1969; *211*
You've Never Been This Far Before: Aug. 1973

You've Really Got A Hold On Me: Jan. 1963
You Waited Too Long: *170*
You Wear It Well: Aug. 1972
(You Were Made For) All My Love: Aug. 1960
You Were Mine: Sep. 1959
You Were On My Mind: Aug. 1965
You Won't See Me: Apr. 1974
You Won't See Me Cry: May 1992

You, You, You: 1953
Yowsah, Yowsah, Yowsah. *See* Dance, Dance, Dance
Yo-Yo: Sep. 1971
Yummy, Yummy, Yummy: May 1968

Zip-A-Dee-Doo-Dah: Nov. 1962
Zippity Zum: Sep. 1954
Zip Zip: Aug. 1957
Zorba The Greek: Jan. 1966

PHOTO ACKNOWLEDGMENTS

This page constitutes a continuation of the copyright page.

ABOUT THE AUTHOR

Norm N. Nite, who is known throughout the United States as "Mr. Music," began his broadcast career at station WGAR in Cleveland. He has been a guest on numerous radio shows around the country and has appeared on dozens of national TV shows, talking about rock music. He hosted a weekend show on WCBS-FM in New York City for 16 years and has developed a database of rock information that is used as a source by many in the recording and music industries. He currently hosts two nationally syndicated radio shows, "The U.S. Hall of Fame" and "Solid Gold Scrapbook." He is the only radio personality who is also a member of the board of directors of the Rock 'n' Roll Hall of Fame. Norm N. Nite is the author of the three-volume Rock On series: *Rock On: The Solid Gold Years, Rock On: The Years of Change,* and *Rock On: The Video Revolution.* He currently divides his time between New York City and Cleveland, Ohio.